Programming in

RPG

IV

by Judy Yaeger

A Division of
DUKE COMMUNICATIONS
INTERNATIONAL

Loveland, Colorado

Library of Congress Cataloging-in-Publication Data

Yaeger, Judy, 1943-
    Programming in RPG IV / by Judy Yaeger.
        p. cm.
    Includes index.
    ISBN 1-882419-24-3
    1. RPG (Computer program language)   I. Title.
    QA76.73.R26Y33 1995
    005. 2'45—dc20   95-34842
                                                                 CIP

Copyright © 1996 by DUKE PRESS
DUKE COMMUNICATIONS INTERNATIONAL
Loveland, Colorado

This book was printed and bound in the United States of America.

Sample screen formats are reproductions of those found on the AS/400.

ISBN 1-882419-24-3

1 2 3 4 5 6 KP 9 8 7 6 5

This one's for the kid.

Acknowledgments

A new version of a book is much like a new version of a programming language: it refines and enhances the previous versions, updating and reorganizing many of the original ideas as well as adding some new ones. Without the help of all the individuals involved in producing *Programming in RPG/400*, *Programming in RPG IV* would not be possible. However, some people deserve special thanks for their work on *Programming in RPG IV*. First, I would like to thank all those instructors who took the time and effort to make suggestions and offer opinions about organization and content. Bryan Meyers, the Director of Information Services for KOA Kampgrounds of America and a technical editor for *NEWS/400*, was most helpful in serving as the technical editor for the project. My special thanks go to Janet Robbins, for her careful job of editing; to Dave Bernard, for his editorial leadership; to Candace Hagel, for the cover design; and to Jan Caufman, for her work in production. I also would like to thank Sunway College, in Petaling Jaya, Malaysia, for its gracious hospitality while I was writing this book.

Table of Contents

Preface XIII

Chapter 1: Introduction to Programming and RPG 1
   Chapter Overview 1
   Programming 1
   History of RPG 1
   Program Variables 4
   Data Files and the Data Hierarchy 5
   Programming Specifications 6
   The Program Development Cycle 9
   Program Entry and Testing 10
   Chapter Summary 12
   Terms 14
   Discussion/Review Questions 14
   Exercises 15

Chapter 2: Getting Started 17
   Chapter Overview 17
   Specifications in RPG IV 17
   Program Specifications for Example Program 18
   File Description Specifications 18
   Input Specifications 21
   Record Identification Entries 21
   Field Description Entries 22
   Output Specifications 23
   Record Identification Entries 24
   Field Description Entries 26
   Calculation Specifications 29
   Indicators and Calculations 31
   RPG IV Operations 32
   Internal Documentation 33
   The Completed Program 35
   Output Editing 36
   Edit Codes 36
   Edit Words 38
   Chapter Summary 39

Terms 41
Discussion/Review Questions 41
Exercises 42
Programming Assignments 42

Chapter 3: Assignment and Arithmetic Operations 45
Chapter Overview 45
Introducing Definition Specifications 45
Numeric Literals 46
Simple Numeric Assignment 47
Arithmetic Operations 47
Using EVAL for Arithmetic 48
Introducing Specific Arithmetic Operators 49
Numeric Truncation and Field Sizes 51
Result Field Size for Addition 52
Result Field Size for Subtraction 53
Result Field Size for Multiplication 53
Result Field Size for Division 53
Rounding 54
Effective Commenting on Calculations 55
Putting It All Together 56
Character Literals 60
Character Assignment 60
Data Type Conversion 61
Figurative Constants 63
Chapter Summary 64
Terms 66
Discussion/Review Questions 66
Exercises 67
Programming Assignments 67

Chapter 4: Top-Down, Structured Program Design 71
Chapter Overview 71
Structured Design 71
Sequential Flow of Control 72
Relational Comparisons 72
Selection Operations 74
IF and Page Overflow 78
Operations for Iteration 80
Loops and Early Exits 84
Top-Down Design 85
Defining Subroutines 86
Control-Break Logic 87
Chapter Summary 92
Terms 94
Discussion/Review Questions 94

Exercises 95
Programming Assignments 96

Chapter 5: Externally Described Files 99
Chapter Overview 99
The AS/400 Approach to Database Files 99
Physical and Logical Files 100
Introduction to DDS 101
Defining Physical Files 102
Data Types and Data Storage 103
Logical Files 106
Simple Logical Files 106
Record Selection/Omission 108
Logical Files with Multiple-Record Formats 110
Join-Logical Files 111
Creating Database Files 113
RPG IV Programming with Externally Defined Files 113
Additional Database File Concepts 114
Externally Described Printer Files 116
Putting It All Together 120
Chapter Summary 122
Terms 123
Discussion/Review Questions 123
Exercises 124
Programming Assignments 124

Chapter 6: File Access and Record Manipulation 129
Chapter Overview 129
Operations for Input Files 129
Sequential Access 129
Random Access 135
Referencing Composite Keys 136
Operations for Output Files 138
Update Files and I/O Operations 140
File and Record Locking 142
I/O Errors 144
Putting It All Together 145
Chapter Summary 148
Terms 150
Discussion/Review Questions 150
Exercises 150
Programming Assignments 151

Chapter 7: Interactive Applications 155
   Chapter Overview 155
   Batch and Interactive Programs 155
   Display Files 155
   Additional DDS Keywords 163
   File-Level Keywords 163
   Record-Level Keywords 164
   Field-Level Keywords 164
   Conditioning Indicators 168
   Interactive File Maintenance 170
   Screen Design and CUA 177
   Chapter Summary 178
   Terms 180
   Discussion/Review Questions 180
   Exercises 180
   Programming Assignments 181

Chapter 8: Tables and Arrays 183
   Chapter Overview 183
   Representing Tables of Data 183
   RPG IV Tables 184
   Table Definition 184
   Compile-Time Tables 186
   Pre-Runtime Tables 187
   Table Look-Ups 188
   Two Related Tables 189
   Multiple Related Tables 191
   Range Tables 194
   Changing Table Values 196
   Arrays 196
   Runtime Arrays and Input Data 197
   Arrays and Indexing 200
   Calculations with Arrays 200
   Using Arrays 205
   Array Look-Ups 208
   Indicators as Array Elements 210
   Output with Arrays 210
   Chapter Summary 211
   Terms 212
   Discussion/Review Questions 212
   Exercises 213
   Programming Assignments 214

Chapter 9: Advanced Data Definition 217
   Chapter Overview 217
   Data Types Revisited 217

Data Types and Time 218
Date/Time Operations 219
The Graphic Data Type 222
Pointer Data Types 222
Named Constants 225
Data Structures 227
Simple Data Structures 228
Multiple-Occurrence Data Structures 232
Initialization and Reinitialization of Variables 235
File-Information Data Structures 239
Program-Status Data Structures 241
Error Handling and *PSSR 242
Chapter Summary 244
Terms 245
Discussion/Review Questions 245
Exercises 246
Programming Assignments 247

Chapter 10: Interactive Programs: Advanced Techniques 251
Chapter Overview 251
Subfiles 251
Subfile Record Formats 253
Subfile Control-Record Formats 254
Loading the Entire Subfile 255
Loading the Subfile a Page at a Time 259
Subfiles and Change 266
Uses of Subfiles 269
On-Line Help 269
Chapter Summary 272
Terms 273
Discussion/Review Questions 273
Exercises 273
Programming Assignments 274

Chapter 11: Working with Bytes and Bits 275
Chapter Overview 275
Field Inspection 275
Inspecting Size 275
Inspecting Bytes 278
Field Character Manipulation 284
Working with Bit Patterns 288
Chapter Summary 290
Terms 291
Discussion/Review Questions 291
Exercises 291
Programming Assignments 292

Chapter 12: Interprogram Communications 295
   Chapter Overview 295
   Modular Programming 295
   Dynamic and Static Binding 296
   Passing Data Between Programs 299
   Using a Modular Approach 302
   APIs 303
   Data Areas 305
   Data-Area Data Structures 306
   Using *NAMVAR DEFINE 306
   Chapter Summary 309
   Terms 310
   Discussion/Review Questions 310
   Exercises 310
   Programming Assignments 311

Chapter 13: Maintaining the Past 315
   Chapter Overview 315
   Compatibility and Conversion 315
   Holdovers from RPG III 316
   Defining Work Fields 316
   Performing Arithmetic and Numeric Assignment 317
   Looping and Selecting 319
   Manipulating Strings 323
   Delimiting Arrays and Tables 324
   Moving Data 325
   RPG II: An Initial Look 326
   RPG's Fixed-Logic Cycle 331
   The Fixed-Logic Cycle and Control Breaks 332
   Decisions in RPG II 336
   Resulting Indicators and Arithmetic 339
   Iteration and RPG II 340
   Chapter Summary 342
   Terms 344
   Discussion/Review Questions 344
   Exercises 344
   Programming Assignments 346

Appendix A: Developing Programs on the AS/400 349
   The Programmer Menu 350
   Programming Development Manager (PDM) 352

Appendix B: Source Entry Utility (SEU) 359
   SEU Overview 359
   Using Prompts 360
   Working Within the Edit Display 362

Function Keys in SEU 363
SEU's Command Line 364
Working with a Split Screen 364
Exiting SEU 366

Appendix C: Program Testing and Debugging 369
Syntax Errors 369
Logic Errors 370
Runtime Errors 370
Diagnosing Abends 371
Diagnosing Infinite Loops 371
Output Errors 372
Detecting Output Errors 372
Correcting Output Errors 373
Debug 376
Breakpoints 376
Trace Commands 377

Appendix D: Data Files 379
Case 1: CompuSell 379
Case 2: Wexler University 383
Case 3: GTC, Inc. 388
Miscellaneous Files 389

Glossary 393

Index 413

Preface

RPG IV, the version of RPG that participates in IBM's Integrated Language Environment (ILE), represents a dramatic step forward in RPG's evolution. RPG IV diverges from its predecessor, RPG III, in significant ways. However, to encourage adoption of the new ILE RPG/400 compiler and to prevent a nightmare for those programmers faced with maintaining older RPG programs, IBM made this latest release largely "backward-compatible" with older versions of RPG. Programs written before 1995 can easily be converted to RPG IV and subsequently modified, without necessitating complete program rewrites. Although such backward-compatibility is a practical solution for language developers, it means the language must retain some components that, in fact, the new features make obsolete.

Writing a textbook about a new version of a language, then, presents the author with a difficult decision: How much should one emphasize those features that, although still available in the language, really represent an outmoded approach to programming? Giving obsolete syntax equal importance with the language's more modern features might inappropriately encourage students to write outdated code; at the very least, equal coverage can unnecessarily complicate the learning process. On the other hand, ignoring those outdated features completely would provide students with an incomplete understanding of the language and would ill prepare them for program maintenance tasks.

This textbook resolves the dilemma by initially presenting students with the most suitable, modern techniques that RPG IV offers to solve typical programming problems. Thus, Chapters 2-12 feature only the appropriate methods and strategies that contemporary programmers use. In recognition of program maintenance needs, however, the final chapter of the book (Chapter 13: Maintaining the Past) details the support features of RPG IV that students must know about when they tackle maintenance tasks in the real world.

Programming in RPG IV, like its predecessor, *Programming in RPG/400*, tries to bridge the gap between academia and the business world by presenting all the facets of RPG IV needed by a professional programmer. The material is introduced incrementally, and the book is organized so that students quickly begin writing complete — though simple — programs. Each successive chapter introduces additional information about RPG IV syntax and fundamental programming methods, so that students become increasingly proficient at developing RPG IV programs — programs that grow in complexity as students progress through the book.

Each chapter includes a brief overview, which orients students to the material contained in the chapter, and a chapter summary, which reviews the chapter's major points. The end-of-chapter sections include discussion/review questions, exercises, and programming assignments designed to help students develop their analytical and problem solving skills, as well as their proficiency with RPG IV syntax. These end-of-chapter sections remain basically unchanged from *Programming in RPG/400*, although they now require solutions in RPG IV, rather than RPG III.

The programming assignments at the end of each chapter are arranged roughly in order of difficulty, so that instructors can assign programs appropriate to their time schedules and their students' abilities. Although none of the program solutions are long by commercial standards, some of the necessary algorithms are quite difficult; the assignments require time and effort on the part of the students to develop correct solutions. Unfortunately, there is no "easy road" to becoming a good programmer, nor can students learn to deal with program complexity by merely reading or talking about it. Programming, as much as any other activity I know, is truly a matter of "learning by doing." Those students interested in becoming MIS professionals must recognize that they have chosen a rewarding — but demanding and challenging — profession, and they need to realize that they must be willing to work hard to succeed in this profession.

To provide students with experience developing application systems, rather than programming in a vacuum, most of the programming assignments relate to three fictitious companies and their application needs (described in Appendix D). By working on these assignments, students should gain a sense of how a company's data files are repeatedly used by numerous applications for different, related purposes.

Although a complete introduction to using the AS/400 is beyond the scope of this text, Appendix A introduces students to working on the system using the Programmer Menu and PDM; Appendix B acquaints students with SEU. Appendix C provides some insights into program testing and debugging, often bewildering processes for beginning programmers.

Depending on the length of the school term and the pace of the course, some instructors may choose to present this material over two terms. Alternately, you may decide to omit some of the more technical chapters of the text or skip those chapters less central to RPG IV. To provide students with the *minimal* information needed by entry-level programmers, you should present Chapters 1-9 and 13.

An instructor's manual is available to those instructors adopting this text for classroom use. The manual includes answers to the review questions and solutions to the exercises. The manual also includes a diskette with the data files for the programming assignments, the source code for the solutions to the programming assignments, and copies of the output produced by the solutions.

Chapter 1

Introduction to Programming and RPG

Chapter Overview

This chapter introduces you to RPG as a programming language and describes how the language has evolved. It also explains general programming and computer-related concepts that you need to know as you begin learning to program in RPG IV.

Programming

Computer programming involves writing instructions for a computer that tell it how to process, or manipulate, data. In many programming languages, these instructions depict a step-by-step procedure needed to produce a specific result or product, such as a sales report. These kinds of languages are called **procedural languages**. Procedural languages require that you explicitly state each processing step or instruction for the computer. Moreover, you must accurately describe the order or sequence in which the computer is to execute these steps for the program to produce correct results.

The computer is a binary device. Designed with electronic components that can depict only two states — on or off, or flow of current or no flow — computers internally store and manipulate instructions (and data) as patterns of **bits**, or **binary digits**. Programmers originally were forced to write computer instructions as strings of 1s and 0s, using machine language. Humans, however, do not function as well at this low representation level. Fortunately, advances in computer science soon led to the development of **high-level languages (HLLs)**.

Programs written in HLLs require translation into the bit patterns of machine language before a computer can actually execute their instructions. The computer itself can accomplish this translation using a special program called a **compile**r. A compiler translates a program written in an HLL into machine language that the computer can understand.

History of RPG

IBM introduced the **Report Program Generator (RPG)** programming language in the early 1960s. RPG filled a niche for providing quick solutions to a common business task: generating reports needed within the business. By designing RPG to be relatively easy to learn and to use, IBM set the stage for today's **Fourth Generation Languages (4GLs)**.

Unlike the procedural languages in use at the time, RPG did not require the programmer to detail each processing step. Instead, the language included a fixed-logic cycle that automatically executed the normal cycle of read-calculate-write found in most report programs. In RPG, the programmer's job was to describe accurately to the computer the files, record layouts, calculations, and output desired for a specific program; the RPG compiler supplied the needed missing steps to provide a standard machine-language program for the computer to execute. RPG required that these descriptive specifications appear in a specific sequence within a program and that entries within a program line appear in fixed locations, or columns, within each line.

Another unique characteristic of RPG was its use of a special class of built-in variables called **indicators**. These variables, many of which simply had numbers for names, were predefined to the computer and could have only one of two values — '1' or '0' (corresponding to "on" or "off"). These indicators could be set on or off in one part of the program; their status would then be referenced in another part of the program to determine what processing was to occur.

By the late 1960s, RPG had gained popularity, especially in small- and medium-sized data processing departments. Programmers were stretching the language beyond its original intended use, using the language for complex computations and complicated file updating, as well as for report generation. Accordingly, IBM introduced an enhanced version of the language, RPG II, when it released its System/3 computer. Although other computer vendors saw the popularity of RPG and developed RPG II compilers for their minicomputers, RPG remained, for the most part, a language associated with IBM installations.

During the 1970s, several trends in data processing became apparent. First, as computers became cheaper and more powerful, and as operating systems became more sophisticated, interest in interactive programs began to mushroom. In **interactive applications**, a user interacts with the computer directly through a terminal or workstation to control the actions of a computer program as it is running. Previously, programs had involved **batch processing**, in which the computer processed a "batch" of data (typically representing business transactions) without user intervention.

A second emerging trend was a growing interest in a database approach to data management. With a database approach, programmers define data independently of programs, in a central data dictionary. The files storing the data are rigorously designed and organized to minimize redundancy and to facilitate accessing data stored in separate files. Any program can use these database files without having to define the data within the program itself.

Finally, a third trend during that decade was an increasing concern with program design. This trend resulted in a methodology called **structured design**. As companies' libraries of developed programs continued to grow, the need to revise those programs to fit evolving business needs grew as well. It became apparent that computer professionals had paid too little attention to the initial design of programs. Poorly designed programs were causing inefficiencies in program maintenance. Experts attributed much of this inefficiency to "spaghetti code"; that is, programs that included undisciplined, haphazard transfer of control from one portion of the program to another.

Advocates of structured design recommended restricting indiscriminate flow of control within a program and using only those operations that kept tight controls on that flow. With this emphasis on structured design, concepts of modular programming and code reusability also began to emerge.

IBM addressed all these trends when it introduced the System/38 minicomputer in 1979. This computer's architecture was unique in that the design of the computer and its operating system had a built-in database approach; the S/38 required data files to be predefined at a system level before a program could reference or use those files. This requirement alone forced IBM to release a new version of RPG to allow external file definition. IBM called this version RPG III.

IBM made several other major changes to RPG at this time as well. First, IBM added features that made it easier for programmers to develop interactive applications. Second, IBM included structured operations for looping and decision logic to address the issues of structured design. Finally, to support modular code and reusability, IBM revamped the language to include the capability to perform calls to other programs and to pass data between programs.

In 1988, IBM announced its successor computer to the S/38 — the Application System/400. With the new computer came a new version of RPG, RPG/400. Despite its changed name, RPG/400 was really just a minor upgrade of RPG III, with a few new operations and enhancements. Following RPG/400's initial release, IBM periodically added additional features to the language, but these changes were also relatively minor. Meanwhile, a growing number of critics accused RPG of being difficult to understand because of its short data names, abbreviated operation codes, and rigidly fixed format. These critics contended that the language was showing its age in its limited choice of data types (e.g., no direct support for date data types), its inability to handle multidimensional arrays, and its patchwork approach to data definition.

To address some of these criticisms, in 1994, concurrent with the release of V3R1 of the AS/400's operating system, IBM introduced a version of RPG sufficiently unlike earlier versions that it warranted a change in name: RPG IV. In addition to trying to address the criticisms mentioned above, IBM included RPG as part of its newly introduced **Integrated Language Environment (ILE)**, which allows program modules to be first compiled and then bound together into executable programs. This change supported the growing interest in developing reusable units of code and improving system performance. Moreover, it allowed the programmer to develop an application using modules written in different languages and then bind these modules into a single application.

These changes have quieted, but not suppressed RPG's critics. However, given the large base of existing RPG applications and IBM's present willingness to support RPG, it is likely that the language will continue to evolve and will remain the primary language for application development on the AS/400 throughout this decade.

If you compared RPG programs written 20 years ago with those written by RPG professionals today, you would be struck by their great design differences. These differences are not due solely to the use of operations unavailable in the past, although the new operations enabled the changes. The biggest change is that RPG, originally a language that emphasized specification instead of procedure, has been transformed by programming practices into a procedural language. Today's programmers virtually ignore RPG's fixed-logic cycle — the feature that made the language unique in the 1960s. And most modern programmers use RPG's indicators only in those instances where the language absolutely requires their use.

Most RPG texts start by instructing students in RPG II, and introduce RPG III or RPG IV only after thoroughly indoctrinating the students in the fixed-logic cycle and the use of indicators. This book begins by teaching RPG as today's programmers use it. Only after you have mastered modern RPG will you become familiar with features of the language common in the past.

You may wonder why, if RPG programming has changed so much, you as a student need to bother learning features of the older versions of RPG. The reason is simple. For better or worse, most companies are still using some programs that were written 10 or more years ago. Because your first job in the computer profession probably will involve maintenance programming, you no doubt will be working with some programs based on RPG III, or even RPG II. Accordingly, you will need to understand the features of these language versions so you can modify such programs when you encounter them. The final chapter of this text points out the important differences between RPG II, RPG III, and RPG IV that you will need to know to complete your understanding of this language.

Now that you have an understanding of RPG's evolution, we can turn to some basic programming concepts that you need to know before you begin to learn RPG IV programming.

Program Variables

Computer programs would be of little value if you needed a different program each time you wanted to change the values of the data to be processed. For example, assume you were developing a payroll program, and one processing step was to multiply hours worked by pay rate. If you had to rewrite this step to state explicitly the number of hours worked and the hourly pay rate for each employee, you would be better off calculating wages by hand or with a calculator. The power and value of computer programming rests in the concept of variables.

A **program variable** represents a location in the memory of the computer that can store data. When a programming instruction involves the manipulation of a variable, the computer checks the value stored at that memory location and uses that value in the calculation. Thus, you can tell the computer to take the value stored in variable Hours and multiply that by the value stored in variable Rate and store the answer in variable GrossPay. If Hours contained 35 and Rate 6, GrossPay would become 210. If Hours contained 40 and Rate 5, GrossPay would become 200.

RPG generally uses the term **field** rather than variable. The language requires that you define all fields by naming them, assigning them a fixed length that determines the amount of memory allocated for storing each field's values, and declaring what type of data the field will contain. You will learn the methods RPG IV uses to define fields and the data types it allows in subsequent chapters of this book.

Data Files and the Data Hierarchy

In the business world, data processing typically centers on processing sets of data from files stored on disk or tape. Files of data of temporary importance, generated during the course of the day's business, are **transaction files**. Once you have processed a transaction file, you typically have no further use for it. In contrast, most companies have sets of data that are of long-term importance to the company. These files, called **master files**, contain vital information about customers, products, accounts, and so on. Although you may update or change master files, companies regard master files as permanent files of data.

All files, transaction or master, are organized into a data hierarchy of file-record-field. A **file** is a collection of data about a given kind of entity or object. For example, a business might have a customer master file that contains information about its customers. A file, in turn, is broken down into **records** that contain data about one specific instance of the entity. Data about customer #20 would be stored in a record within the customer file; data about customer #321 would be stored in a separate record within that file.

Finally, each record contains several discrete pieces of data about each entity instance. For example, a customer record might contain the customer's account number, last name, first name, street address, city, state, zip code, phone number, date of last order, credit limit, and so on. Each of these items is a **field**. A field generally represents the smallest unit of data that we want to manipulate within a program. Figure 1.1 illustrates this data hierarchy.

All records within a file usually contain the same fields of data. Because you define these fields to be fixed in length, if an alphanumeric value (for example, a person's last name) is shorter than the space allocated for it, blanks, or spaces, occupy the unused positions to the right of the value. If a numeric value is smaller than the space allocated for it, the system stores zeros in the unused positions. If quantity-on-hand, for example, was 6 positions long and had a value of 24, the value would be stored in the file as 000024. Note that numeric values are stored as "pure" numbers, without dollar signs, commas, or decimal points.

Figure 1.1
Example of
the Data Hierarchy

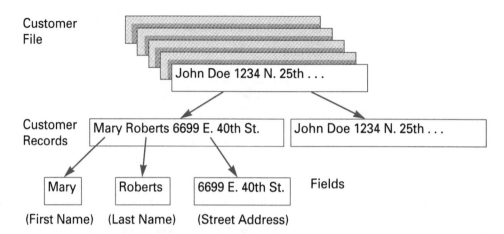

A file occasionally may contain different record types, each with its distinct format. In this case, each record usually contains a code field whose value signals which format that record represents. Figure 1.2 illustrates a data file with multiple record formats.

Figure 1.2
Order File with
Multiple Record Formats

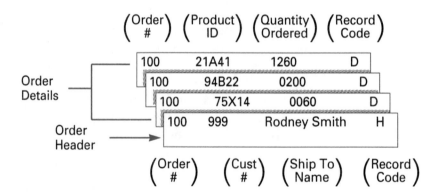

Programming Specifications

In many installations, programmers work from specifications given to them by systems analysts. These specifications detail the desired output of a program, the required input, and a general statement of the processing required. The programmer must then develop the instructions needed to generate the appropriate output from the given input, ensuring that the correct data manipulations take place.

Analysts often provide **record layouts** to describe the record formats of input files to be used by a program. One method of presenting a record layout shows the beginning and ending position of data fields within records; other methods list fields in the order in which they appear in records and give the length of each field or the positions of the fields within records. These methods, illustrated in Figure 1.3, include information about the number of decimal positions of numeric data.

Figure 1.3

Alternate Methods of
Describing Record Layouts

Item Number	Description	Quantity on Hand 0 decimals	Unit Cost 2 decimals	Vendor Code	Reorder Point 0 decimals
1 5	6 25	27 35	36 40	41 43	44 52

Field	Length	Decimal Positions
Item Number	5	
Description	20	
Quantity on Hand	9	0
Unit Cost	5	2
Vendor Code	3	
Reorder Point	9	0

Field	Positions	Decimal Positions
Item Number	1- 5	
Description	6-25	
Quantity on Hand	27-35	0
Unit Cost	36-40	2
Vendor Code	41-43	
Reorder Point	44-52	0

When the desired output includes a report, a **printer spacing chart (PSC)** provides the details of the desired report layout. The position of lines within the chart indicates the desired line spacing for the report. The printer spacing chart shows all constants (report headings or titles, column headings, and so on) that the report should include and where on the report they should appear. Printer spacing charts generally represent variable information with Xs, where each X represents one character of data.

We often want numeric data presented with special formats to facilitate comprehension. The printer spacing chart can depict the desired formatting, or **output editing**. Although there is no single accepted convention for indicating desired output editing, programmers generally recognize the notation presented in this chapter section (and used throughout this book).

Commas, decimal points, and other insertion characters included within the Xs signal that these characters are to appear in the printed output. A zero within the Xs signals that **zero suppression** is desired.

Zero suppression simply means that leading, nonsignificant zeros are not printed. Thus, 000123 would print as ƀƀƀ123 if zero suppression were in effect (ƀ = blank). The location of the 0 within the Xs indicates the extent to which blanks, rather than leading zeros, are to print. X0XX signals "suppress up to and including the hundred's place but no farther." With that format, 0001 should print as ƀƀƀ1. A zero at the end of the format — e.g., XXX0 — signals that zero suppression should continue to the rightmost digit; with that format, a value of 0000 should print as all blanks.

Dollar signs can appear two ways in output: as fixed or as floating dollar signs. A **fixed dollar sign** is positioned in a set column of the output, regardless of the number of significant digits in the number following the sign. A

floating dollar sign prints next to the left-most significant digit of the number; its position varies, or "floats," depending on the value of the number it is associated with. In a printer spacing chart, you can denote a fixed dollar sign by adding a single dollar sign to the immediate left of the Xs representing a numeric field. To signal a floating dollar sign, use two dollar signs, one at the far left of the Xs and the other in place of the zero suppression character.

PSC Notation	Meaning
$XXXX.XX	Fixed dollar sign, no zero suppression, no comma.
$X,XX0.XX	Fixed dollar sign, zero-suppress to unit's place, insert commas.
X,XX.XX	Floating dollar sign, zero-suppress to unit's place, insert commas.
XX0	No dollar sign or decimal; complete zero suppression.

Printer spacing charts also indicate how the analyst wants negative values to print. A single hyphen at the left signals a fixed negative sign. Two hyphens, one to the left and one in place of a zero, indicate a floating negative sign. A single hyphen or CR to the right of the Xs signals a fixed, trailing negative sign or Credit notation.

PSC Notation	Meaning
XXX	No sign to be displayed.
–XX0	Fixed sign, complete zero suppression.
–XX–.XX	Floating sign, zero-suppress to unit's place.
XX0.XX–	Zero-suppress, trailing negative sign.
XX0.XXCR	Zero-suppress, indicate negative value with CR.

Figure 1.4 illustrates a printer spacing chart that includes headings, lines of detailed information, departmental subtotals, and a grand total. Note that the chart indicates that slashes should be inserted within the date and that asterisks are to appear to the right of totals.

Figure 1.4
Sample Printer Spacing Chart

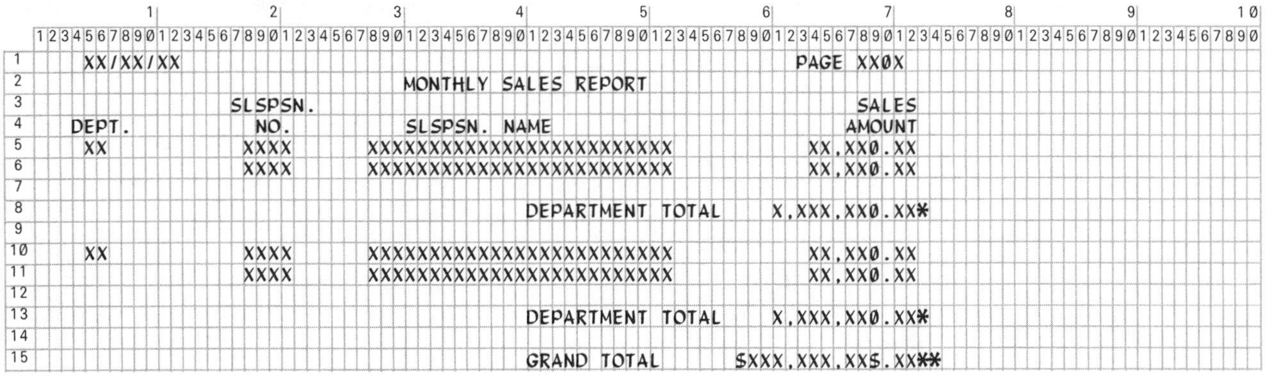

```
              1         2         3         4         5         6         7         8         9         1 0
     1234567890123456789012345678901234567890123456789012345678901234567890123456789012345678901234567890
 1    XX/XX/XX                                                     PAGE XX0X
 2                              MONTHLY SALES REPORT
 3              SLSPSN.                                                SALES
 4    DEPT.      NO.              SLSPSN. NAME                         AMOUNT
 5     XX       XXXX        XXXXXXXXXXXXXXXXXXXXXXXXXX             XX,XX0.XX
 6              XXXX        XXXXXXXXXXXXXXXXXXXXXXXXXX             XX,XX0.XX
 7
 8                                         DEPARTMENT TOTAL       X,XXX,XX0.XX*
 9
10     XX       XXXX        XXXXXXXXXXXXXXXXXXXXXXXXXX             XX,XX0.XX
11              XXXX        XXXXXXXXXXXXXXXXXXXXXXXXXX             XX,XX0.XX
12
13                                         DEPARTMENT TOTAL       X,XXX,XX0.XX*
14
15                                         GRAND TOTAL          $XXX,XXX,XX$.XX**
```

The Program Development Cycle

The programmer's job is to develop a solution to a data processing problem represented by the program specifications. The generally accepted method for achieving this solution is called the **Program Development Cycle**. This cycle, which summarizes the sequence of activities required in programming, can be summarized as follows:

- Define the problem.
- Design the solution.
- Write the program.
- Enter the program.
- Test and debug the program.
- Document the program.
- Maintain the program.

The cycle starts with *problem definition*. It should be obvious that unless you understand the problem, as described in the programming specifications, you have little chance of coming up with a correct solution.

Once you understand the problem, you need to design a solution to the problem. *Program design* requires working out the solution, or **algorithm**, to the problem before expressing the solution in a given programming language. Formal design tools such as program flow charts, Warnier-Orr diagrams, or pseudocode can help clarify and illustrate program logic. Some programmers develop their own methods of sketching out a program solution. Regardless of the method used, the importance of designing a solution *before* writing the program cannot be overemphasized. Developing a correct, well-structured design for a program represents the challenge of programming; this is the stage where most of your thinking should take place. Time spent at the design stage results in time saved fixing problems later in the cycle.

Writing the program is translating the design into a program using a particular programming language. This stage is often called "coding." Beginning programmers may find this task difficult because they are unfamiliar with the rules of the language. Once you have mastered the syntax of a language, however, coding becomes almost a mechanical process that requires relatively little thought. The challenge of programming lies in design.

Entering the program consists of inputting the program statements into the computer. Years ago, program statements were punched onto cards; today, most program entry is done interactively on a terminal, using a system utility called an **editor**.

Testing the program is required to determine the existence of syntax errors or logic errors in your solution. **Syntax errors** are errors in your use of the rules of the language. These errors are flagged by the computer, either as you enter the statements, or later, when the computer tries to translate your statements into machine language. **Logic errors** are errors of design; it is up to the programmer to detect such errors through rigorous program testing by running the program with sets of test data and carefully checking the accuracy of the program's output. **Debugging** means correcting any errors discovered. Testing should continue until you are convinced that the program is working correctly.

Documenting the program refers to providing material useful for understanding, using, or modifying the program. Some documentation, such as system and program flowcharts, user manuals, or operator instructions may be **external** to the program. **Internal documentation** refers to comments included within the code itself. Such comments make the program more understandable to other programmers. Although documentation appears as one of the final stages in the cycle, documentation is best developed as you progress through the stages of the cycle. For example, it is easiest to provide comments within a program as you are actually entering the program, rather than waiting until the program is completely tested and running.

Program maintenance is making modifications once the program is actually being used, or "in production." Estimates are that up to 70 percent of a programmer's time is spent modifying existing programs. The need for maintenance may arise from a "bug" discovered in the program or from changing user needs. Because maintenance is a way of life, any program you develop should be designed with future maintenance ease in mind. This means, among other things, that your code's logic should be clear, the variable names well-chosen, and the internal comments appropriate and sufficient.

Program Entry and Testing

To complete the program entry and testing stages, you need to eliminate all program errors. These errors fall into two general classes: syntax errors and logic errors. Syntax errors represent violation of the rules of the language itself; they are relatively easily detected and corrected. Logic errors are errors in your program that cause the program to produce incorrect results; these problems are detected by extensively testing the program with sets of test data and correcting any program statements that are causing incorrect processing.

As mentioned earlier, you typically enter a program by interacting with the system's editor. Your program statements are called **source code**; the set of statements for one program constitute a **source member** on the AS/400.

The AS/400 editor will detect some syntax errors as you enter your program and will allow you to correct them immediately. Other syntax errors become apparent when you attempt to **compile** your program. Compiling means translating the source code into machine language, or **object code**. The AS/400 has a program, called a compiler, that accomplishes this translation, provided that you have not violated any rules of RPG IV in writing your program. If syntax errors prevent the translation from completing, the compiler provides you with a list of the syntax errors it encountered. All such errors need to be fixed before you can progress to the next stage of testing.

If your program is free of syntax errors, the compiler creates a program module object. You must, in turn, **bind** the module (with other modules, if appropriate) to produce an executable program that can run on the AS/400. If your source code represents an entire program, the AS/400 command, CRTBNDRPG (Create Bound RPG Program), lets you combine compiling and binding into a single step.

Once you have successfully compiled and bound your program, you need to run it with test data to determine whether or not it is working correctly. Note that the computer executes the bound object code, or the translated version of your program. Errors discovered at this stage require that you back up, make changes to the program using the editor, and then recompile your program and bind it again before additional testing.

Figure 1.5 illustrates this iterative process. If you forget to recompile and bind your program after making changes to the source code, the program runs your *old* version of the program, because you have not created a new object incorporating those changes.

Figure 1.5
Flowchart Illustrating Steps
Required to Enter, Test, and
Debug a Program

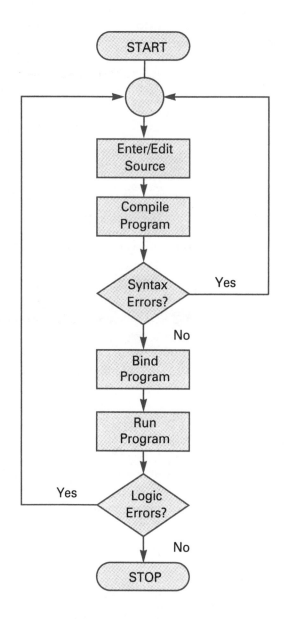

Chapter Summary

RPG (Report Program Generator) is a high-level programming language introduced by IBM in the early 1960s to provide an easy way to produce commonly needed business reports. Since introducing RPG, IBM has added enhancements to expand the language's functionality. Programmers originally used RPG's fixed-logic cycle and built-in indicators to minimize the need for explicit procedural instructions within their programs. As processing requirements have grown more complex and concerns for program understandability have increased, programmers have moved away from the fixed-logic cycle and now tend to explicitly include all processing instructions within their programs.

Variables enable programs to process different sets of data. RPG provides this flexibility through fixed-length fields that may represent character or numeric data. Data is typically organized in a hierarchy of files, records, and fields. Relatively temporary data files that often need to be processed only a single time are called transaction files, while files of data of lasting importance to the company are called master files.

The process of developing a program is often described as the Program Development Cycle. The cycle begins with problem definition. The problem often is presented through programming specifications, which include record layouts of files to be used by the program, printer spacing charts that describe the layout of desired reports, and an overview of needed processing.

In addition to defining the problem, the Program Development Cycle includes designing the solution, writing the program, entering the program, testing and debugging, documenting, and — eventually — maintaining the program once it is in production. Too often, programmers short-cut the design stage and try to develop their logic as they write the program. This approach often leads to programs that are poorly designed or full of errors that must be corrected.

You enter an RPG IV program as source code using the AS/400's editor. The program is stored as a source member within a source file on the system. Because computers actually execute machine language instructions, your source program needs to be translated to an object program of machine language before the computer can run it. A special program called a compiler performs this translation. As part of its translation, the compiler flags any entries in your source program that it cannot understand. These kinds of errors are called syntax errors, because they are caused by your misuse of the rules of the language. Syntax errors prevent the creation of an object program.

Once your program has successfully compiled, you need to bind it into an executable program and then test the program by running it with input data. You need to correct any logic errors in the program that are preventing the program from working correctly to produce the desired results. Each time you use the editor to correct a problem in your program, you must recompile the program and bind it again before running it to incorporate the changes into the executable program.

Terms

algorithm
batch processing
bind
bits (binary digits)
compile
compiler
debugging
editor
external documentation
field
file
fixed dollar sign
floating dollar sign
Fourth Generation
   Languages (4GLs)

high-level languages (HLLs)
indicator
Integrated Language
   Environment (ILE)
interactive applications
internal documentation
logic errors
master files
object code
output editing
printer spacing chart (PSC)
problem definition
procedural languages
program design
Program Development Cycle

program maintenance
program variable
record
record layouts
Report Program Generator
   (RPG)
source code
source member
structured design
syntax errors
transaction files
zero suppression

Discussion/Review Questions

1. What was the original purpose of RPG?

2. What's an indicator?

3. What trends emerged in the 1970s to influence the enhancements included in RPG III?

4. What criticisms influenced IBM's enhancements to RPG in RPG IV?

5. Do you think that a programming language that requires revisions over time is poorly designed in the first place? Why or why not?

6. Give an example of a syntax error and a logic error in your native language (e.g., English).

7. Would it make sense to describe a person's complete address (street address, city, state, zip code) as one field? Why or why not?

8. Would you define each letter in a person's last name as a separate field? Why or why not?

9. Keeping in mind the fact that all records within a file generally have the same, fixed number of fields, how do you think your school handles the problem of storing information about what courses you've taken?

10. Differentiate between source code and object code.

11. How many times do you need to compile a program?

12. Would you build a house without a blueprint? Is this a good analogy to writing a program without first designing it? Why or why not?

Exercises

1. Develop a list of data fields you think your school might store in its student master file. Design a record layout for this file that includes the length needed for each field, an indication of the data type (character or numeric), and the number of decimal positions of numeric fields.

2. For each printer spacing chart (PSC) notation that follows, show how the data value associated with each should appear when printed.

	PSC Notation	Data Value
a.	XXXXX	98100
b.	XXXXX	01254
c.	XX,XX0	31331
d.	XX,XX0	00010
e.	XX,XX0	01000
f.	XX,XX0	00000
g.	$XX,X0X	00872
h.	XX,XX	00298
i.	XX,XX	00000
j.	–XX,X–X	–07254
k.	–XX,X–X	00451
l.	XX,X0XDB	–00923
m.	XX,XX0–	–91486
n.	XX,XX0–	00000

Chapter 2

Getting Started

Chapter Overview

This chapter introduces you to RPG IV specifications. You will learn how to write simple read/write programs using a procedural approach. You will also learn how to include comments within your programs as documentation. Finally, this chapter teaches you RPG's techniques of output editing to control the appearance of values on reports.

Specifications in RPG IV

RPG IV programs consist of different kinds of lines, called specifications; each type of specification has a particular purpose. You use **File Description Specifications**, for example, to identify the files your program uses, and **Calculation Specifications** to detail the arithmetic operations to be performed by your program. Each kind of specification has a different identifier, or form type, which must appear in position 6 of each program line. A File Description Specification line of code, for example, must include an F in position 6.

Not every program requires the use of every kind of specification. However, all those that you use must appear in a specific order, or sequence, within your program, with all program lines representing the same kind of specification grouped together. You will learn this order as you are introduced to the details of each kind of specification.

For the most part, RPG IV programs require fixed-position entries within these specification forms. **Fixed-position**, or **fixed-form**, means that the location of an entry within a program line is critical to its interpretation by the RPG IV compiler. If you use coding sheets to develop your program, the sheets have headings to help you make the correct entries in the correct locations. **Source Entry Utility (SEU)**, the AS/400 editor you use to enter your program, also can provide you with prompts to facilitate making your entries in the proper location. (Appendix B provides more information about SEU.) The code samples in this book use two (or more) header lines to help you determine where to make your entries: the first header line indicates column position, while the other line (or lines) contains "prompts" similar to those given within SEU.

As you begin to work with specifications, don't be overwhelmed by what appear to be hundreds of entries with multiple options. Fortunately, many entries are optional, and you will use them only for complex processing or for achieving specific effects. This book will introduce these entries gradually, initially providing you with just those entries needed to write simple programs. As your mastery of the language grows, you will learn how to use additional specification entries required to develop more complex programs.

When you begin writing your first program, you will notice that an entry does not always take up all the positions allocated for it within a specification. When that happens, a good rule of thumb is that alphabetic entries start at the left-most position of the allocated space, with unused positions to the right; numeric entries are usually right-adjusted, with unused positions to the left.

Program Specifications for Example Program

In this chapter, you will learn the minimal entries needed to procedurally code a simple read/write program. To help you understand how to write such a program, we will walk through writing an RPG IV program to solve the following problem.

You have a file, SalesMast; records in the file are laid out as follows:

Field	Positions	Decimal Positions
Salesperson number	1- 4	0
Salesperson name	5-34	
Item sold	35-50	
Date of sale	51-56	0
Sale price	57-63	2

You want to produce a report laid out as follows:

```
          1         2         3         4         5         6         7         8         9        10
 1234567890123456789012345678901234567890123456789012345678901234567890123456789012345678901234567890
 1
 2   PAGE XX0X                  WEEKLY SALES REPORT           DATE XX/XX/XX
 3
 4 SLSPSN.                                  DATE OF                          SALE
 5 NO.                  NAME                 SALE       ITEM SOLD            PRICE
 6
 7 XXXX    XXXXXXXXXXXXXXXXXXXXXXXXXXXXXX    XX/XX/XX   XXXXXXXXXXXXXXXX    XX.XX0.XX
 8 XXXX    XXXXXXXXXXXXXXXXXXXXXXXXXXXXXX    XX/XX/XX   XXXXXXXXXXXXXXXX    XX.XX0.XX
```

When you compare the desired output to the input record layout, you should note that all the output fields are present on the input records. No data transformation or generation needs to take place within the program. The processing required, then, consists of reading each record from the input file, writing that data to the report with appropriate headings, and formatting the variable data.

File Description Specifications

Generally, RPG IV programs begin with File Description Specifications (also called the shorter name, File Specifications). All File Specifications include an F in position 6. These specifications describe the files your program uses and define how the files will be used within the program. Each file used by a program requires its own File Specification line. In our illustrative problem, file SalesMast contains the data we want to process.

The output of the program is a report. Although you generally think of a report as hard-copy, rather than a file *per se*, on the AS/400 you produce a report through a printer file. We normally use a system-supplied printer file, QPRINT, as the destination file for our report lines. This file then resides as a spooled file in an output queue, where it will wait for you to release it to the printer. Your instructor will tell you which printer file to use in your programs and explain how to work with spooled files in the output queue. Appendix A of this text also contains helpful information about working with output on the AS/400.

You need to code one File Specification for each file the program uses. Although you can describe the files in any order, it is customary to describe the input file first. The figure below shows the layout of a File Specification. Note that in addition to column positions, the layout includes prompts to help you remember where to insert required entries.

```
*.. 1 ...+... 2 ...+... 3 ...+... 4 ...+... 5 ...+... 6 ...+... 7 ...+... 8 ...+... 9 ...+...1Ø
FFilename++IPEASFRlen+LKlen+AIDevice+.Keywords+++++++++++++++++++++++++++++Comments++++++++++++
```

File Name (positions 7-16)
First, in positions 7-16 (labeled Filename on the specification line), enter the name of the file. In RPG IV, file names can be a maximum of 10 characters long. They must begin with an alphabetic character or $, #, or @; the remaining characters may be alphabetic characters, numbers, or any of the four special characters _, #, $, and @. RPG IV allows the use of both upper-case and lowercase alphabetic characters, but the language is not **case sensitive**. Thus, any lowercase letter you use within a file or variable name will be interpreted as its uppercase equivalent by the compiler. A file name cannot contain blanks embedded within the permissible characters.

Our practice problem input file is called SalesMast. The report file is QPRINT. Note that you code file names, like other alphabetic entries, beginning in the left-most position allowed for that entry — in this case, position 7. Simply leave blank any unneeded positions to the right of the name.

File Type (position 17)
Position 17 (labeled I on the specification line), specifies the type of file, or how the file will be used by the program. The two types we will initially work with are input (type I) and output (type O). An **input file** contains data to be read by the program; an **output file** is the destination for writing operations of the program. In our example, SalesMast is an input file, while QPRINT is an output file.

File Designation (position 18; input files only)
Every input file requires an entry for file designation (position 18, labeled P). File designation refers to the way the program will access, or retrieve, the data in the file. In our example, we are going to retrieve data by explicitly reading records within our program, rather than by using the built-in retrieval of RPG's fixed-logic cycle. In RPG terminology, that makes the file **full procedural**, so F is the appropriate entry for position 18.

File Format (position 22)
The next required entry is file format. An F in position 22 (labeled F) stands for fixed format, which means that file records will be described within this program and that each record has the same, fixed length. Although it is preferable to describe files externally, for simplicity's sake we will start with program-described files and progress to externally described files later (Chapter 5). Because our files will be program-described, an F is appropriate for the files of our sample program. All files, regardless of type, require an entry for file format.

Record Length (positions 23-27)
You need to define the record length for each program-described file. Records of data files can be of almost any length; it is important that you code the correct value for this specification. Because SalesMast has a record length of 63, we enter 63 in positions 23-27. Note that record length is coded right-adjusted within the positions allocated for this entry. This is typical of most RPG IV entries requiring a numeric value.

Most printers support a line of 132 characters. As a result, records of printer files (which correspond to lines of report output) are 132 positions long. Accordingly, output file QPRINT is assigned a record length of 132 on its File Specification.

Device (positions 36-42)
A final required entry is Device. Database files are stored on disk. Accordingly, DISK is the appropriate entry for the SalesMast file. The device associated with printer files is PRINTER. These device names are entered left-adjusted in positions 36-42.

No other File Specification entries are required to describe the files used by our sample program. The completed File Specifications for the program are shown below.

```
*.. 1 ...+... 2 ...+... 3 ...+... 4 ...+... 5 ...+... 6 ...+... 7 ...+... 8 ...+... 9 ...+...10
FFilename++IPEASFRlen+LKlen+AIDevice+.Keywords+++++++++++++++++++++++++++++Comments+++++++++++
FSalesMast IF   F  63        DISK
FQPRINT     O   F 132        PRINTER
```

Input Specifications

Input Specifications, identified by an I in position 6, come after File Specifications. Input Specifications describe the records within program-described input files and define the fields within the records. Every program-described input file defined on the File Specifications must be represented by a set of Input Specification lines.

Input Specifications use two types of lines: lines representing record identification entries, which describe the input records at a general level, and lines representing field description entries, which describe the specific fields within the records. The record identification line must precede the field entries for that record. The general layout for these two kinds of Input Specifications is shown below.

```
*.. 1 ...+... 2 ...+... 3 ...+... 4 ...+... 5 ...+... 6 ...+... 7 ...+... 8 ...+... 9 ...+...10
IFilename++SqNORiPos1+NCCPos2+NCCPos3+NCC...................................Comments++++++++++
I......................Fmt+SPFrom+To+++DcField++++++++++L1M1FrP1MnZr......Comments++++++++++
```

Record Identification Entries

File Name (positions 7-16)
A record identification line must contain the name of the input file in positions 7-16 (labeled Filename on the specification line). This name must match the entry on the File Specification, in our case, SalesMast. The file name is a left-adjusted entry.

Sequence (positions 17-18)
The next required record identification entry is Sequence, in positions 17-18 (labeled Sq). This entry signals whether or not the system should check the order of records in the file as the records are read during program execution. Sequence checking is relevant only when a file contains multiple record formats (that is, records with different field layouts). When sequence checking is not appropriate, code any two alphabetic characters in positions 17-18 to signal that sequence checking is not required. Many programmers use NS to signal "no sequence." Because the SalesMast file contains a single record format, we enter NS in positions 17-18.

The complete record identification specification is illustrated below. Note that with the specification coded as shown, the compiler will issue a warning that a record identification indicator is missing from the line. Although record identification indicators are relevant in fixed-logic processing (discussed in Chapter 13), they are not used in modern RPG programming. Simply ignore the compiler warning; it will not prevent your program from successfully compiling.

```
*.. 1 ...+... 2 ...+... 3 ...+... 4 ...+... 5 ...+... 6 ...+... 7 ...+... 8 ...+... 9 ...+...10
IFilename++SqNORiPos1+NCCPos2+NCCPos3+NCC...................................Comments++++++++++
ISalesMast NS
```

Field Description Entries

Field description entries immediately follow the record description entry. You define each field within a record by giving it a valid name, specifying its length, and declaring its data type. Although you can define the fields of a record in any order, convention dictates that fields be described in order from the start of the record to the record's end.

Field Location (positions 37-46)
You define a field's length by specifying the beginning position and ending position of a field within the input record. The beginning position is coded as the "from" location (positions 37-41 of the Input Specifications, labeled From+). The ending position is the "to" location (positions 42-46, labeled To+++). If the field is one byte long, the "from" and "to" entries will be identical, because the field begins and ends in the same location of the record.

Enter the beginning and ending positions right-adjusted within the positions allocated for these entries. You do not need to enter leading, nonsignificant zeros.

Decimal Positions (position 47-48)
The decimal position entry determines the data type of the field it is associated with. To define a field as a **character field**, leave the decimal position entry blank. To define a field as a **numeric field**, include a decimal position entry in positions 47-48 (labeled Dc). In RPG IV, a field must be numeric to be used in arithmetic calculations or to be edited for output, so it is important not to overlook the decimal position entry. If a numeric field represents **integer data** (i.e., whole numbers), the appropriate entry for its decimal positions is 0 (zero). RPG IV numeric fields can contain a maximum of 30 positions to the right of the decimal point. (A more complete discussion of RPG IV data types will occur in Chapter 5).

Field Name (positions 49-62)
The last required entry for a field description specification is a name for the field being described. This name, entered left-adjusted in positions 49-62 (labeled Field+++++++++), must adhere to the rules for valid field names in RPG IV. A valid field name

- contains 10 or fewer characters
- uses alphabetic letters, digits, or the special characters _, #, @, and $
- does not begin with a digit or an underscore
- does not include embedded blanks

The alphabetic characters can be uppercase and/or lowercase. RPG IV does not distinguish between letters on the basis of their case, but using a combination of uppercase and lowercase characters makes your field names easier for others to understand.

Although not a requirement of RPG IV, it is also good programming practice to choose field names that reflect the data that they represent by making full use of the 10-character name limit. LoanNumber is far superior to X for the name of a field that will store loan numbers. Choosing good field names can prevent your accidental use of the wrong field as you write your program and can help clarify your program's processing to others who may have to modify that program.

The field description entries of the Input Specifications for our sample program are shown below.

```
*.. 1 ...+... 2 ...+... 3 ...+... 4 ...+... 5 ...+... 6 ...+... 7 ...+... 8 ...+... 9 ...+...10
I..........................Fmt+SPFrom+To+++DcField++++++++++L1M1FrP1MnZr......Comments++++++++++++
I                            1    4 ØSlspNumber
I                            5   34  SlspName
I                           35   50  ItemNumber
I                           51   56 ØDateOfSale
I                           57   63 2Price
```

In the above Input Specifications for our sample program, we defined SlspNumber (salesperson number), DateOfSale (date of sale) and Price (sale price) as numeric by including decimal position entries in positions 47-48.

Output Specifications

Although Calculation Specifications follow immediately after Input Specifications in RPG programs, we will first discuss **Output Specifications**, because their required entries in many ways parallel those required on Input Specifications. Every program-described output file on the File Specifications needs a set of Output Specifications that provide details about the output required. All Output Specification lines require an O in position 6.

Output Specifications, like Input Specifications, include two kinds of lines: record identification lines, which deal with the output at the record level, and field description lines, which describe the content of a given output record. When output is a report, rather than a data file, "record" translates to "report line." Most reports include several different report-line formats; each needs definition on the Output Specifications.

To refresh your memory, our output file, QPRINT, is to contain a weekly sales report, formatted as shown in the printer spacing chart repeated below.

The desired report includes four different kinds of lines, or record formats. Three of the lines are headings, which should appear at the top of the page of the report, while the fourth is a detail line of variable information. The term **detail line** means that one line is to print for each record in an input file. The line prints detailed information about the data records being processed.

The complete Output Specifications to produce the above report are shown in the following figure. You should refer to this figure again as you read about the required Output Specification entries.

```
*.. 1 ...+... 2 ...+... 3 ...+... 4 ...+... 5 ...+... 6 ...+... 7 ...+... 8 ...+... 9 ...+...10
OFilename++DF..N01N02N03Excnam++++B++A++Sb+Sa+.............................Comments+++++++++++
O.............N01N02N03Field++++++++YB.End++PConstant/editword/DTformat++Comments+++++++++++
OQPRINT    E           Headings      2  2
O                                          8 'PAGE'
O                      PAGE           13
O                                         50 'WEEKLY SALES REPORT'
O                                         64 'DATE'
O                      UDATE         Y  73
O          E           Headings      1
O                                          7 'SLSPSN.'
O                                         48 'DATE OF'
O                                         77 'SALE'
O          E           Headings      2
O                                          3 'NO.'
O                                         21 'NAME'
O                                         46 'SALE'
O                                         61 'ITEM SOLD'
O                                         77 'PRICE'
O          E           Detail        1
O                      SlspNumber        4
O                      SlspName         37
O                      DateOfSale    Y  48
O                      ItemNumber       67
O                      Price         1  79
```

Record Identification Entries

Output Specifications require a record identification entry for each different line of the report. Each of these lines, representing a record format, must be followed with detailed information about what that record format (or report line) contains. Because our report has four different kinds of lines to describe, we have four record-format descriptions in our Output Specifications. The figure below illustrates the layout for record identification entries. The following discussions will refer to this layout.

```
*.. 1 ...+... 2 ...+... 3 ...+... 4 ...+... 5 ...+... 6 ...+... 7 ...+... 8 ...+... 9 ...+...10
OFilename++DF..N01N02N03Excnam++++B++A++Sb+Sa+.............................Comments+++++++++++
```

File Name (positions 7-16)
The first record identification entry requires a file name entry in positions 7-16 (labeled Filename++ on the Output Specifications). This file name serves to associate the record being described with the output file described on the File Specifications. Thus QPRINT, our output file, appears as the file name

entered on the first record-format line of the Output Specifications. Although the Output Specifications include four record-format descriptions, because each describes a format to be written to the same file, QPRINT, you do not have to repeat the file name entry on subsequent record-format entry lines.

Type (position 17)

Each record-format description requires an entry in position 17 (labeled D) to indicate the type of line being described. In this context, "type" refers to how RPG IV is to handle printing the line. Because we will be using procedural techniques to generate the report instead of relying on RPG's fixed-logic cycle, all the record-format lines are Exception lines. As a consequence, we enter an E in position 17 of each record-format line.

Exception Name (position 30-39)

In RPG IV, it is common practice to provide a name in positions 30-39 (labeled Excnam++++) for each exception line. Although not required, such names allow you to control printing without the use of indicators. By using exception names, you can easily reference lines to print from within your Calculation Specifications.

Moreover, you can assign the same name to lines that need to be printed as a group at the same time. Because our report has three lines that should print together at the top of a page, we have given each the name Headings. The fourth line, which will print the variable information from our data file, is identified as Detail. Note that Headings and Detail are arbitrarily assigned names, not RPG-reserved terms. Exception-line names follow the same rules of naming as do field names, and they are coded left-adjusted within the allocated area of the specification form.

Space and Skip Entries (positions 40-51)

One more set of entries is needed to complete the record-format line definitions. These entries describe vertical alignment of a given line within a report page or relative to other report lines. Two kinds of entries control this vertical alignment: Space entries and Skip entries. Each variant offers "before" and "after" options.

For accurate placement of report lines, it is important to understand the differences between Space and Skip entries. Space is analogous to the carriage return on a typewriter, or the Enter key on a computer. Each Space is the equivalent of hitting the Return (or Enter) key. Space before (positions 40-42, labeled B++) is like hitting the Return key before you type a line, while Space after (positions 43-45, labeled A++) equates to hitting Return *after* you type a line.

The same record-format line can include both a Space before and a Space after entry. If both the Space before and Space after entries are left blank within a record-format description, the system defaults to Space 1 after printing, the equivalent of single-spacing. If you have either a Space before or a Space after entry explicitly coded and the other entry blank, the blank entry defaults to 0.

In contrast to Space, Skip entries instruct the printer to "skip to" the designated line on a page. Skip 3 before printing causes the printer to advance to the third line on a page before printing; Skip 20 after printing causes the printer to advance to the twentieth line on the page after printing a line. If the printer is already past that position on a given page, a Skip entry causes the paper to advance to the designated position on the next page. Most often you will have a Skip before entry only for the first heading line of a report. Programmers most often use Skip entries to advance to the top of each new report page.

You code any Skip before entry in positions 46-48 (labeled Sb+), while Skip after entries are made in positions 49-51 (labeled Sa+). If you do not code any skip entries, the system assumes that you do not want any skipping to occur. The maximum value you can specify for any Space or Skip entry is 255.

Because we want the first heading of our report to print on the second line of a page, we code a Skip 2 before entry in positions 46-48 of the record-format line describing that line. The Space 2 after entry (positions 43-45) for that same heading line will advance the printer head to the correct position for the second Headings line. The figure below reproduces the record description entry for the first heading line to show how its entries correspond to the output record description labels.

```
*.. 1 ...+... 2 ...+... 3 ...+... 4 ...+... 5 ...+... 6 ...+... 7 ...+... 8 ...+... 9 ...+...10
OFilename++DF..N01N02N03Excnam++++B++A++Sb+Sa+..............................Comments++++++++++
OQPRINT    E          Headings       2 2
```

The second Headings line, with its Space 1 after entry, positions the printer head for the third Headings line, which in turn, with its Space 2 after entry, positions the printer head for the first Detail line of data to print. Because the report detail lines are to print single-spaced, exception line Detail contains a Space 1 after entry.

Field Description Entries

Each record-format line of the Output Specifications is followed by field description entries that describe the contents of the line. Each field-level specification identifies an item to appear as part of the record format it is associated with, indicates where the item is to appear within the record format, and specifies any special output formatting for that item.

Field-level items to be included within a record format may be entered in any order, although conventionally programmers enter them in the order in which they actually are to appear in the output. The figure below illustrates the layout for these field description entries.

```
*.. 1 ...+... 2 ...+... 3 ...+... 4 ...+... 5 ...+... 6 ...+... 7 ...+... 8 ...+... 9 ...+...10
O.............N01N02N03Field++++++++YB.End++PConstant/editword/DTformat++Comments++++++++++++
```

Field Name (positions 30-43)

The name of each field whose value is to appear as part of the output record is coded in positions 30-43 (labeled Field+++++++++). Any field appearing as part of the Output Specifications must have been defined earlier in the program.

In our sample program, most of the fields to print are part of the Detail record format. These are the same fields — SlspNumber, SlspName, DateOfSale, ItemNumber, and Price — that we defined as part of our input record. By including these field names in the output, each time our program processes a successive record from the input file, each Detail line printed will contain the data values present in those fields of the input record.

In addition to the input fields, two RPG IV reserved words, which function as built-in, predefined fields, appear as part of the report headings. In the first Headings line, notice the field name PAGE. RPG supplies this field to automatically provide the correct page numbers for a report. PAGE, a 4-byte numeric field, has an initial value of 1; that value is automatically incremented by 1 each time the report begins a new page.

The UDATE field, also appearing as part of the first Headings line, is another RPG IV reserved word. UDATE, a 6-byte numeric field, stores the current date in MMDDYY format. Anytime your program needs to access the date on which the program is running, you can simply use UDATE as a field. Reserved words UDAY, UMONTH, and UYEAR allow you to individually access the day, month, and year portions of the current date.

Constants (positions 53-80)

In addition to fields, whose values change through the course of a program's execution, Output Specifications typically contain **constants**, or **literals**: characters that do not change, and instead represent the actual values that are to appear on the report. Enter each constant, enclosed with apostrophes, in positions 53-80 (labeled Constant/editword/DTformat++) of the Output Specifications. The left apostrophe should appear in position 53; that is, enter constants left-adjusted within positions 53-80. A constant cannot appear on the same Output Specification line as a field; each needs its own line.

In our sample program, the first heading is to contain the word PAGE, as well as the page number. Accordingly, 'PAGE' is coded as a constant within the first Heading line. Also, part of this first heading is the title, WEEKLY SALES REPORT. Although several words make up this constant, the group of words is entered as a single constant, enclosed in apostrophes; the spaces between the words form part of the constant.

The second and third report lines, or record formats, consist of column headings for the report. These, too, are handled as constants, with the appropriate values entered in positions 53-80. Notice that the column heading lines are broken up into conveniently sized logical units, and that each unit is then coded as a separate constant.

Note also that you can ignore blank, or unused, positions in output lines, unless they appear within a string of characters you wish to handle as a single constant (e.g., 'DATE OF', or 'ITEM SOLD').

Although they are not appropriate for our current report, output continuation lines introduced in RPG IV let you code long constants as a single entry that spans more than one specification line. The layout for the continuation form of the Output Specification is shown below.

```
*.. 1 ...+... 2 ...+... 3 ...+... 4 ..+... 5 ...+... 6 ...+... 7 ...+... 8 ...+... 9 ...+...10
O.................................................Constant/Editword-continues+Comments+++++++++++
```

Assume, for example, you are defining a report that is to be captioned "ACME EXPLOSIVES SALES REPORT," a constant too long to fit on one specification line. You can code this as a single constant on two (or more) specification lines by using this continuation feature.

Code the ending position for the entire constant on the first line, together with some portion of the constant; then signal that the constant is continued by terminating the entry on the first line with a hyphen (-) or a plus (+). A hyphen signals that the continuation resumes with the *first position* (i.e., position 53) of the continued constant on the next line, while a plus signals that the continuation resumes with the *first non-blank character* encountered in the continued constant on the next line. This output feature is illustrated below. Notice that you use an apostrophe only at the very beginning and very end of the continued constant, rather than needing a set of apostrophes on each line.

```
*.. 1 ...+... 2 ...+... 3 ...+... 4 ...+... 5 ...+... 6 ...+... 7 ...+... 8 ...+... 9 ...+...10
O..............N01N02N03Field++++++++YB.End++PConstant/editword/DTformat++Comments+++++++++++
O.................................................Constant/Editword-continues+Comments+++++++++++
O*The two examples below would produce the same output because of the use of the + and -.
O                                      90 'ACME EXPLOSIVES SALES +
O                                              REPORT'
O                                      90 'ACME EXPLOSIVES SALES -
O                                              REPORT'
```

End Position in Output Record (positions 47-51)
You denote where a field or constant appears within a line by coding its end position (position of its right-most character) within the line. Specify an end position by entering a numeric value that represents the actual position desired for the right-most character of the field or constant. Such an entry should be right-adjusted within positions 47-51 (labeled End++).

For example, because we want the 'E' in constant 'PAGE' to appear in column 8 of the first heading line of our sample report, we coded 8 in position 51 of the specification entry for the constant 'PAGE'. The printer spacing chart indicates that the right-most digit of the page number should appear in column 13 of the report line. Accordingly, 13 is the specified end position for field Page within its Output Specification line.

Our Output Specifications include an end position for each field or constant that is part of our report. If you omit an end position for a field or constant, that item is output immediately adjacent to the previous item with no blanks separating the items.

You can also optionally specify the placement of a field or constant relative to the end position of the previously defined field. To use this alternative method, put a plus sign (+) in position 47 and a numeric value right-adjusted in the remaining positions. The value tells how many blanks you want between the end of the previous field and the beginning position of the current field. The figure below illustrates how you would code the Detail line of our report using this relative notation.

```
*.. 1 ...+... 2 ...+... 3 ...+... 4 ...+... 5 ...+... 6 ...+... 7 ...+... 8 ...+... 9 ...+...10
OFilename++DF..N01N02N03Excnam++++B++A++Sb+Sa+.............................Comments+++++++++++
O.............N01N02N03Field++++++++YB.End++PConstant/editword/DTformat++Comments+++++++++++
O           E          Detail          1
O                      SlspNumber          4
O                      SlspName        +   3
O                      DateOfSale   Y  +   3
O                      ItemNumber      +   3
O                      Price        1  +   3
```

The above code will end field SlspNumber in position 4 and put three blanks between the end of SlspNumber and the start of SlspName, 3 blanks between the end of SlspName and the start of DateOfSale, and so on.

Edit Codes (position 44)
Three of the fields appearing in the output — UDATE, DateOfSale, and Price — have an entry in position 44, Edit Codes (labeled Y). An **edit code** formats numeric values to make them more readable. The Y edit code associated with UDATE and DateOfSale inserts slashes within the date printed. Thus, if DateOfSale has a value of 122093, it will print as 12/20/93.

Edit code 1 causes commas and a decimal point to be inserted within the printed value of Price and signals that if Price is 0, the zero balance should appear on the report, rather than being completely suppressed. RPG IV includes a large selection of editing alternatives to allow you to print or display values with a format most appropriate to your needs. A detailed discussion of these editing features appears at the end of this chapter.

Calculation Specifications

We have now defined the files to be used by our application, the format of the input records to be processed, and the desired output of the application. All we need to complete our program is to describe the processing steps required to obtain the input and write the report. We use Calculation Specifications to describe these processing steps.

Before coding the Calculation Specifications, you need to develop the logic required to produce the desired output. Generally this stage of the Program Development Cycle, designing the solution, would be completed before any program coding, but we delayed program design to introduce you to some of the RPG IV specifications, to give you a taste of the language.

We can sketch out the required processing of our program using pseudocode. **Pseudocode** is simply stylized English that details the underlying logic needed for a program. Although there is no single standard for the format used with pseudocode, key control words generally are capitalized, and indentation is used to show the scope of control of the logic structures. It is always a good idea to work out the design of your program before actually coding it in RPG IV (or in any other language). Pseudocode is language-independent and allows you to focus on what needs to be done, rather than on the specific syntax requirements of a programming language.

Our program exemplifies a simple read/write program in which we want to read a record, write a line on the report, and repeat the process until there are no more records in the file (a condition called **end-of-file**). This kind of application is called *batch processing*, because once the program begins, a "batch" of data, accumulated in a file, directs its execution. Batch programs can run unattended because they do not require control or instructions from a user.

The logic required by our read/write program is quite simple.

Correct Algorithm
Write report headings
Read a record
WHILE there are more records
    Write a detail line
    Read the next record
ENDWHILE
END program

Note that WHILE indicates a repeated process, or loop. Within the loop the processing requirements for a single record are detailed (in this case, simply writing a report line) and then the next record is input. Because we want to print report headings just once at the beginning of the report, rather than once for each record, that step is listed at the beginning of the pseudocode, outside the loop.

You may wonder why there are two read statements in the pseudocode. Why can't there just be a single read, as in the first step within the WHILE loop below?

Incorrect Algorithm
Write report headings
WHILE there are more records
    Read the next record
    Write a detail line
ENDWHILE
END program

The preceding algorithm would work fine as long as each READ operation retrieved a data record from the file. The problem is that eventually the system will try to read an input record and fail because there are no more records in the file to read. Once a program has reached end-of-file, it should not attempt to process any more input data. The incorrect algorithm above would inappropriately write a detail line after reaching end-of-file.

The correct algorithm places the read statement as the last step within the WHILE, so that as soon as end-of-file is detected, no further writing will occur. However, if that were the only read, our algorithm would try to write the first detail line before reading any data. That's why the algorithm also requires an initial read (often called a **priming read**) just before the WHILE to "prime" the processing cycle.

After you have designed the program, it is a simple matter to express that logic in a programming language — once you have learned its syntax. The Calculation Specifications in the following figure show the correct algorithm expressed in RPG IV.

```
*.. 1 ...+... 2 ...+... 3 ...+... 4 ...+... 5 ...+... 6 ...+... 7 ...+... 8 ...+... 9 ...+...10
CLØNØ1Factor1++++++Opcode(E)+Factor2++++++Result++++++++Len++D+HiLoEq....Comments+++++++++++
CLØNØ1Factor1++++++Opcode(E)+Extended-factor2+++++++++++++++++++++++++++++Comments+++++++++++
C                   EXCEPT    Headings
C                   READ      SalesMast                              90
C                   DOW       *IN90 = *OFF
C                   EXCEPT    Detail
C                   READ      SalesMast                              90
C                   ENDDO
C                   EVAL      *INLR = *ON
C                   RETURN
```

Calculation Specifications specify what processing needs to be done. Calculation Specifications include a C in position 6 of the specification line. Each Calculation Specification contains an operation, entered in positions 26-35 (labeled Opcode(E)+). Depending on the operation, specifications may also include a value in factor 1 (positions 12-25), factor 2 (positions 36-49), the result field (positions 50-63), or the extended factor 2 field (positions 36-80). Indicators associated with operations may also appear in positions 71-76, as discussed in the next section.

The Calculation Specifications execute sequentially from beginning to end, unless the computer encounters an operation that redirects flow of control. Our program uses six operations: EXCEPT, READ, DOW, ENDDO, EVAL, and RETURN. Because some of these operations involve indicators, you should learn more about indicators before considering each specific operation.

Indicators and Calculations

An **indicator** in RPG IV is a built-in character variable with only two possible values: '0' (*OFF) and '1' (*ON). Indicators signal whether or not certain events have occurred during processing and can be used, in turn, to control subsequent processing. RPG IV provides 99 numbered indicators (01, 02, 03, ..., 98, 99) for you to use in your program.

Many RPG IV operations can turn on an indicator or indicators, depending on what happens during the operation's execution. These indicators are called *resulting indicators*, because their status depends upon the result of a calculation. You code these indicators in positions 71-76 (labeled HiLoEq) of the Calculation Specifications. As its label implies, this area is actually divided into three two-position areas (positions 71-72, 73-74, and 75-76) for indicator specifications. Many RPG IV operations require coding an indicator in one of these three areas to signal the results or effect of the operation when the program is running; other operations optionally let you associate indicators with their execution.

In turn, you can use these indicators as fields with operations that control subsequent processing. To reference an indicator as a field, you simply add *IN as a prefix to the indicator name. Thus, *IN90 is indicator 90 treated as a field. If the indicator has been turned on, its value will be '1' (also expressed as *ON); otherwise, its value is '0' (or *OFF).

With that overview of indicators, we can look at the specific operations used within the calculations of our program. The intent here is to provide you with sufficient information to understand our basic program and to write similar programs. Several of the operations described in the following section are discussed in more detail in subsequent chapters of this book.

RPG IV Operations

EXCEPT (Calculation Time Output)

An EXCEPT operation directs the program to output an E line or lines from the output specifications. This operation never includes a value in factor 1 (positions 12-25) or the result field (positions 50-63). The use of factor 2 (positions 36-49) is optional. If factor 2 is blank, the operation causes the system to output all *unnamed E lines*. Generally, however, RPG programmers name their E lines and use the EXCEPT operation with an E-line name in factor 2 to state explicitly which line or lines are to be involved in the output operation. In the sample program, the first EXCEPT operation has Headings as a factor 2 entry. As a result, the three heading lines of our report will print. A second EXCEPT specifies Detail in factor 2. When the program executes this line of code, our exception line named Detail prints.

READ (Read Sequentially)

READ is an input operation that instructs the computer to retrieve the next sequential record from the input file named in factor 2 (positions 36-49), in this case, our SalesMast file. To use the READ operation with a file, you must have defined that file as input-capable on the File Specifications.

Notice that each READ statement has a two-digit number entered in positions 75-76, the "Equal" indicator position, toward the right side of the specification. This number — in our case, 90 — designates which indicator we want to turn on when a READ operation encounters end-of-file (runs out of records). You can use any one of RPG's indicators for this purpose, but most programmers use indicators in the 90s for end-of-file signals.

DOW (Do While)
The DOW operation establishes a loop in RPG IV. The end of the loop is signaled by an ENDDO. Note that this DOW and ENDDO correspond to the WHILE and ENDWHILE statements in our pseudocode. The DOW of our program reads, "Do while indicator 90 is off," and is the direct equivalent of the pseudocode statement, "While there are more records...," because indicator 90 will come on only when our READ operation runs out of records.

ENDDO (End Do Group)
This operation serves to mark the end of the scope of a DO operation. All the program statements between the DO operation and its associated ENDDO are repeated as long as the DO operation is in effect.

EVAL (Evaluate Expression)
EVAL is an operation used to assign a value to a variable. In the sample program, by evaluating *INLR=*ON we are assigning *ON to a special indicator called Last Record. *INLR performs a special function within RPG IV. If it is on when our program ends, it signals the computer to close the files and free up the memory associated with this program. If LR is not on, our program continues to tie up some of the system's resources even though the program is no longer running.

RETURN (Return to Caller)
RETURN returns control to the program that called it — either the computer's operating system or perhaps another program. Program execution stops when a RETURN is encountered. Although your program will end correctly without this instruction (provided you have turned on LR), including it is a good practice: RETURN clearly signals the endpoint of your program and allows the program to become part of an application system of called programs. (Chapter 12 deals with called programs in detail.)

Internal Documentation
You might think that once you have a program written and running, you are done with it forever and can move forward, developing new programs. Actually, about 70 percent of all programming is maintenance programming rather than new applications development. Maintenance programming involves modifying existing programs to fix problems, to address changing business needs, or to satisfy user requests for modifications.

Because of the high probability that any program you write will be revised sometime in the future either by yourself or by some other programmer in your company, it is your responsibility to make your program as understandable as possible to facilitate these future revisions.

One good way to help others understand what your program does is to include explanatory documentation internal to your program through the use of **comment lines**. In RPG IV, an asterisk (*) in position 7 of any line, regardless of the specification type, designates that line to be a comment; you can enter any documentation, in any form that you like, within the remaining portion of the line. When the RPG IV compiler encounters a commented line, it skips that line and does not try to translate it into machine code. Comments exist within the program at a source-code level only, for the benefit of programmers who may have to work with the program later. All the specification forms also include a comment area in positions 81-100, so that you can easily add a short comment to any line of code.

In addition to the use of comments, many programmers find that a program's structure is easier to understand if blank lines are used to break the code into logical units. To facilitate using blank lines within your code, RPG IV treats two types of lines as blank: First, any line that is completely blank between positions 6-80 can appear anywhere within your program. Second, if position 6 contains a valid specification type, while positions 7-80 are blank, the line is treated as a blank line; but the line must be located in that portion of the program appropriate for its designated specification type.

Most companies require overview documentation at the beginning of each program. This documentation states the function or purpose of the program, any special instructions or peculiarities of the program that those working with it should know, the program's author, and the date when the program was written. If the program is revised, entries detailing the revisions, including the author and the date of the revisions, usually are added to that initial documentation. If a program uses several indicators, many programmers will provide an indicator "dictionary" as part of their initial set of comments to state the function or role of each indicator used within the program.

In addition to this overview documentation, you should include comments throughout your program as needed to help explain specific processing steps that are not obvious. In adding such comments, assume that anyone looking at your program has at least a basic proficiency with RPG IV; your documentation should help clarify your program to such a person. Documenting trivial, obvious aspects of your program is a waste of time. On the other hand, failing to document difficult-to-grasp processing can cost others valuable time. Inaccurate documentation is worse than no documentation because it supplies false clues that may mislead the person responsible for program modification.

Appropriately documenting a program is an important learned skill. If you are uncertain about what to document, ask yourself, "What would I want to know about this program if I were looking at it for the first time?"

The Completed Program

The completed sample RPG IV program is shown in the figure below. Note that the order of the program statements are File-Input-Calculations-Output. RPG requires this order. Also note that you can use blank comment lines or lines of asterisks to visually break the program into logical units, and that using lowercase lettering within internal documentation helps it stand out from program code.

```
*.. 1 ...+... 2 ...+... 3 ..+... 4 ...+... 5 ..+.. 6 ...+... 7 ...+... 8 ...+... 9 ...+...10
F**********************************************************************
F* This program produces a weekly sales report.  The report data comes   *
F* directly from input file SalesMast.                                    *
F*    Author:  J. Yaeger   Date Written:  12/10/94.                       *
F**********************************************************************
FSalesMast IF   F   63          DISK
FQPRINT     O    F  132         PRINTER
I
ISalesMast NS
I                              1    4 ØSlspNumber
I                              5   34  SlspName
I                             35   50  ItemNumber
I                             51   56 ØDateOfSale
I                             57   63 2Price
C
C              EXCEPT    Headings
C              READ      SalesMast                                90
C
C              DOW       *IN9Ø = *OFF
C              EXCEPT    Detail
C              READ      SalesMast                                90
C              ENDDO
C
C              EVAL      *INLR = *ON
C              RETURN
O
OQPRINT    E            Headings     2  2
O                                          8 'PAGE'
O                       PAGE             13
O                                         50 'WEEKLY SALES REPORT'
O                                         64 'DATE'
O                       UDATE     Y      73
O          E            Headings     1
O                                          7 'SLSPSN.'
O                                         48 'DATE OF'
O                                         77 'SALE'
O          E            Headings     2
O                                          3 'NO.'
O                                         21 'NAME'
O                                         46 'SALE'
O                                         61 'ITEM SOLD'
O                                         77 'PRICE'
O          E            Detail       1
O                       SlspNumber        4
O                       SlspName         37
O                       DateOfSale Y     48
O                       ItemNumber       67
O                       Price      1     79
```

Now that you have seen how to write a complete RPG IV program, we can return to the concept of output editing to learn RPG IV's editing features in greater detail.

Output Editing

Output editing refers to formatting output values by suppressing leading zeros and adding special characters, such as decimal points, commas, and dollar signs, to make the values easier for people looking at the output to comprehend. RPG IV allows numeric fields (but not character fields) to be edited as part of the Output Specifications. You often will use editing to obtain the output format requested in a printer spacing chart.

Editing is used in part because of the way numbers are stored in RPG. For example, if Amount, a field six bytes long with two decimal positions, is assigned the value 31.24, that value is stored as 003124. Although the computer keeps track of the decimal position, a decimal point is not actually stored as part of the numeric value. If you were to specify that Amount print without editing, the number would print as 003124; the non-significant zeros would appear, and there would be no indication of where the decimal point should be.

Edit Codes

To make it easier to specify the most commonly wanted kinds of editing, RPG IV includes several built-in edit codes you can use to indicate how you want a field's value to print. You associate an edit code with a field by entering the code in position 44 of the Output Specification containing that field. All commonly used edit codes automatically result in zero-suppression — that is, printing blanks in place of nonsignificant leading zeros — because that is a standard desired format.

Some editing decisions vary with the application. Do you want numbers to print with commas inserted? How do you want to handle negative values? Ignore them and omit any sign? Print a floating minus sign to the left of a negative value? Print CR immediately after the value? Or print a floating negative sign after the value? And if a field has a value of zero, do you want to print zeros or leave that spot on the report blank? A set of 16 edit codes, 1 through 4, A through D, and J through Q, cover all combinations of these three options (commas, sign handling, and zero balances). The following table details the effects of the 16 codes:

Commas	Zero Balances to Print	No Sign	CR	Right –	Floating –
Yes	Yes	1	A	J	N
Yes	No	2	B	K	O
No	Yes	3	C	L	P
No	No	4	D	M	Q

Thus, if you want commas, zero balances to print, and a floating negative sign, you would use edit code N; if you did *not* want commas or any sign, but did want zero balances to print, you would use edit code 3.

Value	1	2	3	4	A	B	C	D
1234^56	1,234.56	1,234.56	1234.56	1234.56	1,234.56	1,234.56	1234.56	1234.56
1234^56-	1,234.56	1,234.56	1234.56	1234.56	1,234.56CR	1,234.56CR	1234.56CR	1234.56CR
0234^56-	234.56	234.56	234.56	234.56	234.56CR	234.56CR	234.56CR	234.56CR
0000^00	.00		.00		.00		.00	
000000^	0		0		0		0	

To give you a clear understanding of the effects of each of these edit codes, the two parts of this table demonstrate how various values would appear if printed with each of the edit codes. Notice that if you use edit codes 1-4 with a field containing a negative value, that field will print like a positive number.

Value	J	K	L	M	N	O	P	Q
1234^56	1,234.56	1,234.56	1234.56	1234.56	1,234.56	1,234.56	1234.56	1234.56
1234^56-	1,234.56-	1,234.56-	1234.56-	1234.56-	-1,234.56	-1,234.56	-1234.56	-1234.56
0234^56-	234.56-	234.56-	234.56-	234.56-	-234.56	-234.56	-234.56	-234.56
0000^00	.00		.00		.00		.00	
000000^	0		0		0		0	

There are two additional useful edit codes: Y and Z. Edit code Y results in slashes printing as part of a date. Thus, if you run the program on December 11, 1994, UDATE will contain 121194. If edited with edit code Y, this date will print as 12/11/94. Although normally used to edit dates, you can use edit code Y with any field for which slash-insertion is appropriate.

Edit code Z simply zero suppresses leading non-significant zeros. Z does *not* enable the printing of a decimal point or a negative sign, so that if a field contained 0234ʌ56–, the Z edit code would cause it to print as 23456. Z, if used at all, should be limited to integer (whole number) fields.

One additional edit code, X, originally was designed to convert positively signed values to unsigned values; because the AS/400 now does this automatically, this edit code has become obsolete. X is the only edit code that does not suppress leading zeros.

You occasionally will want dollar signs to print as part of your report. As mentioned in Chapter 1, you can position dollar signs in a fixed column of the report, or you can place them just to the left of the first significant digit of the values they are associated with. This latter type of dollar sign is called a *floating dollar sign.*

Fixed Dollar Sign	Floating Dollar Sign
$ 12.34	$12.34
$6,342.11	$6,342.11
$ .00	$.00

Generally, you want to use a dollar sign in addition to one of the editing codes. To specify a floating dollar sign, code '$' in the constant/edit word positions (columns 53-80) of the output specifications *on the same line* as the field and its edit code. To specify a fixed dollar sign, code '$' as a constant *on its own line* with its own end position.

You can use one additional feature along with edit codes. An asterisk, coded in the constant/edit word position (53-80) on the same line as the field and edit code specifies that insignificant leading zeros be replaced by asterisks, rather than simply suppressed. This feature is sometimes called **check-protection**, because its most common use is in printing checks to prevent tampering with the check's face value. For example, a check worth $12.15 might include the amount written as $****12.15.

```
*.. 1 ...+... 2 ...+... 3 ..+... 4 ...+... 5 ...+... 6 ...+... 7 ...+... 8 ..+... 9 ...+...10
O..............N01N02N03Field++++++++YB.End++PConstant/editword/DTformat++Comments++++++++++++
O* The following line illustrates a floating dollar sign.
O                     Amount      1   65 '$'
O* The next two lines illustrate a fixed dollar sign.
O                                 56 '$'
O                     Amount      1   65
O* The following line illustrates asterisk fill.
O                     Amount      1   65 '*'
```

Edit Words

You would think that given the variety of edit codes built into RPG IV, you would be able to find a code to fit your every need. Unfortunately, that is not the case. Social Security and telephone numbers represent good examples of values that we are used to seeing in a format that an edit code cannot supply. RPG IV includes an alternative to edit codes, called **edit words**, that can help in this kind of situation.

An edit word is coded in the constant/edit word portion of the Output Specifications on the same line as the field it is to be used with. Edit words and edit codes are never used together for the same field, because they perform the same function. An edit word supplies a template into which a number is inserted. The template is enclosed with apostrophes. Within the template, a blank position indicates where a digit should appear, while a 0 indicates how far zero-suppression should take place. With no zero in the edit word, the default is to zero-suppress to the first significant digit.

You can use commas *or any other character* as insertion characters within the template. They will print in the specified place, provided they are to the right of a significant digit. A dollar sign at the left of the edit word signals a fixed dollar sign; a dollar sign adjacent to a zero denotes a floating dollar sign. To indicate a blank as an insertion character, use an ampersand (&).

Examine the table below to see how edit words work.

This value	with this edit word	prints as
999999999	'ƀƀƀ-ƀƀ-ƀƀƀƀ'	999-99-9999
999999999	'ƀƀƀ&ƀƀ&ƀƀƀƀ'	999 99 9999
1234123412	'0(ƀƀƀ)ƀƀƀ-ƀƀƀƀ'	(123)412-3412
00012^14	'ƀƀƀƀ$0.ƀƀ'	$12.14
00012^14	'$ƀƀƀƀ0.ƀƀ'	$ 12.14
05612^14	'$ƀƀ,ƀƀ0.ƀƀ'	$ 5,612.14

You can duplicate the effects of any edit code with an edit word. In general, RPG programmers use edit words only when there is not an edit code that provides the format they want for their output.

Chapter Summary

RPG IV programs are written as fixed-form specifications. Different specification forms convey different kinds of information to the RPG IV compiler, which translates the program into machine language.

File Specifications contain descriptions of all files used within a program. Input Specifications provide detailed information about each program-described input file used by a program. There are two kinds of Input Specification lines: one that contains record identification entries, to generally describe a record format within a file, and one that contains field identification entries, to define the fields comprising the record. Each field is described on a separate line.

Calculation Specifications center on operations, or processing steps, to be accomplished by the computer. Each Calculation Specification must include an RPG IV operation and may include additional entries, depending on the specific operation. The computer executes operations in the order they are given on the Calculation Specifications, unless the computer encounters an operation that specifically alters this flow of control.

Output Specifications provide details about each program-described output file. You use two kinds of Output Specification lines: a record identification line, to describe an output record format at a general level, and field description lines, to describe each field or constant that appears as part of a record format. You can use an optional third type of Output Specification to continue constants (or edit words) that are too long to fit on a single line. When the output is a report, you need a record identification line and corresponding field identification entries for each kind of line to appear on the report.

It generally is customary to edit numeric values that are printed. RPG IV supplies ready-made edit codes for common editing requirements and allows you to create special editing formats by using edit words.

An important part of programming is documenting the program. Comment lines, signaled by an * in position 7 of a specification line, can appear anywhere within a program. Such lines are ignored by the RPG IV compiler. Positions 81-100 of all specification lines are also reserved for comments.

Within your code you can insert completely blank lines and lines that are blank except for the specification type to visually break the code into sections.

Terms

Calculation Specifications	end-of-file	numeric field
case sensitive	File Description	output editing
character field	Specifications	output file
check-protection	fixed-position/fixed-form	Output Specifications
comment lines	full procedural	priming read
constants/literals	indicator	pseudocode
detail line	input file	Source Entry Utility (SEU)
edit code	Input Specifications	
edit words	integer data	

Discussion/Review Questions

1. What's a fixed-form language? Can you give an example of a free-form language?

2. Why do reports generated by RPG IV programs need to appear on File Specifications?

3. Why don't you need to enter a File Designation for output files?

4. Which of the following are invalid RPG IV variable names? Why?

```
X              1STQTR         #3
ABC            QTY-OH         CustNo
@end           SALES          $AMT
_YTD_Sales     CUST#          Day1
YR END         YR_END         yearend
InvoiceNumber  avg.sales      cusTnbR
```

5. What is an indicator? What specific methods of turning on indicators were introduced in this chapter? How can you use indicators to control processing?

6. Describe the difference between a skip and a space entry on the Output Specifications.

7. How could you obtain five blank lines between detail lines of a report?

8. What is the advantage of giving the same name to several exception lines of output?

9. What are some fields that are automatically provided by RPG IV for your use?

10. Why do you often need two read statements within a program?

11. What is the correct order of specifications within an RPG IV program?

12. What is the purpose of each kind of RPG IV specification introduced in this chapter?

13. What is LR? Why is it used?

14. What is maintenance programming? What programming techniques can you adopt to facilitate maintenance programming?

15. Why does RPG IV include both edit codes and edit words? What exceptions are there to the rule that an edit code and an edit word or constant should never appear together on the same Output Specification line?

16. What are the programming implications of the fact that RPG IV is not case sensitive?

Exercises

1. A program uses data from file Customers to generate a report that reflects all the data in the file. The record layout of Customers follows:

Description	Positions	(Decimal Positions)
Customer number	1- 5	(0)
Customer name	6-25	
Last order date	26-31	MMDDYY
Balance owed	32-41	(2)

Write the File Specifications for this program.

2. Given the above problem definition, write the Input Specifications.

3. Design a report for the application in Exercise 1, using the printer spacing chart (PSC) notation of Chapter 1.

4. Develop Output Specifications based on your printer spacing chart from Exercise 3 and the File Specifications of Exercise 1.

Programming Assignments

All four of the programming assignments below center on a single company: CompuSell. CompuSell is a mail-order company specializing in computers and computer supplies. A description of the company and the record layouts of its data files appear in Appendix D.

1. The company would like you to write a program to produce a listing of all its customers. Use data file CSCSTP, the customer master file for CompuSell, as your input file. The listing should exactly match the format described in the printer spacing chart below:

```
        XX/XX/XX              COMPUSELL CUSTOMER LISTING              PAGE XX0X
CUST.
NUMBER        FIRST NAME        LAST NAME           LAST ORDER    BALANCE
                                                       DATE          DUE
XXXXXX        XXXXXXXXXX        XXXXXXXXXXXXXXXX    XX/XX/XX      X,XX0.XX
XXXXXX        XXXXXXXXXX        XXXXXXXXXXXXXXXX    XX/XX/XX      X,XX0.XX
```

2. CompuSell wants an inventory listing, formatted as shown in the following printer spacing chart. Write the program to produce this report, exactly matching the printer spacing chart specifications. The input file is CSINVP; its record layout is given in Appendix D.

```
        XX/XX/XX              COMPUSELL INVENTORY LISTING            PAGE XX0X
PROD.                                WEIGHT   QTY. ON   AVERAGE   CURRENT   SELLING
NUM.        DESCRIPTION              LBS. OZS. HAND      COST      COST      PRICE
XXXXXX    XXXXXXXXXXXXXXXXXXXXXXXXX  X0   XX   XX0X    X,XX0.XX  X,XX0.XX  $X,XX$.XX
XXXXXX    XXXXXXXXXXXXXXXXXXXXXXXXX  X0   XX   XX0X    X,XX0.XX  X,XX0.XX  $X,XX$.XX
```

Programming Assignments Continued

Programming Assignments continued

3. CompuSell wants to send out two separate mailings to each of its customers contained in file CSCSTP (see Appendix D for record layout). Accordingly, the company asks you to write a label-printing program that will print 2-across labels. Each of the labels reading across should represent the same customer. The printer will be loaded with continuous label stock when this program is run. Each label is 5 print lines long. The desired format for the labels is shown below. Note that the information in the parentheses is included to let you know what should appear on the label. It should not appear within your output.

```
                    1         2         3         4         5         6         7         8         9         1 0
           1234567890123456789012345678901234567890123456789012345678901234567890123456789012345678901234567890
        1      XXXXXXXXXX XXXXXXXXXXXXXXXX              XXXXXXXXXX XXXXXXXXXXXXXXXX       (FIRST, LAST NAME)
        2      XXXXXXXXXXXXXXXXXXXXXX                   XXXXXXXXXXXXXXXXXXXXXX            (STREET ADDRESS)
        3      XXXXXXXXXXXXXXXX  XX XXXXX-XXXX          XXXXXXXXXXXXXXXX  XX XXXXX-XXXX   (CITY, STATE, ZIP)
        4
        5
        6      XXXXXXXXXX XXXXXXXXXXXXXXXX              XXXXXXXXXX XXXXXXXXXXXXXXXX
        7      XXXXXXXXXXXXXXXXXXXXXX                   XXXXXXXXXXXXXXXXXXXXXX
        8      XXXXXXXXXXXXXXXX  XX XXXXX-XXXX          XXXXXXXXXXXXXXXX  XX XXXXX-XXXX
        9
```

4. CompuSell wants a phone and address listing of all its suppliers. Write a program to produce this listing. Your input file, CSSUPP, is described in Appendix D.

```
                    1         2         3         4         5         6         7         8         9         1 0
           1234567890123456789012345678901234567890123456789012345678901234567890123456789012345678901234567890
        1      COMPUSELL SUPPLIER LIST AS OF XX/XX/XX                    PAGE XX0X
        2
        3    NAME/ADDRESS                    PHONE            CONTACT PERSON
        4
        5  XXXXXXXXXXXXXXXXXXXXXXXXXXX     (XXX) XXX-XXXX    XXXXXXXXXXXXXXXXXXXXXXXXXXXXXXXX
        6  XXXXXXXXXXXXXXXXXXXXXX
        7  XXXXXXXXXXXXXXXX XX XXXXX-XXXX
        8
        9
       10  XXXXXXXXXXXXXXXXXXXXXXXXXXX     (XXX) XXX-XXXX    XXXXXXXXXXXXXXXXXXXXXXXXXXXXXXXX
       11  XXXXXXXXXXXXXXXXXXXXXX
       12  XXXXXXXXXXXXXXXX XX XXXXX-XXXX
       13
       14
       15  XXXXXXXXXXXXXXXXXXXXXXXXXXX     (XXX) XXX-XXXX    XXXXXXXXXXXXXXXXXXXXXXXXXXXXXXXX
       16  XXXXXXXXXXXXXXXXXXXXXX
       17  XXXXXXXXXXXXXXXX XX XXXXX-XXXX
       18
```

Chapter 3

Assignment and Arithmetic Operations

Chapter Overview

Now that you can write simple read/write programs in RPG IV, you're ready to learn how to define work fields, assign values to fields, and perform arithmetic calculations in your programs. RPG was designed as a business language, and as such, its mathematical capabilities don't extend much beyond the four basic arithmetic operations — addition, subtraction, multiplication, and division. You will learn how to express calculations using free-form expressions and appropriate operation codes.

In addition, you will learn how to determine the correct size for fields that store the results of arithmetic operations and how to round calculations to avoid truncation. This chapter also teaches you how to convert data types and how to use numeric and character literals and figurative constants.

Introducing Definition Specifications

RPG IV requires you to define all fields (or variables) used in your program by giving them valid names, specifying their lengths and data types, and — for numeric variables — designating the number of decimal positions they are to have.

At this point, you should have a good understanding of how to use Input Specifications to define fields that will receive values from records of a data file. The programs you have worked with so far simply wrote those field values to reports. Typically, however, program requirements include manipulating input data in other ways and storing the resulting values preparatory to output.

To enable this kind of processing, you need to identify to the computer the additional fields used to store such results. You perform such declarations in RPG IV by defining **stand-alone fields**, so called because these fields are not part of a database record or any other kind of data structure.

You define stand-alone fields in **Definition Specifications**, identified by a D in position 6. If your program uses Definition Specifications, they must follow File Specifications and precede any Input Specifications. The sole purpose of Definition Specifications is to define additional variables your program may need. Because Definition Specifications concentrate data definition to a single group of consecutive statements near the beginning of your program, they facilitate later program maintenance.

To define a stand-alone field, code the name of the field anywhere in positions 7-21 (Name++++++++++) of the line, enter an S (for stand-alone) *left-adjusted* in positions 24-25 (Ds), enter the length of the field right-adjusted in positions 33-39 (To/L+++), and enter the number of decimal positions (for numeric fields) right-adjusted in positions 41-42 (Dc). A decimal position entry signals to the system that the field is numeric; the system interprets blanks in positions 41-42 to mean that the field is of character data type.

```
*.. 1 ...+... 2 ...+... 3 ...+... 4 ...+... 5 ...+... 6 ...+... 7 ...+... 8 ...+... 9 ...+...10
DName++++++++++ETDsFrom+++To/L+++IDc.Keywords+++++++++++++++++++++++++++++++++Comments+++++++++++
D* Field TotalDue defined on a Definition Specification as a stand-alone field seven
D* positions long with two decimal positions.
D TotalDue        S              7 2
D
D* Field CtyStZip defined as a character field 40 positions long.
D CtyStZip        S             40
```

RPG IV allows numeric fields a maximum length of 30 positions, up to 30 of which may be decimal positions. Character fields can be up to 32,767 positions long. All numeric fields are signed and can store negative values without special specification. Recall, however, that negative values will print without a sign unless you use an appropriate edit code with the field on output.

Once you have defined a field in a Definition Specification, you can assign it a value, use it with operations, or print it — just like an input field. Before you learn how to assign values to stand-alone fields, you need to understand another kind of data construct: **numeric literals**.

Numeric Literals

A numeric literal is a number per se; its value remains fixed throughout the program. The literal may include a decimal point and/or a sign. If the numeric literal includes a sign, the sign must be the left-most character of the literal. If the numeric literal does not include a sign, the computer assumes the literal represents a positive number.

Other than a decimal point and a sign, the literal may include only the digits 0 through 9. You should never use commas, dollar signs, or percent signs in a numeric literal. Numeric literals are not enclosed in apostrophes. Some examples of valid numeric literals follow:

–401230.12	0.0715
102	1
+3	–1
3.1416	.123456789

When entered as factor 1 or factor 2 in a Calculation Specification, numeric literals should be *left-adjusted*; this is the one exception to the rule that numeric values are right-adjusted when used as fixed-position entries.

Simple Numeric Assignment

Assigning a value to a field simply means giving a field a value. We used the RPG IV operation EVAL (Evaluate Expression) in the previous chapter to assign the value *ON to an indicator. You can also use EVAL to assign values to numeric fields.

EVAL uses the extended factor 2 format of the Calculation Specification. In this format, EVAL appears as the operation code in positions 26-35, while the extended factor 2 area (positions 36-80) contains a result (target) field, followed by the assignment operator (=), followed by an expression. An EVAL statement says, in effect, "Evaluate the expression to the right of the equal sign and store its value in the result field to the left of the equal sign." The general format for an EVAL statement is shown below.

```
*.. 1 ...+... 2 ...+... 3 ...+... 4 ...+... 5 ...+... 6 ...+... 7 ...+... 8 ...+... 9 ....+...10
CL0N01Factor1+++++++Opcode(E)+Extended-factor2++++++++++++++++++++++++++++++Comments+++++++++++
C                   EVAL      Result field = expression
```

The following examples demonstrate how to use EVAL for simple numeric assignment. In each case, the numeric field that appears to the left of the equal sign receives the value that appears to the right of the sign. The value to the right may be a numeric literal or a numeric field. You cannot define the result field within the EVAL statement; it must be defined elsewhere in the program (e.g., in a Definition Specification).

```
*.. 1 ...+... 2 ...+... 3 ...+... 4 ...+... 5 ...+... 6 ...+... 7 ...+... 8 ...+... 9 ...+...10
CL0N01Factor1+++++++Opcode(E)+Extended-factor2++++++++++++++++++++++++++++++Comments+++++++++++
C                   EVAL      Counter = 0                         Initialize a counter
C                   EVAL      TaxRate = .045                      Assign a value > 0
C                   EVAL      AbslZero = -273.16                  Assign a value < 0
C                   EVAL      AmtOwed  =  BalDue                  Assign a field value
```

Note that the extended factor 2 entry is *free-form*, which means that it can appear anywhere within positions 36 through 80, with as many (or few) blanks between the entry's components as you wish.

Arithmetic Operations

RPG IV does not include a wealth of mathematical operations. The four basic arithmetic operations — add, subtract, multiply, and divide — with a few extras, represent the range of RPG IV's mathematical offerings. Although the language has proven itself adequate to handle most of the mathematical processing required in the business environment, you probably wouldn't want to use RPG IV to calculate rocket trajectories.

The primary operation for arithmetic calculations in RPG IV is the EVAL operation. We will first look at this general-purpose operation and then consider three single-purpose operations that you can use to handle two special calculations EVAL doesn't support.

Using EVAL for Arithmetic

In a previous section we saw how to use EVAL for simple numeric assignment. The EVAL operation also provides a flexible, powerful, relatively free-form method for assigning numeric fields the results of simple or complex arithmetic calculations in a single step.

The expression for evaluation can contain the arithmetic operators + (addition), − (subtraction), ∗ (multiplication), ∕ (division), and ∗∗ (**exponentiation**, or raising a value to a power), as well as parentheses, relational symbols (e.g., <=, >), logical operators (e.g., AND, OR), and built-in functions (discussed later in the text).

A single expression can contain as many arithmetic operators, numeric literals, and numeric fields as are needed to accomplish a desired calculation.

```
*.. 1 ...+... 2 ...+... 3 ...+... 4 ...+... 5 ...+... 6 ...+... 7 ...+... 8 ...+... 9 ...+...10
CLØN01Factor1++++++Opcode(E)+Extended-factor2+++++++++++++++++++++++++++++Comments++++++++++++
C* Examples of calculations using the EVAL operation.
C                   EVAL      WithHold = FICA + StateTax + FedTax
C                   EVAL      NetPay = GrossPay - WithHold
C                   EVAL      GrssProfit = Cost * .6 * QtySold
C                   EVAL      AveAmount = TotAmount / Counter
C                   EVAL      NumSquared = Number ** 2
```

All values used in the arithmetic expression to the right of the equal sign must, of course, be numeric fields or literals. One other restriction arises when division is used in an expression. Remember that division by zero is mathematically impossible. A runtime error occurs if, at the time of the division, the divisor (the part of an expression immediately to the right of the division sign) evaluates to zero.

When the arithmetic expression of an EVAL contains more than one operator, the rules of precedence from mathematics are used to determine the order in which the operations are performed. Exponentiation has the highest precedence, followed by multiplication and division, and then addition and subtraction. When an expression contains operations of equal precedence, the system executes them in order from left to right. You can use parentheses to change the order in which the computer executes these operations; operations within parentheses are performed before any operations outside the parentheses.

```
*.. 1 ...+... 2 ...+... 3 ...+... 4 ...+... 5 ...+... 6 ...+... 7 ...+... 8 ...+... 9 ...+...10
CLØN01Factor1++++++Opcode(E)+Extended-factor2+++++++++++++++++++++++++++++Comments++++++++++++
C* In this example, the multiplication will occur before the subtraction.
C                   EVAL      Answer = A * B - 1
C* In the example below, the parentheses cause the subtraction to take place
C* before the multiplication.
C                   EVAL      Answer = A * (B - 1)
```

Within the extended factor 2 area (positions 36-80), RPG IV lets you use free-form entry, so that you can include as many (or as few) blanks between fields, literals, and operations as you would like to make the expression readable and easy to understand. If it is necessary, you can continue the expression to one or more extended factor 2 continuation lines; these kinds of lines must be blank between positions 7 and 35, with the expression continued in positions 36-80. The figure below illustrates the EVAL operation and the use of a continuation line.

```
*.. 1 ...+... 2 ...+... 3 ...+... 4 ...+... 5 ...+... 6 ...+... 7 ...+... 8 ...+... 9 ...+...10
CLØNØ1Factor1++++++Opcode(E)+Extended-factor2+++++++++++++++++++++++++++Comments+++++++++++
C...........................Extended-factor2-continuation++++++++++++++Comments+++++++++++
C                 EVAL      Pay = HourlyRate * 4Ø +
C                               1.5 * HourlyRate * (HoursWorkd - 4Ø)
```

Those of you who have studied algebra recognize the similarity between EVAL expressions and algebraic equations. Don't be misled by this similarity, however. An algebraic equation is asserting an equality; an EVAL expression instructs the computer to perform the calculation to the right of the equal sign and then assign the result to the field left of the equal sign. In algebra, the equation $x = x + 1$ is a logical impossibility; within an EVAL operation, $X = X + 1$ is a perfectly legitimate instruction that tells the computer to take the value of field X, add 1 to it, and store the result in field X. In fact, this form of EVAL expression is frequently used in RPG IV programming for counting and accumulating. For example, to count the number of customers in a file, you would increment a counter field (i.e., add 1 to it) each time you processed a customer record. Or, to accumulate employees' salaries, you would add each salary to a field representing the grand total of the salaries.

```
*.. 1 ...+... 2 ...+... 3 ...+... 4 ...+... 5 ...+... 6 ...+... 7 ...+... 8 ...+... 9 ...+...10
CLØNØ1Factor1++++++Opcode(E)+Extended-factor2+++++++++++++++++++++++++++Comments+++++++++++
C* Examples of how to increment a counter and how to accumulate a total.
C                 EVAL      Counter = Counter + 1
C                 EVAL      GrandTotal = GrandTotal + EmpSalary
```

You can also decrement a counter or decrease the value of an accumulator by using subtraction.

```
*.. 1 ...+... 2 ...+... 3 ...+... 4 ...+... 5 ...+... 6 ...+... 7 ...+... 8 ...+... 9 ...+...10
CLØNØ1Factor1++++++Opcode(E)+Extended-factor2+++++++++++++++++++++++++++Comments+++++++++++
C                 EVAL      CountDown = CountDown - 1
C                 EVAL      Inventory = Inventory - OrderQty
```

Introducing Specific Arithmetic Operators

The EVAL operation provides an efficient way for programmers to express complex calculations. Also, the free-form entry that EVAL provides in the extended factor 2 resembles the way we express calculations in algebra and the way other modern languages handle calculations. Moreover, using EVAL results in specifications that are easy to understand and maintain. But, although you can use EVAL to accomplish most arithmetic processing, there are two calculations you may occasionally need that EVAL does not directly support: obtaining the square root of a value and capturing the remainder in a division operation. To perform these calculations in RPG IV, you need to use three **specific** (or single-purpose) **arithmetic operations**.

Specific arithmetic operations, like many other RPG IV operations, require the standard form of the Calculation Specifications, rather than the extended factor 2 form:

```
*.. 1 ...+... 2 ...+... 3 ...+... 4 ...+... 5 ...+... 6 ...+... 7 ...+... 8 ...+... 9 ...+...10
CLØNØ1Factor1++++++Opcode(E)+Factor2++++++Result+++++++Len++D+HiLoEq....Comments+++++++++++
```

The operations themselves are coded in positions 26-35 (Opcode(E)+). All require a result-field entry left-adjusted in positions 50-63, and most also include an entry left-adjusted in factor 2 — or entries left-adjusted in both factor 1 (positions 12-25) and factor 2 (positions 36-49). The exact format for each specific operation is described in the following paragraphs.

SQRT (Square Root)

Specific operation SQRT is used for calculating the square root of a numeric value. This operation does not use factor 1. Factor 2 contains a numeric constant or numeric field whose square root you want to calculate, while the result must be a numeric field to store the answer. If the value of factor 2 is 0, the result will be 0; if factor 2 is a negative number, an error condition results, because the square root of a negative value is an imaginary number.

```
*.. 1 ...+... 2 ...+... 3 ...+... 4 ...+... 5 ...+... 6 ...+... 7 ...+... 8 ...+... 9 ...+...10
CLØNØ1Factor1++++++Opcode(E)+Factor2++++++Result+++++++Len++D+HiLoEq....Comments+++++++++++
C                  SQRT      SqFeet        Feet
```

You may recall from algebra that you can express roots by using exponents. Raising a value to the one-half power is equivalent to finding the value's square root. So you might be tempted to use EVAL and the $**$ operator to perform this calculation: EVAL Feet = SqFeet $**$ .5. Unfortunately, this technique does not produce results as accurately as the SQRT operation; and it is, perhaps, not as obvious a technique as operation SQRT if someone else must read or maintain your code.

MVR (Move Remainder) and DIV (Divide)

Occasionally, when dividing, you would like to be able to capture the remainder of a division operation to use in a subsequent calculation or to print. RPG IV provides the MVR operation, which you use in tandem with the specific division operation, DIV, for this purpose.

The DIV operation divides factor 1 by factor 2, storing the quotient in the result field. If it is immediately followed by a MVR operation, the remainder from the division is stored in the result field of the MVR specification. The following example demonstrates a use of this pair of operations:

```
*.. 1 ...+... 2 ...+... 3 ...+... 4 ...+... 5 ...+... 6 ...+... 7 ...+... 8 ...+... 9 ...+...10
CLØNØ1Factor1++++++Opcode(E)+Factor2++++++Result++++++++Len++D+HiLoEq....Comments++++++++++++
C* Convert total minutes to hours and minutes by dividing total minutes by 6Ø to get hours
C* and moving the remainder into a minutes field.
C       TotMinutes    DIV       6Ø            Hours
C                     MVR                     Minutes
```

If you aren't sure what gets divided by what in the division format, mentally substitute a "divided by" sign (/) for the DIV operation to avoid reversing the factors. In algebra, this operation would be expressed as

Result = Factor 1/Factor 2

RPG IV also allows three other specific arithmetic operations — ADD, SUB, and MULT — with formats similar to DIV. Because operation EVAL has made these three specific operations obsolete, you will usually encounter them only when maintaining code developed under previous versions of the language. Accordingly, we'll wait to look at them until Chapter 13.

Numeric Truncation and Field Sizes

With all arithmetic operations, one of your jobs as a programmer is to determine appropriate length and decimal position entries for result fields. It is important to allow sufficient room because otherwise, should a calculation produce an answer too big to store in the result field, a runtime error or **truncation** will occur.

Truncation is the loss of digits from the right or the left ends of a result field. The AS/400 stores the result of any arithmetic operation in the result field based on decimal position alignment. If the value to be stored is too large for the result field, truncation occurs. This digit loss may occur from left-most or right-most digits of the answer (or both), depending on the number of defined digit positions to the left and right of the decimal position in the result field and the operation used. Digit loss from the left is called **high-order truncation**, while loss from the right is **low-order truncation**. The following table illustrates the concept of truncation:

Calculated Value	Result Field Definition		Truncated Result
	Length	**Decimal Position**	
413.29	4	1	413.2
413.29	4	2	13.29
413.29	4	0	0413
413.29	4	3	3.290

From the examples above, you can see that truncation can occur for significant (left-most) or insignificant (right-most) digits, depending on the calculated value and the number of digit positions to the right and the left of the decimal position in the result field. You should also notice that if the answer has fewer digits (left or right of decimal position) than the result field, the system simply zero-fills the unneeded positions.

Truncation is important to understand, because if it occurs during a program's execution, the program may simply continue to run without issuing a warning that digits have been lost, or the program may end abnormally (abend). Losing 1/1000 of a dollar may not be the end of the world (although on a large run it could add up), but losing $10,000 would probably cause your company some distress. Furthermore, program abends reflect poorly on the programmer.

In RPG IV, all arithmetic operations will automatically truncate extra decimal positions (low-order truncation) to fit the value in the result field. EVAL generates a runtime error that causes the program to end abnormally, should high-order truncation be imminent.

How do you determine the size of a result field to ensure that truncation or abends do not inadvertently happen? EVAL keeps track of any intermediate results that occur during the evaluation of its expression, maintaining full precision internally until the expression is completely evaluated and ready to be stored in the result field. However, you must analyze the expression — that is, consider the operations it performs and whether or not it occurs within a loop — to estimate the size needed for the final result. Fortunately, some guidelines exist for result field definition to help you ensure that your result fields are large enough to store the calculated answers. The following sections present some guidelines for determining field sizes of results occurring from two values and an operation. When in doubt, you can always manually perform some representative calculations that mirror what you want the computer to do to guide you in this matter.

Result Field Size for Addition

To avoid truncation when adding two values, you should define the result field with *one more* position *left of the decimal* than the larger of the addends' integer digit positions. Positions to the right of the decimal in the result field should equal the larger of the decimal positions of the addends. For example, if you're adding two fields, one defined as 3 with 2 decimal positions (i.e., 1 to the left, 2 to the right of the decimal) and one defined as 6 with 3 decimal positions (i.e., 3 to the left, 3 to the right of the decimal), your result field should be defined as 7 with 3 decimal positions (4 to the left, 3 to the right).

To see why this rule eliminates the possibility of truncation, simply do the addition with the largest possible values the addends can contain — 9.99 and 999.999 — and you will understand its basis.

When you are using addition to count or accumulate, the value of the result keeps getting larger and larger each time the calculation is performed (for example, when accumulating individuals' calculated gross pay figures to generate a grand total gross pay). In this case, to determine the necessary size of the result field you need to have an approximate idea of how many times the calculation will be performed (i.e., how many employees you will process). Once you have this estimate, follow the rule for multiplication, given below.

Result Field Size for Subtraction

To eliminate the chance of truncation with subtraction, follow the rule given for addition. This advice may seem strange at first, until you realize that you must provide for the possibility of subtracting a negative number, which essentially turns the problem into one of addition. Thus, to avoid high-order truncation when subtracting two values, define the result field to have 1 more digit position to the left of the decimal position than the larger of the high-order positions of the two values. And define the result field to have the same number of decimal positions as the larger of the number of decimal positions of the two values.

Result Field Size for Multiplication

When multiplying, to determine the needed number of digit positions in a result field, add the number of positions to the left of the decimal positions of the two multipliers and use that to determine the number of high-order digits in the result. The sum of the number of positions to the right of the decimal in the multipliers represents the number of positions your result field must have to the right of the decimal. For example, if you were multiplying 999.99 by 99.99, your result field would require 5 places to the left of the decimal and 4 to the right to store the answer without truncation. In RPG IV, this would mean a field 9 positions long, with 4 decimal positions.

Result Field Size for Division

When dividing by a value of 1 or greater, the maximum required positions to the left of the decimal in the result is the number of left-of-decimal positions in the dividend (the value *being* divided). To understand this, recognize that dividing any value by 1 yields the original value; dividing by any value greater than one will give you a value smaller than the original value. When dividing by values less than 1, computing the number of digit positions in the result becomes a more complicated process; the smaller the divisor, the more significant positions needed in the result field. If you are working with divisors less than 1, your safest approach is to hand-calculate with some representative values to get a sense of the size needed to store your answer.

Because few divisions work out evenly, there is no way to guarantee that you will provide enough decimal positions to avoid low-order truncation. Generally, you choose the number of decimal positions for the result field based on the degree of significance, or accuracy, the calculation warrants. Because most business data processing deals with calculations involving dollars and cents, it usually makes sense to carry out intermediate calculations with the maximum needed or the maximum allowable number of decimal positions (whichever is smaller) and then to reduce that to two decimal positions in the final calculation.

When you are using the MVR operation, the definition you give the result field should depend on the definitions of the values and result field of the division operation whose remainder you want to capture. The system will carry out the division until the answer has the same number of decimal positions as the result field; what is left at that point will be moved into the remainder field. To make sure you have your remainder field appropriately defined, hand-calculate some representative samples, because there is no simple rule of thumb to guide you.

Rounding

When you store a value in a result field that has fewer decimal positions than the calculated answer, common business practice dictates that you should always round your answer, rather than allow the system to truncate it. Rounding is sometimes called **half-adjusting** because of the technique computers use to accomplish this feat. The computer adds half the value of your right-most desired decimal position to the digit immediately to the right of that decimal position before storing the answer in the result field. Because the value added is half the value of the least-significant digit position of your result, the term half-adjust came into being.

For example, assume the computer has calculated an answer of 3.14156 that you want to store, in rounded form, in a result field defined as 4 with 3 decimal positions. The computer will add 0.0005 to the answer (i.e., 1/2 of 0.001, the lowest decimal position you are retaining in your result), giving 3.14206. It then stores this value in the result field, truncated to three decimal positions, as 3.142. If you had defined the result as 3 with two decimal positions, the computer would add 0.005 (1/2 of 0.01) to 3.14156, giving 3.14656, and store that answer in the result as 3.14.

Fortunately, even if you don't completely understand how the computer rounds, the method RPG IV uses to specify that rounding should take place is simple: just enter an H, for half-adjust, within parentheses following the operation code of the calculation whose result you want rounded. This directive to round is called an **operation extender** in RPG IV. Although the Calculation Specification prompt lines seem to indicate that you must code such extenders in positions 32-34 (as indicated by (E) in the prompt lines), in fact the extender can float anywhere to the right of the operation, providing it falls within the prescribed positions for the operation as a whole (positions 26-35), as illustrated in the following figure:

```
*.. 1 ...+... 2 ...+... 3 ...+... 4 ...+... 5 ...+... 6 ..+... 7 ...+... 8 ...+... 9 ...+...10
CL0N01Factor1++++++Opcode(E)+Extended-factor2++++++++++++++++++++++++++++++Comments+++++++++++
CL0N01Factor1++++++Opcode(E)+Factor2++++++Result++++++++Len++D+HiLoEq...Comments+++++++++++
C* Samples of calculations specifying that the result should be rounded.
C                 EVAL(H)   Interest = Rate * LoanAmt
C                 EVAL  (H) AvgAmount = TotAmount / Counter
C                 SQRT (H)  SqYards        Yards
```

Note that you need to include the H in every calculation line where you want rounding to occur, even if those calculations use the same result field. The compiler will *not* warn you if you inadvertently omit an H entry.

```
*.. 1 ...+... 2 ...+... 3 ...+... 4 ...+... 5 ...+... 6 ...+... 7 ...+... 8 ...+... 9 ...+...10
CLØN01Factor1++++++Opcode(E)+Extended-factor2++++++++++++++++++++++++++++Comments+++++++++++
C* In the below calcs rounding is specified in each calculation that is to result in
C* a rounded value for Interest.
C                     EVAL (H)  Interest = LoanAmt * StdRate
C                     ...
C                     EVAL (H)  Interest = AltAmt * PrimeRate
```

Although you need to round most often when multiplying or dividing, you can specify rounding for addition and subtraction operations, as well as for multiplication and division. It is important to note that if you want to capture the remainder of a DIV operation with a subsequent MVR operation, you cannot round that division.

Recognize that you do not always need to round when multiplying. Consider the following calculation, for example:

```
*.. 1 ...+... 2 ...+... 3 ...+... 4 ...+... 5 ...+... 6 ...+... 7 ...+... 8 ...+... 9 ...+...10
CLØN01Factor1++++++Opcode(E)+Extended-factor2++++++++++++++++++++++++++++Comments+++++++++++
C                     EVAL      InvtyValue = QtyOnHand * UnitPrice
```

If QtyOnHand is an integer (whole number), and UnitPrice is stored as dollars and cents (e.g., length 4 with 2 decimal positions), the resulting answer will never have more than 2 decimal positions, so you do *not* need to round the answer to store it in InvtyValue, defined as 6 long with 2 decimal positions.

Sometimes students, out of uncertainty or laziness, decide to play it safe by rounding all arithmetic operations, regardless of whether the rounding is needed. Avoid this practice. The RPG IV compiler will issue a warning message about unnecessary half-adjusting, and rounding when uncalled for reflects poorly on your programming skills and/or style.

Effective Commenting on Calculations

One characteristic of good programmers is that they write code realizing that other programmers will have to work with and probably revise the code in the future. In addition to following the guideline to avoid "tricky" code, and to code instead for clarity and straightforwardness, good programmers make liberal use of comments to internally document programs, as discussed in Chapter 2.

In addition to using comment lines to document logic that would otherwise be difficult to follow, most professional RPG IV programmers take advantage of positions 81-100 in Calculation Specifications to add short comments that provide additional explanation about what a given line or block of code accomplishes. This comment area can provide a running commentary of the code, which makes it easier to follow the program's logic.

Putting It All Together

You have learned how to perform arithmetic in RPG IV, and you understand the importance of correctly defining the size of result fields and appropriately rounding calculations. Now it's time to demonstrate the use of these concepts to give you a better flavor of RPG IV's approach to solving arithmetically oriented programming problems.

The following example demonstrates how to use the arithmetic operations of RPG IV to solve a typical business problem. A retail store wants you to write a routine to calculate selling prices for items it has received. The store uses a 60 percent markup for its goods. In addition to the required selling price, the store would like you to generate a projection of gross profit for each item and a grand total projected gross profit for all items received. The gross-profit projections should assume that the store will sell all the items at the price calculated by your program.

An input file, NewItems, contains records with the following format:

Field	Position	Decimal Positions
Item Description	1-30	
Item Cost	31-36	2
Quantity Received	37-40	0

The following printer spacing chart depicts the desired report:

```
          1         2         3         4         5         6         7         8         9        10
 1234567890123456789012345678901234567890123456789012345678901234567890123456789012345678901234567890
 1  XX/XX/XX                      GROSS PROFIT PROJECTION                          PAGE XX0X
 2
 3                                        SELLING            PER UNIT          TOTAL
 4      ITEM                      COST     PRICE     QTY.     PROFIT        GROSS PROFIT
 5
 6 XXXXXXXXXXXXXXXXXXXXXXXXXXXXXX  X.XX0.XX  XX.XX0.XX  X.X0X   X.XX0.XX      XX.XXX.XX0.XX
 7 XXXXXXXXXXXXXXXXXXXXXXXXXXXXXX  X.XX0.XX  XX.XX0.XX  X.X0X   X.XX0.XX      XX.XXX.XX0.XX
 8
 9                       GRAND TOTAL GROSS PROFIT PROJECTED:    $XXX,XXX,XXX.XX$.XX
10
```

Pseudocode of a solution for this problem follows:

```
Print headings
Read a record
WHILE more records exist
      Calculate per unit profit (cost * .6)
      Calculate selling price (cost + per unit profit)
      Calculate total item gross profit (quantity * per unit profit)
      Accumulate grand total gross profit
      Write detail line
      Read a record
ENDWHILE
Print grand total line
END program
```

Notice in the pseudocode that all calculations need to fall within the loop, because each needs to be performed for each data record. Printing headings is done just once before the loop, while printing the grand total line is done just once, following the loop. The pseudocode also shows that the details of the required calculations have been worked out.

The File Specifications for this problem present no new challenges. Note that on the Input Specifications QtyRcvd must include a 0 decimal positions entry, because that field will be used in arithmetic operations.

```
*.. 1 ...+... 2 ...+... 3 ...+... 4 ...+... 5 ...+... 6 ...+... 7 ...+... 8 ...+... 9 ...+...10
FFilename++IPEASFRlen+LKlen+AIDevice+.Keywords+++++++++++++++++++++++++++++Comments+++++++++++
FNewItems  IF   F   40        DISK
FQPrint     O   F  132        PRINTER

*.. 1 ...+... 2 ...+... 3 ...+... 4 ...+... 5 ...+... 6 ...+... 7 ...+... 8 ...+... 9 ...+...10
IFilename++SqNORiPos1+NCCPos2+NCCPos3+NCC....................................Comments+++++++++++
I......................Fmt+SPFrom+To+++DcField++++++++L1M1FrP1MnZr......Comments+++++++++++
INewItems   NS
I                            1   30  Descript
I                           31   36 2ItemCost
I                           37   40 0QtyRcvd
```

Looking at our pseudocode, we realize that we will need four fields that are not part of our input record: one representing unit profit for a given item, one for selling price, one for gross profit for that item, and one for grand total gross profit of all items received. We define these fields as stand-alone fields on Definition Specifications, as shown below.

```
*.. 1 ...+... 2 ...+... 3 ...+... 4 ...+... 5 ...+... 6 ...+... 7 ...+... 8 ...+... 9 ...+...10
DName++++++++++ETDsFrom+++To/L+++IDc.Keywords+++++++++++++++++++++++++++++++Comments+++++++++++
D UnitProfit      S            6  2
D SellPrice       S            7  2
D GrssProfit      S           10  2
D TotProfit       S           14  2
```

The Calculation Specifications that follow show how to solve this problem. Note that the expression used to obtain unit profit (UnitProfit) is rounded, while the one used to calculate gross profit (GrssProfit) is not. This difference is based on the relative number of decimal positions the two multiplication operations generate, given the number of decimal positions in the multipliers.

Also note that to calculate grand total gross profit (TotProfit), in each pass through the loop it is necessary to add the gross profit of the current item (GrssProfit) to the accumulator TotProfit.

The calculations also demonstrate (a bit excessively) how you can use comments in positions 81-100 to clarify the calculations.

```
*.. 1 ...+... 2 ...+... 3 ...+... 4 ...+... 5 ...+... 6 ...+... 7 ...+... 8 ...+... 9 ...+...10
CLØNØ1Factor1++++++Opcode(E)+Factor2++++++Result+++++++Len++D+HiLoEq....Comments+++++++++++
CLØNØ1Factor1++++++Opcode(E)+Extended-factor2+++++++++++++++++++++++++++Comments+++++++++++
C                  EXCEPT    Headings                              Write heading lines
C                  READ      NewItems                        90    Priming read
C
C                  DOW       *IN90 = *OFF                          Start loop
C                  EVAL (H)  UnitProfit = ItemCost * .6            Calc. unit profit
C                  EVAL      SellPrice = ItemCost + UnitProfit     Calc. selling price
C                  EVAL      GrssProfit = UnitProfit * QtyRcvd     Calc. gross profit
C                  EVAL      TotProfit = GrssProfit + TotProfit    Accum. grand total
C                  EXCEPT    Detail                                Write detail line
C                  READ      NewItems                        90    Read next record
C                  ENDDO                                           End of loop
C
C                  EXCEPT    TotalLine                             Write total line
C                  EVAL      *INLR = *ON                           Turn on LR
C                  RETURN
```

All that remains to be completed are the Output Specifications for the program. In the following specification lines, details of the coding for the heading lines are omitted, because they present nothing new to consider. Note that the total line (TotalLine) appears in the output with a Space 1 before entry. That spacing is required to obtain one blank line between the last printed detail line and the total line. Notice that the total line uses a continuation line to express the caption associated with the grand total. Finally, note that a floating dollar sign is associated with field TotProfit, as requested in the printer spacing chart.

```
*.. 1 ...+... 2 ...+... 3 ...+... 4 ...+... 5 ...+... 6 ...+... 7 ...+... 8 ...+... 9 ...+...10
OFilename++DF..NØ1NØ2NØ3Excnam+++B++A++Sb+Sa+...............................Comments+++++++++++
O..............NØ1NØ2NØ3Field++++++++YB.End++PConstant/editword/DTformat++Comments+++++++++++
OQPRINT   E            Headings        1
O                      ...
O         E            Detail          1
O                      Descript             30
O                      ItemCost        1    41
O                      SellPrice       1    53
O                      QtyRcvd         1    62
O                      UnitProfit      1    74
O                      GrssProfit      1    92
O         E            TotalLine    1
O                                      70 'GRAND TOTAL GROSS PROFIT -
O                                         PROJECTED:'
O                      TotProfit       1    92 '$'
```

When we complete the Output Specifications for the heading lines, add some overview documentation, and put all the pieces of code together, we obtain the entire program, as shown in the following figure:

```
*.. 1 ...+... 2 ...+... 3 ...+... 4 ...+... 5 ...+... 6 ...+... 7 ...+... 8 ...+... 9 ...+...10
F*****************************************************************************************
F*  This program calculates selling prices for received items based on a 60% markup over  *
F*  item cost.  It also determines projected gross profit for each item in the shipment    *
F*  and total gross profit for all the items.                                              *
F*     Author:  J. Yaeger                                                                  *
F*     Date Written:  Jan. 1995                                                            *
F*****************************************************************************************
```

```
*.. 1 ...+... 2 ...+... 3 ...+... 4 ...+... 5 ...+... 6 ...+... 7 ...+... 8 ...+... 9 ...+...10
FNewItems IF   F   40          DISK
FQPRINT   O    F  132          PRINTER
F
D***** Definition of all work fields used in program ******
D UnitProfit      S              6 2
D SellPrice       S              7 2
D GrssProfit      S             10 2
D TotProfit       S             14 2
D
I***** Input file of received items defined within the program ******
INewItems   NS
I                                 1   30  Descript
I                                31   36 2ItemCost
I                                37   40 0QtyRcvd
I
C****** Calculations for program ******
C                   EXCEPT    Headings                          Write heading lines
C                   READ      NewItems                    90    Priming read
C
C                   DOW       *IN90 = *OFF                      Start loop
C                   EVAL (H)  UnitProfit = ItemCost * .6        Calc. unit profit
C                   EVAL      SellPrice = ItemCost + UnitProfit Calc. selling price
C                   EVAL      GrssProfit = UnitProfit *  QtyRcvd Calc. gross profit
C                   EVAL      TotProfit = GrssProfit + TotProfit Accum. grand total
C                   EXCEPT    Detail                            Write detail line
C                   READ      NewItems                    90    Read next record
C                   ENDDO                                       End of loop
C
C                   EXCEPT    TotalLine                         Write total line
C                   EVAL      *INLR = *ON                       Turn on LR
C                   RETURN
O****** Output specifications ******
OQPRINT   E            Headings         1
O                      UDATE        Y  11
O                                      55 'GROSS PROFIT PROJECTION'
O                                      82 'PAGE'
O                      PAGE             87
O                      Headings     2  1
O                                      52 'SELLING'
O                                      74 'PER UNIT'
O                                      88 'TOTAL'
O                      Headings     2
O                                      10 'ITEM'
O                                      39 'COST'
O                                      51 'PRICE'
O                                      61 'QTY.'
O                                      73 'PROFIT'
O                                      92 'GROSS PROFIT'
O         E            Detail       1
O                      Descript         30
O                      ItemCost     1   41
O                      SellPrice    1   53
O                      QtyRcvd      1   62
O                      UnitProfit   1   74
O                      GrssProfit   1   92
O         E            TotalLine    1
O                                      70 'GRAND TOTAL GROSS PROFIT -
O                                          PROJECTED:'
O                      TotProfit    1   92 '$'
```

Character Literals

So far, this chapter has focused on assigning values to numeric fields; often you will want to work with character data and fields, as well. Before we look at how to assign values to character fields, one feature of RPG IV not yet mentioned needs to be introduced: **character literals.**

Earlier in this chapter you learned how you could use numeric literals in conjunction with simple assignment and arithmetic operations. RPG IV lets you use character literals in Calculation Specifications when working with character-oriented operations. To indicate that a value is a character literal (and not a field name), simply enclose it within apostrophes. There is no restriction on what characters can comprise the literal; any character that you can represent via the keyboard — including a blank — is acceptable. Some examples of character literals follow:

'John Doe'
'Abc 246 #18w'
'321444'
'45%'

Recognize that you cannot use a character literal — one enclosed within apostrophes — with an arithmetic operation even if all the characters of the literal are digits. Numeric literals do not use apostrophes.

Character Assignment

Now that you understand character literals, let's look at how to assign values to character fields. As you might guess, RPG IV's EVAL operation easily handles this task.

```
*.. 1 ...+... 2 ...+... 3 ...+... 4 ...+... 5 ...+... 6 ...+... 7 ...+... 8 ...+... 9 ...+...10
CL0N01Factor1++++++Opcode(E)+Extended-factor2+++++++++++++++++++++++++++Comments+++++++++++
C                   EVAL      EmailAdd = 'jdoe@rpgiv.com'
```

Just like in numeric assignment operations, the value to be assigned (in this case a character literal) appears to the right of the equal sign, and the receiving field appears to the left. If you need to continue a long literal to another line, use a continuation character (+ or −) to signal to the computer that the literal continues on the next line.

```
*.. 1 ...+... 2 ...+... 3 ...+... 4 ...+... 5 ...+... 6 ...+... 7 ...+... 8 ...+... 9 ...+...10
CL0N01Factor1++++++Opcode(E)+Extended-factor2+++++++++++++++++++++++++++Comments+++++++++++
C...........................Extended-factor2-continuation+++++++++++++++Comments+++++++++++
C                   EVAL      ReportHead = 'Wexler University:  1995 +
C                                         Faculty Directory'
```

Remember when you use the + continuation character, the continuation starts with the first nonblank character in the extended factor 2 of the following line; − directs the continuation to begin with whatever appears in column 36.

The EVAL operation performs the assignment by transferring the literal character by character, starting with the left-most character of the literal. If the result field that receives the literal is defined to be longer than the character literal, EVAL *right-pads* the field with blanks (i.e., the unused positions at the right end of the field contain blanks). If the result field is too small to store the literal, EVAL truncates the extra right-most characters.

```
*.. 1 ...+... 2 ...+... 3 ...+... 4 ...+... 5 ...+... 6 ...+... 7 ...+... 8 ...+... 9 ...+...10
CLØN01Factor1++++++Opcode(E)+Extended-factor2++++++++++++++++++++++++++Comments++++++++++++
C* If the result field and the literal are the same length, all characters are copied
C* to the result field.
C                   EVAL      Example = 'ABCDEFG'
C* Field Example now contains 'ABCDEFG'.
C
C* If the result field is longer than the literal by 5 positions, all characters are copied
C* to the left positions of the result field; the right-most 5 characters are blanks.
C                   EVAL      Example2 = 'ABCDEFG'
C* Field Example2 now contains 'ABCDEFG     '
C
C* If the result field is shorter than the literal by 3 positions, the right-most
C* 3 characters of the literal are not copied to the result field.
C                   EVAL      Example3 = 'ABCDEFG'
C* Field Example3 now contains 'ABCD'.
```

You can also use EVAL to assign the contents of one character field to another. The same rules apply regarding padding and truncation.

```
*.. 1 ...+... 2 ...+... 3 ...+... 4 ...+... 5 ...+... 6 ...+... 7 ...+... 8 ...+... 9 ...+...10
CLØN01Factor1++++++Opcode(E)+Extended-factor2++++++++++++++++++++++++++Comments++++++++++++
C* Suppose PadCourse is 10 positions in length, CourseName contains 'CS365', and
C* Prefix is 2 positions in length.
C                   EVAL      PadCourse = CourseName
C                   EVAL      Prefix = CourseName
C* Field PadCourse now contains 'CS365     ', and field Prefix contains 'CS'.
```

Data Type Conversion
Occasionally, you may need to convert a value's data type from numeric to character, or vice versa, to use the value in operations valid only for a particular data type. For example, you might initially store a numeric value in a character field so that you can check whether or not the value contains a particular digit (how to do this is discussed in Chapter 11). Following this check, you might transfer the value to a numeric field for use in arithmetic calculations or edited output. You cannot use the EVAL operation to perform such data type conversions; EVAL requires that data types match in an assignment statement. You use another assignment operator, MOVE, to carry out data type conversion.

MOVE (Move)
The MOVE operation uses the standard form of the Calculation Specification. Factor 1 is not used with MOVE: the value specified in factor 2 is copied (or assigned) to the result field. The following examples show how to use MOVE to change data types:

```
*.. 1 ...+... 2 ...+... 3 ...+... 4 ...+... 5 ...+... 6 ...+... 7 ...+... 8 ...+... 9 ...+...10
CLØN01Factor1++++++Opcode(E)+Factor2++++++Result+++++++Len++D+HiLoEq....Comments++++++++++++
C* Store a numeric value in character field Alpha (length 4).
C                   MOVE      1234          Alpha
C* Execute desired character operations on Alpha.
C                   ...
C* Then move the value to a numeric field so that it can be used with arithmetic operations or
C* edited for output. Numeric has length 4, with Ø decimal positions.
C                   MOVE      Alpha         Numeric
```

Unlike EVAL, the transfer of characters from the sending field in factor 2 to the receiving field in the result occurs character by character from *right to left*. MOVE disregards the decimal positions of numeric fields, and it does not automatically pad a character field with blanks. (You would need to designate the operation extender (P) for this to occur.)

When changing data types with the MOVE operation, it is good programming practice to match the size of the result field with the size of the factor 2 value to avoid errors in data transfer. Matching sizes with MOVE eliminates inadvertent changes to numeric values; it avoids the truncation of characters or the inclusion of carryover characters from the result field, which can occur if factor 2 is shorter than the result. The following examples demonstrate how errors in data transfer may happen when using MOVE:

```
*.. 1 ...+... 2 ...+... 3 ...+... 4 ...+... 5 ...+... 6 ...+... 7 ...+... 8 ...+... 9 ...+...10
CLØN01Factor1++++++Opcode(E)+Factor2++++++Result+++++++Len++D+HiLoEq....Comments++++++++++++
C* Alpha is a 4-position character field that contains zeros. Numeric is a 5-position
C* numeric field, with 1 decimal position, previously initialized to zero.
C                   MOVE      1.23          Alpha
C                   MOVE      Alpha         Numeric
C* Alpha now contains 'Ø123'; Numeric now contains ØØ12.3.
C
C*                  MOVE      32767         Alpha
C* Alpha now contains '2767'.
C
C                   MOVE      59            Alpha
C* Alpha now contains '2759'.
```

Sometimes programmers use MOVE to split off the right-most portion of a data value that contains both alphabetic characters as well as digits to be treated as numeric data. To split off the left-most portion, you can use another RPG IV assignment operation: MOVEL (Move Left). MOVEL performs identically to MOVE, except that data transfer proceeds from left to right. The following example shows how you can use MOVE and MOVEL to extract parts of a data value:

```
*.. 1 ...+... 2 ...+... 3 ...+... 4 ...+... 5 ...+... 6 ...+... 7 ...+... 8 ...+... 9 ...+...10
CLØN01Factor1++++++Opcode(E)+Factor2++++++Result+++++++Len++D+HiLoEq....Comments++++++++++++
C* StateTax is a 6-byte character field that contains the value 'Ø725CA'; StateID is a
C* 2-byte character field; TaxRate is a numeric field of length 4, with 4 decimal positions.
C                   MOVE      StateTax      StateID
C                   MOVEL     StateTax      TaxRate
C* StateID now contains 'CA'; TaxRate contains .Ø725.
```

In Chapter 13 you will look further at how the MOVE and MOVEL operators were used in previous versions of RPG. You will also learn about other operators that were used before EVAL to carry out specific assignment operations.

Figurative Constants

RPG IV includes a special set of reserved words called figurative constants. **Figurative constants** are implied literals that can be used without a specified length. Figurative constants assume the length and decimal positions of the fields they are associated with. RPG's figurative constants are *BLANK (or *BLANKS), *ZERO (or *ZEROS), *HIVAL, *LOVAL, *OFF, *ON, *ALL, and *NULL.

Assigning *BLANK or *BLANKS causes a character field to be filled with blanks. Assigning *HIVAL fills a character field with X'FFFF...' (all bits on) and a numeric field with all 9s and a plus sign. Assigning *LOVAL fills a character field with X'0000...' (all bits off) and a numeric field with all 9s and a negative sign. Programmers often assign *HIVAL or *LOVAL to a field to ensure that the field's value will be greater than (or less than, for *LOVAL) any other value they may compare to that field.

RPG IV lets you assign *ZERO (or *ZEROS) both to numeric and to character fields to fill the fields with 0s. Assigning figurative constant *ALL, immediately followed by one or more characters within quotes, causes the string within the quotes to be cyclically repeated through the entire length of the result field.

```
*.. 1 ...+... 2 ...+... 3 ...+... 4 ...+... 5 ...+... 6 ...+... 7 ...+... 8 ...+... 9 ...+...10
CL0N01Factor1++++++Opcode(E)+Extended-factor2+++++++++++++++++++++++++++++++Comments+++++++++++
CL0N01Factor1++++++Opcode(E)+Factor2++++++Result++++++++Len++D+HiLoEq....Comments+++++++++++
C* Examples of using figurative constants in assignment operations.
C                   EVAL      *IN50 = *ON
C                   EVAL      LastName = *BLANKS
C                   EVAL      ZeroField = *ZEROS
C                   EVAL      RecordKey = *HIVAL
C                   EVAL      CharField = *ALL'XYZ'
C* If field CharField has length 9, it now contains 'XYZXYZXYZ'
C                   EVAL      UnderLine = *ALL'-'
C* If field UnderLine has length 80, it now contains 80 hyphens
```

Figurative constants *OFF and *ON represent character '0' and character '1', respectively. Although *OFF and *ON can be used with any character field of any length, most often programmers use *OFF and *ON to change the value of an RPG IV indicator or to compare with an indicator's value. *ON is the equivalent of '1', while *OFF equates to '0'. *NULL is used only with pointers, which are discussed later in the text.

Chapter Summary

RPG IV has a limited number of arithmetic operators to use for computations. With the EVAL operation, you can express complex arithmetic calculations in a single, free-form expression that can continue over several lines, if necessary. Such expressions can include the arithmetic operators +, −, *, /, and **; parentheses; numeric fields; and numeric literals. You use the specific arithmetic operations SQRT and MVR (coupled with DIV) to perform calculations that EVAL cannot handle. You can use numeric fields and numeric literals in arithmetic calculations. You do not enclose numeric literals within apostrophes; apostrophes signal to the computer the presence of a character literal, which cannot participate in arithmetic operations.

Calculations often involve creating new fields to store the results of the calculations. You must define these new fields by specifying their data type, length, and number of decimal positions (if numeric) within Definition Specifications. The size of result fields should be large enough to avoid high-order truncation and program abends. If the result of an arithmetic operation contains more decimal positions than you want to store, you should round the calculation.

You can use EVAL to assign values to character fields. EVAL performs character data transfer from left to right and automatically right blank-pads the receiving field if it is longer than the sending field. If the receiving field is shorter than the sending field, EVAL truncates the right-most extra characters.

To change the data type of character or numeric data, use operation MOVE. MOVE transfers data from right to left, doesn't automatically blank-pad, and truncates extra left-most characters. Good programmers match the sizes of fields and/or values in this kind of a MOVE operation to avoid errors in data transfer.

You also can use MOVE and MOVEL to split off the right-most and left-most portions of a data value. MOVEL works like MOVE, except that data transfer proceeds from left to right.

Figurative constants are built-in literals with specified values. The length of a figurative constant automatically adjusts to match that of the field it is used with. Figurative constants include *BLANK, *BLANKS, *ZERO, *ZEROS, *HIVAL, *LOVAL, *OFF, *ON, *ALL, and *NULL.

The following table summarizes the RPG IV operations that have been discussed in this chapter. This table can help you recall the appropriate format for a Calculation Specification based on a particular operation.

Arithmetic and Assignment Operations

Data Types	Factor 1	Operation	Extended Factor 2
character/numeric	—	**EVAL (H)**	RESULT FIELD = EXPRESSION

Data Types	Factor 1	Operation	Factor 2	Result
numeric	field/ literal	**DIV (H)**	FIELD/LITERAL	FIELD
numeric	—	**MVR**	—	FIELD
numeric	—	**SQRT (H)**	FIELD/LITERAL	FIELD
character/numeric	—	**MOVE (P)**	FIELD/LITERAL	FIELD
character/numeric	—	**MOVEL (P)**	FIELD/LITERAL	FIELD

Operation extenders (optional):   H = half-adjust (round) result;
                                                    P = pad result with blanks.

Uppercase entry = required; lowercase entry = optional.

Extended factor 2 entries are free-form.

Terms

assignment operations
character literals
Definition Specifications
exponentiation
figurative constants

half-adjusting
high-order truncation
low-order truncation
numeric fields
numeric literals

operation extender
specific arithmetic operations
stand-alone fields
truncation

Discussion/Review Questions

1. What is a literal? Why would you use a literal within an arithmetic operation? (Give some examples.) Can you think of any disadvantages to using literals in calculations?

2. Which of the values below would *not* constitute valid numeric literals in RPG IV?

+124.22	44%	–10.2
$23.44	1,210.34	.9931
'75.22'	4512	–.012345678

3. Why do you think RPG IV has relatively limited mathematical capabilities ?

4. Why does it make sense that the result of a Calculation Specification cannot be a literal?

5. What two mathematical impossibilities will result in a program error if your program tries to execute them?

6. Summarize the rules of thumb for determining how large to define result fields for arithmetic operations.

7. When should you round an arithmetic operation?

8. Discuss the differences between operations EVAL, MOVE, and MOVEL.

9. Why should you use EVAL rather than MOVE to assign values to numeric fields?

10. What is a figurative constant? What are possible uses for figurative constants? How does *ALL work?

Exercises

1. Write the calculations to discount field OldPrice (6 positions, 2 decimal positions) by 10 percent to give NewPrice.

2. Write the calculations to convert a temperature in Fahrenheit to Centigrade, using the following formula:

   $$C = 5(F - 32)/9$$

   Assume F is 3 positions with 0 decimal positions.

3. Write the calculations to convert a measurement taken in inches (field Inches, 5 positions with 0 decimal positions) into the same measurement expressed as yards, feet, and inches.

4. Code the calculations needed to determine the cost of wall-to-wall carpeting for a room. Field RmLength (3 positions, 1 decimal) contains the room length in feet; field RmWidth (3 positions, 1 decimal) contains the room's width in feet; and field CostPrYard (4 positions, 2 decimals) contains the cost per square yard of the selected carpet.

5. Write the calculations to determine the Economic Order Quantity, EOQ, using the formula

   $$EOQ = \text{square root of } (2DO/C),$$

   where D represents annual demand for product;

   O represents costs to place one order;

   and C represents carrying costs.

   Assume D is 5 positions, 0 decimal positions; O is 5 positions, 2 decimal positions; and C is 6 positions, 2 decimal positions.

Programming Assignments

1. Wexler University wants a program that will produce a student grade report. Input file WUEXAMP (described in Appendix D) contains information about students in a class and five exam grades for each student.

   The program will need to calculate an average exam grade for each student. The school also wants to know the average exam grade for the class as a whole (i.e., the average of the averages). The desired report layout is shown below. Notice that just the initial of the student's first name is to print with the last name.

```
            1         2         3         4         5         6         7         8         9         1 0
   1234567890123456789012345678901234567890123456789012345678901234567890123456789012345678901234567890
 1      XX/XX/XX           WEXLER U. STUDENT GRADE REPORT           PAGE XX0X
 2
 3                                    EXAM  EXAM  EXAM  EXAM  EXAM   AVG.
 4  STUDENT NO.           NAME          1     2     3     4     5   GRADE
 5
 6  XXX-XX-XXXX           X. XXXXXXXXXXXXXX   X0X   X0X   X0X   X0X   X0X   X0X
 7  XXX-XX-XXXX           X. XXXXXXXXXXXXXX   X0X   X0X   X0X   X0X   X0X   X0X
 8  XXX-XX-XXXX           X. XXXXXXXXXXXXXX   X0X   X0X   X0X   X0X   X0X   X0X
 9
10                                          CLASS AVERAGE   X0X
```

Programming Assignments Continued

Programming Assignments continued

2. CompuSell, the computer mail-order company, extends financing to some of its preferred customers. All financing is done for 12 months at a fixed rate of 14 percent. The company charges interest on the total amount financed, rather than on the unpaid balance remaining after each successive payment. Accordingly, the monthly payment is determined by calculating the interest due on the unpaid balance, adding the interest to the unpaid balance, and dividing that sum by 12.

     Write a program for CompuSell that will calculate monthly charges for each customer in the input file CSCSFINP, described in Appendix D.

     The format of the desired report is shown below. Note that purchase date is to print as DD-MM, and that the report requires a count of customers in the file.

```
        1         2         3         4         5         6         7         8         9         10
1234567890123456789012345678901234567890123456789012345678901234567890123456789012345678901234567890
 1  XX/XX/XX                COMPUSELL FINANCE REPORT                          PAGE XXØX
 2
 3  CUST.        PURCHASE      PURCHASE       DOWN          BALANCE         MONTHLY
 4  NUM.         AMOUNT        DATE           PAYMENT       OWED            PAYMENT
 5
 6  XXXXXX       X,XXØ.XX      ØX-XX          X,XXØ.XX      X,XXØ.XX        X,XXØ.XX
 7  XXXXXX       X,XXØ.XX      ØX-XX          X,XXØ.XX      X,XXØ.XX        X,XXØ.XX
 8
 9               TOTALS        $XXX,XX$.XX   $XXX,XX$.XX   $XXX,XX$.XX
10
11  NUMBER OF CUSTOMERS PROCESSED XXØ
```

3. Wexler University wants a program to generate a payroll register for its hourly employees. Appendix D describes the input file for this program: WUHRLYP. The file contains information about regular and over-time hours worked and pay rate for hourly employees.

     The school pays time and a half for overtime hours. Gross pay is the sum of regular and over time pay. Net pay is gross pay less deductions for taxes and FICA. Eighteen percent federal tax is withheld; 5 percent state tax; and 7.51 percent for FICA.

     The format of the desired payroll register is shown below. Note that just the initial of the first name is to print as part of the employee's name.

```
        1         2         3         4         5         6         7         8         9         10
1234567890123456789012345678901234567890123456789012345678901234567890123456789012345678901234567890
 1     PAGE XXØX                                                                    XX/XX/XX
 2
 3                           WEXLER U. PAYROLL REGISTER
 4
 5                                      GROSS        FEDERAL        STATE                    NET
 6     SOC. SEC.       NAME             PAY          TAX            TAX        FICA          PAY
 7
 8  XXX-XX-XXXX   X. XXXXXXXXXXXXXX     X,XXØ.XX     X,XXØ.XX       XXØ.XX     XXØ.XX        X,XXØ.XX
 9  XXX-XX-XXXX   X. XXXXXXXXXXXXXX     X,XXØ.XX     X,XXØ.XX       XXØ.XX     XXØ.XX        X,XXØ.XX
10
11                GRAND TOTALS         $XXX,XX$.XX  $XXX,XX$.XX  $XX,XX$.XX $XX,XX$.XX  $XXX,XX$.XX
12
13
14
15
```

Programming Assignments Continued

Programming Assignments continued

4. Ida Lapeer, Interior Decorator, wants a program that will estimate material costs for interior painting jobs based on data in file BIDS, described at the end of Appendix D.

Coverage per gallon represents the number of square feet of surface area that can be painted by one gallon. All room measurements were taken in terms of feet and inches (e.g., 14'10"). The percent figure given for windows and doors represents Ida's estimate of wall surface that will *not* need paint because of doors or windows. In calculating costs, include the cost of painting the ceiling, as well as all four walls of the room.

Calculate final needed coverage to the nearest square foot and gallons needed to the nearest 100th of a gallon. Paint cost should be based on that figure. Ida has found that 5 percent of her paint costs represents a good estimate of other miscellaneous job costs, such as masking tape, brushes and rollers, and so on.

Your program should produce the report depicted in the printer spacing chart below.

```
          1         2         3         4         5         6         7         8         9         1 0
 1234567890123456789012345678901234567890123456789012345678901234567890123456789012345678901234567890
1      XX/XX/XX                 IDA LAPEER MATERIAL COST ESTIMATES
2
3   JOB       PAINT      COST      COVERAGE     SQ. FEET    GALLONS     ----- ESTIMATED COSTS -----
4   NO.        CODE    PER GAL.    PER GAL.     TO COVER    NEEDED     PAINT      MISC.      TOTAL
5
6   XXXX      XX-XXX    X0.XX        X0X         X,X0X       X0.XX     X,XX0.XX   XX0.XX   XX,XX0.XX
7   XXXX      XX-XXX    X0.XX        X0X         X,X0X       X0.XX     X,XX0.XX   XX0.XX   XX,XX0.XX
```

Chapter 4

Top-Down, Structured Program Design

Chapter Overview

This chapter focuses on program design and introduces you to RPG IV operations that let you write well-designed programs using a top-down, structured approach. Loops, decision logic, and subroutines receive special attention. The chapter applies these design principles by teaching you how to code control-break problems.

Structured Design

Typically, you can solve programming problems in many different ways, each of which might produce correct output. Correct output, however, although an important goal, should not be the only goal of the programmer. Producing code that is readable and easily changed is also important to programmers who are concerned with quality.

Changes in user requirements and processing errors discovered as programs are used dictate that programmers spend a lot of their time maintaining existing programs rather than developing new code. A well-designed, well-documented program facilitates such maintenance, while a poorly designed program can be a maintenance nightmare.

Structured design is one development methodology that has become widely accepted over the past 20 years to facilitate quality program design. One important aspect of structured design is limiting control structures within your program to three basic logic structures: sequence, selection (also called decision), and iteration (also called repetition or looping).

Sequence lets you instruct the computer to execute operations serially. **Selection** lets you establish alternate paths of instructions within a program; which alternate the program executes depends on the results of a test or condition within the program. And **iteration** permits instructions within the program to be repeated until a condition is met or is no longer met. Figure 4.1 illustrates these control structures in flowchart symbols so that you can understand easily how flow of control works with each structure.

Each of these control structures has a single entry point and a single exit point. Together, the structures can serve as basic building blocks to express the complex logic required to solve complicated programming problems, while maintaining the tight control over program flow that facilitates program maintenance. Structured programming sometimes is called

Figure 4.1
Flowcharts Illustrating
Basic Control Structures

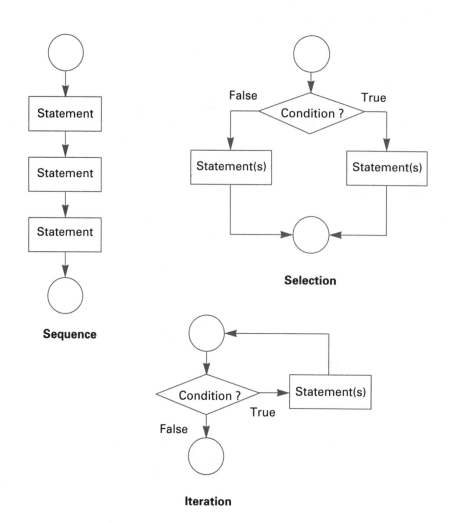

Sequence

Selection

Iteration

"GOTO-less programming," because this methodology discourages the indiscriminate use of GOTOs. GOTOs are the single operation most responsible for "spaghetti code."

Sequential Flow of Control

Sequential flow of control is inherent in RPG IV — and other programming languages — by default. The order in which you describe your operations on the Calculation Specifications determines the order in which the computer executes them. The computer continues to execute the program statements in their order of occurrence unless it encounters an operation that explicitly transfers control to a different location within the program.

Relational Comparisons

To diverge from a sequential flow of control requires the use of explicit operations. RPG IV includes a variety of operations to let you express both decision and iteration logic. Both kinds of operations involve testing a condition to determine the appropriate course of action. This testing involves a **relational comparison** between two values. To express the comparison, RPG IV supports six relational symbols (and six two-letter relational codes) that are used with many of the operations. The symbols, their corresponding two-letter codes, and their meanings are summarized in the table below.

Symbol	Code	Meaning
>	GT	Greater than
<	LT	Less than
=	EQ	Equal to
< >	NE	Not equal to
< =	LE	Less than or equal to
> =	GE	Greater than or equal to

The way the computer evaluates whether or not a comparison is true depends on the data type of the items being compared. If you are comparing two numeric items (whether fields or literals), the system compares them based on algebraic values. The length and number of decimal positions in the items being compared do not affect the outcome of the comparison. For example, 2.25 is equal to 00002.250000, while 00000002.12345 is smaller than 9. A positive value is always larger than a negative value. Only the algebraic values of the data items themselves determine the result of a relational comparison between numeric fields.

You can also perform relational tests between character values. This kind of comparison takes place somewhat differently from numeric comparisons. When you compare two character literals or fields, the system performs a character-by-character comparison, moving from left to right, until it finds an unmatched pair or has finished checking. When it encounters a character difference, the difference is interpreted in terms of the collating sequence of **EBCDIC**, the data-representation format used by IBM. In EBCDIC, A is less than B, B less than C, and so on; lowercase letters are "smaller" than uppercase letters; letters are smaller than digits; and blank is smaller than any other displayable character.

If you are comparing two character items of unequal sizes, the system blank-pads the smaller item to the right before making the character-by-character comparison. To understand character comparisons, consider the examples below. (In the examples, ƀ represents a blank within the data item.)

ART is less than BART
ARTHUR equals ARTHURƀƀƀƀ
ARTƀƀƀƀ is less than ARTHUR
Al is less than AL
123 is greater than ABC

RPG IV does not allow you to compare a numeric data item with a character data item. However, you can use indicators in relational comparisons, provided you preface the indicator with *IN. You can compare one indicator with another (in which case you're trying to determine whether their values are the same), or you can compare an indicator with character literals '1' and '0' or figurative constants *ON and *OFF, all of which represent the possible values an indicator may assume.

Selection Operations

Now that you understand how RPG IV makes relational comparisons, you can learn how the relational operators are used with those RPG IV operations that determine flow of program control. First we will look at the options for sending control to alternate statements within a program — **decision** (or selection) **operations**.

IF (If)

The primary decision operator is IF. The general format of the IF operation is

```
*.. 1 ...+... 2 ...+... 3 ...+... 4 ...+... 5 ...+... 6 ...+... 7 ...+... 8 ...+... 9 ...+...10
CLØNØ1Factor1+++++++Opcode(E)+Extended-factor2++++++++++++++++++++++++++++++++Comments+++++++++++
C                  IF        Conditional expression
C                  ...
C                  ENDIF
```

IF uses the extended factor 2 format of the Calculation Specifications; factor 1 is always blank, while the extended factor 2 contains the conditional expression to be tested. If the result of the conditional expression is true, all the calculations between the IF statement and its ENDIF are executed. If the relationship is not true, those statements are bypassed.

For example, if you wanted to count all senior citizens, you could write the following lines. The IF below can be read, "If Age is greater than or equal to 65, then increment SeniorCnt by one."

```
*.. 1 ...+... 2 ...+... 3 ...+... 4 ...+... 5 ...+... 6 ...+... 7 ...+... 8 ...+... 9 ...+...10
CLØNØ1Factor1+++++++Opcode(E)+Extended-factor2++++++++++++++++++++++++++++++++Comments+++++++++++
C                  IF        Age >= 65
C                  EVAL      SeniorCnt = SeniorCnt + 1
C                  ENDIF
```

You can also use the IF operation with an ELSE to set up an alternate path of instructions, should the IF fail. For example, if you were asked to calculate pay and wanted to pay time-and-a-half for any hours over 40, you could code the following:

```
*.. 1 ...+... 2 ...+... 3 ...+... 4 ...+... 5 ...+... 6 ...+... 7 ...+... 8 ...+... 9 ...+...10
CLØNØ1Factor1+++++++Opcode(E)+Extended-factor2+++++++++++++++++++++++++++++Comments++++++++++++
C                   IF        Hours <= 40
C                   EVAL (H)        TotalPay = Hours * PayRate
C                   ELSE
C                   EVAL (H)        TotalPay = 40 * PayRate +
C                                     (Hours - 40) *PayRate * 1.5
C                   ENDIF
```

Sometimes you want to execute a series of instructions based on multiple tests or conditions. RPG IV includes the binary operators, AND and OR, to allow such multiple conditions. When an AND is used to set up a compound condition, both relationships must be true for the IF to evaluate as true. When you use an OR to connect two relational tests, the IF evaluates to true if one or the other (or both) of the conditions is true.

```
*.. 1 ...+... 2 ...+... 3 ...+... 4 ...+... 5 ...+... 6 ...+... 7 ...+... 8 ...+... 9 ...+...10
CLØNØ1Factor1+++++++Opcode(E)+Extended-factor2+++++++++++++++++++++++++++++Comments++++++++++++
C                   IF        Age >= 65 AND Status = 'R'
C* This block of code executes only if Age >= 65 and Status = R.
C                        ...
C                   ELSE
C* If one or both conditions are not met, this code executes instead.
C                        ...
C                   ENDIF
C
C                   IF        Age >=65 OR Status = 'R'
C* This block executes if one or both conditions are true.
C                        ...
C                   ELSE
C* This block executes only if both conditions are false.
C                        ...
C                   ENDIF
```

You can combine ANDs and ORs to create more complex conditional tests. If the conditional expression requires more room than a single specification offers, you can extend the expression to additional lines by using the extended factor 2 continuation form of the Calculation Specifications. Note that ANDs are evaluated before ORs. However, you can use parentheses to modify the order of evaluation, because parentheses are always evaluated first.

To illustrate how ANDs and ORs are evaluated and to demonstrate the use of parentheses, consider the following scenario. A company wants to print a list of employees eligible for early retirement. Only salaried employees are eligible (code = 'S'); moreover, they must have worked more than 15 years for the company or be 55 (or more) years old. The following figure shows an incorrect way and a correct way to express these conditions:

```
*.. 1 ...+... 2 ...+... 3 ...+... 4 ...+... 5 ...+... 6 ...+... 7 ...+... 8 ...+... 9 ...+...10
CLØNØ1Factor1++++++Opcode(E)+Extended-factor2++++++++++++++++++++++++++++++Comments+++++++++++
C.............................Extended-factor2-continuation+++++++++++++++Comments+++++++++++
C* The IF below would select any employee who was salaried and had worked more than 15 years;
C* it also would incorrectly include any employee at least 55 years old, whether or not
C* (s)he was salaried.
C                   IF        SalaryCode = 'S' AND YrsWorked > 15
C                             OR Age >= 55
C                   ...
C                   ENDIF
C
C* The parentheses in the IF below cause the correct selection of employees who are salaried
C* and who have either worked more than 15 years or are at least 55 years old.
C                   IF        SalaryCode = 'S' AND (YrsWorked > 15
C                             OR Age >= 55)
C                   ...
C                   ENDIF
C
C* The IF below shows a clearer way to enter the correct IF to make the logic more apparent.
C                   IF        SalaryCode = 'S' AND
C                             (YrsWorked > 15 OR Age >= 55)
C                   ...
C                   ENDIF
```

You can combine ANDs and ORs with other operations to form extremely complicated conditional tests. In these cases, order of precedence causes ANDs and ORs to be evaluated last, following the other operations, unless parentheses are used to alter the order of precedence. The figure below illustrates some complex IFs. Note that although such IF logic is permitted in RPG IV, building conditions of such complexity leads to programs that are difficult to understand; the practice should be avoided if at all possible.

```
*.. 1 ...+... 2 ...+... 3 ...+... 4 ...+... 5 ...+... 6 ...+... 7 ...+... 8 ...+... 9 ...+...10
CLØNØ1Factor1++++++Opcode(E)+Extended-factor2++++++++++++++++++++++++++++++Comments+++++++++++
C.............................Extended-factor2-continuation+++++++++++++++Comments+++++++++++
C* In the sample IF below, the order in which the operations would be performed is as follows:
C* first, multiplication (W*X); next, addition (A + B); next, AND; and last, the two ORs,
C* moving from left to right.
C                   IF        A + B > 85 AND X = 10 OR W*X <> G OR
C                             *IN90 = *ON
C                   ...
C                   ENDIF
C
C* The sample IF below includes parentheses that change the order of evaluation.  Now the
C* multiplication (W*X) is done first; next, the second OR is evaluated; next, the first OR;
C* next, the addition; and last, the AND.
C                   IF        A + B > 85 AND (X = 10 OR
C                                     (W*X <> G OR *IN90 = *ON))
C                   ...
C                   ENDIF
```

IFs also can be nested. That is, you can build IFs within IFs, with or without ELSEs. Each IF requires an ENDIF in the appropriate spot to indicate the end point of that IF's influence. The following pseudocode illustrates a nested IF; the code expresses that same logic in RPG IV.

IF age is greater than or equal to 65
    IF sex is female
        life expectancy is 84
    ELSE
        life expectancy is 79
    ENDIF
ELSE
    IF sex is female
        life expectancy is 81
    ELSE
        life expectancy is 78
    ENDIF
ENDIF

```
*.. 1 ...+... 2 ...+... 3 ...+... 4 ...+... 5 ...+... 6 ...+... 7 ...+... 8 ...+... 9 ...+...10
CLØN01Factor1++++++Opcode(E)+Extended-factor2++++++++++++++++++++++++++++Comments+++++++++++
C* This code uses IF and EVAL to assign values to LifeExpect based on age and sex.
C                   IF        Age >= 65
C                   IF          Sex = 'F'
C                   EVAL          LifeExpect = 84
C                   ELSE
C                   EVAL          LifeExpect = 79
C                   ENDIF
C                   ELSE
C                   IF          Sex = 'F'
C                   EVAL          LifeExpect = 81
C                   ELSE
C                   EVAL          LifeExpect = 78
C                   ENDIF
C                   ENDIF
```

Sometimes a program's logic requires that nesting takes place only on the ELSE branches of the decision structure. The following example of assigning commission rates typifies this kind of construct, sometimes called **CASE logic**:

```
*.. 1 ...+... 2 ...+... 3 ...+... 4 ...+... 5 ...+... 6 ...+... 7 ...+... 8 ...+... 9 ...+...10
CLØN01Factor1++++++Opcode(E)+Extended-factor2++++++++++++++++++++++++++++Comments+++++++++++
C* IF used to assign commission rates based on sales level.
C                   IF        Sales <= 5000
C                   EVAL        Rate = .005
C                   ELSE
C                   IF        Sales <= 10000
C                   EVAL        Rate = .0075
C                   ELSE
C                   IF        Sales <= 20000
C                   EVAL        Rate = .01
C                   ELSE
C                   EVAL        Rate = .015
C                   ENDIF
C                   ENDIF
C                   ENDIF
```

Notice in the examples presented so far in this chapter that the free-form entry permitted within the extended factor 2 of the Calculation Specifications lets us indent code to make the logical groupings of conditions and the resulting actions more apparent.

IF and Page Overflow

Before we look at other RPG IV decision operations, one topic remains to be discussed in conjunction with decision logic: page overflow. In the reports we have written up to now, we have included page headings only on the first page. Because most business reports span multiple pages, we need a way to determine when it's time to advance to a new page and reprint heading lines.

RPG IV has built-in indicators called **overflow indicators**. The special indicators that may be used to signal overflow are OA, OB, OC, OD, OE, OF, OG, and OV. If you associate one of them with the report file on the File Specifications, that indicator will automatically come on when the printer reaches the overflow line at the bottom of the page. To make that association, enter keyword OFLIND in the Functions portion of the File Specification (positions 44-80), with the indicator you choose to use specified in parentheses following the keyword.

```
*.. 1 ...+... 2 ...+... 3 ...+... 4 ...+... 5 ...+... 6 ...+... 7 ...+... 8 ...+... 9 ...+...10
FFilename++IPEASFRlen+LKlen+AIDevice+.Keywords+++++++++++++++++++++++++++++Comments+++++++++++
FQPrint    O  F 132          PRINTER OFLIND(*INOF)
```

By referencing the status of that indicator in an IF statement just before printing a detail line, you can advance the page and print headings each time they are needed, as signaled by the overflow indicator. You will also need to turn that indicator off, because it does not go off automatically.

```
*.. 1 ...+... 2 ...+... 3 ...+... 4 ...+... 5 ...+... 6 ...+... 7 ...+... 8 ...+... 9 ...+...10
CL0N01Factor1++++++Opcode(E)+Extended-factor2+++++++++++++++++++++++++++++Comments+++++++++++
CL0N01Factor1++++++Opcode(E)+Factor2++++++Result+++++++Len++D+HiLoEq....Comments+++++++++++
C* Demonstration of how to handle headings within a process loop.
C                   ...
C                   IF        *INOF = *ON
C                   EXCEPT    Headings
C                   EVAL      *INOF = *OFF
C                   ENDIF
C                   EXCEPT    Detail
C                   ...
```

Although you can express even the most complex programming decision with a series of IF operations, nested IFs can be difficult to set up and hard for others to interpret. To overcome this problem, RPG IV has two selection operations to allow you to simplify coding of CASE logic: SELECT and CASxx.

SELECT (Conditionally Select Operations)

The SELECT operation appears on a line alone to identify the start of a CASE construct. The SELECT is followed by one or more WHEN lines, each of which specifies a condition to be tested; each WHEN is followed by one or more calculations to be performed when that condition is met. When the program executes, it checks the WHEN conditions sequentially, starting with the first. As soon as it encounters a true condition, the computer executes the operation(s) following that WHEN statement and then sends control to the end of the SELECT construct, signaled by an ENDSL operation.

The following code uses SELECT· to express the same logic for determining sales commission rates shown previously with nested IFs:

```
*.. 1 ...+... 2 ...+... 3 ...+... 4 ...+... 5 ...+... 6 ...+... 7 ...+... 8 ...+... 9 ...+...10
CLØNØ1Factor1++++++Opcode(E)+Extended-factor2++++++++++++++++++++++++++++Comments++++++++++++
C* Using SELECT and WHEN to assign a value to Rate based on level of sales.
C                   SELECT
C                   WHEN      Sales <= 5000
C                   EVAL          Rate = .005
C                   WHEN      Sales <= 10000
C                   EVAL          Rate = .0075
C                   WHEN      Sales <= 20000
C                   EVAL      Rate = .01
C                   OTHER
C                   EVAL          Rate = .015
C                   ENDSL
```

Notice in the above example that the reserved word OTHER means "in all other cases." OTHER, if used, should be the final "catch-all" condition listed. When a SELECT includes an OTHER, the computer will always perform one of the sets of calculations. When the SELECT is composed only of WHEN conditions, if none of the conditions are met, none of the operations within the SELECT will be performed.

Although not illustrated in the example above, just as in IF operations, multiple operations can follow each WHEN line — as many operations as are needed to accomplish the desired processing on that branch of the CASE structure. You also can couple the WHEN conditions with AND and OR to create compound selection criteria, which can continue on multiple specification lines if needed.

CASxx (Conditionally Select Subroutines)

The CASxx structure is nearly identical to SELECT, with two important differences. First, instead of coding alternate sets of operations in-line following each condition, the CASxx operation sends control to **subroutines** elsewhere in the program. The name of the subroutine to invoke is entered as the result field on the line that specifies the condition to be met to execute the subroutine.

Subroutines will be discussed in detail a little later in this chapter. For now, recognize that a subroutine is a set of operations coded elsewhere within the calculations and invoked as a unit by referencing the subroutine's name. After performing the subroutine, the program returns control to the statement immediately following the one that invoked the routine. In the CASxx operation, control returns to the Calculation Specification immediately following the ENDCS.

The second difference concerns the layout of the CASxx operation. (Here the *xx* represents one of the six two-letter relational codes mentioned earlier in the chapter). Rather than using free-form conditional expressions, CASxx uses a format reminiscent of older versions of RPG to express the conditional test. Consider the following example that uses CASxx to send program control to different subroutines based on the level of sales:

```
*.. 1 ...+... 2 ...+... 3 ...+... 4 ...+... 5 ...+... 6 ...+... 7 ...+... 8 ...+... 9 ...+...10
CL0N01Factor1++++++Opcode(E)+Factor2++++++Result+++++++Len++D+HiLoEq....Comments++++++++++++
C* Using CASxx to send control to different subroutines based on the level of sales;
C* commission rates might be assigned within the subroutines.
C         Sales        CASLE     5000        LowCommSR
C         Sales        CASLE    10000        MedCommSR
C         Sales        CASLE    20000        HighCommSR
C                      CAS                    VHighComSR
C                      ENDCS
```

The value in factor 1 is compared to that in factor 2; if the relationship between the two values matches that specified by the two-letter relational code appending CAS, the subroutine named in the result area is executed. As with SELECT, the first condition that evaluates to true causes the operations associated with that condition (in this case, executing a subroutine) to be performed, and then control jumps to the end of the logic structure to bypass the remaining comparisons. ENDCS signals the end of the CASxx operation. CASxx also lets you specify a subroutine to be performed if none of the tested conditions prove to be true. To include this option, simply use CAS without a relational code, as the final operation within the structure.

Operations for Iteration

The third logical construct of structured programming is iteration. Iteration lets your program repeat a series of instructions, a common necessity in programming. In batch processing, for example, you want to execute a series of instructions repeatedly, once for every record in a transaction file. You already have used one RPG IV operation that enables iteration, or looping: DOW.

DOW (Do While)

The DOW operation establishes a loop, based on a conditional test expression coded in the extended factor 2 of the Calculation Specifications. All the operations coded between this operator and its end statement (ENDDO) are repeated as long as the condition specified in the relational test remains true.

You have already used DOW to repeat processing until an end-of-file indicator is turned on. You can use the DOW for other kinds of repetition as well. Assume you want to add all the numbers between 1 and 100. With a

counter field, Number, and an accumulator, Sum, you can use DOW to easily accomplish this summation, as shown in the following code:

```
*.. 1 ...+... 2 ...+... 3 ...+... 4 ...+... 5 ...+... 6 ...+... 7 ...+... 8 ...+... 9 ...+...10
CLØN01Factor1++++++Opcode(E)+Extended-factor2+++++++++++++++++++++++++++++++Comments++++++++++++
C* This routine adds all the numbers from 1 to 100.
C* Begin by initializing fields Number and Sum to 0.
C                    EVAL      Number = 0
C                    EVAL      Sum = 0
C* Loop while Number is less than 100.
C                    DOW       Number < 100
C* Increment Number by 1.
C                    EVAL           Number = Number + 1
C* Add Number to accumulator Sum.
C                    EVAL           Sum = Sum + Number
C                    ENDDO
```

Like RPG IV's decision operations, the DOW operation lets you use
AND and OR to form compound conditions to control the looping.

```
*.. 1 ...+... 2 ...+... 3 ...+... 4 ...+... 5 ...+... 6 ...+... 7 ...+... 8 ...+... 9 ...+...10
CLØN01Factor1++++++Opcode(E)+Extended-factor2+++++++++++++++++++++++++++++++Comments++++++++++++
C* Any processing specified within the loop would be repeated as long as both indicators
C* 90 and 99 remain off.  Loop is implemented with DOW.
C                    DOW       *IN90 = *OFF AND *IN99 = *OFF
C                    ...
C                    ENDDO
```

DOU (Do Until)

DOU is a structured iteration operation very similar to DOW. Like DOW, it
includes a conditional test expression in the extended factor 2. However, two
major differences exist between a DOW and a DOU. First, the DOW repeats
while the specified condition *remains* true, whereas the DOU operation
repeats *until* the condition *becomes* true. Second, a DOW is a **leading decision
loop**, which means the comparison is made before the instructions within the
loop are executed for the first time. If the comparison evaluates to false, the
computer completely bypasses the instructions within the loop. A DOU, in
contrast, is a **trailing decision loop**. Because the comparison is made after the
instructions within the loop have been executed, the instructions will always
execute at least once. In contrast, instructions within a loop controlled by a
DOW may not be executed at all.

Figure 4.2 presents flowcharts of Do While and Do Until operations to
illustrate their differences.

Figure 4.2

Flowcharts Illustrating the
Difference Between
Do While and Do Until Loops

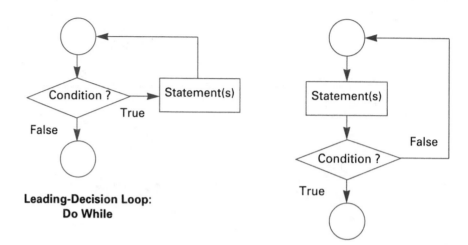

Leading-Decision Loop:
Do While

Trailing-Decision Loop:
Do Until

Do Whiles and Do Untils are often equally suited to setting up a looping structure. For instance, you could use a Do Until to solve the add-the-numbers problem; all you would need to change is the operation and the relational test. The figure below illustrates how to solve this problem using DOU.

```
*.. 1 ...+... 2 ...+... 3 ...+... 4 ...+... 5 ...+... 6 ...+... 7 ...+... 8 ...+... 9 ...+...10
CLØNØ1Factor1+++++++Opcode(E)+Extended-factor2+++++++++++++++++++++++++++++Comments++++++++++++
C* This routine uses DOU to add all the numbers from 1 to 100.
C* Begin by initializing fields Number and Sum to 0.
C                   EVAL      Number = 0
C                   EVAL      Sum = 0
C* Loop until Number equals 100.
C                   DOU       Number = 100
C* Increment Number by 1.
C                   EVAL          Number = Number + 1
C* Add Number to accumulator Sum.
C                   EVAL          Sum = Sum + Number
C                   ENDDO
```

DO (Do)

Often, as in the previous example, you want a loop to execute a specific number of times. To implement this kind of logic with Do Untils or Do Whiles, you need to define a field to serve as a counter. Each time through the loop, you increment the counter as part of your loop instructions and check the value of this counter after each repetition to determine whether or not another iteration is needed.

RPG IV offers an operation designed specifically for count-controlled loops: DO. Like Do Untils and Do Whiles, the end of a DO structure is signaled by ENDDO. Unlike those operations, the DO automatically increments its counter to ensure the repetition is done the desired number of times.

The format of the DO is a little more complicated than that of Do While or Do Until because it provides more options and defaults for the values coded in the factor 1, factor 2, and result field positions. The general layout of a DO loop is shown below.

```
*.. 1 ...+... 2 ...+... 3 ...+... 4 ...+... 5 ...+... 6 ...+... 7 ...+... 8 ...+... 9 ...+...10
CLØN01Factor1+++++++Opcode(E)+Factor2+++++++Result+++++++Len++D+HiLoEq....Comments+++++++++++
C        Start value   DO          Limit value   Counter
C                      ...
C                      ENDDO       Increment value
```

In general, a count-controlled operator in any language lets you specify four things: a field to serve as the counter, the starting value of the counter, the limiting value of the counter for looping to continue, and the amount to be added to the counter at the end of each repetition of the loop.

Although RPG IV gives you the option to specify these four values, you also can omit any of them. You can omit the initial value for the counter and/or the increment value for the counter. RPG IV assumes a default value of one for both. That is, it will start the counter at one and add one to it at the start of each additional pass through the loop, unless you specify differently.

You also can omit designating a field to serve as the counter. In this case, the system still keeps track of the number of repetitions with an internal counter, but you are unable to directly reference the counter's value for calculations or printing.

You can also omit the limit of the counter; again, the default value is one. To specify a different limit, enter a numeric integer field or literal in factor 2. If your factor 2 entry is a field, rather than a literal, the value of the field determines the number of repetitions.

```
*.. 1 ...+... 2 ...+... 3 ...+... 4 ...+... 5 ...+... 6 ...+... 7 ...+... 8 ...+... 9 ...+...10
CLØN01Factor1+++++++Opcode(E)+Factor2+++++++Result+++++++Len++D+HiLoEq....Comments+++++++++++
C* Sample DO loop skeletons.
C
C* The processing within the loop would be done just once.
C                      DO
C                      ...
C                      ENDDO
C
C* The processing within the loop would be done 5Ø times.
C                      DO          5Ø
C                      ...
C                      ENDDO
C
C* This number of repetitions of the loop depends on the value of Iter.
C                      DO          Iter
C                      ...
C                      ENDDO
```

If you need to know which iteration the computer is currently executing — for example, to print the value or to use it in a calculation — you need to designate a field to be used as the counter. You must define this field as an integer numeric field (i.e., a numeric field with 0 decimal positions). To designate that the field is the counter used by the DO, enter it in the result field position of the DO line.

The code below shows the add-the-numbers problem implemented with DO. Number is the counter field that the system automatically increments by one on each pass through the loop.

```
*.. 1 ...+... 2 ...+... 3 ...+... 4 ...+... 5 ...+... 6 ...+... 7 ...+... 8 ...+... 9 ...+...10
CL0N01Factor1++++++Opcode(E)+Extended-factor2+++++++++++++++++++++++++++++Comments++++++++++++
CL0N01Factor1++++++Opcode(E)+Factor2++++++Result+++++++Len++D+HiLoEq....Comments++++++++++++
C* This routine will add all the numbers from 1 to 100 using a DO operation.  Counter Number is
C* automatically incremented each pass through the loop.
C* Initialize accumulator Sum.
C                   EVAL      Sum = 0
C* Loop until Number exceeds 100.
C                   DO        100          Number
C* Add Number to the accumulator.
C                   EVAL           Sum = Sum + Number
C                   ENDDO
```

If you want the counter to start at a value other than 1, you can enter an alternate starting value (as either a literal or a field) in factor 1 of the DO statement. And if you want to use an increment amount other than 1, code this value (again, as a literal or a field) in factor 2 of the ENDDO statement.

For example, we can easily change our sample solution to add all the even numbers from 1 to 100 if we set Number's starting value to 2 and the increment value to 2, as shown in the following figure:

```
*.. 1 ...+... 2 ...+... 3 ...+... 4 ...+... 5 ...+... 6 ...+... 7 ...+... 8 ...+... 9 ...+...10
CL0N01Factor1++++++Opcode(E)+Extended-factor2+++++++++++++++++++++++++++++Comments++++++++++++
CL0N01Factor1++++++Opcode(E)+Factor2++++++Result+++++++Len++D+HiLoEq....Comments++++++++++++
C* This routine will add all the even numbers from 2 to 100 using DO.
C* Initialize accumulator to 0.
C                   EVAL      Sum = 0
C* Start Number at 2 and loop until it exceeds 100.
C     2             DO        100          Number
C* Add Number to accumulator Sum.
C                   EVAL           Sum = Sum + Number
C                   ENDDO     2
C* The 2 in the above ENDDO specifies the increment value for Number.
```

Loops and Early Exits

You sometimes may want to skip the remaining instructions within a loop to begin the next iteration or cycle. In other cases, you may want to exit the loop completely before the repetition is terminated by the relational comparison. Two RPG IV operations — ITER and LEAVE — provide you with these capabilities.

When the computer encounters an ITER within a loop, control skips past the remaining instructions in the loop and causes the next repetition to begin. LEAVE terminates the looping process completely and sends control to the statement immediately following the loop's ENDDO statement. You can use both these statements with all variants of the DO operation: DOW, DOU, and DO.

Assume, for example, you are processing a file of customer records and printing a report line for those customers whose balance due exceeds zero. If amount due equals zero, you simply want to cycle around and read the next record from the file. The following code illustrates a solution that uses LEAVE and ITER:

```
*.. 1 ...+... 2 ...+... 3 ...+... 4 ...+... 5 ...+... 6 ...+... 7 ...+... 8 ...+... 9 ...+...10
CLØNØ1Factor1++++++Opcode(E)+Extended-factor2+++++++++++++++++++++++++++++Comments+++++++++++
CLØNØ1Factor1++++++Opcode(E)+Factor2++++++Result++++++++Len++D+HiLoEq....Comments+++++++++++
C* This routine processes all records in CustFile and prints a detail line for those customers
C* whose AmountDue is not equal to zero.
C                   DOW       *IN90 = *OFF
C                   READ      CustFile                                       90
C                   SELECT
C                   WHEN      *IN90 = *ON
C                   LEAVE
C                   WHEN      AmountDue = 0
C                   ITER
C                   OTHER
C                   EXCEPT    Detail
C                   ENDSL
C                   ENDDO
```

Top-Down Design

Up to now, this chapter has concentrated on structured design. A second design concept, top-down methodology, usually goes hand in hand with a structured approach. **Top-down design** means developing your program solution starting with a broad "outline" and then successively breaking the big pieces into smaller and smaller units. This technique is sometimes called **hierarchical decomposition**.

Hierarchical decomposition is the method your English teacher recommended for writing research papers: Work out an outline, starting with your main topics; then subdivide these into subtopics, and so on, until you have decomposed to a level of sufficient detail to allow you to write the paper (or in programming terms, the individual instructions of your program).

Top-down design lets you handle problems of great complexity by allowing you to initially ignore the detailed requirements of processing. Top-down design works in tandem with modular program development, which advocates that your program be structured into logical units, or modules. In top-down design the first, or upper-level, design modules you develop chiefly concern controlling flow to and from the lower-level modules you develop later.

Each module should be as independent of the others as possible, and the statements within a module should work together to perform a single function. Structural decomposition gives you a way of dealing with complexity; when used with a modular approach, structural decomposition results in programs of functionally cohesive subroutines that are easier to maintain later.

Defining Subroutines

One vehicle for top-down, modular program design in RPG IV is the sub-routine. A subroutine, as mentioned earlier, is a block of code with an identifiable beginning and end. The first line of a subroutine contains the name of the subroutine in factor 1 and the BEGSR operation. The lines of code comprising the executable portion of the subroutine follow. The last line of a subroutine contains ENDSR as the operation code to signal the end of that subroutine. Optionally, the first line (or all lines) of a subroutine may contain the letters SR coded in positions 7-8 to help identify the code as a subroutine. The code that follows shows the skeleton of a subroutine.

```
*.. 1 ...+... 2 ...+... 3 ...+... 4 ...+... 5 ...+... 6 ...+... 7 ...+... 8 ...+... 9 ...+...10
CLØN01Factor1++++++Opcode(E)+Factor2++++++Result++++++++Len++D+HiLoEq....Comments++++++++++++
CSR   CalcTax      BEGSR
C                  ...
C                  ENDSR
```

Subroutines are coded as the last entries on the Calculation Specifications, following all other calculations. The order in which you list the subroutines does not matter, although many programmers prefer to specify them in alphabetical order for easy reference. A program can have an unlimited number of subroutines; each subroutine must have a unique name, based on the same rules that apply to RPG IV fields.

EXSR (Execute Subroutine)

You have already learned one way to send control to a subroutine for execution: the CASxx operation. A second, more common method is to use EXSR. Enter the name of the subroutine to be performed in factor 2, as shown below.

```
*.. 1 ...+... 2 ...+... 3 ...+... 4 ...+... 5 ...+... 6 ...+... 7 ...+... 8 ...+... 9 ...+...10
CLØN01Factor1++++++Opcode(E)+Factor2++++++Result++++++++Len++D+HiLoEq....Comments++++++++++++
CLØN01Factor1++++++Opcode(E)+Extended-factor2+++++++++++++++++++++++++++++Comments++++++++++++
C* The EXSR causes control to drop to SR CalcTax.
C                  EXSR      CalcTax
C* Control returns here when the subroutine finishes executing.
C                  ...
C* Subroutines appear at the end of the calculation specifications.
C     CalcTax      BEGSR
C                  EVAL (H)    FICA = Gross * .0751
C                  EVAL (H)    StateTax = Gross * .045
C                  IF          Gross > 5000
C                  EVAL (H)        FedTax = Gross * .31
C                  ELSE
C                  EVAL (H)        FedTax = Gross * .25
C                  ENDIF
C                  ENDSR
```

When the computer encounters an EXSR operation (or a CASxx), control drops to the named subroutine. Upon completion of the subroutine, control *returns* to the operation immediately following the calculation that invoked the subroutine. The fact that control returns makes it possible to maintain tight control of program flow with CASxx and EXSR.

Subroutines cannot contain other subroutines. Subroutines may execute other subroutines, but a subroutine should never execute itself. This latter coding technique, called **recursion**, is permitted in some programming languages but is treated as an error by the RPG IV compiler.

Control-Break Logic

To demonstrate how top-down, structured design can be used to help develop an easily maintained program, the techniques discussed will be applied to solve a common business programming problem: generating a report that includes subtotals.

Assume you have a file of sales records. Each record contains a salesperson's identification number, department, the amount of a given sale, and the date of the sale. A given salesperson may have many records in the file — depending on how successful a salesperson (s)he is — and the data file is ordered by salesperson, so that all the records for a given salesperson are adjacent to one another in the file. You are asked to write a program that will include the details of each sales transaction and a subtotal of each salesperson's sales. The desired report format is shown in the following illustration:

```
           1         2         3         4         5         6         7         8         9        10
  1234567890123456789012345678901234567890123456789012345678901234567890123456789012345678901234567890
 1        XX/XX/XX     SALES REPORT    PAGE XX0X
 2
 3           SLSPSN.              AMT.
 4
 5           XXXX              X,XX0.XX
 6           XXXX              X,XX0.XX
 7
 8         TOTAL            XX,XX0.XX*
 9
10           XXXX              X,XX0.XX
11           XXXX              X,XX0.XX
12           XXXX              X,XX0.XX
13
14         TOTAL            XX,XX0.XX*
15
16       GRAND TOTAL      XXX,XX0.XX**
17
```

This kind of problem is often referred to as a **control-break problem**, because the solution involves checking the input records for a change, or a "break," in the values of a control field. That occurrence signals the need for a subtotal and triggers special processing associated with printing the subtotal and preparing for the next control group.

Because the computer has only a single record in memory at a time, to determine when a change in the control field's value has occurred, you need to define a stand-alone work field to hold the current value of the control field. Each time a record is read, its control field value can then be compared with that work field; a comparison revealing that the two values are no longer equal signals that the first record of a new group has just been read. Before continuing with the detail processing of that record, it is necessary to "break" away from detail processing and complete any processing required by such a change. Typically, that processing entails printing a subtotal line, rolling over an accumulator, zeroing out that accumulator, and storing the new control field value in the work field.

With that overview of control-break logic, let's develop the pseudocode for the calculations required by the program, using a top-down design strategy. Our design now also will include a provision for printing headings at the top of each page.

```
Do Initialization Routine
WHILE not end-of-file
      IF change in salesperson
            Do Slspbreak Routine
      ENDIF
      Do Detail Process Routine
      Read next record
ENDWHILE
Do Termination Routine
END program
```

The above pseudocode works out the "main-line" logic of the program. Notice that at several spots in the pseudocode, "Do" statements indicate that a number of processing steps need to be performed, but the details are not yet spelled out. That is the essence of top-down design.

Once you determine that the main-line logic is correct, you can develop the logic of the additional modules, or routines. They are shown below.

Initialization Routine
Read first record
Set up hold area
Print headings
END Initialization Routine

Slspbreak Routine
Print salesperson line
Add salesperson's total to grand total
Zero out salesperson's total
Move new value to hold area
END Slspbreak Routine

Detail Process Routine
IF page overflow
      Print headings
ENDIF
Print detail line
Accumulate sales in salesperson's total
END Detail Process Routine

Termination Routine
Do Slspbreak Routine
Print grand total
END Termination Routine

Notice that the processing in Slspbreak is representative of control-break logic in general. Also notice that Slspbreak is invoked from within Termination. The break routine needs to execute one last time to print the very last salesperson's subtotal line before printing the grand total.

The complete RPG IV program, including the calculations reflecting the logic expressed in the pseudocode, is shown in the following example:

```
*.. 1 ...+... 2 ...+... 3 ...+... 4 ...+... 5 ...+... 6 ...+... 7 ...+... 8 ...+... 9 ...+...10
F*****************************************************************
F* This program produces a Sales Report that lists subtotals  *
F* for each salesperson.                                       *
F*  Author: Yaeger      Date Written:  Dec. 1992               *
F*     Modified Jan. 1995 to RPG IV standards. Yaeger.         *
F*****************************************************************
FSalesFile IF   F   19        DISK
FQPRINT    O    F  132        PRINTER OFLIND(*INOF)
D HoldSlsp        S            4
D SlspTotal       S            6 2
D GrandTotal      S            8 2
ISalesFile NS
I                                   1    4  SalesPrsn
I                                   5    7  Dept
I                                   8   13 2SalesAmt
I                                  14   19 ØSaleDate
C*****************************************************************
C*  Calculations required to produce the Sales Report.
C*  Mainline logic.
C*****************************************************************
C                   EXSR      Initial
C
C                   DOW       *IN9Ø = *OFF
C                   IF        HoldSlsp <> SalesPrsn
C                   EXSR      SlspBreak
C                   ENDIF
C                   EXSR      DetailProc
C                   READ      SalesFile                              9Ø
C                   ENDDO
C
C                   EXSR      Terminate
C                   EVAL      *INLR = *ON
C                   RETURN
C*****************************************************************
C* Subroutine to read first record, set up hold, and print
C* first page headings.
C*****************************************************************
C     Initial       BEGSR
C                   READ      SalesFile                              9Ø
C                   EVAL      HoldSlsp = SalesPrsn
C                   EXCEPT    Headings
C                   ENDSR
```

```
*.. 1 ...+... 2 ...+... 3 ...+... 4 ...+... 5 ...+... 6 ..+... 7 ...+... 8 ...+... 9 ...+...10
C****************************************************************
C* Subroutine done when salesperson changes; print subtotal,
C* rollover accumulator, zero out accumulator, and reset hold.
C****************************************************************
C     SlspBreak     BEGSR
C                   EXCEPT      BreakLine
C                   EVAL        GrandTotal = GrandTotal + SlspTotal
C                   EVAL        SlspTotal = 0
C                   EVAL        HoldSlsp = SalesPrsn
C                   ENDSR
C****************************************************************
C* Subroutine executed for each input record.
C****************************************************************
C     DetailProc    BEGSR
C                   IF          *INOF = *ON
C* If end-of-page then print headings.
C                   EXCEPT      Headings
C                   EVAL        *INOF = *OFF
C                   ENDIF
C                   EXCEPT      DetailLine
C                   EVAL        SlspTotal = SlspTotal + SalesAmt
C                   ENDSR
C****************************************************************
C* Subroutine done at end of file; execute SlspBreak one last
C* time and print grand total line.
C****************************************************************
C     Terminate     BEGSR
C                   EXSR        SlspBreak
C                   EXCEPT      TotalLine
C                   ENDSR
O****************************************************************
OQPRINT     E                 Headings        2  1
O                             UDATE         Y    17
O                                                33 'SALES REPORT'
O                                                40 'PAGE'
O                             PAGE               44
O           E                 Headings        2
O                                                20 'SLSPSN.'
O                                                37 'AMT.'
O           E                 DetailLine      1
O                             SalesPrsn          18
O                             SalesAmt        1  39
O           E                 BreakLine       1  2
O                                                24 'TOTAL'
O                             SlspTotal       1  39
O                                                40 '*'
O           E                 TotalLine
O                                                26 'GRAND TOTAL'
O                             GrandTotal      1  39
O                                                41 '**'
```

Programmers often are faced with coding solutions to multiple-level control-break problems, in which two or more different control fields of the input file are to be associated with subtotal lines. For example, our sample problem could have specified a need for department subtotals in addition to the salesperson subtotals. If the input file were ordered by department, and within department by salesperson, producing the desired report would take little additional programming effort, because the logic of multiple-level control-break problems follows directly from that of a single-level problem.

To code a multiple-level control-break problem, set up a stand-alone work field for each control field to hold the value of the group being processed. Code a separate break subroutine for each level; typically, the same processing steps take place in each kind of break (e.g., printing a subtotal line, rolling over an accumulator, zeroing out the accumulator, and moving the new control field value into the work field), but using variables appropriate to that level.

Then, before the detail processing of each record, check each control field to see if its value has changed, checking from major (biggest grouping) to minor (smallest grouping); if a break has occurred, execute the appropriate break subroutines, starting with the minor (smallest grouping) and finishing with the break routine that corresponds to the control field that triggered the break processing.

The pseudocode that follows illustrates the logic of a two-level control-break problem.

Mainline Logic for Two-Level Control Break
Do Initialization Routine
WHILE not end-of-file
    IF change in department
        Do Slspbreak Routine
        Do Deptbreak Routine
    ELSE
        IF change in salesperson
            Do Slspbreak Routine
        ENDIF
    ENDIF
    Do Detail Process Routine
    Read next record
ENDWHILE
Do Termination Routine
END program

Initialization Routine
Read first record
Set up hold areas for department and salesperson
Do headings
END Initialization Routine

Slspbreak Routine
Print salesperson line
Add salesperson's total to department's total
Zero out salesperson's total
Move new salesperson to salesperson hold area
END Slspbreak Routine

Deptbreak Routine
Print department line
Add department's total to grand total
Zero out department's total
Move new department to department hold area
END Deptbreak Routine

Detail Process Routine
IF page overflow
        Print headings
ENDIF
Print detail line
Add sales to salesperson's total
END Detail Process Routine

Termination Routine
Do Slspbreak Routine
Do Deptbreak Routine
Print grand total
END Termination Routine

Especially notice the order in which the pseudocode checks for changes in the control fields, the order in which it executes the break subroutines, and the parallels between the Slspbreak and Deptbreak routines. Once you understand the logic of a two-level break problem, you could write a program with any number of level breaks, because the required processing steps can be exactly modeled on those required for a two-level control break.

Chapter Summary

The goal for this chapter has been to give you a basic understanding of structured design and how it is often used with a top-down, modular approach to program development. Structured program design means developing your program logic with flow of control tightly managed, by using structured operations. Top-down methodology requires that you approach designing your program hierarchically, working out its broad logic first — concentrating primarily on flow of control — and later attending to the detailed processing requirements. Both design concepts encourage a modular approach to programming, in which you design your program around subroutines of statements that form functionally cohesive units of code.

RPG IV provides structured operations IF, SELECT WHEN, and CASxx to implement decision logic, and structured operations DOW, DOU, and DO to implement looping logic. IF, SELECT WHEN, DOW, and DOU let you express the conditional test associated with the operation as a free-form logical expression.

The *xx* in structured operation CASxx indicates that the operation requires the use of one of the six relational codes to express the conditional test controlling the operations' execution. These relational codes are GT, LT, EQ, NE, LE, and GE.

All the structured operations mentioned above have a single entry point and a single exit point that help maintain tight flow of control within a program. The following table can help you remember the formats for the operations presented in this chapter.

Decision and Iteration Operations

Factor 1	Operation	Extended Factor 2
—	**IF**	CONDITIONAL EXPRESSION
—	**ELSE**	—
—	**ENDIF**	—
—	**SELECT**	—
—	**WHEN**	CONDITIONAL EXPRESSION
—	**OTHER**	—
—	**ENDSL**	—
—	**DOW**	CONDITIONAL EXPRESSION
—	**DOU**	CONDITIONAL EXPRESSION
—	**ENDDO**	—
—	**ITER**	—
—	**LEAVE**	—

Factor 1	Operation	Factor 2	Result
FIELD/LITERAL	**CASxx**	FIELD/LITERAL	SRNAME
—	**ENDCS**	—	—
field/literal	**DO**	field/literal	field
—	**ENDDO**	field/literal	—
—	**EXSR**	SRNAME	—
SRNAME	**BEGSR**	—	—
—	**ENDSR**	—	—

Uppercase entry = required; lowercase entry = optional.

Extended factor 2 expressions are free-form.

xx = one of the six relational codes.

Terms

CASE logic
control-break problem
decision operations
EBCDIC
hiearchical decomposition
iteration

leading-decision loop
overflow indicators
recursion
relational codes
relational comparison
selection

sequence
structured design
subroutines
top-down design
trailing-decision loop

Discussion/Review Questions

1. Characterize structured design.

2. If RPG IV did not include a relational symbol or code to check for "not equal," what alternate way could you express the following logic in RPG IV? "If balance due <> 0, execute the calculation routine."

3. What does "tight" flow of control mean?

4. Describe how RPG IV compares numeric values.

5. Describe how RPG IV compares character values.

6. Now that RPG has a SELECT operation, can you always avoid writing nested IF statements? Explain your answer.

7. What's the difference between AND and OR?

8. How would you decide whether to use SELECT or CASxx?

9. Why does RPG IV need looping operations other than DO? Are both DOW and DOU essential from a logical standpoint?

10. Describe how ITER and LEAVE work. Would they be considered structured options? Explain.

11. Characterize a control-break problem.

12. In control-break processing, why is a "hold" or work field needed to store the value of the control field?

13. Can you think of an alternative way to handle page advance other than referencing an overflow indicator?

Exercises

1. Use IF to code the calculations needed to determine property tax based on a property's value, stored in Value (6 positions, 0 decimal positions). Use the information in the table below as the basis for your calculations:

Property Value	Property Tax
$0- $50,000	1% of value
$50,001- $75,000	$50 plus 2% of value
$75,001-$100,000	$70 plus 2.5% of value
over $100,000	$100 plus 3% of value

2. Solve the problem described in Exercise 1 using operation SELECT.

3. Write a routine to determine traffic fines based on the values of two input fields: MphOver (miles over speed limit) and NbrOffense (number of offenses). Fines are to be determined as follows:

MPH Over Limit	Fine
1-10	$25
11-20	$40
21-30	$70
over 30	$100

If the speeder is a first-time offender, there is no additional fine. However, second-time offenders are fined an additional $25 if they are no more than 20 miles over the limit and an additional $50 if they are more than 20 miles over the limit. Third-time offenders are fined an additional $50 if they are no more than 20 miles over the limit and an additional $100 if they are going more than 20 miles over the limit.

4. Use DO to write the calculations needed to obtain the squares, cubes, and square roots of all numbers from 1 to 50.

5. A program to update a master file needs a routine that checks the update code stored in Code and sends control to one of three different subroutines (AddSR, ChangeSR, and DeleteSR), depending on whether the code is A, C, or D (Add, Change, or Delete records). Invalid codes should cause subroutine ErrorSR to execute. Write this routine twice, each time using a different structured operator.

Programming Assignments

1. Wexler University wants a summary report of its student population that shows how many in-district, out-of-district, and international students there are at the freshman, sophomore, junior, senior, and graduate levels. The input file for this program is the school's student master file WUSTDP. The record layout for this file is given in Appendix D. The records in the file are ordered by Social Security number.

    Note that district code is a code field where I = in-district, O = out-of-district, and F = international student status. The classification field differentiates G (graduate) from U (undergraduate) students. The school subdivides undergraduates based on earned credits: Students with fewer than 30 credits are freshmen; those with 30-59 credits are sophomores; those with 60-89 credits are juniors; and those with 90 or more credits are seniors.

    The school wants the summary report to be formatted as shown in the printer spacing chart below.

```
          1         2         3         4         5         6         7         8         9         10
 1234567890123456789012345678901234567890123456789012345678901234567890123456789012345678901234567890
1   XX/XX/XX                        WEXLER U.                                PAGE XX0X
2                        STUDENT POPULATION SUMMARY REPORT
3
4                          ------------------RESIDENCY--------------
5       CLASSIFICATION     IN-DISTRICT   OUT-OF-DISTRICT   INTERNATIONAL      TOTAL
6       --------------     -----------   ---------------   -------------      -----
7           FRESHMEN         X,X0X          X,X0X             X,X0X          XX,X0X
8           SOPHOMORES       X,X0X          X,X0X             X,X0X          XX,X0X
9           JUNIORS          X,X0X          X,X0X             X,X0X          XX,X0X
10          SENIORS          X,X0X          X,X0X             X,X0X          XX,X0X
11
12          TOTAL           XX,X0X         XX,X0X            XX,X0X          XX,X0X
13
```

2. Wexler University needs a report to determine how equitable its faculty salaries are across sexes. Because salaries vary with academic rank and length of employment, they want average salaries broken down by rank, as well as by sex, and they also would like average-length-of-employment figures. The input file, WUINSTP, is described in Appendix D. The desired report is shown below.

```
          1         2         3         4         5         6         7         8         9         10
 1234567890123456789012345678901234567890123456789012345678901234567890123456789012345678901234567890
1    WEXLER UNIVERSITY FACULTY SALARY REPORT  XX/XX/XX
2
3
4                     AVERAGE SALARIES AND LENGTH OF EMPLOYMENT
5                         MALE                       FEMALE
6  RANK                 SALARY    YEARS    N        SALARY    YEARS    N
7  ----------           ---------------------       ---------------------
8  INSTRUCTOR           XXX,XX0.XX   0X  (0X)       XXX,XX0.XX   0X  (0X)
9  ASSISTANT            XXX,XX0.XX   0X  (0X)       XXX,XX0.XX   0X  (0X)
10 ASSOCIATE            XXX,XX0.XX   0X  (0X)       XXX,XX0.XX   0X  (0X)
11 PROFESSOR            XXX,XX0.XX   0X  (0X)       XXX,XX0.XX   0X  (0X)
12
13 ALL                  XXX,XX0.XX   0X (X0X)       XXX,XX0.XX   0X (X0X)
14
15
16       NOTE: N=NUMBER IN EACH CATEGORY
17
```

Programming Assignments Continued

Programming Assignments continued

3. The municipal water company needs a program that will calculate monthly water charges. The rates for city residents are:

> $.035 per unit for the first 500 units
> $.030 per unit for the next 500 units
> $.027 per unit for all units beyond 1,000

In addition, there is a service fee of $10.00 per month for all customers, regardless of usage. Water users who are not residents of the city pay 1.5 times the total bill.

An input file, MWC001P, described in Appendix D, contains customer information and old and new meter readings. Determine usage from the old and new meter readings. Note that the meters are like car odometers; when they reach their maximum value (9,999), the next unit's usage causes them to read 0000. You must take this feature into account in your calculations. You may assume that no one will ever use more than 9,999 units of water per month.

Output should appear as shown on the printer spacing chart below.

```
        1         2         3         4         5         6         7         8         9        10
123456789012345678901234567890123456789012345678901234567890123456789012345678901234567890
1  XX/XX/XX                                                   PAGE XX0X
2                  GOTHAM CITY WATER BILLING REPORT
3
4  CUST.                        RES.  OLD    NEW            AMOUNT
5   NUM.        NAME            CODE  METER  METER  USAGE    OWED
6
7  XXXXX  XXXXXXXXXXXXXXXXXXXX   X    XXXX   XXXX   X,X0X   X,XX0.XX
8  XXXXX  XXXXXXXXXXXXXXXXXXXX   X    XXXX   XXXX   X,X0X   X,XX0.XX
9
```

4. ACME manufacturing company wants you to write a payroll program. Each record in the input file, ACP001, described in Appendix D, represents *one day's* work for an employee. Records are accumulated for a week, so there will be several records per employee. Records in the file are ordered by Social Security number.

The company uses both an hourly rate and a piece rate to pay its employees. Everyone gets $5.50 per hour worked. Additionally, if a person produces 0-500 units during the week, (s)he receives 25 cents per unit; if (s)he produces 501-1,000 units, (s)he receives 30 cents per unit; if over 1,000 units, 40 cents per unit. After using these figures to calculate gross pay, a 4.6 percent state tax and a 15 percent federal tax must be subtracted from gross pay to obtain net pay.

Your program is to generate the report illustrated in the printer spacing chart on the following page.

Programming Assignments Continued

Programming Assignments continued

```
        1         2         3         4         5         6         7         8         9        10
1234567890123456789012345678901234567890123456789012345678901234567890123456789012345678901234567890
1  XX/XX/XX                         ACME PAYROLL REPORT                            PAGE XXØX
2
3                              HOURS              GROSS      STATE     FED.        NET
4  SOC. SEC.       NAME        WORKED    UNITS     PAY        TAX      TAX        PAY
5
6  XXX-XX-XXXX  XXXXXXXXXXXXXXXX  ØX     X,XØX   X,XXØ.XX   XØ.XX   XXØ.XX    X,XXØ.XX
7  XXX-XX-XXXX  XXXXXXXXXXXXXXXX  ØX     X,XØX   X,XXØ.XX   XØ.XX   XXØ.XX    X,XXØ.XX
8  XXX-XX-XXXX  XXXXXXXXXXXXXXXX  ØX     X,XØX   X,XXØ.XX   XØ.XX   XXØ.XX    X,XXØ.XX
9
10           AVERAGE GROSS PAY:  $X,XXØ.XX
11           AVERAGE UNITS PER EMPLOYEE:  X,XØX
12           AVERAGE UNITS PER HOUR:  X,XØX
13
```

5. Wexler University's faculty members run a credit union. They want you to write a program to calculate monthly payments for loan applicants. The monthly payment is to be calculated using the formula shown below. Note that I represents **monthly interest rate** and N represents number of **months** for the loan. Also note that the N in the formula is an exponent, not a multiplier. The formula to be used in calculating payment amount is:

$$\text{Payment} = \text{LoanAmt} * (I * (1+I)^N) / ((1+I)^N - 1)$$

Records in input file WULOANP, described in Appendix D, contain information about the loan amounts, interest rates, and length of loan. Generate a report formatted as shown below.

```
        1         2         3         4         5         6         7         8         9        10
1234567890123456789012345678901234567890123456789012345678901234567890123456789012345678901234567890
1  DATE XX/XX/XX         WEXLER U. FACULTY CREDIT UNION           PAGE XXØX
2                          NEW LOAN APPLICANTS REPORT
3
4  LOAN         CUSTOMER            LOAN       ANNUAL     NO. OF      MONTHLY
5  NUM.          NAME              AMOUNT    INT. RATE    MONTHS      PAYMENT
6
7  XXXXX    XXXXXXXXXXXXXXX       XX,XXØ.XX    XØ.XX%      XØX       XX,XXØ.XX
8  XXXXX    XXXXXXXXXXXXXXX       XX,XXØ.XX    XØ.XX%      XØX       XX,XXØ.XX
9
10             GRAND TOTALS     X,XXX,XXØ.XX                      X,XXX,XXØ.XX
11
```

Chapter 5

Externally Described Files

Chapter Overview

In this chapter you will learn how the AS/400 handles database files. The chapter explains the differences between physical and logical files and discusses field-reference files. You will be introduced to the AS/400's data types and the storage implications of numeric and character data types. You will learn how to define database files at a system level and how to access these definitions from within RPG IV programs. You will also learn about externally described printer files.

The AS/400 Approach to Database Files

The AS/400, like its predecessor the S/38, is unique in the way it handles data. Unlike other systems, which require additional, costly software to provide them with database capabilities, the AS/400 was designed with database applications in mind. Its operating system automatically treats all data files as part of a large relational database system. One consequence of this approach is that all data files need to be defined to the system independently of application programs. Even those applications that on the surface seem to be "creating" files are actually creating records and storing them in a file that must have been defined to the AS/400 before program execution.

These files may be defined on the system at a record level (i.e., not broken down into individual fields) or at a field level. If you define a file only to the record level, any RPG IV program that uses that file must subdivide that record into the appropriate logical fields in the Input or Output Specifications. On the other hand, if you have externally defined the file at a field level (i.e., created an **externally described file**), you do not need to code those field definitions within your application programs that use the file; the definitions will be brought into the program at compile time. The use of externally defined files is almost universally practiced by RPG IV programmers today.

There are several advantages to defining data files external to application programs. First, if you design the files using database design principles, externally defined files can reduce the need for duplication of data across files. (This kind of duplication is called **redundancy.**) Because all programs using a given file use the same field definitions and names, externally defined files impose a standardization among programmers and across applications.

External file description increases programmer efficiency, because programmers don't need to duplicate the file definition effort each time they need to reference a file within a program. And finally, if it is necessary to add a field to a file's records or to change a field's definition (e.g., expand zip code to 9 digits), these changes need to be made only in a single place (in the external file definition), rather than in every program using that file. This feature simplifies system maintenance.

Physical and Logical Files

The AS/400 lets you define two kinds of database files: **physical files** and **logical files**. Physical files actually store data records. If you define the physical file at a field level and one of those fields is designated the key, you subsequently can access records stored in that file in either **key sequence** or **arrival sequence** (first-in, first-out). If you do not define a **key field**, access is limited to arrival sequence.

Logical files describe how data *appears* to be stored in the database. Logical files do not actually contain data records; instead, they store access paths, or pointers, to records in physical files. Because you generally want these access paths to be based on values of key fields, logical files typically have one or more fields designated as a key. A logical file is always based on one or more physical files. Depending on which fields are specified and which are named as keys, the apparent record images and processing order of a logical file may vary greatly from that of the physical file(s) underlying it. Logical files correspond to users' views of data, or **subschemas**, in database terminology.

To understand the relationship between physical and logical files, consider the example below, which shows records of an employee master physical file and two logical files based on the physical file. Employee number is the key field to the physical file. One of the logical files is keyed on a **composite**, or **concatenation**, of department and employee number, while the other has zip code as the key field.

The example shows the order in which the records would appear to an application program for each file if you stipulated sequential retrieval by key.

```
Physical File EMPMST (keyed on employee number)
Emp. no.    Last Name  First Name  Dept.  Salary  Street         City       St  Zip
111111111   Jones      Mary        MKT    54000   123 W. 45th    Decatur    MI  49065
222222222   Smith      Sam         ACT    61500   4422 N. Oak    Paw Paw    MI  49045
333333333   Adams      Arnold      MKT    34950   1120 W. Main   Kalamazoo  MI  49008
444444444   Houston    Wanda       MIS    29500   290 S. State   Kalamazoo  MI  49007
555555555   Jacobs     David       ACT    43275   9911 S. 88th   Mattawan   MI  49069
666666666   Salinger   Carol       MIS    38500   1300 Maple Lk. Paw Paw    MI  49065
777777777   Riley      Thomas      MKT    24600   8824 E. Drake  Kalamazoo  MI  49008
```

```
Logical File EMPMSTL1 (keyed on department and employee number)
222222222  Smith     Sam         ACT    61500
555555555  Jacobs    David       ACT    43275
444444444  Houston   Wanda       MIS    29500
666666666  Salinger  Carol       MIS    38500
111111111  Jones     Mary        MKT    54000
333333333  Adams     Arnold      MKT    34950
777777777  Riley     Thomas      MKT    24600


Logical File EMPMSTL2 (keyed on zip code)
Houston   Wanda    290 S. State    Kalamazoo  MI  49007
Adams     Arnold   1120 W. Main    Kalamazoo  MI  49008
Riley     Thomas   8824 E. Drake   Kalamazoo  MI  49008
Smith     Sam      4422 N. Oak     Paw Paw    MI  49045
Jones     Mary     123 W. 45th     Decatur    MI  49065
Salinger  Carol    1300 Maple Lk.  Paw Paw    MI  49065
Jacobs    David    9911 S. 88th    Mattawan   MI  49069
```

Although the actual data records are stored *only in the physical file* (remember that the logical files store only access paths to records), programs can use logical files just as though the logical files themselves contained the data.

You might use the first logical file to produce a salary report of employees, broken down by department, while the second logical file could be used to print mailing labels for employees, ordered by zip code. Note that logical file records do not need to include all the fields present in the physical records upon which they are based; what fields appear within a logical file depend on the logical file's definition.

Introduction to DDS

The procedure for creating database file definitions is similar to that of creating an RPG IV program. The first step is to use SEU to create a source member of definition statements. Most installations use a special file, QDDSSRC, to store members representing externally described files. The source type of a physical file member is PF, whereas that of a logical file member is LF. SEU automatically provides prompts appropriate to the member type you specify.

A fixed-format language that you can use to code the source definitions for physical and logical database files, as well as for display and printer files, is called **Data Description Specifications (DDS)**. The format for DDS definitions resembles RPG specifications — for a good reason: AS/400 file definitions were closely modeled after RPG. All DDS lines include an A in position 6. As in RPG IV, an asterisk in position 7 of a DDS source line signals a comment line. You can use comment lines throughout the file definition. Minimally, you should include a few comment lines at the beginning of each file definition to identify the nature of the file.

In addition to comment lines, DDS includes *record format descriptions*, which define a record type within the file; *field definition lines*, which describe fields within records; and perhaps *key specifications*, which designate which fields are to serve as keys to the file. The particular nature of these specifications depends on whether you are defining a physical file or a logical file.

DDS also extensively uses a variety of **keywords**, each with a special meaning. Some keywords, which apply to the file as a whole, are called **file-level keywords**; some apply to a specific record format within the file and are called **record-level keywords**; and some, which are associated only with a specific field, are called **field-level keywords**.

Although all externally defined files share those general features mentioned above, the details of a DDS definition depend on the type of file you are defining. Accordingly, let's first look at using DDS to define physical files.

Defining Physical Files

A physical file's source statements define the data contents that file will have. Physical files can contain only a single record format, or type. That means that every record within a physical file must have an identical record layout. Because of this requirement, a physical file's DDS may contain only one record type, or format. The record format is signaled by an R in position 17 (Name Type), and a name for the record format is entered in positions 19-28 (Name).

Following the record-format specification, you must enter lines to define each field the record contains. Following the field definitions, you optionally can designate a key for the file. A K in position 17 denotes a key field. If you list a key field, its contents determine the sequence in which you can retrieve records from the file. The example below illustrates the DDS code for the employee master file EMPMST.

```
*.. 1 ...+... 2 ...+... 3 ...+... 4 ...+... 5 ...+... 6 ...+... 7 ...+... 8
A..........T.Name++++++RLen++TDpB......Functions+++++++++++++++++++++++++++++
A* Employee master physical file EMPMST
A                                       UNIQUE
A          R EMPREC
A            EMPNO         9S 0         TEXT('Employee number')
A            LNAME        15A           TEXT('Last name')
A            FNAME        10A           TEXT('First name')
A            DEPT          3A           TEXT('Department')
A            SALARY        6P 0         TEXT('Annual salary')
A            STREET       15A           TEXT('Street address')
A            CITY         15A           TEXT('City')
A            STATE         2A           TEXT('State')
A            ZIP           5S 0         TEXT('Zip code')
A          K EMPNO
```

Let's look at the details of that definition. First, UNIQUE is a file-level keyword. (All file-level keywords appear at the beginning of the DDS, before the record-format specification line.) UNIQUE stipulates that the file cannot contain records with duplicate key values. When you include this keyword, attempts to write a record to the file with a key value identical to a record already in the file will cause the system to generate an error message. Use of UNIQUE is optional; without its use, the system permits records with duplicate key values.

The record-format line is next. Note the R in position 17, and the format name, EMPREC, left-justified in positions 19-28. The AS/400 allows record-format names (and field names, for that matter) to be up to 10 characters long. These names must begin with an alphabetic character (A through Z, @, $, or #); the remaining characters can be any of the alphabetic characters, any of the digits 0 through 9, or the underscore character (_). Unlike RPG IV, DDS source code cannot contain lowercase alphabetic characters, so all record format and field names in DDS source are entered as uppercase.

You define the fields of a record on successive lines below the record-format line. The field name begins in position 19. Next, you specify the length of the field, right-adjusted in positions 30-34 (Length). As in RPG IV, any numeric field definition must include a decimal position entry (positions 36-37). You use position 35 (Data Type) to specify data type, a concept we'll explore in detail in the next section.

Following the definition of all the fields to appear within the record, you may designate one or more fields as the record key by coding a K in position 17 and specifying the name of the key field in positions 19-28. In our example, EMPNO is named as the key field of the file. Notice that you must define the key field as part of the record prior to the K specification.

If you list more than one key line, you are specifying a composite or concatenated key. For composite keys, list the key fields in order from major to minor. Note that fields need not be adjacent to one another within the record to be key components.

The TEXT keyword entries are optional ways to provide documentation. In our example, TEXT is used with each field to explain what the field represents. You must enclose text comments with apostrophes and surround them with parentheses. Although text comments are not required, it makes good sense to include them, especially if your field names are somewhat cryptic. TEXT also can appear as a record-level keyword to document the record format.

Programmers new to DDS are sometimes confused by the fact that the name of the file is not included within the DDS (except, perhaps, within a comment line). The file name is determined by what you call the source member, which by default becomes the name of the compiled object, or database file.

Data Types and Data Storage

As mentioned a few paragraphs ago, you must assign a data type to each field of a physical file. The data type assigned to a field determines how the field's values are stored, how much storage the field occupies, and what kinds of operations can be performed on the field when it is used within a program.

From previous chapters of this text, you are already familiar with two general types of data — character and numeric. To denote that a field is to contain **character** (or alphanumeric) data, you code an A for its type; if you leave the type entry blank and also leave the decimal position entry blank, the system assumes that the data type of the field is character.

Numeric fields (signaled by non-blank decimal position entries) are a little more complicated. The numeric class of data types actually contains three different numeric data types: **zoned decimal** (type S), **packed decimal** (type P), and **binary** (type B). RPG IV does not differentiate among numeric data types in determining what kinds of operations you can perform on a field or what kinds of output editing are possible; however, the data type of a numeric field — zoned decimal, packed decimal, or binary — determines how that field is represented and stored within the database. If you leave the type entry blank for a numeric field, the system defaults to the packed decimal data type for the field.

An explanation of data representation must begin with EBCDIC. You know that computers manipulate data in binary form. You also probably know that any numeric value can be converted from its familiar decimal, or base 10, value to a corresponding value in binary, or base 2, notation. At first glance, then, data representation should be a simple matter of converting values from one base to another. The problem is that many characters and values that we want to represent to the computer are not numbers — letters of the alphabet, for example, or $ and {.

IBM developed a coding scheme to allow any data character — numeric or non-numeric — to be represented to the computer. This coding scheme is called EBCDIC (Extended Binary Coded Decimal Interchange Code). EBCDIC assigns a unique 8-bit binary pattern to each representable character. Capital A, for example, is 11000001 in EBCDIC, while the digit 1 is represented as 11110001. The left-most four bits are often called **zone** or **high-order bits**, while the right-most four bits are **digit** or **low-order bits**. Because eight bits comprise a byte, it takes one byte of storage to store each character in EBCDIC. All non-numeric, or character, data values are stored this way.

Numbers can be handled slightly differently. The EBCDIC codes for the digits 0-9 are shown below.

Digit	EBCDIC
0	11110000
1	11110001
2	11110010
3	11110011
4	11110100
5	11110101
6	11110110
7	11110111
8	11111000
9	11111001

The first thing you should notice is that the zone bits of all digits are identical — 1111. This means that the zone portion is redundant for numeric data; that is, if the system knows the data is numeric, it knows that the zones of the data are all 1s. Two forms of numeric data storage take advantage of this redundancy.

The first form, zoned (or signed) decimal, takes a full byte to store each digit of a numeric value, except that the zone of the right-most digit is used to store the sign of the data: 1111 represents a plus sign (+), while 1101 represents a negative sign (–). Zoned-decimal representation, then, is almost identical to character representation, except that the sign is represented as part of the right-most digit's byte.

The second form of numeric representation, packed decimal, takes greater advantage of the redundancy built into digit representation by simply not bothering to store the zones of numbers. Data in packed format can take as little as half the amount of storage it would take to store the same number in zoned-decimal format. In packed format, only the digit, or low-order, bits of a number are stored, with the sign of the number represented by an additional four bits. These sign bits always occupy the right-most four-bit positions of a packed-decimal value.

Study the figure below to understand the differences in data representation between these two formats. Notice the location of the signs in both representations, and the elimination of the zone bits in the packed format.

Value to Represent	Zoned Decimal
+ 136	11110001 11110011 11110110
– 136	11110001 11110011 11010110
	(sign)

	Packed Decimal
+ 136	00010011 01101111
– 136	00010011 01101101
	(sign)

The third form for representing numbers, binary format, dispenses completely with EBCDIC and stores the number as its direct binary equivalent. This format can result in the greatest savings in storage: It takes just two bytes of storage to store any number 1-4 digits long, and four bytes of storage to store any number 5-9 digits long.

Programmers seldom use binary format, however. It adds overhead during processing, because the computer must convert the binary values to packed decimal before the values can be used in calculations. The system also converts zoned-decimal values to packed decimal before using them in calculations. Although some programmers prefer to define numeric fields as zoned decimal (type S) because it's easier to print or view the raw data in the file when the data is stored in this format, the AS/400 works most effi-ciently with numbers stored in packed-decimal format.

The length of the entry you give a field in DDS represents the number of digit positions in the value to be represented, but the number of bytes of stor-age it will take to actually store the value may vary, given the data type. Packed fields take $(n+1)/2$ bytes of storage (rounded to the nearest whole byte), where n = number of digit positions in the data value. The formula derives from the fact that in packed format, the sign and each digit require a half-byte of storage; you need to round up to the nearest whole byte because data stor-age is allocated in byte-sized units. A number eight positions long would have a length of 5 if stored in packed format. (So would a number nine positions long. Because it takes the same amount of storage, many programming experts recommend that you always define packed numeric fields with an odd number of digit positions.) An 8-digit number would have a storage length of 4 if binary was the type specified for it. For zoned-decimal format, storage length corresponds exactly to digit positions in the value to be stored.

DDS recognizes other data types besides A, S, P, and B, although these were the only types recognized within RPG until the introduction of RPG IV. We will look at the additional RPG IV data types in Chapter 9: Advanced Data Definition. For now, we'll limit our scope to the character and numeric types presented above so that we can turn our attention to logical files.

Logical Files

Although you could, in theory, "get by" using only physical files to define your data, you are just scratching the surface of the AS/400's database capa-bilities until you begin to use logical files.

As discussed in the introduction of this chapter, logical files define access paths to data actually stored in physical files. You can use a logical file to restrict user views to a subset of fields contained in a physical file, to change the retrieval order of records from a file (by changing the designated key field), or to combine data stored in two or more separate physical files into a single logical file. Although the data actually is stored in physical files, once you have defined logical files to the system you can reference these logical files in RPG IV programs as though the logical files themselves actually contained records. The advantage of using logical files is that they can provide alternate ways to look at data, including different orders of record access, without redundantly storing the actual data on the system.

Simple Logical Files

A logical file based on a single physical file is called a simple logical file. The method of defining simple logical files is similar to that of defining physical files: You first specify a record format, follow that with a list of fields (option-al), and follow that with one or more (optional) key fields. Because logical files provide views of physical files, you must include the keyword PFILE beginning in position 45 (Functions) on the record-format line, followed, in parentheses, by the name of the physical file upon which the logical record format is based.

The easiest way to code a simple logical file is to use the same record-format name within the logical file as the record-format name in the physical file the logical file is based on. With this method, the system assumes the record layouts of the files are identical. As a result, you do not need to include fields within your logical record description. However, you can still designate one or more fields as a key, and this key does not have to match the key of the physical file. The following example shows a logical file based on employee master file EMPMST:

```
*.. 1 ...+... 2 ...+... 3 ...+... 4 ...+... 5 ...+... 6 ...+... 7 ...+... 8
A..........T.Name++++++.Len++TDpB......Functions++++++++++++++++++++++++++++
A* Logical file EMPMSTL3, keyed on last name
A          R EMPREC                    PFILE(EMPMST)
A          K LNAME
```

With this definition, all the fields defined within the physical file are included within the logical file. Because the logical file is keyed on last name, keyed sequential access of this logical file will retrieve the employee records in alphabetic order by last name. This kind of logical file definition is widely used to change the retrieval order of records in a file. Its effects are identical to that of physically sorting file records into a different order, but without the system overhead that a physical sort requires.

If you want to restrict the logical file so that it includes only some of the fields from the physical file, provide the logical file with a record-format name different from that of the record name in the physical file and then list just those fields to be included in the logical file. Again, you may designate one or more of these fields to serve as the key to the file. The logical file defined below would produce the logical view of employee data organized by department and employee number illustrated earlier in the chapter.

```
*.. 1 ...+... 2 ...+... 3 ...+... 4 ...+... 5 ...+... 6 ...+... 7 ...+... 8
A..........T.Name++++++.Len++TDpB......Functions++++++++++++++++++++++++++++
A* Logical file EMPMSTL1, keyed on department and, within department,
A* on employee number.  Only those fields listed are accessible
A* through the logical file.
A          R EMPRECL1                  PFILE(EMPMST)
A            EMPNO
A            LNAME
A            FNAME
A            DEPT
A            SALARY
A          K DEPT
A          K EMPNO
```

Notice that you do not need to specify length, type, and decimal positions for the fields in a logical file; these field attributes are already given in the physical file on which the logical file is based.

If you wanted to limit access to only name and address information in the employee master file and retrieve the records in zip-code order, you could define a logical file like the one that follows. Again, the data view resulting from this logical file was illustrated earlier.

```
*.. 1 ...+... 2 ...+... 3 ..+... 4 ...+... 5 ..+... 6 ...+... 7 ...+... 8
A.........T.Name+++++.Len++TDpB.....Functions++++++++++++++++++++++++++++++
A* Logical file EMPMSTL2, keyed on zip code.
A           R EMPRECL2                  PFILE(EMPMST)
A             LNAME
A             FNAME
A             STREET
A             CITY
A             STATE
A             ZIP
A           K ZIP
```

Record Selection/Omission

You can define logical files to exclude certain records contained in the physical file, or to include only a subset of the records contained in the physical file, by using Omit or Select specifications. You can use this feature only if the logical file contains a key specification. Your specifications base record exclusion or inclusion on actual data values present in selected fields of the physical file records. For example, assume you want to omit the MIS department from the salary report. You simply designate department as an omit field (O in position 17) and then in position 45 provide the basis for the omission. In this case, because you want to omit a specific department, simply use the field-level keyword VALUES, followed by the value or values you want to omit. If the field type is character, you must enclose each value with apostrophes.

```
*.. 1 ...+... 2 ...+... 3 ...+... 4 ...+... 5 ...+... 6 ..+... 7 ...+... 8
A.........T.Name+++++.Len++TDpB......Functions+++++++++++++++++++++++++++++++
A* Logical file EMPMSTL4, keyed on department, and within department,
A* on employee number.  MIS department employees are excluded from
A* the file.
A           R EMPRECL4                  PFILE(EMPMST)
A             EMPNO
A             LNAME
A             FNAME
A             DEPT
A             SALARY
A           K DEPT
A           K EMPNO
A           O DEPT                       VALUES('MIS')
```

If you wanted to *include only* the MIS and ACT departments, you could change the O in position 17 of the select/omit field to an S, and specify MIS and ACT as values. In that case, the logical file would *contain* only employees of the MIS and ACT departments. Other departments would be excluded.

```
*.. 1 ...+... 2 ...+... 3 ...+... 4 ...+... 5 ...+... 6 ...+... 7 ...+... 8
A..........T.Name+++++.Len++TDpB.....Functions++++++++++++++++++++++++++++++
A* Logical file EMPMSTL5, keyed on department, and within department,
A* on employee number.  Only MIS and ACT departments are included
A* within the file.
A          R EMPRECL5                   PFILE(EMPMST)
A            EMPNO
A            LNAME
A            FNAME
A            DEPT
A            SALARY
A          K DEPT
A          K EMPNO
A          S DEPT                        VALUES('MIS' 'ACT')
```

Besides VALUES, two additional keywords let you specify the basis of record inclusion or exclusion: RANGE and COMP. Keyword RANGE, followed by parentheses containing two values, lets you specify the beginning value and the ending value of a *range* of values upon which the selection or omission is to be based. In the example that follows, only employees with zip codes 49400 through 50000 will be included in the logical file.

```
*.. 1 ...+... 2 ...+... 3 ...+... 4 ...+... 5 ...+... 6 ...+... 7 ...+... 8
A..........T.Name+++++.Len++TDpB.....Functions++++++++++++++++++++++++++++++
A* Logical file EMPMSTL6, selecting specified records based on a
A* range of zip codes.
A          R EMPRECL6                   PFILE(EMPMST)
A            LNAME
A            FNAME
A            STREET
A            CITY
A            STATE
A            ZIP
A          K ZIP
A          S ZIP                         RANGE(49400 50000)
```

With keyword COMP, you can specify a comparison between a field's value and a given value to serve as the basis of selection or omission. You specify the nature of the comparison by using one of eight relational operators: EQ (equal to), NE (not equal to), LT (less than), NL (not less than), GT (greater than), NG (not greater than), LE (less than or equal to), and GE (greater than or equal to). To use this feature, enter field-level keyword COMP; follow the keyword with parentheses containing first the relational operator and then a literal indicating the comparison value. In the following example, employees with zip codes below 49500 would be omitted from the logical file:

```
*.. 1 ...+... 2 ...+... 3 ...+... 4 ...+... 5 ...+... 6 ...+... 7 ...+... 8
A.........T.Name+++++.Len++TDpB.....Functions++++++++++++++++++++++++++++++
A* Logical file EMPMSTL7, omitting those employees whose zip codes
A* are less than 49500.
A          R EMPRECL7                   PFILE(EMPMST)
A            LNAME
A            FNAME
A            STREET
A            CITY
A            STATE
A            ZIP
A          K ZIP
A          O ZIP                        COMP(LT 49500)
```

You can designate multiple select and/or omit fields, set up alternate criteria using ORs (O in position 7), or list multiple criteria using ANDs (A in position 7) so that several specifications must hold true for record inclusion/exclusion to occur. (See IBM's *DDS Reference*, SC41-3712, for additional details.)

Logical Files with Multiple-Record Formats

You also can define logical files based on two or more physical files. One way to do this is to define logical files with multiple-record formats, where each format is based on a different physical file.

Consider the following scenario. You have a student master physical file that contains student number, name, major, date admitted (and so on). As students take courses, each course is recorded in a second physical file containing student number, course identification, semester taken, grade received, and so on. Partial definitions of these physical files are shown below.

```
*.. 1 ...+... 2 ...+... 3 ...+... 4 ...+... 5 ...+... 6 ...+... 7 ...+... 8
A.........T.Name+++++RLen++TDpB.....Functions++++++++++++++++++++++++++++++
A* Physical file definition for student master file STUDMAST.
A          R STUDREC
A            STUD_NO      9S 0          TEXT('Student Number')
A            LNAME       20A            TEXT('Last Name')
A            FNAME       10A            TEXT('First Name')
A            MAJOR        6A            TEXT('Major')
A            ADM_DTE      6S 0          TEXT('Date Admitted')
A          K STUD_NO

*.. 1 ...+... 2 ...+... 3 ...+... 4 ...+... 5 ...+... 6 ...+... 7 ...+... 8
A.........T.Name+++++RLen++TDpB.....Functions++++++++++++++++++++++++++++++
A* Physical file definition of student courses taken, file STUDCRSE.
A          R CRSEREC
A            STUD_NO      9S 0          TEXT('Student Number')
A            CRSE_ID      6A            TEXT('Course Identifier')
A            SEMESTER     3A            TEXT('Semester Taken')
A            GRADE        2A            TEXT('Grade Received')
A          K STUD_NO
A          K CRSE_ID
```

Now assume you want to produce a report that shows the name, number, and major for each student, followed immediately with a list of all the courses (s)he has taken and the grade received in each course. One way to handle this would be to define a logical file based on the two physical files. The logical file definition is shown below.

```
*.. 1 ...+... 2 ...+... 3 ...+... 4 ...+... 5 ...+... 6 ...+... 7 ...+... 8
A..........T.Name++++++.Len++TDpB......Functions++++++++++++++++++++++++++++
A* Logical file over STUDMAST and STUDCRSE physical files.
A          R STUDREC                    PFILE(STUDMAST)
A          K STUD_NO
A          R CRSEREC                     PFILE(STUDCRSE)
A          K STUD_NO
A          K SEMESTER
```

Notice that the logical file contains two record formats: one based on physical file STUDMAST and the other on physical file STUDCRSE. Both record formats use the student number as the major key; the second format, CRSEREC, also has semester as the minor portion of a concatenated key.

With this definition, sequentially reading the logical file will retrieve first a student record (that student with the lowest student number); then, one by one, each record from the course file for that student, arranged in semester order; then the next student's record, followed by the courses, in semester order, for that student; and so on. The logical file gives the appearance that the two physical files have been merged together, with records grouped by student, and within that grouping arranged by semester. In reality, the data remains in the two separate physical files. The logical file interconnects them by building access paths to the records in both files.

Join-Logical Files

You can define a second kind of logical file based on two or more physical files: a **join-logical file**. In contrast to a logical file with multiple-record formats, in which data from different physical files remain on separate records in the logical file, a join-logical file combines fields from different physical files into a single record. To use this format, there must be a matching field across the physical files upon which the join can be based.

Take, for example, the case where you want to generate invoice lines based on an inventory physical file whose records contain part number, description, unit cost, and selling price and an order physical file that contains order number, part number and quantity ordered. You could set up a logical file to combine the description and price information from the inventory file with the order number and quantity ordered information from the order file by joining the two files on part number.

```
*.. 1 ...+... 2 ...+... 3 ...+... 4 ...+... 5 ...+... 6 ...+... 7 ...+... 8
A.........T.Name+++++RLen++TDpB.....Functions++++++++++++++++++++++++++++++
A* Physical file of inventory, INVENT
A          R INVREC
A            PART_NO        6A              TEXT('Part Number')
A            DESCRPT       30A              TEXT('Part Description')
A            UNIT_COST      5P 2            TEXT('Unit Cost')
A            SELL_PRICE     5P 2            TEXT('Selling Price')
A            OH_QTY         5P 0            TEXT('On-hand Quantity')
A          K PART_NO

*.. 1 ...+... 2 ...+... 3 ...+... 4 ...+... 5 ...+... 6 ...+... 7 ...+... 8
A.........T.Name+++++RLen++TDpB.....Functions++++++++++++++++++++++++++++++
A* Physical file of orders, ORDERS
A          R ORDREC
A            ORDER_NO       6A              TEXT('Order Number')
A            CUST_NO        5A              TEXT('Customer Number')
A            PART_NUM       6A              TEXT('Part Number')
A            QTY_ORD        3P 0            TEXT('Quantity Ordered')
A          K ORDER_NO
A          K PART_NUM

*.. 1 ...+... 2 ...+... 3 ...+... 4 ...+... 5 ...+... 6 ...+... 7 ...+... 8
A.........T.Name+++++.Len++TDpB.....Functions++++++++++++++++++++++++++++++
A* Join logical file connecting files INVENT and ORDERS
A          R ORDLINE                        JFILE(ORDERS INVENT)
A          J                                JOIN(ORDERS INVENT)
A                                           JFLD(PART_NUM PART_NO)
A            ORDER_NO
A            CUST_NO
A            PART_NO
A            DESCRPT
A            SELL_PRICE
A            QTY_ORD
```

In the logical file above, keyword JFILE signals which physical files are used by the logical file. The next two lines specify the nature of the join. Notice that the join specification requires a J in position 17 of the specification line. Keyword JOIN designates which files are used in this join. Because we expect every record from ORDERS to appear in the logical file, we list that file first. (It is likely that many of the parts represented in file INVENT are not part of anyone's current order, and accordingly would not appear in the join logical file.)

The JFLD keyword indicates which fields' values are to be matched across the physical files named in the JOIN parameter. Following the join-level entries are the fields comprising the logical record. Notice that some fields within the logical record come from INVENT, while others come from ORDERS. Records from these two files are "joined" together to create a single, logical-record image. Any record (from either physical file) that does not have a corresponding record in the other file (based on a match of the part number fields) will not appear in the join-logical file.

Creating Database Files

The first step in actually creating a physical or logical file is to enter the DDS statements using SEU. As mentioned earlier, it is standard practice to use source file QDDSSRC for storing database source members. Also recall that the source type is PF for physical file and LF for logical file.

Once you have entered your DDS code, you must compile it to create the file as an object on the system. If you are working from PDM or the Programmer's Menu, follow the same procedure to compile a database object that you use to create a program module object.

If you compile by directly entering a command at a command line, rather than by working through menus, the appropriate commands are CRTPF (Create Physical File) and CRTLF (Create Logical File).

If the system encounters syntax errors while trying to create your file, you will receive a message indicating that the creation was not successful. Otherwise, the system will tell you the job completed normally and that the database object now exists. Once the file object exists, you may use it to store data. You can enter data into physical files by using a system utility called **Data File Utility (DFU)**, by writing values to the file through a program, or by copying records to the file from another file.

Note that you must create a physical file before you can create logical files based on that physical file; failure to do so will result in error messages. If you want to change the definition of a physical file after you have created a logical file based on that definition, you must first delete the logical file object (though not the source) before the system will allow you to delete the physical file object and create a new one.

You should be aware of one additional caveat: If you want to change a physical file's definition after you have stored data in the file, deleting the file deletes the data in the file as well. You can avoid such data loss by copying it temporarily to a different file; your instructor can provide you with this information, should you need it.

RPG IV Programming with Externally Defined Files

Now that you understand how to define and create files on the AS/400, you will find that it is simple to reference these external definitions within your programs. Basically, all you need to do is make a few minor modifications to your File Specifications and eliminate your Input Specifications.

On the File Specifications in position 22, instead of an F for Fixed Format, code an E for Externally Defined. Next, omit a record-length entry, because the system will supply that information automatically, based on the external definition. And finally, if the file is keyed and you want to access records based on keys, code a K in position 34. Omitting the K results in record retrieval based on arrival sequence (i.e., the order in which the records were originally written to the file). The following figure illustrates a File Specification for an externally described file:

```
*.. 1 ...+... 2 ...+... 3 ...+... 4 ...+... 5 ...+... 6 ...+... 7 ...+... 8 ...+... 9 ...+...10
FFilename++IPEASFRlen+LKlen+AIDevice+.Keywords+++++++++++++++++++++++++++++++Comments+++++++++++
FEmpMaster IF   E          K DISK
```

EmpMaster is a physical file. If you wanted to use a logical file, you would enter the logical file name; the remaining entries would be identical to those shown for the physical file. At a program level, there is no distinction made between physical and logical files.

If your input file is externally described, you do not need to code Input Specifications for that file. When you compile your program, the system will copy the file's definition into your source listing where the input specifications would normally appear. Obviously then, when you use external definition, the file must exist before your program will successfully compile.

Less obviously, if you make changes in a physical or logical file definition after you have compiled a program using that file, you must recompile the program before the system will allow the program to run. This feature, called **level checking**, prevents you from running a program based on an obsolete or inaccurate definition of a database file.

Calculation and Output Specifications may use any fields defined as part of the externally described input file just as though the fields were defined internally as part of the Input Specifications. You also can externally describe database files used as output; in that case, Output Specifications are unnecessary and writing to the file can take place directly from your calculations. Chapter 6 explores this concept in detail.

Additional Database File Concepts

The purpose of this chapter has been to provide the beginning RPG IV programmer with a basic understanding of externally defined files on the AS/400. The AS/400 provides features for defining data far beyond what has been covered here. Variants on join-logical files, for instance, can be much more complex than the simple examples illustrated. In addition to the keywords used in this chapter, the AS/400 offers 30 or so other keywords used with data file definition. Some of these keywords allow you to establish data validity checks for interactive data entry, while others allow you to specify how the field will be edited upon output to the screen.

Finally, the AS/400 lets you create a physical file that serves as a centralized **data dictionary** of fields used within an application system. Such a physical file is called a **field-reference file**. You never actually use this kind of file for data storage; its sole purpose is to provide field definitions for use in subsequent physical file creation. Once you have created a field-reference file, you can define the fields that comprise your physical files by simply referring to the definitions contained in the field-reference file.

Consider the examples of physical files that were part of the student records application system illustrated earlier in this chapter. Instead of defining each field within the physical database files, we could have first created a physical file containing the definitions of *all* the fields that the student record system will need to store. This file — a field-reference file — is illustrated in the following figure:

```
*.. 1 ...+... 2 ...+... 3 ...+... 4 ...+... 5 ...+... 6 ...+... 7 ...+... 8
A..........T.Name+++++RLen++TDpB......Functions++++++++++++++++++++++++++++++
A* Field reference file STUDREF for the student records system.
A          R RECORD
A            STUD_NO       9S 0        TEXT('Student Number')
A            LNAME        20A          TEXT('Last Name')
A            FNAME        10A          TEXT('First Name')
A            MAJOR         6A          TEXT('Major')
A            ADM_DTE       6S 0        TEXT('Date Admitted')
A            CRSE_ID       6A          TEXT('Course Identifier')
A            SEMESTER      3A          TEXT('Semester Taken')
A            GRADE         2A          TEXT('Grade Received')
A            ...
```

Once you have created the reference file, you can create physical database files whose field definitions are obtained from the reference file. To use this feature, simply include in your physical file the file-level keyword REF, with the name of the field-reference file in parentheses. You can then define any field in this physical file whose definition already exists in the reference file by simply coding an R in position 29 (Reference) and omitting the length, type, decimal entry, and relevant keyword information for that field. The two physical files that follow illustrate the use of the field-reference file to supply field definitions:

```
*.. 1 ...+... 2 ...+... 3 ...+... 4 ...+... 5 ...+... 6 ...+... 7 ...+... 8
A..........T.Name+++++RLen++TDpB......Functions++++++++++++++++++++++++++++++
A* Physical file definition for student master file STUDMAST.
A                                     REF(STUDREF)
A          R STUDREC
A            STUD_NO       R
A            LNAME         R
A            FNAME         R
A            MAJOR         R
A            ADM_DTE       R
A          K STUD_NO
```

```
*.. 1 ...+... 2 ...+... 3 ...+... 4 ...+... 5 ...+... 6 ...+... 7 ...+... 8
A..........T.Name+++++RLen++TDpB......Functions++++++++++++++++++++++++++++++
A* Physical file definition of student courses taken, file STUDCRSE.
A                                     REF(STUDREF)
A          R CRSEREC
A            STUD_NO       R
A            CRSE_ID       R
A            SEMESTER      R
A            GRADE         R
A          K STUD_NO
A          K CRSE_ID
```

Field-reference files can enforce a uniformity and consistency throughout an application system that facilitates program development and maintenance. Using such files, however, requires a thoughtful, structured approach to application system development, because your data needs should be determined before any file creation or application development. The casual approach that many companies take toward developing new systems does not allow them to take advantage of field-reference files.

Another related topic of concern to programmers is database design. A crucial step in application system development is determining the file structure for the system. What data fields will you need to store? What physical and logical files will you need? How do you determine what fields belong in what files? Whole books have been written on the subject of relational database design. Although this topic is beyond the scope of this book, realize that every professional programmer should have a solid understanding of relational database design.

As systems become complex and the number of files used in a system grows, it becomes increasingly important for an IS department to have file-naming conventions that provide some information about the function and type of each file. Although working with a maximum of 10-character file names poses some restrictions on your ability to assign good file names, many installations use an agreed-upon mnemonic prefix to denote the system within which the file was designed to be used and a short alphabetic mnemonic code — often related to the key of the file — to uniquely identify each file within the system. Some companies also use a suffix of P, L, or F to denote whether the file is a physical, logical, or field-reference file and a number to differentiate between similar files.

Externally Described Printer Files

In addition to allowing the external definition of database files, RPG IV lets you define reports externally. Although programmers use this feature less often than they use externally described database files, a significant number of programmers prefer to handle all their report programs by externally describing the reports.

There are two primary advantages to externally describing printer files. First, this method lets you modify a report format without changing the source code of the program that produces the report, a wise approach to application maintenance. Second, if you externally define printer files, you can use a system utility, **Report Layout Utility (RLU)**, to help you design the layout of the report visually on the terminal; you don't need to use paper and printer spacing chart forms. RLU then generates the DDS required to describe the report so you don't have to do the grunt work of figuring out line position and spacing entries. (The details of using RLU fall outside the scope of this text; those persons interested in developing printer files with this method should consult the IBM manual *Application Development ToolSet/400: Report Layout Utility*, SC09-1767.)

You use DDS to define printer files at the source level, the same as you do for database files. The source members of printer files, like database files, are generally stored in QDDSSRC; a printer file's type, however, is PRTF. Once you have entered the source code through SEU (or via RLU), you compile the source to create a printer file object. Once the object exists, it can receive output from a program for printing. The DDS code for a printer file is analogous to that of a database file, except that its focus is the definition of record formats of information to be sent to the printer. Printer files, like logical files, may contain multiple record formats, each defining a different set of output lines. The DDS may also include keyword entries at the file level, the record level, and/or the field level to define the position and/or appearance of the output.

To illustrate how you would externally define a printer file, let's reconsider the sales report from Chapter 4. Recall that the desired report includes headings, individual sales figures, a sales total for each salesperson, and a grand total for all salespersons. The printer spacing chart for the report is reproduced below.

```
           1         2         3         4         5         6         7         8         9        10
  1234567890123456789012345678901234567890123456789012345678901234567890123456789012345678901234567890
 1        XX/XX/XX    SALES REPORT    PAGE XX0X
 2
 3            SLSPSN.              AMT.
 4
 5                XXXX          X,XX0.XX
 6                XXXX          X,XX0.XX
 7
 8            TOTAL         XX,XX0.XX*
 9
10                XXXX          X,XX0.XX
11                XXXX          X,XX0.XX
12                XXXX          X,XX0.XX
13
14            TOTAL         XX,XX0.XX*
15
16         GRAND TOTAL     XXX,XX0.XX**
17
```

The RPG IV program in Chapter 4 defined five exception lines, grouped as Headings, DetailLine, BreakLine, and TotalLine, to generate this output. You would follow much the same procedure to externally describe this report in DDS.

The following figure illustrates the DDS for the sales report. First, you need to define one record format for each line or group of lines to be printed in a single output operation. Then, for each of those record formats, you need to specify what fields and/or literals are to print as part of that format, what line spacing each format should follow, where within a line the variable or constant data should appear, and what editing (if any) should be associated with the numeric fields.

```
*.. 1 ...+... 2 ...+... 3 ...+... 4 ...+... 5 ...+... 6 ...+... 7 ...+... 8
AAN01N02N03T.Name++++++RLen++TDpBLinPosFunctions++++++++++++++++++++++++++++
A* Printer file SALESRPT, externally describing the sales report.
A             R HEADINGS                    SKIPB(1)
A                                         10DATE EDTCDE(Y)
A                                         22'SALES REPORT'
A                                         37'PAGE'
A                                         42PAGNBR EDTCDE(3)
A                                           SPACEA(2)
A                                         14'SLSPSN.'
A                                         34'AMT.'
A                                           SPACEA(2)
A             R DETAILLINE                   SPACEA(1)
A               SALESPRSN      4           15
A               SALESAMT       6 2         32EDTCDE(1)
A             R BREAKLINE                    SPACEB(1) SPACEA(2)
A                                         20'TOTAL'
A               SLSPTOTAL      6 2         31EDTCDE(1)
A                                         40'*'
A             R TOTALLINE
A                                         16'GRAND TOTAL'
A               GRANDTOTAL     8 2         30EDTCDE(1)
A                                         40'**'
```

You must begin each record-format definition with an R in position 17, followed by the name of the format in positions 19-28. Next, for each record format, you need to define all the information that is to print as part of that format. Specify fields in positions 19-28, just as for database files. Constants are coded in positions 45-80 and must be enclosed in apostrophes.

To define each field within the DDS, provide its length in positions 30-34 and, for numeric fields, its number of decimal positions in positions 36-37; blanks in the decimal position columns signal a character field. Thus, in our example, SALESPRSN is defined as a 4-byte character field, while SALESAMT is a 6-byte numeric field with two decimal positions. Literals 'SALES REPORT' and 'PAGE' are simply entered starting in position 45.

You also need to specify where within the report line each piece of information is to appear. Use positions 42-44 for this purpose. Note that in DDS, unlike in RPG IV, you must specify the field or constant's *beginning position* (where it starts within the line), rather than its *ending position*. Thus, in our example, because SALES REPORT begins in column 22 of the first heading, you code 22 in positions 43-44 of the DDS line for that constant.

DDS handles the system date and the report page numbers a little bit differently than RPG IV does. RPG IV includes two built-in variables, UDATE and PAGE, which supply the system date and page number, respectively. In DDS the same information is accessible through the keywords DATE and PAGNBR. As shown in the example, you enter these keywords on their own lines in DDS.

The same edit codes and edit words available in RPG IV to modify the appearance of numeric output are available within DDS. However, you indicate desired editing through the use of keywords EDTCDE or EDTWRD, followed by the appropriate edit code or word enclosed within parentheses. In our example, DATE will print with slashes as a result of the EDTCDE(Y) entry, while fields SALESAMT, SLSPTOTAL, and GRANDTOTAL will print with commas and zero balances because of keyword EDTCDE(1). EDTCDE(3) specifies that PAGNBR, a 4-digit numeric value, should be zero-suppressed and printed without commas.

The easiest way to specify line positioning on a page in DDS is to use four keywords: SPACEA, SPACEB, SKIPA, and SKIPB. The meaning of these keywords — space after or before and skip after or before — corresponds exactly to the meaning of those terms in RPG IV. The number of lines to space (for SPACEA or SPACEB) or the line to skip to (for SKIPA and SKIPB) is designated within parentheses following the keyword. You can use these keywords at the record level or at the field level. If you want line positioning to change *within* a record format, you would use the appropriate keyword at a field level; whereas if line positioning is to change for the record format as a whole, use the keyword at the record level.

In our previous example, because we want the headings to begin on the first line of each new page, we use the keyword entry SKIPB(1) at the record-format level (that is, on the line containing the R entry or the lines immediately following that entry and before any field or constant entry). But recall that record format HEADINGS contains information about two heading lines for our report, and we want to position the second line two lines below the first heading. The SPACEA(2) keyword entry immediately following the PAGNBR keyword entry produces the desired line spacing; immediately following the printing of the page number, the paper would advance two lines. Printing would then continue with the constant 'SLSPSN.'. Note that multiple keywords can appear on the same code line, as shown by the record-level entry SPACEB(1) SPACEA(2) for record format BREAKLINE.

Other optional features of externally described printer files (e.g., changing fonts, printing bar codes, using indicators, defining fields by reference) are beyond the scope of this text. But with this introduction, you should be able to use DDS to externally describe most common types of printed output.

How does external definition of printed output affect an RPG IV program? First, in the File Specification entry for the report file, include the actual name of the printer file, rather than the generic output file QPRINT. In addition, change the file format entry (position 22) to E — for Externally Described. And finally, omit any entry for record length. You can associate an indicator (but not OA-OF or OV) with this file to signal page overflow by using keyword OFLIND and your selected indicator enclosed within parentheses. The following figure illustrates a File Specification for an externally described printer file:

```
*.. 1 ...+... 2 ...+... 3 ...+... 4 ...+... 5 ...+... 6 ...+... 7 ...+... 8 ...+... 9 ...+...10
FFilename++IPEASFRlen+LKlen+AIDevice+.Keywords+++++++++++++++++++++++++++++Comments+++++++++++
FSalesRept O   E             PRINTER OFLIND(*IN10)
```

The externally described printer file eliminates the need for Output Specifications in your program. How then do you direct the computer to print at the appropriate times as it executes your program? Instead of using the EXCEPT operation, which references lines defined on Output Specifications, use the WRITE operation, with the name of the appropriate record format of your printer file specified in factor 2. The figure below illustrates the WRITE operation.

```
*.. 1 ...+... 2 ...+... 3 ...+... 4 ...+... 5 ...+... 6 ...+... 7 ...+... 8 ...+... 9 ...+...10
CLØN01Factor1++++++Opcode(E)+Factor2++++++Result+++++++Len++D+HiLoEq....Comments+++++++++++
C* Sample calculation showing output to an externally described printer file.
C                    WRITE     Headings
```

Putting It All Together

Now that you have seen how database files and printer files can be externally described and you have a sense of how this approach to file definition affects RPG IV programs, we can rewrite our control-break program from Chapter 4 to take advantage of external definition. First, let's externally define the input file SALESFILE. The DDS for this file is shown in the following example. Because the file is keyed on SALESPRSN, data records later stored in the file will be kept ordered by salesperson number, a necessary condition for our control break report.

```
*.. 1 ...+... 2 ...+... 3 ...+... 4 ...+... 5 ...+... 6 ...+... 7 ...+... 8
A..........T.Name+++++RLen++TDpB......Functions++++++++++++++++++++++++++++++
A* Definition of physical file SALESFILE.
A          R SALESREC
A            SALESPRSN      4A         TEXT('Salesperson number')
A            DEPT           3A         TEXT('Department')
A            SALESAMT       6S2        TEXT('Sales amount')
A            SALEDATE       6SØ        TEXT('Date of sale')
A          K SALESPRSN
```

We have already developed the DDS for the printer file SALESRPT. Remember that you must compile or create an object of each externally described file before it can be used. (Also remember that the physical file initially is empty; you would need to put actual data records into the file before it could meaningfully be used as input.) With those files externally described, our RPG IV program becomes considerably shorter. In addition, we can now make changes to our report layout or to our data file definition without having to modify the RPG IV program, except to recompile it.

```
*.. 1 ...+... 2 ...+... 3 ...+... 4 ...+... 5 ...+... 6 ...+... 7 ...+... 8 ...+... 9 ...+...10
F******************************************************************
F* This program produces a Sales Report that lists subtotals   *
F* for each salesperson.                                        *
F*  Author: Yaeger       Date Written:  Dec. 1992               *
F*                                                              *
F* Modified, Nov., 1994, by Yaeger                              *
F*   Changed program-described files to externally described.   *
F* Modified, Feb., 1995, by Yaeger                              *
F*   Incorporated RPG IV features.                              *
F******************************************************************
```

```
*.. 1 ...+... 2 ...+... 3 ...+... 4 ...+... 5 ...+... 6 ...+... 7 ...+... 8 ...+... 9 ...+...10
FSalesFile IF   E           K DISK
FSalesRpt  O    E              PRINTER OFLIND(*IN1Ø)
D HoldSlsp       S             4
D SlspTotal      S             6 2
D GrandTotal     S             8 2
C***********************************************************
C*  Calculations required to produce the Sales Report.
C*  Mainline logic.
C***********************************************************
C                 EXSR      Initial
C
C                 DOW       *IN9Ø = *OFF
C                 IF        HoldSlsp <> SalesPrsn
C                 EXSR      SlspBreak
C                 ENDIF
C                 EXSR      DetailProc
C                 READ      SalesFile                              90
C                 ENDDO
C
C                 EXSR      Terminate
C                 EVAL      *INLR = *ON
C                 RETURN
C***********************************************************
C* Subroutine to read first record, set up hold, and print
C* first page headings.
C***********************************************************
C     Initial     BEGSR
C                 READ      SalesFile                              90
C                 EVAL      HoldSlsp = SalesPrsn
C                 WRITE     Headings
C                 ENDSR
C***********************************************************
C* Subroutine done when salesperson changes; print subtotal,
C* rollover accumulator, zero out accumulator, and reset hold.
C***********************************************************
C     SlspBreak   BEGSR
C                 WRITE     BreakLine
C                 EVAL      GrandTotal = GrandTotal + SlspTotal
C                 EVAL      SlspTotal = Ø
C                 EVAL      HoldSlsp = SalesPrsn
C                 ENDSR
C***********************************************************
C* Subroutine executed for each input record.
C***********************************************************
C     DetailProc  BEGSR
C                 IF        *IN1Ø = *ON
C* If end-of-page then print headings
C                 WRITE     Headings
C                 EVAL      *IN1Ø = *OFF
C                 ENDIF
C                 WRITE     DetailLine
C                 EVAL      SlspTotal = SlspTotal + SalesAmt
C                 ENDSR
C***********************************************************
C* Subroutine done at end of file; execute SlspBreak one last
C* time and print grand total line.
C***********************************************************
C     Terminate   BEGSR
C                 EXSR      SlspBreak
C                 WRITE     TotalLine
C                 ENDSR
```

Chapter Summary

The AS/400 defines data files independently of your programs. Such files, defined through DDS statements, exist as objects on the system and may be used by any program as externally described files. Physical files contain data records, while logical files provide access paths, or pointers, to the physical file records. A logical file is always associated with one or more physical files. Both physical and logical files may contain a key that lets you retrieve records based on the value of the key. The key can consist of one or several data fields; in the latter case, the key is called a composite, or concatenation.

A physical file may contain only a single-record format or type. Logical files may contain multiple record formats, based on records from two or more physical files. A logical file also may contain a single-record format that actually combines data fields stored in different physical files; this kind of file is called a join-logical file. You can also use logical files to specify which records should be selected for inclusion or omitted from inclusion based on data values of the records in the physical file upon which the logical file is based.

You can use a special kind of physical file, a field-reference file, to record field definitions. Physical database files then can reference this file rather than having the field definitions included directly within the physical files themselves.

The AS/400 requires you to specify the type of data to be stored within fields. Two data types the AS/400 recognizes are character, or alphanumeric, and numeric. Furthermore, three distinct numeric data formats exist: zoned decimal, packed decimal, and binary. Zoned decimal is easiest to view but takes up the most room on disk. Packed decimal, the data format native to the AS/400, eliminates redundant high-order bits in storing digit values. Both zoned-decimal and packed-decimal formats use EBCDIC representation. Binary format stores the binary equivalent of a numeric value without first representing the number in EBCDIC.

Database design is an important part of application system design and development. A well-planned database can facilitate application development and maintenance; a poorly designed database can plague programmers for years. Once database files exist, using them within RPG IV programs is simple: Reference the file as Externally Described on the File Specifications. The system then will import the file's record definition to your program when you compile the program.

Some programmers use externally described printer files to define report formats. This practice offers several advantages: You can change report formats without modifying programs, you can use RLU to design the reports and generate the DDS, and you can eliminate Output Specifications from your programs.

Terms

arrival sequence
binary data type
character data type
composite key
concatenation
Data Description
    Specifications (DDS)
data dictionary
Data File Utility (DFU)
externally described file

field-level keywords
field-reference file
file-level keywords
high-order bits
join-logical file
key field
key sequence
keywords
level checking
logical files

low-order bits
packed-decimal data type
physical files
record-level keywords
redundancy
Report Layout Utility (RLU)
subschemas
zoned-decimal data type

Discussion/Review Questions

1. Explain the advantages of externally describing database files. Do externally described printer files share the same advantages?

2. Explain the difference between a logical file and a physical file.

3. What does concatenation mean? What is a concatenated key?

4. What are the advantages of logical files? Why not just create lots of physical files to store records in different orders or to present different combinations of data fields?

5. How does the system know whether you intend a keyword to be a file-level, record-level, or field-level keyword?

6. Why might you use UNIQUE as a keyword in a physical file?

7. Express the following values in zoned-decimal and packed-decimal format: +362 and −51024

8. How many bytes will it take to store 389,241,111 in zoned decimal? In packed decimal? In binary?

9. Provide several practical examples for using logical files.

10. Explain the differences between keywords COMP, RANGE, and VALUES.

11. If Select and Omit specifications were not available in logical file definitions, how could you produce a report that included only the employees of the ACT and MIS departments and excluded other employees?

12. What is a join-logical file?

13. Explain the difference between arrival sequence and key sequence of sequential record retrieval.

14. Assume you wanted to write a program that used an externally described logical file that was based on a join of two physical files. What order would you use to create the four objects required to execute the program? Why?

15. Some programmers argue that standards in file and field naming and the use of features like field-reference files reduces their opportunities to be creative and should not be enforced. How would you respond to them?

Exercises

1. A library wants a database file to store book title; author's last name, first name, and middle initial; catalog number; publisher; date published; number of pages; and number of copies owned. Code a physical-file definition to store this data after determining what you believe to be the appropriate fields, and the length and type for each field. Consider what the key field (if any) should be, and whether UNIQUE is appropriate.

2. The library wants to be able to access the catalog information described in Exercise 1 based on author's name. Among other things, they want to be able to print out listings by author such that all books by the same author will appear together. Define a logical file that will enable this kind of access.

3. The library also wants to store a description of each book. Because the books' descriptions vary greatly in length, from a few words to a long paragraph, the person designing the library's database suggested storing the descriptions in a separate physical file, where each record contained the catalog number, a description line number, and 40 characters of description. Define this physical file.

4. Define a multiple-record-format logical file that will combine the information in the physical files from Exercises 1 and 3 such that the initial book information will be followed sequentially by the lines of description, in order, for that book.

5. Define a field-reference file for the library based on the data requirements of Exercises 1 and 3 and then rewrite the physical-file definitions to take advantage of the field-reference file.

Programming Assignments

Note: All of the following assignments involve producing reports that either can be defined as part of your RPG IV program or described externally; your instructor will tell you which technique to use.

1. This assignment includes several parts.
   a) Create a physical file for Wexler University's student master file (file WUSTDP, in Appendix D). Key this file on student number and specify that keys be unique.
   b) Enter records in the file, following your instructor's directions.
   c) Design a report for Wexler University that provides a listing of student information. Include student number, first and last name, credits earned, major, date admitted, and grade-point average in your report layout.
   d) Write a program to produce the report you designed in part c, with your input file the externally described file you defined in part a. The report should show students listed in order by Social Security number.
   e) Create a logical file over WUSTDP with last name and first name as a concatenated key.

Programming Assignments Continued

Programming Assignments continued

    f) Modify your program from part d to use this logical file as the input file. The resulting report should list the students in alphabetical order by last name, and within last name, by first name.

2. This assignment includes several parts.

    a) Create a physical file for CompuSell's customer master file (CSCSTP in Appendix D). Key the file on customer number and specify that keys be unique.

    b) Enter records in the file, following your instructor's directions.

    c) Write a program using the file you created as input to produce the report shown below. All the customers should be listed, in order of customer number.

    d) Create a logical file over the customer file keyed on last name, and within last name, by first name.

    e) Modify your program to use the file you created in part d as the input file. The report should now list customers in name order.

    f) Create another logical file over the customer file, this time keyed on balance due and selecting only those customers with a balance greater than zero.

    g) Modify your program to use the file you created in part f as the input file. The report should now list customers in balance-owed order and include only those customers who owe the company money.

```
          1         2         3         4         5         6         7         8         9         1Ø
 1234567890123456789012345678901234567890123456789012345678901234567890123456789012345678901234567890
 1  XX/XX/XX    COMPUSELL REPORT OF CUSTOMER BALANCES        PAGE XXØX
 2
 3     CUST. NO.    FIRST NAME    LAST NAME          BALANCE OWED
 4
 5       XXXXXX     XXXXXXXXXX    XXXXXXXXXXXXXXX      -X.XX-.XX
 6       XXXXXX     XXXXXXXXXX    XXXXXXXXXXXXXXX      -X.XX-.XX
 7       XXXXXX     XXXXXXXXXX    XXXXXXXXXXXXXXX      -X.XX-.XX
 8
 9                                      TOTAL         $XXX.XX$.XX
1Ø
```

3. This assignment includes several parts.

    a) Create a physical file for Wexler University's student master file (file WUSTDP, in Appendix D). Key this file on student number and specify that keys be unique.

    b) Create a physical file for Wexler University's department file (WUDPTP, in Appendix D), keyed on department code.

    c) Enter records in both files, following the directions of your instructor.

    d) Create a multiple-record-format logical file based on the department file and the student master file, with formats keyed on department code, and department of major and earned credits, respectively.

    e) Use the logical file from part d as an input file to produce the report shown below. *Hint*: you will have to use control-break logic. You may assume that the student major has been validated so there will never be a student who does not belong within an existing department. However, there may be departments that

Programming Assignments Continued

Programming Assignments continued

do not currently have students enrolled in their programs. In that case, print the message shown in the printer spacing chart. Note that the date admitted should print in MM/DD/YY format.

```
          1         2         3         4         5         6         7         8         9         10
 1234567890123456789012345678901234567890123456789012345678901234567890123456789012345678901234567890
 1  XX/XX/XX              WEXLER U.  DEPARTMENTAL LISTING OF STUDENTS              PAGE XX0X
 2
 3
 4 DEPARTMENT                        STUDENTS
 5         SOC. SEC.    NAME: LAST      FIRST      CREDITS    GPA    DATE ADMIT.
 6
 7 XXXXXXXXXXXXXXXXXXXXXX
 8        XXX-XX-XXXX  XXXXXXXXXXXXXXX XXXXXXXXXX     X0X      0.XX    XX/XX/XX
 9        XXX-XX-XXXX  XXXXXXXXXXXXXXX XXXXXXXXXX     X0X      0.XX    XX/XX/XX
10        XXX-XX-XXXX  XXXXXXXXXXXXXXX XXXXXXXXXX     X0X      0.XX    XX/XX/XX
11
12 XXXXXXXXXXXXXXXXXXXXXX
13        (NO MAJORS AT THIS TIME)
14
15 XXXXXXXXXXXXXXXXXXXXXX
16        XXX-XX-XXXX  XXXXXXXXXXXXXXX XXXXXXXXXX     X0X      0.XX    XX/XX/XX
17        XXX-XX-XXXX  XXXXXXXXXXXXXXX XXXXXXXXXX     X0X      0.XX    XX/XX/XX
18        XXX-XX-XXXX  XXXXXXXXXXXXXXX XXXXXXXXXX     X0X      0.XX    XX/XX/XX
19
```

4. Wexler University wants you to put together a University Catalog that lists all the courses of all departments. The format of the catalog is shown on the following page. You will need to do the following to generate the catalog:

   a) Create three physical files: one for the department file (WUDPTP), one for the course file (WUCRSP) and one for the course description file (WUCRSDSP). Appendix D describes the layouts of these files.

   b) Put records in the files, following your instructor's directions.

   c) Create a multiple-record-format logical file over the three physical files.

   d) Use the file to generate the catalog. You can assume that every course belongs to a department, and that every department offers at least one course. However, some courses may not have a description.

Start each department on a new page. Use the system year in the catalog heading. Each course is identified by a course identification consisting of the department code and the course number; the course title follows the identification

Programming Assignments continued

```
            1         2         3         4         5         6         7         8         9         10
   1234567890123456789012345678901234567890123456789012345678901234567890123456789012345678901234567890
 1    XXØX
 2                  WEXLER UNIVERSITY CATALOG
 3                         19XX
 4
 5 DEPARTMENT
 6 XXXXXXXXXXXXXXXXXXXXX  CHAIR: XXXXXXXXXXXXXXXXXXXXXXXXXX
 7       FOR INFORMATION CALL (XXX)XXX-XXXX OR VISIT ROOM XXXXXXXXXX
 8
 9
10 COURSES:
11    XXXXXX  XXXXXXXXXXXXXXXXXXXXXXXXXX     X CREDITS
12       XXXXXXXXXXXXXXXXXXXXXXXXXXXXXXXXXXXXXXXXXXXXXXXXX
13       XXXXXXXXXXXXXXXXXXXXXXXXXXXXXXXXXXXXXXXXXXXXXXXXX
14       XXXXXXXXXXXXXXXXXXXXXXXXXXXXXXXXXXXXXXXXXXXXXXXXX
15
16    XXXXXX  XXXXXXXXXXXXXXXXXXXXXXXXXX     X CREDITS
17       XXXXXXXXXXXXXXXXXXXXXXXXXXXXXXXXXXXXXXXXXXXXXXXXX
18       XXXXXXXXXXXXXXXXXXXXXXXXXXXXXXXXXXXXXXXXXXXXXXXXX
19       XXXXXXXXXXXXXXXXXXXXXXXXXXXXXXXXXXXXXXXXXXXXXXXXX
20       XXXXXXXXXXXXXXXXXXXXXXXXXXXXXXXXXXXXXXXXXXXXXXXXX
21       XXXXXXXXXXXXXXXXXXXXXXXXXXXXXXXXXXXXXXXXXXXXXXXXX
22
23    XXXXXX  XXXXXXXXXXXXXXXXXXXXXXXXXX     X CREDITS
24       XXXXXXXXXXXXXXXXXXXXXXXXXXXXXXXXXXXXXXXXXXXXXXXXX
25       XXXXXXXXXXXXXXXXXXXXXXXXXXXXXXXXXXXXXXXXXXXXXXXXX
```

Chapter 6

File Access and Record Manipulation

Chapter Overview

This chapter introduces you to RPG IV's operations for reading, writing, and updating records. You will learn both sequential and random file access techniques. The chapter also discusses file maintenance — adding, deleting, and changing records in a file — and record locking considerations in update procedures.

Operations for Input Files

File access refers to how records can be retrieved, or read, from an input file. RPG IV offers several alternative operations for accessing data from full procedural database files. Several of these operations are appropriate for sequential processing; you can use others for random access processing.

Sequential Access

In **sequential access**, records are retrieved in either key order, if the file is keyed and so noted in position 31 on the File Specifications, or in arrival or FIFO order (First-In-First-Out) for non-keyed files. Reading generally starts with the first record in the file, with each subsequent read operation retrieving the next record in the file until eventually you reach end-of-file. This kind of sequential access is especially suited for batch processing.

READ (Read a Record)
As you know, the READ operation retrieves records sequentially. A file name in factor 2 designates which file the READ accesses. An indicator in positions 75-76 (Eq) comes on to signal end-of-file when the READ finds no additional records in the file.

```
*..1 ...+... 2 ...+... 3 ...+... 4 ...+... 5 ...+... 6 ...+... 7 ...+... 8 ...+... 9 ...+...10
CL0N01Factor1++++++Opcode(E)+Factor2++++++Result+++++++Len++D+HiLoEq....Comments++++++++++++
C                   READ      CustMast                                90
```

For externally described files, factor 2 can actually be a record-format name, rather than a file name. However, if the read encounters a record format different from that named in factor 2 — as could be the case when the input file is a logical file with multiple formats — the operation ends in error. You optionally can code an indicator in positions 73-74 (Lo) to detect such errors and appropriately handle them, as shown below, or you can use other error-handling techniques (discussed in Chapter 9).

```
*.. 1 ...+... 2 ...+... 3 ...+... 4 ...+... 5 ...+... 6 ...+... 7 ...+... 8 ...+... 9 ...+...10
CLØN01Factor1++++++Opcode(E)+Factor2++++++Result+++++++Len++D+HiLoEq....Comments++++++++++++
CLØN01Factor1++++++Opcode(E)+Extended-factor2+++++++++++++++++++++++++++Comments++++++++++++
C                  READ      CustRecord                            8090
C                  IF        *IN80 = *ON
C                  EXSR      ErrorSR
C                  ENDIF
```

If your program does not include some way to handle this kind of error, however, the program will terminate before reaching its normal ending point after issuing an error message. (This kind of abnormal ending is often called an **abend**). Accordingly, unless you have a specific reason for reading a record format, rather than the file, and unless you explicitly want to include an error handler, you are better off using a file name as factor 2.

RPG IV includes additional operations that provide variations on sequential record access. Some of these operations control where in the file sequential reading will next occur, while others determine the nature of the reading itself.

SETLL (Set Lower Limit)

The SETLL operation provides flexibility related to where sequential reading occurs within a file. SETLL allows you to begin sequential processing at a record other than the first one in the file. It also can be used to reposition the file once end-of-file has been reached. The general format of a SETLL follows:

```
*.. 1 ...+... 2 ...+... 3 ...+... 4 ...+... 5 ...+... 6 ...+... 7 ...+... 8 ...+... 9 ...+...10
CLØN01Factor1++++++Opcode(E)+Factor2++++++Result+++++++Len++D+HiLoEq....Comments++++++++++++
C* General format of SETLL.
C       Factor1    SETLL     Factor2
```

SETLL positions a file at the first record whose *key* is greater than or equal to the value specified in factor 1. Factor 1 can be a literal, field name, figurative constant, or KLIST (discussed shortly). Factor 2 can be a file name or record format name (if the file is externally described). Notice that no indicator is required in conjunction with this operation. You can, however, use any or all three resulting indicator positions, if you wish. Each indicator position signals a different outcome of the SETLL operation.

An indicator in the Hi position (71-72) comes on if the value of factor 1 is greater than the highest key in the file. An indicator in the Lo position (73-74) comes on if some system error occurs upon execution of the operation. An indicator in the Eq position (75-76) comes on if a record is found in the file whose key exactly matches the value of factor 1.

```
*.. 1 ...+... 2 ...+... 3 ...+... 4 ...+... 5 ...+... 6 ...+... 7 ...+... 8 ...+... 9 ...+...10
CLØNØ1Factor1++++++Opcode(E)+Factor2++++++Result++++++++Len++D+HiLoEq....Comments+++++++++++
CLØNØ1Factor1++++++Opcode(E)+Extended-factor2+++++++++++++++++++++++++++++Comments+++++++++++
C* Demonstrating the use of indicators with SETLL.
C     CustIn        SETLL     CustMast                              9Ø5Ø75
C                   SELECT
C                   WHEN      *IN5Ø = *ON
C                   EXSR      SystemErr
C                   WHEN      *IN9Ø = *ON
C                   EXSR      ValueTooHi
C                   WHEN      *IN75 = *ON
C                   EXSR      ExactMatch
C                   OTHER
C                   EXSR      GTMatch
C                   ENDSL
```

The SETLL does *not* actually retrieve a record; it simply positions the file to determine what record the next sequential read will access. An unsuccessful SETLL causes the file to be positioned at end-of-file.

SETLL has two common uses in RPG IV programming. The first is to reposition the file to the beginning during processing by using figurative constant *LOVAL as factor 1. The next sequential read operation then retrieves the first record in the file.

```
*.. 1 ...+... 2 ...+... 3 ...+... 4 ...+... 5 ...+... 6 ...+... 7 ...+... 8 ...+... 9 ...+...10
CLØNØ1Factor1++++++Opcode(E)+Factor2++++++Result++++++++Len++D+HiLoEq....Comments+++++++++++
C* Using SETLL to position pointer to first record in file for subsequent read.
C     *LOVAL        SETLL     CustMast
C                   READ      CustMast                              90
```

The second common use of SETLL is to position the file to the first record of a group of records with identical key values preparatory to processing that group of records. (Details of this use are described in conjunction with the READE operation.)

You also can use SETLL to determine whether or not a record exists in a file without actually reading it. If you simply need to check for the presence of a record with a given key, without accessing the data contained in the record, using a SETLL is more efficient than doing a READ operation.

```
*.. 1 ...+... 2 ...+... 3 ...+... 4 ...+... 5 ...+... 6 ...+... 7 ...+... 8 ...+... 9 ...+...10
CLØNØ1Factor1++++++Opcode(E)+Factor2++++++Result++++++++Len++D+HiLoEq....Comments+++++++++++
CLØNØ1Factor1++++++Opcode(E)+Extended-factor2+++++++++++++++++++++++++++++Comments+++++++++++
C* Using SETLL to determine whether or not a record exists in a file.
C     CustIn        SETLL     CustMast                              10
C                   IF        *IN10 = *ON
C                   EXSR      CustFound
C                   ELSE
C                   EXSR      NoCustomer
C                   ENDIF
```

SETGT (Set Greater Than)

The SETGT operation works similarly to SETLL. The primary difference is that this operation positions the file to a record whose key value is *greater* than the value of factor 1, rather than greater than or equal to the value of factor 1.

```
*.. 1 ...+... 2 ...+... 3 ...+... 4 ...+... 5 ...+... 6 ...+... 7 ...+... 8 ...+... 9 ...+...10
CLØN01Factor1++++++Opcode(E)+Factor2++++++Result++++++++Len++D+HiLoEq....Comments++++++++++++
C* General format of SETGT.
C       Factor1         SETGT     Factor2
```

As with the SETLL operation, factor 1 can be a field, literal, figurative constant, or KLIST; factor 2 can be a file name or record format name. Like SETLL, SETGT does not require the use of resulting indicators. You can, however, include indicators in the Hi and/or Lo positions. An indicator in the Hi position (71-72) comes on with SETGT if the positioning is *not* successful (in which case the file would be positioned at end-of-file); an indicator in the Lo position (73-74) comes on if an error occurs during the operation. You cannot use an indicator in the Eq position (75-76) with the SETGT operation.

```
*.. 1 ...+... 2 ...+... 3 ...+... 4 ...+... 5 ...+... 6 ...+... 7 ...+... 8 ...+... 9 ...+...10
CLØN01Factor1++++++Opcode(E)+Factor2++++++Result++++++++Len++D+HiLoEq....Comments++++++++++++
CLØN01Factor1++++++Opcode(E)+Extended-factor2+++++++++++++++++++++++++++++Comments++++++++++++
C* Demonstrating the use of indicators with SETGT.
C       CustIn          SETGT     CustMast                          9050
C                       SELECT
C                       WHEN      *IN50 = *ON
C                       EXSR      SystemErr
C                       WHEN      *IN90 = *ON
C                       EXSR      ValueTooHi
C                       OTHER
C                       EXSR      GTMatch
C                       ENDSL
```

To understand the value of this operation, assume you have a logical file over your orders file, keyed on order date in YYMMDD format, and you want to generate a report of orders from the last six months of 1994. By using the SETGT operation with June 30 as the factor 1 value, the system will position the file to the first record of July, regardless of what date that happens to be. The code below illustrates this example.

```
*.. 1 ...+... 2 ...+... 3 ...+... 4 ...+... 5 ...+... 6 ...+... 7 ...+... 8 ...+... 9 ...+...10
CLØN01Factor1++++++Opcode(E)+Factor2++++++Result++++++++Len++D+HiLoEq....Comments++++++++++++
CLØN01Factor1++++++Opcode(E)+Extended-factor2+++++++++++++++++++++++++++++Comments++++++++++++
C* Orders file keyed on date; code uses SETGT to process all orders placed
C* after June 30, 1994.
C       940630          SETGT     Orders
C                       READ      Orders                                      90
C                       DOW       *IN90 = *OFF
C                       ...
C                       READ      Orders                                      90
C                       ENDDO
C                       ...
```

SETGT also is used with *HIVAL to position the file to end-of-file preparatory to a READP operation (discussed in the next section). Remember that a SETGT, like a SETLL, merely positions the file; it does not actually retrieve a record from the database.

READE (Read Equal Key)
The READE operation sequentially reads the next record in a full procedural file if the key of that record matches the value in factor 1. If the record's key does not match, or if the file is at end-of-file, the indictor you specify in the Eq position (75-76) comes on. The operation requires an indicator in this position. You may also use an indicator in the Lo position (73-74) to signal the occurrence of an error during the operation.

Factor 1 can be a field, literal, figurative constant, or KLIST name (KLISTs are described later in this chapter). Factor 1 also may be omitted, provided that the file previously has been positioned using SETLL, SETGT, READ, READE (with factor 1 specified), or other input-related operations that position the file. Factor 2 may be a file name or a record-format name.

Programmers use this operation within a loop to identically process sets of records with duplicate keys in a file. Programmers often precede the first READE with a SETLL operation to position the file initially, preparatory to processing those records with keys identical to that specified by the SETLL.

Assume, for example, that you want to list all orders received on a specific date, and that the order file is keyed on date. Further assume that the date whose orders are to print is stored in field InDate. The following processing would be appropriate:

```
*.. 1 ...+... 2 ...+... 3 ...+... 4 ...+... 5 ...+... 6 ...+... 7 ...+... 8 ...+... 9 ...+...10
CLØNØ1Factor1++++++Opcode(E)+Factor2++++++Result+++++++Len++D+HiLoEq....Comments++++++++++++
CLØNØ1Factor1++++++Opcode(E)+Extended-factor2+++++++++++++++++++++++++++Comments++++++++++++
C* Code to list all orders placed on InDate.
C      InDate       SETLL     Orders                              50
C                   IF        *IN50 = *ON
C      InDate       READE     Orders                              90
C                   DOW       *IN90 = *OFF
C                   EXCEPT    OrderLine
C      InDate       READE     Orders                              90
C                   ENDDO
C                   ELSE
C                   EXCEPT    NoOrders
C                   ENDIF
```

The code above uses the value of InDate to position the Orders file to a key value that matches that of InDate. If the match exists, indicator 50 comes on. If indicator 50 is on, the program does an initial READE of the file and then sets up a loop with DOW; within the loop the program uses EXCEPT to write an order line and then reads the next equal record. The loop continues as long as the READE is successful. If the initial SETLL failed (signaled by indicator 50 remaining off), flow bypasses the loop, drops down to the ELSE, and writes a "no orders" line using EXCEPT.

READP (Read Prior Record) and READPE (Read Prior Equal)
The READP and READPE operations are sequential reading operations that
have their parallels in READ and READE, respectively. The only difference
between READP and READ, and between READPE and READE, is direc-
tionality; the PRIOR operations move "backwards" through the file. You do
not use a factor 1 entry with READP; a factor 1 entry is optional for
READPE, subject to the same constraints as READE. Both PRIOR operations require a factor 2 entry, which may be a file or record-format name.

Like READ and READE, both READP and READPE *require* the use of an
indicator in the Eq position (75-76). This indicator comes on at beginning-of-
file for the READP, or when the key of the prior sequential record does not
match the factor 1 value for READPE. With both operations, you have the
option to use an indicator in the Lo position (73-74) to signal an error.

You must first position the file with some input operation before using
READP or READPE with a blank factor 1. Programmers often use a SETGT for
this initial positioning before beginning the reverse transversal through the file.

The concept of "backwards" sequential access is relatively easy to grasp;
it is harder to visualize why such processing might be desired. Let's consider
an example to get a sense of when these operations might be appropriate.

Imagine the following scenario. As part of an order-processing program, the program is to assign order numbers sequentially. Each day the
program is run, the number assigned to the first order number is to be one
larger than the number of the last order processed the previous day. Assume
also that the order file is keyed on order number. The following code will
determine the appropriate starting value for the day's orders:

```
*...1 ...+... 2 ...+... 3 ...+... 4 ...+... 5 ...+... 6 ...+... 7 ...+... 8 ...+... 9 ...+...10
CL0N01Factor1++++++Opcode(E)+Factor2++++++Result+++++++Len++D+HiLoEq....Comments++++++++++++
CL0N01Factor1++++++Opcode(E)+Extended-factor2+++++++++++++++++++++++++++++Comments++++++++++++
C* Code using SETGT and READP to determine the next order number to use.
C* Orders file is keyed on field Order#.
C        *HIVAL         SETGT     Orders
C                       READP     Orders                                      90
C                       IF        *IN90 = *OFF
C                       EVAL      Order# = Order# + 1
C                       ELSE
C                       EXSR      Error
C                       ENDIF
```

In the above code, SETGT positions the file at end-of-file. The READP
operation retrieves the last record in the file (e.g., the record with the highest order number). Adding 1 to Order#, then, gives you the value for the
first new order of the day. If indicator 90 comes on, it indicates that you are
at beginning-of-file, which means that there are no records in the order file;
in this case, an error routine should be performed.

In general, the PRIOR read operations might be used any time you
want to process files in descending key order, because ordinarily the AS/400
organizes keyed files in sequence by ascending key value.

Random Access

All the operations discussed so far in this chapter have dealt with retrieving database records sequentially. Often, however, you want to be able to read a specific record, determined by its key value, without having to read through the file sequentially to reach that record. This kind of access is called **random access**. Random access lets you "reach into" a file and extract just the record you want.

CHAIN (Random Retrieval from a File)

RPG IV supports random access of full procedural database files through the CHAIN operation. CHAIN requires a factor 1 entry. The literal or data item name of factor 1 contains the key value of the record to be randomly read. Factor 2, also required, contains the name of the file (or record format) from which the record is to be randomly retrieved. A required indicator in the Hi position (71-72) comes on if the random read is *unsuccessful*; that is, if no record in the file matches the specified key value of factor 1. You have the option of including an error indicator in the Lo position (73-74).

```
*.. 1 ...+... 2 ...+... 3 ...+... 4 ...+... 5 ...+... 6 ...+... 7 ...+... 8 ...+... 9 ...+...10
CLØNØ1Factor1++++++Opcode(E)+Factor2++++++Result++++++++Len++D+HiLoEq....Comments+++++++++++
CLØNØ1Factor1++++++Opcode(E)+Extended-factor2++++++++++++++++++++++++++++Comments+++++++++++
C     CustNbr       CHAIN     CustMaster                          90
C                   IF        *IN90 = *ON
C                   EXSR      NoCust
C                   ELSE
C                   EXSR      CustFound
C                   ENDIF
```

In the example shown above, CustNbr contains the key value of the CustMaster record you want to read. If the CHAIN does not find a record with that key value, indicator 90 comes on and the program executes subroutine NoCust; if the record is found, indicator 90 stays off and the program executes subroutine CustFound.

When the file contains records with duplicate keys, such that more than one record would qualify as a match, the system retrieves the first record that matches.

If the CHAIN is successful (signaled by the resulting indicator remaining *OFF), the system positions the file to the record immediately following the retrieved record. Accordingly, issuing a READ or READE to the file following a successful CHAIN results in sequentially accessing the file starting with the record *immediately following* the CHAINed record. Because of this, the CHAIN operation can be used to position the file in a manner similar to SETLL. The primary difference between these two approaches is that a successful CHAIN actually reads a record, whereas a successful SETLL merely repositions the file without retrieving a record.

If a CHAIN operation is unsuccessful, it cannot be followed with a sequential read operation without first successfully repositioning the file with another CHAIN, SETLL, or SETGT operation.

Referencing Composite Keys

As discussed in Chapter 5, both physical and logical files can have keys based on more than one field. This kind of key is called a **composite** or **concatenated key**. The existence of composite keys raises a puzzling question: What can you use as a factor 1 search argument for CHAIN, SETLL, READE, etc., when the records in the file you are trying to access are keyed on more than a single field value? That is, how can you indicate a corresponding composite value in a single data-item entry? RPG IV solves this problem with the KLIST operation.

KLIST (Define a Composite Key) and KFLD (Define Parts of a Key)
The KLIST operation lets you define a field for accessing records based on a composite key. Factor 1 specifies the name you wish to give the KLIST. No entries other than factor 1 are used with KLIST.

At least one KFLD operation must immediately follow a KLIST operation. Each KFLD entry declares a field that is to participate in the concatenation; the field is entered as the result field of the operation. The order in which the KFLDs are listed determines the order in which they are concatenated to form the KLIST.

To understand how to form and use KLISTs, consider the following example. Assume you have a database file of student grades, StudGrades, which contains one record per student per course taken. The records contain four fields — StudNbr, CrseNbr, Grade, and Semester — and the file has a composite key based on StudNbr, Semester, and CrseNbr. You are writing a program that requires you to randomly access the StudGrades file to retrieve a grade that a given student received in a given class. The student, semester, and course you want to find are stored in fields Student, Smster, and Course, respectively.

```
*.. 1 ...+... 2 ...+... 3 ...+... 4 ...+... 5 ...+... 6 ...+... 7 ...+... 8 ...+... 9 ...+...10
CL0N01Factor1+++++++Opcode(E)+Factor2+++++++Result++++++++Len++D+HiLoEq....Comments+++++++++++
C     StdSemCrs     KLIST
C                   KFLD                      Student
C                   KFLD                      Smster
C                   KFLD                      Course
C                   ...
C     StdSemCrs     CHAIN     StudGrades                         90
```

In the above example, StdSemCrs is the KLIST name that stores the combined values of student number (Student), semester (Smster), and course (Course). That KLIST is then used to chain to the StudGrades file.

The KFLDs may have, but do not need to have, the same names as those of the file records' composite key. However, each KFLD field must agree in length, type, and decimal positions with the field it corresponds to in the file's composite key. Each KFLD is associated with a composite key field based on the ordinal positions of the corresponding fields. That is, the first KFLD field is matched to the first (or high-order) field of the composite key, and so on.

KLIST and KFLD are declarative operations, providing definitions rather than executable operations. You can declare a KLIST anywhere within a program, but it is good programming practice to include it at the beginning of the calculations or as part of an initialization subroutine. You can use the same KLIST name to access different database files — provided it is appropriate to do so. You can also use one KLIST multiple times to access the same file within a program. A KLIST name can serve as the factor 1 value in CHAIN, READE, READPE, SETLL, SETGT, and DELETE operations.

Partial Key Lists

KLIST offers an additional feature that makes processing groups of logically associated records relatively simple. Use the example above, but this time instead of wanting information about a grade for one course for one student, assume you want to be able to access *all* the records in StudGrades for a particular student for a given semester, perhaps to print out his/her grades earned that semester.

```
*.. 1 ...+... 2 ...+... 3 ...+... 4 ...+... 5 ...+... 6 ...+... 7 ...+... 8 ...+... 9 ...+...10
CL0N01Factor1+++++++Opcode(E)+Factor2++++++Result+++++++Len++D+HiLoEq....Comments++++++++++++
CL0N01Factor1+++++++Opcode(E)+Extended-factor2+++++++++++++++++++++++++++Comments++++++++++++
C* Define a partial KLIST.
C     StudSmster    KLIST
C                   KFLD                    Student
C                   KFLD                    Smster
C* Use KLIST to access correct student and semester.
C     StudSmster    CHAIN     StudGrades                  90
C                   IF        *IN90 = *OFF
C *Loop through records for that student/semester.
C                   DOW       *IN90 = *OFF
C                   EXSR      PrintGrade
C* READE fails when no more records are found for that student/semester.
C     StudSmster    READE     StudGrades                  90
C                   ENDDO
C                   ELSE
C                   EXSR      NoGrades
C                   ENDIF
```

The above code accomplishes the desired processing. First, it defines KLIST StudSmster with only the student number and semester as the KFLDs of the list. StudSmster, then, is a partial KLIST, because the file it will be used with is keyed on a composite of student number, semester, and course number.

Using StudSmster, the program chains to the StudGrades file to read the first course for the given student in the given semester. If the CHAIN is successful (signaled by indicator 90 remaining off), the program sets up a loop that continues until indicator 90 comes on. Within the loop, the program executes subroutine PrintGrade to print grades and then executes a READE to bring in the next course for the student being processed. If the original CHAIN fails, control drops to the ELSE and the program executes subroutine NoGrades to indicate that the student/semester was not in the file.

Note that the same effects could have been achieved by issuing a SETLL to position the file and then, provided the operation was successful, using a READE to read the first record of the set. A successful CHAIN reads a record and positions the file to the desired location in one operation.

RPG IV lets you access a database file based on a partial key list, provided the portion you want to use is the major, or high-order, key field(s). That is, given StudGrades keyed on StudNbr + Semester + CrseNbr, we can access the records with a partial key of student, or student and semester, but not with a partial key of course or semester. Thus, we can get a list of all courses for a given student, but not a list of all students who have taken a given course; the database file would need to be keyed differently to allow this kind of access.

Operations for Output Files

The operations we've looked at so far are appropriate for input files. A few I/O operations deal with output — that is, writing records to database files. Until now, the output of your programs has been reports. You may also designate a database file as program output. The File Specification entries in this case require the file name in positions 7-16, the type, O for output, in position 17, E in position 22 (assuming the file is externally described), K in position 34 (if the file is accessed via a key) and DISK, the device specification, in positions 36-42.

```
*.. 1 ...+... 2 ...+... 3 ...+... 4 ...+... 5 ...+... 6 ...+... 7 ...+... 8 ...+... 9 ...+...10
FFilename++IPEASFRlen+LKlen+AIDevice+.Keywords+++++++++++++++++++++++++++++Comments+++++++++++
F* File specification for a program that writes records to a new file.
FCustMast  O   E          K DISK
```

You may need to make one additional entry to the File Specifications, depending on whether your program is performing an initial file load — that is, putting records into the file for the first time — or adding records to a file that already contains records. If you are adding records to an output file that already contains records, you must signal that fact by entering an A in position 20 of the File Specification, as shown below.

```
*.. 1 ...+... 2 ...+... 3 ...+... 4 ...+... 5 ...+... 6 ...+... 7 ...+... 8 ...+... 9 ...+...10
FFilename++IPEASFRlen+LKlen+AIDevice+.Keywords+++++++++++++++++++++++++++++Comments+++++++++++
F* File specification for a program that adds records to those already in a file.
FCustMast  O  A E          K DISK
```

Once you have defined a database file as output, two RPG IV operations let you output records to the file: EXCEPT and WRITE.

EXCEPT (Calculation Time Output)

You already have used the EXCEPT operation to write to printer files; you can also use EXCEPT to write records to a database file. The form of the EXCEPT statement that is used to write to database files is no different than the form used for printer files.

The EXCEPT operation optionally can designate a named E line on the output. When the program reaches the EXCEPT operation, it writes the named E lines (if the EXCEPT includes a line name in factor 2) or all unnamed E lines (if the EXCEPT operation appeared alone on the Calculation Specification) from the Output Specifications.

In the Output Specifications, you need to enter the record format name of the externally described file, rather than the file name itself, in positions 7-16. Then list either all the fields comprising the record, or simply *ALL. Omitting a field or fields from the list causes zeros or blanks, depending on the data type, to be written to the record for that field. Rather than listing all the fields, you can simply code *ALL, which has the same effect as including all the field names.

```
*.. 1 ...+... 2 ...+... 3 ...+... 4 ...+... 5 ...+... 6 ...+... 7 ...+... 8 ...+... 9 ...+...10
CLØN01Factor1+++++++Opcode(E)+Factor2+++++++Result++++++++Len++D+HiLoEq....Comments+++++++++++
C*  Writing to a database file with EXCEPT.
C                       ...
C                     EXCEPT    Record

*.. 1 ...+... 2 ...+... 3 ...+... 4 ...+... 5 ...+... 6 ...+... 7 ...+... 8 ...+... 9 ...+...10
OFilename++DF..NØ1NØ2NØ3Excnam++++B++A++Sb+Sa+..........................:....Comments+++++++++++
O* Exception lines for an initial file load.
OCustRecordE          Record
O                     *ALL
```

The above code examples show how you could write records to the customer file for an initial file load. If you want to add records to records already in a file, besides entering an A in position 20 of the File Specification, you need to include an ADD entry in positions 18-20 of the Output Specification E line, as shown below.

```
*.. 1 ...+... 2 ...+... 3 ...+... 4 ...+... 5 ...+... 6 ...+... 7 ...+... 8 ...+... 9 ...+...10
OFilename++DF..NØ1NØ2NØ3Excnam++++B++A++Sb+Sa+..........................:....Comments+++++++++++
O* Exception line for adding records to an existing file.
OCustRecordEADD       Record
O                     *ALL
```

WRITE (Write a Record to a File)

Today's RPG IV programmers generally output database records more directly in their calculations by using the WRITE operation. The WRITE operation must designate a record-format name, rather than a file name. If the writing is adding records to a file that already contains records, the A in position 20 of the File Specification for that file is required.

```
*.. 1 ...+... 2 ...+... 3 ...+... 4 ...+... 5 ...+... 6 ...+... 7 ...+... 8 ...+... 9 ...+...10
CLØNØ1Factor1++++++Opcode(E)+Factor2++++++Result+++++++Len++D+HiLoEq....Comments++++++++++++
C* Writing a record to database file CustMaster.
C                   WRITE     CustRecord
C                   ...
```

With a WRITE operation, the current program values for all the fields comprising the record definition are written to the file. You may include an optional indicator in the Lo position (73-74) for this operation to signal an error.

Update Files and I/O Operations

A common data processing task is file maintenance. File maintenance, or updating, involves adding or deleting records from database files, or changing the information in database records, to keep the information current and correct. Records that do not exist cannot be changed or deleted; if a file has unique keys, a second record with the same key should not be added to the file. Accordingly, file maintenance routines typically require first determining whether or not the record exists in the file (through a CHAIN or SETLL), and then determining what update option is valid, given the record's found status.

RPG IV includes an update file type, signaled by U in position 17 of the File Specifications, which allows you to read, change, and then rewrite records to the file, as well as to add and delete entire records. Any database file can be used as an update file simply by coding it as such in the File Specifications. If the maintenance procedure involves adding new records, you need to signal that fact in the File Specifications by entering an A (for Add) in position 20.

An update file supports both input and output operations. If you define a file as an update full procedural file, you can use all the input operations discussed so far — CHAIN, READ, READE, READPE, READP, SETLL, and SETGT — to access records in the file. You also can use KLIST for externally described update files. If you defined the file for add capability (the A on the File Specifications), you can use the WRITE operation to add new records to the file. Two additional I/O operations exist that you can use only for update files: DELETE and UPDATE.

DELETE (Delete Record)

The DELETE operation deletes a single record from the file specified in factor 2. Factor 2 can be a file name or, if the file is externally described, a record-format name. The use of factor 1 is optional. If you leave factor 1 blank, the system deletes the record most recently read. If you use factor 1 to specify which record is to be deleted, you may enter a field name, a literal, or a KLIST name. If duplicate records based on the factor 1 value exist in the file, the system deletes only the first record.

An entry in factor 1 requires the use of an indicator in positions 71-72 (Hi). This indicator comes on if the record to be deleted is not found in the file. An optional indicator in the Lo position (73-74) signals other I/O error conditions.

```
*.. 1 ...+... 2 ...+... 3 ...+... 4 ...+... 5 ...+... 6 ...+... 7 ...+... 8 ...+... 9 ...+...10
CL0N01Factor1++++++Opcode(E)+Extended-factor2+++++++++++++++++++++++++++++++Comments+++++++++++
CL0N01Factor1++++++Opcode(E)+Factor2++++++Result+++++++Len++D+HiLoEq....Comments+++++++++++
C* This code deletes the record of customer 100 if the record exists in the file.
C                   EVAL      CustNbr = '100'
C        CustNbr    CHAIN     CustMaster                           90
C                   IF        *IN90 = *OFF
C                   DELETE    CustMaster
C                   ENDIF
C* The lines below produce the same result as the code above.
C                   EVAL      CustNbr = '100'
C        CustNbr    DELETE    CustMaster                           90
```

Note that if you use DELETE with factor 1 blank without first retrieving a record from the file, you will get a system error message. The DELETE operation logically deletes records from a file, rather than physically removing them. Although as a result of DELETE, a record is no longer accessible to programs or queries, the record actually remains on disk until the file containing the deleted record is reorganized.

UPDATE (Modify Existing Record)

The UPDATE operation modifies the record most recently read. You can use this operation only with files defined for update. This operation does not use factor 1; factor 2 must contain a record-format name, not a file name, if the file is externally described. Moreover, your program must have successfully completed a READ, READE, READP, READPE, or CHAIN operation to retrieve that record format before it executes an UPDATE.

UPDATE causes the current program values of all the record's fields to be rewritten to the file. The typical procedure involving UPDATE is to retrieve a record, change one or more of its fields' values, and then UPDATE to rewrite the record with its new values. You cannot issue multiple UPDATEs for a single read operation; each UPDATE must be preceded by a record retrieval.

```
*.. 1 ...+... 2 ...+... 3 ...+... 4 ...+... 5 ...+... 6 ...+... 7 ...+... 8 ...+... 9 ...+...10
CL0N01Factor1++++++Opcode(E)+Factor2++++++Result+++++++Len++D+HiLoEq....Comments+++++++++++
CL0N01Factor1++++++Opcode(E)+Extended-factor2+++++++++++++++++++++++++++++++Comments+++++++++++
C* Retrieve the customer record, add the current invoice amount to the customer's balance due,
C* and rewrite the record to the file.  If the customer is not in the file, perform
C* an error routine.
C        CustNbr    CHAIN     CustMaster                           90
C                   IF        *IN90 =*OFF
C                   EVAL      BalanceDue = BalanceDue + InvoiceAmt
C                   UPDATE    CustRecord
C                   ELSE
C                   EXSR      NoCustomer
C                   ENDIF
```

Updating Through EXCEPT

The UPDATE operation rewrites *all* of a database record's fields to a file. In the above example, the current value of BalanceDue *and every other field in CustRecord* is incorporated into the record by the UPDATE. If your program logic has resulted in changes in field values that you do not wish to be updated, you can use EXCEPT to designate which fields are to be rewritten.

```
*.. 1 ...+... 2 ...+... 3 ...+... 4 ...+... 5 ...+... 6 ...+... 7 ...+... 8 ...+... 9 ...+...10
CL0N01Factor1++++++Opcode(E)+Factor2++++++Result+++++++Len++D+HiLoEq....Comments+++++++++++
CL0N01Factor1++++++Opcode(E)+Extended-factor2+++++++++++++++++++++++++++++Comments+++++++++++
C* Retrieve the customer record, add the current invoice amount to the customer's balance due,
C* and rewrite via EXCEPT.  If the customer is not in the file, perform an error routine.
C     CustNbr       CHAIN     CustMaster                              90
C                   IF        *IN90 = *OFF
C                   ...
C                   EVAL      BalanceDue = BalanceDue + InvoiceAmt
C                   EXCEPT    CustRewrit
C                   ELSE
C                   EXSR      NoCustomer
C                   ENDIF
```

```
*.. 1 ...+... 2 ...+... 3 ...+... 4 ...+... 5 ...+... 6 ...+... 7 ...+... 8 ...+... 9 ...+...10
OFilename++DF..N01N02N03Excnam++++B++A++Sb+Sa+........................................Comments+++++++++++
O* Only the balance due field is updated to the file; other fields of the customer record
O* will retain whatever values they originally had when the record was read, regardless of
O* how their values have been changed within the program.
OCustRecordE          CustRewrit
O                     BalanceDue
```

File and Record Locking

Any multiuser system needs to address the problems related to simultaneous use of the same database file. Otherwise, it is possible that if two users access the same record for update, make changes in the record, and then rewrite it to the file, one of the user's changes might get lost — a condition sometimes called **phantom updates**. Two approaches you can use to deal with this type of problem are **file locking** and **record locking**.

The easiest kind of locking is to limit access to a file to one user at a time — a condition known as file locking. Although OS/400 permits you to lock files at a system level by issuing CL commands, most of the time you want to allow multiple users access to the same files at the same time. RPG IV includes built-in, automatic locking features at a record level.

If your program designates a file as an update file, RPG IV automatically places a lock on a record when it is read within your program. Updating that record or reading another record releases the record from its locked state. While the record is locked, other application programs can access that record if they have defined the file as an input file, but not if they, too, have defined the file as an update file. This solution eliminates the problem of lost updates.

However, record locking can cause waiting and access problems for users if programmers don't structure their code to avoid locks except when absolutely necessary. The nightmare scenario you should keep in mind when designing update programs is that of the user who keys in a request to update a record, pulls up the screen of data preparatory to making changes in the record, and then realizes it's lunch time and disappears for an hour. Meanwhile, the record lock prevents all other users from accessing that record.

A common solution programmers used in the past to avoid this problem was to read the record to obtain its field values and then immediately write an exception line to that record format with no fields listed. This exception output would release the record from its locked state. Then, once the program had obtained all needed update values, it would again read the same record and immediately update that record with the new values.

More recently (V2R2 of OS/400), IBM added enhancements to RPG to deal more easily with this record-locking problem. First, IBM added operation extender (N), which can be used with READ, READE, READP, READPE, and CHAIN, to specify that the input operation to an update file be done without locking the record. You can use this feature to avoid unnecessary locking. Second, IBM added operation UNLOCK. If you've read a record with a lock and want to release the lock, you can use this operation along with a file name in factor 2 to release all locks to that file.

```
*.. 1 ...+... 2 ...+... 3 ...+... 4 ...+... 5 ...+... 6 ...+... 7 ...+... 8 ...+... 9 ...+...10
CLØN01Factor1++++++Opcode(E)+Factor2++++++Result++++++++Len++D+HiLoEq....Comments+++++++++++
C* Random read of an update file automatically locks the record.
C       CustNbr        CHAIN     CustMaster                       90
C
C* Random read of an update file with operation extender N keeps the record unlocked.
C       CustNbr        CHAIN (N) CustMaster                       90
C
C* Release all current record locks for CustMaster.
C                      UNLOCK    CustMaster
```

If you start releasing record locks in update procedures, however, be aware that you can easily code yourself right back into the phantom-update problem that caused systems to incorporate record-locking in the first place. If you aren't including some provision that checks to make certain another user has not updated a record between the time you first accessed the record and the time you are about to rewrite the record with the values from your program, leave all record locking in place.

Beyond record-locking considerations, generally accepted programming practice dictates that a program should not keep a file open any longer than it needs to access the required data from the file. RPG IV automatically opens your files at the beginning of processing and then closes them all at the end of processing. If your program needs access to a file for only a portion of its total running time, you should take control of the file opening and closing, rather than allowing RPG IV to manage those tasks for you. RPG IV includes two operations to give you this capability: OPEN and CLOSE.

```
*.. 1 ...+... 2 ...+... 3 ...+... 4 ...+... 5 ...+... 6 ...+... 7 ...+... 8 ...+... 9 ...+...10
CLØN01Factor1++++++Opcode(E)+Factor2++++++Result++++++++Len++D+HiLoEq....Comments+++++++++++
C* Explicitly opening file CustMaster.
C                   OPEN      CustMaster
C* Explicitly closing file CustMaster.
C                   CLOSE     CustMaster
```

You can close a file that RPG IV opened automatically. If you want to control the file opening with the OPEN operation, you must make an additional entry within the File Specification for the file you wish to open. Keyword USROPN (User Open), coded in the Keywords area of the specification line, prevents the file from being implicitly opened by RPG IV and signals that the opening of the file will be explicitly coded within the program.

```
*.. 1 ...+... 2 ...+... 3 ...+... 4 ...+... 5 ...+... 6 ...+... 7 ...+... 8 ...+... 9 ...+...10
FFilename++IPEASFRlen+LKlen+AIDevice+.Keywords+++++++++++++++++++++++++++++Comments+++++++++++
F* File is an update file, with record addition possible. File opening is user-controlled.
FCustMasterUF A E           K DISK     USROPN
```

Trying to open a file that's already open causes an error. However, you can open a given file more than once within a program, provided the file is closed before each successive open.

I/O Errors

Many of the I/O operations discussed above use resulting indicators to signal commonly expected results of the operation, such as reaching end-of-file or CHAINing to a record not in the file. All the operations include the optional use of an indicator to detect errors of input or output, such as trying to read a record locked by another program or issuing a read to a record format not next in the file. You can trap such errors as part of your operation by including an indicator in the Lo resulting indicator position (73-74).

```
*.. 1 ...+... 2 ...+... 3 ...+... 4 ...+... 5 ...+... 6 ...+... 7 ...+... 8 ...+... 9 ...+...10
CLØN01Factor1++++++Opcode(E)+Factor2++++++Result++++++++Len++D+HiLoEq....Comments+++++++++++
CLØN01Factor1++++++Opcode(E)+Extended-factor2++++++++++++++++++++++++++++++Comments+++++++++++
C* Indicator 80 is used with the UPDATE operation to detect I/O errors.
C                   UPDATE    CustRecord                      80
C                   IF        *IN8Ø = *ON
C                   EXSR      IOError
C                   ENDIF
```

Chapter 9 will show you additional ways to detect these and other kinds of errors. Errors not handled by a program cause the program to end abnormally (abend). Abends upset users and operators and often result in frantic phone calls to the programmer, usually at 3 a.m. Good, defensive programmers always design programs to minimize the possibility of errors and then trap for unexpected errors to ensure their reputations and minimize middle-of-the-night wake-up calls.

Putting It All Together

Now that you have learned about RPG IV's input and output operations, you might find some sample programs helpful to demonstrate how to apply these operations. Accordingly, read the scenarios that follow and study the program solutions to develop a sense of when to use the various I/O operations.

In the first scenario, a company has decided to give all its employees a five percent pay raise. Assume that an externally described master file of employees (EmpMaster) exists, that the record format within the database file is EmpRecord, and that the pay field is Pay. The file is keyed on employee ID. Externally described printer file ErrReport contains two record formats: ReadProb, to signal problems that occur when reading, and UpdateProb, to signal problems that occur when updating. A solution for this problem is shown below.

```
*.. 1 ...+... 2 ...+... 3 ...+... 4 ...+... 5 ...+... 6 ...+... 7 ...+... 8 ...+... 9 ...+...10
F***************************************************************************
F* This program gives each employee in the EmpMaster file a 5% raise.    *
F* Any I/O errors are recorded in ErrReport.                             *
F*   Author: Yaeger.  Feb. 1995.                                         *
F***************************************************************************
FEmpMaster UF   E           K DISK
FErrReport O    E             PRINTER OFLIND(*IN10)
C                READ      EmpMaster                      5099
C                DOW       *IN99 = *OFF
C                IF        *IN50 = *ON
C                EXSR      Error
C                ELSE
C                EVAL (H)  Pay = Pay * 1.05
C                UPDATE    EmpRecord                      60
C                IF        *IN60 = *ON
C                EXSR      Error
C                ENDIF
C                ENDIF
C                READ      EmpMaster                      5099
C                ENDDO
C                EVAL      *INLR = *ON
C                RETURN
C* Subroutine to write I/O errors to a report.
C     Error      BEGSR
C                IF        *IN10 = *ON
C                WRITE     ErrHeads
C                EVAL      *IN10 = *OFF
C                ENDIF
C                SELECT
C                WHEN      *IN50 = *ON
C                WRITE     ReadProb
C                WHEN      *IN60 = *ON
C                WRITE     UpdateProb
C                ENDSL
C                ENDSR
```

In the above solution, the file is declared as an update file, but because we are not asked to add new records to the file, the program does not specify that record addition should be enabled. Because all employees are to receive the raise, the calculations consist of a simple loop that sequentially reads through the file, calculates the new pay for each employee, and updates the employee's record. IF logic is included to detect I/O errors and write such problems to a report.

Now let's complicate the problem a little. Instead of giving every employee a raise, the company wants to give only selected employees a five percent raise; those employees' IDs (field EmpID) are contained in a transaction file called RaiseTrans.

The processing requirements of this problem vary from the first scenario, because now we need to access only those employees in EmpMaster who appear in file RaiseTrans. Every record in RaiseTrans, however, must be processed. Accordingly, we want to sequentially process RaiseTrans and use the information on each record to randomly access an EmpMaster record to update. To provide for the possible error where RaiseTrans contains one or more employee IDs not found in the master file, assume that the error report file includes an additional error line: NoEmpProb.

```
*.. 1 ...+... 2 ...+... 3 ...+... 4 ...+... 5 ...+... 6 ..+... 7 ...+... 8 ...+... 9 ...+...10
F*******************************************************************************
F* This program updates employees' pay by 5% based on employee IDs contained in  *
F* file RaiseTrans.  Problems of incorrect IDs and I/O errors are recorded in     *
F* Err Report.                                                                     *
F*  Author: Yaeger.  Feb. 1995.                                                    *
F*******************************************************************************
FRaiseTransIF   E              DISK
FEmpMaster UF   E            K DISK
FErrReport O    E              Printer OFLIND(*IN1Ø)
C                READ      RaiseTrans                          5Ø99
C                DOW       *IN99 = *OFF
C                IF        *IN5Ø = *ON
C                EXSR      Error
C                ELSE
C       EmpID    CHAIN     EmpMaster                           9Ø5Ø
C                IF        *IN5Ø = *ON OR *IN9Ø = *ON
C                EXSR      Error
C                ELSE
C                EVAL (H)  Pay = Pay * 1.Ø5
C                UPDATE    EmpRecord                           6Ø
C                IF        *IN6Ø = *ON
C                EXSR      Error
C                ENDIF
C                ENDIF
C                ENDIF
C                READ      RaiseTrans                          5Ø99
C                ENDDO
C                EVAL      *INLR = *ON
C                RETURN
C* Subroutine to write I/O errors to a report.
C       Error    BEGSR
C                IF        *IN1Ø = *ON
C                WRITE     ErrHeads
C                EVAL      *IN1Ø = *OFF
C                ENDIF
C                SELECT
C                WHEN      *IN5Ø = *ON
C                WRITE     ReadProb
C                WHEN      *IN6Ø = *ON
C                WRITE     UpdateProb
C                WHEN      *IN9Ø = *ON
```

```
*.. 1 ...+... 2 ...+... 3 ...+... 4 ...+... 5 ...+... 6 ...+... 7 ...+... 8 ...+... 9 ...+...10
C                   WRITE     NoEmpProb
C                   ENDSL
C                   ENDSR
```

Now let's change the problem again, complicating it further. This time, the employers want to give raises to all the employees in certain departments; DeptTrans is a file that contains the names of the departments to receive the raise.

The best way to solve this problem is to define a logical file over the EmpMaster file, keyed on department, and then use this file for updating the employees. This approach lets you use SETLL to locate the appropriate departments within the file and then use READE to process all the employees within each department. The program below shows a solution using this approach. Note that the error handling has been omitted to let you focus more easily on the file accessing used in the program.

```
*.. 1 ...+... 2 ...+... 3 ...+... 4 ...+... 5 ...+... 6 ...+... 7 ...+... 8 ...+... 9 ...+...10
F*****************************************************************************
F* This program updates employees' pay by 5% based on departments contained in   *
F* file DeptTrans.  EmpMasterL is a logical file of employees, keyed on department. *
F*   Author:  Yaeger.  Feb. 1995.                                                *
F*****************************************************************************
FDeptTrans IF   E            DISK
FEmpMasterLUF   E          K DISK
C                   READ      DeptTrans                              99
C* Loop to process each department.
C                   DOW       *IN99 = *OFF
C     Dept          SETLL     EmpMasterL                            80
C                   IF        *IN80 = *ON
C     Dept          READE     EmpMasterL                            90
C* Loop for all the employees within a department.
C                   DOW       *IN90 = *OFF
C                   EVAL (H)  Pay = Pay * 1.05
C                   UPDATE    EmpRecordL
C                   READE     EmpMasterL                            90
C                   ENDDO
C                   ENDIF
C                   READ      DeptTrans                              99
C                   ENDDO
C                   EVAL      *INLR = *ON
C                   RETURN
```

As you begin to write programs that require you to access several files, try to decide how to handle access to each file. Ask yourself how many records in each file will you need to process. If you need to access all the records in the file or a subset (or subsets) of the records based on a common value of a field, sequential access, using READ or READE (for subsets of sequential records) is appropriate. If you need to select only certain records from the file, random access, using CHAIN, would be best. And don't forget that the AS/400's facility for defining keyed logical files lets you retrieve records based on any field. Often, defining logical files goes hand-in-hand with developing programs.

Chapter Summary

In this chapter you learned many I/O operations appropriate to input, output, and update files. READ, READE, READP, and READPE are input operations used to access records sequentially from a full procedural file whose type is declared as input or update. You can use SETLL and SETGT to position the file before a sequential read operation. CHAIN randomly retrieves a record and also positions the file for subsequent sequential reading, if desired.

The KLIST and KFLD operations let you position the file or retrieve a record based on a composite key. By using a partial KLIST, you can initiate access to sets of records that share a common value on the first field(s) of a composite key.

You can use WRITE or EXCEPT to put records into an output file or an update file. Operations UPDATE and DELETE are specific to update files. You cannot UPDATE a record without having first read it; you may, however, DELETE a record without first retrieving it if you indicate the key of the record to delete in factor 1 of the DELETE operation.

The AS/400 includes built-in record locking to prevent the problem of phantom updates. Techniques — including use of the UNLOCK operation — exist to minimize record locking, but they should not be used if their implementation might cause lost updates to occur.

You have read about a large number of operations dealing with input and output. Although it is not difficult to remember what each operation does, it is hard to keep from confusing what indicator goes where to signal what, and whether the operation uses a file name or a record-format name. The table that follows summarizes the operations for you, to help you see more clearly the differences among the operations and to serve as a quick reference as you write your programs.

Input/Output Operations

File Types	Factor 1	Operation	Factor 2	Result	Indicators		
					Hi	**Lo**	**Eq**
I,U	—	**READ (N)**	FILE/RFMT	dtastr	—	err	EOF
I,U	flck	**READE (N)**	FILE/RFMT	dtastr	—	err	EOF
I,U	—	**READP (N)**	FILE/RFMT	dtastr	—	err	BOF
I,U	flck	**READPE (N)**	FILE/RFMT	dtastr	—	err	BOF
I,U	FLCK	**SETLL**	FILE/RFMT	—	nr	err	eq
I,U	FLCK	**SETGT**	FILE/RFMT	—	nr	err	—
I,U	FLCK	**CHAIN (N)**	FILE/RFMT	dtastr	NR	err	—
O,U	—	**WRITE**	RFMT	dtastr	—	err	—
O,U	—	**EXCEPT**	ename	—	—	—	—
U	—	**UPDATE**	RFMT	dtastr	—	err	—
U	flck	**DELETE**	FILE/RFMT	—	nr	err	—
U	—	**UNLOCK**	FILE	—	—	err	—
I,O,U	—	**OPEN**	FILE	—	—	err	—
I,O,U	—	**CLOSE**	FILE	—	—	err	—
I,U	NAME	**KLIST**	—	—	—	—	—
I,U	—	**KFLD**	—	FIELD	—	—	—

Operation extender (optional): N = do not lock record.

Uppercase entry = required; lowercase entry = optional.

Indicators:	eof = end-of-file; bof = beginning-of-file; nr = no record; err = error; eq = equal match found.
flck	May be a field, literal, constant, or KLIST.
FILE/RFMT	May be a file name or a record format name (for externally described files).
RFMT	Must be a record format name for externally descibed files.
FILE	Must be a file name.
dtastr	Data structure — used only with program-described files.
ename	Exception line name on output.

Terms

abend   file access   random access
composite key   file locking   record locking
concatenated key   phantom updates   sequential access

Discussion/Review Questions

1. Describe the difference between sequential and random record retrieval.

2. What does "position the file" mean?

3. What are the differences between the SETGT and SETLL operations?

4. Since READE and READPE imply reading records with matching keys, would you ever use them in programs accessing files with UNIQUE keys? Explain your answer.

5. When is it appropriate to use a READE, as opposed to a READ operation?

6. When can you omit an A in position 20 of the File Specification of an output file? Why don't you need this A on printer files?

7. What does the term "file maintenance" mean? What kinds of files are likely to need maintenance?

8. Is there any difference possible in the results when you update a file with EXCEPT rather than UPDATE?

9. Because designating a file type as update allows you maximum flexibility in which I/O operations you can use with that file, why don't programmers designate all their files as update files, just in case? That is, why bother with input and output files?

10. What is the difference between a file lock and a record lock? Which technique do you think is easier for an operating system to implement? Why? Which technique is preferable from a user standpoint? Why?

11. What is defensive programming? What defensive programming technique is described in this chapter? Name several other ways to be a defensive programmer.

Exercises

1. Assume you had a logical file of customers, CustLZip, keyed on zip code. Write the Calculation Specifications that would allow you to print an exception line CustLine for every customer whose zip code matched ZipIn. If no customers have that zip code, print exception line NoCust.

2. Your company sequentially assigns a unique customer number to each new customer. Assume customer file CustMaster is keyed on customer number, field CustNbr. Write the Calculation Specifications necessary for determining what number should be assigned to the next new customer.

3. You have a sales file, SalesFile, keyed on a composite key of store, department, and salesperson. (Duplicate keys are present, since each record represents a single sale.) Write the Calculation Specifications needed to total all the sales for a given department within a given store. Field Dept contains the

Exercises Continued

Exercises continued

desired department, field Store holds the store. The sales field that you want to accumulate is SalesAmt. Modify your code so that it totals all the sales of the store represented in Store.

4. Write the File Specifications and Calculation Specifications needed to let you randomly retrieve a customer in file CustMast based on the customer number in CustNbr, subtract Payment from BalanceDue, and rewrite the record. Execute subroutine NoCust if the customer is not found in the file.

5. You have a transaction file CustTrans of records to be added, deleted, or changed in the CustMaster master file. The Code field of the transaction record contains an A, D, or C, denoting whether the record is to be added, deleted, or changed, while the number of the customer to add, delete, or change is contained in transaction field CustNo. Write the File Specifications and Calculation Specifications that will allow you to appropriately process each record in the transaction file. Add is a valid option if the customer does not already exist in CustMaster; Change or Delete is valid only if the customer does exist in CustMaster. Execute subroutine AddRecord for valid adds, ChgRecord for valid changes, and DltRecord for valid deletions; for all invalid transactions, execute subroutine TransError. (Don't code the details of these subroutines; stop at the point of coding the EXSR statements.)

Programming Assignments

1. GTC Telephone Company wants a program to update its Customer Master File (GTCSTP) based on data contained in the Payments Transaction File (GTPAYP). Data files are described in Appendix D. For each record in the payment file, randomly retrieve the appropriate customer, subtract the payment amount from amount owed, change the date of last payment field, and rewrite the customer record. Also prepare the audit report shown below. Notice that if a customer in the payment file is not found in the customer file, an error notation should appear on the report.

```
             1         2         3         4         5         6         7         8         9         10
    1234567890123456789012345678901234567890123456789012345678901234567890123456789012345678901234567890
 1   XX/XX/XX      GTC PAYMENTS PROCESSED   PAGE XX0X
 2                          AUDIT REPORT
 3
 4      CUSTOMER        DATE RECEIVED      AMOUNT
 5
 6    (XXX)XXX-XXXX       XX/XX/XX       X,XX0.XX
 7    (XXX)XXX-XXXX       XX/XX/XX       X,XX0.XX  ERROR
 8    (XXX)XXX-XXXX       XX/XX/XX       X,XX0.XX
 9
10                         TOTAL      XXX,XX0.XX
11
12      X0X CUSTOMERS NOT IN MASTER FILE
13
```

Programming Assignments Continued

Programming Assignments continued

2. CompuSell wants a program that will generate purchase orders for those items in the inventory file that need reordering — that is, if their quantity on hand is less than or equal to their reorder point. For any inventory item that meets this criterion and that has not already been reordered (the reorder code field is still blank), include that item on a purchase order and rewrite the record to the inventory file with an R in the reorder code field to signal that it has been reordered.

   Only one purchase order should be completed per supplier — that is, all items to be purchased from the same supplier should appear on the same purchase order. The format of the purchase order is shown below. Note that the item number is the *supplier's* product number, not CompuSell's. The unit cost is the current cost figure and the quantity is the reorder quantity in the inventory file.

   You will need to use data from CompuSell's Inventory File (CSINVP) and Supplier File (CSSUPP), described in Appendix D. You will also need to create a logical file so that the inventory records can be processed in supplier number order.

```
        1         2         3         4         5         6         7         8         9         1 0
1234567890123456789012345678901234567890123456789012345678901234567890123456789012345678901234567890
 1    XX/XX/XX                    COMPUSELL
 2                               5260 HAWORTH
 3                          KALAMAZOO  MI  49008-0010
 4
 5  PURCHASE ORDER TO:
 6
 7   SUPPLIER: XXXXXXXXXXXXXXXXXXXXXXXXXXX   CONTACT: XXXXXXXXXXXXXXXXXXXXXXXXXXXXXXXXX
 8             XXXXXXXXXXXXXXXXXXXXXX                  (XXX)XXX-XXXX
 9             XXXXXXXXXXXXXXX   XX  XXXXX-XXXX
10
11   ITEM NUMBER          DESCRIPTION          UNIT COST    QTY        EXTENSION
12    XXXXXXXX    XXXXXXXXXXXXXXXXXXXXXXXXXXX   X,XXØ.XX   X,XØX   XX,XXX,XXØ.XX
13    XXXXXXXX    XXXXXXXXXXXXXXXXXXXXXXXXXXX   X,XXØ.XX   X,XØX   XX,XXX,XXØ.XX
14    XXXXXXXX    XXXXXXXXXXXXXXXXXXXXXXXXXXX   X,XXØ.XX   X,XØX   XX,XXX,XXØ.XX
15
16                                           ORDER TOTAL     $XXX,XXX,XXØ.XX
17
18
19
20              AUTHORIZED SIGNATURE_____
21
```

3. CompuSell wants you to write a program to process goods received from suppliers. As ordered goods are received from suppliers, the items are added to inventory and a record of the item received is added to the Goods Received file CSRCVP. The contents of this file are then run in batch to update the Inventory file, CSINVP. Appendix D describes these files. Note that you will need to create a logical file to access the records in CSINVP by supplier product ID.

   For each item in CSRCVP, the following changes must be made in the corresponding record of CSINVP: a) the quantity on hand must be changed to reflect the additional goods; b) the reorder code should be changed to spaces; c) if the current charge from the supplier is not identical to the current and average cost stored in the inventory file, two changes must be made. First, the Inventory file's current cost must be changed to reflect the new cost. Second, the average cost must be recalculated and updated.

Programming Assignments Continued

Programming Assignments continued

To calculate new average cost, multiply the old average cost by the old quantity on hand, add this to the cost of the items that have just come in, and divide by the new total quantity on hand. Thus, if you had 10 units in stock with an average cost of $3 and received 20 more units at a cost of $4, the new average cost would be $(10*3 + 20*4)/30 = \$3.67$.

In addition to updating the Inventory file, your program should produce the following report to serve as an audit trail of the updating. Note that if there is an error in an item number in CSRCVP, so that a corresponding item does not exist in CSINVP, that fact should be noted on the report printing two special lines, as shown. The second line contains an image of the problem record from CSRCVP.

```
          1         2         3         4         5         6         7         8         9        10
 1234567890123456789012345678901234567890123456789012345678901234567890123456789012345678901234567890
 1  XX/XX/XX              COMPUSELL INVENTORY UPDATE REPORT              PAGE XX0X
 2                        RECEIVED GOODS PROCESSED
 3
 4 SUPPLIER     ITEM     QTY     NEW QTY     OLD          NEW          OLD AVG.     NEW AVG.
 5   ID         NO       RCVD    ON HAND     COST         COST         COST         COST
 6
 7 XXXXXXXX   XXXXX     XX0X     XX0X      X,XX0.XX     X,XX0.XX     X,XX0.XX     X,XX0.XX
 8 XXXXXXXX   XXXXX     XX0X     XX0X      X,XX0.XX     X,XX0.XX     X,XX0.XX     X,XX0.XX
 9 XXXXXXXX   ITEM NOT FOUND IN INVENTORY FILE; RECHECK SUPPLIER ID
10          XXXXXXXXXXXXXXXXXXXX   RECORD NOT PROCESSED
11 XXXXXXXX   XXXXX     XX0X     XX0X      X,XX0.XX     X,XX0.XX     X,XX0.XX     X,XX0.XX
12
```

4. Wexler University wants you to write a program that will generate a transcript of completed courses for each student in the transcript request file WUTRANSP. This program will also require the use of the Student Master File (WUSTDP), the Course File (WUCRSP) and the Earned Credits File (WUCRDP). All files are described in Appendix D.

Note that the line showing graduation date and degree granted should print only if the student has, in fact, graduated, as signaled by non-blank values in those fields of the student's master record.

Courses should be listed in chronological order. Note that under semester, the school wants WIN to print for semester code 1, SUM for semester code 2, and FAL for semester code 3; the right-most *XX* represents the year the course was taken.

```
          1         2         3         4         5         6         7         8         9        10
 1234567890123456789012345678901234567890123456789012345678901234567890123456789012345678901234567890
 1                    WEXLER UNIVERSITY OFFICIAL TRANSCRIPT
 2                    DATE ISSUED: XX/XX/XX
 3
 4 STUDENT:   XXXXXXXXXXXXXX XXXXXXXXXX     DATE ADMITTED: XX/XX/XX
 5            XXX-XX-XXXX                   MAJOR: XXX
 6
 7            CREDITS EARNED: X0X           GRADE POINT AVERAGE: 0.XX
 8            GRADUATED:  XX/XX/XX          DEGREE GRANTED: XXX
 9
10    COURSE           TITLE              SEMESTER    CREDITS     GRADE
11    XXXXXX   XXXXXXXXXXXXXXXXXXXXXXXX    XXX XX        X          XX
12    XXXXXX   XXXXXXXXXXXXXXXXXXXXXXXX    XXX XX        X          XX
13    XXXXXX   XXXXXXXXXXXXXXXXXXXXXXXX    XXX XX        X          XX
14
```

Programming Assignments Continued

Programming Assignments continued

5. Wexler University wants you to write a program that will generate class lists to distribute to all instructors. The class lists should be formatted as shown in the following printer spacing chart. Because these lists are sent to the instructors, begin each instructor's list on a new page. You will need to access data from several files to obtain the output: the Current Enrollment file (WUENRLP), the Student Master file (WUSTDP), the Current Sections File (WUSCTP), the Course File (WUCRSP), and the Instructor File (WUINSTP). These data files are described in Appendix D. Follow your instructor's directions for accessing these files of data. *Hint*: You will need to use logical files to solve this problem.

```
                        WEXLER U. CLASS LIST19XX

INSTRUCTOR: XXXXXXXXXXXXXXX DEPT: XXX

    DEPT  COURSE     TITLE                    CREDITS      SECTION
    XXX   XXX    XXXXXXXXXXXXXXXXXXXXXXXXX        X        XXXXX

          STUDENT                 SOC. SEC.      DCODE     MAJOR
          XXXXXXXXXXXXXXX XXXXXXXXXX   XXX-XX-XXXX    X       XXX
          XXXXXXXXXXXXXXX XXXXXXXXXX   XXX-XX-XXXX    X       XXX
          XXXXXXXXXXXXXXX XXXXXXXXXX   XXX-XX-XXXX    X       XXX

              SECTION ENROLLMENT: X0X STUDENTS


    DEPT  COURSE     TITLE                    CREDITS      SECTION
    XXX   XXX    XXXXXXXXXXXXXXXXXXXXXXXXX        X        XXXXX

          STUDENT                 SOC. SEC.      DCODE     MAJOR
          XXXXXXXXXXXXXXX XXXXXXXXXX   XXX-XX-XXXX    X       XXX
          XXXXXXXXXXXXXXX XXXXXXXXXX   XXX-XX-XXXX    X       XXX
          XXXXXXXXXXXXXXX XXXXXXXXXX   XXX-XX-XXXX    X       XXX
          XXXXXXXXXXXXXXX XXXXXXXXXX   XXX-XX-XXXX    X       XXX

              SECTION ENROLLMENT: X0X STUDENTS
```

Chapter 7

Interactive Applications

Chapter Overview

In this chapter you will learn how to define display files and how to use them to develop interactive applications.

Batch and Interactive Programs

So far, the applications you have written were designed to run in batch. In **batch processing**, once a program begins to run, it continues to execute instructions without human intervention or control. Most batch applications in the business environment involve processing one or more transaction files sequentially; the programs end when the transaction files reach end-of-file.

Interactive applications, in contrast, are user driven. As the program runs, a user at a workstation interacts with the computer — selecting options from menus, entering data, responding to prompts, and so on. The sequence of instructions the program executes is determined in part by the user; the program continues until the user signals (s)he is ready to quit.

This dialogue between the user and the computer is mediated through what, on the AS/400, are called **display files**. Display files define the screens that the program presents as it runs. Display files allow values keyed by the user in response to the screen to be input as data to the program. Thus, display files serve as the mechanism that allows the user and program to interact.

Display Files

Display files are defined externally to the program that uses them. The procedure for creating a display file is similar to the procedure followed for creating a physical or logical file. You code display files using DDS, enter the specifications using SEU to create a source member (with type DSPF), and then compile the source code to create an object. IBM also provides a utility called Screen Design Aid (SDA), which automatically generates the DDS source code as you design and create display screens in an interactive environment.

Display files include entries at a file, record, and field level, just like database and printer file definitions. File-level entries appear at the very beginning of the definition, and apply to all the record formats within the file. Record-level entries are associated with a single record format, while field-level entries are coded for specific fields or constants within a record format. Each record format defines what is written to or read from the workstation in a single I/O operation. On an output operation, the record may fill an entire screen with prompts and/or values, or, on an input operation, the record may read several values keyed from the workstation.

Unless you make special provisions, only one screen displays at a time. When a different record format is written, the first screen is erased prior to the display of the second.

As an introduction to DDS coding for display files, consider the following situation: A school identifies each of its semester offerings through a section number. For each section, the school stores information about the course this section is associated with, the days and time it meets, the assigned room, the section enrollment, and the instructor. This data is stored in file SECTIONS; its physical file definition is shown below.

```
*.. 1 ...+... 2 ...+... 3 ...+... 4 ...+... 5 ...+... 6 ...+... 7 ...+... 8
A..........T.Name+++++RLen++TDpB......Functions++++++++++++++++++++++++++++++
A* Physical file SECTIONS definition.
A          R SECREC
A            SECTNO         5              TEXT('Section Number')
A            DAYS           3              TEXT('Days class meets')
A            BEGTIME        4  0           TEXT('Time class starts')
A            ROOM           4  0           TEXT('Classroom')
A            ENROLL         3  0           TEXT('Current enrollment')
A            INSTR         15              TEXT('Instructor')
A            COURSE         6              TEXT('Course Identifier')
A          K SECTNO
```

The school wants a simple online inquiry program that will let a user enter a section number and display information about that section. The input, or entry, screen for this application is shown below.

```
                         Section Inquiry

       Type value, then Enter.

            Section number . . _____




       F3=Exit
```

The DDS of the display-file record format needed to produce the above screen is shown below.

```
*.. 1 ...+... 2 ...+... 3 ...+... 4 ...+... 5 ...+... 6 ...+... 7 ...+... 8
AAN01N02N03T.Name++++++RLen++TDpBLinPosFunctions++++++++++++++++++++++++++++
A           R SECT1
A                                          CA03(03 'F3=Exit')
A                                        1 28'Section Inquiry'
A                                        3  2'Type value, then Enter.'
A                                        5  5'Section number . .'
A             SECTION       5A   I       5 24
A                                       23  2'F3=Exit'
```

Notice that each record format begins with an identifier, an R in position 17, followed by a name for that format, in this case, SECT1, beginning in position 19 (Name++++++). Below the record format line appear all the fields and literals that are to make up that format. You must indicate the location of each literal and field on this screen by specifying the screen line on which it is to appear (in positions 39-41, Lin) and its *starting* column position within that line (coded in positions 42-44, Pos).

Code the literals themselves, such as 'Section Inquiry', in positions 45-80 (Functions) of the DDS line. You must enclose them in apostrophes.

You enter field names left-adjusted in positions 19-28 (Name). Each field needs an assigned usage, coded in position 38 (B). Usage codes include I for input, O for output, or B for both input and output. SECTION, the only field in the sample definition, is an input field, because its value is to be entered by the user and read by (input to) the program. Its usage is I.

You must further define each field by specifying its length in positions 30-34 (Len), data type in position 35 (T), and — for numeric fields — decimal positions in positions 36-37 (Dp).

Actually, column 35 for display files is more appropriately called data type/keyboard shift, because it allows many more possible values than are permitted for field definitions of physical files. These additional values affect the **keyboard-shift attribute** of different workstations to limit what characters the user can enter. Although a complete description of allowable values is beyond the scope of this text, four commonly used values are described in the following table.

Keyboard-Shift Value	Description
A (Alphanumeric shift)	Used for character fields; puts keyboard in lower shift; lets user enter any character.
X (Alphabetic only)	Used for character fields; lets user enter only A-Z, commas, periods, dashes, and spaces; sends lowercase letters as uppercase.
S (Signed numeric)	Used for numeric fields; lets user enter digits 0-9, but no signs; uses Field- key for entering negative values.
Y (Numeric only)	Used for numeric fields; lets the user enter digits 0-9, plus or minus signs, periods, commas, and spaces.

One very important distinction between S and Y is that Y lets edit codes and edit words be associated with the field, while S does not.

Because our example application treats SECTION as a character field, a decimal-position entry is not appropriate. Type is A, or character; we could have omitted the A, because A is the default type for character fields. The default type for numeric fields is S, unless you associate an edit code or word with that field; in this latter case, the system assumes a default value of Y.

The line below the record format definition, CA03(03 'F3 = Exit'), establishes a connection between function key F3 and the 03 indicator. When coding interactive applications, indicators communicate between the screen and the program that uses the screen. Control generally returns from the screen to the program when the user presses the Enter key or a function key that has been assigned a special meaning. In this screen, for instance, the user is prompted to press F3 to exit the program. But because the function key cannot be referenced directly within an RPG IV program, an indicator must serve as a mediator.

The DDS line CA03(03 'F3 = Exit') accomplishes three things. First, the CA03 portion establishes F3 as a valid command key in this application; only those function keys explicitly referenced within the DDS are valid, or enabled, during program execution. Second, the 03 within the parentheses associates indicator 03 with F3, so that when F3 is pressed, indicator 03 comes on. Although you can associate any indicator (01-99) with any function key, it makes good programming sense to associate a function key with its corresponding numeric indicator to avoid confusion. And finally, by referencing the function key as CA (Command Attention) rather than CF (Command Function), the code is saying to return control to the program without the input data values (if any) that the user has just entered. If the line were coded CF03(03 'F3 = Exit'), control would return to the program *with* the input data.

The information within apostrophes — 'F3 = Exit' — serves only as documentation. You could omit it (e.g., code only CA03(03)) without affecting how the screen functions. Good programming practice, however, suggests including such documentation.

We can now look at the design of the second screen the application needs. It's an information screen, or panel, to display the requested information. The specific values shown give you a sense of what the screen might look like when the program is running.

```
        Section Information

Section number . . . . . . 12435
Course . . . . . . . . . . BIS350
Instructor . . . . . . . . Johnson
Room . . . . . . . . . . . 1120
Meets on days  . . . . . . MWF
Starting time  . . . . . . 10:30
Enrollment . . . . . . . . 36








Press Enter to continue.

F3=Exit  F12=Cancel
```

This screen will require a second record format within the display file. The DDS for this record format is shown below.

```
*.. 1 ...+... 2 ...+... 3 ...+... 4 ...+... 5 ...+... 6 ...+... 7 ...+... 8
AAN01N02N03T.Name+++++RLen++TDpBLinPosFunctions+++++++++++++++++++++++++++++
A                                   REF(SECTIONS)
A          R SECT2
A                                   CA03(03 'F3=Exit')
A                                   CA12(12 'F12=Cancel')
A                                 1 10'Section Information'
A                                 3  2'Section number . . . . . . .'
A            SECTNO    R         0 3 29
A                                 4  2'Course . . . . . . . . . .'
A            COURSE    R         0 4 29
A                                 5  2'Instructor . . . . . . . .'
A            INSTR     R         0 5 29
A                                 6  2'Room . . . . . . . . . . .'
A            ROOM      R         0 6 29
A                                 7  2'Meets on days  . . . . . .'
A            DAYS      R         0 7 29
A                                 8  2'Starting time  . . . . . .'
A            BEGTIME   R         0 8 29
A                                 9  2'Enrollment . . . . . . . .'
A            ENROLL    R         0 9 29
A                                21  2'Press Enter to continue.'
A                                23  2'F3=Exit'
A                                23 11'F12=Cancel'
```

The previous code represents a "bare bones" record format to describe the screen. Note that the fields represented are given an O, for Output, usage. That's because their values are going to be sent from the program to the screen. Instead of including length and decimal-position entries, these field entries contain an R in position 29. This R (for Reference) signals that the fields are defined elsewhere, and that their definitions can be obtained from that source. The source, in this case, is the file SECTIONS, as indicated by the first line containing keyword REF, followed by the file name in parentheses. REF is a file-level keyword that should appear at the beginning of the DDS, before *any* record-format definitions.

If you define a field through referencing, and if the referenced database field includes an edit code or edit word associated with it in the database file, that editing is automatically incorporated into the display file. (If the referenced field is unedited, or if the field is defined within the display file itself, you can add editing within the display file, as discussed later in this chapter.)

Notice that record format SECT2 enables F12, as well as F3. Generally accepted AS/400 screen design standards use F12, Cancel, to signal that the user wants to back up to the previous screen, while F3, Exit, means exit the entire application.

Putting the two format definitions together completes the DDS for the display file, called SECTINQR.

```
*.. 1 ...+... 2 ...+... 3 ...+... 4 ...+... 5 ...+... 6 ...+... 7 ...+... 8
AAN01N02N03T.Name+++++RLen++TDpBLinPosFunctions++++++++++++++++++++++++++++++
A* Display file SECTINQR, containing 2 record formats.
A                                       REF(SECTIONS)
A          R SECT1
A                                       CA03(03 'F3=Exit')
A                                    1 28'Section Inquiry'
A                                    3  2'Type value, then Enter.'
A                                    5  5'Section number . .'
A            SECTION      5A  I      5 24
A                                   23  2'F3=Exit'
A          R SECT2
A                                       CA03(03 'F3=Exit')
A                                       CA12(12 'F12=Cancel')
A                                    1 10'Section Information'
A                                    3  2'Section number . . . . . .'
A            SECTNO       R      O   3 29
A                                    4  2'Course . . . . . . . . . .'
A            COURSE       R      O   4 29
A                                    5  2'Instructor . . . . . . . .'
A            INSTR        R      O   5 29
A                                    6  2'Room . . . . . . . . . .'
A            ROOM         R      O   6 29
A                                    7  2'Meets on days . . . . . .'
A            DAYS         R      O   7 29
A                                    8  2'Starting time . . . . . .'
A            BEGTIME      R      O   8 29
A                                    9  2'Enrollment . . . . . . . .'
A            ENROLL       R      O   9 29
A                                   21  2'Press Enter to continue.'
A                                   23  2'F3=Exit'
A                                   23 11'F12=Cancel'
```

Before looking at some of the many additional features available for defining display files, let's develop the section inquiry program to see how display files are used in interactive programs. Recall that the user wants to enter a section number to request section information from the SECTIONS file. The program should display the retrieved information on the screen. The user may then enter another section number or signal that (s)he is finished by pressing F3.

In writing the program, you must define display file SECTINQ, like any other kind of file, on the File Specifications. Display files are full procedural, externally described files. However, because the concept of "key" is not applicable to this kind of file, leave position 34 blank. What about type (position 17)? You have worked with input files (I), output files (O), and update files (U). Display files represent a new type: combined (C). A **combined file** supports both input and output, but as independent operations. You cannot update a combined file. Finally, the device is WORKSTN. Below are the complete File Specifications for the section inquiry program.

```
*.. 1 ...+... 2 ...+... 3 ...+... 4 ...+... 5 ...+... 6 ...+... 7 ...+... 8 ...+... 9 ...+...10
FFilename++IPEASFRlen+LKlen+AIDevice+.Keywords+++++++++++++++++++++++++++++Comments+++++++++++
FSections  IF   E           K DISK
FSectInqr  CF   E             WORKSTN
```

Because both the files are externally described, the program will have no Input Specifications, nor Output Specifications, for that matter. The only portion of the program left to code is the Calculation Specifications. Before jumping into this coding, however, it pays first to think through the logic of a solution. Interactive programs are extremely prone to "spaghetti coding," primarily because flow of control is less straight line; depending on which function key a user presses, you may need to repeat, back up, or early-exit out of different routines.

The present program will need to loop until the user presses F3 in response to either screen 1 or screen 2. If the user presses F12 at screen 2 to back up, that effectively is the same in this program as hitting the Enter key, because in both cases the user should next see screen 1 again.

A rough solution written in pseudocode is shown on the following page.

WHILE user wants to continue (no Exit)
    Display first screen
    Obtain user's response to the screen
    IF user wants to continue (no Exit)
        Random read section file to get section information
        IF record found
            Display second screen
            Obtain user's response
        ENDIF
    ENDIF
ENDWHILE

You can easily develop the RPG IV calculations from the pseudocode, except that you don't know how to send screens of data to the user or read user input. The allowable operations for screen I/O are WRITE, READ, and EXFMT (Execute Format). All three operations require a record-format name in factor 2.

The READ operation sends control to the currently displayed screen, waits for the end of user input (signaled by the user's pressing either the Enter key or any other enabled special key), and returns control to the program. The WRITE operation displays a screen and returns control to the program without waiting for user input.

EXFMT combines the features of WRITE and READ; it first writes a record to the screen and then waits for user input to that screen. When the user has finished inputting, the system reads the data back from the screen and returns control to the program. Because in most screen I/O you want to display some information and then wait for a user response, EXFMT is the operation you will use most frequently in your interactive programs.

The figure below shows an RPG IV implementation of the pseudocode solution to the section inquiry problem.

```
*.. 1 ...+... 2 ...+... 3 ..+... 4 ...+... 5 ...+... 6 ...+... 7 ...+... 8 ...+... 9 ...+...10
CLØNØ1Factor1++++++Opcode(E)+Extended-factor2+++++++++++++++++++++++++++++++Comments+++++++++++
CLØNØ1Factor1++++++Opcode(E)+Factor2++++++Result+++++++Len++D+HiLoEq....Comments+++++++++++
C                  DOW       *INØ3 = *OFF
C                  EXFMT     Sect1
C                  IF        *INØ3 = *OFF
C        Section   CHAIN     Sections                            90
C                  IF        *IN9Ø = *OFF
C                  EXFMT     Sect2
C                  ENDIF
C                  ENDIF
C                  ENDDO
C                  EVAL      *INLR = *ON
C                  RETURN
```

In that code, indicator 03, which comes on when the user presses F3, controls the main program loop. Because the user can signal "Exit" at screen SECT1, the calculations need an IF following the return from the SECT1 screen to check for this possibility. Because the user may have keyed in a wrong section number, which would cause the CHAIN operation to fail (indicator 90 on), the program executes the information panel, SECT2, only if the chaining worked.

Additional DDS Keywords

Although the DDS definition for the example above would work, it represents a minimalist approach to screen design. It contains no "bells-and-whistles." More importantly, perhaps, as the DDS is presently coded, numeric fields would be displayed without editing, and information about a possible important program event — a section not found in the file — is not conveyed to the user. You can include these and other kinds of special effects by using keywords.

You already have been introduced to three keywords used with display files (REF, CAnn, and CFnn). The AS/400 includes a long list of permissible keywords for display files to modify the screen's appearance or the screen/user interaction. This section discusses some of the major keywords. Refer to IBM's manual *DDS Reference* (SC41-3712) for additional detail.

Keywords are always coded in positions 45-80 (Functions) of the DDS line. Keywords apply at a file, record, or field level. Some keywords can be used with two levels, while others are appropriate to just one level. Where you code the keyword determines which level it is associated with.

File-Level Keywords

File-level keywords always must appear as the first lines in the DDS before any record-format information. If you have several file-level keywords, the order in which they are coded does not matter. You have already encountered one file-level keyword, REF, used to indicate a database file that contains definitions of fields used in the screen.

MSGLOC (Message Location) specifies the position of the message line for error and other messages. The keyword's format is MSGLOC(line number). Without this keyword, the message-line position defaults to the last screen line (line 24 on a standard 24 x 80 screen).

The CAnn (Command Attention) and CFnn (Command Function) keywords, already discussed, enable the use of function keys and associate the keys with program indicators. You can use as many function keys as are appropriate to your application by including a CAnn or CFnn keyword for each.

If you code these keywords at a file level, they apply to *all* the record formats within the file. Alternately, they can be associated with individual record formats, as in our example above. In that case, the keys are valid only during input operations for the screen or screens with which they are associated.

A commonly used file-level keyword is PRINT. This keyword enables the PRINT key during the interactive application to let the user print the current screen. Without this keyword, the print key is disabled. You can also use PRINT as a record-level keyword to enable the key for some screens but not others.

VLDCMDKEY is a file-level or record-level keyword used to turn on an indicator when the user presses any valid (enabled) command key. Note that command keys include any special key, such as the ROLLUP key, in addition to function keys. The format for this keyword is VLDCMDKEY(indicator ['text']). The indicator can be any numbered indicator (01-99); the text description is optional and serves only as documentation.

VLDCMDKEY is useful because it lets the program differentiate between control returned as a result of the Enter key and control returned by any other key. You often need to set up separate logic branches based on this distinction.

Record-Level Keywords

Record-level keywords appear on the line on which the record format is named and/or on lines immediately following that line, *preceding* any field or literal definition. These kinds of keywords apply only to the screen with which they are associated. They do not carry over or influence other record formats defined within the file.

You can use keywords CAnn, CFnn, PRINT, and VLDCMDKEY as record-level keywords, as well as file-level keywords. Keyword BLINK, on the other hand, is strictly a record-level keyword. BLINK causes the cursor to blink during the display of the record format with which it is associated.

OVERLAY is a record-level keyword specifying that the record format be displayed without clearing the previous display. OVERLAY works only when the record formats involved do not overlap lines on the screen.

```
*.. 1 ...+... 2 ...+... 3 ...+... 4 ...+... 5 ...+... 6 ...+... 7 ...+... 8
AANØ1NØ2NØ3T.Name++++++RLen++TDpBLinPosFunctions+++++++++++++++++++++++++++
A* Sample DDS showing record-level keywords.
A          R SAMPLE             PRINT
A                               CAØ3(Ø3 'F3=Exit')
A                               CA12(12 'F12=Cancel')
A                               VLDCMDKEY(3Ø 'Any valid key')
A                               OVERLAY
```

Field-Level Keywords

A field-level keyword applies only to the specific field with which it is associated. A field can have several keywords. The first keyword appears on the same line as the field definition or on the line immediately following the definition. You can code additional keywords on the same line (provided there is room) or on successive lines. All keywords for a field must be coded before the next field definition line.

Two field-level keywords control the format of numeric output fields on the display: EDTCDE (Edit Code) and EDTWRD (Edit Word). Recall that only numerically defined fields may be edited, and that the field type specification in column 35 of the DDS must be Y or blank to use editing for a displayed field.

Edit codes and edit words match those used within RPG IV itself and have the same meaning as in RPG IV. EDTCDE's format is EDTCDE(edit-code [*|$]); the parentheses should contain a valid edit code, such as 1, optionally followed by a single * to provide asterisk protection or a single $ to supply a floating dollar sign. The format for EDTWRD is EDTWRD('edit-word'). To review RPG IV edit words and edit codes, see Chapter 2.

The following DDS sample shows the use of EDTWRD and EDTCDE. Note that because editing is a concept related to output, the use of EDTWRD and EDTCDE is appropriate for fields defined for output usage or fields used for both input and output, but not for fields defined to be used for input only.

```
*.. 1 ...+... 2 ...+... 3 ...+... 4 ...+... 5 ...+... 6 ...+... 7 ...+... 8
AAN01N02N03T.Name++++++RLen++TDpBLinPosFunctions+++++++++++++++++++++++++++++++
A* Sample DDS showing the use of editing keywords.
A          R SAMPLE
A            SOCSEC        9Y 00   4 10EDTWRD('   -  -    ')
A            NAME         20   0   5 10
A            BILLDATE      6Y 00   6 10EDTCDE(Y)
A            AMOUNTDUE     7Y 20   7 10EDTCDE(1 $)
```

Another field-level keyword, DSPATR, or Display Attribute, determines the appearance of fields on the screen. You can use DSPATR more than once for a given field, and you can include more than one attribute with the same keyword. The keyword is followed by parentheses containing the codes of the desired attributes. The following attributes can be assigned to all types of fields (input, output, or both).

Attribute	Meaning
BL	Blinking field
CS	Column separator (a vertical bar separating each position within a field)
HI	High intensity
ND	Nondisplay (keyed characters don't appear on screen)
PC	Position cursor (position cursor to the first character of this field)
RI	Reverse image
UL	Underline

The sample code on the next page illustrates the use of **display attributes**. This sample is not intended to set a style standard to be followed, because a screen with so many "bells and whistles" would be distracting for the user. In general, use such features sparingly and consistently to draw attention to specific fields on the screen or to problems the user must deal with.

```
*.. 1 ...+... 2 ...+... 3 ...+... 4 ...+... 5 ...+... 6 ...+... 7 ...+... 8
AAN01N02N03T.Name+++++RLen++TDpBLinPosFunctions+++++++++++++++++++++++++++++++
A* DDS sample code illustrating display attributes.
A           R SAMPLE
A             SOCSEC          9Y 00  4 10DSPATR(ND)
A                                       DSPATR(UL)
A             NAME           20   0  5 10DSPATR(BL UL)
A             BILLDATE        6Y 00  6 10EDTCDE(Y)
A                                       DSPATR(RI)
A                                       DSPATR(PC HI BL)
```

Another important set of field-level keywords concerns **data validation**. Every programmer should recognize the extreme importance of preventing invalid data from entering the system; corrupt data files can cause abnormal endings or incorrect processing. Although no way exists to completely ensure that values a user enters are correct, by validating data as tightly as possible, you can eliminate some kinds of errors.

The four major keywords used for validating user entry are VALUES, COMP, RANGE, and CHECK. Each lets you place restrictions on what the user may enter. Violating these restrictions causes the system to display an appropriate error message on the message line and to display the field in reverse image to force the user to change the entered value.

The VALUES keyword lets you specify the exact valid values allowed for a field. The keyword format is VALUES(value1 value2 ...). Up to 100 values can be entered. Character values must be enclosed in apostrophes.

The RANGE keyword lets you specify a range within which the user's entry must fall to be considered valid. The format for this keyword is RANGE(low-value high-value). If you use the RANGE keyword with character fields, the low and high values must each be enclosed in apostrophes. The valid range includes the low and high values, so the entered value must be greater than or equal to the low value and less than or equal to the high value to be considered valid.

COMP lets you specify a relational comparison to be made with the user's entered value to determine validity. This keyword's format is COMP(relational-operator value). The relational operator can be one of the following:

Operator	Meaning
EQ	Equal to
NE	Not equal to
GT	Greater than
NG	Not greater than
LT	Less than
NL	Not less than
GE	Greater than or equal to
LE	Less than or equal to

CHECK is a field-level keyword that you can use for validity checking. Its format is CHECK(code [...]). That is, one or more validity checking codes can be associated with a single CHECK entry. Some of these validity codes are ME (Mandatory Enter), MF (Mandatory Fill), and AB (Allow blanks).

For Mandatory Entry fields, the user must enter at least one character of data (that character could be a blank); the user cannot simply bypass that field. Mandatory Fill specifies that each position in the field have a character in it. (A blank is considered a character.) AB provides the user with an override option for a field that fails a validity check. For example, if a field has a VALUES keyword associated with it and the user is not certain which value is appropriate to the record (s)he is entering, (s)he can simply enter blanks and the value will be accepted.

```
*.. 1 ...+... 2 ...+... 3 ...+... 4 ...+... 5 ...+... 6 ...+... 7 ...+... 8
AAN01N02N03T.Name++++++RLen++TDpBLinPosFunctions+++++++++++++++++++++++++++++
A* Sample DDS illustrating the use of keywords for data validation.
A          R SAMPLE
A            DEPT          3  I  4 10VALUES('CIS' 'DPR' 'MGT')
A                                   CHECK(MF AB)
A            MONTH        2Y 0I  6 10RANGE(1 12)
A            REGHOURS     3Y 1I  7 10COMP(LE 40)
```

The CHECK keyword includes parameter values concerned with functions other than validity checking. CHECK(LC), for example, lets the user enter lowercase letters (as well as uppercase) for character fields. Without this keyword, all user-entered alphabetic characters are returned to the program as uppercase. You can use CHECK at a field, record, or file level, depending on how broadly you want to enable lowercase data entry.

One field-level keyword of major importance is ERRMSG (Error Message). When an error message is in effect for a field, the message displays on the message line of the screen, and the field with which it is associated appears on the screen in reverse image. The format for the ERRMSG keyword is ERRMSG('message text' [indicator]). If you include an indicator, that indicator is turned off as part of the input operation that follows the display of the error message. Error messages are useful for conveying information about program-processing problems to the user's screen.

Finally, two field-level keywords serve as built-in variables to display the date and/or time on the screen. TIME, entered as a keyword, along with screen line and column position values, causes the system time to be displayed in HHMMSS format (hours, minutes, seconds). The time is displayed with default edit word '0ƀ:ƀƀ:ƀƀ' unless you specify an alternate display format. You can display the current date by using keyword DATE, along with line and column entries. DATE appears as a six-position, unedited value unless you associate an edit code or word with it.

```
*.. 1 ...+... 2 ...+... 3 ...+... 4 ...+... 5 ...+... 6 ...+... 7 ...+... 8
AAN01N02N03T.Name++++++RLen++TDpBLinPosFunctions+++++++++++++++++++++++++++++
A* Sample DDS illustrating the use of DATE and TIME keywords.
A          R SAMPLE
A                                     1  5TIME
A                                     1 60DATE EDTCDE(Y)
```

Conditioning Indicators

So far, field-level keywords have been discussed as though they are always in effect. However, if this were the case, many would be of little value. Why, for instance, would you want an error message to display each time a field appears on the screen? In fact, you can condition most individual field-level keywords by one or more indicators. The status of these indicators when the screen displays determines whether or not the keywords are in effect. Actually, not only can you condition keywords, you can also associate fields and literals with indicators, to control whether or not the field or literal appears on the screen.

Moreover, you can use multiple indicators, in AND and/or in OR relationships, to condition screen events. You can include up to three indicators on a DDS line; these indicators are in an AND relationship with one another, such that all the indicators on the line would need to be on for the event they are conditioning to occur. If you need to use more than three indicators to control an event, you can signal an AND by coding A in position 7 of the DDS line.

If you want an event to occur if one of several indicators is on (i.e., you wish to express an OR relationship), code one indicator per line, with an O in position 7 of the second (and successive) lines; the keyword, field, or literal conditioned by these indicators should appear on the last line of the set.

```
*.. 1 ...+... 2 ...+... 3 ...+... 4 ...+... 5 ...+... 6 ...+... 7 ...+... 8
AAN01N02N03T.Name++++++RLen++TDpBLinPosFunctions+++++++++++++++++++++++++++++
A* Sample DDS showing the use of indicators.
A          R SAMPLE
A   10      FLDA         10  0  4 15
A  N10      FLDB         12  0  4 30
A           FLDC          5  0  6  5
A   20 25                               DSPATR(HI)
A   30
AO  40                                  DSPATR(UL)
A*  10                           15  5'Indicator 10 is on'
```

In the previous code, FLDA displays if indicator 10 is on, while FLDB displays only if indicator 10 is off (signaled by the N in position 8). FLDC will always appear, but it will be displayed in high intensity only if indicators 20 and 25 are both on; it will be underlined if either indicator 30 or indicator 40 is on. The literal 'Indicator 10 is on' will display only if indicator 10 is, in fact, on.

Because you can turn indicators on or off as part of your program logic, they provide a way for program events to control screen display. For example, in our sample program, if the user-entered section number didn't exist in the SECTIONS file, it would be nice to not just return the user to the first screen, but to return with the erroneous section number in reverse video, with a message "Section not found" at the bottom of the screen, and with the cursor positioned on the field. We can easily cause that to happen by making a few changes in the first screen format. Because the program is already turning on indicator 90 when an unsuccessful chain occurs, we simply need to use indicator 90 to condition the ERRMSG keyword.

```
*.. 1 ...+... 2 ...+... 3 ...+... 4 ...+... 5 ...+... 6 ...+... 7 ...+... 8
AAN01N02N03T.Name+++++RLen++TDpBLinPosFunctions+++++++++++++++++++++++++++++
A* Display file SECTINQR, containing 2 record formats.
A                                         REF(SECTIONS)
A                                         PRINT
A           R SECT1
A                                         BLINK
A                                         CA03(03 'F3=Exit')
A                                       1 28'Section Inquiry'
A                                       3  2'Type value, then Enter.'
A                                       5  5'Section number . .'
A             SECTION      5A  B  5 24
A N90                                      DSPATR(UL)
A N90                                      DSPATR(HI)
A  90                                      ERRMSG('Section not found' 90)
A                                        23  2'F3=Exit'
A           R SECT2
A                                         CA03(03 'F3=Exit')
A                                         CA12(12 'F12=Cancel')
A                                       1 10'Section Information'
A                                       3  2'Section number . . . . . .'
A             SECTNO       R     0  3 29
A                                       4  2'Course . . . . . . . . .'
A             COURSE       R     0  4 29
A                                       5  2'Instructor . . . . . . . .'
A             INSTR        R     0  5 29
A                                       6  2'Room . . . . . . . . . .'
A             ROOM         R     0  6 29EDTCDE(Z)
A                                       7  2'Meets on days . . . . . .'
A             DAYS         R     0  7 29
A                                       8  2'Starting time  . . . . . .'
A             BEGTIME      R     0  8 29EDTWRD(' 0:  ')
A                                       9  2'Enrollment . . . . . . . .'
A             ENROLL       R     0  9 29EDTCDE(3)
A                                      21  2'Press Enter to continue.'
A                                      23  2'F3=Exit'
A                                      23 11'F12=Cancel'
```

Note that one of the changes includes changing the usage of SECTION to B (both) so the erroneous section number will be returned to the screen. If indicator 90 is off, SECTION displays as an underlined field in bold, or high intensity. If 90 is on, the error message appears and the field automatically appears in reverse image. A few extra keywords were added to give the display file more functionality: PRINT (to enable the Print key) and BLINK (to cause the cursor to blink).

The only additions to record format SECT2 were to add editing to ROOM, DAYS, and ENROLL to achieve the format shown in the sample screen shown earlier in the chapter (page 157).

Interactive File Maintenance

A common data processing task is file maintenance — that is, adding, deleting, and changing records in a company's database files. Over the past decade an increasing amount of such updating has been implemented through interactive, rather than batch, processing.

In a typical updating program, the user specifies the key of a record and signals whether that record is to be added, changed, or deleted. Because businesses typically want key-field values to master records to be unique (e.g., they would not want the same customer number to be assigned to two customers), a user request to add a record with a key that matches the key of a record already in the file generally is handled as an error. Similarly, it is impossible to change or delete a record that does not exist in the file.

As a result, the first tasks of an updating program are to accept the user's update option request (add, delete, or change) and the key of the record to be maintained, and to check the file for the existence of a record with that key before giving the user the chance to actually enter data values.

A critical concern of interactive updates is how to detect invalid data entries to prevent corrupting the business' database files. On the AS/400, you have three methods of safeguarding against invalid data: by using validation keywords within the database definitions themselves, provided those fields are displayed for input and reference back to the database file; by including validation keywords within the display file; or by validating field values within the program, after they are read from the screen.

Some validation is handled automatically for you by the AS/400's operating system. For example, the system will not let you enter a non-numeric value for a numerically defined field. Or, if you have specified type X for a character field, the system will permit alphabetic entries only. The use of validation keywords also automatically limits what the user can enter without the need for further programming on your part. For example, if you specify VALUES('A' 'C' 'D') for field CODE, attempts by the user to enter any other value will automatically cause an error message to appear on the bottom line of the screen and CODE to display in reverse video.

Always validate your data as tightly as possible, given the nature of the data. For some fields (e.g., name), the best you can do is ensure that the user enters some value, rather than skipping over the field; for other fields (e.g., sex code), you will be able to specify permissible values for the entered data. Never overlook validating data at any point where it enters the system.

To illustrate screen and program design for interactive updating, we will develop a program to update the university's SECTIONS file. To refresh your memory, the file definition is shown below.

```
*.. 1 ...+... 2 ...+... 3 ...+... 4 ...+... 5 ...+... 6 ...+... 7 ...+... 8
A.........T.Name+++++RLen++TDpB......Functions++++++++++++++++++++++++++++++
A* Physical file SECTIONS definition.
A          R SECREC
A            SECTNO         5                TEXT('Section Number')
A            DAYS           3                TEXT('Days class meets')
A            BEGTIME        4   Ø            TEXT('Time class starts')
A            ROOM           4   Ø            TEXT('Classroom')
A            ENROLL         3   Ø            TEXT('Current enrollment')
A            INSTR         15                TEXT('Instructor')
A            COURSE         6                TEXT('Course Identifier')
A          K SECTNO
```

The first screen of the application is shown below. The user keys in a section number and an action code to specify whether (s)he wants to add, change, or delete the section.

```
                        Section File Maintenance

    Type values, then Enter.

        Section number . . _____
        Action Code  . . . _        A=Add
                                    C=Change
                                    D=Delete

    F3=Exit
```

If the user tries to enter an invalid action code, an error message appears. If (s)he enters a section with an action code inappropriate for that section — that is, trying to add a section already in the file, or trying to change or delete a section *not* in the file — an appropriate error message appears on the screen.

If the user's entries are valid and appropriate, screen 2 displays, with blank fields if the user is in Add mode, or with the field values from the selected record displaying if the mode is Change or Delete. A prompt appropriate to each mode displays at the bottom of the screen. Some data validation takes place as values are entered. When the user presses Enter, the program performs the appropriate action and then returns the user to the first screen. If the user presses F12 at the second screen, no maintenance is done for that record and the user returns to the first screen. Pressing F3 at the second screen causes a program exit without maintenance of the last displayed data.

```
                        Section File Maintenance        ADD

   Section number . . . . . .  XXXXX
   Course . . . . . . . . . .  XXXXXX
   Instructor . . . . . . . .  XXXXXXXXXXXXXX
   Room . . . . . . . . . . .  XXXX
   Meets on days  . . . . . .  XXX
   Starting time  . . . . . .  XX:XX
   Enrollment . . . . . . . .  XXX




   Press Enter to add

   F3=Exit   F12=Cancel
```

The DDS for the display file, SECTMAIN, is shown on the following page. It contains a DSPATR entry not yet introduced. DSPATR(PR) protects input-capable fields (i.e., usage I or B) from input keying. Because you can condition display attributes with indicators, this attribute can be used to permit or prevent a user from keying a value into a field, depending on processing needs at that point in time. The maintenance program on page 187 uses DSPATR(PR) to prevent the user from changing field values within a record when (s)he has selected the delete option.

```
*.. 1 ...+... 2 ...+... 3 ...+... 4 ...+... 5 ...+... 6 ...+... 7 ...+... 8
AAN01N02N03T.Name++++++RLen++TDpBLinPosFunctions+++++++++++++++++++++++++++++++
A* Display file SECTMAIN, used for interactively maintaining the
A* SECTIONS file.
A                                       REF(SECTIONS)
A                                       PRINT
A                                       CA03(03 'F3=Exit')
A                                       VLDCMDKEY(10)
A           R SCREEN1
A                                     1 28'Section File Maintenance'
A                                     3  2'Type values, then Enter.'
A                                     5  5'Section number . .'
A             SECTION     5   B  5 24
A 30
AO 31
AO 32
AO 91                                   DSPATR(PC)
A 30                                    ERRMSG('Record already exists' 30)
A 31                                    ERRMSG('No record for change' 31)
A 32                                    ERRMSG('No record for delete' 32)
A 91                                    ERRMSG('I/O error' 91)
A                                     6  5'Action Code . . .'
A             ACTION      1   I  6 24VALUES('A' 'C' 'D')
A                                     6 30'A=Add'
A                                     7 30'C=Change'
A                                     8 30'D=Delete'
A                                    24  2'F3=Exit'
A           R SCREEN2                   CA12(12 'F12=Cancel')
A                                     1 28'Section File Maintenance'
A             MODE        6   O  1 60DSPATR(HI)
A                                     3  2'Section number . . . . . .'
A             SECTNO      R      O  3 29
A                                     4  2'Course . . . . . . . . .'
A             COURSE      R   B  4 29
A 40                                    DSPATR(PR)
A                                     5  2'Instructor . . . . . . .'
A             INSTR       R   B  5 29
A 40                                    DSPATR(PR)
A                                     6  2'Room . . . . . . . .'
A             ROOM        R   B  6 29EDTCDE(Z)
A 40                                    DSPATR(PR)
A                                     7  2'Meets on days  . . . . .'
A             DAYS        R   B  7 29VALUES('MWF' 'TTH')
A 40                                    DSPATR(PR)
A                                     8  2'Starting time  . . . . .'
A             BEGTIME     R   B  8 29EDTWRD(' 0:  ')
A 40                                    DSPATR(PR)
A                                     9  2'Enrollment . . . . . . .'
A             ENROLL      R   B  9 29EDTCDE(3)
A 40                                    DSPATR(PR)
A                                    21  2'Press Enter to '
A             MODE2       6   O 21 17DSPATR(HI)
A                                    23  2'F3=Exit'
A                                    23 11'F12=Cancel'
```

Notice in the above DDS for record format SCREEN2 that SECTNO is
Output only, to prevent the user from modifying that field. Also, record format SCREEN1 uses indicators to display error messages differentially, depending on processing outcomes within the program. Because SECTION should
display in reverse image with the cursor positioned to that field for any file
error, DSPATR(PC) is conditioned by four indicators in an "OR" relation; if

any one of the four indicators is on, the display attributes will be in effect. DSPATR(PR), or protected, is enabled for all SCREEN2 input-capable fields during the deletion mode to prevent the user from modifying these fields.

Before jumping into the RPG IV code required to implement this interactive application, let's work out the logic of what the application should do. Typically this "think-before-acting" approach to programming leads to more structured code. And remember, when coding for interactive applications, it is hard to resist falling into the GOTO habit. The pseudocode below illustrates the logic needed for this maintenance program. Notice that the pseudocode breaks the program into separate modules based on the function the code performs.

Program Mainline
WHILE user wants to continue
    Display screen 1
    Read screen 1
    SELECT
        WHEN user signals exit
            Leave
        WHEN action is Add
            Do subroutine AddRecord
        WHEN action is Change
            Do subroutine ChngRecord
        WHEN action is Delete
            Do subroutine DeltRecord
    ENDSELECT
ENDWHILE
END program

Subroutine AddRecord
Chain to Section file
IF record found
    Set on error indicator
ELSE
    Zero and blank all record fields except section number
    Display screen 2
    Read screen 2
    IF not valid command key
        Write record to file
    ENDIF
ENDIF
END Subroutine

Subroutine ChngRecord
Chain to Section file
IF record not found
    Set on error indicator
ELSE
       Display screen 2
       Read screen 2
       IF not valid command key
           Update record to file
       ENDIF
ENDIF
END Subroutine

Subroutine DeltRecord
Chain to Section file
IF record not found
    Set on error indicator
ELSE
       Display screen 2
       Read screen 2
       IF not valid command key
           Delete record from file
       ENDIF
ENDIF
END Subroutine

Once you have the pseudocode worked out, coding the RPG IV is simple. In the program below, notice that indicators turned on within the program to control screen display may need to be turned off. Those indicators associated with error messages in the screen are set off automatically.

```
*.. 1 ...+... 2 ...+... 3 ...+... 4 ...+... 5 ...+... 6 ...+... 7 ...+... 8 ...+... 9 ...+...10
F*****************************************************************
F* This program interactively maintains file SECTIONS.          *
F*    Author: Judy Yaeger.   Date Written: 11-92.               *
F*    Revised 2-95 for RPG IV by Yaeger.                        *
F*                                                              *
F*   Indicators:                                               *
F*      03 -- F03; exit                                         *
F*      10 -- Valid command key pressed                         *
F*      12 -- F12; cancel                                       *
F*      30 -- Invalid add; record already exists                *
F*      31 -- Invalid change; no record for change              *
F*      32 -- Invalid delete; no record for delete              *
F*      40 -- Protect screen fields on delete                   *
F*      90 -- No record in file                                 *
F*      91 -- I/O failure on WRITE, UPDATE, or DELETE           *
F*****************************************************************
FSections  UF A E            K DISK
FSectMain  CF   E              WORKSTN
C                   DOW       *IN03 = *OFF                        Loop until exit.
```

```
*.. 1 ...+... 2 ...+... 3 ...+... 4 ...+... 5 ...+... 6 ...+... 7 ...+... 8 ...+... 9 ...+...10
C                   EVAL      *IN40 = *OFF
C                   EVAL      *IN12 = *OFF
C                   IF        *IN91 = *OFF AND                      If no error, blank
C                             *IN30 = *OFF AND                      out section number.
C                             *IN31 = *OFF AND
C                             *IN32 = *OFF
C                   EVAL      Section = *BLANKS
C                   ENDIF
C                   EXFMT     Screen1                               Display 1st screen.
C                   SELECT
C                   WHEN      *IN03 = *ON                           If F3, then
C                   LEAVE                                           exit loop.
C                   WHEN      *IN12 = *ON
C                   ITER
C                   WHEN      Action = 'A'                          Add requested.
C                   EXSR      AddRecord
C                   WHEN      Action = 'C'                          Change requested.
C                   EXSR      ChngRecord
C                   WHEN      Action = 'D'                          Delete requested.
C                   EXSR      DeltRecord
C                   ENDSL
C                   ENDDO
C                   EVAL      *INLR = *ON
C                   RETURN
C*****************************************************************
C*  Subroutine AddRecord:  Processes an Add action request       *
C*****************************************************************
C     AddRecord     BEGSR
C     Section       CHAIN     Sections                    90
C                   IF        *IN90 = *OFF                          If section exists,
C                   EVAL      *IN30 = *ON                            then Add error.
C                   ELSE
C                   EVAL      Mode = 'ADD   '
C                   EVAL      Mode2 = 'add   '
C                   EVAL      SectNo = Section
C                   EXSR      Initial                               Initialize.
C                   EXFMT     Screen2                               Get values.
C                   IF        *IN10 = *OFF                          If not VLDCMDKEY,
C                   WRITE     SecRec                      91           add record.
C                   ENDIF
C                   ENDIF
C                   ENDSR
C*****************************************************************
C*  Subroutine ChngRecord:  Processes a Change request           *
C*****************************************************************
C     ChngRecord    BEGSR
C     Section       CHAIN     Sections                    90
C                   IF        *IN90 = *ON                           If no section,
C                   EVAL      *IN31 = *ON                            then Change error.
C                   ELSE
C                   EVAL      Mode = 'CHANGE'
C                   EVAL      Mode2 = 'change'
C                   EXFMT     Screen2                               Get values.
C                   IF        *IN10 = *OFF                          If not VLDCMDKEY,
C                   UPDATE    SecRec                      91           rewrite record.
C                   ENDIF
C                   ENDIF
C                   ENDSR
C*****************************************************************
C*  Subroutine DeltRecord:  Processes a Delete request           *
C*****************************************************************
C     DeltRecord    BEGSR
C     Section       CHAIN     Sections                    90
```

```
*.. 1 ...+... 2 ...+... 3 ...+... 4 ...+... 5 ...+... 6 ...+... 7 ...+... 8 ...+... 9 ...+...10
C                   IF        *IN90 = *ON                              If no section,
C                   EVAL      *IN32 = *ON                                then Delete error.
C                   ELSE
C                   EVAL      Mode = 'DELETE'
C                   EVAL      Mode2 = 'delete'
C                   EVAL      *IN40 = *ON                              Protect fields.
C                   EXFMT     Screen2                                  Get confirmation.
C                   IF        *IN10 = *OFF                             If not VLDCMDKEY,
C                   DELETE    SecRec                       91            delete record.
C                   ENDIF
C                   ENDIF
C                   ENDSR
C*********************************************************************
C* Subroutine Initial: Initializes record fields to blanks *
C* and zeros preparatory to an Add.                        *
C*********************************************************************
C     Initial       BEGSR
C                   EVAL      Course = *BLANKS
C                   EVAL      Instr = *BLANKS
C                   EVAL      Room = *ZEROS
C                   EVAL      Days = *BLANKS
C                   EVAL      BegTime = *ZEROS
C                   EVAL      Enroll = *ZEROS
C                   ENDSR
```

Many RPG IV programmers feel that the fields used in the display file should not be the same as the database fields, and in some applications, depending on the program design, such separate definition in fact may be necessary to prevent losing values input by the user (or read from the database).

To implement this approach, simply define the display file fields independently, giving them new names. Then, in your RPG IV program add two subroutines — one that assigns the screen field values to the database fields, and one that does the reverse (assigns the database fields to the screen fields). Before you add or update a record, execute the subroutine that assigns the screen fields to the database fields. Before you display the data entry screen for a change or delete, execute the subroutine that assigns the database fields to the screen fields.

Screen Design and CUA

The screens illustrated in this chapter were based on a set of design standards called **CUA**, or **Common User Access**. IBM developed and promotes CUA as a way of standardizing user interfaces across platforms. All the AS/400 screens follow these standards.

Screens can be classified into one of four panel types: menu, list, entry, and information. Under CUA, all panels have the same general layout: a panel title on the first screen line, an optional information area, an instruction area, a panel body area (where either the menu, list, data entry fields, or informational output occur), and at the bottom of the screen, a command area, a list of function keys, and a message line. The following screen illustrates the layout for these types of panels:

```
/  Panel ID                          Panel Title

   Optional Information Area (on menu, list, or info)
     and/or controlling fields for list panel

   Instruction Area (on menu, entry, or list)

   Panel Body Area
     □    Menu choices on Menu Panel
     □    List area on List Panel
     □    Entry prompts on Entry Panel
     □    Information prompts on Information Panel




   Optional Command Area
   Function Key Area
   Message Area
\
```

CUA has specific guidelines for row and column placement of screen items, vertical alignment of screen columns, capitalization and punctuation, function key use, error-condition handling, and so on. Although you may think such standards stifle creativity, there are two excellent reasons for standardizing the user interface.

First, a standardized interface makes it easier for a user to learn new applications, because the interface is consistent with other applications. If F3 is always the Exit key across applications, for instance, and F12 always backs up to the previous screen, the user does not have to learn new commands counter to those used in other applications.

A second major reason for adopting CUA (or other) standards is that such standards can improve programmer productivity. If you adopt a set of design standards, you can easily develop a set of generic DDS descriptions — one for each panel type — that can then easily be tailored to your specific applications.

Chapter Summary

Display files, defined in DDS, are the mechanism that allows a user and a program to interact. Each record screen format of a display file defines a screen. The screen format may include literals to display and fields for output, input, or both. Each data item is positioned on the screen based on line and column DDS entries.

DDS relies on keywords to achieve specific desired effects. You can associate some keywords with the entire file, others with a specific record format, and others yet with specific fields. Keywords enable function keys, determine the appearance and format of displayed items, control what the user can enter as input values, and associate error messages with fields.

You can condition most keywords, as well as fields and literals, by indicators. If the indicator is on at display time, the keyword is in effect (or the field or literal displays); if the indicator is off, the effect or data item the indicator is associated with is suppressed. The indicators are turned on within a program to control screen display. On the display side, you can associate valid command keys with indicators to convey information back to the program.

Today's businesses frequently use interactive applications to display database information or the results of processing data; more and more companies also use interactive applications for file maintenance. In this latter case you should pay special attention to validating the user's entries, to maintain data file integrity.

IBM has developed a set of screen-design guidelines, called CUA (Common User Access), that can standardize AS/400 interactive applications. Such standards of screen design can make it easier for users to learn new applications and for programmers to develop new applications more efficiently.

Terms

batch processing   data validation   interactive applications
combined file   display attributes   keyboard-shift attribute
CUA (Common User Access)   display file

Discussion/Review Questions

1. Contrast batch and interactive applications.

2. What are the permissible I/O operations that can be used with record formats of display files? What are the effects of each?

3. Describe how a combined file differs from an update file.

4. What allows the system to determine whether you are using a keyword as a file-, record-, or field-level keyword?

5. What's the difference between referring to a function key as CA (Command Attention) and CF (Command Function)? How does each affect your program?

6. Explain the meaning of each of the following display-attribute codes: BL, CS, ND, HI, UL, RI, PC.

7. Why might you want to know in general whether the user pressed an enabled function key or a special key (i.e., use the VLDCMDKEY keyword), when each valid key has its own indicator whose status can be checked within your program?

8. What are the relational codes used with COMP in DDS display files?

9. What's the difference between Mandatory Enter and Mandatory Fill?

10. What happens when an Error Message (ERRMSG) is in effect for a field? Describe the screen effects.

11. How can program events influence screen display, and how can screen input influence program flow of control?

12. Describe how a record's existence affects the validity of adding, deleting, or changing the record when maintaining a file with unique keys.

13. Discuss the pros and cons of adopting IBM's CUA standards in your screen design.

14. What impact do you think Graphical User Interfaces (GUIs), as typified by Microsoft's Windows environment, will have on future AS/400 interactive applications?

Exercises

1. Assume that your school has a student file containing name, sex, total credits accumulated, residency code, grade point average, major (or degree program), and student classification. Write the DDS for a record format that prompts the user to enter values for these fields, including as many validation keywords as are appropriate.

2. Write a DDS record format that would prompt the user to enter salesperson number, date of sale, and amount of sale. The cursor should blink, salesperson number should be underlined with column separators, date of sale should display in high intensity, and amount of sale should be in reverse image and blinking.

Exercises Continued

Exercises continued

3. Rewrite the DDS from Exercise 2 so that the salesperson number is underlined if indicator 10 *and* 12 are on, and displayed with column separators if 10 *or* 12 is on. Date of sale should display in high intensity only if indicator 10 is on. Amount of sale should be in reverse image and blinking if 10 *and* 12 are on *or* if 14 *and* 16 are on.

4. Write the pseudocode for a program to allow interactive processing of received goods. The program should let a user enter a product number (on Screen1), determine whether or not that product number exists in the file, and either display an error message (on Screen1) if the product number is incorrect, or display a second screen (Screen2) that asks the user to enter the quantity of that product received. The amount entered should be added to the current quantity on hand, and the product record then updated. Include provisions for exiting and canceling.

5. Write the RPG IV for the pseudocode of Exercise 4. Don't code the DDS. Make up whatever file and field names you need. Document whatever indicators you use.

Programming Assignments

1. CompuSell wants you to develop an interactive application that will allow the company to enter its product number for an item and display a screen of information about the supplier of that product. The screen should include all the information in the supplier file CSSUPP. You also must use inventory file CSINVP to obtain the correct supplier number for the item in question. The data files are described in Appendix D; follow your instructor's directions for obtaining the files.

    Develop the DDS and the RPG IV program for this application. Design your application with two screens: one inquiry screen and one informational display. Write your program to loop so that, following the display of the requested information, the program prompts the user for a new product number; continue until (s)he signals that (s)he is finished. Follow your instructor's directions for testing this program.

2. CompuSell wants you to write an interactive file maintenance program for its Customer Master File CSCSTP (see Appendix D). If the user wants to add a new customer, your program must determine the appropriate number to assign the customer (numbers are sequentially assigned) and provide the number automatically for the user; also automatically use the system date for the date of last order and assign balance due a value of zero. For a change request, allow the user to change any field except the customer number. Do not allow the user to delete a record if the customer has a balance greater than zero. Follow your instructor's directions for testing this program.

3. Wexler University wants you to write an interactive file maintenance program for its instructor file WUINSTP (see Appendix D). Design screens as appropriate for the application. Allow the users to add, delete, or change instructor records. Do not allow them to change the Social Security number or add a record with a duplicate Social Security number. Include as much data validation as you can, given the nature of the data fields being entered. Follow your instructor's directions for testing this program.

Programming Assignments Continued

Programming Assignments continued

4. CompuSell wants you to write an interactive application to enter customer orders. The application should begin by determining the appropriate starting order number, based on the last order number in Order File CSORDP. The main process loop should then begin by requesting the customer number; only orders for established customers (those in the Customer Master File CSCSTP) may be processed. If the customer exists, then the program should set up a loop to let the user enter ordered items until the order is complete.

   For each item, the user should enter the product number and the quantity desired. If the product is not in the Inventory File CSINVP, or if the quantity on hand is less than the quantity desired, inform the user through error messages that the item cannot be ordered; otherwise, update the quantity-on-hand field of the inventory file to reflect the new, lower quantity on hand and write a record to the Orders File (CSORDPRP) for that item.

   When the user has finished entering items for a customer, determine whether payment was included in the order, and if so, for how much. A record should be written to the CSORDP file, leaving the amount due zero. (The files CSORDP and CSORDPRP will be used by different programs to generate pick-lists and invoices.)

5. Wexler University wants you to write a program that will provide an online registration system for its students. The registration system should work as follows:

   a) The student should be prompted to enter his/her Social Security number. If the student is not found in the student master file, the program should not allow him/her to proceed.

   b) If the student is in the file, (s)he should be allowed to register for courses until (s)he signals that (s)he is finished.

   c) For each desired course, the student will enter the section number. If the section number is invalid, the student should be informed. If the number is valid, the course identification, title, and credits should display on the screen, along with the time and days the section meets and an indication of whether the section is full or not full (current enrollment < cap).

   d) If the section is not full, and if the student indicates that this is, in fact, the course and section into which (s)he wishes to enroll, the program should confirm the enrollment to the user, update the current enrollment figure in the Current Section record by adding 1 to it, and add a record to the Current Enrollment File for this student in this section.

   When a student has finished enrolling, the program should return to the initial screen to let the next student enroll. This process should continue until the user presses F3 to exit the application completely.

   Your program will use files WUSTDP, WUSCTP, WUCRSP, and WUENRLP (see Appendix D). Follow your instructor's directions for testing this program.

Chapter 8

Tables and Arrays

Chapter Overview

In this chapter you will learn how to create, store, and access tables of data. You will also learn how to define and use arrays, data structures that can simplify repetitive processing of similar data.

Representing Tables of Data

In common usage, a **table** is a collection of data organized into columns and rows. Similar kinds of data are stored within a column, and the data elements within a row of the table are related, or "belong" together. Typically, the data elements in the first column of a table are organized sequentially in ascending order to facilitate finding an item. Once you find the item you want in column 1, you then read across the row to extract the data related to that item.

The three-column table below, for example, would let you look up a state code to extract the name and sales tax of the state associated with that state code. (Note that the full table would include 50 codes and their corresponding names and tax rates, not just the eight shown.)

State Code	State Name	Tax Rate
AK	Alaska	.0000
AL	Alabama	.0400
AR	Arkansas	.0000
AZ	Arizona	.0500
CA	California	.0725
CO	Colorado	.0300
CT	Connecticut	.0600
DE	Delaware	.0000
...	...	...

RPG IV provides two data structures that you can use to represent such collections of data: tables and arrays. Originally, RPG included only tables; arrays were added later to allow greater flexibility than tables could offer. Although tables and arrays have several similarities, the capabilities of arrays go beyond those of tables. In fact, some RPG programmers no longer use tables; they prefer to use arrays for any solution that requires addressing multiple data values with a single field name. In this chapter we'll look at basic tables first, and then investigate the added power arrays provide.

RPG IV Tables

RPG IV lets you define table data structures so that your program can extract data in a way analogous to how you use tables. The major difference between an RPG IV table and tables as we are used to thinking about them is that one RPG IV table represents only a single column of data. In RPG IV terms, our table above is actually *three* related tables.

Table Definition

Data elements within an RPG IV table need to have the same length, the same data type, and the same number of decimal positions (if numeric data). In the above table, state codes are all 2-byte-long character data; the state names, however, have different lengths. To use the names in an RPG IV table, you would have to determine the length of the longest state name (South Carolina and North Carolina both have 14 characters) and pad the names of the other states with trailing blanks to make them all 14 characters long.

Definition Specifications are used to define tables. When your program uses Definition Specifications, recall that these specifications must follow the File Specifications and precede the Input Specifications. The Definition Specification entries required to define a table vary, depending on the complexity and layout of the data you are storing in table format and where the table data values are coming from. However, table definitions always require the use of one or more keywords, coded in positions 44-80 (Keywords+++...) of the Definition Specification. Within this area, keywords can be entered separated by one or more spaces in any order, with several keywords on the same line.

You can use a Definition Specification continuation line to complete a list of required keywords, if additional room is needed. If you use a continuation line, simply enter it immediately following the initial Definition Specification with the additional keywords specified in positions 44-80. Other than leaving positions 7-43 of the continuation line blank, you need to give no additional signal that the line completes the previous statement. The figure below shows the layout of a Definition Specification and a Definition Specification continuation line.

```
*.. 1 ...+... 2 ...+... 3 ...+... 4 ...+... 5 ...+... 6 ...+... 7 ...+... 8 ...+... 9 ...+...10
DName++++++++++ETDsFrom+++To/L+++IDc.Keywords+++++++++++++++++++++++++++++++Comments+++++++++++
D.................................Keywords-continuation++++++++++++++++Comments+++++++++++
```

With that overview completed, let's now look at how to define various kinds of tables. Consider first how RPG IV would handle a very simple table — a table of 50 state codes. Once you understand definitional requirements for this table, you can expand your understanding to more complex examples. The table of state codes appears below.

State Code
AK
AL
AR
AZ
CA
CO
CT
DE
...

An RPG IV table name must begin with the characters TAB (uppercase, lowercase, or mixed-case), followed by up to seven additional characters. You can enter the table name anywhere in positions 7-21 (Name++++++++++) of the Definition Specifications. An S, coded left-adjusted in positions 24-25 (Ds) declares the table to be a stand-alone field. Unlike other stand-alone fields we have worked with, however, a table stores multiple values. To indicate how many values, or elements, the table contains, you must include keyword DIM (for Dimension) in positions 44-80 (Keywords+++...), with the number of table elements specified within parentheses after the keyword.

You also must indicate the length of each table element right-adjusted in positions 33-39 (To/L+++) of the specification line, along with the number of decimal positions within each element (for numeric table data) in positions 41-42 (Dc). If the table data is arranged in order, you should indicate this order by including keyword ASCEND (for ascending data) or DESCEND (for descending data), although this entry is optional for most tables.

```
*.. 1 ...+... 2 ...+... 3 ...+... 4 ...+... 5 ...+... 6 ...+... 7 ...+... 8 ...+... 9 ...+...10
DName++++++++++ETDsFrom+++To/L+++IDc.Keywords++++++++++++++++++++++++++++++++Comments++++++++++++
D TabCode         S              2    DIM(50) ASCEND
```

The Definition Specification above associates the table name TabCode with our state codes, and states that it contains 50 elements of two-position-long character data in ascending order. This table definition allocates memory so that the entire table of data can remain in memory throughout a program's execution.

Additional entries are required to complete the above definition. These entries depend on the source of the data values to be stored in the table and the layout of this original data. You can put data values into a table in two ways: You can either hard-code the data within your program (this kind of table is often called a **compile-time table**), or you can instruct the computer to obtain the data from a separate disk file each time the program runs (a **pre-runtime**, or **pre-execution table**).

Compile-Time Tables

A compile-time table obtains its data from the program's source code; the data is bound to the table when you compile the program. The table data must be entered at the very end of the program, following the last program entries (most often the last output specification).

RPG IV uses what is called a ****CTDATA record** as a delimiter (or separator line) to explicitly identify the table whose data follows. To code this delimiter, place asterisks in positions 1 and 2 of a line following the last line of program code; in positions 3-8 enter CTDATA (for compile-time data); leave position 9 blank; and, starting in position 10, enter the name of the table whose data follows.

The actual table data follows this separator line. How you enter the data at this point is up to you. You could put one table entry per line, two per line, three per line, and so on. In our example, because each state code is two bytes long, we could code all 50 state codes on a single line, if we wanted to. The only stipulations are that the values must begin in the first position of each line, that they must be entered in the order you want them to appear in the table, that multiple entries per line be entered contiguously (without spaces separating them), and that you are consistent in the number of entries you put on each line.

If the number of entries per line is not an even multiple of the number of total table entries, the odd number of entries goes on the last line. For example, assume that you decide to enter four state codes on one line. There would be 12 lines of four codes, with a final thirteenth line containing only two codes. The coding would look like this:

```
*.. 1 ...+... 2 ...+... 3 ...+... 4 ...+... 5 ...+... 6 ...+... 7 ...+... 8 ...+... 9 ...+...10
OFilename++DAddN01N02N03Excnam++++.........................................Comments+++++++++++
O            ...
O            ...
**CTDATA TabCode
AKALARAZ
CACOCTDE
...
WVWY
```

Every compile-time table requires a keyword, CTDATA, included within its Definition Specification to signal that the table data appears at the end of the program. Additionally, you may need to use keyword PERRCD to indicate how the data values are entered. Each program line in your source member is a record in the source file. Accordingly, if you have entered four state codes per line, there are four table entries per record. If you had entered only one state code per line, there would be one table entry per record. Including the PERRCD keyword with the number of table entries per record (or code line) indicated within parentheses after the keyword, lets the system correctly obtain the data to load within the table. If you omit the PERRCD keyword for a compile-time table, the system assumes the data is entered with one entry per record.

The figure below shows the Definition Specification for the state-code table as a compile-time table with four entries per record.

```
*.. 1 ...+... 2 ...+... 3 ...+... 4 ...+... 5 ...+... 6 ...+... 7 ...+... 8 ...+... 9 ...+...10
DName++++++++++ETDsFrom+++To/L+++IDc.Keywords+++++++++++++++++++++++++++++++Comments+++++++++++
D* Compile-time table of 50 state codes, entered in ascending sequence, 4 per record.
D TabCode         S             2    DIM(50) ASCEND CTDATA PERRCD(4)
```

Compile-time tables are useful for relatively small tables whose data are not likely to change over time. With large tables, it would be a waste of a programmer's time to enter the data as part of the program. Moreover, if the table data is **volatile** (i.e., frequently changing), a programmer would have to go back to the source program, change the table data at the end of the program, and recompile the program each time the data needed updating. You should avoid this practice, because each time you enter SEU to modify your source code, you run the risk of inadvertently introducing errors into the program.

Pre-Runtime Tables

An alternate way to handle data values required by a table is to store the data in a database file that is loaded into the table each time the program is run. This kind of table is called a pre-runtime or pre-execution table, because RPG IV automatically retrieves all the table data from the file before the program's procedural processing begins.

The Definition Specification for a pre-runtime table varies slightly from that of a compile-time table. Instead of using keyword CTDATA, pre-runtime tables require you to include keyword FROMFILE, with the name of the file containing the table data included within parentheses following the keyword. The value indicated with keyword PERRCD should indicate how many table entries are coded per record within the table file; if only one value appears per record, the PERRCD keyword can be omitted.

```
*.. 1 ...+... 2 ...+... 3 ...+... 4 ...+... 5 ...+... 6 ...+... 7 ...+... 8 ...+... 9 ...+...10
DName++++++++++ETDsFrom+++To/L+++IDc.Keywords+++++++++++++++++++++++++++++++Comments+++++++++++
D* Pre-runtime table of 50 state codes, entered one per record in ascending order.
D TabCode         S             2    DIM(50) FROMFILE(StateCodes) ASCEND
```

Because the data for a pre-runtime table is obtained from a file, a definition of this file must be included within the File Specifications of the program using the table. The File Specification for a file that contains table data differs somewhat from that of other files you have worked with. The file type (position 17) is I (Input), because the data is read by the program, but the file's designation (position 18) is T (Table); this entry directs the system to read all the data into a table automatically at the program's start. Because the table is

defined internally within the program, rather than externally, code an F
(Fixed format) in position 22, and include the appropriate record length in
positions 23-27.

```
*.. 1 ...+... 2 ...+... 3 ...+... 4 ...+... 5 ...+... 6 ...+... 7 ...+... 8 ...+... 9 ...+...10
FFilename++IPEASFRlen+LKlen+AIDevice+.Keywords+++++++++++++++++++++++++++++++Comments++++++++++++
F* Input table file of state codes, with one code per record.
FStates    IT  F   2         DISK
```

If you want to write the table back to a file at the end of program execution, perhaps because your program has modified some of the table values
and you want to update the file to reflect these changed values, you need to
include keyword TOFILE as part of the table's Definition Specification, along
with the name of the target file in parentheses after the keyword. If the
FROMFILE is different from the TOFILE, you would need an additional File
Specification defining the TOFILE as an output file. If the table data is to be
written back to the same file from which it was initially read, the file type
should be C (for combined).

```
*.. 1 ...+... 2 ...+... 3 ...+... 4 ...+... 5 ...+... 6 ...+... 7 ...+... 8 ...+... 9 ...+...10
FFilename++IPEASFRlen+LKlen+AIDevice+.Keywords++++++++++++++++++++++++++++++ Comments++++++++++++
F* Table file of 50 state codes, with one code per record; records to be rewritten at
F* end of processing.
FStates    CT  F   2         DISK
```

```
*.. 1 ...+... 2 ...+... 3 ...+... 4 ...+... 5 ...+... 6 ...+... 7 ...+... 8 ...+... 9 ...+...10
DName++++++++++ETDsFrom+++To/L+++IDc.Keywords+++++++++++++++++++++++++++++++Comments++++++++++++
D...................................Keywords-continuation+++++++++++++++++Comments++++++++++++
D* Pre-runtime table of 50 state codes, entered one per record in ascending order. Table
D* file to be rewritten at end of processing.
D TabCode         S         2    DIM(50) FROMFILE(States) ASCEND
D                                 TOFILE(States)
```

Table Look-Ups

Tables are used for one primary purpose: to look up data values using the
LOOKUP operation. Typically, you have a field, either from an input file or a
result field from a calculation, that you want to find in the table; this value goes
in factor 1 of a standard Calculation Specification. The name of the table goes
in factor 2. The LOOKUP operation requires an indicator to serve as a signal
for the type of match you want to find between the table value and the factor
1 value. Most of the time you want an equal match, so you put the indicator in
the Eq position (75-76).

When a LOOKUP is successful, the resulting indicator comes on and an
internal pointer is positioned at the matching table value. You can use the
indicator's status to control subsequent processing within the program. The
code below illustrates a simple **table look-up**.

```
*.. 1 ...+... 2 ...+... 3 ...+... 4 ...+... 5 ...+... 6 ..+... 7 ...+... 8 ...+... 9 ...+...10
CLØNØ1Factor1++++++Opcode(E)+Factor2++++++Result+++++++Len++D+HiLoEq....Comments+++++++++++
CLØNØ1Factor1++++++Opcode(E)+Extended-factor2+++++++++++++++++++++++++Comments+++++++++++
C* Use input field CodeIn as the search argument of a look-up within TabCode. Indicator 50
C* comes on if an equal match is found.
C     CodeIn        LOOKUP    TabCode                            50
C                   IF        *IN5Ø = *ON
C                   EXSR      CodeFound
C                   ELSE
C                   EXSR      BadCode
C                   ENDIF
```

A table look-up involving a single table is of limited value. Its primary purpose would be to validate the value of an input field. The more common use of tables — to look up a value in one column of a table to extract a related value from a second column — requires some additional table definition in RPG IV and a slight modification of the LOOKUP operation.

Two Related Tables

Recall that in RPG IV a table corresponds to one column of information. Assume you wanted to represent the information in the following example in table format within RPG IV.

State Code	State Name
AK	Alaska
AL	Alabama
AR	Arkansas
AZ	Arizona
CA	California
CO	Colorado
CT	Connecticut
DE	Delaware
...	...

To represent both the state codes and the state names within RPG IV requires defining two tables. The form of those definitions depends on how you have entered the data supplying the table values. When you are entering pairs of related table data, it is often convenient to enter the pairs together, as shown on the following page.

```
*.. 1 ...+... 2 ...+... 3 ...+... 4 ...+... 5 ...+... 6 .+... 7 ...+... 8 ..+... 9 ...+...10
OFilename++DAddNØ1NØ2NØ3Excnam++++........................................Comments+++++++++++
O           ...
O           ...
**CTDATA TabCode
AKAlaska
ALAlabama
ARArkansas
AZArizona
CACalifornia
COColorado
CTConnecticut
DEDelaware
...
```

This form of table data entry is called **alternating format**. The state *codes* would be considered the primary table, alternating with the state *names* in the data. To reflect this data organization, the Definition Specification for the primary table remains identical to how it would be defined if it were a stand-alone table. A second Definition Specification is required to define the table that is in alternating format. In this definition, you must include keyword ALT, followed by the name of the primary table enclosed in parentheses. Keyword DIM is also a required entry for the alternating table. However, you cannot include the CTDATA, FROMFILE, TOFILE, or PERRCD keywords in the alternating table's definition; the alternating table "inherits" these keywords from the table with which it alternates.

```
*.. 1 ...+... 2 ...+... 3 ...+... 4 ...+... 5 ...+... 6 .+... 7 ...+... 8 ..+... 9 ...+...10
DName++++++++++ETDsFrom+++To/L+++IDc.Keywords+++++++++++++++++++++++++++++++Comments+++++++++++
D* Two compile-time tables are defined in alternating format; each table has 5Ø elements,
D* entered 1 per record.  TabCode is in ascending sequence.
D TabCode         S              2    DIM(5Ø) CTDATA ASCEND PERRCD(1)
D TabName         S             14    DIM(5Ø) ALT(TabCode)
```

In the tables defined above, the state names are stored in TabName and the length of each name is stated as 14 — the length of the longest name. Note that the number of entries per record specification in keyword PERRCD is one, because only *one pair* of values is coded on each line. If the data had been laid out so that several pairs of data were entered on the same line, that keyword entry would need to be adjusted to accurately reflect the data layout.

Although the example above deals with alternating-format, compile-time tables, pre-runtime tables can be in alternating format, too. Simply make sure the data is entered in alternating format in the file records and include the file definition in the File Specifications; then, in the Definition Specification of the primary table include the FROMFILE and TOFILE (if needed) keywords rather than keyword CTDATA. The table in alternating format with the primary table would require only the DIM and ALT keywords.

```
*.. 1 ...+... 2 ...+... 3 ...+... 4 ...+... 5 ...+... 6 ...+... 7 ...+... 8 ...+... 9 ...+...10
FFilename++IPEASFRlen+LKlen+AIDevice+.Keywords+++++++++++++++++++++++++++++Comments++++++++++++
F* Table file of state codes and state names in alternating format.
FStates    IT  F   16         DISK

*.. 1 ...+... 2 ...+... 3 ...+... 4 ...+... 5 ...+... 6 ...+... 7 ...+... 8 ...+... 9 ...+...10
DName++++++++++ETDsFrom+++To/L+++IDc.Keywords+++++++++++++++++++++++++++++Comments++++++++++++
D.....................................Keywords-continuation+++++++++++++++Comments++++++++++++
D* Two pre-runtime tables whose data is stored in alternating format in file States.
D TabCode         S              2    DIM(50) PERRCD(1) FROMFILE(States)
D                                      ASCEND
D TabName         S             14    DIM(50) ALT(TabCode)
```

You can then use the tables to look up a state code to extract a state name. To extract the name related to the state code, TabName must appear in the result field of the LOOKUP operation. A successful code look-up causes the internal pointer to be positioned in TabName at the name that corresponds to the matched code in TabCode. The result is that TabName contains the desired state name, and you can print or display TabName or use it in any other operation for which you need the appropriate state name.

If the look-up of TabCode is not successful, TabName will contain the state name from the last successful look-up. Good programming practice suggests that you should always provide for the possibility of unsuccessful look-ups within your code.

```
*.. 1 ...+... 2 ...+... 3 ...+... 4 ...+... 5 ...+... 6 ...+... 7 ...+... 8 ...+... 9 ...+...10
CL0N01Factor1++++++Opcode(E)+Factor2++++++Result++++++++Len++D+HiLoEq....Comments++++++++++++
CL0N01Factor1++++++Opcode(E)+Extended-factor2+++++++++++++++++++++++++++Comments++++++++++++
C* Look up CodeIn in TabCode to extract TabName.
C       CodeIn        LOOKUP    TabCode       TabName                 50
C* *IN50 is on if the look-up located an equal match.
C                     IF        *IN50 = *ON
C                     EXSR      PrintName
C                     ELSE
C                     EXSR      BadCode
C                     ENDIF
```

Multiple Related Tables

RPG IV lets you define only one table in alternating format with a primary table. How, then, can you represent the following data so you can look up a state code to extract both the state name and the sales tax rate?

State Code	State Name	Tax Rate
AK	Alaska	.0000
AL	Alabama	.0400
AR	Arkansas	.0000
AZ	Arizona	.0500
CA	California	.0725
CO	Colorado	.0300
CT	Connecticut	.0600
DE	Delaware	.0000
...	...	...

This problem has two solutions. The appropriate one depends on how your table data values are actually entered. Assume your data values are entered in alternating format, as shown below.

```
*.. 1 ...+... 2 ...+... 3 ...+... 4 ...+... 5 ...+... 6 ...+... 7 ...+... 8 ...+... 9 ...+...10
OFilename++DAddN01N02N03Excnam++++.......................................Comments++++++++++++
O                    ...
O                    ...
**CTDATA TabCode
AKAlaska        0000
ALAlabama       0400
ARArkansas      0000
AZArizona       0500
CACalifornia    0725
COColorado      0300
CTConnecticut   0600
DEDelaware      0000
...
```

Because RPG IV lets you define only two tables in alternating format, you would need to define the state names and tax rates as a single table and then split apart the two pieces after a successful look-up.

```
*.. 1 ...+... 2 ...+... 3 ...+... 4 ...+... 5 ...+... 6 ...+... 7 ...+... 8 ...+... 9 ...+...10
DName++++++++++++ETDsFrom+++To/L+++IDc.Keywords++++++++++++++++++++++++++++++Comments++++++++++++
D* Two tables defined for the compile-time data; TabTwo actually contains both the state name
D* and the state tax rate.
D TabCode          S              2    DIM(50) PERRCD(1) ASCEND CTDATA
D TabTwo           S             18    DIM(50) ALT(TabCode)
```

```
*.. 1 ...+... 2 ...+... 3 ...+... 4 ...+... 5 ...+... 6 ...+... 7 ...+... 8 ...+... 9 ...+...10
CLØN01Factor1++++++Opcode(E)+Factor2++++++Result++++++++Len++D+HiLoEq....Comments+++++++++++
CLØN01Factor1++++++Opcode(E)+Extended-factor2+++++++++++++++++++++++++++++Comments+++++++++++
C* Calculations to look up TabCode to extract the correct TabTwo value and split that value
C* into its name and tax rate components.  The rate is used to calculate TaxDue.  Rate is
C* a 4-digit numeric field with 4 decimal positions, while StateName is defined as a 14-byte
C* character field.
C       CodeIn       LOOKUP    TabCode        TabTwo                     50
C                    IF        *IN5Ø = *ON
C                    MOVE      TabTwo         Rate
C                    MOVEL     TabTwo         StateName
C                    EVAL (H)  TaxDue = Amount * Rate
C                    ELSE
C                    EXSR      BadCode
C                    ENDIF
```

A MOVE operation to a result field of the appropriate length and decimal positions lets you split off the right-most portion of the table data — in this case the tax rate — while a MOVEL operation gives you the left-most data — state name.

An alternate way to handle multicolumn table data is to first enter all the data from one column, then all the data from the next, and so on. A **CTDATA record must appear between each set of data.

```
*.. 1 ...+... 2 ...+... 3 ...+... 4 ...+... 5 ...+... 6 ...+... 7 ...+... 8 ...+... 9 ...+...10
OFilenam++DAddNØ1NØ2NØ3Excnam++++.................................Comments+++++++++++
O                ...
O                ...
**CTDATA TabCode
AK
AL
AR
AZ
...
**CTDATA TabName
Alaska
Alabama
Arkansas
Arizona
...
**CTDATA TabRate
ØØØØ
Ø4ØØ
ØØØØ
Ø5ØØ
...
```

With this data layout, you define each table independently on the Definition Specifications, as shown in the following example:

```
*.. 1 ...+... 2 ...+... 3 ...+... 4 ...+... 5 ...+... 6 ...+... 7 ...+... 8 ...+... 9 ...+...10
DName++++++++++ETDsFrom+++To/L+++IDc.Keywords++++++++++++++++++++++++++++Comments+++++++++++
D* Three tables independently defined.
D TabCode        S             2    DIM(5Ø) PERRCD(1) CTDATA ASCEND
D TabName        S            14    DIM(5Ø) PERRCD(1) CTDATA
D TabRate        S             4  4 DIM(5Ø) PERRCD(1) CTDATA
```

The calculations would then require two separate look-ups, one to extract the appropriate state name and the other to extract the tax rate. Notice that if the look-up is successful, you can use TabRate directly as a factor in a calculation. You do not need to first move it to a non-table field.

```
*.. 1 ...+... 2 ...+... 3 ...+... 4 ...+... 5 ...+... 6 ...+... 7 ...+... 8 ...+... 9 ...+...10
CLØNØ1Factor1++++++Opcode(E)+Factor2++++++Result++++++++Len++D+HiLoEq....Comments+++++++++++
CLØNØ1Factor1++++++Opcode(E)+Extended-factor2+++++++++++++++++++++++++++++Comments+++++++++++
C* Look up state name and tax rate based on code; then use the tax rate to calculate tax due.
C       CodeIn      LOOKUP    TabCode       TabName                50
C       CodeIn      LOOKUP    TabCode       TabRate                50
C                   IF        *IN50 = *ON
C                   EVAL (H)  TaxDue = Amount * TabRate
C                   ELSE
C                   EXSR      BadCode
C                   ENDIF
```

Although the sample coding above used compile-time tables, the same techniques of entering multicolumn data and performing look-ups apply to pre-runtime tables as well, where the data is stored in a table file.

There are trade-offs between these two techniques of handling multicolumn tables. When you enter data values column by column, you increase the chance of data entry errors or of associating incorrect values; when you enter data values a row at a time, with all related data adjacent to each other, you decrease the chance of errors.

On the other hand, if you handle multicolumn data as two alternating tables, with the second table a concatenation of several data values that need to be split apart in the calculations, the calculations are less obvious and more error-prone.

Range Tables

One final kind of table needs to be considered: a **range table**. Consider the following table of shipping charges:

Package Weight (lb)	Shipping Charge ($)
0- 1	2.50
2- 5	4.25
6- 10	7.50
11- 20	9.00
21- 40	12.00
41- 70	16.00

You would use this table to look up a package weight to determine the shipping charges for the package. Unlike the previous tables, in this table the weight column entries represent a range of values rather than discrete values.

How should these values be represented, and how should the LOOKUP be performed? One solution is to represent this data as two tables, storing only the *upper* end of the range of weights in the table along with the charges, as shown below.

```
*.. 1 ...+... 2 ...+... 3 ...+... 4 ...+... 5 ...+... 6 ...+... 7 ...+... 8 ...+... 9 ...+...10
OFilename++DAddN01N02N03Excnam++++.................................................Comments++++++++++
O              ...
O              ...
**CTDATA TabWeight
010250
050425
100750
200900
401200
701600
```

```
*.. 1 ...+... 2 ...+... 3 ...+... 4 ...+... 5 ...+... 6 ...+... 7 ...+... 8 ...+... 9 ...+...10
DName++++++++++ETDsFrom+++To/L+++IDc.Keywords+++++++++++++++++++++++++++++++++++Comments++++++++++
D TabWeight       S              2 0 DIM(6) ASCEND CTDATA PERRCD(1)
D TabCharge       S              4 2 DIM(6) ALT(TabWeight)
```

The above Definition Specifications define TabWeight as a table of six elements, with one entry per record and each entry a 2-byte numeric value with no decimal positions, and TabCharge as a table in alternating format with TabWeight, with each TabCharge entry a 4-byte numeric value with two decimal positions. Range tables *require* a sequence entry; the weights are in ascending sequence, so keyword ASCEND appears as part of TabWeight's definition.

You use the LOOKUP operation to access range tables. Because you are no longer looking for an exact match between an input value and a table value, you enter a resulting indicator in two positions for the LOOKUP operation; given the sample table's layout, the indicator is entered in the Hi and Eq positions (71-72 and 75-76).

```
*.. 1 ...+... 2 ...+... 3 ...+... 4 ...+... 5 ...+... 6 ...+... 7 ...+... 8 ...+... 9 ...+...10
CL0N01Factor1++++++Opcode(E)+Factor2++++++Result+++++++Len++D+HiLoEq....Comments++++++++++
CL0N01Factor1++++++Opcode(E)+Extended-factor2+++++++++++++++++++++++++++Comments++++++++++
C* A table look-up to find a weight in the table of weights to determine the appropriate
C* shipping charge for a package.
C     WeightIn    LOOKUP    TabWeight    TabCharge            50 50
C                 IF        *IN50 = *ON
C                 EVAL      TotCharge = PkgCharge + TabCharge
C                 ELSE
C                 EXSR      CannotShip
C                 ENDIF
```

The look-up statement above translates to "Find the first table weight that is greater than or equal to the input weight and extract the shipping charge that corresponds to that table weight." Because the maximum table weight is 70, failure of the look-up indicates an input weight over the 70-pound limit. In such cases, the program executes an error routine to indicate that the package cannot be shipped.

Changing Table Values

Tables are generally used for extracting values. It is possible, however, to change table values — either intentionally or accidentally — during program execution. Anytime you specify a table name as the result of a mathematical or an assignment operation, the value of the entry where the table is currently positioned will be changed. Failing to understand this can sometimes lead to inadvertent program errors.

For example, consider the shipping weight problem. Assume that in the application developed, you want to add and print either the appropriate shipping charge, or, for packages weighing more than 70 pounds, to add and print 0 to indicate that the package can't be shipped. The following incorrect solution may tempt you:

```
*.. 1 ...+... 2 ...+... 3 ...+... 4 ...+... 5 ...+... 6 ...+... 7 ...+... 8 ...+... 9 ...+...10
CLØN01Factor1++++++Opcode(E)+Factor2++++++Result++++++++Len++D+HiLoEq....Comments+++++++++++
CLØN01Factor1++++++Opcode(E)+Extended-factor2+++++++++++++++++++++++++++++Comments+++++++++++
C* This incorrect solution may change some of the values in TabCharge to zero.
C        WeightIn     LOOKUP    TabWeight     TabCharge              50 50
C                     IF        *IN50 = *OFF
C                     EVAL         TabCharge = Ø
C                     ENDIF
C                     EVAL      TotCharge = PkgCharge + TabCharge
```

The result of the above code would be that each time a package weighing more than 70 pounds is processed, the TabCharge value of the most recently successful look-up would be set to 0. The next time a package of that lower weight was processed, its shipping charge would incorrectly be extracted as 0.

You can deliberately change table values, if you wish, by first executing a LOOKUP to position the table correctly and then moving the new value into the table. If the table data came from a file and you want to store the table with its revised values back in the file at the end of processing, you can accomplish this task quite simply with a few modifications of the File and Definition Specifications.

First, designate the table file as a combined file, rather than an input file. Then include the file name with keyword TOFILE (as well as with FROMFILE) on the Definition Specification. These two changes will cause the (changed) table values to be written back to the file upon program completion.

Arrays

An **array** is a data structure similar to a table, in that it contains multiple elements, all defined with a common name. Like a table, each element within an array must be the same data type, with the same length and number of decimal positions (if the elements are numeric). Arrays are defined on Definition

Specifications; the required entries are the same as those required for tables. Like tables, you may load data into arrays at compile time, with values entered at the end of the program, or at pre-runtime, with values obtained from a table file. Array data may be obtained in alternating format, again, like tables.

Basically the only *definition* differences between **compile-time arrays** and tables and **pre-runtime arrays** and tables is that array names *cannot* begin with TAB. For reasons soon explained, programmers keep array names shorter than 10 characters, usually no more than 6-8 characters long. Examine the definitions below and you will see that other than the names, these are identical to table definitions.

```
*.. 1 ...+... 2 ...+... 3 ...+... 4 ...+... 5 ...+... 6 ...+... 7 ...+... 8 ...+... 9 ...+...10
FFilename++IPEASFRlen+LKlen+AIDevice+.Keywords++++++++++++++++++++++++++++++Comments+++++++++++
F* Table file ZipCodes contains alternating arrays Zip and City.
FZipCodes  IT   F  20         DISK

*.. 1 ...+... 2 ...+... 3 ...+... 4 ...+... 5 ...+... 6 ...+... 7 ...+... 8 ...+... 9 ...+...10
DName++++++++++ETDsFrom+++To/L+++IDc.Keywords++++++++++++++++++++++++++++++Comments+++++++++++
D.................................Keywords-continuation++++++++++++++++++Comments+++++++++++
D* Definitions of arrays from file ZipCodes: Zip contains 500 numeric elements, each 5 digits
D* long, with 0 decimals; City contains 500 character elements, each 15 bytes long.
D Zip            S              5 0 FROMFILE(ZipCodes) DIM(500) ASCEND
D                                   PERRCD(1)
D City           S             15   ALT(Zip) DIM(500)
D
D* Array Charge is a compile-time array, with three elements per record; it contains 100
D* elements, each 6 digits long with 2 decimal positions.
D Charge         S              6 2 CTDATA DIM(100) PERRCD(3)
```

One major difference between arrays and tables is that unlike tables, arrays can be loaded with values during the course of program execution. This kind of array is called a **runtime array**.

A runtime array is signaled on the Definition Specifications by the *omission* of both the CTDATA and FROMFILE keywords from the array definition; keyword PERRCD is also not used with runtime arrays.

```
*.. 1 ...+... 2 ...+... 3 ...+... 4 ...+... 5 ...+... 6 ...+... 7 ...+... 8 ...+... 9 ...+...10
DName++++++++++ETDsFrom+++To/L+++IDc.Keywords++++++++++++++++++++++++++++++Comments+++++++++++
D* The system recognizes the arrays defined below as runtime arrays.
D TaxAry         S              7 2 DIM(12)
D SlsAry         S             13 2 DIM(12)
D Names          S             20   DIM(200)
```

Data values for a runtime array can come from records read during program execution or from calculations performed within the program.

Runtime Arrays and Input Data

It is common for programmers to want to define some fields within an input record as an array to facilitate coding repetitive operations. Although you cannot directly define fields as array elements within an externally described file, a method of data redefinition does exist that lets you convert separately defined input fields into elements of a single runtime array. This method involves an advanced data definition feature called a **data structure**, a topic that we will extensively explore in the next chapter. For now, we'll introduce only enough information about data structure definition to let you define runtime arrays from input data.

Assume you have a file of sales records from all the company's sales staff. Each record contains the salesperson's identification number and the total sales for each month during the past year — 12 sales figures in all. Each sales figure is 10 digits long, with two decimal positions. Because you plan to redefine the sales figures as an array, you have defined the sales as a single, large character field, as shown below.

```
*.. 1 ...+... 2 ...+... 3 ...+... 4 ...+... 5 ...+... 6 ...+... 7 ...+... 8
A..........T.Name++++++RLen++TDpB......Functions++++++++++++++++++++++++++++
A* Externally described file SalesFile with 12 sales figures defined as
A* a single field.
A          R SALESREC
A            SLSNBR         5A          TEXT('Salesperson Number')
A            SALES        120A          TEXT('Twelve Months Sales')
```

You are writing a program that uses SalesFile as input, and you want to refer to the 12 sales figures within each record as elements of an array. To do this, you must include within the program's Definition Specifications a data structure definition that references the sales input field and redefines it as an array. The specifications below illustrate such a data structure.

```
*.. 1 ...+... 2 ...+... 3 ...+... 4 ...+... 5 ...+... 6 ...+... 7 ...+... 8 ...+... 9 ...+...10
DName++++++++++ETDsFrom+++To/L+++IDc.Keywords+++++++++++++++++++++++++++++++++Comments+++++++++++
D                 DS
D Sales                    1     120A
D SalAry                   1     120S 2 DIM(12)
```

The DS entry in positions 24-25 of the first line declares that what follows is a data structure definition. The second line says that the character field Sales (from SalesFile) occupies bytes 1 through 120 of the data structure, as indicated by the From+++ and To/L+++ entries. The third line defines SalAry as an array of 12 zoned-decimal elements, each with two decimal positions. Since SalAry also occupies bytes 1 through 120 of the data structure, it represents an **overlay**, or a redefinition, of the Sales field; as a result, SalAry breaks that big field down into 12 array elements, each 10 bytes long.

Some programmers prefer to explicitly specify the length of the array elements in the Definition Specification, instead of using positional length notation, when overlaying a field with an array. One way to do this is to define the array first, followed by the field it overlays.

```
*.. 1 ...+... 2 ...+... 3 ...+... 4 ...+... 5 ...+... 6 ...+... 7 ...+... 8 ...+... 9 ...+...10
DName++++++++++ETDsFrom+++To/L+++IDc.Keywords+++++++++++++++++++++++++++++++++Comments+++++++++++
D                 DS
D SalAry                         10S 2 DIM(12)
D Sales                    1     120A
```

An alternate way to externally describe the sales file is to define each month's sales figure separately.

```
*.. 1 ...+... 2 ...+... 3 ...+... 4 ...+... 5 ...+... 6 ..+... 7 ...+... 8
A.........T.Name++++++RLen++TDpB......Functions++++++++++++++++++++++++++++
A* Externally described file SalesFile.
A           R SALESREC
A             SLSNBR        5A          TEXT('Salesperson Number')
A             JANSALES     10S 2        TEXT('January Sales')
A             FEBSALES     10S 2        TEXT('February Sales')
A             MARSALES     10S 2        TEXT('March Sales')
A             APRSALES     10S 2        TEXT('April Sales')
A             MAYSALES     10S 2        TEXT('May Sales')
A             JUNSALES     10S 2        TEXT('June Sales')
A             JULSALES     10S 2        TEXT('July Sales')
A             AUGSALES     10S 2        TEXT('August Sales')
A             SEPSALES     10S 2        TEXT('September Sales')
A             OCTSALES     10S 2        TEXT('October Sales')
A             NOVSALES     10S 2        TEXT('November Sales')
A             DECSALES     10S 2        TEXT('December Sales')
```

Given the above file definition, you must slightly modify the data structure to manipulate the sales figures as array elements.

```
*.. 1 ...+... 2 ...+... 3 ...+... 4 ...+... 5 ...+... 6 ..+... 7 ...+... 8 ...+... 9 ...+...10
DName++++++++++ETDsFrom+++To/L+++IDc.Keywords+++++++++++++++++++++++++++++Comments+++++++++++
D                 DS
D SalAry                         10S 2 DIM(12)
D JanSales            1          10S 2
D FebSales           11          20S 2
D MarSales           21          30S 2
D AprSales           31          40S 2
D MaySales           41          50S 2
D JunSales           51          60S 2
D JulSales           61          70S 2
D AugSales           71          80S 2
D SepSales           81          90S 2
D OctSales           91         100S 2
D NovSales          101         110S 2
D DecSales          111         120S 2
```

In the above data structure, each month's sales is defined as a successive 10-byte area within the data structure; array SalAry, occupying the same 120 bytes of memory, redefines the 12 sales figures as its 12 elements. A more thorough discussion of data structures occurs in the next chapter; for now, simply understand that you can use data structures to convert database fields to elements within an array.

With either method of defining the input file and its associated data structure, each time you read a record from SalesFile, the 12 sales figures from that record will be stored in array SalAry. When a new input record is read, the sales figures from that record replace the previous contents of the array. Thus, the contents of SalAry change as the program is running, and that's the reason why we call SalAry a runtime array.

In addition to loading runtime arrays through input operations, you can also assign values to arrays through calculations performed by your program.

Before looking at this method of loading a runtime array, you must learn about array indexes.

Arrays and Indexing

Unlike table elements, you can directly reference and manipulate individual elements of an array using an **index**, or pointer. To indicate an array element in RPG IV, use the array name followed by a set of parentheses that contains the location number of the element within the array. Thus, SalAry(3) means the third element in the array SalAry. TaxAry(10) is the tenth element in the array TaxAry. When you use an array name without an index, the system infers that you wish to reference or manipulate the entire array — that is, all its elements.

The index that you use to reference an element of an array does not have to be a numeric literal. Instead, you can use a field as an index, provided you have defined the field as numeric, with 0 decimal positions. If the index is a field, the current value of that field determines which element of the array is referenced. Thus, if Index has a value of 3, TaxAry(Index) is the third element of TaxAry. If Index's value is 10, TaxAry(Index) is the tenth element of the array.

Because you often need to fit an array element name into the 14 spaces provided for factor 1, factor 2, and result field entries on Calculation Specifications, programmers frequently restrict array names to fewer than 10 characters. Our example, TaxAry(Index), occupies 13 positions. By using a shorter name for the index field, we could use a longer array name: TaxArray(N) occupies only 11 positions. Experienced programmers anticipate how they may use fields within a program and choose appropriate-length names.

Calculations with Arrays

You can use any of the arithmetic or assignment operations (e.g., EVAL, SQRT, MOVE) with arrays or their elements. If you just reference individual elements in your calculations, the effects are the same as if you were using fields.

```
*.. 1 ...+... 2 ...+... 3 ...+... 4 ...+... 5 ...+... 6 ...+... 7 ...+... 8 ...+... 9 ...+...10
CL0N01Factor1++++++Opcode(E)+Extended-factor2+++++++++++++++++++++++++++++++Comments+++++++++++
CL0N01Factor1++++++Opcode(E)+Factor2++++++Result++++++++Len++D+HiLoEq....Comments+++++++++++
C* Sample calculations involving array elements.
C
C* Add the values of two elements and store the result in a third element.
C                   EVAL      Ary(12) = Ary(6) + Ary(3)
C
C* Assign the contents of numeric element Ary(5) to character element CharAry(5).
C                   MOVE      Ary(5)         CharAry(5)
C
C* Divide the third element of Ary by 60 and store the remainder in RemAry(3).
C     Ary(3)        DIV       60             Quotient
C                   MVR                      RemAry(3)
```

You can also use entire arrays, rather than just individual elements of the arrays, in calculations. In this case, the result field *must always* be an array name.

If all the factors involved in the operation are arrays, then the operation is performed successively on *corresponding elements* of the arrays until the array with the fewest number of elements has been completely processed.

```
*.. 1 ...+... 2 ...+... 3 ...+... 4 ...+... 5 ...+... 6 ...+... 7 ...+... 8 ...+... 9 ...+...10
CL0N01Factor1++++++Opcode(E)+Extended-factor2+++++++++++++++++++++++++++++Comments+++++++++++
CL0N01Factor1++++++Opcode(E)+Factor2++++++Result+++++++Len++D+HiLoEq....Comments+++++++++++
C* Multiply corresponding elements of AryA and AryB, storing the products in AryC.
C                   EVAL (H)  AryC = AryA * AryB
C
C* Assign the values of AryB to AryA.
C                   EVAL      AryA = AryB
C
C* Take the square root of each element of AryA and store the result in the corresponding
C* element of AryB.
C                   SQRT (H)  AryA        AryB
```

When you combine non-array values and arrays in calculations, the operation works with corresponding elements of the arrays, along with the non-array values in each case, and continues until all the elements in the shortest array have been processed.

```
*.. 1 ...+... 2 ...+... 3 ...+... 4 ...+... 5 ...+... 6 ...+... 7 ...+... 8 ...+... 9 ...+...10
CL0N01Factor1++++++Opcode(E)+Factor2++++++Result+++++++Len++D+HiLoEq....Comments+++++++++++
CL0N01Factor1++++++Opcode(E)+Extended-factor2+++++++++++++++++++++++++++++Comments+++++++++++
C* Calculate gross pay for employees that work overtime; arrays Rate and Hours contain
C* employee values; array GPay stores results.
C                   EVAL      GPay = 40 * Rate + ((Hours - 40) * 1.5 * Rate)
C
C* Store 'ABCDE' in each element of array AryD
C                   EVAL      AryD = 'ABCDE'
```

In addition to the standard operations already presented in this text, three operations apply only to arrays: XFOOT, SORTA, and MOVEA.

XFOOT (Sum the Elements of an Array)

XFOOT, called "crossfoot," sums the elements of an array. This operation does not use factor 1 of the standard Calculation Specification. Factor 2 contains the name of the array whose elements are to be added together, and the result field contains the field where the answer is to be stored. If you half-adjust this operation, the rounding takes place just before the final answer is stored in the result field. **Crossfooting** is a term used in accounting to sum across a row of figures to develop a total for that row. The XFOOT operation is very useful in such applications, provided the figures to be added are array elements.

```
*.. 1 ...+... 2 ...+... 3 ...+... 4 ...+... 5 ...+... 6 ..+... 7 ...+... 8 ...+... 9 ...+...10
CL0N01Factor1++++++Opcode(E)+Factor2++++++Result+++++++Len++D+HiLoEq....Comments++++++++++++
C* Sum the elements of array AryA and store the answer in field Total.
C                   XFOOT(H)  AryA          Total
```

SORTA (Sort an Array)

SORTA is a simple but useful operation that re-arranges the values of the
elements of an array into ascending or descending sequence. The order used
depends on the sequence keyword (ASCEND or DESCEND) specified within
the array's definition on the Definition Specifications. If the definition
includes neither keyword, the SORTA operation sorts the values in ascending sequence, the default order. The Calculation Specification for this operation includes just the operation and the name of the array to be sorted,
entered in factor 2.

```
*.. 1 ...+... 2 ...+... 3 ...+... 4 ...+... 5 ...+... 6 ..+... 7 ...+... 8 ...+... 9 ...+...10
CL0N01Factor1++++++Opcode(E)+Factor2++++++Result+++++++Len++D+HiLoEq....Comments++++++++++++
C* AryA is an array of 5 numeric elements, each 2 bytes long, with no decimals.
C* Before SORTA, the array element values, in order, are 10 92 33 85 12.
C                   SORTA     AryA
C* Following SORTA, the array contains, in order, 10 12 33 85 92.
```

MOVEA (Move Array)

The MOVEA (Move Array) operation transfers values from factor 2 to the
result field of the operation. At least one of these entries — factor 2 or the
result — must contain an array name. Generally MOVEA is used with character data, although it can be used with numeric values if the entries in factor 2
and the result have the same numeric length (though not necessarily the
same number of decimal positions).

```
*.. 1 ...+... 2 ...+... 3 ...+... 4 ...+... 5 ...+... 6 ...+... 7 ...+... 8 ...+... 9 ...+...10
CL0N01Factor1++++++Opcode(E)+Factor2++++++Result+++++++Len++D+HiLoEq....Comments++++++++++++
C* Sample showing the format of the MOVEA operation.  Note that at least one of the
C* data items used in the operation must be an array.
C                   MOVEA     Factor2       Result
```

What makes MOVEA unusual is that the operation ignores the element
boundaries of the array and moves the values, character by character, from
the sending to the receiving field or array until either there is nothing left to
send or there is no more room in the receiving field.

The easiest way to understand how a MOVEA operation works is to
look at some examples. Assume you have two arrays: AryA, a four-element
character array, with each element three characters long; and AryB, a character array of five elements, each two characters long. FieldA is a field five
characters long.

The following examples illustrate the effects of different MOVEA operations using the arrays defined above. Notice especially that the data movement

takes place *from left to right* and that portions of the receiving field or array not used in the operation retain their original values.

Example 1:
MOVEA used with two arrays containing elements of different lengths; the target array elements are shorter than those of the sending array.

```
*.. 1 ...+... 2 ...+... 3 ...+... 4 ...+... 5 ...+... 6 ...+... 7 ...+... 8 ...+... 9 ...+...10
CLØNØ1Factor1++++++Opcode(E)+Factor2++++++Result+++++++Len++D+HiLoEq....Comments+++++++++++
C                 MOVEA     AryA          AryB
```

	AryA	**AryB**
Before MOVEA:	abc def ghi jkl	mn op qr st uv
After MOVEA:	abc def ghi jkl	a b cd ef gh ij

Example 2:
MOVEA used with two arrays containing elements of different lengths; the target array elements are longer than those of the sending array.

```
*.. 1 ...+... 2 ...+... 3 ...+... 4 ...+... 5 ...+... 6 ...+... 7 ...+... 8 ...+... 9 ...+...10
CLØNØ1Factor1++++++Opcode(E)+Factor2++++++Result+++++++Len++D+HiLoEq....Comments+++++++++++
C                 MOVEA     AryB          AryA
```

	AryB	**AryA**
Before MOVEA:	mn op qr st uv	abc def ghi jkl
After MOVEA:	mn op qr st uv	mno pqr stu vkl

Example 3:
MOVEA used to send the value of a field to a target array.

```
*.. 1 ...+... 2 ...+... 3 ...+... 4 ...+... 5 ...+... 6 ...+... 7 ...+... 8 ...+... 9 ...+...10
CLØNØ1Factor1++++++Opcode(E)+Factor2++++++Result+++++++Len++D+HiLoEq....Comments+++++++++++
C                 MOVEA     FieldA        AryA
```

	FieldA	**AryA**
Before MOVEA:	ZYXWV	abc def ghi jkl
After MOVEA:	ZYXWV	ZYX WVf ghi jkl

Example 4:
MOVEA used to send an array to a target field.

```
*.. 1 ...+... 2 ...+... 3 ...+... 4 ...+... 5 ...+... 6 ...+... 7 ...+... 8 ...+... 9 ...+...10
CLØNØ1Factor1++++++Opcode(E)+Factor2++++++Result+++++++Len++D+HiLoEq....Comments+++++++++++
C                 MOVEA     AryA          FieldA
```

	AryA	**FieldA**
Before MOVEA:	abc def ghi jkl	ZYXWV
After MOVEA:	abc def ghi jkl	abcde

Factor 2 and/or the result field can specify an array element, rather than an entire array. In that case, the data movement *starts* at that array element; elements preceding the specified element are not involved in the MOVEA operation. Data movement continues until there is nothing left to move or until the receiving array or field has no more room. The examples below illustrate this kind of data movement.

Example 5:
MOVEA used to send an array element to a target array.

```
*.. 1 ...+... 2 ...+... 3 ...+... 4 ...+... 5 ...+... 6 ...+... 7 ...+... 8 ...+... 9 ...+...10
CL0N01Factor1++++++Opcode(E)+Factor2++++++Result+++++++Len++D+HiLoEq....Comments++++++++++++
            MOVEA     AryA(3)     AryB
```

	AryA	**AryB**
Before MOVEA:	abc def ghi jkl	mn op qr st uv
After MOVEA:	abc def ghi jkl	g h ij kl st uv

Example 6:
MOVEA used to send an array to a target array element.

```
*.. 1 ...+... 2 ...+... 3 ...+... 4 ...+... 5 ...+... 6 ...+... 7 ...+... 8 ...+... 9 ...+...10
CL0N01Factor1++++++Opcode(E)+Factor2++++++Result+++++++Len++D+HiLoEq....Comments++++++++++++
            MOVEA     AryA        AryB(4)
```

	AryA	**AryB**
Before MOVEA:	abc def ghi jkl	mn op qr st uv
After MOVEA:	abc def ghi jkl	mn op qr ab cd

Example 7:
MOVEA used to send an array element to a target array element.

```
*.. 1 ...+... 2 ...+... 3 ...+... 4 ...+... 5 ...+... 6 ...+... 7 ...+... 8 ...+... 9 ...+...10
CL0N01Factor1++++++Opcode(E)+Factor2++++++Result+++++++Len++D+HiLoEq....Comments++++++++++++
            MOVEA     AryA(3)     AryB(2)
```

	AryA	**AryB**
Before MOVEA:	abc def ghi jkl	mn op qr st uv
After MOVEA:	abc def ghi jkl	mn gh ij kl uv

As you probably noticed, those positions within the result field that did not have new values moved to them by MOVEA retained their old values. By using extender (P) with the MOVEA operation, you can specify that the unused, right-most bytes of the target data item be blank-padded. The following sample code illustrates this feature:

Example 8:
MOVEA used to send an array element to an array element, with padding specified.

```
*.. 1 ...+... 2 ...+... 3 ...+... 4 ...+... 5 ...+... 6 ..+... 7 ...+... 8 ...+... 9 ...+...10
CLØNØ1Factor1++++++Opcode(E)+Factor2++++++Result+++++++Len++D+HiLoEq....Comments+++++++++++
             MOVEA(P)  AryA(3)         AryB(2)
```

	AryA	**AryB**
Before MOVEA:	abc def ghi jkl	mn op qr st uv
After MOVEA:	abc def ghi jkl	mn gh ij kl ƀƀ

The MOVEA operation can be extremely useful for manipulating portions of data fields and combining bits and pieces from different data sources into a single data item.

Using Arrays

Now that you understand how to define arrays and how to use them in different calculations or special array operations, you are ready to see how arrays can simplify or expedite solutions to different kinds of programming problems. The ability to index an array with a field, rather than a literal, adds tremendous flexibility to your ability to manipulate arrays and makes arrays the preferred data structure to handle problems requiring identical processing of similar data items.

Recall, for example, the SalesFile file described earlier, in which each record contained a salesperson's number and 12 monthly sales totals for that salesperson.

```
*.. 1 ...+... 2 ...+... 3 ..+... 4 ...+... 5 ...+... 6 ...+... 7 ...+... 8
A.........T.Name+++++RLen++TDpB......Functions++++++++++++++++++++++++++++
A* Externally described file SalesFile.
A           R SALESREC
A             SLSNBR        5A           TEXT('Salesperson Number')
A             JANSALES     1ØS 2         TEXT('January Sales')
A             FEBSALES     1ØS 2         TEXT('Februrary Sales')
A             MARSALES     1ØS 2         TEXT('March Sales')
A             APRSALES     1ØS 2         TEXT('April Sales')
A             MAYSALES     1ØS 2         TEXT('May Sales')
A             JUNSALES     1ØS 2         TEXT('June Sales')
A             JULSALES     1ØS 2         TEXT('July Sales')
A             AUGSALES     1ØS 2         TEXT('August Sales')
A             SEPSALES     1ØS 2         TEXT('September Sales')
A             OCTSALES     1ØS 2         TEXT('October Sales')
A             NOVSALES     1ØS 2         TEXT('November Sales')
A             DECSALES     1ØS 2         TEXT('December Sales')
```

Assume that the file is to be used in a program to help a company determine the end-of-year bonuses to be paid to the sales force. The bonuses are determined on a monthly basis by the sales for that month; anytime the monthly sales exceeds $50,000, the bonus for that month is one-half percent of the sales; otherwise, there is no bonus for that month. The company wants to calculate the total annual bonus for each salesperson, but also print the individual monthly bonuses. The figure below shows a printer spacing chart for the desired report.

To program a solution without using arrays would require writing a set of calculations that would be replicated 12 times, each time with a different set of fields representing each of the 12 months. With sales for different salespersons handled as elements of an array and with another array to store the salesperson's bonus for each of the 12 months, you can considerably shorten the calculations.

First, recall that we can define the 12 monthly sales as elements of an array by using a data structure. The Definition Specifications that follow illustrate the data structure, as well as define an additional array, Bonus, and some stand-alone work fields that we require for our solution.

```
*.. 1 ...+... 2 ...+... 3 ...+... 4 ...+... 5 ...+... 6 ...+... 7 ...+... 8 ...+... 9 ...+...10
DName++++++++++ETDsFrom+++To/L+++IDc.Keywords+++++++++++++++++++++++++++++++++Comments++++++++++
D* Data structure for converting sales fields to array elements.
D                 DS
D SlsAry                        10S 2 DIM(12)
D JanSales               1      10S 2
D FebSales              11      20S 2
D MarSales              21      30S 2
D AprSales              31      40S 2
D MaySales              41      50S 2
D JunSales              51      60S 2
D JulSales              61      70S 2
D AugSales              71      80S 2
D SepSales              81      90S 2
D OctSales              91     100S 2
D NovSales             101     110S 2
D DecSales             111     120S 2
D* Array for bonuses
D Bonus           S              6S 0 DIM(12)
D* Stand-alone work fields
D GrandTotal      S             11S 0
D TotBonus        S              8S 0
D I               S              2S 0
D* I is a loop counter and the index for the sales and bonus arrays.
```

Given the above array definitions, the calculations for solving our problem are relatively short, as shown below.

```
*.. 1 ...+... 2 ...+... 3 ...+... 4 ...+... 5 ...+... 6 ...+... 7 ...+... 8 ...+... 9 ...+...10
CLØNØ1Factor1++++++Opcode(E)+Extended-factor2+++++++++++++++++++++++++++++++++Comments++++++++++
CLØNØ1Factor1++++++Opcode(E)+Factor2++++++Result+++++++Len++D+HiLoEq....Comments++++++++++++
C* Specifications for calculating and printing bonuses for all salespersons in SalesFile.
C                 EVAL      GrandTotal = 0
C                 EXCEPT    Headings
C                 READ      SalesFile                                  90
C                 DOW       *IN90 = *OFF
C* Use DO to loop through the 12 sales figures for the salesperson.
C                 DO        12            I
C                 IF        SlsAry(I) > 50000
C                 EVAL (H)      Bonus(I) = SlsAry(I) * .005
C                 ELSE
C                 EVAL          Bonus(I) = 0
C                 ENDIF
C                 ENDDO
C                 XFOOT     Bonus         TotBonus
C                 EVAL      GrandTotal = GrandTotal + TotBonus
C                 IF        *INOF = *ON
C                 EXCEPT    Headings
C                 EVAL      *INOF = *OFF
C                 ENDIF
C                 EXCEPT    Detail
C                 READ      SalesFile                                  90
C                 ENDDO
C                 EXCEPT    TotalLine
C                 EVAL      *INLR = *ON
C                 RETURN
```

The beauty of handling data with arrays and variable indexes, as shown in the example, is that if there were 1,200 sales figures for each salesperson, instead of 12, the calculations to determine bonuses and totals would be no longer; the only required changes would be to increase the number of iterations of the DO loop from 12 to 1,200 and to increase the lengths of the work fields to avoid truncation.

Array Look-Ups

This chapter began with a discussion of tables and operation LOOKUP. LOOKUP also can be used to access arrays. There are two variants of the array LOOKUP: one that uses an index and one that doesn't.

If you simply want to know whether or not a value exists as an element in an array, but you don't need to access the element or know its location within the array, you can use LOOKUP without an index.

```
*.. 1 ...+... 2 ...+... 3 ...+... 4 ...+... 5 ...+... 6 ...+... 7 ...+... 8 ...+... 9 ...+...10
CLØNØ1Factor1++++++Opcode(E)+Factor2++++++Result+++++++Len++D+HiLoEq....Comments+++++++++++
CLØNØ1Factor1++++++Opcode(E)+Extended-factor2+++++++++++++++++++++++++++++Comments+++++++++++
C* This LOOKUP simply indicates whether or not an array element exists that matches Value.
C           Value         LOOKUP    Ary                                  50
C                         IF        *IN50 = *ON
C                         EXSR      ValueFound
C                         ELSE
C                         EXSR      NotFound
C                         ENDIF
```

If, on the other hand, you want to know not only whether a value exists in the array but also its location in the array, you need to use an index. To start the look-up at the beginning of the array, you must initialize the index to one prior to LOOKUP.

```
*.. 1 ...+... 2 ...+... 3 ...+... 4 ...+... 5 ...+... 6 ...+... 7 ...+... 8 ...+... 9 ...+...10
CLØNØ1Factor1++++++Opcode(E)+Extended-factor2+++++++++++++++++++++++++++++Comments+++++++++++
CLØNØ1Factor1++++++Opcode(E)+Factor2++++++Result+++++++Len++D+HiLoEq....Comments+++++++++++
C* This LOOKUP, if successful, assigns index I the value that points to the array element
C* whose value matches Value.
C                         EVAL      I = 1
C           Value         LOOKUP    Ary(I)                                    50
```

If indicator 50 is on following the look-up, it means that the value was found in the array. Moreover, index I's value points to the location of the array element with the same value as Value. Thus, if the third element of Ary had the same value as Value, after the LOOKUP index I would be three.

To understand how arrays and the LOOKUP operation can be used to extract data from a "table" (in the popular sense), let's reconsider our three-column table of state codes, state names, and sales tax rates discussed earlier in this chapter. Let's assume that the three columns of data are entered successively at the end of our program, as shown below, but as compile-time *arrays*, rather than compile-time *tables*.

```
*.. 1 ...+... 2 ...+... 3 ...+... 4 ...+... 5 ...+... 6 ...+... 7 ...+... 8 ...+... 9 ...+...10
OFilename++DAddNØ1NØ2NØ3Excnam+++.......................................Comments+++++++++++
O                  ...
O                  ...
**CTDATA Code
AK
AL
AR
AZ
...
**CTDATA Name
Alaska
Alabama
Arkansas
Arizona
...
**CTDATA Rate
ØØØØ
Ø4ØØ
ØØØØ
Ø5ØØ
...
```

The Definition Specifications for these arrays would be identical to those used in the RPG IV table solution, except for the data names.

```
*.. 1 ...+... 2 ...+... 3 ...+... 4 ...+... 5 ...+... 6 ...+... 7 ...+... 8 ...+... 9 ...+...10
DName++++++++++ETDsFrom+++To/L+++IDc.Keywords++++++++++++++++++++++++++++++Comments+++++++++++
D* Three arrays independently defined.
D Code           S              2    DIM(5Ø) PERRCD(1) CTDATA ASCEND
D Name           S             14    DIM(5Ø) PERRCD(1) CTDATA
D Rate           S              4  4 DIM(5Ø) PERRCD(1) CTDATA
```

Using arrays, however, the calculations would require only a single LOOKUP of the primary array to determine the appropriate value for the index; you can then use that index to point to the corresponding element in each additional "table" column.

```
*.. 1 ...+... 2 ...+... 3 ...+... 4 ...+... 5 ...+... 6 ...+... 7 ...+... 8 ...+... 9 ...+...10
CLØNØ1Factor1++++++Opcode(E)+Extended-factor2+++++++++++++++++++++++++++++++Comments+++++++++++
CLØNØ1Factor1++++++Opcode(E)+Factor2++++++Result+++++++Len++D+HiLoEq....Comments+++++++++++
C* Look-up code based on CodeIn. If the look-up is successful, Name(I) will refer to the
C* correct state name and Rate(I) to the correct tax rate.
C                   EVAL      I = 1
C        CodeIn     LOOKUP    Code(I)                                  5Ø
C                   IF        *IN5Ø = *ON
C                   EVAL (H)  TaxDue = Amount * Rate(I)
C                   ELSE
C                   EXSR      BadCode
C                   ENDIF
C                   ...
```

Indicators as Array Elements

One special, predefined array exists in RPG IV: array *IN. *IN is an array of 99
one-position character elements that represent the indicators 01-99. Thus,
*IN(1) and *IN01 are both references to indicator 01. Note that the non-
numbered indicators (e.g, *INLR or *INOF) are not represented within this
array. The elements of *IN can contain only the character values '0' (*OFF)
or '1' (*ON). Any operations valid for an array of character elements are valid
to use with *IN. RPG IV programmers sometimes use this feature of indicators
to turn off or on a consecutive block of indicators in a single calculation.

```
*.. 1 ...+... 2 ...+... 3 ...+... 4 ...+... 5 ...+... 6 ...+... 7 ...+... 8 ...+... 9 ...+...10
CLØN01Factor1++++++Opcode(E)+Factor2++++++Result++++++++Len++D+HiLoEq....Comments+++++++++++
C* The following calculation turns off indicators 31-35.
C                   MOVEA     '00000'       *IN(31)
```

In general, it is best to avoid using this feature of RPG IV. It's easy to
make mistakes in its use, and it results in code that is less understandable
than other methods of manipulating indicator values.

Output with Arrays

When you specify a table name as part of an Output Specification, the current instance of the table (the value to which the table is positioned) prints.
In contrast, when you specify an array name to print, *all* the elements appear,
separated with two blanks, with the last element ending in the ending position specified for the array. Any editing associated with the array applies to
each element. Depending on the printer spacing chart you are following, you
may be able to use this shortcut; the alternative is to list each element of the
array individually, with an index, and give each its own ending position.

If you need to print all the elements of an array but require more than
two blanks separating the elements on the report, you can use an edit word
that includes blanks (&) to increase the distance between the elements. In the
following examples, array Ary stores seven numeric values (each of length
six with two decimal positions), which will be printed so that the last element ends in position 76.

```
*.. 1 ...+... 2 ...+... 3 ...+... 4 ...+... 5 ...+... 6 ...+... 7 ...+... 8 ...+... 9 ...+...10
O..............N01N02N03Field++++++++YB.End++PConstant/editword/DTformat++Comments+++++++++++
O* Given the specification below, all the elements of Ary will print, separated with two
O* spaces and containing commas.  The last element will end in position 76.
O                          ...
O                          Ary           1    76
O                          ...
O* Alternately, each element could be listed individually.
O                          ...
O                          Ary(1)        1    16
O                          Ary(2)        1    26
O                          Ary(3)        1    36
O                          ...
O                          Ary(7)        1    76
O                          ...
O* If you need more than two blanks between elements, you can still use the array
O* name without an index by using an edit word.  The code below results in 3 blanks
O* separating Ary's elements.
O                          ...
O                          Ary                76 '&  ,  0.  '
```

Chapter Summary

You can use both tables and arrays to store sets of similar elements in RPG IV. You can load both tables and arrays at compile time, from data hard-coded at the end of the source program, or at pre-execution time, from data contained in a table file. You can also load arrays during runtime, from values contained on input records or as the result of calculations.

RPG IV tables are useful for performing look-ups with the LOOKUP operation. You can look up a value in one table to extract information from a parallel table, provided that table is named as the result of the LOOKUP operation. Using a table name in a calculation or printing operation causes the element to which the table is currently positioned to be used.

Arrays offer more flexibility and power than tables. You can explicitly reference an individual array element by using an index, or you can manipulate the array as a whole by using the array name without an index. You may use a numeric literal or field as an index to point to a specific array element. You can use three special RPG IV operations with arrays: XFOOT, SORTA, and MOVEA. You also can use LOOKUP with one array to extract information from other arrays parallel to that array. However, you most often use arrays to simplify processing of identical kinds of data or to manipulate portions of data fields.

You can access RPG IV's numbered indicators as elements of a built-in array, *IN, although this technique is not generally recommended. Specifying an array name and an end position on Output Specifications causes all the array elements to print, separated by two spaces, with the last element finishing in the designated end position.

Terms

alternating format	data structure	range table
array	index	runtime array
compile-time array	overlay	table
compile-time table	pre-runtime array	table look-up
crossfooting	pre-runtime (pre-execution)	volatile
**CTDATA record	table	

Discussion/Review Questions

1. If you wanted to describe the phone book as a table in RPG IV, how many tables would you define?

2. If a program uses tables, what additional specification form is required and where should these specifications appear in your program?

3. What is the difference between the "number of entries per table" and "number of entries per record" entries on the Definition Specifications?

4. What factors would you use to determine whether to hard-code a table or store the table data in a disk file?

5. What are the two techniques that can be used to define tables of more than two columns? What are the advantages and disadvantages of each technique?

6. What is a "range" table? Give an example of one.

7. When would you need to use keyword FROMFILE as part of a table or array definition on the Definition Specifications?

8. What are RPG IV's requirements for naming tables and arrays? What practical considerations add additional constraints to array names?

9. What do the terms *compile time, pre-runtime,* and *runtime* refer to when used to describe tables or arrays?

10. Give four ways that arrays can obtain data values.

11. What is the difference between using a table name and an array name (without an index) in a calculation (i.e., what data is being represented)?

12. How are the effects of standard arithmetic operations dependent upon whether array elements or arrays are entered as factors in the calculations?

13. What RPG IV operations are used only with arrays? What does each do?

14. Compare and contrast how MOVE, MOVEL, and MOVEA work in RPG IV.

15. Describe appropriate uses for tables and arrays. How would you decide which (if either) to use in a given application?

Exercises

1. You are writing an application to process orders. Records include date ordered in YYMMDD format, but you want the *name* of the month ordered, rather than the number of the month, to print. a) Show how you would hard-code data for a two-column table relating month number to month name. b) Code the Definition Specifications for these compile-time tables, matching the definitions to the way in which you've laid out your data. c) Write the calculations needed to look up OrdMonth(order month) in one table to extract the appropriate month name.

2. Modify your work in Exercise 1 by using arrays, rather than tables. Don't require your program to do more work than needed. (*Hint:* Can you think of a way to obtain the correct month name without performing a look-up?)

3. An input file contains records of sales. Each record represents one week of sales, with seven sales figures, each 10 with two decimal positions, in positions 21-90 of the input record. Code the Definition, Input, and portion of the Calculation Specifications needed to generate a weekly sales total and also to separately accumulate sales for each day of the week as input to the file is processed.

4. Assume the IRS wants you to use the following table to determine how much salary to withhold for federal taxes:

| | Tax Rate | |
If weekly salary is	Single	Married
0- $150	.18	.15
$151- $250	.25	.18
$251- $500	.28	.25
$501-$1000	.31	.28
over $1000	.33	.31

a) Hard-code this information so it can be handled with RPG IV tables. b) Define the Definition Specifications to reflect your hard coding. c) Write the calculations needed to assign the proper value to field Rate based on Salary (salary) and MrtStatus (marital status: S = single, M = married) of an employee's input record. d) Modify your code as needed if the table data were stored in a table file, rather than hard-coded.

Programming Assignments

1. Wexler University wants a program that will produce a student grade report and assign final grades. An input file, WUEXAMP (Appendix D) contains student records with five exam grades per student.

   The program will need to calculate an average exam grade for each student. The school also wants to know class averages for each exam and for the course as a whole. The program should also assign final grades based on the following criteria:

Average Grade	Final Grade
93 - 100	A
88 - 92	BA
83 - 87	B
75 - 82	CB
70 - 74	C
65 - 69	DC
60 - 64	D
< 60	F

   The desired report layout is shown below. Notice that the students' first and last names are to print together, with one blank between the last character of the first name and the first character of the last name.

```
         1         2         3         4         5         6         7         8         9         1 0
123456789012345678901234567890123456789012345678901234567890123456789012345678901234567890123456789012345678 90
 1    XX/XX/XX              WEXLER U. STUDENT GRADE REPORT          PAGE XX0X
 2
 3                                      EXAM EXAM EXAM EXAM EXAM   AVG.  FINAL
 4   STUDENT ID.         NAME            1    2    3    4    5    GRADE GRADE
 5
 6  XXX-XX-XXXX   XXXXXXXXXXXXXXXXXXXXXXXXXX  X0X  X0X  X0X  X0X  X0X   X0X   XX
 7  XXX-XX-XXXX   XXXXXXXXXXXXXXXXXXXXXXXXXX  X0X  X0X  X0X  X0X  X0X   X0X   XX
 8  XXX-XX-XXXX   XXXXXXXXXXXXXXXXXXXXXXXXXX  X0X  X0X  X0X  X0X  X0X   X0X   XX
 9
10               CLASS AVERAGE:             X0X  X0X  X0X  X0X  X0X   X0X
11
```

2. CompuSell wants you to write an interactive program that can be used by its shipping department to calculate shipping charges based on destination and weight of package.

   Two files of table information related to shipping exist: the Zip/Zone Table File (CSZPZNP) and the Charges Table File (CSCHGP). These files are described in Appendix D.

   Your program should allow a user to enter the first three digits of the zip code of a package's destination and the pounds and ounces of the package weight, and based on the entered information, calculate the appropriate shipping charge and display the charge to the user.

   Note that any package with ounces greater than zero should get charged the rate appropriate for the next pound. That is, a package weighing 7 pounds 3 ounces should get charged at the 8-pound rate.

Programming Assignments Continued

Programming Assignments continued

3. Wexler University wants you to write a program to score student tests. Each test is a 50-question, multiple-choice test. (Possible answers for each question are A, B, C, D, and E). Student responses are scanned and stored in a database file WUTSTP. The format of these records is described in Appendix D; each record includes information about the course, the test, the student, and the student's test responses. The file is keyed on Course ID, Test, and Section number. An answer key to each test is prepared and stored in database file WUKEYP (Appendix D); this file is keyed on Course ID and Test.

There will be several sets of tests, possibly from different sections and different courses, in WUTSTP. The same key may be used to grade different sections' tests, provided the test number and course ID of the key record of WUKEYP matches those of the records to be graded.

You want to grade every record in WUTSTP; there may be keys in WUKEYP that don't match any of the current batches of tests, but there should not be any student test that does not have a corresponding key in WUKEYP.

Use arrays to do the scoring. Then use a compile-time table to assign letter grades. The table should reflect the following scale:

Score	Letter Grade
< = 29	F
30 - 34	D
35 - 39	C
40 - 44	B
45 - 50	A

Prepare a report as shown below. Start each new section and/or each new test on a new page with all headings. If a section takes more than one page, repeat all headings on successive pages. Note that an average grade for each section is required.

```
          1         2         3         4         5         6         7         8         9         10
 1234567890123456789012345678901234567890123456789012345678901234567890123456789012345678901234567890
 1                    WEXLER U. GRADE REPORT
 2
 3  COURSE ID:  XXXXXX    TEST:  XXXX              DATE:   XX/XX/XX
 4
 5  SECTION:   XXXXXX   INSTRUCTOR:  XXXXXXXXXXXXXXX
 6
 7          STUDENT ID              TEST SCORE      LETTER GRADE
 8         XXX-XX-XXXX                 ØX               X
 9         XXX-XX-XXXX                 ØX               X
10         XXX-XX-XXXX                 ØX               X
11
12             SECTION AVERAGE         ØX
13
```

4. GTC, a local telephone company, wants you to write a program to calculate costs of calls as part of a billing system. A Calls Transaction File (GTCLSP) is generated automatically as part of the company's switching system. Call data accumulates in this file during the course of the month. At the end of the month, the file is first used with this program and then used to print bills before being cleared for the next month's accumulation of call

Programming Assignments Continued

Programming Assignments continued

data. Note that the file includes a cost-of-call field, but the value for that field will be supplied by this program when it updates each record. When the record is read initially, this field contains zeros.

Cost of calls depends on two things: the area code and exchange of the number called, and the time of the call. Base daytime rates for all area codes and exchanges are contained in a rates file, GTCRATP. Each record contains the cost for the first minute and the per-minute charge for each additional minute for calls made to that area code/exchange. This file should be loaded into a table that can be used to look up the appropriate charges for each call in the calls file.

Time of call affects cost, based on the table below. This table should be incorporated into a hard-coded table so it can be used for look-ups during processing. The percents are *discounts* to the standard costs contained in the rate file.

Hours	Mon-Fri	Sat	Sun
8:00 a.m. - 4:59 p.m.	0%	60%	60%
5:00 p.m. - 10:59 p.m.	35%	60%	35%
11:00 p.m. - 7:59 a.m.	60%	60%	60%

Notice that the time of call in the calls file is based on a 24-hour clock, such that 2:15 p.m. would be stored as 1415. To apply the discount, you need to know the day of the week. The algorithm below first converts a date to a sequential century-day and then from that figure derives a value (day-of-week) from 1-7 to represent the day of week from Sunday thru Saturday, respectively. Where the algorithm says INTEGER, truncate the value to a whole number (no rounding); where it says REMAINDER, use the MVR operation.

```
IF month > 2
        Add 1 to month
ELSE
        Add 13 to month
        Subtract 1 from year
ENDIF
century-day = INTEGER(years * 365.25) + INTEGER(month * 30.6) + days – 63
day-of-week = REMAINDER(century-day / 7) + 1
```

Your program is to determine the cost of each call in GTCLSP, based on the area code and exchange of the *called* number and the time of the call; each call record should be updated with the cost calculated by your program.

Chapter 9

Advanced Data Definition

Chapter Overview

This chapter provides you with more detail about RPG IV data types and shows you how to perform "date arithmetic" using date operations. The chapter also covers a variety of RPG IV features that let you define data in ways that facilitate data manipulation, error trapping and debugging, and program maintenance. Although all the topics included in this chapter deal with data, they are basically independent, stand-alone concepts. You can incorporate any or all of these concepts within your programs to improve your programming style.

Data Types Revisited

You are already familiar with the use of Definition Specifications for defining stand-alone work fields, tables, and arrays. Definition Specifications consolidate the definitions of all data items used by your program within a single place within your source code for ease of understanding and program maintenance.

RPG IV, as you recall, requires that you define each data item used within your program by giving it a name, declaring its **data type**, and allocating a fixed amount of memory for storing that data item's value. In Chapter 5 you learned about some of the data types available in RPG IV: the character data type and the three numeric data types — zoned decimal, binary, and packed decimal. RPG IV supports additional data types, organized within data classes. The table below shows all of RPG IV's data classes, the data types within those classes, and the code used to signal the data type within a definition.

Data Class	Data Type	Code
Character	Fixed length	A
Numeric	Zoned decimal	S
	Packed decimal	P
	Binary	B
Date	Date	D
Time	Time	T
Timestamp	Timestamp	Z
DBCS	Graphic	G
Basing pointer	Basing pointer	*
Procedure pointer	Procedure pointer	*

Data Types and Time

Three data types exist for dealing with time: **date**, **time**, and **timestamp**. Each data type has a default length and display format (*ISO), based on the International Standards Organization standards. The default display format for type date (D) is a 10-byte long field with format yyyy-mm-dd. Time (T) has a default length of 8 bytes, with format hh.mm.ss. The default display format for timestamp (Z) has a length of 26 bytes, with format yyyy-mm-dd-hh.mm.ss.mmmmmm.

The date and time data types allow alternate display formats to the defaults. Date, for instance, supports eight different formats, including *MDY (mm/dd/yy), *DMY (dd/mm/yy), and *EUR (dd.mm.yyyy). Time supports five different formats, including *HMS (hh:mm:ss) and *USA (hh:mm AM or hh:mm PM). To specify an alternate format for a date field, use keyword DATFMT on the Definition Specification with the desired format code (e.g., *MDY, *EUR) as the parameter value; for time fields, use keyword TIMFMT and the desired format code (e.g., *HMS, *USA). (You can also change the default display format of date and time fields for the program as a whole, or for all fields of date or time type within a file: Refer to IBM's *ILE RPG/400 Reference* (SC09-1526) for complete instructions about how to do this.)

Each display format includes a default separator character: for example, the separator character for the *ISO date format is –. To further complicate matters, several of the formats let you change the separator character by specifying an alternate separator. For example, acceptable separator characters for the *MDY and *DMY date formats are the slash (/), the hyphen (–), the period (.), the comma (,), and the ampersand (& — displays as a blank). Acceptable separator characters for the *HMS time format are the colon (:), the period (.), the comma (,), and the ampersand (& — for blank). To change from the default separator, simply insert the separator character you want to use after the format code (e.g., *MDY– or *HMS,).

When defining data items with any of the date/time data types, you do not need to specify length, because the length is determined by the format associated with the field. The code below illustrates how to define these kinds of fields. Note that some of the definitions use the default display formats while others specify alternate formats.

```
*.. 1 ...+... 2 ...+... 3 ...+... 4 ...+... 5 ...+... 6 ..+... 7 ...+... 8 ...+... 9 ...+...10
DName++++++++++ETDsFrom+++To/L+++IDc.Keywords+++++++++++++++++++++++++++++Comments+++++++++++
D* Definitions of stand-alone fields with various date/time data types.
D
D* Define a date field in default format (*ISO):  e.g., 1995-03-15.
D TodaysDate      S              D
D* Define a date field in *YMD format, with the default separator (/):  95/03/15.
D DueDateA        S              D    DATFMT(*YMD)
D* Define a date field in *YMD format with an alternate separator (.):  95.03.15.
D DueDateB        S              D    DATFMT(*YMD.)
D
D* Define a time field in default format (*ISO):  e.g., 14.45.24.
D TimeA           S              T
D* Define a time field in *USA format: 2:45 PM.
D TimeB           S              T    TIMFMT(*USA)
D* Define a time field in *HMS format with an alternate separator (blank): 14 45 24.
D TimeC           S              T    TIMFMT(*HMS&)
D
D*Define a timestamp field:  e.g., 1995-03-15-06.15.37.000000.
D TimeStmp        S              Z
```

Date/Time Operations

Three operations let you use these data types in calculations involving time and/or dates. You code the operations on standard Calculation Specifications. All three operations use the duration codes *YEARS (or *Y), *MONTHS (or *M), *DAYS (or *D), *HOURS (or *H), *MINUTES (or *MN), *SECONDS (or *S), and *MSECONDS (or *MS) to indicate which portion of the date/time data you want to manipulate. The operations are detailed below.

ADDDUR (Add Duration)

The ADDDUR operation lets you add a duration coded in factor 2 to the time specified in factor 1 and store the answer in the date, time, or time-stamp field specified as the result field. If factor 1 is blank, the factor 2 duration is simply added to the result field. If factor 1 is present, it may contain any data item representing one of the three time data types, but its type must match that of the result field.

Factor 2 must contain an integer field (or literal), which represents the number to add, and one of the seven duration codes listed above, which indicates the kind of duration the number represents. You separate these two portions of factor 2 with a colon (:). If the numeric portion of factor 2 represents a negative value, the duration is subtracted, rather than added.

The following code illustrates the use of ADDDUR. Assume that fields BillDate, StartDate, and EndDate were defined as type D (date), and fields StartTime and EndTime were defined as type T (time).

```
*.. 1 ...+... 2 ...+... 3 ...+... 4 ...+... 5 ...+... 6 ...+... 7 ...+... 8 ...+... 9 ...+...10
CLØN01Factor1++++++Opcode(E)+Factor2++++++Result+++++++Len++D+HiLoEq....Comments++++++++++++
C* Add 30 days to BillDate to determine DueDate.
C     BillDate      ADDDUR    30:*DAYS       DueDate
C* Add field Min, containing a number of minutes, to StartTime to determine EndTime.
C     StartTime     ADDDUR    Min:*MN        EndTime
C* Add 5 years to DueDate.
C                   ADDDUR    5:*YEARS       DueDate
C* Subtract 5 months from EndDate to get StartDate.
C     EndDate       ADDDUR    -5:*MONTHS     StartDate
```

SUBDUR (Subtract Duration)

Operation SUBDUR has two uses: One is to subtract a date/time duration from a date/time value (similar to ADDDUR); the second is to calculate the duration between two date/time units. To subtract a factor 2 duration from a date/time data item in factor 1 and store the answer in the result field, code the operation the same as you would ADDDUR. To calculate the duration between two date/time units, place data items of compatible types in both factor 1 and factor 2 and place an integer receiving field, followed by a duration code that denotes the unit of time involved in the operation, in the result field. Again, a colon (:) separates these two subfactors. Both uses of SUBDUR are shown in the code below.

```
*.. 1 ...+... 2 ...+... 3 ...+... 4 ...+... 5 ...+... 6 ...+... 7 ...+... 8 ...+... 9 ...+...10
CLØN01Factor1++++++Opcode(E)+Factor2++++++Result+++++++Len++D+HiLoEq....Comments++++++++++++
C* Subtract 30 days from DueDate to determine BillDate.
C     DueDate       SUBDUR    30:*DAYS       BillDate
C* Subtract 5 years from DueDate.
C                   SUBDUR    5:*Y           DueDate
C* Subtract a birthdate from today to get age in years.
C     TodayDate     SUBDUR    BirthDate      Age:*YEARS
C* Determine the number of days left to study for a test.
C     ExamDate      SUBDUR    TodayDate      CramTime:*D
```

EXTRCT (Extract Part of a Date/Time Item)

EXTRCT, the third operation for manipulating dates and times, extracts a portion of a date, time, or timestamp data item and stores it in a result field, which can be any numeric or character receiving field. The factor 2 date/time data item must be coupled with a duration code to signal which portion of the date/time unit is to be extracted. Factor 1 is always blank for EXTRCT operations.

```
*.. 1 ...+... 2 ...+... 3 ...+... 4 ...+... 5 ...+... 6 ...+... 7 ...+... 8 ...+... 9 ...+...10
CLØN01Factor1++++++Opcode(E)+Factor2++++++Result+++++++Len++D+HiLoEq....Comments++++++++++++
C* Determine the birthyear of a birthdate.
C                   EXTRCT    BirthDate:*Y BirthYear
C*Extract the month of a loan.
C                   EXTRCT    LoanDate:*M  LoanMonth
```

If you want to use any of the date data types with literals, you must use what IBM calls a **typed literal**. A typed literal begins with the code representing the data type of the literal; the code, in turn, is followed by the literal value enclosed in apostrophes. The value should include the appropriate separator characters. Examples of typed literals are

D'1995-03-15'	(date data type)
T'08.56.20'	(time data type)
Z'1995-03-15-08.58.000000'	(timestamp data type)

The following example demonstrates how you can use date/time literals in calculations:

```
*.. 1 ...+... 2 ...+... 3 ...+... 4 ...+... 5 ...+... 6 ..+... 7 ...+... 8 ...+... 9 ...+...10
CL0N01Factor1++++++Opcode(E)+Factor2++++++Result+++++++Len++D+HiLoEq....Comments+++++++++++
C* Calculate times for late arrival or early leaving.
C      T'08:00:00'  ADDDUR    15:*MN        LateArrive
C      T'16:30:00'  SUBDUR    15:*MN        EarlyLeave
```

RPG IV lets you use EVAL to assign values to date/time fields, but you cannot use EVAL to perform date/time arithmetic with + and −; you must use ADDDUR and SUBDUR. RPG IV also supports operations MOVE, MOVEL, and MOVEA to move values between date/time data types and numeric or character fields. The rules for these movements depend on the kinds of data types involved in the move and can be somewhat complicated. Consult *ILE RPG/400 Reference* for details on how to use these operations.

RPG IV does not include an operation that determines the day of the week from a date field, but you can code a short routine that uses other RPG IV operations to perform this task. By comparing a given date with a known Sunday (e.g., December 31, 1899), you can determine the day of the week for any twentieth century (or later) date. The following code produces a number between 0 and 6 (to represent the weekdays from Sunday to Saturday) and demonstrates some of the date/time data type concepts described in this chapter:

```
*.. 1 ...+... 2 ...+... 3 ...+... 4 ...+... 5 ...+... 6 ..+... 7 ...+... 8 ...+... 9 ...+...10
DName++++++++++ETDsFrom+++To/L+++IDc.Keywords+++++++++++++++++++++++++++++++Comments+++++++++++
CL0N01Factor1++++++Opcode(E)+Extended-factor2+++++++++++++++++++++++++++++++Comments+++++++++++
CL0N01Factor1++++++Opcode(E)+Factor2++++++Result+++++++Len++D+HiLoEq....Comments+++++++++++
D* Fields needed for day-of-week identification.
D KnownDate       S              D
D ThisDate        S              D
D WorkField       S              5 0
D Weekday         S              1 0
C* Initialize KnownDate to December 31, 1899, using *ISO format.
C                   EVAL      KnownDate = D'1899-12-31'
C     ThisDate      SUBDUR    KnownDate     WorkField:*D         Calc. number of days
C                   DIV       7             WorkField            Calc. whole weeks
C                   MVR                     Weekday              Remainder = 0-6
```

The Graphic Data Type

DBCS (Double-Byte Character Set) is a graphic data type in which two bytes are required to represent any one character of the character set. This data type provides easy manipulation and display of graphic characters and is especially suited for languages whose character sets are more complicated than that of English, such as Japanese.

As you will recall, the original encoding scheme developed by IBM, EBCDIC, uses one 8-bit byte to represent a single character to the computer. Because each of the eight bits can be 0 or 1, there are 256 (or 2^8) different possible bit arrangements within a single byte. Therefore, EBCDIC has an upper limit of 256 different representable characters.

As computer technology advanced, however, and interest in manipulating and displaying graphics grew, the limits of single-byte character representation became apparent. Before RPG IV, IBM used a work-around to let the AS/400 represent graphic data. The data to be interpreted as graphic was surrounded by SO (shift-out, or hexadecimal value X'0E') and SI (shift-in, or X'01') to differentiate the enclosed characters from simple EBCDIC. With the DBCS data type, this work-around is no longer needed.

Data defined as DBCS (type G) will automatically be treated as graphic by the computer, with two bytes representing a single character. In the definition of a graphic data item, the length entry should reflect the number of graphic characters (not the number of single bytes) the field will store.

```
*.. 1 ...+... 2 ...+... 3 ...+... 4 ...+... 5 ...+... 6 ...+... 7 ...+... 8 ...+... 9 ...+...10
DName++++++++++ETDsFrom+++To/L+++IDc.Keywords+++++++++++++++++++++++++++++++++Comments++++++++++++
D* Sample definition of a DBCS field capable of storing 4 graphic characters.
D SampField      S              4G
```

You can manipulate DBCS data with EVAL, MOVE, and MOVEL operations, use it as the basis for tests of looping or branching, and write it to or read it from data files. In general, you can use DBCS data within a program in the same ways that you can use single-byte character data. Further investigation of the DBCS data type beyond this brief introduction falls outside the scope of this text. For more information about using DBCS data in RPG IV programs, refer to *ILE RPG/400 Reference*.

Pointer Data Types

RPG IV includes two kinds of pointer data types: **basing pointers** and **procedure pointers**. Both kinds of pointers are used to access storage that is allocated dynamically throughout the program, rather than once at the beginning of the program. Pointers store addresses of memory locations, rather than data values. A pointer tells you where to find something, not what is stored there. Basing pointers reference storage locations of variables, while procedure pointers reference storage locations of program modules.

You define pointers on Definition Specifications. You can define them explicitly as stand-alone data items, subfields of a data structure (discussed later in this chapter), or elements of an array. You can also implicitly define a based pointer by naming it as the pointer upon which an entity is "based." Some examples of pointer definitions are shown below. Both basing and procedure pointers are type *, with a fixed length of 16 bytes. To indicate a procedure pointer, you must include the keyword PROCPTR as part of its definition.

```
*.. 1 ...+... 2 ...+... 3 ...+... 4 ...+... 5 ...+... 6 ...+... 7 ...+... 8 ...+... 9 ...+...10
DName++++++++++ETDsFrom+++To/L+++IDc.Keywords++++++++++++++++++++++++++++++Comments+++++++++++
D* Definitions of pointers in RPG IV.
D Ptr1            S                   *
D Ptr2            S                   *     PROCPTR
D ArrayPtr        S                   *     DIM(10)
D BField          S                  8A     BASED(Ptr3)
```

In the above definitions, Ptr1 is a basing pointer and Ptr2 is a procedure pointer, as indicated by keyword PROCPTR. ArrayPtr is an array of 10 pointers. (Note that because all pointers are 16 bytes long, you do not need to include a length entry as part of a pointer's definition; the * in position 40 denoting the pointer data type suffices.) Ptr1, Ptr2, and ArrayPtr are explicitly defined pointers; Ptr3 is an implicitly defined pointer, because it is the pointer upon which the character field BField is "based."

BField is an example of a type of variable called a **based field**. You use based fields to access the *contents* of the address (or storage location) to which a basing pointer "points." The Definition Specifications below illustrate definitions of basing pointers and their associated based fields.

```
*.. 1 ...+... 2 ...+... 3 ...+... 4 ...+... 5 ...+... 6 ...+... 7 ...+... 8 ...+... 9 ...+...10
DName++++++++++ETDsFrom+++To/L+++IDc.Keywords++++++++++++++++++++++++++++++Comments+++++++++++
D* Definitions of pointers and based fields in RPG IV.
D Ptr1            S                   *
D FieldX          S                  8 2  BASED(Ptr1)
D FieldY          S                  6 2  BASED(Ptr2)
D Array1          S                 10    DIM(20) BASED(Ptr3)
D Array2          S                 20    DIM(10) BASED(Ptr4)
```

In the above example, FieldX and FieldY are both based fields, while Array1 and Array2 are based arrays. You can use FieldX to access the contents of any numeric storage location Ptr1 points to. FieldY accesses the contents of Ptr2's address. Array1 and Array2 access the contents of storage locations pointed to by Ptr3 and Ptr4, respectively.

Pointers acquire values in several ways. The default value of a pointer is *NULL, which means that the pointer does not point to any storage location. You can use EVAL to assign a pointer the value of another pointer. Moreover, you can use the **built-in function** %ADDR, which automatically returns the address of any field specified as its argument, to assign a value to a basing pointer.

Pointer concepts can be difficult to grasp for beginning programmers. To get a feeling for how based fields and basing pointers operate, study Figure 9.1.

Figure 9.1
Manipulating Basing Pointers
and Based Fields

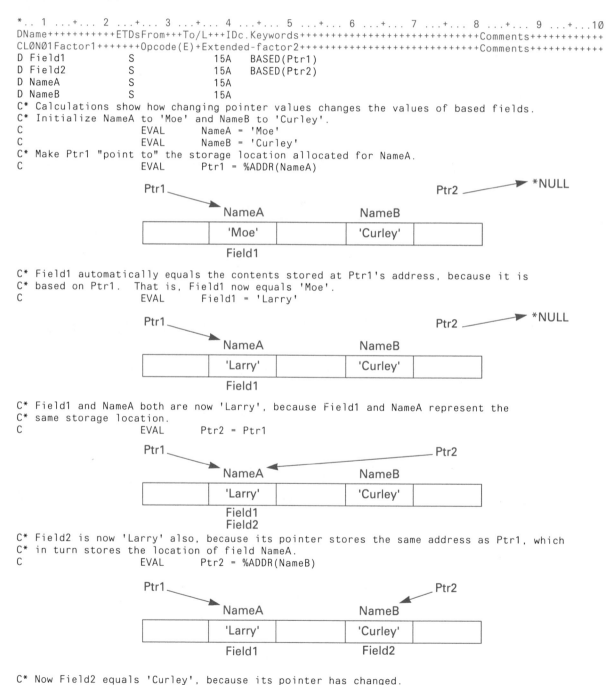

```
*.. 1 ...+... 2 ...+... 3 ...+... 4 ...+... 5 ...+... 6 ...+... 7 ...+... 8 ...+... 9 ...+...10
DName++++++++++ETDsFrom+++To/L+++IDc.Keywords+++++++++++++++++++++++++++++++Comments+++++++++++
CLØNØ1Factor1+++++++Opcode(E)+Extended-factor2++++++++++++++++++++++++++++++Comments+++++++++++
D Field1          S             15A    BASED(Ptr1)
D Field2          S             15A    BASED(Ptr2)
D NameA           S             15A
D NameB           S             15A
C* Calculations show how changing pointer values changes the values of based fields.
C* Initialize NameA to 'Moe' and NameB to 'Curley'.
C                   EVAL      NameA = 'Moe'
C                   EVAL      NameB = 'Curley'
C* Make Ptr1 "point to" the storage location allocated for NameA.
C                   EVAL      Ptr1 = %ADDR(NameA)
```

C* Field1 automatically equals the contents stored at Ptr1's address, because it is
C* based on Ptr1. That is, Field1 now equals 'Moe'.
```
C                   EVAL      Field1 = 'Larry'
```

C* Field1 and NameA both are now 'Larry', because Field1 and NameA represent the
C* same storage location.
```
C                   EVAL      Ptr2 = Ptr1
```

C* Field2 is now 'Larry' also, because its pointer stores the same address as Ptr1, which
C* in turn stores the location of field NameA.
```
C                   EVAL      Ptr2 = %ADDR(NameB)
```

C* Now Field2 equals 'Curley', because its pointer has changed.

You should see from Figure 9.1 that based variables have no storage assigned directly to them; instead, they dynamically access various storage locations depending on the value of their pointers. You can use a based entity within a program anywhere you can use a non-based data item — provided its pointer has been assigned some address (i.e., it is not *NULL).

Pointers have proven very useful for languages like C, but their use in RPG is not yet widespread because of the newness of this data type to the language. Chapter 12 discusses the use of procedure pointers.

Named Constants

You are already familiar with the concept of a constant (or literal). RPG IV lets you associate a data name with a constant so that you can reference the constant by its name throughout your program. Unlike a field, a **named constant** cannot change its value during program execution.

You define a named constant on Definition Specifications by entering its name anywhere in positions 7-21 (Name++++++++++); this name must follow the rules governing field names. C, for constant, must appear in position 24 (Ds) of the specification. You enter the value of the constant in positions 44-80 (Keywords+++...), or you can code the keyword CONST, followed by the constant enclosed within parentheses. Enter numeric constant values with a decimal point or sign if appropriate, but never with commas. Enclose character constant values within apostrophes and express date/time constants as typed literals.

A named constant can be at most 1,024 bytes long; a numeric constant can contain up to 30 decimal positions. To enter a named constant too long to fit on a single line, continue the value onto the Keywords area (positions 44-80) of one or more Definition Specification continuation lines. Recall that a hyphen (−) at the end of a line to be continued indicates that the constant continues in the first position of the Keywords area of the continuation line. A plus sign (+) signals that the constant resumes with the first non-blank character in the continuation line.

```
*.. 1 ...+... 2 ...+... 3 ...+... 4 ...+... 5 ...+... 6 ...+... 7 ...+... 8 ...+... 9 ...+...10
DName++++++++++ETDsFrom+++To/L+++IDc.Keywords++++++++++++++++++++++++++++++++Comments+++++++++++
D.....................................Keywords-continuation+++++++++++++++++Comments+++++++++++
D* Examples of valid named constants.
D FICA            C                   CONST(.0751)
D*
D Pi              C                   3.142
D*
D ExVicePres      C                   CONST('Dan Quayle')
D*
D LongWord        C                   'ANTIDISESTABLISHMENTARIANISM'
D*
D Example         C                   CONST('This long constant has -
D                                     blanks where you would expect them-
D                                      to appear in a sentence.')
D*
D PhoneEdtWd      C                   '(   )    -    '
D*
D IndpnDay        C                   D'1776-07-04'
```

Once you have defined a named constant, you can use it in calculations appropriate to its type, or as a constant or edit word in the Output Specifications. The value of a named constant is fixed; you cannot change it during the course of program execution.

Named constants have three primary uses. The most obvious is to let you use within your calculations a value that is too long to directly enter as a literal in factor 1 or factor 2 on the Calculation Specifications. A second use of named constants is to define an edit word that is to be applied to several different output fields. By defining the edit word once as a named constant, you can use it repeatedly on the Output Specifications simply by entering the constant's name, instead of entering the edit word itself.

Perhaps the most important advantage of named constants is that they let you define constants in one place near the beginning of your program, rather than coding them as literals throughout your calculations. This practice is a standard of good programming, because it facilitates maintenance programming. If a value, such as FICA rate, needs to be changed, it is much easier and less error-prone to locate the named constant and change its value in that one place, rather than to search through an entire program looking for every calculation in which the literal value .0751 occurs.

LIKE (Field Definition)

RPG IV lets you define one field's length and type by referencing a second field that provides the definition; that is, it lets you say that one field is "like" another field. This practice can help simplify and standardize your work field definitions, and more importantly, it can also make program maintenance more efficient.

The field being defined appears anywhere in positions 7-21 (Name++++++++++) of the Definition Specification. If it is a stand-alone field, code an S in position 24 (Ds). You include the field providing the definition as a parameter of keyword LIKE, coded in positions 44-80 (Keywords+++...). The field providing the definition can itself be defined internally or externally to the program. It can be a field, an array, or a table; if it is an array or a table, the attributes of one of the elements of the array or table provide the definition for the new field.

```
*.. 1 ...+... 2 ...+... 3 ...+... 4 ...+... 5 ...+... 6 ...+... 7 ...+... 8 ...+... 9 ...+...10
DName++++++++++ETDsFrom+++To/L+++IDc.Keywords+++++++++++++++++++++++++++++++Comments++++++++++++
D NewField         S                 LIKE(OldField)
```

The specification above defines NewField by giving it the type, length, and decimal positions (if type is numeric) of OldField. A variant of this basic format lets you lengthen or shorten the field being defined by entering a "signed" number (e.g., +4, –3), right-adjusted within positions 33-39 (To/L+++), to indicate that the field being defined should be larger or smaller than the defining field. The entered number signals the extent of the increase (+) or decrease (–) in field length. You cannot change the number of decimal positions of the field being defined.

Assume you are writing a payroll program and that Gross is an externally defined salary field. As part of your program, you need to define fields to store NetPay, FedTax, and StateTax, as well as four accumulators for storing grand totals for each of the above four fields. The example below shows how you could use LIKE to define the needed data items.

```
*.. 1 ...+... 2 ...+... 3 ...+... 4 ...+... 5 ...+... 6 ...+... 7 ...+... 8 ...+... 9 ...+...10
DName++++++++++ETDsFrom+++To/L+++IDc.Keywords++++++++++++++++++++++++++++++Comments+++++++++++
D NetPay          S                       LIKE(Gross)
D FedTax          S                -2     LIKE(Gross)
D StateTax        S                -2     LIKE(Gross)
D TotalGross      S                +4     LIKE(Gross)
D TotalNet        S                +4     LIKE(NetPay)
D TotalFdTax      S                +4     LIKE(FedTax)
D TotalStTax      S                +4     LIKE(StateTax)
```

This example illustrates the value of defining fields with LIKE for easy program maintenance. Assume that the payroll program containing these definitions is put into production, and that, after a few years, inflation causes salaries to become so high that the original definition for Gross is too small. Accordingly, you modify the definition of Gross in the database file to make it large enough to hold new salary figures.

If you had defined the work fields in this program without using LIKE, and instead had given each an absolute fixed length, you would need to carefully check the program's field definitions and manually modify any work field whose length needs to be increased. But because you used LIKE for those work fields, all you need to do is recompile the program; the work field lengths will be adjusted automatically based on the new length of Gross.

Another common use of LIKE is in the definition of display fields for interactive applications. Rather than directly referencing database fields within a display file, many programmers use work fields in their screen definitions to handle screen input and output; then, they transfer the data values between the work fields and the database fields within their RPG IV programs. By using LIKE to define an alternate field for each database field to be displayed, the programmer assures that any future changes to the database field definitions will not create maintenance problems for programs containing such display fields.

Data Structures

You have already extensively used stand-alone fields for defining work fields, tables, and arrays. **Data structures** represent an additional option for defining data within RPG IV. Data structures can give you flexibility in your handling of data by letting you subdivide fields into subfields, restructure records with different field layouts, change field data types, and add a second dimension to arrays. Thinking of a data structure as a contiguous portion of memory, which is then subdivided and referenced in different ways by the data structure's subfields, can help you conceptualize how data structures work.

You were introduced to data structures in Chapter 8 as a method of redefining externally described fields as elements of a runtime array. This section of the text will extend your understanding of how to define and use data structures. Although you can define data structures externally, this discussion focuses on program-defined data structures, because that is the kind used most often by RPG IV programmers.

Simple Data Structures

You use Definition Specifications to define data structures. DS, coded in positions 24-25 (Ds), signals the beginning of a data structure. You also may enter a name for the data structure in positions 7-21 (Name+++++++++++); this name entry is optional, but it is required if you plan to reference the data structure as a whole elsewhere in your program. Data structure names follow the same rules as field names. Although you can enter the length of the entire data structure in positions 33-39 (To/L+++) of the DS line, this entry is optional. If you omit it, the system derives the length of the structure as a whole from the lengths of its subfields.

Subfields comprising the data structure follow the DS header line. Define each subfield entry by giving it a name (positions 7-21). The name can float within its prescribed positions to make the hierarchical layout of the data structure easily visible. Two methods exist for specifying the length of a subfield, which you can also conceptualize as the location of the subfield within the data structure as a whole. The first method involves using positions 26-32 (From+++) and positions 33-39 (To/L+++) to indicate the beginning and ending positions of the subfield within the data structure. This method, called *absolute notation*, is similar to the method you used to define program-described input records in the beginning chapters of this text. The second method entails leaving the From+++ entry blank and entering the subfield's length in the To/L+++ positions, an approach called *length notation*. These alternative methods are demonstrated below.

```
*.. 1 ...+... 2 ...+... 3 ...+... 4 ...+... 5 ...+... 6 ...+... 7 ...+... 8 ...+... 9 ...+...10
DName++++++++++ETDsFrom+++To/L+++IDc.Keywords+++++++++++++++++++++++++++++++Comments+++++++++++
D* Defining subfields of a data structure using absolute notation.
D OptName         DS
D   SubfieldA                  1      3 0
D   SubfieldB                  4      8 2
D* Defining the same structure using length notation.
D OptName         DS
D   SubfieldA                         3 0
D   SubfieldB                         5 2
```

Regardless of the method used, numeric subfields require a decimal position entry in positions 41-42 (Dc), as shown above. Code the data type of the subfield in position 40 (I). If type is blank, the default is packed decimal for numeric fields (fields with a decimal position entry) and character for fields with a blank decimal position entry.

Subfields can be unique to the data structure itself, or they can be fields defined elsewhere in the program — as part of an input record, for example. If defined elsewhere, the two definitions must match, because they define the same data item and reference the same area of memory. A subfield can itself be an array, or it can be defined in terms of another field by using keyword LIKE.

The locations of subfields within a data structure can overlap, and the same position within a data structure can fall within the location of several subfields. When using absolute notation to define subfields, such overlapping is clearly indicated by the From and To position entries.

As an illustration of the concept of overlapping, or defining subfields within subfields, assume that your externally described input file contains fields FirstName (15 bytes) and Phone (10 digits). Your program needs to work with just the initial of the first name and with the area code, exchange, and local portions of the phone number as separate data items. Data structures let you easily access the data that way.

```
*.. 1 ...+... 2 ...+... 3 ...+... 4 ...+... 5 ...+... 6 ...+... 7 ...+... 8 ...+... 9 ...+...10
DName++++++++++ETDsFrom+++To/L+++IDc.Keywords+++++++++++++++++++++++++++++++Comments++++++++++++
D* Data structures to "split up" input fields into subfields.
D                 DS
D FirstName              1     15
D   Initial              1      1
D                 DS
D Phone                  1     10  0
D   AreaCode             1      3  0
D   Exchange             4      6  0
D   LocalNbr             7     10  0
```

Because the data structure subfields FirstName and Phone are identical to fields of the input record, each time a record is read those values will be stored in the data structure. Subfield Initial will contain the first letter of the value of FirstName, and the phone number of Phone will be broken into three pieces accessible through subfields AreaCode, Exchange, and LocalNbr.

If we want to use length notation to describe the above data definition, we need a way of indicating that Initial is supposed to be a part of FirstName, rather than a subfield adjacent to it. RPG IV includes keyword OVERLAY to supplement length notation for this purpose. The format of the keyword is OVERLAY(name{:pos}). OVERLAY indicates that the subfield overlays the storage of "name," starting in the position within "name" indicated by "pos." Note that {:pos} indicates that the position entry is optional; if you omit it, OVERLAY defaults to the first position of "name." The code below reworks our example using length notation and OVERLAY.

```
*.. 1 ...+... 2 ...+... 3 ...+... 4 ...+... 5 ...+... 6 ..+.. 7 ...+... 8 ...+... 9 ...+...10
DName++++++++++ETDsFrom+++To/L+++IDc.Keywords+++++++++++++++++++++++++++++Comments+++++++++++
D* Data structures to "split up" input fields into subfields.
D                 DS
D FirstName                    15
D   Initial                     1      OVERLAY(FirstName)
D                 DS
D Phone                        10  0
D   AreaCode                    3  0   OVERLAY(Phone)
D   Exchange                    3  0   OVERLAY(Phone:4)
D   LocalNbr                    4  0   OVERLAY(Phone:7)
```

When using OVERLAY, the data name within the parentheses must be a
subfield already defined within the current data structure, and the subfield
being defined must be completely contained within the subfield it overlays. If
the data item within parentheses is an array, then OVERLAY applies to each
element of the array; thus, the overlaid subfield itself becomes an array, without any explicit dimensioning.

```
*.. 1 ...+... 2 ...+... 3 ...+... 4 ...+... 5 ...+... 6 ...+... 7 ...+... 8 ...+... 9 ...+...10
DName++++++++++ETDsFrom+++To/L+++IDc.Keywords+++++++++++++++++++++++++++++Comments+++++++++++
D* Given the definitions below, BigArray is an array of 300 elements, each 10 characters
D* long; because of the OVERLAY, SubArray is also an array of 300 elements, each 2
D* characters long.  Each element of SubArray is identical to the first two bytes
D* of the corresponding elements in BigArray.
D                 DS
D BigArray                     10      DIM(300)
D   SubArray                    2      OVERLAY(BigArray)
```

Another use of a data structure is to group fields from non-adjacent
locations on a data record. The physical file definition below contains fields
WareHouse and PartNbr, but the fields are not adjacent to one another in
the record.

```
*.. 1 ...+... 2 ...+... 3 ...+... 4 ...+... 5 ...+... 6 ...+... 7 ...+... 8
A..........T.Name+++++RLen++TDpB......Functions++++++++++++++++++++++++++++++
A          R PARTREC
A            PARTNBR          5  0
A            DESCRPT         20
A            QTY              7  0
A            WAREHOUSE        3  0
A          K PARTNBR
```

By defining the following data structure, you can access WareHouse
and PartNbr as a concatenation, or combined field, using the data structure
name WarePart.

```
*.. 1 ...+... 2 ...+... 3 ...+... 4 ...+... 5 ...+... 6 ..+... 7 ...+... 8 ...+... 9 ...+...10
DName++++++++++ETDsFrom+++To/L+++IDc.Keywords+++++++++++++++++++++++++++++Comments+++++++++++
D WarePart         DS
D   WareHouse                1   3  0
D   PartNbr                  4   8  0
```

Or consider another example. An externally described file contains student answers for a 100-problem, multiple-choice exam, and a second externally described file contains a key for the exam. You want to write a program to grade the exams, using array manipulation to compare each student's answers one at a time with the correct answer for that problem.

Because externally described files do not allow fields to be defined as arrays, the student answers have been defined as one large field, StdAns, while the answers on the key have been defined as one large field, KeyAns. A data structure can be used to convert these answer fields to arrays, preparatory to processing.

```
*.. 1 ...+... 2 ...+... 3 ...+... 4 ...+... 5 ...+... 6 ...+... 7 ...+... 8 ...+... 9 ...+...10
DName++++++++++ETDsFrom+++To/L+++IDc.Keywords++++++++++++++++++++++++++++++Comments++++++++++++
D* Data structure redefining StdAns and KeyAns as arrays, using mixed notation.
D                 DS
D StdAns                    1    100
D StdAry                    1    100    DIM(100)
D KeyAns                         100
D KeyAry                           1    OVERLAY(KeyAns) DIM(100)
```

Array StdAry provides a redefinition of field StdAns, using a technique we introduced in Chapter 8. Array KeyAry redefines KeyAns, using keyword OVERLAY. Note that the data structure uses both absolute notation and length notation to define its subfields. When length notation is used for an array, the length entry refers to the length of each element of the array — 1 for KeyAry in this example.

Although you can also overlap field definitions or include the same positions in several fields within program-defined records in a way that looks identical to data structure subfield definitions, the results of these kinds of definitions are different than for data structures. When you define overlapping fields in a program-defined input record, the system establishes a separate storage location for each field, so that changing the value of one field does not affect the value of any of the other fields. With data structures, in contrast, overlapping subfields reference the same memory locations.

```
*.. 1 ...+... 2 ...+... 3 ...+... 4 ...+... 5 ...+... 6 ...+... 7 ...+... 8 ...+... 9 ...+...10
I.......................Fmt+SPFrom+To+++DcField++++++++L1M1FrP1MnZr......Comments++++++++++++
IInRecord  NS
I                              1   15  FirstName
I                              1    1  Initial
```

Given the input record definition above, if FirstName were 'JACK' and our program assigned 'M' to Initial, FirstName would still remain 'JACK'. In contrast, a data structure's overlapping subfields reference the same area of storage, so that changing the value of one of the subfields also changes the value of any fields that overlap it. Thus, if the above were a data structure and FirstName was 'JACK', Initial would be 'J'; if we then assigned 'M' to Initial, FirstName would become 'MACK'.

Multiple-Occurrence Data Structures

You can define a "repeated" data structure by declaring it as a **multiple-occurrence data structure**. Keyword OCCURS signals this kind of data structure, and the numeric value you enter as the parameter of OCCURS determines how many times the structure is repeated in storage. (The maximum number of occurrences is 32,767). A multiple-occurrence data structure is similar to an array or a table, because it enables the computer to store many values for a given field name. But because the entire data structure is repeated, you can build a much more complex collection of elements than you can with RPG IV arrays or tables.

Consider the problem of the state tax data discussed in Chapter 8. We wanted to access the state name and the sales tax rate based on the state code, and we solved the problem two ways: once using tables, and once using arrays. Each solution required us to define three separate tables or arrays. As the number of data items increases, however, implementing such access through tables or arrays becomes more and more awkward. If, for example, you wanted to access the state's capital, its lowest zip code, and its highest zip code in addition to the state name and the tax rate (based on the state code), you would need to define six separate tables or arrays. If you used tables, you would also need to perform five separate look-ups to obtain the information. A data structure handles this problem more simply.

```
*.. 1 ...+... 2 ...+... 3 ...+... 4 ...+... 5 ...+... 6 ...+... 7 ...+... 8 ...+... 9 ...+...10
DName++++++++++ETDsFrom+++To/L+++IDc.Keywords+++++++++++++++++++++++++++++++++Comments+++++++++++
D DSState          DS                  OCCURS(50)
D   Code                        2
D   Name                       15
D   SalesTax                    4    4
D   Capital                    15
D   LowZip                      5    0
D   HiZip                       5    0
```

The data structure above occurs 50 times; each occurrence contains Code, Name, SalesTax, Capital, LowZip, and HiZip, which are the same names as the field names within file StatesFile. To load the data structure with the data from StatesFile, it is necessary to read each successive record from the file into a successive occurrence of the data structure. (This loading operation is illustrated in detail shortly.)

Multiple-occurrence data structures do not use subscripts or pointers directly to indicate which occurrence you want to work with. Instead, the OCCUR operation establishes which occurrence of the data structure is to be used next within the program.

In an OCCUR operation (coded on the standard Calculation Specification), factor 1 specifies which occurrence should be made active, while factor 2 contains the name of the data structure whose occurrence is being set. Factor 1 may contain a literal, a numeric field, or a named constant. Alternately, factor 1 may contain the name of a different multiple-occurrence data structure; in this case, the current occurrence of *that* data structure determines the occurrence of the data structure named in factor 2. (An optional indicator can be coded in positions 73-74 (Lo); this indicator comes on if the specified occurrence is outside the range of the data structure.)

```
*.. 1 ...+... 2 ...+... 3 ...+... 4 ...+... 5 ...+... 6 ...+... 7 ...+... 8 ...+... 9 ...+...10
CLØNØ1Factor1+++++++Opcode(E)+Factor2++++++Result++++++++Len++D+HiLoEq....Comments++++++++++++
C* Make the fifth occurrence of DSState active.
C     5           OCCUR     DSState
C* Make the Nth occurrence of DSState active.
C     N           OCCUR     DSState
```

If you want to determine which occurrence of a data structure is active, you can leave factor 1 blank and code an entry (which must be an integer numeric field) in the result-field position; the result field will be given the value of the current occurrence.

```
*.. 1 ...+... 2 ...+... 3 ...+... 4 ...+... 5 ...+... 6 ...+... 7 ...+... 8 ...+... 9 ...+...10
CLØNØ1Factor1+++++++Opcode(E)+Factor2++++++Result++++++++Len++D+HiLoEq....Comments++++++++++++
C* After the following line executes, field S's value will indicate which occurrence of
C* DSState is currently active.
C                 OCCUR     DSState       S
```

The following calculations illustrate how the state data could be obtained from a full procedural input file to load the values into the multiple-occurrence data structure defined earlier.

```
*.. 1 ...+... 2 ...+... 3 ...+... 4 ...+... 5 ...+... 6 ...+... 7 ...+... 8 ...+... 9 ...+...10
CLØNØ1Factor1+++++++Opcode(E)+Factor2++++++Result++++++++Len++D+HiLoEq....Comments++++++++++++
CLØNØ1Factor1+++++++Opcode(E)+Extended-factor2+++++++++++++++++++++++++++++Comments++++++++++++
C* Loop 50 times to load DDState from StatesFile.  Exit early if the file contains fewer
C* than 50 records.
C                 DO        50            I
C     I           OCCUR     DSState
C                 READ      StatesFile                              90
C                 IF        *IN90 = *ON
C                 EXSR      FileErr
C                 LEAVE
C                 ENDIF
C                 ENDDO
```

Once the data structure is loaded, the information is available for "look-ups." To access the data structure information based on a match between an input state code (CodeIn) and the state codes in the data structure, you can code a loop to change the occurrence until a match is found; at that point, all the data structure fields contain values appropriate for CodeIn. The following calculations illustrate this technique:

```
*.. 1 ...+... 2 ...+... 3 ...+... 4 ...+... 5 ...+... 6 ...+... 7 ...+... 8 ...+... 9 ...+...10
CLØN01Factor1++++++Opcode(E)+Extended-factor2+++++++++++++++++++++++++++++Comments+++++++++++
CLØN01Factor1++++++Opcode(E)+Factor2++++++Result+++++++Len++D+HiLoEq....Comments+++++++++++
C* Code to look up information when data is stored in a multiple-occurrence data structure.
C
C* Set DSState to its first occurrence.
C                   EVAL      I = 1
C        I          OCCUR     DSState                              99
C* Then loop, changing the occurrence, until either a match is found or the last occurrence
C* of the data structure has been examined.
C                   DOW       CodeIn <> Code AND *IN99 = *OFF
C                   EVAL      I = I + 1
C        I          OCCUR     DSState                              99
C                   ENDDO
C* If indicator 99 is on, CodeIn was not found among the Code values in the data structure.
C                   IF        *IN99 = *ON
C                   EXSR      BadCode
C                   ELSE
C                   EXSR      Found
C                   ENDIF
```

Another use of a multiple-occurrence data structure is to provide capabilities equivalent to those of **two-dimensional arrays**. Unlike most other programming languages, RPG IV only allows single-dimensional arrays. Sometimes this limitation makes programming a solution to a problem more difficult than if the language included the capability to define arrays in two (or more) dimensions.

A simple analogy can help you understand the concept of a two-dimensional array. Most of you are familiar with spreadsheets. Each spreadsheet cell is addressed by a row position and a column position. The row represents one dimension, the column represents a second. Although most spreadsheets implement this addressing with an alphabetic "pointer" for the column and a numeric "pointer" for the row (e.g., cell B4), you can see how each cell is uniquely addressed by the combination of row and column values. Changing either the row address or the column address changes which cell (array element) you are referencing.

Although RPG IV does not directly support two-dimensional arrays, you can achieve the same effect by including an array within a multiple-occurrence data structure. The array subscripts would point to a value in one dimension (the "column"), while the occurrence of the data structure would point to the second dimension (the "row").

Consider the following problem. A company has an externally described file of sales transactions for the year; each record includes Amount (amount of sale), Date (date of sale in YYMMDD format), and LocateIn (numeric value, 1-50, designating the location at which the sale took place). The company wants a report that shows total monthly sales broken down by location.

One solution to this problem uses a multiple-occurrence data structure with 50 occurrences (each representing a location), where each occurrence contains an array of 12 elements (representing each month). The portion of the program defining the data structure and showing the calculations to accumulate the sales follows:

```
*.. 1 ...+... 2 ...+... 3 ...+... 4 ...+... 5 ...+... 6 ...+... 7 ...+... 8 ...+... 9 ...+...10
DName++++++++++ETDsFrom+++To/L+++IDc.Keywords+++++++++++++++++++++++++++++++++++++Comments+++++++++++
CL0N01Factor1++++++Opcode(E)+Factor2++++++Result++++++++Len++D+HiLoEq....Comments+++++++++++
CL0N01Factor1++++++Opcode(E)+Extended-factor2+++++++++++++++++++++++++++++++++++Comments+++++++++++
D* A multiple-occurrence data structure with 50 occurrences; each occurrence is an array.
D Location       DS                    OCCURS(50) INZ
D   Total                      10  2 DIM(12)
D* Data structure to access the month portion of input field Date.
D                 DS
D Date            1   6  0
D   Yr            1   2  0
D   Mon           3   4  0
D   Day           5   6  0
D
C* Calculations to process SalesFile to accumulate sales within the appropriate accumulator
C* of the data structure.
C               READ      SalesFile                              90
C               DOW       *IN90 = *OFF
C* Set the occurrence of the data structure based on Location's value.
C    LocateIn   OCCUR     Location                              55
C* Check for an invalid location or an invalid month value.
C               IF        *IN55 = *ON OR Mon < 1 OR Mon > 12
C               EXSR      Error
C               ELSE
C               EVAL      Total(Mon) = Total(Mon) + Amount
C               ENDIF
C               READ      SalesFile                              90
C               ENDDO
```

At the end of the above routine, the year's sales have been accumulated within data structure Location, with each of the 50 occurrences of Location containing the 12 monthly sales totals for that location. You could then print the totals in a row/column format.

Initialization and Reinitialization of Variables

Data structures are considered character fields regardless of the data type of their subfields; as a result, they will contain blanks at the start of your program unless you explicitly initialize their subfields. In our sample code for accumulating sales, if we had not initialized all the elements within all the occurrences of Total to 0 (indicated by INZ in Location's header line), our program would have ended abnormally when we tried to add Amount to a Total element.

You initialize a data structure *globally* when you include keyword INZ in the Keywords area of the data structure header line. This use of INZ causes all subfields in the entire data structure to be automatically initialized to the default value appropriate for their data types (e.g., all numeric subfields are set to zero, all character fields to spaces, all pointers to *NULL).

Alternately, you can initialize specific subfields of a data structure by including keyword INZ as part of their definitions. If you want to initialize the subfield to a value other than the default, you can include the desired value within parentheses following INZ. You can express this value as a literal or a named constant, but it must fit the data type of the subfield; moreover, it cannot be longer than the subfield or have more decimal positions than the subfield (if the type is numeric). If the value is too long to fit on one line, it can be continued over several lines in the same way that values for named constants can be continued.

The use of keyword INZ is not limited to data structures; you can use it to initialize stand-alone fields and arrays, as well. The rules for using INZ with data structure subfields also apply to these kinds of data items. Study the figure below to gain a sense of how to use INZ.

```
*.. 1 ...+... 2 ...+... 3 ...+... 4 ...+... 5 ...+... 6 ...+... 7 ...+... 8 ...+... 9 ...+...10
DName++++++++++ETDsFrom+++To/L+++IDc.Keywords++++++++++++++++++++++++++++++++Comments+++++++++++
D..................................Keywords-continuation++++++++++++++++++Comments+++++++++++
D* The lines below define two named constants.
D NbrK            C                   CONST(14419)
D CharK           C                   'ACCOUNTING'
D
D* The entire data structure below is globally initialized.
D Example1        DS                  INZ
D   CharSubFld               30
D   NbrSubFld                 9 4
D
D* Specific subfield initialzation is illustrated below. Two subfields are initialized
D* to named constants.
D Example2        DS
D   Nbr1            1      4 0 INZ
D   Nbr2            5      8 2 INZ(12.3)
D   Char1           9     18   INZ
D   Char2          19     28   INZ('ABCDEFG')
D   Char3          29     69   INZ('This is an initial value +
D                                   for Char3.')
D   Nbr3           70     74 0 INZ(NbrK)
D   Char4          75     89   INZ(CharK)
D
D* Stand-alone fields can also be initialized using INZ.
D Example3        S             15 6 INZ
D Example4        S              5 1 INZ(1234.5)
D Example5        S             20   INZ(CharK)
D DateExmp        S              D   INZ(D'1995-03-15')
D PtrExmp         S              *   INZ
D
D* And even array elements can be assigned initial values.
D NbrAry          S              5 2 DIM(20) INZ(123.45)
D ChrAry          S             50   DIM(10) INZ(*ALL'-')
```

In the sample code above, keyword INZ initializes the entire Example1 data structure, such that any of its numeric subfields (e.g., NbrSubFld) are 0 and any character subfields (e.g., CharSubFld) are blank. All Example2 data structure subfields are initialized individually. Nbr1 is initialized to zero and Char1 is initialized to blanks, because no alternate values are provided for those fields. Char2's initial value is 'ABCDEFG', and Char3's is 'This is an initial value for Char3.' Nbr3's value becomes 14419 and Char4's value becomes 'ACCOUNTING   ', because they are initialized to named constants with those values. Note that in the stand-alone field definitions, DateExmp, a field of type date, is initialized to March 15, 1995; PtrExmp, a basing pointer, is initialized to *NULL. All the elements of array NbrAry are initialized to 123.45, while the figurative constant used to initialize array ChrAry fills each element with all hyphens.

An alternate way to handle initialization of data structure subfields, and of fields in general, is to explicitly assign them initial values within a subroutine that the program performs just once at the start of execution. RPG IV actually provides such a subroutine, named ***INZSR**. If you include a subroutine with this name within your program, the subroutine is invoked automatically immediately after the program completes its other start-up tasks, such as opening the files and loading any arrays or tables. Although you can include other kinds of operations within *INZSR, good programming practice suggests that all operations within this subroutine focus on a single function — initializing variables.

```
*.. 1 ...+... 2 ...+... 3 ...+... 4 ...+... 5 ...+... 6 ...+... 7 ...+... 8 ...+... 9 ...+...10
CL0N01Factor1+++++++Opcode(E)+Factor2+++++++Result+++++++Len++D+HiLoEq....Comments+++++++++++
CL0N01Factor1+++++++Opcode(E)+Extended-factor2+++++++++++++++++++++++++++++Comments+++++++++++
C* Sample code initializing variables using the built-in subroutine *INZSR.
C     *INZSR        BEGSR
C                   EVAL      RecordCnt = 0
C                   EVAL      Adds = 0
C                   EVAL      Changes = 0
C                   EVAL      Deletes = 0
C                   EVAL      ErrorCnt = 0
C                   ...
C                   ENDSR
```

Although RPG IV automatically initializes all numeric fields to 0; all character fields to blanks; all date, time, and timestamp fields to *LOVAL; and all pointers to *NULL at the start of a program, there are good reasons to *explicitly* initialize variables in an initialization subroutine or through the Definition Specifications. This practice makes the processing steps within your program more evident. Moreover, it relies less on the automatic features of RPG, in keeping with the movement toward complete procedural implementation of the language.

You often need to reinitialize field values during processing. For instance, in control-break programs, you need to set subtotal accumulators back to 0. Or in interactive maintenance programs, you may want to clear data fields when you add new records. RPG IV provides two operations — CLEAR and RESET — to let you reinitialize variables.

CLEAR (Clear to Default Value)
CLEAR changes the values of the data items it is used with to their appropriate default values, based on data type (0 for numeric fields; blanks for character fields; *LOVAL for date, time, and timestamp fields; *NULL for pointers). You can CLEAR individual fields or whole structures (data structures, arrays, tables, record formats). A CLEAR operation requires an entry in the result area of the specification that tells which data item is to be cleared. If you specify an array, the system clears the entire array. If, however, you specify a

multiple-occurrence data structure or a table for clearing, only the current occurrence or table element is cleared, unless you use keyword *ALL in factor 2; in that case, all the occurrences or the entire table are cleared.

If the data item to be cleared is a database file-record format, you can specify *NOKEY in factor 1 to signal that all the record's fields except the record key are to be cleared. When you CLEAR a display record format, only fields that are output in that record format are affected. This means that if you clear a display-file record format, only those fields with usage O (output) or B (both) would be reinitialized.

```
*.. 1 ...+... 2 ...+... 3 ...+... 4 ...+... 5 ...+... 6 ...+... 7 ...+... 8 ...+... 9 ...+...10
CLØN01Factor1++++++Opcode(E)+Factor2++++++Result++++++++Len++D+HiLoEq....Comments+++++++++++
C* Examples of the CLEAR operation.
C* The numeric field is reinitialized to 0.
C                   CLEAR                   NbrFld
C* The character field is reinitialized to blanks.
C                   CLEAR                   CharFld
C* The data structure subfields are set to the default values appropriate
C* for their individual data types.
C                   CLEAR                   DataStr
C* All record fields except the key are set to the field's default values.
C    *NOKEY         CLEAR                   Record
C* All array elements are cleared.
C                   CLEAR                   Arry
C* Only the current occurrence of the multiple-occurrence DS is cleared.
C                   CLEAR                   MultOcrDS
C* All occurrences of the multiple-occurrence DS are cleared because of *ALL.
C                   CLEAR      *ALL         MultOcrDS
```

RESET (Reset to Initial Value)

The RESET operation is similar to CLEAR, except that instead of automatically reinitializing values to their appropriate default values based on data type, RESET restores the elements to whatever values they had at the end of the initialization step at the program's start. If you initialized data structure subfields to specific values, turned on indicators, or assigned values to fields in *INZSR, and these values subsequently changed during the program's execution, you can easily reassign those initial values with RESET.

The format of RESET is identical to that of CLEAR: The result entry can be a data structure, a record format, an array, a table, or a variable (field, subfield, or indicator). As with CLEAR, only the current occurrence of a data structure or the current element of a table is reset, unless keyword *ALL appears in factor 2. If the result item is a display-file record format, only those fields with usage O (output) or B (both) are reinitialized to their starting values.

```
*.. 1 ...+... 2 ...+... 3 ...+... 4 ...+... 5 ...+... 6 ...+... 7 ...+... 8 ...+... 9 ...+...10
CLØNØ1Factor1++++++Opcode(E)+Factor2++++++Result+++++++Len++D+HiLoEq....Comments+++++++++++
C* All data structure subfields are reset to their originally initialized values or to
C* blanks, if no explicit INZ values were present.
C                   RESET                   DataStr
C* All record fields except key are set to initialized values or to default
C* values, if not explicitly initialized to another value.
C     *NOKEY        RESET                   Record
C* All array elements are reset to initialized value.
C                   RESET                   Arry
C* Only the current occurrence of the multiple-occurrence DS is reset.
C                   RESET                   MultOcrDS
C* All occurrences of the multiple-occurrence DS are reset, because of *ALL.
C                   RESET     *ALL          MultOcrDS
```

File-Information Data Structures

A **file-information data structure** is a special data structure that you can define for each file used by your program. A file-information data structure contains predefined subfields that can provide information to your program about the file and the outcomes of input and/or output operations to the file. Because much of this information details exception or error information, using a file-information data structure can be helpful in debugging programs.

A file-information data structure must be linked to the file it is associated with by making a required entry on that file's File Specification description. Use keyword INFDS, with the name of the data structure serving as that file's file-information data structure noted in parentheses following the keyword.

```
*.. 1 ...+... 2 ...+... 3 ...+... 4 ...+... 5 ...+... 6 ...+... 7 ...+... 8 ...+... 9 ...+...10
FFilename++IPEASFRlen+LKlen+AIDevice+.Keywords+++++++++++++++++++++++++++++++Comments+++++++++++
F* File specification declaring data structure SampleDS as the file-information
F* data structure file.
FSample   UF  E         K DISK    INFDS(SampleDS)
```

The above code defines data structure SampleDS as the file-information data structure for file Sample. Each such data structure is 528 positions long and is subdivided into predefined segments or subfields, each of which automatically will contain information about the file the data structure is associated with. Your data structure needs only to include those subfields that contain data you want to reference within your program; you can ignore the others. To reference a particular subfield of information, you need to know its From and To positions within the data structure. You can look these positions up in *ILE RPG/400 Reference.*

Alternately, IBM has provided keywords, which are more easily remembered, to represent the location of those subfields most often referenced. For these subfields, you can substitute the keyword for the subfield's actual location within the data structure. You must supply a name for the subfield, regardless of whether you reference its location through actual positions or through a keyword.

Although a complete discussion of file-information data structures is beyond the scope of this text, the following paragraph describes some of the subfields and what they represent to give you a sense of the potential usefulness of file-information data structures.

The subfield in positions 1-8 (keyword *FILE) contains the name of the file. Positions 16-21 (keyword *OPCODE) contain the name of the most recent operation processed on the file, such as READ. Positions 11-15 (keyword *STATUS) contain a five-digit numeric field (0 decimal positions) that contains the status code of the most recent input/output (I/O) operation.

Status codes are predefined values that signal specific I/O events. Status code 00000 reflects no error or exception. Status code 00002 indicates that a function key was used to end a display. Status code 00011 signals an end-of-file on a read. Status code 00012 signals a no-record-found condition on a chain operation. Any status code greater than 00099 is an error. Different error codes signal precisely what kind of error occurred. For example, 01211 indicates an attempt at I/O to a closed file, while status code 01021 indicates an attempt was made to write a record with a duplicate key to a file that is supposed to have unique keys.

Some of the subfields, such as the status-code subfield, are useful for testing and debugging programs. Other subfields may provide information needed by your program as part of its normal processing. For example, if you are trying to develop an interactive application that is cursor-sensitive, your program will need to be able to determine the cursor's location on the screen; positions 370-371 of the file-information data structure contain (in binary representation) the row and column coordinates of the cursor upon return from a screen.

Other subfields of the file-information data structure include information about the position of the file "pointer," or current relative record number (positions 397-400); a count of the total number of records in the file (positions 156-159); or what function key was used to end a display (position 369).

The following example shows a sample file-information data structure. Notice the use of keywords in place of location in three of the subfields. Rather than *FILE, you could access the file name by coding From 1 To 8.

```
*.. 1 ...+... 2 ...+... 3 ...+... 4 ...+... 5 ...+... 6 ...+... 7 ...+... 8 ...+... 9 ...+...10
DName++++++++++ETDsFrom+++To/L+++IDc.Keywords+++++++++++++++++++++++++++++++++Comments++++++++++++
D* Sample file-information data structure.
D SampleDS        DS
D   FileName         *FILE
D   FileStatus       *STATUS
D   OpCode           *OPCODE
D   RelRecNbr        397    400B 0
D   RecCnt           156    159B 0
```

In general, anytime you write a program for which you need "behind-the-scenes" information about the files used by the program, remember file-information data structures. Chances are that you can obtain the data you need from a subfield within such a data structure.

Program-Status Data Structures

Just as you can define file-information data structures to provide information about data or events associated with the files used by your program, you can also define a **program-status data structure** to provide information about the program itself and about exceptions/errors that occur during program execution.

Like a file-information data structure, a program-status data structure has predefined subfields that automatically acquire values during the course of your program's execution. Some of these subfields are useful in testing and debugging to determine what went wrong in the program, while others provide information that might be needed to implement the logic of the program itself.

For example, a program-status data structure can supply you with the name of the program, the job name and job number, the name of the user who called the program, and the specific number of any runtime exception or error that occurs while the program is running. A status code subfield also can provide information about program problems. To give you a sense of what kinds of errors the status code can report, below is a sample of some of the possible values for the status code subfield:

Code	Meaning
00000	No error occurred
00101	Negative square root
00102	Divide by 0
00121	Array index not valid
00122	OCCUR outside range
00907	Decimal data error

An S in position 23 (T) of a data structure initial definition line identifies a program-status data structure. Any subfield of the data structure that you want to access must be defined within the data structure. The definition includes the location of the subfield, a decimal entry (if appropriate), and a name you assign to the subfield. IBM has provided keywords that can substitute for the location of those subfields most commonly used. A sample program-status data structure is illustrated below. For more information about program-status data structures, see *ILE RPG/400 Reference.*

```
*.. 1 ...+... 2 ...+... 3 ...+... 4 ...+... 5 ...+... 6 ...+... 7 ...+... 8 ...+... 9 ...+...10
DName++++++++++ETDsFrom+++To/L+++IDc.Keywords+++++++++++++++++++++++++++++Comments+++++++++++
D* Sample program status data structure.
D PSDS            SDS
D   PrgStatus     *STATUS           0
D   ErrType          40     42
D   ErrCode          43     46
D   JobName         244    253
D   JobNumber       264    269 0
D   UserName        354    363
```

Error Handling and *PSSR

Without explicit error handling within your program, regardless of whether you include file-information and program-status data structures, any runtime error will cause the system to suspend the program and send a message to the interactive user or the system operator (when the program is running in batch). Assume you want to handle errors internally within your program, rather than letting the errors cause a program **abend** (abnormal ending). You could use one of several alternative methods to handle errors.

One technique is to code an error indicator in positions 73-74 (Lo) of those operations that permit such an entry. If an error occurs during an operation that includes such an error indicator, the indicator comes on and the program simply continues to the next sequential instruction.

```
*.. 1 ...+....2 ...+... 3 ...+... 4 ...+... 5 ..+... 6 ...+... 7 ...+... 8 ...+... 9 ...+...10
CL0N01Factor1++++++Opcode(E)+Factor2++++++Result++++++++Len++D+HiLoEq....Comments+++++++++++
CL0N01Factor1++++++Opcode(E)+Extended-factor2+++++++++++++++++++++++++++++Comments+++++++++++
C* Error indicator 56 causes the program to simply continue if an error occurs with any
C* of the operations using the indicator.
C                   READ      Sample                            5690
C                   DOW       *IN90 = *OFF
C         Samp      CHAIN     OtherFile                         9556
C                   EXSR      Calcs
C                   READ      Sample                            5690
C                   ENDDO
```

Although this method prevents an abend of your program, it simply ignores the error — a potentially dangerous practice. A better method would be to include an error routine that the program executes immediately upon encountering an error. By checking the status of your error indicator after each operation that uses it, your program could appropriately execute a special routine should any error occur.

```
*.. 1 ...+... 2 ...+... 3 ...+... 4 ...+... 5 ..+... 6 ...+... 7 ...+... 8 ...+... 9 ...+...10
CL0N01Factor1++++++Opcode(E)+Factor2++++++Result++++++++Len++D+HiLoEq....Comments+++++++++++
CL0N01Factor1++++++Opcode(E)+Extended-factor2+++++++++++++++++++++++++++++Comments+++++++++++
C* Error indicator 56 is checked and subroutine Error executed if an error occurs.
C                   READ      Sample                            5690
C                   IF        *IN56 = *ON
C                   EXSR      Error
C                   ENDIF
C                   DOW       *IN90 = *OFF
C         Samp      CHAIN     OtherFile                         9556
C                   IF        *IN56 = *ON
C                   EXSR      Error
C                   ENDIF
C                   EXSR      Calcs
C                   READ      Sample                            5690
C                   IF        *IN56 = *ON
C                   EXSR      Error
C                   ENDIF
C                   ENDDO
```

Including all these checks, however, greatly increases the length of your program and still doesn't solve the problem of errors generated by operations (such as DIV) that do not permit the use of an error indicator.

Fortunately, an alternate method of error trapping exists. RPG IV provides a built-in subroutine name, *PSSR. If you include a subroutine named ***PSSR** within your program, that subroutine will automatically receive control when a *program* error occurs. To send control to this subroutine for *file* exceptions/errors, as well, you must explicitly designate *PSSR as the error handler for the files. This assignment is quite straightforward; simply use keyword INFSR as part of the file definition and include *PSSR in parentheses following the keyword.

```
*.. 1 ...+... 2 ...+... 3 ...+... 4 ...+... 5 ...+... 6 ...+... 7 ...+... 8 ...+... 9 ...+...10
FFilename++IPEASFRlen+LKlen+AIDevice+.Keywords++++++++++++++++++++++++++++++Comments+++++++++++
F* File definition with a file-information data structure and the *PSSR error handler
F* defined for the file.
FSample    UF  E          K DISK     INFDS(SampleDS) INFSR(*PSSR)
```

Keyword INFSR signals that its parameter is to serve as the error routine automatically invoked when a file exception/error occurs. Although any subroutine could be used for file error handling, most programmers prefer to combine program error handling and file error handling within a single subroutine, named *PSSR. With this method, any kind of error encountered while your program is running will cause control to be transferred to subroutine *PSSR — without the need for including and checking error indicators.

```
*.. 1 ...+... 2 ...+... 3 ..+... 4 ...+... 5 ...+... 6 ...+... 7 ...+... 8 ...+... 9 ...+...10
CL0N01Factor1++++++Opcode(E)+Factor2++++++Result++++++++Len++D+HiLoEq....Comments+++++++++++
CL0N01Factor1++++++Opcode(E)+Extended-factor2+++++++++++++++++++++++++++++Comments+++++++++++
C* Error routine *PSSR is automatically invoked if any error occurs, without the need
C* for error indicators.
C                   READ      Sample                           90
C                   DOW       *IN90 = *OFF
C     Samp          CHAIN     OtherFile                        95
C                   EXSR      Calcs
C                   READ      Sample                           90
C                   ENDDO
C                   ...
C     *PSSR         BEGSR
C                   ...
C                   ENDSR
```

Within *PSSR, you could check the status codes and other subfields of the file-information and program-status data structures to determine the best response to the error — perhaps ignoring the error and continuing, perhaps writing a line to an error report and continuing, or perhaps noting the error and bringing the program to a normal ending. The optimal design of *PSSR logic is beyond the scope of this text. As a programmer new to RPG IV, you should be aware of the need for error detection and understand the function and value of a *PSSR subroutine. As you gain more experience with the language, you will no doubt begin to incorporate such error handling within your programs.

Chapter Summary

In addition to character and numeric types of fields, RPG IV offers other data types useful for specific purposes. Time, date, and timestamp data types let you declare that variables will hold date-/time-related data. Once so declared, you can manipulate the data using special operations ADDDUR, SUBDUR, and EXTRCT, to facilitate date computations.

The DBCS graphic data type lets you define and manipulate graphics data, where two bytes represent a single graphic character. The basing pointer and procedure pointer data types let you dynamically access storage for the data items associated with the pointers.

Named constants let you assign literal values to data names, which you then can use throughout your program. Named constants can represent data values too long to hard-code as factors within your calculations, and they concentrate program maintenance to a single line of code when a constant value needs to be changed.

You can define fields relative to other field definitions using keyword LIKE. A field defined in this way can exactly match its length to that of the field supplying the definition; alternately, you can specify its length to be longer (+ a number of positions) or shorter (− a number of positions) than the length of the second field.

You can define data structures that represent complex definitions of a given area of memory. A data structure is composed of subfields. These subfields can represent overlapping areas of storage or subdivisions of fields. A multiple-occurrence data structure establishes repetitions of the data structure in memory to let you perform data manipulation more complex than what simple arrays or tables offer. Arrays can appear as subfields of multiple-occurrence data structures, a feature that provides the equivalent function of two-dimensional arrays in other languages.

You can easily initialize data structures or subfields of data structures in the data structure definition by using keyword INZ. RPG IV also provides subroutine *INZSR, which, if included within your program, automatically executes at the program's startup. Programmers often use *INZSR to explicitly initialize fields and other data items. You can use operation CLEAR to initialize or reinitialize data items to the default values associated with their data types. RESET, on the other hand, reinitializes data items to whatever values they were given at the beginning of the program.

Two special data structures of predefined subfields exist in RPG IV to provide information about the status of files used by the program or about the processing of the program itself: file-information data structures and program-status data structures. You often access these data structures within RPG IV's *PSSR error subroutine to determine the cause of an execution error.

Terms

abend
based field
basing pointer
built-in function
data structure
data type
date data type

DBCS graphic data type
file-information data structure
*INZSR
multiple-occurrence
   data structure
named constant
procedure pointer

program-status data structure
*PSSR
time data type
timestamp data type
two-dimensional array
typed literal

Discussion/Review Questions

1. What are the primary advantages offered by RPG IV's various date data types?

2. Compare and contrast RPG IV's basing pointers and array indexes.

3. What is a named constant?

4. What are the advantages of using named constants in a program?

5. What is the purpose of defining fields with keyword LIKE? Why might you use this RPG IV feature?

6. What kinds of capabilities can you gain by using data structures?

7. What is a multiple-occurrence data structure? Compare and contrast it to an RPG IV table.

8. Data structures use OCCUR; what parallel for OCCUR do you have when you are working with arrays? With tables?

9. What is variable initialization? What techniques are available in RPG IV to let you initialize fields and other data items?

10. Describe the difference between the CLEAR and RESET operations.

11. What built-in subroutines does RPG IV provide for your use? When is each executed?

12. Compare and contrast a file-information data structure with a program-status data structure.

13. How many file-information data structures can you have within a program? How many program-status data structures?

14. Discuss different options for trapping errors (or not trapping errors) within a program, giving the pros and cons of each method.

Exercises

1. Code the following values as named constants: a commission rate of 2.5%; the company name "Acme Explosives Company"; the FICA cut-off income of $58,000; an edit word for editing Social Security numbers; and the date January 1, 1980.

2. A retail business' SALES file contains field DAYSALES, eight positions long with two decimal positions, that represents the store's sales from one day. Use LIKE to define fields that will hold the sales tax for a day's sales, a week's worth of sales, a week's sales tax, annual sales, and annual sales tax.

3. Data file WUTSTP contains student answers to 50-item, multiple-choice tests. The format of these records is shown below.

Field	Description	Positions
TEST	Test number	1- 4
SECT	Section number	5- 9
CRSE	Course ID	10-15
STID	Social Security number	16-24
ANS	Answers 1-50	25-74

Code a data structure that does the following: subdivides CRSE into two three-position fields (the first represents the department offering the course, the second the course number); subdivides STID — Social Security number — into three-, two-, and four-position subfields; and defines ANS as an array, with each answer a separate element of the array.

4. To determine shipping charges, CompuSell uses a table file that contains shipping charges based on weight and zone. Each record contains a weight and six charges (one each for zones 2-7).

There are 70 records in the file, sequentially reflecting weights 1-70. The record layout of CSCHGP is:

Field	Positions	(Decimal positions)
Weight (pounds)	1- 2	(0)
Charge zone 2	3- 6	(2)
Charge zone 3	7-10	(2)
Charge zone 4	11-14	(2)
Charge zone 5	15-18	(2)
Charge zone 6	19-22	(2)
Charge zone 7	23-26	(2)

Define a multiple-occurrence data structure that will hold the contents of this file and allow you to store all the table information at once within the data structure as an alternative to storing it in tables.

5. Write the calculations that would be needed to load the data structure from Exercise 4 with the contents of CSCHGP. Make up whatever data names you need, in addition to those of the data structure.

6. Write the calculations needed to locate the appropriate charge from the data structure of Exercises 4 and 5 based on an input weight — field WTIN — and zone — field ZIN. (That is, do the equivalent of a table look-up, using your data structure.)

7. Write the code needed to determine whether or not a bill is more than 30 days past due. The due date field, DateIn, and the system date, UDATE, are 8-byte numeric fields with 0 decimal positions. (Hint: Define two date data type fields, assign to them the values of DateIn and UDATE, and use one of the date operations to determine the difference between the two dates.)

Programming Assignments

1. Acme Explosive Company tracks its product sales by month. This sales information is stored in file PRDSLSP, described in Appendix D. There is only one record per product manufactured by the company. Each record includes sales totals for that product for each month of the previous year.

   The company wants you to write a program to produce a summary report of sales, highlighting the month with the lowest sales and the month with the highest sales for each product. The name of the months, rather than the month number, is to appear on the report. At the end of the report the company wants the overall product sales for each month.

   To facilitate processing the sales figures, define the input record as a data structure containing an array. Define all work variables with LIKE. Handle the names of the months as a compile-time array.

```
         1         2         3         4         5         6         7         8         9         10
1234567890123456789012345678901234567890123456789012345678901234567890123456789012345678901234567890
1  XX/XX/XX      ACME EXPLOSIVES ANNUAL SALES SUMMARY      PAGE XX0X
2
3  PRODUCT             BEST MONTH          WORST MONTH
4  XXXXXX         XXX,X0X JANUARY     XXX,X0X SEPTEMBER
5  XXXXXX         XXX,X0X MAY         XXX,X0X AUGUST
6  XXXXXX         XXX,X0X JUNE        XXX,X0X DECEMBER
7
8  TOTAL MONTHLY SALES:
9  JANUARY      $XX,XXX,X$X
10 FEBRUARY     $XX,XXX,X$X
11 MARCH        $XX,XXX,X$X
12 ...
13 DECEMBER     $XX,XXX,X$X
```

2. Honest John's Used Cars employs 20 salespeople; each salesperson has a number assigned to him/her (numbers range from 1-20). During the course of a week, each sale a salesperson makes is recorded in a transaction file, HJSLSP (see Appendix D). Each record includes information about the salesperson number, the invoice number, and the amount of the sale. Each input record in the transaction file contains a record of a single sale. The file records are not sorted in any way. There may be several input records for a given salesperson, depending on how many successful sales (s)he has had during the week.

   A salesperson file is also available, HJSLPP, keyed on salesperson number and including the salesperson's name and weekly base pay (see Appendix D).

   Honest John wants you to determine weekly pay due each salesperson. Pay is based on the weekly base pay plus a commission based on total weekly sales for each salesperson. If total sales is greater than $50,000, use a 3% commission rate; if it's between $25,000 and $50,000, use a 2% commission rate; if it's less than $25,000, use a 1% commission rate. It is possible that not every salesperson has had at least one sale this week; however, each should get paid at least his/her base pay.

   Write a program to generate the report shown below, with the following restrictions on your program: 1) Do not define a logical file over HJSLSP. Instead, use a multiple-occurrence data structure to accumulate sales for each sales person. 2) Do not hard-code commission levels or rates in your calculations; instead, handle them as named constants. 3) Use LIKE to define any work variables needed within your program.

Programming Assignments Continued

Programming Assignments continued

```
                  1         2         3         4         5         6         7         8         9         1 0
   1234567890123456789012345678901234567890123456789012345678901234567890123456789012345678901234567890
 1     XX/XX/XX                    HONEST JOHN'S USED CARS
 2                            WEEKLY SALESMAN PAY SCHEDULE
 3
 4     SLSP.                           BASE                          TOTAL
 5      NO.          NAME              PAY           COMMIS.          PAY
 6
 7       1     XXXXXXXXXXXXXXXXXXXXXXXXX    X.XX0.XX       X.XX0.XX       XX.XX0.XX
 8       2     XXXXXXXXXXXXXXXXXXXXXXXXX    X.XX0.XX       X.XX0.XX       XX.XX0.XX
 9       3     XXXXXXXXXXXXXXXXXXXXXXXXX    X.XX0.XX       X.XX0.XX       XX.XX0.XX
10                                            ...
11
12                    TOTALS         $XXX,XX$.XX    $XXX,XX$.XX    $X,XXX,XX0.XX
```

3. Piper, a small commuter airline, runs three flights a day between two cities, seven days a week. Its plane holds 20 passengers. The airline wants an online reservation system that will do the following:

Allow the user to enter a day (1-7) *, representing Monday-Sunday, a flight number (1-3), and the number of requested seats. If that many seats are available, allow the user to enter the name and phone number of the person making the reservation and reserve that many seats by adding a record to the reservation file. Confirm the reservation and then redisplay the original entry screen with no values showing. If that flight does not have enough vacant seats, display a message on the screen that tells how many seats are available and allow the user to change all or part of the reservation (i.e., redisplay with the old data).

A physical file, PIPRESP, exists for use by your program (Appendix D). The file contains information about reservations for the flights for the week, including information about the person who made the reservation and the number of seats (s)he reserved. This file should be updated as customers place reservations and should be used to determine availability of seats.

Hint: Load a multiple-occurrence data structure from the file at the beginning of the program before taking reservations. As you take reservations, make sure you update the data structure to keep it current, and also write a record to the reservation file.

*To simplify the problem, assume that Piper does not take reservations more than a week in advance, nor does it take reservations on the day of the flight. Thus, if today is Tuesday, a reservation for day 2 would be interpreted to be for next Tuesday. Also assume that the first thing each morning a program runs that transfers all reservation records for that day's flight to another file, so you don't need to worry about mixing up today's reservations with those for a week from now.

4. Wexler University wants you to write a program to prepare tuition bills for students based on their current enrollment. You will need to use four files: WUENRLP, WUSTDP, WUCRSP, and WUSCTP. (See Appendix D). You may create whatever logical files you need to facilitate processing.

Each record in WUENRLP, which represents student current enrollment, should be processed in student order. For each section a student is enrolled in, you will need to determine the course identification and credits. Accumulate credits for the student. Then bill the student based on the total number of credits (s)he is enrolled for and the student's residency and status, using the following per-credit-hour tuition figures:

Programming Assignments Continued

Programming Assignments continued

	Indistrict ($)	Out-of-District ($)	International ($)
Lower Division (<61 credits)	77.50	155.25	200.50
Upper Division (>60 credits)	87.25	195.50	225.75
Graduate	111.50	250.50	276.00

In addition to tuition fees, the school levies the following fees:

a) Enrollment fee: An enrollment fee will be charged to all students. Students enrolled in seven or more credit hours will be charged $194.00. Those enrolled in fewer than seven credit hours will be charged $72.50.

b) Student Activity fee: $8.00 is a Student Organization's assessment.

c) MCC Fee: Michigan Collegiality Congress fee of $.50.

Define all fees and charges as named constants in your program, because as a student you know these charges are bound to change soon. Use whatever other features discussed in this chapter (such as *INZSR) that you feel will make your job easier.

Prepare a student tuition bill for each student, formatted as follows:

```
          1         2         3         4         5         6         7         8         9         10
 1234567890123456789012345678901234567890123456789012345678901234567890123456789012345678901234567890
 1  WEXLER U. TUITION BILL      BILLING DATE: XX/XX/XX
 2
 3 TO: XXXXXXXXXXXXXXX XXXXXXXXXX
 4      XXXXXXXXXXXXXXX
 5      XXXXXXXXXXXXXXX XX XXXXX-XXXX
 6
 7 ACCORDING TO OUR RECORDS, YOU HAVE ENROLLED IN THE
 8 FOLLOWING COURSES:
 9 COURSE       SECTION     DAYS    TIME       CREDITS
10 XXXXXX       XXXXXX      XXX     X0:XX         X
11 XXXXXX       XXXXXX      XXX     X0:XX         X
12 XXXXXX       XXXXXX      XXX     X0:XX         X
13                         TOTAL CREDITS     X0
14
15                         AMOUNT DUE
16         TUITION:        $X,XX$.XX
17         ENROLLMENT FEE:    XX0.XX
18         ACTIVITY FEE:      X0.XX
19         MCC FEE:            .XX
20
21         TOTAL DUE:      $X,XX$.XX
22
23 FAILURE TO PAY TOTAL WITHIN 21 DAYS OF BILLING
24 WILL RESULT IN YOUR BEING DROPPED FROM ALL
25 CLASSES.
```

Programming Assignments Continued

Programming Assignments continued

5. Wexler University wants a report showing faculty earnings and number of years of employment. The data is contained in physical file WUINSTP (see Appendix D). The printer spacing chart of the desired report is shown below. Note that you are to list the faculty members in order of increasing salary within their respective departments. Also note that the names on the report represent a trimmed concatenation of last name, comma, and first name (e.g., Doe, John). The number of years employed should represent the number of whole years completed when considering date of hire and the current system date.

```
         1         2         3         4         5         6         7         8         9         10
1234567890123456789012345678901234567890123456789012345678901234567890123456789012345678901234567890
 1  XX/XX/XX                        WEXLER UNIVERSITY                      PAGE XX0X
 2                               FACULTY EARNINGS REPORT
 3
 4                                                                  NO. YEARS
 5      DEPT.           NAME                    RANK  SEX   SALARY   EMPLOYED
 6
 7      XXX    XXXXXXXXXXXXXXXXXXXXXXXXXXXXX      X    X   XXX,XX0.XX    0X
 8             XXXXXXXXXXXXXXXXXXXXXXXXXXXXX      X    X   XXX,XX0.XX    0X
 9
10      XXX    XXXXXXXXXXXXXXXXXXXXXXXXXXXXX      X    X   XXX,XX0.XX    0X
11             XXXXXXXXXXXXXXXXXXXXXXXXXXXXX      X    X   XXX,XX0.XX    0X
12             XXXXXXXXXXXXXXXXXXXXXXXXXXXXX      X    X   XXX,XX0.XX    0X
13
```

6. GTC needs a listing of all customers who owe a balance and have not sent in a payment within the past 30 days. The company wants this listing to be in descending order by amount owed, so they can concentrate on collecting from those customers who owe them the most money first. The data upon which the report is to be based is stored in GTC's customer master file GTCSTP (Appendix D). The desired listing format is shown below; the customer name should be a trimmed concatenation of first name followed by last name (with a blank separator).

```
         1         2         3         4         5         6         7         8         9         10
1234567890123456789012345678901234567890123456789012345678901234567890123456789012345678901234567890
 1      XX/XX/XX             GTC OVERDUE PAYMENTS LISTING        PAGE XX0X
 2
 3      CUSTOMER                     PHONE            AMOUNT      DAYS SINCE
 4        NAME                       NUMBER            OWED      LAST PAYMENT
 5
 6    XXXXXXXXXXXXXXXXXXXXXXXXXXX  (XXX) XXX-XXXX    X,XX0.XX         X0X
 7    XXXXXXXXXXXXXXXXXXXXXXXXXXX  (XXX) XXX-XXXX    X,XX0.XX         X0X
 8    XXXXXXXXXXXXXXXXXXXXXXXXXXX  (XXX) XXX-XXXX    X,XX0.XX         X0X
 9    XXXXXXXXXXXXXXXXXXXXXXXXXXX  (XXX) XXX-XXXX    X,XX0.XX         X0X
10
```

Chapter 10

Interactive Programs: Advanced Techniques

Chapter Overview

This chapter extends your ability to write interactive applications by introducing you to two new concepts: subfiles and on-line help.

Subfiles

In Chapter 7 you were introduced to interactive programs. You learned how to write inquiry and maintenance programs where the program logic required the display of information one record at a time. Some kinds of applications require the use of **list panels**, in which data from many records is displayed on a screen for review, selection, or update. RPG IV has a special feature called **subfiles** to handle this kind of program requirement.

A subfile is a collection of records that is handled as a unit for screen I/O. Although subfile processing can get quite complicated, you can learn basic subfile processing techniques without great difficulty. As a prelude to discussing coding requirements for subfiles, consider the following problem description.

In Chapter 7 we worked with a file of course section information and developed an interactive application to display detailed section information based on an entered section number. The record layout of that file, SECTIONS, is repeated below.

```
*.. 1 ...+... 2 ...+... 3 ...+... 4 ...+... 5 ...+... 6 ...+... 7 ...+... 8
A..........T.Name+++++RLen++TDpB......Functions++++++++++++++++++++++++++++
A* Physical file SECTIONS definition.
A          R SECREC
A            SECTNO         5             TEXT('Section Number')
A            DAYS           3             TEXT('Days class meets')
A            BEGTIME        4  0          TEXT('Time class starts')
A            ROOM           4  0          TEXT('Classroom')
A            ENROLL         3  0          TEXT('Current enrollment')
A            INSTR         15             TEXT('Instructor')
A            COURSE         6             TEXT('Course Identifier')
A          K SECTNO
```

Now assume that the same school wants an application in which it can enter a course name to see a list of all the sections offered for that course.

The desired screen layouts are shown below. Notice that the second screen contains information from many section records, rather than just a single one. This fact means that you will need to use subfiles to implement the solution.

```
                        Course Inquiry

Type value, then Enter.

   Course number . .  _____










F3=Exit
```

```
                   XXXXXX Course Information

         Section     Instructor       Room   Days    Time    Enroll.
          XXXXX   XXXXXXXXXXXXXX       XXXX   XXX    XX:XX    XØX
          XXXXX   XXXXXXXXXXXXXX       XXXX   XXX    XX:XX    XØX
          XXXXX   XXXXXXXXXXXXXX       XXXX   XXX    XX:XX    XØX








Press Enter to continue.

F3=Exit   F12=Cancel
```

The first step before beginning the screen definition is to create a logical file over the SECTIONS file to access the records in order by course, and within course by section. The definition for that logical file, SECTIONL, is shown below.

```
*.. 1 ...+... 2 ...+... 3 ...+... 4 ...+... 5 ...+... 6 ...+... 7 ...+... 8
A..........T.Name+++++.Len++TDpB......Functions+++++++++++++++++++++++++++++
A* Definition of SECTIONL, a logical file over SECTIONS physical file.
A          R SECREC                    PFILE(SECTIONS)
A          K COURSE
A          K SECTNO
```

Now consider the display file, SECTINQ. The first screen definition is identical to the layout from the screen in Chapter 7; only the literals need to be changed. Note, though, that CA03 has been moved to make it a file-level keyword.

```
*.. 1 ...+... 2 ...+... 3 ...+... 4 ...+... 5 ...+... 6 ...+... 7 ...+... 8
AAN01N02N03T.Name++++++RLen++TDpBLinPosFunctions+++++++++++++++++++++++++++++
A                                      CA03(03 'F3=Exit')
A          R CRSEINQ
A                                      BLINK
A                                  1 28'Course Inquiry'
A                                  3  2'Type value, then Enter.'
A                                  5  5'Course number . .'
A            COURSENO      6A  B   5 24
A N90                                  DSPATR(UL)
A N90                                  DSPATR(HI)
A  90                                  ERRMSG('Course not found' 90)
A                                 23  2'F3=Exit'
```

The second screen will require subfile definition. To use a subfile to display multiple records on a screen requires two record formats: one to define a subfile record and one to control the subfile and its display.

Subfile Record Formats

The **subfile record format** describes the fields that are to appear on the screen. Because in this example the screen and database fields are the same, the database file containing the field definitions is noted with record-level keyword REF.

A new record-level keyword is required, SFL (Subfile), which identifies this format as a subfile. The remaining information in the subfile record format describes the fields to appear, their locations on the screen, and any editing or other special keywords if desired. The line number associated with each field represents the line on which the first record of the subfile is to appear.

The DDS on the following page illustrates the subfile record format of our application.

```
*.. 1 ...+... 2 ...+... 3 ...+... 4 ...+... 5 ...+... 6 ...+... 7 ...+... 8
AAN01N02N03T.Name++++++RLen++TDpBLinPosFunctions+++++++++++++++++++++++++++
A                                          REF(SECTIONS)
A           R SFLSECT                       SFL
A             SECTNO     R         0  4 14
A             INSTR      R         0  4 23
A             ROOM       R         0  4 41
A             DAYS       R         0  4 49
A             BEGTIME    R     Y   0  4 57EDTWRD('0  :   ')
A             ENROLL     R     Y   0  4 66EDTCDE(3)
```

Subfile Control-Record Formats

The **subfile control-record format** must immediately follow the subfile record format. This record format controls the display of the subfile records through the use of special record-level keywords. In addition, programmers often include the column headings for the subfile display as part of this record format.

The subfile control-record format *requires* several record-level keywords. These required keywords and their functions are as follows:

SFLCTL (Subfile Control): This keyword identifies this as the subfile control record for the subfile named within the parentheses of the keyword.

SFLDSP (Subfile Display): If this keyword is active when an output operation is performed on the subfile control record, the subfile itself is also displayed. This keyword generally is conditioned by an indicator to control whether or not the subfile displays on a given output operation.

SFLPAG (Subfile Page): This keyword defines how many subfile records are to be displayed at one time on the screen. The number follows the keyword and is enclosed in parentheses. You generally determine this number by calculating the number of available screen lines after all other lines to be displayed along with the subfile are taken into account.

SFLSIZ (Subfile Size): This value, enclosed in parentheses immediately following the keyword, should be either equal to or greater than the SFLPAG value. If the value is greater, you may make it large enough to accommodate the maximum number of records you would normally have in the subfile. (If you underestimate, however, the subfile will automatically be extended to make room for the additional records.) A subfile cannot be greater than 9,999 records. If SFLSIZ is greater than SFLPAG, OS/400 automatically handles paging through the subfile when the user presses the roll keys, and displays a + on the bottom of the screen to indicate there are subfile records not yet displayed.

Subfile control record-level keywords that are optional but usually used include the following:

SFLDSPCTL (Subfile Display Control): This keyword enables the display of any output fields or constants described within the control-record format. This keyword generally is conditioned with the same indicator used for the SFLDSP keyword.

SFLCLR (Subfile Clear): If this keyword is active when an output operation is performed on the subfile control record, the subfile itself is cleared of records. An option indicator is required for this keyword, or the system would clear the subfile on every output operation to the control record. The indicator often is the reverse of the indicator used for SFLDSP and SFLDSPCTL, so that you clear the subfile in one output operation and display the subfile and the control-record information in a second output operation.

The DDS below illustrates a subfile control-record format. Notice that when indicator 50 is on, the system will clear the subfile; when 50 is off, the system will display both the subfile record format and the subfile control-record format. Also note that the control-record format includes screen column headings for the subfile.

```
*.. 1 ...+... 2 ...+... 3 ...+... 4 ...+... 5 ...+... 6 ...+... 7 ...+... 8
AAN01N02N03T.Name++++++RLen++TDpBLinPosFunctions++++++++++++++++++++++++++++
A* Subfile control record format for course inquiry application.
A           R CTLSECT                     SFLCTL(SFLSECT)
A                                          SFLPAG(15)
A                                          SFLSIZ(80)
A  50                                      SFLCLR
A N50                                      SFLDSPCTL
A N50                                      SFLDSP
A             COURSENO       6A  0  1 28
A                                       1 35'Course Information'
A                                       3 12'Section'
A                                       3 24'Instructor'
A                                       3 41'Room'
A                                       3 49'Days'
A                                       3 57'Time'
A                                       3 64'Enroll.'
```

As mentioned above, the relationship between subfile size and subfile page can be varied. There are several different approaches to defining this interrelationship and loading data into the subfile. The method used depends in part on the program's anticipated processing requirements. We will develop our sample program using four different techniques, to give you a sense of the variation and rationale for each method.

Loading the Entire Subfile

The first method involves defining the subfile size large enough to hold the maximum expected number of records and then loading all the appropriate data into the subfile before any record display. This method is the easiest to code but results in the slowest initial response time. Once the display begins, however, paging through the subfile is fast. This method is least appropriate when there are a large number of records to be loaded and the user is unlikely to want to see most of them.

The following figure shows the complete DDS for this application method. Notice the inclusion of a footer-record definition, which contains prompts about active function keys. This record format is needed because the control-record format cannot reference screen lines that would fall both above the subfile display (i.e., the column headings) and below the subfile (the function key prompts). The control-record format includes the record-level keyword OVERLAY so that the footer-record format will not be erased when the subfile is displayed.

```
*.. 1 ...+... 2 ...+... 3 ...+... 4 ...+... 5 ...+... 6 ...+... 7 ...+... 8
AAN01N02N03T.Name+++++RLen++TDpBLinPosFunctions++++++++++++++++++++++++++++
A* Display file SECTINQ, coded for loading the entire subfile at once.
A                                          CA03(03 'F3=Exit')
A                                          CA12(12 'F12=Cancel')
A                                          REF(SECTIONS)
A* Record format of initial inquiry screen.
A         R CRSEINQ
A                                          BLINK
A                                      1 28'Course Inquiry'
A                                      3  2'Type value, then Enter.'
A                                      5  5'Course number . .'
A           COURSENO     6A  B  5 24
A N90                                      DSPATR(UL)
A N90                                      DSPATR(HI)
A  90                                      ERRMSG('Course not found' 90)
A                                     23  2'F3=Exit   F12=Cancel'
A* Record format for subfile.
A         R SFLSECT                        SFL
A           SECTNO       R      0  4 14
A           INSTR        R      0  4 23
A           ROOM         R      0  4 41
A           DAYS         R      0  4 49
A           BEGTIME      R   Y  0  4 57EDTWRD('0 :  ')
A           ENROLL       R   Y  0  4 66EDTCDE(3)
A* Record format for subfile control.
A         R CTLSECT                        SFLCTL(SFLSECT)
A                                          SFLPAG(15)
A                                          SFLSIZ(80)
A  50                                      SFLCLR
A N50                                      SFLDSPCTL
A N50                                      SFLDSP
A                                          OVERLAY
A           COURSENO     6A  O  1 28
A                                      1 35'Course Information'
A                                      3 12'Section'
A                                      3 24'Instructor'
A                                      3 41'Room'
A                                      3 49'Days'
A                                      3 57'Time'
A                                      3 64'Enroll.'
A* Footer record format.
A         R FOOTER
A                                     21  2'Press Enter to continue.'
A                                     23  2'F3=Exit   F12=Cancel'
```

With the display-file definition complete, we can turn to the requirements for the program that will use it.

First, for all subfile applications, RPG IV requires that you identify a subfile within the File Specification of the display file with which you want to associate the subfile. In addition, as part of the display file's definition, you need to identify a field that your program will use to represent a subfile record's **relative record number**. Relative record number simply means the position of the record within the subfile (e.g., first subfile record, second subfile record). This field is needed because RPG IV writes records to a subfile (and retrieves records from a subfile) based on the value of the relative record number.

You associate the subfile and relative record number field with a workstation file by using keyword SFILE in the Keywords area. The subfile record format name (e.g., SFLSECT), a colon (:), and the field to be used to store the relative record number (e.g., RRN) appear within parentheses following the keyword, as shown below.

```
*.. 1 ...+... 2 ...+... 3 ..+... 4 ...+... 5 ...+... 6 ...+... 7 ...+... 8 ...+... 9 ...+...10
FFilename++IPEASFRlen+LKlen+AIDevice+.Keywords+++++++++++++++++++++++++++++Comments+++++++++++
FSECTIONL  IF   E         K DISK
FSECTINQ   CF   E           WORKSTN SFILE(SFLSECT:RRN)
```

Next, you need to design the calculations. In our application, once the user has entered the desired course, the program needs to use that value to access the appropriate records in SECTIONL and write them to the subfile; loading the subfile continues until there are no more appropriate records (i.e., no more sections for that course). Then the subfile can be displayed by executing the subfile control-record format. Because SLFPAG is less than SLFSIZ, the system will handle any user request to roll up or roll down. Upon return the program should either end or request another course, depending on whether the user pressed F3 or Enter. The pseudocode below illustrates the logic needed for this application.

```
WHILE user wants to continue
      Display inquiry screen
      IF user doesn't want to exit
            Access start of appropriate sections
            IF section not found
                  Turn on error indicator
            ELSE
                  Clear subfile
                  Load subfile
                  Display subfile
            ENDIF
      ENDIF
ENDWHILE
```

The pseudocode for loading the subfile using this method of handling subfiles is as follows:

```
Read a matching section record
WHILE there are more appropriate section records
      Increment relative record number
      Write a record to the subfile
      Read a matching section record
ENDWHILE
```

The following code illustrates the RPG IV implementation of the design depicted in pseudocode:

```
*.. 1 ...+... 2 ...+... 3 ...+... 4 ...+... 5 ...+... 6 ...+... 7 ...+... 8 ...+... 9 ...+...10
CL0N01Factor1++++++Opcode(E)+Factor2++++++Result+++++++Len++D+HiLoEq....Comments+++++++++++
CL0N01Factor1++++++Opcode(E)+Extended-factor2+++++++++++++++++++++++++++Comments+++++++++++
C* Calculations for subfile application when entire subfile is loaded before any display
C* takes place.
C
C* Partial key list to access SectionL file by course number.
C        CourseKey     KLIST
C                      KFLD                        CourseNo
C* Process loop until user wants to exit.
C                      DOW         *IN03 = *OFF
C                      EXFMT       CrseInq
C                      IF          *IN03 = *OFF
C        CourseKey     SETLL       SectionL                         10
C                      IF          *IN10 = *OFF
C* If no matching section in file, turn on error indicator.
C                      EVAL        *IN90 = *ON
C                      ELSE
C* Otherwise clear and then load subfile.
C                      EXSR        ClearSF
C                      EXSR        LoadSF
C* Write footer to screen and then display subfile via control record format.
C                      WRITE       Footer
C                      EXFMT       CtlSect
C                      ENDIF
C                      ENDIF
C                      ENDDO
C                      EVAL        *INLR = *ON
C                      RETURN
C
C* Subroutine to clear the subfile and reset RRN to 0.
C        ClearSF       BEGSR
C                      EVAL        *IN50 = *ON
C                      WRITE       CtlSect
C                      EVAL        *IN50 = *OFF
C                      EVAL        RRN = 0
C                      ENDSR
C
C* Subroutine to load the subfile until no more section records.
C        LoadSF        BEGSR
C        CourseKey     READE       SectionL                         95
C                      DOW         *IN95 = *OFF
C                      EVAL        RRN = RRN + 1
C                      WRITE       SFLSect
C        CourseKey     READE       SectionL                         95
C                      ENDDO
C                      ENDSR
```

Note in the above calculations that the subfile is loaded by writing records to the subfile record format based on the relative record number field, which is incremented before each successive write operation. The program displays the subfile by executing the subfile control-record format. A WRITE to the control format clears the subfile (as long as the indicator for SFLCLR is on); the program also uses WRITE — rather than EXFMT — to display the Footer format because a user response to that display is not required. The KLIST lets you access the file by a partial key.

In the subfile application above, subfile size was greater than subfile page, and the size was large enough to handle the maximum number of records the subfile normally would be expected to hold. The program stored all relevant database records in the subfile before any display. With this approach, OS/400 automatically enables the roll keys and signals through a + in the lower screen corner that more subfile records are available for viewing. From a programmer's viewpoint, this technique is the simplest to code. Unfortunately, this method can result in poor response time when the application is used.

The cause of the slow system response is that this technique requires the system to access all the records that meet the selection criterion and store them in the subfile before displaying the first page of the subfile. If the subfile size is small, the performance will be satisfactory, but as the subfile size increases, response time will degrade noticeably. In that case, especially if the user typically does not roll much throughout the subfile, it may make sense to build the subfile a page at a time, as the user requests additional pages.

Loading the Subfile a Page at a Time
The other methods of subfile building load the subfile a page at a time. Three variations exist for this technique.

Variation #1 — Subfile Size One Greater than Page
This method of subfile handling relies on the fact that the system will automatically expand a subfile, regardless of its stated size, as your program adds more records to it. Because this additionally allocated room is not contiguous on disk, performance degrades as the number of pages in the subfile increases, but the technique works well when the number of records usually required within the subfile is small.

This method entails loading the subfile one page at a time, based on the user's request for additional pages. Rolling within the subfile records already loaded is handled automatically by the operating system. When the user attempts to roll up past the last page in the subfile, however, control returns to the program, which must load an additional page (if more appropriate records exist).

To use this method, you must add three additional keywords to the subfile control-record format. First, the ROLLUP keyword must be associated with an indicator to let the system send control back to the program when a roll-up request exceeds the current limits of the subfile. You must also add the SFLEND (Subfile End) keyword, conditioned by an indicator.

Keyword SFLEND, its associated indicator, and the Rollup key work in conjunction with one another to determine what happens when the user tries to roll past the current limits of the subfile. If the SFLEND indicator is off, the system displays a + sign and returns control to your program to load the next page; if the SFLEND indicator is on, the plus sign is not displayed, and control is not returned to your program for additional loading. Thus, your program should turn on the SFLEND indicator when no additional records remain to be put into the subfile. The system will then prohibit user attempts to roll past the last page of records in the subfile.

The third keyword needed is SFLRCDNBR (subfile record number), coded within the subfile control-record format opposite a hidden field. The value of the hidden field determines which page of the subfile is displayed when the subfile control format is written. Without this keyword and its associated field, when your program writes the control record after loading a new page into the subfile, it will by default display the first page of the subfile, rather than the newly loaded page. Using parameter value CURSOR with SFLRCDNBR causes the cursor to be positioned on that record upon display.

Note that you signify a field is hidden by entering an H in position 38 (Usage) of the DDS specifications. Hidden fields do not include a screen-location specification, because although they are part of the screen, they are not displayed. Your program can write a value to the field and read the field's value, but the user cannot see or change the value of a hidden field.

The changes this method requires in the subfile control-record format are shown below. Note that the illustrative DDS does not repeat the initial inquiry screen, the portion of the control-record format defining the column headings, or the footer-record format, because those lines remain unchanged from our first example.

```
*.. 1 ...+... 2 ...+... 3 ...+... 4 ...+... 5 ...+... 6 ...+... 7 ...+... 8
AAN01N02N03T.Name++++++RLen++TDpBLinPosFunctions++++++++++++++++++++++++++++
A* Display file SECTINQ, coded for loading the subfile one page at a time,
A* with subfile size one greater than page.
A                                        CA03(03 'F3=Exit')
A                                        CA12(12 'F12=Cancel')
A                                        REF(SECTIONS)
A* Record format for subfile.
A          R SFLSECT                     SFL
A            SECTNO      R        O  4 14
A            INSTR       R        O  4 23
A            ROOM        R        O  4 41
A            DAYS        R        O  4 49
A            BEGTIME     R      Y O  4 57EDTWRD('0 : ')
A            ENROLL      R      Y O  4 66EDTCDE(3)
A* Record format for subfile control.
A          R CTLSECT                     SFLCTL(SFLSECT)
A                                        SFLPAG(15)
A                                        SFLSIZ(16)
A 50                                     SFLCLR
A N50                                    SFLDSPCTL
A N50                                    SFLDSP
A                                        OVERLAY
A                                        ROLLUP(21 'Rollup')
A 95                                     SFLEND
A            SFLRCD      4S  0H          SFLRCDNBR(CURSOR)
A            COURSENO    6A   O   1 28
A            ...
```

The major logic changes in the program center on loading the subfile a page at a time. Each time control returns to the program from the screen, if the return was triggered by the roll key, the program must load the next page of the subfile and return control back to the screen.

When there are no more records left to load, the program should turn on the SFLEND indicator to disable rolling past the last subfile page. To determine whether additional pages can be built, the program needs to read one additional record after loading an entire subfile page before displaying the new page. The following code illustrates this technique. Note that the ClearSF subroutine is not included, because it is identical to that of our first example.

```
*.. 1 ...+... 2 ...+... 3 ...+... 4 ...+... 5 ...+... 6 ...+... 7 ...+... 8 ...+... 9 ...+...10
CLØNØ1Factor1++++++Opcode(E)+Factor2++++++Result+++++++Len++D+HiLoEq....Comments++++++++++++
CLØNØ1Factor1++++++Opcode(E)+Extended-factor2+++++++++++++++++++++++++++++Comments++++++++++++
C* Calculations for subfile application when subfile is built one page at a time.
C
C* Partial key list to access SectionL file by course number.
C     CourseKey     KLIST
C                   KFLD                      CourseNo
C* Process loop until user wants to exit.
C                   DOW       *INØ3 = *OFF
C                   EXFMT     CrseInq
C                   IF        *INØ3 = *OFF
C     CourseKey     CHAIN     SectionL                        10
C                   IF        *IN10 = *ON
C* If no matching section in file, turn on error indicator.
C                   EVAL      *IN90 = *ON
C                   ELSE
C* Otherwise clear and then load subfile.
C                   EXSR      ClearSF
C                   EXSR      LoadSF
C* Initialize SFLEND indicator to off.
C                   EVAL      *IN95 = *OFF
C* Write footer to screen and then display subfile via control record format.
C                   WRITE     Footer
C                   EXFMT     CtlSect
C* Loop to load page and display as long as user presses rollkey (*IN21).
C                   DOW       *IN21 = *ON
C                   EXSR      LoadSF
C                   EXFMT     CtlSect
C                   ENDDO
C                   ENDIF
C                   ENDIF
C                   ENDDO
C                   EVAL      *INLR = *ON
C                   RETURN
C* Subroutine to load one page of subfile or until no more records exist.
C     LoadSF        BEGSR
C                   EVAL      SflRcd = RRN + 1
C* Loop 15 times to load the page.
C                   DO        15
C                   EVAL      RRN = RRN + 1
C                   WRITE     SFLSect
C     CourseKey     READE     SectionL                        95
C                   IF        *IN95 = *ON
```

```
*.. 1 ...+... 2 ...+... 3 ...+... 4 ...+... 5 ...+... 6 ...+... 7 ...+... 8 ...+... 9 ...+...10
CLØN01Factor1++++++Opcode(E)+Factor2++++++Result+++++++Len++D+HiLoEq....Comments++++++++++++
CLØN01Factor1++++++Opcode(E)+Extended-factor2+++++++++++++++++++++++++++Comments++++++++++++
C* Early exit if no more matching records.
C                   LEAVE
C                   ENDIF
C                   ENDDO
C                   ENDSR
```

Notice that in the above code, in contrast to the code of the first method, the subroutine LoadSF reads and writes only 15 records to the subfile — that is, one page. If no more appropriate sections remain before the page is full, the looping ends. In the mainline, a loop of load-and-display continues until the user presses some key other than the rollup key (*IN21).

Variation #2 — Size Much Bigger Than Page
This method of building subfiles a page at a time, setting size much bigger than page, is really just a variant of loading the entire subfile at once. However, like variation #1, this method builds the subfile just a page at a time, instead of putting all the appropriate records in the subfile before any display.

This method is appropriate when a large number of records need to be stored in a subfile, because the large specified size allocates adjacent disk space for faster access during subfile processing. Although each user request for an additional page still requires loading that page of the subfile, the system does not have to allocate additional disk space before each page load (unless the subfile begins to exceed the declared size). You should probably not use this method if the expected subfile size exceeds 100 records.

To use this technique, you need only to make slight modifications to the display file; the program logic for this implementation remains identical to that of variation #1. In the display file, you merely need to change the subfile size and move the ROLLUP keyword from the subfile control-record format to the subfile record format. These changes are illustrated on the following page; note that the figure does not repeat the footer record or that portion of the subfile control record that describes the screen file headings, because these entries remain unchanged.

```
*.. 1 ...+... 2 ...+... 3 ...+... 4 ...+... 5 ...+... 6 ...+... 7 ...+... 8
AAN01N02N03T.Name+++++RLen++TDpBLinPosFunctions++++++++++++++++++++++++++++
A* Display file SECTINQ, coded for loading the entire subfile one page
A* at a time, with subfile size much greater than page.
A                                          CA03(03 'F3=Exit')
A                                          CA12(12 'F12=Cancel')
A                                          REF(SECTIONS)
A* Record format for subfile.
A          R SFLSECT                       SFL
A                                          ROLLUP(21 'Rollup')
A            SECTNO    R       0  4 14
A            INSTR     R       0  4 23
A            ROOM      R       0  4 41
A            DAYS      R       0  4 49
A            BEGTIME   R     Y 0  4 57EDTWRD('0 : ')
A            ENROLL    R     Y 0  4 66EDTCDE(3)
A* Record format for subfile control.
A          R CTLSECT                       SFLCTL(SFLSECT)
A                                          SFLPAG(15)
A                                          SFLSIZ(80)
A  50                                      SFLCLR
A N50                                      SFLDSPCTL
A N50                                      SFLDSP
A                                          OVERLAY
A  95                                      SFLEND
A            SFLRCD    4S 0H                SFLRCDNBR(CURSOR)
A            COURSENO  6A  0  1 28
A            ...
```

Variation #3 — Subfile Size Equals Page

Setting subfile size equal to page is most appropriate when the user is likely to want to roll through a large number of records; for example, to do generic searches. Response time is medium and consistent, regardless of the number of records viewed.

With this method, the subfile stores only one page of records. Rolling forward requires replacing the existing page with the next page through loading; because rolling backward requires replacing the existing page with records already read, the program logic required by this technique is more complicated than that of the other methods. Moreover, the method of backward rolling used will depend on whether you are accessing records by unique keys, non-unique keys, partial keys, or relative record numbers. As an alternative to enabling ROLLDOWN, often programmers require users to restart the subfile at the beginning to review records already displayed. This is the method illustrated here.

The DDS for this implementation is similar to that used when subfile size is one greater than subfile page, except that subfile size equals subfile page and keyword SFLRCDNBR is not used. (Because the subfile is only one page long, positioning the subfile upon redisplay is not a problem with this technique.) Note that the control-record format includes keywords ROLLUP and SFLEND, and function key 04 is enabled to signal restarting the course display. Also note that the illustration omits the initial inquiry screen and the screen column headings from the subfile control-record format, which remain identical to those of the previous methods. The footer prompt line now indicates that F04 restarts the subfile.

```
*.. 1 ...+... 2 ...+... 3 ...+... 4 ...+... 5 ...+... 6 ...+... 7 ...+... 8
AAN01N02N03T.Name+++++RLen++TDpBLinPosFunctions++++++++++++++++++++++++++++++
A* Display file SECTINQ, where subfile size equals subfile page.
A                                           CA03(03 'F3=Exit')
A                                           CA12(12 'F12=Cancel')
A                                           REF(SECTIONS)
A* Record format for subfile.
A            R SFLSECT                       SFL
A              SECTNO    R        0  4 14
A              INSTR     R        0  4 23
A              ROOM      R        0  4 41
A              DAYS      R        0  4 49
A              BEGTIME   R     Y  0  4 57EDTWRD('0 :  ')
A              ENROLL    R     Y  0  4 66EDTCDE(3)
A* Record format for subfile control.
A            R CTLSECT                       SFLCTL(SFLSECT)
A                                           SFLPAG(15)
A                                           SFLSIZ(15)
A  50                                       SFLCLR
A N50                                       SFLDSPCTL
A N50                                       SFLDSP
A                                           OVERLAY
A                                           ROLLUP(21 'Rollup')
A  95                                       SFLEND
A                                           CA04(04 'Restart course')
A                                           VLDCMDKEY(05)
A              COURSENO        6A  0  1 28
A                 ...
A* Footer record format.
A            R FOOTER
A                                        21  2'Press Enter to continue.'
A                                        23  2'F3=Exit  F4=Restart Sections'
A                                        23 32'F12=Cancel'
```

This method does require some major changes to the RPG IV program, however. First, before each loading of the subfile, the subfile must be cleared, because the new records should completely replace the previously displayed records. Second, the program must check the roll-key indicator and indicator 04 upon return from the screen to determine whether to put the next set of section records into the subfile or to chain to the first section record again and load the first set of records back into the subfile.

```
*.. 1 ...+... 2 ...+... 3 ...+... 4 ...+... 5 ...+... 6 ...+... 7 ...+... 8 ...+... 9 ...+...10
CLØNØ1Factor1++++++Opcode(E)+Factor2++++++Result+++++++Len++D+HiLoEq....Comments+++++++++++
CLØNØ1Factor1++++++Opcode(E)+Extended-factor2+++++++++++++++++++++++++++++Comments+++++++++++
C* Calculations for subfile application when subfile size equals page.
C
C* Partial key list to access SectionL file by course number.
C     CourseKey    KLIST
C                  KFLD                      CourseNo
C* Process loop until user wants to exit.
C                  DOW          *INØ3 = *OFF
C                  EXFMT        CrseInq
C                  IF           *INØ3 = *OFF
C     CourseKey    CHAIN        SectionL                    10
C                  IF           *IN1Ø = *ON
C* If no matching section in file, turn on error indicator.
C                  EVAL         *IN9Ø = *ON
C                  ELSE
C* Loop until user no longer wants to roll or restart the section.
C                  DOU          *INØ4=*OFF AND *IN21 = *OFF
C* If user wants to restart section, chain and reload subfile.
C                  IF           *INØ4 = *ON
C     CourseKey    CHAIN        SectionL                    10
C                  ENDIF
C* Clear and load subfile, then write footer and display subfile page.
C                  EXSR         ClearSF
C                  EXSR         LoadSF
C                  WRITE        Footer
C                  EXFMT        CtlSect
C                  ENDDO
C                  ENDIF
C                  ENDIF
C                  ENDDO
C                  EVAL         *INLR = *ON
C                  RETURN
C
C* Subroutine to clear the subfile and reset RRN to Ø.
C     ClearSF      BEGSR
C                  EVAL         *IN5Ø = *ON
C                  WRITE        CtlSect
C                  EVAL         *IN5Ø = *ON
C                  EVAL         RRN = Ø
C                  ENDSR
C
C* Subroutine to load one page of subfile or until no more records. First record of page
C* already read by CHAIN or previous READE.
C     LoadSF       BEGSR
C                  DO           15
C                  EVAL         RRN = RRN + 1
C                  WRITE        SFLSect
C     CourseKey    READE        SectionL                    95
C                  IF           *IN95 = *ON
C* Early exit if no more matching records.
C                  LEAVE
C                  ENDIF
C                  ENDDO
C                  ENDSR
```

Subfiles and Change

Assume you wanted to list sections of a course not just to inspect the data, but to make changes in the data; perhaps you need to assign different instructors to sections, or to reschedule some sections to different rooms. An RPG IV operation — READC (Read Next Changed Record) — used only with subfiles, lets you develop such an application.

The READC operation requires a subfile name in factor 2 and an indicator in positions 75-76 to signal end-of-subfile. Generally used within a loop, the READC operation will read only those records from a subfile that have been modified during a prior EXFMT operation; when no changed subfile records remain to be read, the indicator associated with the operation comes on.

Because of the READC operation, a user can make as many changes as are necessary to various records in the subfile in a single display; all these changes can then be processed when control returns to the program.

You can use READC regardless of the technique used to load and display the subfile. For simplicity's sake, we'll modify the first version of the program, in which all the relevant records are loaded into the subfile at one time, to demonstrate how to use this operation.

We need to make a few changes in the display file. First, the subfile fields need to be different from the database fields. Without this change, rereading a database record preparatory to updating it would obliterate any changes to subfile field values. Also, the usage of most of the subfile fields needs to be B, to let users modify their values; section number remains output only, to prevent changes to the key. Finally, some of the screen captions and prompts require changes to better suit the new application.

```
*.. 1 ...+... 2 ...+... 3 ...+... 4 ...+... 5 ...+... 6 ...+... 7 ...+... 8
AAN01N02N03T.Name++++++RLen++TDpBLinPosFunctions++++++++++++++++++++++++++++
A* Display file SECTUPDT, coded for loading the entire subfile at once.
A                                      CA03(03 'F3=Exit')
A                                      CA12(12 'F12=Cancel')
A                                      REF(SECTIONS)
A* Record format of initial inquiry screen.
A          R CRSEINQ
A                                      BLINK
A                                    1 28'Course Section Update'
A                                    3  2'Type value, then Enter'
A                                    5  5'Course number . .'
A          COURSENO      6A B  5 24
A N90                                  DSPATR(UL)
A N90                                  DSPATR(HI)
A  90                                  ERRMSG('Course not found' 90)
A                                   23  2'F3=Exit  F12=Cancel'
A* Record format for subfile.
A          R SFLSECT                    SFL
A          SECTNO      R     0  4 14
A          SINSTR        15  B  4 23
A          SROOM          4 0B  4 41
A          SDAYS          3  B  4 49
A          SBEGTIME      4Y 0B  4 57EDTWRD('0 :  ')
A          SENROLL       3Y 0B  4 66EDTCDE(3)
```

```
*.. 1 ...+... 2 ...+... 3 ...+... 4 ...+... 5 ...+... 6 ...+... 7 ...+... 8
AAN01N02N03T.Name++++++RLen++TDpBLinPosFunctions+++++++++++++++++++++++++++++
A* Record format for subfile control.
A             R CTLSECT                    SFLCTL(SFLSECT)
A                                          SFLPAG(15)
A                                          SFLSIZ(80)
A  50                                      SFLCLR
A N50                                      SFLDSPCTL
A N50                                      SFLDSP
A                                          OVERLAY
A               COURSENO      6A  0  1 28
A                                       1 35'Course Information'
A                                       3 12'Section'
A                                       3 24'Instructor'
A                                       3 41'Room'
A                                       3 49'Days'
A                                       3 57'Time'
A                                       3 64'Enroll.'
A* Footer record format.
A             R FOOTER
A                                      21  2'Change values as desired;-
A                                          ' press Enter to continue.'
A                                      23  2'F3=Exit  F12=Cancel'
```

The program requires a few changes to enable the updating to take place. First, remember that the database file will be an update type, so that records can be read and then rewritten to the file with any changes.

The program logic will remain basically the same. The major difference occurs when control returns to the program following the subfile display. At that point, provided the user did not press F3 or F12, the program needs to loop, using READC to read any modified subfile record and use that data to update the data file. The loop should continue until there are no more changed records.

Because specific database records need to be accessed by their complete key, the program needs a second KLIST, with both course and section as KFLDs. Finally, because the subfile and database fields are different, the program needs to move values back and forth between corresponding fields at appropriate times.

```
*.. 1 ...+... 2 ...+... 3 ...+... 4 ...+... 5 ...+... 6 ...+... 7 ...+... 8 ...+... 9 ...+...10
F********************************************************************************
F* This interactive program displays sections of a course entered by the user
F* and lets the user update the section information.
F*    Author: Yaeger   Date Modified:  Mar. 1995.
F********************************************************************************
FSectionL  UF   E    K      DISK
FSectUpdt  CF   E           WORKSTN SFILE(SFLSECT:RRN)
D RRN         S           2 0
C* Partial key list to access SectionL file by course number.
C      CourseKey    KLIST
C                   KFLD                CourseNo
C      FullKey      KLIST
C                   KFLD                CourseNo
C                   KFLD                SectNo
```

```
*.. 1 ...+... 2 ...+... 3 ...+... 4 ...+... 5 ...+... 6 ...+... 7 ...+... 8 ...+... 9 ...+...10
C* Process loop until user wants to exit.
C                   DOW       *IN03 = *OFF
C                   EXFMT     CrseInq
C                   IF        *IN03 = *OFF
C     CourseKey     SETLL     SectionL                              10
C                   IF        *IN10 = *OFF
C* If no matching section in file, turn on error indicator.
C                   EVAL      *IN90 = *ON
C                   ELSE
C* Otherwise clear and then load subfile.
C                   EXSR      ClearSF
C                   EXSR      LoadSF
C* Write footer to screen and then display subfile via control record format.
C                   WRITE     Footer
C                   EXFMT     CtlSect
C                   IF        *IN03 = *OFF and *IN12 = *OFF
C                   EXSR      UpdateSR
C                   ENDIF
C                   ENDIF
C                   ENDIF
C                   ENDDO
C                   EVAL      *INLR = *ON
C                   RETURN
C
C* Subroutine to clear the subfile and reset RRN to 0.
C     ClearSF       BEGSR
C                   EVAL      *IN50 = *ON
C                   WRITE     CtlSect
C                   EVAL      *IN50 = *OFF
C                   EVAL      RRN = 0
C                   ENDSR
C
C* Subroutine to load the subfile until no more section records exist.
C     LoadSF        BEGSR
C     CourseKey     READE     SectionL                              95
C                   DOW       *IN95 = *OFF
C                   EVAL      RRN = RRN + 1
C                   EXSR      MoveDB
C                   WRITE     SFLSect
C     CourseKey     READE     SectionL                              95
C                   ENDDO
C                   ENDSRC
C
C* Subroutine to read changed records in the subfile and update the database records.
C     UpdateSR      BEGSR
C                   READC     SFLSect                               99
C                   DOW       *IN99 = *OFF
C     FullKey       CHAIN     SectionL                      10
C                   IF        *IN10 = *OFF
C                   EXSR      MoveSF
C                   UPDATE    SecRec
C                   ENDIF
C                   READC     SFLSect                               99
C                   ENDDO
C                   ENDSR
C
C* Subroutine to transfer values from database fields to subfile fields.
C     MoveDB        BEGSR
C                   EVAL      SDays = Days
C                   EVAL      SBegTime = BegTime
C                   EVAL      SRoom = Room
C                   EVAL      SEnroll = Enroll
C                   EVAL      SInstr = Instr
C                   ENDSR
```

```
*.. 1 ...+... 2 ...+... 3 ...+... 4 ...+... 5 ...+... 6 ...+... 7 ...+... 8 ...+... 9 ...+...10
C* Subroutine to transfer values from subfile fields to database fields.
C     MoveSF        BEGSR
C                   EVAL      Days = SDays
C                   EVAL      BegTime = SBegTime
C                   EVAL      Room = SRoom
C                   EVAL      Enroll = SEnroll
C                   EVAL      Instr = SInstr
C                   ENDSR
```

Uses of Subfiles

You can use subfiles in a variety of ways. They can simply display data, when the user only needs to review information. You can use them for display with selection, so the user can select one of the entries for more detailed information about the selected record; the user can then update the selected record, if (s)he wishes to.

You can use subfiles for data entry of new records to database files, with or without validity checking. You can associate multiple subfiles with a given workstation file. You can display two subfiles simultaneously on the screen. You can transfer data between the program and the subfile by using CHAIN, UPDATE, and WRITE operations, as well as READC; such processing is always based on relative record numbers of the subfile records. Finally, you can display system messages through special message subfiles.

It should be obvious from the above discussion that subfile processing can become complex, and that mastery of programming with subfiles, like any kind of programming, comes with practice and experience.

On-Line Help

Well-designed interactive applications often let the user obtain additional information about what (s)he is supposed to do. This kind of information, called *help*, normally does not appear on the standard display because of space limitations, but can be evoked by pressing the Help key.

The AS/400 lets you build such help into your applications as part of your display file DDS. The actual help text may reside in an Office-Vision/400 document, in records within a separate display file, through panel groups defined within UIM (User Interface Manager), or as records within the display file used in the interactive application. We will look at only this last technique; for information on the other techniques, consult IBM's AS/400 manual *DDS Reference* (SC41-3712).

To build on-line help into your display file, you first need to include the keyword HELP, at either the file or record level, to enable the Help key. With the Help key enabled, pressing it will display help information associated either with the entire display or with a specific area of the display, depending on how you have implemented this feature. The simplest kind of help to code is help associated with the entire screen. For this kind of implementation, all you need in addition to the keyword HELP is file-level keyword HLPRCD, coupled with the name of the record format containing the help text.

```
*.. 1 ...+... 2 ...+... 3 ...+... 4 ...+... 5 ...+... 6 ...+... 7 ...+... 8
AAN01N02N03T.Name+++++RLen++TDpBLinPosFunctions+++++++++++++++++++++++++++++
A* Sample DDS demonstrating global help.
A                                               HELP
A                                               HLPRCD(RCD02)
A          R RCD01
A            ...
A          R RCD02
A                                       4  5'This is the record format'
A                                       5  5'containing the help text'
A                                       6  5'that will display when the'
A                                       7  5'user presses the Help key.'
```

You often want to be able to associate specific help text with specific portions of the screen, rather than having global help. You can provide such cursor-sensitive help by including a new kind of format within your DDS — the **help-specification format** — which will associate a specific portion of the screen with a specific record of help text. Signal this kind of specification by entering an H in position 17 and the keyword HLPARA in positions 45-80. Help specifications are associated with standard record formats; the H line must appear after any record-level keywords but before any fields of the associated record.

The HLPARA (Help area) associated with the help specification defines a rectangular area on the screen; if the cursor is within this area when the user presses the Help key, the text of the record associated with this help specification is displayed. Define the rectangular area by specifying within parentheses four numeric values representing the line and column positions of the upper-left corner of the rectangular area and the line and column positions of the lower-right corner of the area.

In addition to the HLPARA, the help specification includes keyword HLPRCD to designate which record should be displayed when the user requests help from within the designated screen area.

```
*.. 1 ...+... 2 ...+... 3 ...+... 4 ...+... 5 ...+... 6 ...+... 7 ...+... 8
AAN01N02N03T.Name+++++RLen++TDpBLinPosFunctions+++++++++++++++++++++++++++++
A* Sample DDS demonstrating cursor-sensitive help.
A                                               CA03(03 'F3=Exit')
A                                               HELP
A                                               HLPRCD(GENHLP)
A          R INQREC
A        H                                      HLPARA(2 10 4 40)
A                                               HLPRCD(REC1)
A        H                                      HLPARA(5 15 20 70)
A                                               HLPRCD(REC2)
A            ...
A          R REC1
A                                       1  5'Help text 1'
A          R REC2
A                                       1  5'Help text 2'
A          R GENHLP
A                                       1  5'General help'
```

In the generic example above, two different help areas are associated with record format INQREC. Each help area, in turn, evokes a different help record. If the user presses the Help key while viewing INQREC and his/her cursor is in the rectangular area defined by screen line 2, column 10 and line 4, column 40, the contents of REC1 display; if the cursor is within the area defined by line 5, column 15 and line 20, column 70, REC2 displays. If the cursor is outside both these areas, record GENHLP displays.

To further demonstrate on-line help, the display file from the course-inquiry application is partially duplicated below with the addition of specific help (if the user's cursor is on the screen line asking for course input) and general help instructions (if the cursor is anywhere else on the screen).

```
*.. 1 ...+... 2 ...+... 3 ...+... 4 ...+... 5 ...+... 6 ...+... 7 ...+... 8
AAN01N02N03T.Name++++++RLen++TDpBLinPosFunctions+++++++++++++++++++++++++++++++
A                                       CA03(03 'F3=Exit')
A                                       CA12(12 'F12=Cancel')
A                                       HELP
A                                       HLPRCD(GENHLP)
A* Record format of initial inquiry screen.
A          R CRSEINQ
A                                       BLINK
A          H                            HLPARA(5 5 5 24)
A                                       HLPRCD(CORHLP)
A                                     1 28'Course Section Update'
A                                     3  2'Type value, then Enter.'
A                                     5  5'Course number . .'
A            COURSENO      6A  B      5 24
A N90                                   DSPATR(UL)
A N90                                   DSPATR(HI)
A  90                                   ERRMSG('Course not found' 90)
A                                    23  2'F3=Exit   F12=Cancel'
A          R GENHLP
A                                     4  5'To get Help, position the'
A                                     4 30' cursor within the item f'
A                                     4 55'or which you want more   '
A                                     5  5'information and press Hel'
A                                     5 30'p.'
A          R CORHLP
A                                     5  5'Enter the 6 character ID '
A                                     5 30'of the course whose secti'
A                                     5 55'ons you want to see.     '
A                                     6  5'(For example, BIS264)'
```

You can have as many help specifications, each describing a different screen area, as you need. The area can be as big or small as you wish to make it. If the user presses the Help key outside all defined help areas, the file-level help record is displayed, if you have included one; otherwise, the system informs the user that no help is available. You cannot use help specifications within subfile record formats but may include them as part of subfile control-record formats.

Chapter Summary

Subfiles let users work with more than one database record at a time in an interactive application. Records stored in a subfile are displayed in a single output operation to the workstation file; changes made to subfile records are returned to the program in a single input operation.

To define subfiles within DDS requires two kinds of record formats: one that defines the fields within the subfile and describes the field locations within a screen line; and a second format, called a subfile control-record format, that actually manages the displaying of the subfile information.

You use several required keywords with subfiles: Record-level keyword SFL identifies a record format as a subfile record, while record-level keyword SFLCTL identifies a format as a subfile control-record format. Additional required keywords determine how many records appear on the screen at the same time, how much total storage the system allocates to the subfile, and when the subfile and its control record are displayed.

Several different techniques exist for loading and displaying subfiles. These methods differ in the relationship they establish between subfile page and subfile size and in when they write records to the subfile relative to when the subfile display begins. Regardless of the technique you use, all applications involving subfiles require additional entries on the File Specifications for the workstation files using the subfiles. You do all input to and output from a subfile through relative record numbers. The READC operation lets your application program process just those subfile records that the user has changed.

The AS/400 lets you associate on-line help with an entire screen or with specific areas of the screen that the user can access through the Help key.

Terms

help-specification format
list panels

relative record number
subfiles

subfile record format
subfile control-record format

Discussion/Review Questions

1. What is a subfile?

2. What are the functions of a subfile record format and a subfile control-record format in a display file?

3. What are the meanings of the following display file keywords, and which record format is each used with? SFL, SFLCTL, SFLPAG, SFLSIZ, SFLDSP, SFLCLR, SFLDSPCTL.

4. In subfile processing, how are column headings for the subfile and screen footings (i.e., information to display below the subfile) generally handled?

5. What is a File Specification continuation line? What information is required on a continuation line when you develop an application using subfiles?

6. What is a hidden field?

7. When do you need to use the keyword SFLRCDNBR?

8. Discuss the relative merits of different approaches to subfile definition and loading.

9. Discuss roll-key control and action with the different approaches to subfile definition and loading.

10. How does the READC operation differ from the other read operations of RPG IV?

11. In using subfiles for updating, why do you need to use fields for the subfile that are different from the fields of the database file you are updating?

12. How do you establish cursor-sensitive help?

Exercises

1. Design the screens and write the DDS for an interactive application that lets the user enter a zip code and lists the names of all the company's customers residing within that zip code. Create whatever fields you may need and make subfile size much greater than page.

2. Write the RPG IV for Exercise 1. Make up whatever file and field names you need, but be consistent with definitions used in Exercise 1. Use the technique of loading the entire subfile prior to display.

3. Revise the DDS from Exercise 1 to make subfile size and page equal. Modify the RPG IV code from Exercise 2 to suit this change.

4. Write the pseudocode for an interactive application that will display a list of all a company's product numbers and their descriptions and let the user place an X in front of those products for which (s)he wants more information. The program should then display a screen of detailed production information (quantity on hand, cost, selling price, reorder point, reorder quantity) for each product selected by the user.

5. Write the generic pseudocode needed to use subfiles for data entry (i.e., for adding large numbers of records to a file).

Programming Assignments

1. Write an interactive application for Wexler University that will let the user enter a department number to display all the instructors working within that department. Use a logical file built over WUINSTP (see Appendix D).

2. Write an interactive application for CompuSell that will let a user locate a customer based on a generic name search. That is, the user can enter one or more starting letters of the last name and the program will display the customers by last name, starting with the first customer whose name meets the generic specification and ending when a customer's name no longer matches that specification.

   The subfile of customers displayed should include just the last name, first name, and identification of the customers, plus a selection field. If the user chooses (selects) one of the records, the program then should display all the detailed information about that customer (all the data fields of the customer master file). You will need to use CSCSTP and a logical file keyed on last name built over CSCSTP (see Appendix D). Include a generic help screen in your application.

3. Write an application for Wexler University that will let a user interactively add or change (but not delete) a course and/or its description in files WUCRSP and WUCRSDSP (see Appendix D). Do not let the user change the course identification, or add a duplicate identification. All other fields of either file may be changed. Do not display the line numbers of the description on the screen.

4. GTC Telephone Company wants you to develop an interactive application to process payments from customers. The program should let the user enter a screen full of payments at one time by entering for each payer his phone number and amount paid. This information should be used for two purposes: 1) to update the Customer Master File (GTCSTP) amount-owed and data-of-last-payment fields; and 2) to write a record to the Payments Archive File (GTPAYP). Use the system date for date fields. See Appendix D for file layouts.

Chapter 11

Working with Bytes and Bits

Chapter Overview

This chapter introduces you to several RPG IV built-in functions and operations that let you inspect or manipulate individual positions or bytes within a field. You will also learn how to work with bit patterns and when such manipulations are needed.

Field Inspection

Often a field is defined as "the smallest unit of data that can be manipulated within a program." It would be more accurate to say that a field is the unit most often manipulated by a program. In fact, RPG IV offers a way to access data at subfield levels through data structures. Additionally, RPG IV includes **built-in functions (BIFs)** and operations that let you inspect or manipulate individual bytes, or even bits of bytes, within data fields. Although these features are not needed as often as other operations discussed so far, they do provide options for processing data at a level that otherwise would be beyond our capabilities.

Two RPG IV built-in functions let you inspect the size of data items, while several RPG IV operations let you check, or test, individual positions, or bytes, within a character field.

Inspecting Size

In Chapter 9 we discussed built-in function %ADDR, which you can use to assign a value to a basing pointer. RPG IV offers two built-in functions that return values associated with the size of fields, literals, named constants, arrays, tables, and data structures. Like %ADDR, these functions return specific values based on evaluation of their arguments (parameters within parentheses following the function).

You can use these functions to help define data items within Definition Specifications, or you can use them within calculations. When used in Calculation Specifications, the functions can only appear within an extended factor 2 entry.

%SIZE (Number of Bytes)
%SIZE returns the number of bytes, or length, of its argument. The function
requires at least one parameter, which represents the data item whose size you
want. You can use %SIZE to determine the size of a field, literal, named constant, data structure, subfield, array, or table. If the argument has only a single
parameter, and that parameter is the name of an array, table, or multiple-
occurrence data structure, the value returned is the size of a single element or
occurrence. If a second parameter, *ALL, follows the first, the returned value
is the size of the entire table, array, or data structure. Below are some examples demonstrating how to use %SIZE. Notice that the argument containing
two parameters uses a colon (:) to separate them.

```
*.. 1 ...+... 2 ...+... 3 ...+... 4 ...+... 5 ...+... 6 ...+... 7 ...+... 8 ...+... 9 ...+...10
CLØNØ1Factor1++++++Opcode(E)+Extended-factor2++++++++++++++++++++++++++++Comments++++++++++++
C* Examples demonstrating how to use BIF %SIZE.
C
C* Obtain the size of a field.
C                   EVAL      SIZ = %SIZE(FIELDA)
C* Obtain the size of one array element.
C                   EVAL      SIZ = %SIZE(ArrayX)
C* Obtain the size of an entire table.
C                   EVAL      SIZ = %SIZE(TableX:*ALL)
C* Obtain the size of a literal.
C                   EVAL      SIZ = %SIZE('gurubesar')
```

When you use %SIZE to determine the length of a packed-decimal value
or a binary value, remember it returns the number of bytes used to store the
value, *not* the number of digits in the value. Consider the following examples:

```
*.. 1 ...+... 2 ...+... 3 ...+... 4 ...+... 5 ...+... 6 ...+... 7 ...+... 8 ...+... 9 ...+...10
DName++++++++++ETDsFrom+++To/L+++IDc.Keywords+++++++++++++++++++++++++++++Comments++++++++++++
CLØNØ1Factor1++++++Opcode(E)+Extended-factor2++++++++++++++++++++++++++++Comments++++++++++++
D Salary          S              5P 0
D BNumber         S              3B 0
D NumOfBytes      S              2  0
C                   EVAL      NumOfBytes = %SIZE(Salary)
C* Suppose Salary stores 48600; NumOfBytes = (number of digits + 1)/2 = (5 + 1)/2 = 3,
C* applying the formula from Chapter 5.
C                   EVAL      NumOfBytes = %SIZE(BNumber)
C* Suppose BNumber stores 750; NumOfBytes = 2, because 750 requires two bytes to store
C* its base 2 representation (1011101110).
```

As mentioned previously, you sometimes find this function helpful
when defining other data items, as shown in the next set of examples.

```
*.. 1 ...+... 2 ...+... 3 ...+... 4 ...+... 5 ..+... 6 ...+... 7 ...+... 8 ..+... 9 ...+...10
DName++++++++++ETDsFrom+++To/L+++IDc.Keywords++++++++++++++++++++++++++++++Comments+++++++++++
D* Definition Specifications showing BIF %SIZE used to define data items.
D FieldA          S             25
D
D* Number of elements of ArrayA based on the length of FieldA.
D ArrayA          S              3    DIM(%SIZE(FieldA))
D
D* Initial value of Indx set to length of FieldA.
D Indx            S              2 0  INZ(%SIZE(FieldA))
D
D* Constant MaxVal equals the entire length of ArrayA.
D MaxVal          C                   CONST(%SIZE(ArrayA:*ALL))
```

%ELEM *(Number of Elements)*

The second size-related built-in function RPG IV supports is %ELEM, which returns the number of elements in an array or a table, or the number of occurrences in a multiple-occurrence data structure. Like %SIZE, you can use %ELEM in calculations or when defining other fields. This latter use can result in code that is self-documented and easy to maintain, as demonstrated by the following example:

```
*.. 1 ...+... 2 ...+... 3 ...+... 4 ...+... 5 ...+... 6 ...+... 7 ...+... 8 ...+... 9 ...+...10
DName++++++++++ETDsFrom+++To/L+++IDc.Keywords++++++++++++++++++++++++++++++Comments+++++++++++
D* Example showing how to use BIF %ELEM within field definitions.
D NumLocats       C                   CONST(100)
D NumMonths       C                   CONST(12)
D Location        S              4 0  DIM(NumLocats)
D MonthSales      DS                  OCCURS(NumMonths)
D   LocatTotal                  10 2  DIM(%ELEM(Location))
D Projection      DS                  OCCURS(%ELEM(MonthSales))
D   LocatProj                   10 2  DIM(%ELEM(LocatTotal))
```

In this example, array Location stores four-digit code numbers for 100 shop locations. MonthSales is a multiple-occurrence data structure that contains an array of monthly sales totals for each location. Projection is the same type of data structure, but it stores monthly sales projections for each location. If the number of shop locations changes over time or the number of months per sales cycle changes, updating only the named constants and recompiling the program will automatically adjust the number of elements allocated for MonthSales and Projection.

The following example shows how you might use %ELEM within Calculation Specifications:

```
*.. 1 ...+... 2 ...+... 3 ...+... 4 ...+... 5 ...+... 6 ...+... 7 ...+... 8 ...+... 9 ...+...10
CL0N01Factor1+++++++Opcode(E)+Extended-factor2+++++++++++++++++++++++++++++Comments+++++++++++
C* Assume field Indx was defined as a 4-digit integer value.
C                   EVAL      Indx = 1
C                   DOW       Indx <= %ELEM(LocatTotal)
C                   ...
C                   EVAL        Indx = Indx + 1
C                   ENDDO
```

In this example, we've matched the number of passes through the loop to the number of elements in LocatTotal. Should the number of locations change over time, you would not have to make any changes to these Calculation Specifications — the number of loop passes would automatically adjust to the updated number of elements of LocatTotal.

Inspecting Bytes

RPG IV provides several operations to test the value or individual bytes of a field. These operations — TESTN, TEST, SCAN, CHECK, and CHECKR — are described in the sections that follow.

TESTN (Test Numeric)

You can use the TESTN operation to determine whether a character field contains all numeric characters, leading blanks followed by all numeric characters, or all blanks. The operation is useful for validating fields before you use them in mathematical operations or attempt to edit the fields to prevent an abnormal program ending that would occur if the data were non-numeric. Because you can use the TESTN operation only with character fields, you would need to move the field's value to a numeric field following validation or redefine the field as a numeric variable within a data structure, before you use it for arithmetic or editing.

The TESTN operation does not use factors 1 and 2 of the standard Calculation Specification; the field to be tested occurs as the result field. You must use at least one resulting indicator with this operation. Where you position that indicator depends on what you are trying to test for. You can, if you wish, use indicators in all three resulting indicator positions.

An indicator specified in positions 71-72 (Hi) comes on if all the characters within the field are numeric. An indicator in positions 73-74 (Lo) comes on if the result field contains numeric characters and one or more leading blanks. An indicator in positions 75-76 (Eq) comes on if the result field contains all blanks.

Because of the way RPG IV handles signed numbers, the right-most character of the field may contain the EBCDIC representation of A-R and still be considered numeric, since these are the same representations as signed (+ or –) digits 0-9.

Study the following examples to understand the use of indicators with this operation:

```
*.. 1 ...+... 2 ...+... 3 ...+... 4 ...+... 5 ...+... 6 ..+... 7 ...+... 8 ...+... 9 ...+...10
CL0N01Factor1++++++Opcode(E)+Factor2++++++Result+++++++Len++D+HiLoEq....Comments+++++++++++
C* TESTN with an indicator in the Hi position.
C                    TESTN                   FieldA            10
```

Given the TESTN coded above, indicator 10, entered in the Hi resulting indicator position, would be off or on, depending on the value of FieldA.

FieldA	*IN10	Explanation
'123'	ON	Every character is numeric.
'1A3'	OFF	A is not numeric.
'12C'	ON	C interpreted as positively signed 3.

If you include several indicators along with the TESTN operation, at most one would turn on as a result of the check.

```
*.. 1 ...+... 2 ...+... 3 ...+... 4 ...+... 5 ...+... 6 ...+... 7 ...+... 8 ...+... 9 ...+...10
CL0N01Factor1++++++Opcode(E)+Factor2++++++Result++++++++Len++D+HiLoEq....Comments+++++++++++
C* TESTN with three resulting indicators specified.
C                   TESTN               FieldA                    102030
```

The table below shows what the status of indicators 10, 20, and 30 would be following the TESTN above, given different values for FieldA.

FieldA	*IN10	*IN20	*IN30	Explanation
'123'	ON	OFF	OFF	All characters are digits.
' 23'	OFF	ON	OFF	Leading blank is present.
' 3'	OFF	ON	OFF	Both blanks are leading.
'1 3'	OFF	OFF	OFF	Blank is not leading.
' '	OFF	OFF	ON	All characters are blanks.
'A2C'	OFF	OFF	OFF	A is not a digit.

TEST (Test Date/Time/Timestamp)
The TEST operation is similar to TESTN, except it checks the validity of date, time, or timestamp fields. You code the field to be tested as the result field, and leave factor 1 and factor 2 blank. A resulting indicator coded in positions 73-74 (Lo) comes on if the result field contains an invalid date/time value. The examples below demonstrate this use of the TEST operation.

```
*.. 1 ...+... 2 ...+... 3 ...+... 4 ...+... 5 ...+... 6 ...+... 7 ...+... 8 ...+... 9 ...+...10
CL0N01Factor1++++++Opcode(E)+Factor2++++++Result++++++++Len++D+HiLoEq....Comments+++++++++++
C* Fields TodaysDate and StartTime are date (D) and time (T) data types, respectively.
C                   TEST                TodaysDate                    90
C                   TEST                StartTime                     90
```

To use TEST to check character and numeric fields for valid date/time data, you must include an operation extender (D for date, T for time, and Z for timestamp) to identify which test you want to perform. Factor 1 contains the date/time display format (e.g., *MDY, *USA) you want to compare to your data. If it is blank, RPG IV compares your data to the default *ISO format. Consider the following examples, where UserDate and UserTime are numeric fields:

```
*.. 1 ...+... 2 ...+... 3 ...+... 4 ...+... 5 ...+... 6 ...+... 7 ...+... 8 ...+... 9 ...+...10
CL0N01Factor1++++++Opcode(E)+Extended-factor2+++++++++++++++++++++++++++++++++Comments+++++++++++
CL0N01Factor1++++++Opcode(E)+Factor2++++++Result+++++++Len++D+HiLoEq....Comments+++++++++++
C                   EVAL      UserDate = 19950315
C                   TEST (D)            UserDate              90
C* Factor 1 is blank, so UserDate is checked to see if it stores a valid *ISO date;
C* indicator 90 is set off because the value is a valid date for the default format.
C                   EVAL      UserTime = 180000
C     *HMS          TEST (T)            UserTime              90
C* UserTime is a valid *HMS time value, so indicator 90 is set off.
C                   EVAL      UserDate = 12311995
C     *EUR          TEST (D)            UserDate              90
C* Now UserDate is tested to see if it is a valid *EUR date value (dd.mm.yyyy);
C* because it is not a valid date in this format, indicator 90 is set on.
```

When testing the date/time validity of character fields, RPG IV also checks to see that valid separator characters are included in the field. Assume UserDate is a 10-byte character field and UserTime is an 8-byte character field in the following examples:

```
*.. 1 ...+... 2 ...+... 3 ...+... 4 ...+... 5 ...+... 6 ...+... 7 ...+... 8 ...+... 9 ...+...10
CL0N01Factor1++++++Opcode(E)+Extended-factor2+++++++++++++++++++++++++++++++++Comments+++++++++++
CL0N01Factor1++++++Opcode(E)+Factor2++++++Result+++++++Len++D+HiLoEq....Comments+++++++++++
C                   EVAL      UserDate = '1995-03-15'
C                   TEST (D)            UserDate              90
C* Indicator 90 is set off because UserDate is a valid *ISO date.
C                   EVAL      UserTime = '18-00-00'
C     *HMS          TEST (T)            UserTime              90
C* The hypehn (-) is not a valid separator for *HMS format, so indicator 90 is set on.
```

SCAN (Scan Character String)

The SCAN operation lets you look for a character or a string of characters within a character field. The direction of the SCAN is left to right. SCAN is case sensitive; that is, 'A' is not the same as 'a'. If the string you are looking for includes blanks, whether leading, trailing, or embedded, the blanks are considered part of the pattern to find. Similarly, blanks within the field searched are not ignored. SCAN requires entries in both factor 1 and factor 2. An optional result indicator in positions 75-76 (Eq) comes on if the SCAN is successful.

```
*.. 1 ...+... 2 ...+... 3 ...+... 4 ...+... 5 ...+... 6 ...+... 7 ...+... 8 ...+... 9 ...+...10
CL0N01Factor1++++++Opcode(E)+Factor2++++++Result+++++++Len++D+HiLoEq....Comments+++++++++++
C* Sample format of the SCAN operation.  Look for FieldA's contents within FieldB and
C* turn on indicator 50 if the string is found.
C     FieldA        SCAN      FieldB                          50
```

Factor 1 contains the string you are looking for, sometimes called the **compare string**. This may be represented by a character field, an array element, a named constant, a data structure name, a literal, or a table name. Moreover, you can specify that only a portion of that data item be used as the string to search for by following the data item with a colon (:), followed by an integer length, expressed either as a literal, field, named constant, array element, or table name. The length determines how much of the factor 1 entry the operation scans for.

For example, factor 1 could be Code, in which case the entire value of the Code field would be the compare string, or it could be Code:3, in which case the first three characters of the Code field would be the compare string. If factor 1 were Code:X, the value of X would determine how many characters of Code comprised the compare string.

Factor 2 contains the string to be scanned, sometimes called the **base string**. The base string may be a character field, array element, named constant, data-structure name, literal, or table name. The base string may be followed by a colon (:), followed in turn by an integer literal, field, named constant, or array element that represents the *starting location* for the SCAN within the string. For example, if factor 2 contains Name, the entire Name field will be scanned, whereas if it contains Name:4, the scan will begin at the fourth character in the Name field.

```
*.. 1 ...+... 2 ...+... 3 ...+... 4 ...+... 5 ...+... 6 ...+... 7 ...+... 8 ...+... 9 ...+...10
CL0N01Factor1++++++Opcode(E)+Factor2++++++Result+++++++Len++D+HiLoEq....Comments++++++++++++
C* SCAN operations showing variant formats of Factor1 and Factor2.
C
C* Search for FieldA within FieldB.
C     FieldA        SCAN      FieldB                        50
C
C* Search string begins with the 4th character of FieldA; scan all of FieldB.
C     FieldA:4      SCAN      FieldB                        50
C
C* Look for all of FieldA in FieldB, beginning with the 3rd position of FieldB.
C     FieldA        SCAN      FieldB:3          50
C
C* Look for a portion of FieldA within a portion of FieldB; the length of FieldA's substring
C* and the starting position within FieldB are based on variables.
C     FieldA:X      SCAN      FieldB:Y          50
```

You can also include an optional result field with SCAN. If used, the result may be a field, an array element, an array name, or a table name, but it must be defined as a numeric data type with no decimal positions (i.e., an integer). If a result field is present and it is anything other than an array name, the SCAN operation will stop as soon as it locates an occurrence of the compare string within the base string, and a number representing the starting position of the compare string within the base string will be stored in the result field. If the compare string is not found within the base string, the result field is set to 0.

To get a feeling for how SCAN works with a result field, consider the following example:

```
*.. 1 ...+... 2 ...+... 3 ...+... 4 ...+... 5 ...+... 6 ...+... 7 ...+... 8 ...+... 9 ...+...10
CL0N01Factor1++++++Opcode(E)+Factor2++++++Result+++++++Len++D+HiLoEq....Comments++++++++++++
C* Sample SCAN with result field, Found, a numeric integer field.
C     LookFor       SCAN      LookIn        Found           50
```

The table below shows the effects the previous SCAN operation would have on the contents of Found and indicator 50, where LookFor = 'my' and LookIn takes on various values.

Field Values		Results		
LookFor	LookIn	Found	*IN50	Explanation
'my'	'Do it my way'	7	ON	Match of 'my' and 'my'.
'my'	'Amy knows best.'	2	ON	Match of 'my' and 'my'.
'my'	'It may harm you.'	0	OFF	'my' is not 'may' or 'm y'.
'my'	'My way is best.'	0	OFF	'my' is not 'My'.
'my'	'Amy knows my dad.'	2	ON	Stops at first 'my' match.

If the result field is an array name, the SCAN does not stop when it finds the first match, but instead continues to the end of the base field. The starting locations of each occurrence of the compare string within the base string are stored in successive elements of the array. If the array contains more elements than the number of compare string occurrences within the base string, the unneeded array elements are set to 0.

```
*.. 1 ...+... 2 ...+... 3 ...+... 4 ...+... 5 ...+... 6 ...+... 7 ...+... 8 ...+... 9 ...+...10
CLØN01Factor1++++++Opcode(E)+Factor2++++++Result++++++++Len++D+HiLoEq....Comments+++++++++++
C* In the examples below, assume that FieldA's value is 'abcde', while FieldB is
C* 'mabcdeabczab'.  The comment below each example explains the results of the SCAN.
C
C      FieldA:3      SCAN      FieldB        FieldC                     50
C* FieldC is 2, and 50 is on, because compare value 'abc' is found in FieldB at position 2.
C
C      FieldA:3      SCAN      FieldB:3      FieldC                     50
C* FieldC is 7 and 50 is on, because SCAN starts in position 3 of FieldB.
C
C      FieldA:4      SCAN      FieldB:3      FieldC                     50
C* FieldC is 0 and 50 is off, because 'abcd' not found from position 3 to the end of FieldB.
C
C      FieldA:2      SCAN      FieldB        Arry                       50
C* Arry is a 5-element array.  Its values are 2, 7, 11, 0, and 0, because 'ab' was found
C* in positions 2, 7, and 11 of FieldB.  50 is on.
```

When coding the SCAN operation, you optionally may include an indicator in positions 73-74 (Lo), which will come on if an error occurs during the operation.

The SCAN operation is useful for inspecting text data. It could be used, for example, to scan addresses to locate all businesses or customers residing on the same street. Text retrieval software uses operations like SCAN to index text based on the presence of keywords within the text.

CHECK (Check)
The format of the CHECK operation is similar to that of SCAN. Factor 1 contains a character compare field, and factor 2 contains a source or base string, while the result field contains a numeric field or array name.

Significant differences exist between CHECK and SCAN, however. SCAN looks for the *presence* of the *entire* compare string within the base string and notes the location of its occurrence in the result field. CHECK notes *discrepancies* between the *individual characters* of the compare field and the base string and signals the *absence* of a base character from the set of compare characters by storing its location in the result field.

SCAN is used for locating substrings within a base string, while CHECK is useful for verification of characters within the base string.

```
*.. 1 ...+... 2 ...+... 3 ...+... 4 ...+... 5 ...+... 6 ...+... 7 ...+... 8 ...+... 9 ...+...10
CL0N01Factor1++++++Opcode(E)+Factor2++++++Result++++++++Len++D+HiLoEq....Comments+++++++++++
C* Example showing format of CHECK.
C     LookIn     CHECK     LookFor     NotFound
```

The factor 1 value of CHECK, represented in a character field, literal, named constant, data structure, array element, or table name, contains a list of valid characters. Factor 2 contains the character field, literal, named constant, data structure, array element, or table name whose characters you want checked against those of the data item in factor 1. The result field contains a numeric field, array element, data structure name, table name, or array name.

The CHECK operation proceeds from left to right as it checks the characters of the base string against those in the compare string. If the result field is anything other than an array name, CHECK stores in it the position of the first character of the base string not found in the compare string. If all the base string characters are present in the compare string, the result field is set to 0. If the result field is an array name, the CHECK operation does not stop at the first mismatch, but continues to store the positions of unmatched base-string characters in successive elements of the named array. Unneeded array elements are set to 0.

As with the SCAN operation, you can use the colon notation with the base string to specify the position within the base string where the CHECK operation is to begin; the value represented by the field or literal following the colon determines the starting location for the CHECK.

If you don't need to know the position of invalid characters but simply want to know whether the base string contains one or more invalid characters, you can omit a result-field entry and code an indicator in positions 75-76 (Eq) of the specification. This indicator will come on if CHECK finds one or more unmatched characters in the base string.

```
*.. 1 ...+... 2 ...+... 3 ...+... 4 ...+... 5 ...+... 6 ...+... 7 ...+... 8 ...+... 9 ...+...10
CL0N01Factor1++++++Opcode(E)+Factor2++++++Result++++++++Len++D+HiLoEq....Comments+++++++++++
C* Examples illustrating the CHECK operation.
C
C* Assume field Code contains 'X'.
C     'ABCDE'       CHECK     Code                            50
C* 50 comes on, because X is not a character within factor 1.
C
C* Assume Digits contains '0123456789' and Amount contains '$125.50'.
C     Digits        CHECK     Amount       Reslt              50
C* 50 comes on, and Reslt is 1, because the 1st position character of Amount, the $, is
C* not contained within Digits.
C
C* Assume Digits contains '0123456789', Amount contains '$125.50', and Arry is a
C* 5-element numeric array.
C     Digits        CHECK     Amount       Arry               50
C* Arry(1) is 1 (position of $); Arry(2) is 5 (position of the decimal point);the remaining
C* array elements' values are 0.  50 is on.
C
C* Assume Digits contains '0123456789', Amount contains '$125.50', and Arry is a
C* 5-element numeric array.
C     Digits        CHECK     Amount:2     Arry               50
C* Arry(1) is 5 (position of the decimal point); all other elements are 0. The position
C* of the $ is not noted because the CHECK begins with the 2nd position of Amount.
```

CHECKR (Check Reverse)

CHECKR works exactly like CHECK, except that it checks the base string from right to left, rather than from left to right. You can use this operation to locate the right-most invalid character in a string or to determine the length of a string of non-blank characters within a field.

```
*.. 1 ...+... 2 ...+... 3 ...+... 4 ...+... 5 ...+... 6 ...+... 7 ...+... 8 ...+... 9 ...+...10
CL0N01Factor1++++++Opcode(E)+Factor2++++++Result++++++++Len++D+HiLoEq....Comments+++++++++++
C* Examples of CHECKR.
C     'ABCDE'       CHECKR    Code                            50
C* 50 comes on, because X is not a character within factor 1.
C
C* Assume Digits contains '0123456789' and Amount contains '$125.50'.
C     Digits        CHECKR    Amount       Reslt              50
C* 50 comes on, and Reslt is 5, because the 5th position character of Amount, the decimal
C* point, is not contained within Digits.
C
C* Assume Digits contains '0123456789', Amount contains '$125.50', and Arry is a
C* 5-element numeric array.
C     Digits        CHECKR    Amount       Arry               50
C* Arry(1) is 5 (position of the decimal point); Arry(2) is 1 (position of $); the
C* remaining array elements' values are 0.  50 is on.
C
C* Assume Name contains 'Jones         '
C     ' '           CHECKR    Name         Length
C* Length has a value of 5, the position of the right-most non-blank character of Name.
```

Field Character Manipulation

The built-in functions and operations we've discussed so far in this chapter let you look at (or inspect) size, individual characters, and substrings of character fields.

RPG IV also provides several features that enable string manipulation: the + operator used with EVAL for concatenating (i.e., combining) strings; the built-in functions %TRIM, %TRIML, and %TRIMR for removing leading and/or trailing blanks from strings; the built-in function %SUBST for extracting substrings; and operation XLATE for converting characters within a string. These operations and functions let you change individual characters or strings of characters within a field.

+ (Concatenate Character Strings)

Using + with EVAL is a convenient way to concatenate two (or more) strings to form a new string. You can combine string literals, named constants, and character fields in a free-form expression using one or more occurrences of +, coded in the extended factor 2 region of the Calculation Specification. The examples below demonstrate how to use + to concatenate strings.

```
*.. 1 ...+... 2 ...+... 3 ...+... 4 ...+... 5 ...+... 6 ...+... 7 ...+... 8 ...+... 9 ...+...10
CLØNØ1Factor1++++++Opcode(E)+Extended-factor2++++++++++++++++++++++++++++Comments+++++++++++
C* Examples of string concatenation using + with EVAL.
C
C                   EVAL      Greeting = 'Hello ' + 'World'
C* Greeting now contains 'Hello World'
C
C                   EVAL      FullName = FirstName + ' ' +
C                             MidInitial + '. ' +
C                             LastName
C* FullName contains the contents of field FirstName followed immediately by a space,
C* the contents of MidInitial, a period and another space, and the contents of LastName.
```

In the example above, if Firstname contained the value 'Susan', MidInitial contained the value 'B', and LastName contained 'Anthony', then FullName's value would be 'Susan B. Anthony'. However, if FirstName and LastName were both of length 10 and right-padded with blanks, FullName would retain the extra blanks: 'Susan   B. Anthony   '. To eliminate such unneeded blanks, RPG IV provides three built-in functions, which we'll discuss in the next section.

If the concatenated string is smaller than the result field it is assigned to, EVAL right-pads the result field with blanks. If the concatenated string is too large to fit in the result field it is assigned to, truncation occurs from the right end of the string.

```
*.. 1 ...+... 2 ...+... 3 ...+... 4 ...+... 5 ...+... 6 ...+... 7 ...+... 8 ...+... 9 ...+...10
CLØNØ1Factor1++++++Opcode(E)+Extended-factor2++++++++++++++++++++++++++++Comments+++++++++++
C* The examples below are based on FName (5 positions), with a value of 'John ';
C* LName (12 positions), with a value of 'Jackson III '; WholeName (25 positions); and
C* ShortName (1Ø positions).
C
C                   EVAL      WholeName = FName + LName
C* WholeName contains 'John Jackson III        ', with blanks appearing in its unused
C* right-most positions.
C
C                   EVAL      ShortName = FName + LName
C* ShortName contains 'John Jacks', because it can store only 1Ø characters.
```

%TRIM, %TRIML, and %TRIMR (Trim Blanks)

Three built-in functions — %TRIM, %TRIML, and %TRIMR — remove leading and/or trailing blanks from their arguments. These functions each require a single argument, which must be a data item of either character or graphic data type. %TRIML removes leading, or left-most blanks from the argument; %TRIMR removes trailing, or right-most blanks; and %TRIM removes both leading and trailing blanks. The value returned by these functions is the trimmed result, a character string. You can use these functions with character variables, constants, or expressions. You can see how these trimming functions work from the examples below.

Function	Returned Value
%TRIML(' 1234 N. 25th St. ')	'1234 N. 25th St. '
%TRIMR(' 1234 N. 25th St. ')	' 1234 N. 25th St.'
%TRIM(' 1234 N. 25th St. ')	'1234 N. 25th St.'

```
*.. 1 ...+... 2 ...+... 3 ...+... 4 ...+... 5 ...+... 6 ...+... 7 ...+... 8 ...+... 9 ...+...10
CL0N01Factor1++++++Opcode(E)+Extended-factor2++++++++++++++++++++++++++Comments++++++++++++
C* Examples applying the %TRIMx BIFs.
C
C* Perform left-justification using %TRIML.
C                   EVAL      LeftText = %TRIML(TextLine)
C
C* Concatenate first and last name, with one space in between.
C                   EVAL      FullName = %TRIMR(FirstName) + ' ' +
C                                        %TRIM(LastName)
C
C* Determine the length of the name of the city.
C                   EVAL      CharCnt = %SIZE(%TRIM(City))
```

%SUBST (Substring)

Built-in function %SUBST extracts a substring, or portion, of a character string. The argument parameters of %SUBST are, in order, the string from which the extraction is to occur; the position within that string where the substring is to start; and, optionally, the length of the substring. If you omit this third parameter, the substring will include all the bytes from the starting position to the final, rightmost byte of the string. Thus, the format of the substring function is

%SUBST(string:start{:length})

As shown above, you use colon separators between parameters. You can represent the starting position and the optional length by numeric variables, constants, or expressions that evaluate to integers greater than zero. If the length is too big given the starting position (i.e., the substring would extend beyond the end of the string), a runtime error will occur.

```
*.. 1 ...+... 2 ...+... 3 ...+... 4 ...+... 5 ...+... 6 ...+... 7 ...+... 8 ...+... 9 ...+...10
CL0N01Factor1++++++Opcode(E)+Extended-factor2+++++++++++++++++++++++++++++++Comments+++++++++++
CL0N01Factor1++++++Opcode(E)+Factor2++++++Result+++++++Len++D+HiLoEq....Comments+++++++++++
C* Examples of accessing portions of character string Phone (e.g., '9705551212') using %SUBST.
C                   EVAL      AreaCode = %SUBST(Phone:1:3)
C* AreaCode contains the first three characters of Phone.
C                   EVAL      Exchange = %SUBST(Phone:4:3)
C* Exchange contains the 4th, 5th, and 6th characters of Phone.
C                   EVAL      Local = %SUBST(Phone:7)
C* Local contains all the characters of Phone from position 7 through the end of the string.
C
C* Example demonstrating how to change Name from the form 'Yaeger, Judy' to 'Judy Yaeger'.
C       ','         SCAN      Name          CommaPlace
C                   EVAL      FirstName = %SUBST(Name:CommaPlace + 2)
C                   EVAL      LastName = %SUBST(Name:1:CommaPlace - 1)
C                   EVAL      NewName = FirstName + ' ' + LastName
```

Like the other built-in functions already discussed, you can use %SUBST to return a value needed within a calculation, as shown in the above examples. Unlike the other functions, you can also use %SUBST as the target (or result) of an EVAL assignment operation to change the value of a designated substring. For this usage, the designated string must be a variable that can be assigned a value; a constant, for example, would be inappropriate. The figure below illustrates this use of %SUBST.

```
*.. 1 ...+... 2 ...+... 3 ...+... 4 ...+... 5 ...+... 6 ...+... 7 ...+... 8 ...+... 9 ...+...10
CL0N01Factor1++++++Opcode(E)+Extended-factor2+++++++++++++++++++++++++++++++Comments+++++++++++
C* In this example, '616' replaces the first three characters of Phone.
C                   EVAL      %SUBST(Phone:1:3) = '616'
```

XLATE (Translate Characters)

XLATE is an operation that lets you translate, or convert, characters within a string to other characters. Factor 2 contains the source string to be converted, and the result field specifies where the results of the translation should be placed; this field can be the same as the source field. This effectively means that the conversion can take place within the string field itself, without using an additional target field. You can use a colon and a value to designate the position where the translation is to begin. If you do not specify a starting location, the conversion starts at the first position of the factor 2 string.

How do you specify which characters should be translated and what they should be changed to? A factor 1 entry supplies this information by including first a From string, then a colon, and then a To string. The From and To strings serve as translation tables. The two strings must have the same number of characters, with the characters ordered so that each character in the From string has a corresponding character in the To string that represents the desired substitute for the From character.

```
*.. 1 ...+... 2 ...+... 3 ...+... 4 ...+... 5 ...+... 6 ...+... 7 ...+... 8 ...+... 9 ...+...10
CL0N01Factor1++++++Opcode(E)+Factor2++++++Result+++++++Len++D+HiLoEq....Comments+++++++++++
C* Sample format of XLATE operation.
C       From:To     XLATE     Source        Changed
```

During the XLATE operation, any character in the source string found in the From string is converted to the corresponding character in the To string and stored in the result field. If a source string character does not appear in the From string, the character is transferred unchanged to the result field.

The factor 2 source string and the result field can be character fields, array elements, or table names. The factor 1 From and To strings can be named constants, fields, literals, array elements, or table names. You can optionally use operation extender (P) to ensure that residual characters are not left in the result field, should its length be larger than that of the source string.

If this sounds confusing, looking at the examples below should help clarify how the operation works. The examples convert uppercase letters to lowercase letters and vice versa; this kind of translation is the most frequent application of XLATE. The From and To strings of alphabetic characters are defined through named constants UC and LC.

```
*.. 1 ...+... 2 ...+... 3 ...+... 4 ...+... 5 ...+... 6 ...+... 7 ...+... 8 ...+... 9 ...+...10
DName++++++++++ETDsFrom+++To/L+++IDc.Keywords++++++++++++++++++++++++++++++++Comments+++++++++++
CL0N01Factor1++++++Opcode(E)+Factor2++++++Result+++++++Len++D+HiLoEq....Comments+++++++++++
CL0N01Factor1++++++Opcode(E)+Extended-factor2+++++++++++++++++++++++++++++++Comments+++++++++++
D* Two named constants to serve as translation "tables".
D UC              C                   'ABCDEFGHIJKLMNOPQRSTUVWXYZ'
D LC              C                   'abcdefghijklmnopqrstuvwxyz'
D
C* LName (15 bytes) contains 'BYRNE-SMITH     '; Name (20 bytes) contains
C* 'XXXXXXXXXXXXXXXXXXXX'.
C
C     UC:LC         XLATE     LName         Name
C* Name now is 'byrne-smith     XXXXX'; all uppercase letters of LName have been changed
C* to lowercase; the hyphen is unchanged; the X's remain as residual characters,
C* because padding was not stated.
C
C     UC:LC         XLATE (P) LName:2       Name
C* Name now is 'Byrne-smith         '; the starting position of 2 leaves the B unchanged,
C* and padding removes trailing residual characters.
C
C     UC:LC         XLATE (P) LName:2       LName
C* LName now contains 'Byrne-smith, because the source field was also designated
C* as the result.
C
C* Assume that FieldA in the next example has a value of 'abc123ABC'.
C     LC:UC         XLATE     FieldA        FieldA
C* FieldA now is 'ABC123ABC', because LC is the "from" string and UC the "to" string.
C* Had they been reversed (i.e., UC:LC), FieldA would now be 'abc123abc'.
```

Working with Bit Patterns

Sometimes as a programmer you need to work with EBCDIC values that you cannot directly enter from the keyboard. Many of these values represent display attributes (e.g., reverse image, blinking) for screen output or control characters for printers. These values generally have binary representations (or bit patterns) below 01000000 (or hexadecimal 40). RPG IV provides a way to assign such values directly to fields, via the hexadecimal number system.

Hexadecimal is a system of representing values based on powers of 16, in contrast to **binary** representation, based on powers of 2, and **decimal** representation, based on powers of 10. The binary system requires only two digits (0 and 1), while the decimal system uses 10 digits (0-9). The hexadecimal system needs 16 digits: The digits 0-9 plus the letters A-F make up the hexadecimal digit set, which represents the decimal values 0-15. Thus, hexadecimal A is the equivalent of decimal 10, hexadecimal B is the equivalent of decimal 11, and so on.

Hexadecimal representation often is used with computers because of the convenient relationship between hexadecimal and binary representation: You can represent four binary digits as a single hexadecimal digit. Thus, the bits of a byte can always be translated into exactly two hexadecimal digits: 0011 1110, for example, is hexadecimal 3E.

Because you can represent the bits of any character — displayable or non-displayable — with two hexadecimal characters (provided it is not a double-byte (DBCS) graphic character), you can manipulate hexadecimal values to achieve a specific bit pattern that represents a desired attribute or control character. To signal to the computer that a value is a hexadecimal value, express the value as a hex literal: Simply code an X, followed by the hexadecimal digits enclosed within apostrophes. Hexadecimal 3E, then, is entered as X'3E'.

You can manipulate hex literals within your calculations, or you can define them as named constants and then work with the named constants within your calculations. The example below uses a hex literal to assign the binary value 00111000 (or X'38') to a field.

```
*.. 1 ...+... 2 ...+... 3 ...+... 4 ...+... 5 ...+... 6 ...+... 7 ...+... 8 ...+... 9 ...+...10
CL0N01Factor1+++++++Opcode(E)+Extended-factor2+++++++++++++++++++++++++++++Comments+++++++++++++
C* Example of using a hex literal to assign a value to a field.
C                   EVAL      FieldA = X'38'
C* FieldA is now 00111000, or X'38'.
```

To alter a bit pattern to achieve a different attribute, code the hex literal representing the new pattern and reassign the field the new hex literal. For example, if we wanted bit pattern 00110011 (or X'33'), we would reassign FieldA as follows:

```
*.. 1 ...+... 2 ...+... 3 ...+... 4 ...+... 5 ...+... 6 ...+... 7 ...+... 8 ...+... 9 ...+...10
CL0N01Factor1+++++++Opcode(E)+Extended-factor2+++++++++++++++++++++++++++++Comments+++++++++++++
C                   EVAL      FieldA = X'33'
C* FieldA is now 00110011, or X'33'.
```

Chapter Summary

RPG IV includes several operations and built-in functions to inspect fields and/or manipulate characters within fields. With the exception of the size-related functions, which you can use with a variety of data items, you primarily use these operations and functions with character fields.

Function %SIZE lets you determine the length (or number of bytes) of a data item, while %ELEM returns the number of elements in an array or table, or the number of occurrences in a multiple-occurrence data structure. You can use these functions within Definition Specifications or Calculation Specifications.

TESTN determines whether the characters within a field are all numeric, all blanks, or leading blanks followed by numeric characters. The most common use of this operation is to validate fields to make sure they contain numeric data.

You can use operation TEST in two ways: to check date/time fields for valid date/time data, or to test numeric and character fields for valid date/time data. When checking numeric/character fields, an operation extender (D, T, or Z) tells the computer which date/time test to perform.

SCAN, CHECK, and CHECKR are operations that let you inspect the contents of character fields. SCAN looks for the presence of a specified character or string of characters, while CHECK and CHECKR detect the presence of non-specified characters. All three operations let you store the position of the located character or string within the field for subsequent use.

The + concatenation operator, the %TRIMx and %SUBST built-in functions, and the XLATE operation let you change or manipulate characters within a field. You combine two fields' values into a third field by using + within an EVAL statement; you trim leading and/or trailing blanks from a field's contents with %TRIM, %TRIML, and %TRIMR. %SUBST extracts a substring from within a field, and XLATE converts characters based on a translation table you provide.

RPG IV also lets you manipulate the bit patterns of fields by directly assigning hexadecimal literal values in an EVAL operation. This feature is useful when you need to represent characters that you cannot enter from the keyboard.

Terms

base string   built-in function (BIF)   decimal
binary   compare string   hexadecimal

Discussion/Review Questions

1. Do you need to use TESTN to assure that input fields entered interactively are numeric? Why or why not?

2. What does "case sensitive" mean?

3. Discuss the differences between SCAN, CHECK, and CHECKR.

4. Explain the differences between %SUBST, XLATE, and the concatenation operator +.

5. Which operation(s) would you use if you wanted to determine whether or not data fields included lowercase letters?

6. Which operation(s) would you use if you wanted to guarantee that a data field contained only uppercase letters?

7. Could you "trim" (i.e., remove leading/trailing blanks) from a character field if RPG IV did not include the %TRIMx built-in functions? Explain your answer.

8. Why might you want to know the size of a field within your program (i.e., why does RPG IV include the %SIZE built-in function)?

9. Discuss the relationship between hexadecimal values and binary values.

10. Many companies that send out mass mailings are plagued with duplicates on their mailing lists. Why is this often the case? Describe specifically how some of the operations discussed in this chapter help eliminate the duplication. Do you think you could eliminate all duplication? Why or why not?

Exercises

1. Use TESTN to determine whether PayIn (8-byte character) is numeric or blank. If all characters are numeric, move the value to a numeric field; if all characters are blank, execute subroutine MissingSR; otherwise, execute subroutine ErrorSR.

2. Write the code needed to determine whether or not PrtDsc (part description) contains the word "washer."

3. Assume you have two character fields, Zip and Zip4, and that you want a third field, Zip10, to include the zip code in the form '12345-6789' if Zip4 is not blank or zero, but '12345   ' if the Zip4 value is blank. Write the code to accomplish this processing.

4. Write the code needed to change a date stored in OldDate in YYMMDD format to NewDate in the new format of name of month, day, 4-digit year (examples: June 1, 1995 and January 31, 1992). Note that extra trailing blanks following the month name should be trimmed, and that non-significant leading zeros in the day should not be stored.

5. Write the code needed to assign field Fld the bit pattern 01001001.

Programming Assignments

1. Wexler University needs a program to print mailing labels for its instructors (file WUINSTP, Appendix D). Depending on the instructor's preferred mode of address, the label should be addressed to "DR.," "MR.," "MRS.," or "MS.," followed by the name. As shown in the example below, all trailing blanks should be trimmed from first name and city. Note that the form of the zip code depends on whether or not the plus-4 digits are present. The university uses 3-across labels, each of which is 30 characters wide and five print lines long. The printer spacing chart shows the desired format for the labels.

```
 1  DR. HAL HOLLOWAY              MRS. DONNA SMITH              DR. JO ANNE CERTAIN
 2  3345 N. WESTERN AVE.          213 E. WILSON BLVD.           19000 S. WOODLAND DR.
 3  KALAMAZOO, MI   49005-1010    PAW PAW, MI   49045           MATTAWAN, MI   49069
 4
 5
 6  MR. ARNOLD VON RIEGLE
 7  1221 E. BROAD ST.
 8  PORTAGE, MI   49008-0010
 9
10
```

2. Wexler University is very embarrassed. It seems that the user who entered the course descriptions didn't know how to spell "receive," and as a result, the word is misspelled "RECIEVE" in several places within the description file WUCRSDSP. (See Appendix D.) Write a program that will check through the records of WUCRSDSP and change any misspelled instances of "RECEIVE." Note that your code should correct "RECIEVING," "RECIEVES," and "RECIEVED," as well as "RECIEVE."

3. The president of Wexler University has just seen the labels from Program 1 (above) and he says they're not elegant enough. He doesn't want all the lettering to appear in uppercase. You point out that this is going to take a lot more programming effort, but he is adamant. Read the specifications for Program 1, but incorporate lowercase lettering within your labels, as shown below, to produce mailing labels for the instructors in WUINSTP.

```
 1  Dr. Hal Holloway              Mrs. Donna Smith              Dr. Jo Anne Certain
 2  3345 N. Western Ave.          213 E. Wilson Blvd.           19000 S. Woodland Dr.
 3  Kalamazoo, MI   49005-1010    Paw Paw, MI   49045           Mattawan, MI   49069
 4
 5
 6  Mr. Arnold Von Riegle
 7  1221 E. Broad St.
 8  Portage, MI   49008-0010
 9
10
```

4. Wexler University is even more embarrassed. They just realized that the person who didn't know how to spell "receive" also consistently misspelled "QUANTITY" as "QUANITY" throughout the course descriptions. This error also appears as "QUANITATIVE" and "QUANITIES." Write a program that will check through the records of WUCRSDSP (Appendix D) and change any of these misspellings.

Programming Assignments Continued

Programming Assignments continued

Note that because you are adding a letter, in some instances this might make your description line too long for the 50-position field and you will need to word-wrap to the next description line. This wrapping may have to continue until you encounter a line with enough trailing blanks to include the wrapped word. Conceivably, you might even have to enter an additional description line for that course to handle the wrapping. Assume that hyphenation was not used in the original descriptions.

Chapter 12

Interprogram Communications

Chapter Overview

This chapter discusses modular programming and shows you how RPG IV programs can communicate with one another by passing data values as parameter arguments. It also introduces you to two other RPG IV capabilities: calling APIs from within an RPG IV program, and sharing data among programs through data areas.

Modular Programming

As concern about program development and maintenance efficiencies has grown, programmers have become increasingly interested in developing small, stand-alone units of code (rather than writing monolithic programs thousands of lines long). There are many advantages to this approach, which is often called **modular programming**.

First, if you develop code in small, independent units, you often can reuse these units, because it is common for several applications to share identical processing requirements for some portions of their logic. Furthermore, small programs are easier to test than large programs. Moreover, changes made to code are less likely to cause unexpected — and unwanted — side effects if the changes are made within a small, stand-alone module, rather than in a routine that is embedded within a gigantic program. And finally, because you can separately develop and test such modules, a modular approach to programming makes it easier to divide an application development project among members of a programming team, each with responsibilities for developing different modules.

RPG IV provides two operations that let you adopt this modular approach to program development: CALL and CALLB. Before comparing and contrasting these two operations in detail, you need to understand how call operations affect flow of control.

When program execution reaches a call statement (either CALL or CALLB), control passes to the called program, which in turn begins to execute. The called program continues to execute until it reaches a RETURN statement; at this point, control returns to the calling program, at the statement immediately following the call. Figure 12.1 illustrates this flow of control among calling and called programs.

Figure 12.1
Flow of Control with Calls

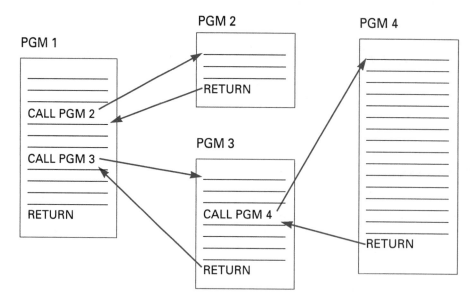

As you can see, the flow of control with a call is like that of an EXSR, except that a call invokes an external program or module, rather than a subroutine internal to the program. A called program may in turn call other programs, but it should not recursively call its calling program.

Flow of control operates identically for CALL and CALLB, and indeed, on the surface these two operations appear very similar. However, one important difference exists between these two operations, based on when the calling and called programs (or modules) are *linked*, or bound, together. You use CALL for programs that are dynamically bound, while CALLB is appropriate for programs that are statically bound.

Dynamic and Static Binding

Until RPG IV, CALL with **dynamic binding** was the only option for programmers wishing to adopt a modular approach to their code. With this method, programmers compiled each program separately to create individual, executable *PGM objects. When you ran a program that used CALL to invoke another program (*PGM object), the system then went "looking" for the called program and bound it to the calling program dynamically, during runtime. Although this method worked, this dynamic binding took time and degraded system performance — in some instances, severely — compared to performance if the programmer handled the called programs as subroutines internal to the calling program.

When IBM introduced the Integrated Language Environment (ILE), it included the option of connecting program modules before runtime; this **static binding** eliminates the performance degradation found with dynamic binding.

Here is how static binding works. When you compile source code with the CL command CRTRPGMOD (Create RPG Module), the compiler creates a *MODULE object, rather than an executable program object (*PGM). To form the *PGM object, you must carry out a separate binding procedure, invoked through the CRTPGM (Create Program) command. If some *MODULEs are to call others, you can, if you want, link them together during this binding step to form a single executable *PGM object. When the program runs, the binding has already been completed, so performance is not affected.

To call modules (*MODULE) that are to be statically bound, you use the RPG IV operation CALLB; you use CALL when you want to call programs (*PGM) that are dynamically bound. Note that if you want to create an executable program from RPG IV source that does not require binding with other modules, you can complete the compiling and binding procedures in one step by using CL command CRTBNDRPG (Create Bound RPG Program).

With this brief overview of binding completed, let's now look at the details of CALL and CALLB.

CALL (Call a Program)
The CALL operation passes control to the program object (*PGM) named in factor 2. Factor 2 may contain a literal specifying the program to be executed (the *called program*). Alternately, factor 2 may contain a field, an array element, or a named constant that specifies the name of the program to be called. You can also include an optional indicator in the Lo position (73-74) to signal that an error occurred when the program attempted the call.

When you use a variable to represent the program name in a CALL operation, the program to be called is not fixed, or constant; it may change from one call to the next, depending on the value of the variable.

```
*.. 1 ...+... 2 ...+... 3 ...+... 4 ...+... 5 ...+... 6 ...+... 7 ...+... 8 ...+... 9 ...+...10
CL0N01Factor1++++++Opcode(E)+Factor2++++++Result+++++++Len++D+HiLoEq....Comments++++++++++++
C* A call to a program whose name is specified as a literal.
C                   CALL      'GL001R'
C* A call to a program whose name is the value of a variable.
C                   CALL      ProgName
```

Assume ProgName is a 10-position character field, with value 'GL001R'. In that case, the two CALL statements in the above examples will have identical effects: the execution of program GL001R. However, with the second method the value of ProgName could change during execution so that a repetition of that CALL statement could invoke a different program.

Calling a program by supplying its name as a field value rather than as a literal causes more system overhead than coding its name as a literal. Accordingly, you should use a literal unless the program to be called actually may change within a run or between runs of the calling program.

The system returns control from the called program to the calling program when it encounters the RETURN statement in the called program. If the LR indicator is also on when the RETURN is executed, the system's resources tied up by the called program are released; a subsequent call to that program causes the program to start up again as though for the first time. On the other hand, if LR is not on within the called program upon return, the called program remains activated. As a result, a subsequent call to that program will find all the fields and indicators of the called program to have the values they had at the time of the previous RETURN. Moreover, any files used by the called program also will still be open as a result of the previous call.

```
*.. 1 ...+... 2 ...+... 3 ...+... 4 ...+... 5 ...+... 6 ...+... 7 ...+... 8 ...+... 9 ...+...10
CL0N01Factor1++++++Opcode(E)+Extended-factor2+++++++++++++++++++++++++++++++Comments+++++++++++
CL0N01Factor1++++++Opcode(E)+Factor2++++++Result++++++++Len++D+HiLoEq....Comments+++++++++++
C* Portion of a calling program, which calls SAMPPRG within a loop.
C                   DOW          *IN40 = *OFF
C                   ...
C                   CALL         'SAMPPRG'
C                   ...
C                   ENDDO

*.. 1 ...+... 2 ...+... 3 ...+... 4 ...+... 5 ...+... 6 ...+... 7 ...+... 8 ...+... 9 ...+...10
CL0N01Factor1++++++Opcode(E)+Extended-factor2+++++++++++++++++++++++++++++++Comments+++++++++++
CL0N01Factor1++++++Opcode(E)+Factor2++++++Result++++++++Len++D+HiLoEq....Comments+++++++++++
C* Portion of called program SAMPPRG where RETURN is executed without LR turned on;
C* the program will remain active, and field Count will be 1 greater each time the called
C* program is entered from the calling program.
C                   ...
C                   EVAL         Count = Count + 1
C                   ...
C                   RETURN

*.. 1 ...+... 2 ...+... 3 ...+... 4 ...+... 5 ...+... 6 ...+... 7 ...+... 8 ...+... 9 ...+...10
CL0N01Factor1++++++Opcode(E)+Extended-factor2+++++++++++++++++++++++++++++++Comments+++++++++++
CL0N01Factor1++++++Opcode(E)+Factor2++++++Result++++++++Len++D+HiLoEq....Comments+++++++++++
C* In this version of SAMPPRG, where LR is turned on before the RETURN, the program is
C* deactivated, and Count will be 0 each time SAMPPRG is called.
C                   ...
C                   EVAL         Count = Count + 1
C                   ...
C                   EVAL         *INLR = *ON
C                   RETURN
```

Whether or not you should turn on LR before returning from a called program, then, depends on whether you want the called program to start afresh each time the calling program evokes it, or you want the called program to pick up where it had left off on the previous call (within a given run). Failure to correctly handle the LR indicator can cause undesired effects in the called program.

CALLB (Call a Bound Module)
As mentioned earlier, the CALLB operation is appropriate for invoking a program module (*MODULE) that has been statically bound with the calling program module. The factor 2 specification must reference a *MODULE procedure that is contained within the same *PGM object as the calling program. CALLB cannot call a separately bound program (*PGM object type).

The format of CALLB is identical to CALL; however, factor 2 must contain a literal, a named constant, or a procedure pointer. It *cannot* contain a field whose value is the procedure name. The figure below illustrates CALLB.

```
*.. 1 ...+... 2 ...+... 3 ...+... 4 ...+... 5 ...+... 6 ...+... 7 ...+... 8 ...+... 9 ...+...10
DName++++++++++ETDsFrom+++To/L+++IDc.Keywords+++++++++++++++++++++++++++++++Comments+++++++++++
CL0N01Factor1++++++Opcode(E)+Factor2++++++Result++++++++Len++D+HiLoEq....Comments+++++++++++
CL0N01Factor1++++++Opcode(E)+Extended-factor2++++++++++++++++++++++++++++++Comments+++++++++++
D ProcName         C                   'ProcXYZ'
C* Examples of CALLB: one where the called procedure is specified as a literal, one where
C* a constant is used to specify the called procedure, and one where a procedure pointer,
C* PPtr, is used to indicate the called procedure.
C                   CALLB     'ProcXYZ'
C                   ...
C
C                   CALLB     ProcName
C                   ...
C
C                   EVAL      PPtr = %PADDR('ProcXYZ')
C                   CALLB     PPtr
C                   ...
```

Notice the use of %PADDR in the above example. %PADDR is a built-in function similar to %ADDR (discussed in Chapter 9), except it returns the address of a procedure (*MODULE) entry point, instead of the address of a variable's storage location. Calling a statically bound procedure using a procedure pointer is usually somewhat faster than using either a literal or a constant.

You can also use %PADDR to initialize a procedure pointer to the address of a procedure you will call later. You do this within the Definition Specification for the procedure pointer, as shown in the following example. This practice facilitates program maintenance, because you can easily change the called procedure in one place in your program, without searching through Calculation Specifications for all the calls to that procedure.

```
*.. 1 ...+... 2 ...+... 3 ...+... 4 ...+... 5 ...+... 6 ...+... 7 ...+... 8 ...+... 9 ...+...10
DName++++++++++ETDsFrom+++To/L+++IDc.Keywords+++++++++++++++++++++++++++++++Comments+++++++++++
CL0N01Factor1++++++Opcode(E)+Factor2++++++Result++++++++Len++D+HiLoEq....Comments+++++++++++
D PPtr            S            *    PROCPTR INZ(%PADDR('ProcXYZ'))
D
C                   CALLB     PPtr
C                   ...
```

Within a CALLB operation you can include an optional indicator in the Lo position (73-74) to signal that an error occurred when the program attempted the call, just like you can with operation CALL. Also, the status of LR (i.e., whether it is on or off) affects operation CALLB the same way it affects CALL.

Passing Data Between Programs

A call would be of limited value if it did not permit the called and calling programs to share data. Within a single RPG IV program, all variables are globally defined; that is, you can access the value of any variable from anywhere within the program. This global feature of variables does not extend across program or procedure boundaries, however. That means if you want a called program to process some data and send the results of the processing back to the calling program, you need to make special provisions to let this sharing take place. Both CALL and CALLB use parameters to pass values between caller and callee. The discussion below, then, applies to both of these operations, and the word "program" in this discussion stands for "module" or "procedure," as well.

RPG IV uses the PARM (Identify Parameters) operation to indicate which field's values are to be shared between programs. A list of **PARMs** in the calling program must have a list of corresponding PARMs in the called program.

Each PARM requires an entry in the result field of the standard Calculation Specification. This entry can be a field, a data structure, or an array that is to serve as the parameter. It cannot be an indicator, a literal, a label, a constant, or a table name. If the field is a multiple-occurrence data structure, all occurrences of the data structure are passed as a single field.

Although the data names of the PARMs used in the calling and called programs do not need to be the same, corresponding PARMs in the two programs should have the same type and length, because in fact these corresponding parameters are referencing the same storage location within the computer.

You can list PARMs immediately following a call operation. Alternately, you can use a PLIST (Identify a Parameter List) operation, which can precede or follow the call operation. PLIST is merely a declarative operation that identifies a list of parameters to be shared between programs. PLIST requires an identifying entry in factor 1; that entry should be a PLIST name, if the PLIST is within a calling program, or *ENTRY, if the PLIST is within the called program. Reserved word *ENTRY signals that this PLIST contains the parameter arguments the called program is to receive upon its invocation by the calling program. If a PLIST is used within a calling program, the name of the PLIST must appear as the result field entry of the call associated with the list.

Before we discuss PARMs in more detail, let's clarify the relationship between calling and called programs, PLISTs, and PARMs by looking at some examples. In the illustration below, the calling program calls Prog2, passing it PARMs FldA, FldB, and FldC. Because the PARMs appear immediately following a call operation, they do not require a PLIST header preceding them.

```
*.. 1 ...+... 2 ...+... 3 ...+... 4 ...+... 5 ...+... 6 ...+... 7 ...+... 8 ...+... 9 ...+...10
CL0N01Factor1++++++Opcode(E)+Factor2++++++Result++++++++Len++D+HiLoEq....Comments++++++++++++
C* This is a sample of a calling program.  Notice how the PARMs follow the CALL without a
C* PLIST operation.
C                   CALL      'Prog2'
C                   PARM                    FldA
C                   PARM                    FldB
C                   PARM                    FldC
```

An alternate way to code the same logic is to include the PARMs within a PLIST and specify that PLIST within the call operation, as shown below. Both examples accomplish the same effect — passing the addresses of FldA, FldB, and FldC to the called program, Prog2.

```
*.. 1 ...+... 2 ...+... 3 ...+... 4 ...+... 5 ...+... 6 ...+... 7 ...+... 8 ...+... 9 ...+...10
CLØNØ1Factor1++++++Opcode(E)+Factor2++++++Result+++++++Len++D+HiLoEq....Comments+++++++++++
C* This is a sample of a calling program.  The PARMs appear in a PLIST, which is referenced
C* in the CALL operation.  The effect is identical to that of the previous example.
C     PlistA        PLIST
C                   PARM                    FldA
C                   PARM                    FldB
C                   PARM                    FldC
C                   ...
C                   CALL      'Prog2'       PlistA
                    ...
```

To access those storage locations passed by the calling program, the called program also must include PARMs. These PARMs occur within a PLIST labeled *ENTRY, as shown below. A called program can contain only one *ENTRY PLIST.

```
*.. 1 ...+... 2 ...+... 3 ...+... 4 ...+... 5 ...+... 6 ...+... 7 ...+... 8 ...+... 9 ...+...10
CLØNØ1Factor1++++++Opcode(E)+Factor2++++++Result+++++++Len++D+HiLoEq....Comments+++++++++++
C* This is the called program, Prog2.  It includes an *ENTRY PLIST.
C     *ENTRY        PLIST
C                   PARM                    FldX
C                   PARM                    FldY
C                   PARM                    FldZ
C                   ...
```

Note that although the variable names in the corresponding PARMs of the calling and called programs may be different, they must agree in data type and length, because they reference the same storage location. You must define the variables declared as PARMs within their respective programs on Definition Specifications.

Because RPG IV passes parameter arguments by passing the address of the storage location represented by the field (called *passing by reference*), rather than by passing the field's value (*passing by value*), changes in the parameter fields within the called program result in the same changes in the parameter fields of the calling program. For example, assume in the above illustration that FldA had a value of 150 before the call to Prog2, and that as part of its processing, Prog2 changed the value of FldX to 0. Upon return to the calling program, FldA now would have a value of 0, because that field and FldX of the called program reference the same storage location.

If this possible change in parameter field values could cause undesired effects, you can use factor 2 with the PARM operation to eliminate this side effect. Simply enter the field whose value you want passed to the called program as factor 2 and enter a different field as the result field. When the call takes place, the system copies the value of the factor 2 field into the result field and passes the address of the result field to the called program. Upon return from the called program the result field's value may be changed, but the factor 2 field value remains undisturbed.

```
*.. 1 ...+... 2 ...+... 3 ...+... 4 ...+... 5 ...+... 6 ...+... 7 ...+... 8 ...+... 9 ...+...10
CL0N01Factor1++++++Opcode(E)+Factor2++++++Result+++++++Len++D+HiLoEq....Comments++++++++++++
C* Example showing how to pass FldA's value to Prog1 without the possibility of FldA's
C* value being changed by Prog1.
C                     CALL      'Prog1'
C                     PARM      FldA            FldX
```

As mentioned earlier, both CALL and CALLB can use PARMs to share data. In addition, when using CALLB, you can define variables whose values are available across modules. You must define the variable on Definition Specifications within each relevant procedure. Then specify keyword EXPORT within the variable's definition in the module that will allocate storage. Finally, specify keyword IMPORT in the variable's definition in all remaining modules that reference it. Data items so defined should not be included as PARMs. The procedure exporting the data item is responsible for any initialization of that variable.

```
*.. 1 ...+... 2 ...+... 3 ...+... 4 ...+... 5 ...+... 6 ...+... 7 ...+... 8 ...+... 9 ...+...10
DName++++++++++ETDsFrom+++To/L+++IDc.Keywords++++++++++++++++++++++++++++++Comments++++++++++++
CL0N01Factor1++++++Opcode(E)+Factor2++++++Result+++++++Len++D+HiLoEq....Comments++++++++++++
D* Example of a calling program EXPORTing a variable to the ProgA procedure.
D FldA            S              9 2 EXPORT INZ(200)
C                     ...
C                     CALLB     'ProgA'
C                     ...
```

```
*.. 1 ...+... 2 ...+... 3 ...+... 4 ...+... 5 ...+... 6 ...+... 7 ...+... 8 ...+... 9 ...+...10
DName++++++++++ETDsFrom+++To/L+++IDc.Keywords++++++++++++++++++++++++++++++Comments++++++++++++
CL0N01Factor1++++++Opcode(E)+Factor2++++++Result+++++++Len++D+HiLoEq....Comments++++++++++++
D* ProgA, which imports FldA's value from the calling program.
D FldA            S              9 2 IMPORT
C                     ...
```

Using a Modular Approach

You will find a wide variation in the extent to which different companies make use of RPG IV's calling features. Some companies incorporate calls within menu programs that present application choices to users; the menu programs will then call the selected programs to perform the desired processing. Typically, this kind of program does not require passing data between the calling program and the programs it calls.

Another application of RPG IV's calling features is to access a routine that performs a specific task, without recoding the routine every time you need it. For example, in Chapter 9 we looked at a routine to determine the day of the week for a given date in *ISO format. You could perform this day-of-the-week "calculation" within a called program.

The calling program would include two parameters — one to contain the given date and one to store the calculated day of the week. The called program determines the day of the week of the value represented in the first parameter, stores the result in the second parameter, and returns control to the calling program.

Another example of a routine that might be called by many programs is one that converts a numeric value representing dollars and cents (e.g., 123.43) to its representation in words (e.g., one hundred twenty-three dollars and 43 cents). The logic required for such a conversion is not trivial, and companies do not want to continually reinvent that particular wheel.

Calling an external routine offers one additional significant advantage over an EXSR operation: The routine called (whether by CALLB or CALL) does not have to be an object created from RPG IV source. You can write a program in any high-level language (HLL) supported by the AS/400, or in OS/400's CL, compile it, and then call it from an RPG IV program.

Similarly, you can call an RPG IV program from a CL program or from a program written in a different HLL supported by the AS/400. The RPG IV program's RETURN statement returns control to whatever program called it.

This flexibility lets you break a problem down into logical units, write each unit in the language best suited for developing the algorithm required by that unit, and then call the units to perform their processing as needed. Although this multilanguage approach to program development is not widely used in the AS/400 world today, its use will grow as cooperative processing and the use of Graphical User Interfaces (GUIs) demand more sophisticated capabilities than those RPG IV alone can offer.

In general, many programmers once reluctant to use CALL because of the decreased performance of the AS/400 associated with these calls are beginning to take advantage of CALLB and static binding. As a result, modular programming is becoming more common in MIS departments that use RPG IV.

APIs

You have learned how an RPG IV program can call another program (or module) written in RPG IV (or any other AS/400 language) by using CALL or CALLB. You can also use CALL to access **APIs** (application programming interfaces). APIs are programs or commands built into the operating system that let you access lower-level machine functions or system data not otherwise available within an HLL program.

There are many different APIs: Each provides you with a different, specific capability. For example, API QUSRLSPL builds a list of spooled files from an output queue; a related API, QUSRSPLA, retrieves this data into your program. You can use APIs to obtain information about a job, a database file, a library, or any other kind of object on the system. Almost all APIs have a required, specific set of PARMs used to pass values from your program, return values to your program, or both. Many APIs also require a special kind of storage area, called a **user space**, to receive their output or to supply their input. User spaces are defined, permanent locations in storage;

they are similar to data areas, which are described in detail later in this chapter. How do user spaces originate? An API, QUSCRTUS, creates a user space for use by other APIs.

Although a complete discussion of APIs is beyond the scope of this text, we will take a closer look at two often used APIs to give you a sense of how you might use APIs within your RPG IV programs.

The first API we'll consider is QUSCMDLN. This API presents an AS/400 system command line as a pop-up window within your program. Say, for example, that you were writing an interactive application in which you wanted to give the user access to the system command line so (s)he can check the status of a spooled file, send a message to another user, or whatever. In your display file, you would enable a function key (e.g., F21) to signal the user's request for a command line and include a prompt at the bottom of the screen to inform the user of this feature (e.g., 'F21 = command line'). Then, within your RPG IV program upon return from the display, you would check the status of the indicator associated with that function key. If its value indicates the user has pressed the function key, your program would call the API to pop up the command line on the current screen.

```
*.. 1 ...+... 2 ...+... 3 ...+... 4 ...+... 5 ...+... 6 ...+... 7 ...+... 8 ...+... 9 ...+...10
CLØNØ1Factor1++++++Opcode(E)+Factor2++++++Result+++++++Len++D+HiLoEq....Comments++++++++++++
CLØNØ1Factor1++++++Opcode(E)+Extended-factor2+++++++++++++++++++++++++++Comments++++++++++++
C* Example showing a portion of an interactive program that lets the user access a CL
C* command line.
C                   ...
C                   EXFMT     Screen1
C                   IF        *IN21 = *ON
C                   CALL      'QUSCMDLN'
C                   ELSE
C                   ...
```

When the user finishes with the command line and exits from it, control returns to your program, which resumes processing from the point of the call. Notice that QUSCMDLN, unlike most APIs, uses no parameters. The second API we'll look at, QCMDEXC, is more typical in its format.

What does QCMDEXC do? Occasionally within an RPG IV program, you would like to communicate directly with the operating system to issue a CL command. You might, for example, want to override one database file with another or send a message reporting on the program's progress to the user. API QCMDEXC lets you execute such a CL command from within an HLL program.

Any program can call QCMDEXC. QCMDEXC expects to receive arguments for two parameters: The first parameter should contain the command the system is to execute, and the second should contain the command's length. (The variable representing this length must be defined as a numeric field with 15 positions, 5 of which are decimal positions.)

The EVAL operation easily completes the job of assigning a command to a parameter, as shown on the following page:

```
*.. 1 ...+... 2 ...+... 3 ...+... 4 ...+... 5 ...+... 6 ...+... 7 ...+... 8 ...+... 9 ...+...10
FFilename++IPEASFRlen+LKlen+AIDevice+.Keywords++++++++++++++++++++++++++++++++Comments++++++++++++
DName++++++++++ETDsFrom+++To/L+++IDc.Keywords++++++++++++++++++++++++++++++++++Comments++++++++++++
CL0N01Factor1++++++Opcode(E)+Extended-factor2+++++++++++++++++++++++++++++++++Comments++++++++++++
CL0N01Factor1++++++Opcode(E)+Factor2+++++++Result++++++++Len++D+HiLoEq....Comments++++++++++++
F* Example showing the use of QCMDEXC to override a display file.
F* Override command is assigned to the PARM field through EVAL.
FScreen1   CF   E           WORKSTN
F                   ...
D OvrCmd         S             23
D Len            S             15  5
C                   EVAL      OvrCmd = 'OVRDSPF SCREEN1 SCREEN2'
C                   CALL      'QCMDEXC'
C                   PARM                    OvrCmd
C                   PARM      23            Len
C                   ...
```

You can see that APIs provide you with a variety of callable routines to access the resources of the AS/400 in ways not possible with RPG IV alone. If you are interested in learning more details about APIs, see the IBM manual *System API Reference* (SC41-3801).

Data Areas

PARMs let calling and called programs share data. **Data areas** also are AS/400 objects that represent storage locations used to share data between programs within a job or between jobs. However, one program does not have to call another to share the data if the data resides in a data area. You can use data areas to store information of limited size (up to 2,000 bytes), independent of database files or programs.

The system automatically creates a **local data area (LDA)** for each job in the system. Each LDA is 1,024 positions long, with type character; initially, blanks fill the LDA. When you submit a job with the SBMJOB command, the value of your LDA is copied into the LDA of the submitted job, so that the submitted job can access any data values stored in the LDA by your initial job. When a job ends, its LDA ceases to exist.

You also can create more permanent data areas with the CL command CRTDTAARA (Create Data Area). A data area created in this way remains an object on the system until it is explicitly removed; such a data area can be accessed by any program regardless of its job.

Programmers use data areas for storing small quantities of data that are frequently used by several programs or by the same program each time it is run. For example, they might prefer storing within a data area the next order number or customer number to be assigned, to avoid having to retrieve that information from a database file of orders or customers. Programmers sometimes use a data area to store constant values used by several programs, such as tax rates or discounts, or to transfer the processing results of one program to another.

Data-Area Data Structures

As a programmer, you should understand how you can access data areas from within an RPG IV program. One way to make a data area accessible to an RPG IV program is to define a data structure for the data area. A U in position 23 (T) of a data structure identifies it as a **data-area data structure**.

If you do not provide a name for a data-area data structure, the data structure automatically represents the LDA. If you want the data structure to contain data from a different data area, you must provide a program name for the data structure that matches the name of the data area in the system. The figure below illustrates two data-area data structures.

```
*.. 1 ...+... 2 ...+... 3 ...+... 4 ...+... 5 ...+... 6 ...+... 7 ...+... 8 ...+... 9 ...+...10
DName++++++++++ETDsFrom+++To/L+++IDc.Keywords+++++++++++++++++++++++++++++++Comments++++++++++++
D* The data structure below represents the Local Data Area (LDA).
D                 UDS
D InvNo                         8 0
D
D* The data structure below represents data area Receipts.
D Receipts         UDS
D    Store1                    10 2
D    Store2                    10 2
D    Store3                    10 2
```

The contents of any data area defined via a data structure, as in the above examples, are read into the program at program initialization. The data area is then locked to prevent other programs from accessing it. When the program ends, the system writes the contents of the data structure from the program back to the data area and removes the lock.

Using *NAMVAR DEFINE

You do not have to define a data-area data structure to access data areas within your program. Contents of a data area are also accessible through the *NAMVAR DEFINE operation. This operation requires *NAMVAR in factor 1, while the result field must contain a variable that is to receive the data area's contents. This variable can be a field, a data-structure subfield, or a data structure (but *not* a data-area data structure — that is, no U in position 23). You must define this result variable within your program, and the definition must match that of the data area itself.

Factor 2 normally contains the external name of the data area whose contents you want to access. If you leave factor 2 blank, the result field must contain the external data-area name and also serve as the name you use to represent the data area within your program. If you want to use this operation with the LDA, code *LDA in factor 2.

```
*.. 1 ...+... 2 ...+... 3 ...+... 4 ...+... 5 ...+... 6 ...+... 7 ...+... 8 ...+... 9 ...+...10
DName++++++++++ETDsFrom+++To/L+++IDc.Keywords+++++++++++++++++++++++++++++++Comments++++++++++++
CL0N01Factor1+++++++Opcode(E)+Factor2+++++++Result+++++++Len++D+HiLoEq....Comments++++++++++++
D* Examples of using *NAMVAR DEFINE to access data areas.  Data items used to receive the
D* data areas' data are defined on Definition Specifications below.
D
D* Stand-alone field InvNo.
D InvNo           S               8 0
D* Stand-alone field CheckNo.
D CheckNo         S               6 0
D* Data structure Receipts.
D Receipts        DS
D   Store1                       10 2
D   Store2                       10 2
D   Store3                       10 2
C
C* Data area Check associated with field CheckNo.
C     *NAMVAR       DEFINE    Check         CheckNo
C* Data area Receipts associated with data structure Receipts.
C     *NAMVAR       DEFINE                  Receipts
C* Local Data Area associated with InvNo.
C     *NAMVAR       DEFINE    *LDA          InvNo
```

There are two important differences between accessing a data area with *NAMVAR DEFINE and accessing it through a data-area data structure. First, the contents of the data area are not automatically retrieved into the result variable at the start of the program with *NAMVAR DEFINE, the way they are with a data-area data structure. Second, the result field's contents are not automatically written back out to the data area at program termination. Instead, you must explicitly "read" and "write" the contents of the data area within your calculations. Specific operations (IN, OUT, and UNLOCK) let you control this explicit I/O of data areas. If you want to use these explicit operations with a data-area data structure, that structure must also appear as the result field of a *NAMVAR DEFINE statement, with the factor 2 entry blank.

IN (Retrieve a Data Area)

IN "reads" the contents of the data area into your program. Factor 2 must contain the result field of a *NAMVAR DEFINE statement. By including the optional entry *LOCK as a factor 1 entry, you can lock the data area from update by another program. If you leave factor 1 blank and the data area has been retrieved previously, the locked status associated with the previous retrieval remains in effect. That is, if the data area was locked before this IN operation, it remains locked; if it was not locked, it remains unlocked. *LOCK cannot be used with the LDA.

```
*.. 1 ...+... 2 ...+... 3 ...+... 4 ...+... 5 ...+... 6 ...+... 7 ...+... 8 ...+... 9 ...+...10
CLØNØ1Factor1++++++Opcode(E)+Factor2++++++Result+++++++Len++D+HiLoEq....Comments+++++++++++
C* Examples showing *NAMVAR DEFINE and subsequent use of IN.
C* Data area Check associated with field CheckNo.
C     *NAMVAR     DEFINE    Check         CheckNo
C* Data area Receipts associated with Data Structure Receipts.
C     *NAMVAR     DEFINE              Receipts
C* Local Data Area associated with InvNo.
C     *NAMVAR     DEFINE    *LDA          InvNo
C
C* Retrieves the contents of the LDA into InvNo.
C                IN        InvNo
C* Retrieves the contents of data area Check into CheckNo with lock.
C     *LOCK      IN        CheckNo
C* Retrieves data area Receipts into data-area data structure Receipts.
C                IN        Receipts
```

OUT (Write Out a Data Area)

OUT "writes" data back to (or updates) the data area referenced in factor 2. Factor 2 must contain the result field of a *NAMVAR DEFINE statement. Moreover, the operation cannot be used unless the data area already has been retrieved — either through the execution of an IN operation, or through the implicit retrieval that results for data-area data structures.

If you include the optional entry *LOCK in factor 1, a lock remains in effect for the data area following the OUT operation; if you leave factor 1 blank, the data area is unlocked after it is updated. As with the IN operation, you cannot include a *LOCK entry for the LDA.

```
*.. 1 ...+... 2 ...+... 3 ...+... 4 ...+... 5 ...+... 6 ...+... 7 ...+... 8 ...+... 9 ...+...10
CLØNØ1Factor1++++++Opcode(E)+Factor2++++++Result+++++++Len++D+HiLoEq....Comments+++++++++++
C* Examples showing the use of OUT.
C
C* LDA is updated.
C                OUT       InvNo
C* Receipts is updated but the lock remains in effect.
C     *LOCK      OUT       Recepts
C* Data area Check is updated and the lock is removed.
C                OUT       CheckNo
```

UNLOCK (Unlock a Data Area)

UNLOCK unlocks the data area referenced in factor 2. This factor 2 entry must be the result field of a *NAMVAR DEFINE statement. Executing an UNLOCK operation on a data area already unlocked does not cause a system error. You cannot use the UNLOCK operation with the LDA.

```
*.. 1 ...+... 2 ...+... 3 ...+... 4 ...+... 5 ...+... 6 ...+... 7 ...+... 8 ...+... 9 ...+...10
CLØNØ1Factor1++++++Opcode(E)+Factor2++++++Result+++++++Len++D+HiLoEq....Comments+++++++++++
C* Examples showing the unlocking of data areas.
C* Unlocks data area Receipts.
C                UNLOCK    Receipts
C* Unlocks data area Check.
C                UNLOCK    CheckNo
```

For all three data area operations — IN, OUT, and UNLOCK — if you enter *NAMVAR as the factor 2 entry, instead of a specific variable, *all* the

data areas appearing as result fields in *NAMVAR DEFINE operations participate in the operation. All three operations also let you include an optional
error indicator in positions 73-74 (Lo) to signal that an error occurred during the operation.

Chapter Summary

Programming experts advocate a modular approach to programming, in
which you break complex processing down into separate programs or modules, each focused on accomplishing a single function. These programs then
can be called by other programs. If a procedure is compiled and bound into a
separate *PGM object, you must use operation CALL to invoke that program
— a process called dynamic binding. If, on the other hand, separately compiled program modules are connected to one another to form a single *PGM
object — static binding — you use the CALLB operation to invoke a bound
module. Static binding results in better system performance at runtime than
does dynamic binding. The AS/400 lets you write calling and called programs
in any mix of languages available on the system, including CL.

In RPG IV, all variables are global within a program, but local to the program. To share data between a calling and called program or module, both
programs use PARMs to define the shared data. These PARMS immediately follow a CALL or CALLB operation, appear as part of a named PLIST in the calling program, or appear within an *ENTRY PLIST in the called program. The
corresponding PARM variables in the calling and called programs share a common storage location. As a result, changes to a parameter's value in one of the
programs affects that corresponding parameter's value in the other program.

IBM offers several built-in system programs (APIs), which you can call
from your RPG IV program, to accomplish various lower-level processing. API
QUSCMDLN presents an AS/400 system command line for use within a program, while API QCMDEXC lets you execute a CL command from within
your program. You simply pass the command as a parameter to QCMDEXC,
along with another parameter that specifies the command's length.

The AS/400 also provides data areas (special storage areas defined on
the system) for sharing values between programs. The programs do not have
to call one another to access the same data area. A temporary local data area
(LDA) is automatically available for each job; you also can define permanent data areas that any program can subsequently access. You access the
contents of a data area within an RPG IV program by defining a special data
structure — a data-area data structure — or by referencing the data area in
a *NAMVAR DEFINE statement.

Data contained in data-area data structures is automatically retrieved at
the start of a program and written back to the data area at the end of the program. To retrieve data from data areas referenced only through *NAMVAR
DEFINE, you must explicitly use the IN operation. OUT writes data values
back to a data area, while UNLOCK can release a lock on a data area to allow
its access for update by other programs.

Terms

APIs	local data area (LDA)	passing by value
data area	modular programming	static binding
data-area data structure	PARMs	user space
dynamic binding	passing by reference	

Discussion/Review Questions

1. What does "modular programming" mean?

2. What are the advantages of a modular approach to application development?

3. What effect does LR have on a called program?

4. Although static binding leads to improved system performance, when might you still want to use dynamic binding to CALL a program?

5. What is the function of a PARM operation?

6. When do PARMs need to occur as part of a PLIST?

7. When is *ENTRY used as a PLIST name?

8. Explain the difference between API QUSCMDLN and API QCMDEXC.

9. What is an LDA?

10. Why might you use a data area rather than a database file to store values?

11. What is an advantage of accessing data areas through a data-area data structure?

12. What are the two uses of the DEFINE operation that you have encountered in this text?

Exercises

1. Write the RPG IV code to call either ProgA, ProgB, or ProgC, depending on whether field Option is 1, 2, or 3. No parameters are needed with any of the calls.

2. Write that portion of a calling program that passes a date of numeric data type in YYMMDD format to a called program to convert the date to a date in month-name, day, 4-digit-year format (e.g., January 1, 1993).

3. Write the entire RPG IV program that would be called in Exercise 2 to convert the date to the desired format.

4. Assume a data area named CheckValue contains a 6-position number representing the last check number used, a 6-position date reflecting the most recent date on which the check-writing program was run, 10 positions containing the name of the last user running the check-writing program, and four positions reflecting the number of checks written during the last program run. Code a data-area data structure to enable access to this data area.

5. At a certain point in an RPG IV program you need to delete a database file. The name of the file to be deleted is contained in field FileName, a 10-position character field. The CL command to delete a file is:

```
DLTF FILE(*CURLIB/XXXXXXXXXX)
```

where *XXXXXXXXXX* represents where a file name should appear.

Write the RPG IV code to incorporate the file name from FileName in the proper location within the command and then call QCMDEXC to carry out the command.

Programming Assignments

1. Develop an interactive menu application that presents the user with a choice for executing one of four programs you have written this semester. (Your instructor may tell you which applications to include; preferably, the programs will be part of the same application system and include at least one interactive application.) Your program should call the appropriate program based on the user's choice. Upon return from the called program, the user should again see the menu for another selection. This should continue until the user signals Exit at the menu. Design your menu to be user friendly and to include informational messages signaling the results of processing for non-interactive applications, so that the user knows the selected program has executed. Also, let the user access a CL command line from the menu by pressing F21.

2. As part of its billing procedure, GTC needs to convert military time to standard time in several programs. The company decides to do this conversion through a called program. Write such a called program that will receive as a parameter argument the time in HHMM format, where the hours are based on a 24-hour clock (i.e., military time), convert that value to time expressed on a 12-hour clock, with a.m. or p.m. noted, and pass that converted value back to the calling program. For example, if the called program was passed 1530, it should convert that value to 3:30 p.m.

   To test your program, use GTC's Calls Transaction File (GTCLSP) as the input file to a calling program that passes the time-of-call value from each record to the called program and generates the following report to reflect the converted time returned by the called program:

```
        1|        2|        3|        4|        5|        6|        7|        8|        9|       10|
1234567890123456789012345678901234567890123456789012345678901234567890123456789012345678901234567890
 1  XX/XX/XX                    PAGE  XX0X
 2     GTC TIME CONVERSION TEST REPORT
 3
 4     MILITARY TIME  CONVERTED TIME
 5
 6          XXXX       0X:XX A.M.
 7          XXXX       0X:XX P.M.
 8          XXXX       0X:XX A.M.
 9
```

3. GTC needs to convert time from military to standard time and determine the day of the week from a given date, both as part of its billing procedure. The programmers decide to implement each of these conversions as called programs. Write two called programs to accomplish these tasks. More details of the time conversion are described in Assignment 2 above. For the called program that determines the day of the week, use the algorithm below, which extends the routine presented in Chapter 9 that compared a given date to a known Sunday (December 31, 1899). *Hint*: To convert a numeric date in YYMMDD format to a *ISO date, use operation MOVE: enter *YMD in factor 1, the given date in factor 2, and a *ISO date field in the result.

   Algorithm for determining the day of the week from a date stored in YYMMDD numeric format:

   Initialize known date

   Convert given date to date data type

   Calculate number-of-days from known date to converted date

Programming Assignments Continued

Programming Assignments continued

Calculate day-of-week (remainder from number-of-days/7)

```
IF day-of-week = 0
    name-of-day = "Sunday"
ELSE
IF day-of-week = 1
    name-of-day = "Monday"
ELSE
IF day-of-week = 2
    name-of-day = "Tuesday"
ELSE
...
ENDIF
```

Test your two called programs by generating the report shown below, using the date-of-call and time-of-call fields of GTC's Call Transaction File (GTCLSP) for your test data. For the report column "DAY", print the appropriate name of the day (e.g., SUNDAY).

```
         1          2          3          4          5          6          7          8          9         10
1234567890123456789012345678901234567890123456789012345678901234567890123456789012345678901234567890
1 XX/XX/XX                              PAGE XX0X
2   GTC DATE AND TIME CONVERSION TEST REPORT
3
4 DATE          DAY       MILITARY TIME   CONVERTED TIME
5
6 XX/XX/XX    XXXXXXXXX       XXXX          0X:XX A.M.
7 XX/XX/XX    XXXXXXXXX       XXXX          0X:XX P.M.
8 XX/XX/XX    XXXXXXXXX       XXXX          0X:XX A.M.
9
```

4. CompuSell wants you to write a label-printing program for its customers in file CSCSTP (Appendix D); the company wants your program to print 2-across labels. Each of the labels reading across should represent the same customer. The printer will be loaded with continuous-label stock when this program is run. Each label is five print lines long. The desired format for the labels is shown below. Note that the information within parentheses is included to let you know what should appear on the label, but that information should not appear within your output.

```
         1          2          3          4          5          6          7          8          9         10
1234567890123456789012345678901234567890123456789012345678901234567890123456789012345678901234567890
1
2     XXXXXXXXXX XXXXXXXXXXXXXXX          XXXXXXXXXX XXXXXXXXXXXXXXX       (first, last name)
3     XXXXXXXXXXXXXXXXXXXX                XXXXXXXXXXXXXXXXXXXX             (street address)
4     XXXXXXXXXXXXXX  XX XXXXX-XXXX        XXXXXXXXXXXXXX  XX XXXXX-XXXX    (city, state, zip)
5
6
7     XXXXXXXXXX XXXXXXXXXXXXXXX          XXXXXXXXXX XXXXXXXXXXXXXXX
8     XXXXXXXXXXXXXXXXXXXX                XXXXXXXXXXXXXXXXXXXX
9     XXXXXXXXXXXXXX  XX XXXXX-XXXX        XXXXXXXXXXXXXX  XX XXXXX-XXXX
10
```

Programming Assignments Continued

Programming Assignments continued

This is a repeat of program assignment 2.3, except that now management has decided the labels will look nicer if the names, addresses, and city print in lowercase (except for the first letter of each word). Rather than writing a conversion routine repeatedly for each of the fields, you decide to write the routine once as a called program so that it will be available for use in other programs as well.

Write a called program that converts a string of uppercase letters to a string in which the first character in the field and any other character immediately following a blank remains uppercase, but all other letters are converted to lowercase. Include as parameters two character fields each 25 positions long. The program should process the value passed in the first parameter and store the converted string in the second PARM field prior to returning.

Once you have written the called program, in your label program successively call that program to convert first name, last name, street address, and city to the desired format for each customer before printing the label.

Chapter 13

Maintaining the Past

Chapter Overview

This chapter discusses the migration of older RPG programs to RPG IV. It also introduces you to features and operations extensively used in earlier versions of the language, but now obsolete (though still supported) in RPG IV. It familiarizes you with the fixed-logic cycle, as well as the use of conditioning, resulting, and level indicators.

Compatibility and Conversion

As RPG evolved, IBM's language developers tried to keep the language *backward-compatible*, so that old program source code would successfully compile and then execute with each new version of RPG. Typically, modifications to RPG consisted of "add-ons," rather than replacements to older features, so that although the new version of the language might offer a better way to accomplish some programming task, the older method of accomplishing the task would still work. Thus, for example, RPG II programs would compile under RPG III with only slight, if any, modification to the source code.

RPG IV, however, introduced fundamental changes to the language. For example, source code lines were lengthened to 100 characters, where previous versions of the language used 80-column specifications. Moreover, RPG IV increased the permitted field name length from six to ten characters, allowed mixed-case entry and blank lines, changed the maximum length of operation names from five to six characters, shifted the location of some fixed-position entries, and changed some code requirements from fixed-position entries to more free-form keywords. All the specification types changed; some were eliminated, and a new one (the Definition Specification) was introduced. As a result, source code of programs written before RPG IV require a "face-lift" to be compatible with the RPG IV compiler.

To let RPG shops migrate code as effortlessly as possible to RPG IV, IBM supplies a command, CVTRPGSRC (Convert RPG Source), that converts pre-RPG IV source code to RPG IV syntax. This conversion utility automatically rearranges fixed-position entries to new locations, changes obsolete positional entries to appropriate keywords, creates Definition Specifications for tables and arrays to replace the eliminated Extension Specifications, substitutes new six-character operation codes for their obsolete five-character equivalents (e.g., LOOKUP for LOKUP, EXCEPT for EXCPT), and so on.

Generally, companies using AS/400s traditionally stored RPG programs within source file QRPGSRC. As companies use command CVTRPGSRC to convert their old programs to RPG IV syntax, many choose to store the converted source code in the default source file QRPGLESRC. Depending on a company's approach to program migration, the business may have converted all its source code shortly after adopting RPG IV, or it may have taken a more leisurely approach, converting code on a member-by-member basis, only as program maintenance needs require it.

But when you begin working as an RPG IV programmer (regardless of whether you need to convert source code to RPG IV or you are put to work on source code already converted), you need to understand the programming conventions and styles appropriate to earlier versions of the language to thoroughly understand the programs you encounter. CVTRPGSRC modifies only those syntactical variants that are no longer valid under RPG IV. In converted RPG IV source code you can still find many coding styles and syntactical usage once necessary and/or appropriate for earlier versions of RPG. Consequently, the code you maintain may not look very much like the code you'd write from scratch in RPG IV.

Holdovers from RPG III

First, don't be surprised to see variable names that are very short, and written in all uppercase letters. Versions of RPG before RPG IV did not permit mixed-case entry, and they imposed a maximum length of six characters on field names. To give you a sense of what these earlier programs might look like migrated to RPG IV, all the code in this chapter illustrating pre-RPG IV techniques uses only uppercase characters and field names no longer than six characters. Program documentation, of course, does not extend beyond column 80.

Defining Work Fields

In RPG III, Definition Specifications did not exist. As a result, programs written during the RPG III era (and before it) defined each work field within the Calculation Specification in which that field appeared as a result. With this method, the length of the result field is right-adjusted in positions 64-68 (Len++). If the field is numeric — as it must be if it is the result of an arithmetic operation — the appropriate number of decimal positions is right-adjusted in positions 69-70 (D+). (Note that all Calculation Specifications in pre-RPG IV versions of the language were *standard* form, rather than *extended factor 2* form.)

```
*.. 1 ...+... 2 ...+... 3 ...+... 4 ...+... 5 ...+... 6 ...+... 7 ...+... 8 ...+... 9 ...+...1Ø
CLØNØ1Factor1++++++Opcode(E)+Factor2++++++Result++++++++Len++D+HiLoEq....Comments++++++++++++
C* A division calculation that shows result field definition.
C      DAYS        DIV (H)  7          WEEKS              9 Ø
```

RPG III did let programmers define one variable "like" another, but in the absence of Definition Specifications, this feature was implemented via a Calculation Specification: *LIKE was the factor 1 value, DEFINE was the operation, the reference field was factor 2, and the field being defined was the result. You could stipulate that the new field be longer or shorter than the defining field by including an entry in the length position: + signaled the new field should be longer than the defining field, while − meant it should be shorter than the defining field. The value following the sign indicated the amount of increase or decrease. The code below illustrates this RPG III feature.

```
*.. 1 ...+... 2 ...+... 3 ...+... 4 ...+... 5 ...+... 6 ...+... 7 ...+... 8 ...+... 9 ...+...10
CL0N01Factor1++++++Opcode(E)+Factor2++++++Result+++++++Len++D+HiLoEq....Comments++++++++++++
C* Older method of defining one field like another.
C        *LIKE     DEFINE    OLDFLD         NEWFLD
C        *LIKE     DEFINE    SALES          SLSTOT        +  5
C        *LIKE     DEFINE    SLSTAX         SLSTOT        -  2
```

Performing Arithmetic and Numeric Assignment

The EVAL operation, with its free-form extended factor 2 capabilities, was also not available before RPG IV. As a result, programmers used various fixed-form operations to express assignment and arithmetic logic. You have already learned how the specific arithmetic operation DIV works to divide one numeric value by another. There are three other specific arithmetic operations that enable basic calculation: ADD, SUB, and MULT. Like DIV, you can apply these operations to numeric fields or numeric literals, and the results of the operation must be stored in a numeric field designated as the result field. Also like DIV, all three operations can result in high- or low-order truncation, depending on the size of the answer relative to that of the result field. You can specify rounding, or half-adjusting, for any of the operations by using the operation extender (H).

In its basic form, operation ADD adds the values of factor 1 and factor 2, storing the answer in the result field. Programmers used two different methods with ADD when counting or accumulating. With the older method, the result field also had to appear in factor 1 or factor 2. With RPG III, programmers could omit repeating the result field as a factor and simply include the incrementing value in factor 2. The following code illustrates various forms and uses of ADD.

```
*.. 1 ...+... 2 ...+... 3 ...+... 4 ...+... 5 ...+... 6 ...+... 7 ...+... 8 ..+... 9 ...+...10
CLØN01Factor1++++++Opcode(E)+Factor2++++++Result+++++++Len++D+HiLoEq....Comments++++++++++++
C* Sample calculations using the ADD operation to add two numeric values.
C* The result fields are defined within the specifications.
C           REGPAY        ADD       OVRPAY        TOTPAY          9 2
C           25            ADD       QTY           NEWQTY          7 0
C           RATE1         ADD (H)   .045          RATE2           4 2
C* Calculations showing two equivalent ways of incrementing a counter.
C           COUNT         ADD       1             COUNT           3 0
C                         ADD       1             COUNT           3 0
C* Calculations showing two equivalent ways of accumulating net pay.
C           NETPAY        ADD       TOTNET        TOTNET          9 2
C                         ADD       NETPAY        TOTNET          9 2
```

The SUB operation subtracts factor 2 from factor 1, storing the answer in the result field. Unlike ADD, the order of the factors is significant. In algebra, the SUB operation would be expressed as

$$Result = Factor1 - Factor2$$

You can also decrement a counter or decrease the value of an accumulator by omitting factor 1. This format of SUB says, in effect, "Subtract factor 2 from the result field and store the answer in the result field." The code below illustrates the SUB operation.

```
*.. 1 ...+... 2 ...+... 3 ...+... 4 ...+... 5 ...+... 6 ...+... 7 ...+... 8 ...+... 9 ...+...10
CLØN01Factor1++++++Opcode(E)+Factor2++++++Result+++++++Len++D+HiLoEq....Comments++++++++++++
C* Examples of the use of SUB.
C           GROSS         SUB       WTHHLD        NETPAY          7 2
C           65            SUB       AGE           WRKYRS          2 0
C                         SUB       1             COUNT           5 0
C                         SUB       AMT           RMDR            5 2
```

The MULT operation lets you multiply the contents of factor 1 and factor 2 and store the answer in the result field. MULT also supports a second format, in which you omit factor 1. With this format, the value of the result field is multiplied by factor 2 and the product is stored in the result field. This form of MULT, used within a loop, was sometimes used to accomplish exponentiation, because before RPG IV there was no direct way to raise a number to a power.

```
*.. 1 ...+... 2 ...+... 3 ...+... 4 ...+... 5 ...+... 6 ...+... 7 ...+... 8 ...+... 9 ...+...10
CLØN01Factor1++++++Opcode(E)+Factor2++++++Result+++++++Len++D+HiLoEq....Comments++++++++++++
C* Examples of the MULT operation.
C           SALES         MULT (H)  TAXRAT        SLSTAX          5 2
C           60            MULT      HOURS         MINUTE          5 0
C           GROSS         MULT (H)  .0751         FICA            6 2
C                         MULT (H)  VALUE         EXPVAL         15 9
```

The advantage of RPG IV's EVAL over the individual arithmetic operators is obvious, especially when a complex calculation needs to be executed. A calculation that might take dozens of specification lines using the fixed-form arithmetic operation codes can be accomplished with a single EVAL. The following example illustrates this contrast:

```
*.. 1 ...+... 2 ...+... 3 ...+... 4 ...+... 5 ...+... 6 ...+... 7 ...+... 8 ...+... 9 ...+...10
CLØNØ1Factor1++++++Opcode(E)+Extended-factor2+++++++++++++++++++++++++++++++++Comments+++++++++++
CLØNØ1Factor1++++++Opcode(E)+Factor2++++++Result+++++++Len++D+HiLoEq....Comments+++++++++++
C* The formula for converting a Fahrenheit temperature to Centigrade is
C*     C = 5(F - 32)/9. The EVAL below accomplishes this conversion.
C                 EVAL(H)   C = 5 * ( F - 32 ) / 9
C
C* Here's the same conversion using fixed-form arithmetic operations.
C       F         SUB       32            WRKFLD          4 Ø
C       WRKFLD    MULT      5             WRKFLD
C       WRKFLD    DIV(H)    9             C               4 Ø
```

Two additional operations — Z-ADD (Zero and Add) and Z-SUB (Zero and Subtract) — were commonly used to assign values to numeric variables before the introduction of EVAL. You can interpret Z-ADD, which requires a factor 2 value and a result field, as "Zero out the result field and add factor 2 to it." The effect of this operation was to assign the value of factor 2 to the result field. The most common use of this operation was to initialize or reinitialize a counter or accumulator to zero, but you could use Z-ADD to assign the value of any numeric literal or numeric field to the result field.

Like Z-ADD, Z-SUB requires a factor 2 entry and a result field entry. The Z-SUB operator works similarly to Z-ADD, except that after zeroing out the result field, it subtracts the value of factor 2 from the result field. Because this operation assigns the negative value of factor 2 to the result field, its effect is to reverse the sign of a field.

```
*.. 1 ...+... 2 ...+... 3 ...+... 4 ...+... 5 ...+... 6 ...+... 7 ...+... 8 ...+... 9 ...+...10
CLØNØ1Factor1++++++Opcode(E)+Factor2++++++Result+++++++Len++D+HiLoEq....Comments+++++++++++
C* Examples showing uses of Z-ADD and Z-SUB.
C* Set COUNT to zero.
C                 Z-ADD     Ø             COUNT           3 Ø
C* Assign COUNT the same value as NBR.
C                 Z-ADD     NBR           COUNT
C* Set MAXMUM to 20.
C                 Z-ADD     20            MAXMUM          2 Ø
C* After the below calculation, MINMUM has a value of -20.
C                 Z-SUB     20            MINMUM          2 Ø
C* After the below calculation, X has a value of +15.
C                 Z-SUB     -15           X               3 Ø
C* In general, Z-SUB reverses signs.
C                 Z-SUB     POSVAL        NEGVAL          5 2
C                 Z-SUB     NEGVAL        POSVAL          5 2
```

Looping and Selecting

Another set of obsolete operators you may encounter in maintenance programming are DOWxx, DOUxx, IFxx, and WHENxx. These fixed-form structured operators function identically to their modern counterparts: DOW, DOU, IF, and WHEN. The major difference is that the older operations do not use free-form conditional expressions. Instead, each operation requires an entry in factor 1, an entry in factor 2, and a relational code (replacing the *xx* in the operation) to specify the way in which the two factor entries are to be compared. The table below, duplicated from Chapter 4, lists these relational codes and their meanings.

Symbol	Code	Meaning
>	GT	Greater than
<	LT	Less than
=	EQ	Equal to
<>	NE	Not equal to
<=	LE	Less than or equal to
>=	GE	Greater than or equal to

Like their RPG IV counterparts, these RPG III structured operations require scope terminators to indicate their end-points. Although the operation-specific terminators (e.g., ENDIF, ENDSL) were available in later versions of RPG III, initially only a generic END was used with these operations.

Because these older structured operations do not allow free-form expressions, to express a compound condition to check two (or more) relationships, you couple the comparisons with ANDxx and/or ORxx operations to build complex conditional tests.

Carefully examine the examples below, which include converted RPG III code segments and their RPG IV equivalents, to understand how these RPG III structured operations work.

```
*.. 1 ...+... 2 ...+... 3 ...+... 4 ...+... 5 ...+... 6 ...+... 7 ...+... 8 ...+... 9 ...+...10
CL0N01Factor1++++++Opcode(E)+Factor2++++++Result+++++++Len++D+HiLoEq....Comments+++++++++++
CL0N01Factor1++++++Opcode(E)+Extended-factor2++++++++++++++++++++++++++++Comments+++++++++++
C* Decision logic using IFxx.
C     MILES         IFLE      50000
C     MONTHS        ANDLT     36
C                   EXSR      WRRNTY
C                   ELSE
C                   EXSR      YOUPAY
C                   END
C
C* Equivalent decision logic using IF.
C                   IF        Mileage <= 50000 AND Months < 36
C                   EXSR      WarrantySR
C                   ELSE
C                   EXSR      YouPaySR
C                   ENDIF
```

```
*.. 1 ...+... 2 ...+... 3 ...+... 4 ...+... 5 ...+... 6 ..+... 7 ...+.. 8 ...+... 9 ...+...10
CL0N01Factor1++++++Opcode(E)+Factor2++++++Result++++++++Len++D+HiLoEq....Comments+++++++++++
CL0N01Factor1++++++Opcode(E)+Extended-factor2+++++++++++++++++++++++++++++Comments+++++++++++
C* Decision logic using SELECT and WHENxx.
C                   SELECT
C         ADJGRS    WHENLE    8000
C                   Z-ADD     .00        RATE            2 2
C         ADJGRS    WHENLE    18000
C                   Z-ADD     .10        RATE
C         ADJGRS    WHENLE    35000
C                   Z-ADD     .21        RATE
C                   OTHER
C                   Z-ADD     .28        RATE
C                   END
C
C* Equivalent logic using SELECT and WHEN.
C                   SELECT
C                   WHEN      AdjstGross <=8000
C                   EVAL      Rate = .00
C                   WHEN      AdjstGross <= 18000
C                   EVAL      Rate = .10
C                   WHEN      AdjstGross <= 35000
C                   EVAL      Rate = .21
C                   OTHER
C                   EVAL      Rate = .28
C                   ENDSL


*.. 1 ...+... 2 ...+... 3 ...+... 4 ...+... 5 ...+... 6 ..+... 7 ...+.. 8 ...+... 9 ...+...10
CL0N01Factor1++++++Opcode(E)+Factor2++++++Result++++++++Len++D+HiLoEq....Comments+++++++++++
CL0N01Factor1++++++Opcode(E)+Extended-factor2+++++++++++++++++++++++++++++Comments+++++++++++
C* Iteration implemented with DOWxx.  Any processing specified within the
C* loop would be repeated as long as both indicators 90 and 99 remain off.
C     *IN90         DOWEQ     *OFF
C     *IN99         ANDEQ     *OFF
C                   ...
C                   END
C
C* The same iteration logic implemented with DOW.
C                   DOW       *IN90 = *OFF AND *IN99 = *OFF
C                   ...
C                   ENDDO


*.. 1 ...+... 2 ...+... 3 ...+... 4 ...+... 5 ...+... 6 ..+... 7 ...+.. 8 ...+... 9 ...+...10
CL0N01Factor1++++++Opcode(E)+Factor2++++++Result++++++++Len++D+HiLoEq....Comments+++++++++++
CL0N01Factor1++++++Opcode(E)+Extended-factor2+++++++++++++++++++++++++++++Comments+++++++++++
C* Iteration implemented with DOUxx.  Any processing specified within the
C* loop would be repeated until either indicator 90 or 99 turned on.
C     *IN90         DOUEQ     *ON
C     *IN99         OREQ      *ON
C                   ...
C                   END
C
C* The same iteration logic implemented with DOU.
C                   DOU       *IN90 = *ON OR *IN99 = *ON
C                   ...
C                   ENDDO
```

In addition to the above structured operations, when maintaining older programs you may encounter two *unstructured* operations: CABxx and GOTO. These operations are unstructured because neither has built-in constraints to limit how it directs flow of control.

The GOTO operation diverts control to a different location within a program. Factor 2 of the GOTO contains a label that identifies the location to which control should transfer. That same label must appear as the factor 1 entry of a TAG operation somewhere within the program. TAG, a non-executable operation, simply marks a program line as a label statement that identifies a location in the program. The same rules for forming RPG field names apply to RPG labels.

You can use GOTO to branch around a sequence of instructions if the TAG is below the GOTO, or to set up a loop if the TAG is above the GOTO.

```
*.. 1 ...+... 2 ...+... 3 ...+... 4 ...+... 5 ...+... 6 ...+... 7 ...+... 8 ...+... 9 ...+...10
CLØN01Factor1++++++Opcode(E)+Factor2++++++Result++++++++Len++D+HiLoEq....Comments++++++++++++
C* This GOTO branches around instructions by sending control to SKIP.
C                   GOTO      SKIP
C                   ...
C     SKIP          TAG
C                   ...
C
C     LOOP          TAG
C                   ...
C* This GOTO creates a loop by sending control back up to LOOP.
C                   GOTO      LOOP
```

The above instructions show the GOTO used to set up *unconditional* transfer of control. You will seldom, if ever, find unconditional transfer of control within a program; if you always want to bypass a set of instructions, why include them in the first place? And unconditional transfer to set up a loop results in an infinite loop that would cause a program to run forever. Accordingly, most often GOTOs are used with IF logic or conditioned by indicators (discussed later in this chapter) to transfer control based on some conditional test.

The CABxx (Compare and Branch) operation is simply a GOTO in disguise. CABxx combines a conditional test and the transfer of control in a single operation. CABxx compares the value of factor 1 with the value of factor 2 based on the relational code included in the CABxx operation; if the comparison is true, control is transferred to the TAG label designated in the result field.

```
*.. 1 ...+... 2 ...+... 3 ...+... 4 ...+... 5 ...+... 6 ...+... 7 ...+... 8 ...+... 9 ...+...10
CLØN01Factor1++++++Opcode(E)+Factor2++++++Result++++++++Len++D+HiLoEq....Comments++++++++++++
C* This CABxx branches around instructions by sending control to SKIP
C* if A is greater than B.
C     A             CABGT     B             SKIP
C                   ...
C     SKIP          TAG
C                   ...
C
C     LOOP          TAG
C                   ...
C* This CABxx creates a loop by sending control back up to LOOP
C* if indicator 40 is on.
C     *IN40         CABEQ     *ON           LOOP
```

With both CABxx and GOTO, transfer of control is unidirectional; flow simply continues on from the tag. Use of GOTO and CABxx often makes programs harder to follow, because these operators do not keep as tight a rein on flow of control as do the structured operators, with their single-entry, single-exit points.

Manipulating Strings

In Chapter 11 you were introduced to RPG IV's techniques of string manipulation. You may still encounter two RPG III operations that no longer need to be used for handling strings: SUBST (Substring), which has been superseded by the built-in function %SUBST, and CAT (Concatenate), made obsolete by the + operator used within an EVAL operation.

The SUBST operation copies a portion of a character string into a different field. Factor 2, required for this operation, contains the base character string *to be copied*. The result field serves as the receiving field for the SUBST operation. And factor 1, also required, indicates the length of the string to be copied. The copying begins with the left-most character of the base string, unless the data item representing the base string is followed by a colon and a start location.

An optional indicator in positions 73-74 (Lo) comes on if the length specified in factor 1 causes the substring to extend beyond the end of factor 2. If the specified starting location is greater than the actual length of the base character string, the SUBST operation does not take place. If the substring is shorter than the result field, the unused positions of the result field will retain their previous contents unless you use operation extender (P) — pad — to blank-fill the unused portion of the result field.

Some examples demonstrating the use of SUBST are explained below.

```
*.. 1 ...+... 2 ...+... 3 ...+... 4 ...+... 5 ...+... 6 ...+... 7 ...+... 8 ...+... 9 ...+...10
CL0N01Factor1++++++Opcode(E)+Factor2++++++Result+++++++Len++D+HiLoEq....Comments+++++++++++
C* All the examples below are based on FIELDA with value 'abcdefgh'
C* and RESULT with value '12345' before the SUBST operation.
C
C        3         SUBST     FIELDA        RESULT              90
C* RESULT now contains 'abc45', because just the first 3 characters of
C* FIELDA are copied.  Indicator 90 is off.
C
C        3         SUBST (P) FIELDA        RESULT              90
C* RESULT is 'abc  ', because the operation specifies padding.
C
C        4         SUBST (P) FIELDA:3      RESULT              90
C* RESULT is 'cdef ', because 4 characters are copied, beginning with the
C* third character of FIELDA.  Indicator 90 is off.
C
C        3         SUBST     FIELDA:9      RESULT              90
C* The operation is not executed, because the starting position exceeds
C* the length of FIELDA.
C
C        6         SUBST     FIELDA:5      RESULT              90
C* Indicator 90 comes on, because the specified substring length, in
C* conjunction with the starting position, exceeds the length of FIELDA.
```

The CAT operation was used for combining the values of two strings to form a third string. The two character items to be combined are specified in factor 1 and factor 2; the result-field entry specifies where the results of the concatenation are to be placed.

You have the option of specifying the number of blanks you want to appear between the non-blank characters of the concatenated fields by appending a colon (:) to the factor 2 item, followed by a data item that specifies the desired number of blanks. If you do not specify the number of desired blanks, all the trailing blanks (if they exist) within factor 1 are included in the concatenation.

If the concatenation is too large to fit in the result field, truncation occurs from the right of the string. No indicators are used with the CAT operation. As was the case for SUBST, CAT leaves residual characters in the unused left-most positions of the result field unless you indicate through use of operation extender (P) that you want to pad those unused positions with blanks.

You can get a sense of how CAT works by examining the examples below.

```
*.. 1 ...+... 2 ...+... 3 ...+... 4 ...+... 5 ...+... 6 ...+... 7 ...+... 8 ...+... 9 ...+...10
CLØNØ1Factor1++++++Opcode(E)+Factor2++++++Result++++++++Len++D+HiLoEq....Comments+++++++++++
CLØNØ1Factor1++++++Opcode(E)+Extended-factor2+++++++++++++++++++++++++++++Comments+++++++++++
C* The examples below are all based on FNAME (10 positions) with a value of
C* 'John      ', LNAME (12 positions) with a value of 'Jackson     ', and
C*  WHLNAM (25 positions) with a value of 'abcdefghijklmnopqrstuvwxy'.
C
C        FNAME         CAT       LNAME       WHLNAM         25
C* WHLNAM contains 'John      Jackson     rstuvwxy', since nothing
C* about blanks or padding was specified.
C
C        FNAME         CAT       LNAME:1     WHLNAM
C* WHLNAM contains 'John Jackson      rstuvwxy', because 1 blank was
C* requested.
C
C        FNAME         CAT (P)   LNAME:1     WHLNAM
C* WHLNAM contains 'John Jackson             ', because 1 blank and
C* padding were requested.
C
C        FNAME         CAT (P)   LNAME:Ø     WHLNAM
C* WHLNAM contains 'JohnJackson              ', because Ø blanks
C* were requested.
C
C* SMLNAM, in the example below, is 10 bytes long.
C        FNAME         CAT (P)   LNAME:1     SMLNAM
C* SMLNAM contains 'John Jacks', because it can store only 10 characters.
```

Delimiting Arrays and Tables

There is one additional RPG III feature you may encounter when working with older programs that include compile-time arrays or tables: The required delimiter line between the end of the source code and the array/table data contains **Ƀ, rather than **CTDATA and the array/table name. Because this older delimiter gives no indication of which array/table follows it, programs with multiple compile-time arrays or tables must define the arrays/tables in the same order as the data appears at the program's end.

Moving Data

Before we turn the clock even further back to consider RPG II, to complete our discussion of RPG III requires that we take a second look at MOVE, MOVEL, and MOVEA. Although these three operations have already appeared in this text as integral to RPG IV, in maintaining RPG III programs you will find that the operations were used much more extensively for accomplishing a wider variety of processing needs than the earlier discussions in this text would lead you to believe. For example, before operation EVAL, programmers used MOVE and MOVEL for all character assignment operations; they also used these two operations to split fields into smaller units or to rearrange subfields within fields. The following example typifies this use of MOVE and MOVEL: A "legacy" date (i.e., a date stored as a number or a character string, rather than a date data type value) stored in YYMMDD format is switched to MMDDYY format.

```
*.. 1 ...+... 2 ...+... 3 ...+... 4 ...+... 5 ...+... 6 ...+... 7 ...+... 8 ...+... 9 ...+...10
CL0N01Factor1++++++Opcode(E)+Factor2++++++Result+++++++Len++D+HiLoEq....Comments+++++++++++
C* Assume YRMNDY is a date, 950329, in YYMMDD format. Extract month & day.
C                   MOVE      YRMNDY        MNDY          4
C* The above MOVE stores '0329' in field MNDY.  Extract the year.
C                   MOVEL     YRMNDY        YR            2
C* The above MOVEL stores '95' in field YR. Store month & day.
C                   MOVEL (P) MNDY          MNDYYR        6
C* The above MOVEL puts '0329 ' in field MNDYYR.  Now move year.
C                   MOVE      YR            MNDYYR
C* MNDYYR now contains '032995'.
```

Before the introduction of string operations and built-in functions in RPG IV, programmers used arrays and the MOVEA operation to inspect and manipulate characters within string fields. This approach involved using MOVEA to move field values into an array of one-character-long elements. By looping through the elements of the array, you could check each of the characters in the array, while the array index served as a positional locator of the character. In this way, you could count, modify, or rearrange characters within a string.

To illustrate this concept, assume that a customer file contains records with a first name field FNAME, 12 positions long, and a last name field LNAME, 15 positions long. You want to use the file to generate letters to the customers, but you want the letter salutation to read

"Dear Judy Yaeger:" — not
"Dear Judy   Yaeger   :"

The code that follows uses MOVEA and arrays to trim trailing blanks from the names and concatenate the desired string. ARY is a runtime array of 35 character elements, each 1 byte long. Read the comment lines carefully to understand how the program uses the array to build the salutation.

```
*.. 1 ...+... 2 ...+... 3 ...+... 4 ...+... 5 ...+... 6 ...+... 7 ...+... 8 ...+... 9 ...+...10
CL0N01Factor1++++++Opcode(E)+Factor2++++++Result+++++++Len++D+HiLoEq....Comments+++++++++++
C* Move "Dear" into the leftmost positions of ARY.
C                   MOVEA(P)  'Dear'          ARY
C* ARY now contains 'Dear                              '.
C
C* Now move FNAME into ARY, leaving a blank before the name.
C                   MOVEA     FNAME           ARY(6)
C* ARY now contains 'Dear Judy                         '.
C
C* Now loop to inspect the characters of ARY, moving backwards from the
C* last possible position for the last character of FNAME, until a
C* non-blank character is found.
C                   Z-ADD     17              I                 2 0
C     ARY(I)        DOWEQ     ' '
C                   SUB       1               I
C                   END
C* Given the example, I now has a value of 9.
C
C* Add 2 to I so it points to where LNAME should begin.
C                   ADD       2               I
C* Move LNAME to array, beginning at that position.
C                   MOVEA     LNAME           ARY(I)
C* ARY now contains 'Dear Judy Yaeger                  '.
C
C* Now loop to move backwards from end of array, looking for the last
C* non-blank character.
C                   Z-ADD     35              I
C     ARY(I)        DOWEQ     ' '
C                   SUB       1               I
C                   END
C* Given the example, I now has a value of 16.

C* Add 1 to I for the colon position.
C                   ADD       1               I
C                   MOVEA     ':'             ARY(I)
C* ARY now contains 'Dear Judy Yaeger:                 '.
```

RPG II: An Initial Look

Because some RPG shops may be in a transitional stage between RPG III and RPG IV, you might find that some programmers still use the features discussed so far in this chapter. You will also frequently encounter these features in any maintenance programming you do. However, you may wonder, "Why bother with RPG II, a language version that IBM officially retired more than fifteen years ago?" The primary reason why you should be familiar with RPG II is that you often will be asked to maintain programs that have been based in part — or perhaps entirely — on features from this version of the language. Some of the programs may be old, written before RPG III existed; others may be more recent, but written by programmers who had not entirely embraced more modern styles of programming. If you don't understand how these RPG II features work, you will have little chance of success modifying programs that rely on them.

Recognize that the inclusion of RPG II in this book is not an endorsement of these methods. However, you can implement all the features discussed in this section in RPG IV, because of the backward-compatibility of the language. Also note that all RPG II examples that follow are showing code as it would look *after* CVTRPGSRC conversion, because that would always be the first step in the maintenance of older programs.

To demonstrate the differences between RPG IV and RPG II, let's revisit the first program we wrote in Chapter 2 to see how it would be implemented in RPG II. The program is reproduced below as it appeared in the earlier chapter, except that an overflow indicator and check for page-advance has been added.

```
*.. 1 ...+... 2 ...+... 3 ...+... 4 ...+... 5 ...+... 6 ...+... 7 ...+... 8
F********************************************************************************
F* This program produces a weekly sales report.  The report data comes     *
F* directly from input file SalesMast.                                      *
F*      Author:  J. Yaeger    Date Written:  12/10/94.                      *
F********************************************************************************
FSalesMast IF   F   63          DISK
FQPRINT    O    F  132          PRINTER OFLIND(*INOF)
I
ISalesMast NS
I                                     1    4 ØSlspNumber
I                                     5   34  SlspName
I                                    35   50  ItemNumber
I                                    51   56 ØDateOfSale
I                                    57   63 2Price
C
C                    EXCEPT    Headings
C                    READ      SalesMast                              9Ø
C
C                    DOW       *IN9Ø = *OFF
C                    IF        *INOF = *ON
C                    EXCEPT    Headings
C                    EVAL      *INOF = *OFF
C                    ENDIF
C                    EXCEPT    Detail
C                    READ      SalesMast                              9Ø
C                    ENDDO
C
C                    EVAL      *INLR = *ON
C                    RETURN
O
OQPRINT    E          Headings        2  2
O                                               8 'PAGE'
O                                 PAGE         13
O                                              50 'WEEKLY SALES REPORT'
O                                              64 'DATE'
O                                 UDATE      Y 73
O          E          Headings        1
O                                               7 'SLSPSN..'
O                                              48 'DATE OF'
O                                              77 'SALE'
O          E          Headings        2
O                                               3 'NO.'
O                                              21 'NAME'
O                                              46 'SALE'
O                                              61 'ITEM SOLD'
O                                              77 'PRICE'
O          E          Detail          1
O                                 SlspNumber     4
O                                 SlspName      37
O                                 DateOfSale  Y 48
O                                 ItemNumber    67
O                                 Price       1 79
```

The program represents a simple read/write program. The calculations of the program focus on setting up a loop to read records and write report lines. To express this logic in RPG II will require a few modifications to our program.

First, RPG II programs rely on RPG's **fixed-logic cycle**. All versions of RPG (including RPG IV) have had a built-in read-process-write cycle that you could use to automate part of the processing requirements, but use of this cycle fell out of favor with the adoption of RPG III. This read-process-write cycle repeats until all the desired records have been processed. To plug into the automated reading portion of the fixed-logic cycle, you need to designate the main input file as P (for Primary), rather than F (Full procedural). RPG automatically handles the reading of records from a primary file, so you do not (in fact, you cannot) explicitly issue an input instruction to that file. The File Specifications for our revised program appear below.

```
*.. 1 ...+... 2 ...+... 3 ..+... 4 ...+... 5 ...+... 6 ...+... 7 ...+... 8 ...+... 9 ...+...10
FFilename++IPEASFRlen+LKlen+AIDevice+.Keywords+++++++++++++++++++++++++++++++Comments++++++++++++
FSalesMast IP   F  63          DISK
FQPRINT     O   F 132          PRINTER OFLIND(*INOF)
```

We also need to make a minor addition to the Input Specifications of our program: adding a **record identifying indicator** in positions 21-22 of the record identification line of the input file description. The indicator that we designate as the record identifying indicator will come on each time RPG successfully reads a record from the file; the indicator is automatically turned off just before the next automatic attempt to read another record. If the system retrieves another record, the indicator comes back on. On the other hand, if the system detects end-of-file, the record identifying indicator remains off and indicator LR automatically comes on instead.

You can use any one of RPG's numbered indicators (01-99) to serve as a record identifying indicator. In our sample program, indicator 01 will serve this purpose. Note that you enter all indicators as two-digit numbers, even if the first digit is a zero.

```
*.. 1 ...+... 2 ...+... 3 ...+... 4 ...+... 5 ...+... 6 ...+... 7 ...+... 8 ...+.., 9 ...+...10
IFilename++SqNORiPos1+NCCPos2+NCCPos3+NCC....................................Comments++++++++++++
ISalesMast NS  01
I                              1   4 ØSlspNumber
I                              5  34  SlspName
I                             35  50  ItemNumber
I                             51  56 ØDateOfSale
I                             57  63 2Price
```

To automate the output portion of the cycle, so that writing is done automatically without explicit output operations, you need to change the record format type on the Output Specifications from E to the type appropriate for a given line: H for heading lines, D for detail, or T for total. Also remove the line names, because names are permitted only for exception lines.

In addition to changing the line types and removing the line names, you now also will need to use indicators to condition whether or not a given line should print during the output portion of the fixed-logic cycle. Associating an indicator with an output line means that the indicator must be on for the line to print during the output phase of the current pass of the fixed-logic cycle. Enter indicators in positions 21-29 of the Output Specifications. Multiple indicators on a line are in an AND relationship, such that they all must be on for the line to print. To express an OR relationship between indicators, code one indicator on a line, drop down a line and enter OR in positions 16-17, and enter the second indicator on this second line.

In the sample program, you want headings each time the overflow indicator OF comes on. There is also a special indicator, 1P (First page), which is on for a very brief time at the beginning of the program. This indicator normally is used to produce headings on the first page, because the overflow indicator does not come on until the first page is full. You condition heading lines, then, with 1P or OF. With the fixed-logic cycle, OF turns off automatically after use; you do not need to explicitly turn it off within your calculations.

Because you want a detail line to print each time an input record is processed, use indicator 01, the record identifying indicator, to condition the detail line. These modified output specifications are illustrated below.

```
*.. 1 ...+... 2 ...+... 3 ...+... 4 ...+... 5 ...+... 6 ...+... 7 ...+... 8 ...+... 9 ...+...10
OFilename++DF..NØ1NØ2NØ3Excnam++++B++A++Sb+Sa+..........................Comments+++++++++++
O.............NØ1NØ2NØ3Field++++++++YB.End++PConstant/editword/DTformat++Comments+++++++++++
OQPPRINT    H    1P              2  2
O          OR    OF
O                                           8 'PAGE'
O                        PAGE              13
O                                         50 'WEEKLY SALES REPORT'
O                                         64 'DATE'
O                        UDATE     Y       73
O          H     1P              1
O          OR    OF
O                                           7 'SLSPSN.'
O                                         48 'DATE OF'
O                                         77 'SALE'
O          H     1P              2
O          OR    OF
O                                           3 'NO.'
O                                         21 'NAME'
O                                         46 'SALE'
O                                         61 'ITEM SOLD'
O                                         77 'PRICE'
O          D     Ø1              1
O                        SlspNumber         4
O                        SlspName          37
O                        DateOfSale  Y     48
O                        ItemNumber        67
O                        Price       1     79
```

What changes are required in the Calculation Specifications? Because this is a simple read/write program, there would be no calculations! In the RPG IV version of the program, the calculations consisted of setting up a processing loop, reading, and writing. All those steps are built into the fixed-logic cycle, so that none of them need to be explicit in your RPG II program. And when you use the fixed-logic cycle with a primary input file, indicator LR comes on automatically at end-of-file; this signal serves to end the program automatically.

If the program had required arithmetic operations, decision processing, or repetitive processing for a given input record, these operations would appear on Calculation Specifications. In general, for a simple detailed report, the only Calculation Specifications needed are those that describe the processing required for each input record. Remember that the record retrieval, writing, and main process looping occurs automatically with the fixed-logic cycle.

The entire RPG II version of the sample program is shown below. (Notice that field names have been shortened and capitalized to conform to RPG's earlier standards.)

```
*.. 1 ...+... 2 ...+... 3 ...+... 4 ...+... 5 ...+... 6 ...+... 7 ...+... 8 ...+... 9 ...+...10
F******************************************************************
F* This program produces a weekly sales report using RPG's fixed logic   *
F* cycle.                                                                 *
F*    Author:  J. Yaeger   Date Written:  12/10/94.                       *
F******************************************************************
FSALESMST  IP   F   63        DISK
FQPRINT     O   F  132        PRINTER OFLIND(*INOF)
I********************Input Specifications************************
ISALESMST  NS   01
I                                  1    4 0SLPNBR
I                                  5   34  SLPNAM
I                                 35   50  ITMNBR
I                                 51   56 0SLSDAT
I                                 57   63 2PRICE
O********************Output Specifications***********************
OQPRINT    H   1P                 2  2
O          OR   OF
O                                          8 'PAGE'
O                     PAGE               13
O                                        50 'WEEKLY SALES REPORT'
O                                        64 'DATE'
O                     UDATE        Y     73
O          H   1P                 1
O          OR   OF
O                                          7 'SLSPSN.'
O                                        48 'DATE OF'
O                                        77 'SALE'
O          H   1P                 2
O          OR   OF
O                                          3 'NO.'
O                                        21 'NAME'
O                                        46 'SALE'
O                                        61 'ITEM SOLD'
O                                        77 'PRICE'
O          D   01                 1
O                     SLPNBR              4
O                     SLPNAM             37
O                     SLSDAT       Y     48
O                     ITMNBR             67
O                     PRICE        1     79
```

RPG's Fixed-Logic Cycle

As mentioned above, the fixed-logic cycle provides a built-in logical process of read-process-write that automatically overlays the descriptions that you enter through your program specifications. The steps of the logic cycle are described in the pseudocode below.

> *Pseudocode of RPG's Fixed-Logic Cycle*
> Turn on 1P indicator
> WHILE LR is off
>   Print detail output (H and D lines)
>   Turn off 1P, record identifying, and level indicators
>   Read record from primary file
>   IF end of file
>   Turn on LR and all level indicators
>   ELSE
>   Turn on record identifying indicator
>   IF change in control field
>   Turn on level indicator(s)
>   ENDIF
>   ENDIF
>   Perform total calculations
>   Perform total output (T lines)
>   IF LR is not on
>   IF overflow indicator is on
>   Print lines conditioned by overflow
>   ENDIF
>   Move data into input fields
>   Perform detail calculations
>   ENDIF
> ENDWHILE

If you examine the above cycle carefully, you see that characterizing the fixed-logic cycle as read-calculate-write is a simplification. For one thing, at various points in the cycle different indicators automatically come on or are turned off. For another, the calculations and writing each are actually broken down into two segments — total time and detail time, with total-time calculations and output preceding detail calculations and output. A more accurate characterization, then, would be read-calculate-write-calculate-write.

Total-time calculations are characterized by special indicators, called level indicators, coded in positions 7-8 of the Calculation Specifications; calculations without an indicator in positions 7-8 are treated as detail calculations. On the Calculation Specifications, all detail calculations should be coded first, followed by total-time calculations, with subroutines appearing last within the calculations.

On the output, total-time output is represented by those lines designated as T lines, while H and D lines are considered detail output.

The Fixed-Logic Cycle and Control Breaks

The primary reason for breaking the fixed-logic cycle into two segments — total-time and detail-time — is to facilitate the automatic preparation of control-break reports. You'll recall from Chapter 4 that control-break reports require detecting a change in a control-field value, and when such a change is detected, executing special break processing: printing a subtotal line, rolling over accumulators, zeroing out accumulators, and resetting the hold field.

The example below reprints the control-break program developed procedurally in Chapter 4.

```
*.. 1 ...+... 2 ...+... 3 ...+... 4 ...+... 5 ...+... 6 ...+... 7 ...+... 8 ...+... 9 ...+...10
F****************************************************************
F* This program produces a Sales Report that lists subtotals   *
F* for each salesperson.                                        *
F* Author:  Yaeger      Date Written:  Dec. 1992               *
F*      Modified Jan. 1995 to RPG IV standards. Yaeger.        *
F****************************************************************
FSalesFile IF   F   19          DISK
FQPRINT    O    F  132          PRINTER OFLIND(*INOF)
D HoldSlsp        S             4
D SlspTotal       S             6 2
D GrandTotal      S             8 2
ISalesFile NS
I                                   1    4  SalesPrsn
I                                   5    7  Dept
I                                   8   13 2SalesAmt
I                                  14   19 ØSaleDate
C****************************************************************
C*  Calculations required to produce the Sales Report.
C*  Mainline logic.
C****************************************************************
C                   EXSR      Initial
C
C                   DOW       *IN9Ø = *OFF
C                   IF        HoldSlsp <> SalesPrsn
C                   EXSR      SlspBreak
C                   ENDIF
C                   EXSR      DetailProc
C                   READ      SalesFile                          90
C                   ENDDO
C
C                   EXSR      Terminate
C                   EVAL      *INLR = *ON
C                   RETURN
C****************************************************************
C* Subroutine to read first record, set up hold, and print
C* first page headings.
C****************************************************************
C     Initial       BEGSR
C                   READ      SalesFile                          90
C                   EVAL      HoldSlsp = SalesPrsn
C                   EXCEPT    Headings
C                   ENDSR
```

```
*.. 1 ...+... 2 ...+... 3 ...+... 4 ...+... 5 ...+... 6 ...+... 7 ...+... 8 ...+... 9 ...+...10
C****************************************************************
C* Subroutine done when salesperson changes; print subtotal,
C* rollover accumulator, zero out accumulator, and reset hold.
C****************************************************************
C     SlspBreak     BEGSR
C                   EXCEPT      BreakLine
C                   EVAL        GrandTotal = GrandTotal + SlspTotal
C                   EVAL        SlspTotal = Ø
C                   EVAL        HoldSlsp = SalesPrsn
C                   ENDSR
C****************************************************************
C* Subroutine executed for each input record.
C****************************************************************
C     DetailProc    BEGSR
C                   IF          *INOF = *ON
C* If end-of-page then print headings.
C                   EXCEPT      Headings
C                   EVAL        *INOF = *OFF
C                   ENDIF
C                   EXCEPT      DetailLine
C                   EVAL        SlspTotal = SlspTotal + SalesAmt
C                   ENDSR
C****************************************************************
C* Subroutine done at end of file; execute SlspBreak one last
C* time and print grand total line.
C****************************************************************
C     Terminate     BEGSR
C                   EXSR        SlspBreak
C                   EXCEPT      TotalLine
C                   ENDSR
O****************************************************************
OQPRINT    E            Headings      2  1
O                       UDATE         Y     17
O                                           33 'SALES REPORT'
O                                           40 'PAGE'
O                       PAGE                44
O          E            Headings      2
O                                           20 'SLSPSN.'
O                                           37 'AMT.'
O          E            DetailLine    1
O                       SalesPrsn           18
O                       SalesAmt      1     39
O          E            BreakLine     1  2
O                                           24 'TOTAL'
O                       SlspTotal     1     39
O                                           40 '*'
O          E            TotalLine
O                                           26 'GRAND TOTAL'
O                       GrandTotal    1     39
O                                           41 '**'
```

Let's rework this program using the fixed-logic cycle. First, you need to know that RPG has special **level indicators**, L1-L9, that can be associated with control fields and that come on automatically when a change in the value of these fields is detected. Level indicators eliminate the need for explicit hold fields, because RPG automatically detects changes in control fields' values and turns on the appropriate level indicator(s) when it detects a change.

You can use those level indicators to condition any calculations that would need to be done as part of break processing and also to condition the appropriate subtotal line to print when a change in the control field occurs.

Again, you will recall that when you procedurally code a control-break problem, when a break occurs you need to complete the processing for the prior group before continuing with the detail processing of the record that triggered the break. It is for this reason that the fixed-logic cycle performs total calculations and output before detail calculations and output. It is also why, once end-of-file is detected, the cycle runs through total-time before ending. These final steps allow the wrap-up for the very last group in the report and the printing of grand totals, if the report requires them.

Because all total calculations are performed before total output, you cannot zero out a level's accumulator as part of total-time calculations; otherwise, the subtotals would always print as 0. RPG provides an alternate method of zeroing out these fields in the Output Specifications. By coding a B in position 45, for Blank after printing, the field is automatically set to zeros (if its type is numeric) or blanks (if its type is character) immediately after its value is printed.

The code below represents the sales report program written using the fixed-logic cycle and indicators. Fields SlspTotal and GrandTotal are defined on the Calculation Specifications, rather than on Definition Specifications, because the latter did not exist until RPG IV. Notice that the sales amount is rolled over into the grand-total accumulator as a total-time calculation conditioned by L1. As a result, the program executes that calculation each time SalesPrsn changes. Also note that the grand-total line is conditioned by LR, so that it prints just once, just before the program ends.

```
*.. 1 ...+... 2 ...+... 3 ...+... 4 ...+... 5 ...+... 6 ...+... 7 ...+... 8 ...+... 9 ...+...10
F*****************************************************************
F* This program produces a Sales Report that lists subtotals  *
F* for each salesperson.                                       *
F* Author: Yaeger      Date Written:  Mar. 1995               *
F*****************************************************************
FSalesFile IP   F   19          DISK
FQPRINT     O   F  132          PRINTER OFLIND(*INOF)
ISalesFile NS  01
I                           1    4  SalesPrsn     L1
I                           5    7  Dept
I                           8   13 2SalesAmt
I                          14   19 0SaleDate
C*****************************************************************
C*  Calculations required to produce the Sales Report.
C*****************************************************************
C             ADD    SalesAmt    SlspTotal      6 2
CL1           ADD    SlspTotal   GrandTotal     8 2
O*****************************************************************
OQPRINT    H   1P              2 1
O          OR  OF
O                    UDATE         Y    17
O                                       33 'SALES REPORT'
O                                       40 'PAGE'
O                    PAGE               44
```

```
*.. 1 ...+... 2 ...+... 3 ...+... 4 ...+... 5 ...+... 6 ...+... 7 ...+... 8 ...+... 9 ...+...10
O            H    1P                    2
O            OR   OF
O                                              20 'SLSPSN.'
O                                              37 'AMT.'
O            D    01                    1
O                      SalesPrsn             18
O                      SalesAmt     1        39
O            T    L1                  1 2
O                                              24 'TOTAL'
O                      SlspTotal    1B        39
O                                              40 '*'
O            T    LR
O                                              26 'GRAND TOTAL'
O                      GrandTotal   1         39
O                                              41 '**'
```

If the sales file were sorted by department, and within department by salesperson, we could easily convert this program to a two-level control-break problem by associating L2 with department and adding a department accumulator and a department total line (printed when L2 is on). Calculation modifications would be minimal: Instead of rolling SlspTotal into GrandTotal, we'd roll it into DeptTotal when L1 was on; when L2 came on, we'd roll DeptTotal into GrandTotal.

Note that a file does not have to be program-described to use level indicators. If SalesFile were externally described, we could still use level indicators; all we would need to do is include just those input specifications necessary to make the association between the control field and L1.

Although RPG did not make use of externally described files until RPG III, as a maintenance programmer you may encounter any mix of techniques from different versions of the language.

The examples below show all the File and Input Specifications needed for our program if SalesFile were externally described. Notice that on the Input Specifications you use the record format name, not the file name, and the positions 17-18 (Sq) are left blank. Also notice that From and To positions are omitted from the SalesPrsn field definition, because that field is externally described.

```
*.. 1 ...+... 2 ...+... 3 ...+... 4 ...+... 5 ...+... 6 ...+... 7 ...+... 8 ...+... 9 ...+...10
FFilename++IPEASFRlen+LKlen+AIDevice+.Keywords+++++++++++++++++++++++++++++Comments+++++++++++
F* Example showing SalesFile externally described.
FSalesFile IP   E           K Disk
FQPRINT    O    E 132         Printer OFLIND(*INOF)

*.. 1 ...+... 2 ...+... 3 ...+... 4 ...+... 5 ...+... 6 ...+... 7 ...+... 8 ...+... 9 ...+...10
IFilename++SqNORiPos1+NCCPos2+NCCPos3+NCC.....................Comments+++++++++++
I......................Fmt+SPFrom+To+++DcField++++++++L1M1FrPlMnZr......Comments+++++++++++
I* Example showing association of level indicator L1 with control
I* field SalesPrsn from externally described file SalesFile.
ISalesRec      01
I                                        SalesPrsn     L1
```

At this point, you may be wondering why RPG II techniques, and especially the fixed-logic cycle, are no longer used much. After all, they seem to let you write code that is a lot shorter, and the code doesn't seem so difficult to understand. However, RPG II had many drawbacks. One of its major problems was its heavy reliance on indicators; as indicator use proliferates within a program, the code becomes increasingly difficult to understand. Indicators in RPG substituted for more sophisticated ways of controlling flow of execution within a program.

Decisions in RPG II

Originally, RPG had no operations to handle decision logic. Without IF, IFxx, CASxx, SELECT, or CABxx operators, RPG II still needed some way to perform a relational test between two values and then perform alternate courses of action based on the outcome of that test. To provide that function, earlier versions of RPG relied on the COMP (Compare) operation and indicators.

COMP compares the values of factor 1 and factor 2 and turns on an indicator in the Hi (positions 71-72), Lo (positions 73-74), or Eq (positions 75-76) columns, depending on whether factor 1 is greater than, less than, or equal to factor 2. You can enter an indicator in just one or several of those locations, and use one, two, or three different indicators, depending on the kind of comparison you are trying to make.

You then used those indicators in calculations following the COMP to condition whether or not the operation was to be performed. The original 80-column RPG Calculation Specification let you code up to three **conditioning indicators** on a single line; RPG IV's 100-column Calculation Specification has room for only a single indicator, in positions 9-11, but you can use multiple code lines to condition a given calculation. Any calculation so conditioned is executed only if its associated indicators are on at that time.

Consider the following IF logic:

```
*.. 1 ...+... 2 ...+... 3 ...+... 4 ...+... 5 ...+... 6 ...+... 7 ...+... 8 ...+... 9 ...+...10
CL0N01Factor1++++++Opcode(E)+Extended-factor2++++++++++++++++++++++++++++++Comments+++++++++++
C* RPG IV example of decision logic.
C                   IF        Age >= 65
C                   EVAL      SeniorCnt = SeniorCnt + 1
C                   ENDIF
```

To express that same logic in RPG II syntax would require the following lines. Indicator 65 turns on if AGE is greater than or equal to 65; indicator 65 conditions the addition operation. (Notice that in keeping within RPG II limitations, field names are all capital letters and work fields are defined within the calculations that reference them.)

```
*.. 1 ...+... 2 ...+... 3 ...+... 4 ...+... 5 ...+... 6 ...+... 7 ...+... 8 ...+... 9 ...+...10
CL0N01Factor1++++++Opcode(E)+Factor2++++++Result++++++++Len++D+HiLoEq....Comments+++++++++++
C* Example of decision logic using RPG II methods.
C     AGE           COMP      65                                    65 65
C   65SNRCNT        ADD       1             SNRCNT          3 0
```

That doesn't look too bad, does it? But let's make the decision logic a little more complex. In the example below, the AN in positions 7-8 stands for "and," and means that the indicator in the preceding line, as well as the one in the current line, must be on for the calculation to be executed. Also note that if an indicator is preceded by N, it means the indicator must be off for the calculation to be performed.

```
*.. 1 ...+... 2 ...+... 3 ...+... 4 ...+... 5 ...+... 6 ...+... 7 ...+... 8 ...+... 9 ...+...10
CLØNØ1Factor1++++++Opcode(E)+Factor2++++++Result+++++++Len++D+HiLoEq....Comments++++++++++++
C* Example showing compound decision logic using RPG II techniques.
C     AGE       COMP      65                                      65 65
C     SEX       COMP      'F'                                        70
C  65
CAN 70          Z-ADD     84            LIFE               3 Ø
C  65
CANN70          Z-ADD     79            LIFE
C  N65
CAN 70          Z-ADD     81            LIFE
C  N65
CANN70          Z-ADD     70            LIFE
```

The example below shows the same decision logic expressed using RPG IV's IF operation to clarify the code.

```
*.. 1 ...+... 2 ...+... 3 ...+... 4 ...+... 5 ...+... 6 ...+... 7 ...+... 8 ...+... 9 ...+...10
CLØNØ1Factor1++++++Opcode(E)+Extended-factor2+++++++++++++++++++++++++++++Comments++++++++++++
C* Example showing compound decision logic using RPG IV methods.
C               IF        Age >= 65 AND Sex = 'F'
C               EVAL          LifeExpect = 84
C               ELSE
C               IF        Age >= 65 AND Sex = 'M'
C               EVAL          LifeExpect = 79
C               ELSE
C               IF        Age < 65 AND Sex = 'F'
C               EVAL          LifeExpect = 81
C               ELSE
C               EVAL          LifeExpect = 78
C               ENDIF
C               ENDIF
C               ENDIF
```

You have seen that RPG indicator logic can become complex when you combine indicators in "and" relations and use an indicator's "off status" as a condition for a calculation (e.g., N75). You can also combine indicators in "or" relations, such that the calculation is performed if at least one of the indicators is on. The code below demonstrates this option.

```
*.. 1 ...+... 2 ...+... 3 ...+... 4 ...+... 5 ...+... 6 ...+... 7 ...+... 8 ...+... 9 ...+...10
CLØNØ1Factor1++++++Opcode(E)+Factor2++++++Result+++++++Len++D+HiLoEq....Comments++++++++++++
C* Example showing the use of OR and indicator conditioning; A and B
C* will be added if either indicator Ø5 or indicator 10 (or both) is on.
C  Ø5
COR 10A         ADD       B             C                  5 2
```

As the decision logic's complexity increases, the number of indicators needed to express that logic in RPG II increases, along with the difficulty of understanding the code. For example, can you figure out what the following code is trying to do?

```
*.. 1 ...+... 2 ...+... 3 ...+... 4 ...+... 5 ...+... 6 ...+... 7 ...+... 8 ...+... 9 ...+...10
CL0N01Factor1++++++Opcode(E)+Factor2++++++Result++++++++Len++D+HiLoEq....Comments+++++++++++
C                   Z-ADD     .15          RATE           2 2
C        SALARY      COMP      25000                           602030
C      60SALARY      COMP      40000                           603060
C      20SALARY      COMP      15000                           20  20
C      20            Z-ADD     .18          RATE
C      30            Z-ADD     .25          RATE
C      60            Z-ADD     .31          RATE
```

A conditioning indicator applies only to the line of code with which it is associated. If each of three calculations, for example, is to be executed only if indicator 10 is on, indicator 10 must appear with each calculation. Programmers sometimes tried to avoid this repetitive use of indicators on calculations by using the GOTO operation to branch around, or bypass, a group of calculations. The example below demonstrates how GOTO was sometimes used with decision logic in RPG II.

```
*.. 1 ...+... 2 ...+... 3 ...+... 4 ...+... 5 ...+... 6 ...+... 7 ...+... 8 ...+... 9 ...+...10
CL0N01Factor1++++++Opcode(E)+Factor2++++++Result++++++++Len++D+HiLoEq....Comments+++++++++++
C* Example showing use of GOTO with indicators.
C        SALARY      COMP      15000                           10
C      10            Z-ADD     .15          RATE           2 2
C      10            GOTO      EXTTAG
C        SALARY      COMP      25000                           20
C      20            Z-ADD     .18          RATE
C      20            GOTO      EXTTAG
C        SALARY      COMP      40000                           603060
C      30            Z-ADD     .25          RATE
C      60            Z-ADD     .31          RATE
C        EXTTAG      TAG
```

The two preceding examples both express the same logic using RPG II techniques. You can see that using the structured operations and methods of RPG IV, as shown in the next example, results in code that is much easier to understand.

```
*.. 1 ...+... 2 ...+... 3 ...+... 4 ...+... 5 ...+... 6 ...+... 7 ...+... 8 ...+... 9 ...+...10
CL0N01Factor1++++++Opcode(E)+Extended-factor2+++++++++++++++++++++++++++++Comments+++++++++++
C* Example of RPG IV solution to previous example.
C                   SELECT
C                   WHEN      Salary < 15000
C                   EVAL         Rate = .15
C                   WHEN      Salary < 25000
C                   EVAL         Rate = .18
C                   WHEN      Salary < 40000
C                   EVAL      Rate = .25
C                   OTHER
C                   EVAL         Rate = .31
C                   ENDSL
```

Resulting Indicators and Arithmetic

Another common use of indicators in RPG II was to include them as **resulting indicators** in conjunction with arithmetic operations. You can associate resulting indicators with any arithmetic or assignment operation; they are commonly used with ADD, SUB, MULT, and DIV.

Resulting indicators will go on or off automatically when the operation with which they are associated is executed, depending on the value of the result of that operation. If the result is a positive value, an indicator in positions 71-72 will come on; if the result is negative, an indicator in positions 73-74 will come on; and if the result is zero, an indicator in positions 75-76 will come on. Any resulting indicator in a position that does not reflect the sign of the result goes off (or stays off). The example below demonstrates the use of resulting indicators.

```
*.. 1 ...+... 2 ...+... 3 ...+... 4 ...+... 5 ...+... 6 ...+... 7 ...+... 8 ...+... 9 ...+...10
CLØNØ1Factor1++++++Opcode(E)+Factor2++++++Result++++++++Len++D+HiLoEq....Comments++++++++++++
C* Examples showing how resulting indicators work.
C* Indicator 1Ø comes on if C is Ø.
C     A         MULT      B         C                   1Ø
C
C* Indicator 1Ø comes on if C is less than Ø; otherwise 2Ø comes on.
C     A         DIV       B         C                   2Ø1Ø2Ø
C
C* Indicator 1Ø comes on if C is greater than Ø, 2Ø if C is less than
C* Ø, and 3Ø if C equals Ø.
C     A         SUB       B         C                   1Ø2Ø3Ø
```

As you can see from the examples above, you can use one or more of these indicator positions in a given calculation, with the same indicator repeated (e.g., if you want it to signal that the result is greater than or equal to zero) or with a unique indicator in each position.

The main use of resulting indicators was to eliminate the need for a COMP operation in RPG II, in which the result field would be compared to zero. In later versions of RPG, sometimes programmers would use resulting indicators to eliminate the need for an IFxx operation involving the result field's value.

```
*.. 1 ...+... 2 ...+... 3 ...+... 4 ...+... 5 ...+... 6 ...+... 7 ...+... 8 ...+... 9 ...+...10
CL0N01Factor1++++++Opcode(E)+Factor2++++++Result+++++++Len++D+HiLoEq....Comments+++++++++++
C* Examples showing three logically equivalent ways of specifying that if
C* taxable income is less than zero, reset taxable income to zero.
C
C* Method using resulting indicator.
C        GROSS         SUB       DEPEND        TAXINC        7 2 20
C   20                  Z-ADD     0             TAXINC
C
C* Method using COMP.
C        GROSS         SUB       DEPEND        TAXINC        7 2
C        TAXINC        COMP      0                                      20
C   20                  Z-ADD     0             TAXINC
C
C* Method using IFxx.
C        GROSS         SUB       DEPEND        TAXINC        7 2
C        TAXINC        IFLT      0
C                      Z-ADD     0             TAXINC
C                      ENDIF
```

Iteration and RPG II

Just as RPG II had no decision operations, it also had no operations to allow iteration. Without DO, DOW, DOU, DOWxx, and DOUxx, even with its built-in processing cycle RPG II still needed a way to create loops to perform repetitive processing for a single input record. In RPG II, programmers implemented loop logic with COMP and indicators; the indicators conditioned a GOTO that sent control back to prior calculations to repeat processing steps.

The following example illustrates an RPG II technique of adding all the numbers from 1 to 100:

```
*.. 1 ...+... 2 ...+... 3 ...+... 4 ...+... 5 ...+... 6 ...+... 7 ...+... 8 ...+... 9 ...+...10
CL0N01Factor1++++++Opcode(E)+Factor2++++++Result+++++++Len++D+HiLoEq....Comments+++++++++++
C* Example showing RPG II techniques of adding the numbers from 1 to 100.

C* Initialize NUM and SUM to 0.
C                      Z-ADD     0             NUM           3 0
C                      Z-ADD     0             SUM           4 0
C* Loop while NUM is less than 100.
C        LOOP          TAG
C        NUM           ADD       1             NUM
C        SUM           ADD       NUM           SUM
C        NUM           COMP      100                                    50
C   50                 GOTO      LOOP
```

Another pair of operations often used in RPG II was SETON and SETOFF. Because RPG II did not let you reference indicators directly as fields (e.g., *IN10), the only way to change the value of an indicator directly was to SETON or SETOFF the desired indicator(s).

With these operations, factor 1, factor 2, and the result are always blank; but, you can specify up to three indicators in positions 71-76 of the specification line.

```
*.. 1 ...+... 2 ...+... 3 ...+... 4 ...+... 5 ...+... 6 ...+... 7 ...+... 8 ...+... 9 ...+...10
CLØN01Factor1++++++Opcode(E)+Factor2++++++Result+++++++Len++D+HiLoEq....Comments++++++++++++
CLØN01Factor1++++++Opcode(E)+Extended-factor2+++++++++++++++++++++++++++Comments++++++++++++
C* Turn on indicators 10, 20, and 30 using RPG II methods.
C                     SETON                                        102030
C
C* Equivalent results using RPG IV.
C                     EVAL      *IN10 = *ON
C                     EVAL      *IN20 = *ON
C                     EVAL      *IN30 = *ON
C
C* Turn off indicators 10 and 20 using RPG II methods.
C                     SETOFF                                       1020
C
C* Equivalent results using RPG IV.
C                     EVAL      *IN10 = *OFF
C                     EVAL      *IN20 = *OFF
```

As you have seen, most of the features discussed in this chapter — features that at one time in RPG's history were the only means to accomplish a given programming solution — have alternate, more modern counterparts to accomplish the same result in RPG IV. Specifically, you should avoid using conditioning indicators, arithmetic resulting indicators, COMP, and GOTOs, RPG's legacy from RPG II. Moreover, EVAL and the new structured operators that let you write conditional tests as free-form expressions are preferable to using the older specific arithmetic operations, assignment operations, and fixed-format decision and iteration operations. Furthermore, data definition should *always* take place on Definition Specifications, rather than within Calculation Specifications.

Whether or not to completely abandon the fixed-logic cycle is an interesting question. RPG's fixed-logic cycle still underlies every RPG program written, but more and more, today's programmers are ignoring its automatic features in favor of taking complete procedural control over program logic. Figure 13.1 contrasts program flow using the fixed-logic cycle with the procedural approach favored today. Rather than "riding" the basic process loop built into RPG, contemporary RPG programmers structure their own loops that execute repeatedly during the first (and only) pass through RPG's cycle.

Figure 13.1
The Fixed-Logic Cycle Versus
Modern Process Logic

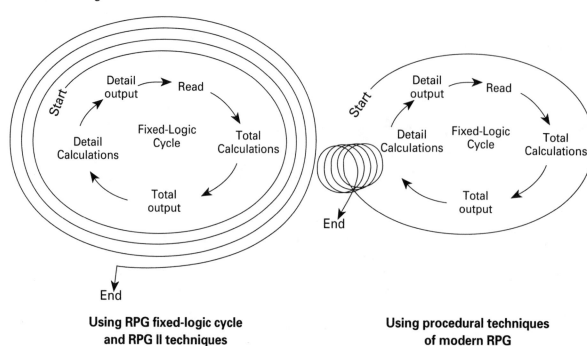

**Using RPG fixed-logic cycle
and RPG II techniques**

**Using procedural techniques
of modern RPG**

The fixed-logic cycle truly is worthless for interactive applications, because the cycle presupposes that you have a primary data file that you want to sequentially process from beginning to end-of-file. On the other hand, when all you require is a straightforward report of a data file's contents — with or without subtotals — using RPG's fixed-logic cycle may result in somewhat shorter programs, perhaps more quickly developed than if you coded full procedural programs. Whether or not these shorter programs are as easy to maintain as procedural programs is open to debate.

Ultimately more important than whether or not you incorporate the fixed-logic cycle into your report programs, regardless of the method you use, is that you think before you code and that your work reflects a structured, modular approach to program design.

Chapter Summary

RPG has evolved since its introduction in the early 1960s. With the introduction of RPG IV, IBM supplied a CL command, CVTRPGSRC, to convert source code written in earlier versions of RPG to a form that is compatible with the new RPG IV syntax. Nonetheless, the language still lets you use operations and features once necessary but now obsolete by modern programming standards.

Use of the fixed-logic cycle upon which RPG is based has also diminished through time. The fixed-logic cycle automatically retrieved and processed records sequentially from a file designated as primary. The cycle automatically wrote output described on the Output Specifications. The cycle actually consists of two separate calculate-and-write segments — one called "total time," appropriate for control-break processing and grand totals, and one called "detail time," for the calculations and output associated with each input record.

Although today's programmers should avoid outdated or obsolete techniques in their own code, they still must understand how such methods and operations work. Knowledge of the capabilities and techniques of previous versions of the language will better enable programmers to maintain older programs that used those features of RPG.

Terms

conditioning indicator   level indicator   resulting indicator
fixed-logic cycle   record identifying indicator

Discussion/Review Questions

1. Describe RPG's fixed-logic cycle.

2. What is a primary input file?

3. How does RPG differentiate between detail output and total output?

4. How does RPG differentiate between detail calculations and total calculations?

5. Why did RPG II include a COMP operation?

6. Give several contemporary alternatives to conditioning calculation lines with indicators.

7. What is a resulting indicator?

8. Describe the general steps of the fixed-logic cycle.

9. Why is the fixed-logic cycle inappropriate for most interactive applications?

10. The CL command CVTRPGSRC has been characterized as a "dumb" conversion program, because it simply mechanically substitutes obsolete RPG syntax with its RPG IV equivlent. What additional services might a "smarter" conversion program provide?

Exercises

For each of the exercises below, rewrite the RPG IV code to include just those features available in RPG II.

1.

```
*.. 1 ...+... 2 ...+... 3 ...+... 4 ...+... 5 ...+... 6 ...+... 7 ...+... 8 ...+... 9 ...+...10
CLØNØ1Factor1++++++Opcode(E)+Extended-factor2++++++++++++++++++++++++++++++Comments+++++++++++++
C* This code uses nested IFs to assign a value to Rate based on level of Sales.
C                   IF        Sales <= 5000
C                   EVAL        Rate = .005
C                   ELSE
C                   IF        Sales <= 10000
C                   EVAL        Rate = .0075
C                   ELSE
C                   IF        Sales <= 20000
C                   EVAL        Rate = .01
C                   ELSE
C                   EVAL        Rate = .015
C                   ENDIF
C                   ENDIF
C                   ENDIF
```

Exercises Continued

Exercises continued

2.

```
*.. 1 ...+... 2 ...+... 3 ...+... 4 ...+... 5 ...+... 6 ...+... 7 ...+... 8 ...+... 9 ...+...10
CLØNØ1Factor1++++++Opcode(E)+Factor2++++++Result+++++++Len++D+HiLoEq....Comments+++++++++++
C* This code uses CASxx to send control to different subroutines based on the
C* level of gross sales.
C       Gross         CASGT     40000          HighSR
C       Gross         CASGE     30000          MediumSR
C       Gross         CASGT     15000          LowSR
C                     CAS                       VeryLowSR
C                     ENDCS
```

3.

```
*.. 1 ...+... 2 ...+... 3 ...+... 4 ...+... 5 ...+... 6 ...+... 7 ...+... 8 ...+... 9 ...+...10
CLØNØ1Factor1++++++Opcode(E)+Extended-factor2+++++++++++++++++++++++++++++Comments+++++++++++
C* If no overtime hours, total pay is hours * rate.
C                     IF        Hours <= 40
C                     EVAL (H)  TotalPay = Hours * Rate
C                     ELSE
C* Otherwise pay time-and-a-half for overtime hours.
C                     EVAL (H)  TotalPay = 40 * Rate +
C                                          (Hours - 40) * Rate * 1.5
```

4.

```
*.. 1 ...+... 2 ...+... 3 ...+... 4 ...+... 5 ...+... 6 ...+... 7 ...+... 8 ...+... 9 ...+...10
CLØNØ1Factor1++++++Opcode(E)+Extended-factor2+++++++++++++++++++++++++++++Comments+++++++++++
CLØNØ1Factor1++++++Opcode(E)+Factor2++++++Result+++++++Len++D+HiLoEq....Comments+++++++++++
C* Reorder, depending on region, code, and number of spare parts.
C                     IF        (Region = 'W' OR Region = 'S')
C                     AND Code = 12
C                     AND (Reorder - QtyOnHand) <= 0
C                     EXSR      OrderSR
C                     ENDIF
```

5.

```
*.. 1 ...+... 2 ...+... 3 ...+... 4 ...+... 5 ...+... 6 ...+... 7 ...+... 8 ...+... 9 ...+...10
CLØNØ1Factor1++++++Opcode(E)+Extended-factor2+++++++++++++++++++++++++++++Comments+++++++++++
CLØNØ1Factor1++++++Opcode(E)+Factor2++++++Result+++++++Len++D+HiLoEq....Comments+++++++++++
C* This routine processes all records in CustFile and prints a detail line for those
C* customers whose AmtDue is not equal to Ø.
C                     DOW       *IN90 = *OFF
C                     READ      CustFile                              90
C                     SELECT
C                     WHEN      *IN90 = *ON
C                     LEAVE
C                     WHEN      AmtDue = 0
C                     ITER
C                     OTHER
C                     EXCEPT    Detail
C                     ENDSL
C                     ENDDO
```

Programming Assignments

1. Wexler University wants a department directory. Write a program using the fixed-logic cycle to develop this directory, shown below.

```
          1         2         3         4         5         6         7         8         9         1 0
 1234567890123456789012345678901234567890123456789012345678901234567890123456789012345678901234567890
1                              WEXLER UNIVERSITY
2                              DIRECTORY OF DEPARTMENTS
3                                    19XX
4
5 DEPT.      NAME                     CHAIR                    OFFICE       PHONE
6
7 XXX    XXXXXXXXXXXXXXXXXXXX     XXXXXXXXXXXXXXXXXXXXXXXXXXX  XXXXXXXXXX  (XXX)XXX-XXXX
8 XXX    XXXXXXXXXXXXXXXXXXXX     XXXXXXXXXXXXXXXXXXXXXXXXXXX  XXXXXXXXXX  (XXX)XXX-XXXX
9
```

2. CompuSell wants a report that shows the current value of its inventory based on the product costs. For each record in the Inventory Master File (CSINVP), multiply quantity on hand by average cost to get the inventory value for that product. Use the report layout shown below. Implement this program using the fixed-logic cycle.

```
          1         2         3         4         5         6         7         8         9         1 0
 1234567890123456789012345678901234567890123456789012345678901234567890123456789012345678901234567890
1   XX/XX/XX                    COMPUSELL            PAGE XX0X
2                            INVENTORY REPORT
3
4  PROD.       DESCRIPTION            QUANTITY  AVERAGE      TOTAL
5  NUMBER                             ON HAND    COST        VALUE
6
7  XXXXXX  XXXXXXXXXXXXXXXXXXXXXXXXX   XX0X    X,XX0.XX   X,XXX,XX0.XX
8  XXXXXX  XXXXXXXXXXXXXXXXXXXXXXXXX   XX0X    X,XX0.XX   X,XXX,XX0.XX
9
10                                   GRAND TOTAL   $XXX,XXX,XX$.XX
11
```

3. At the end of the semester Wexler University distributes mark-sensitive grade reports to its instructors based on the records in the Current Enrollment File; these reports are scanned to add the final grade to each record in file WUENRLP. Wexler University wants you to write a program that updates students' grade-point-average and credits-earned fields of the Student Master File (WUSTDP) based on the credits and grades earned by each student represented in the Current Enrollment File.

    The school uses the following grade values to determine grade points:

    A: 4.0   CB: 2.5   D: 1.0
    BA: 3.5   C: 2.0   F: 0
    B: 3.0   DC: 1.5

    Build a logical file over WUENRLP keyed on student number and use RPG II's fixed-logic cycle and control-break features to update the Student Master File.

4. GTC wants you to write a program that prepares customers' phone bills and updates two fields in the Customer Master File: current billing amount and balance owed. For current billing amount, replace previous contents with the amount due calculated for this month's charges; for the balance owed, add this month's charges to the previous amount.

Programming Assignments Continued

Programming Assignments continued

Billing charges:

There is a set monthly charge for local service of $15.00 per month, regardless of calls made. Additionally, there is an intrastate access charge of $4.39 per month, regardless of calls. A 3 percent federal excise tax applies to the total *cost of calls only*, but not to service charges. A 4 percent state sales tax applies to the cost of calls and the services charges.

You will need to use files GTCSTP (Customer Master) and GTCLSP (Calls Transaction) for this application; you can create whatever logical files you find helpful. Note that because of the monthly service charges, you will need to bill every customer, even if (s)he has made no calls this month.

If you have written program 12.2, call that program to convert the time from military time to standard time for printing; if you have not written that program, change the printer spacing chart to reflect military time (HHMM as stored in GTCLSP).

Implement this program using either RPG IV or RPG II, based on your instructor's directions.

Your bills should be formatted as shown below:

```
          1          2          3          4          5          6          7          8          9          10
 1234567890123456789012345678901234567890123456789012345678901234567890123456789012345678901234567890
 1 GTC INC    PO BOX 123  LAWRENCE  MI  49067
 2
 3    BILL FOR:  X. XXXXXXXXXXXXXXX
 4               XXXXXXXXXXXXXXXXXXXXX
 5               XXXXXXXXXXXXXX XX XXXXX
 6               (XXX)XXX-XXXX
 7
 8 GTC CURRENT CHARGES
 9      LOCAL SERVICE                              15.00
10      INTRASTATE ACCESS                           4.39
11
12 DATE       CALLS MADE      MIN    TIME         COST
13 MMMDD      XXX-XXX-XXXX    XX0    HHMMA.M.     XX0.XX
14 MMMDD      XXX-XXX-XXXX    XX0    HHMMP.M.     XX0.XX
15 MMMDD      XXX-XXX-XXXX    XX0    HHMMP.M.     XX0.XX
16
17                                    CALLS TOTAL  X,XX0.XX
18
19      3% FEDERAL EXCISE TAX ON X,XX0.XX              XX0.XX
20      4% STATE TAX ON X,XX0.XX                       XX0.XX
21                                                -------------------
22 CHARGES FOR THIS BILLING PERIOD                   X,XX0.XX
23 BALANCE PAST DUE                                  X,XX0.XX
24 AMOUNT DUE                                        X,XX0.XX
25
```

Appendix A

Developing Programs on the AS/400

As described in Chapter 1, once you have written a program, you must enter it on the system, compile it, bind it, and then run the program. This appendix is designed to introduce you to those features of the AS/400 that you need to know to complete the above tasks.

The AS/400 has a set of commands, called Control Language (CL), that lets you direct its activities. It also has a series of menus that let you work on the AS/400 without knowing CL. This appendix introduces you to two alternate menus — the Programmer Menu and Programming Development Manager — that you can use to complete your assignments.

Before you look at these menus, you need a basic understanding of AS/400 terminology. The AS/400 uses libraries to organize stored information, called objects. A library is analogous to a PC directory (and is itself an object). The AS/400 stores many kinds of objects — data files, job descriptions, commands, output queues, programs, and so on. The type associated with an object determines what kinds of actions you can perform on the object. All object types begin with an asterisk (*).

You will be working with three primary kinds of objects: *MODULE, *PGM, and *FILE. *MODULE objects result from successful program compiling and contain the machine language version of your source code. An object with type *PGM is a bound program of executable code, based on one or more *MODULEs. When you call an object of type *PGM, you are telling the computer to carry out the instructions contained in the object.

Objects with type *FILE are files; files are further differentiated by attributes, which categorize the nature of the file: The attribute PF-SRC indicates the file is a source physical file that contains source code. Attribute PF-DTA indicates that the object is a physical database file; attribute LF indicates that the object is a logical database file.

The contents of all files, regardless of attribute, can be organized into members. A member is like a subdivision of a file. A file must exist before members can be added to it. Each program that you enter will be stored as a member within a source physical file; when you compile that member (or program), you will create a *MODULE object with the same name as the member.

Generally, most companies use source file QRPGLESRC to store RPG IV source code. It is not unusual for installations to store their source code in libraries separate from their object (executable) code, although in the typical school environment each student has a single library for storing all his/her own work. Your instructor will supply you with the name of the source file and the library name within which you will be working.

The Programmer Menu

The **Programmer Menu** is easy to use, although it is not as versatile as the **Programming Development Manager**. How you reach this menu will depend on how your user profile is set up; if you see the AS/400 Main Menu upon sign-on, select Option 5 (Programming), and then at the resulting Programming panel select Option 1 (Programmer Menu). You should see the following display:

```
                              Programmer Menu
                                                      System:    S1Ø34373
         Select one of the following:
            1. Start AS/400 Data File Utility
            2. Work with AS/4ØØ Query
            3. Create an object from a source file      object name, type, pgm for CMD
            4. Call a program                           program name
            5. Run a command                            command
            6. Submit a job                             (job name), , ,(command)
            7. Go to a menu                             menu name
            8. Edit a source file member               (srcmbr), (type)
            9. Design display format using SDA          (srcmbr), ,(mode)
           9Ø. Sign off                                 (*nolist, *list)

         Selection . . . . .  ___          Parm . . . .  _____
         Type  . . . . . . .  _____      Parm 2 . . .  _____
         Command . . . . . .  _____

         Source file . . . .  _____   Source library . . . . . . .  *LIBL
         Object library  . .  _____   Job description . . . . . .   *USRPRF


         F3=Exit        F4=Prompt          F6=Display messages    F1Ø=Command entry
         F12=Cancel     F14=Work with submitted jobs              F18=Work with output
```

The **Programmer Menu** presents a list of options. You need to use just three of these options to enter, compile, bind, and run your program.

Enter/Edit a Program

Select Option 8 (Edit a source file member) from the menu. Key the name you wish to call your program (the member name) on the line to the right of the first Parm prompt. Before pressing the Enter key, make sure that the following entries on the bottom of the screen are complete: Source library, Source file, Object library, and Type. Use the arrow, tab, or field-exit keys to position your cursor to the proper location for entry. (Enter RPGLE for type of RPG IV source members; obtain information about which source file, source library, and object library to use from your instructor.)

Compile and Create an Executable Program

Select Option 3 (Create an object from a source file) from the menu. The Member name, Type, Source file, Source library, and Object library entries must be present on the screen before you press the Enter key.

Although compiling and binding are actually two separate processes, if you want to create an executable program from a single source member, you can choose this option to combine the processes into a single directive. Option 3 causes the system to first compile the program to create a temporary *MODULE object; if the compiling is successful, the system then binds the module into a *PGM object and deletes the *MODULE object.

Most systems are set up to compile in batch, so that your workstation is free for other tasks while the system is compiling and binding your program. However, your program will not be ready to run until the processing has completed. Wait for a message-waiting sign at the bottom of your screen and make sure the compiling has successfully completed before trying to run the program. The compiler generates a compile listing of your program (and errors, if any were found) that will be in your output queue when the compiling has completed.

If you have previously successfully compiled and bound this source code, so that a *PGM object already exists for the program, the system will prompt you to delete the object by pressing F11; you must then reissue the Option 3 command.

Run a Program

Select Option 4 (Call a program) from the menu. Because this option is interactive, your workstation will be locked up until the program completes.

In addition to the three menu options described above, you will use some of the function keys noted at the bottom of the Programmer Menu screen.

View or Print Output

Pressing F18 will display your output queue. The output queue contains reports generated by the system or by your programs. These reports are called spooled files, because they are stored temporarily on disk rather than automatically being sent to the printer. You can display these reports, delete them, or release them to the printer by entering the appropriate number to the left of the spooled file. For more detailed information on printing, refer to the printing instructions within the next section.

Display Messages

F6 shows you a list of any messages the system has sent you.

Programming Development Manager (PDM)

PDM is a little more complex to use than the Programmer Menu, but it provides you with much more flexibility for accessing and manipulating libraries, objects, and members. This discussion focuses only on those features of PDM you need to complete your assignments.

To access PDM from the Main Menu of the AS/400, first select Option 5 (Programming); at the resulting Programming panel, select Option 2 (Programming Development Manager). You will see the following PDM menu:

```
                   AS/400 Programming Development Manager (PDM)

    Select one of the following:

          1. Work with libraries
          2. Work with objects
          3. Work with members

          9. Work with user-defined options




    Selection or command
    ===>_____

    F3=Exit       F4=Prompt       F9=Retrieve        F10=Command entry
    F12=Cancel    F18=Change defaults
```

Enter/Edit a Program

Select Option 3 (Work with members) from the PDM menu. You will see the resulting display:

```
                  Specify Members to Work With

Type choices, press Enter

  File  . . . . . . . . .   CMD*_____   Name, F4 for list

    Library . . . . . . .   ATEST_____  *LIBL, *CURLIB, name

  Member:
    Name  . . . . . . . .   *ALL_____   *ALL, name, *generic*
    Type  . . . . . . . .   *ALL_____   *ALL, type, *generic*, *BLANK




F3=Exit     F4=Prompt     F5=Refresh     F12=Cancel
```

You may either enter the desired source file or position your cursor on the file prompt and press F4 to get a list of the possible files. Once you have entered or selected the desired file, the system will display all the members of that file.

```
                  Work with Members Using PDM

 File  . . . . . .   QCLSRC____
   Library . . . .   WORKLIB___              Position to  . . . . .   _____

 Type options, press Enter.
  2=Edit          3=Copy  4=Delete 5=Display     6=Print     7=Rename
  8=Display description  9=Save  13=Change text 14=Compile  15=Create module...

 Opt  Member      Type        Text
 __   AP0010C     CLP_____  Audit report on daily entries_____
 __   ATTNPGM     CLP_____  ATTN pgm for group jobs_____
 __   CAMON       CLP_____  message monitor_____
 __   CHGPRTFC    CLP_____  Find/then change print files on System_____
 __   CL0010C     CLP_____  Chg security on selected files_____
 __   CLCMPSRC    CLP_____  check source last change dates in version libs___
 __   COMPC       CLP_____  Compare_2_files_up_to_1024_in_length_____
 __   CONFIG      CLP_____  _____
                                                                  More...

 Parameters or command
 ===> _____
 F3=Exit          F4=Prompt          F5=Refresh          F6=Create
 F9=Retrieve      F10=Command entry  F23=More options    F24=More keys
```

From this screen you can select a source member to edit, print, or compile by keying in a 2, 6, or 14 adjacent to the member you want to work with. Note that Option 14 does not appear on the initial screen; pressing F23 (More options) reveals this and other options for working with members.

However, an option does not have to appear on the screen to use it — provided it is a valid option.

Edit/Enter a Member
To edit an existing member, enter a 2 to the left of the member name to bring that member into SEU and continue work on it. If you are creating a new member, pressing F6 (Create) will take you to the Start SEU screen. You will need to enter the source file name, the member name, and the type.

Compile a Member and Create an Executable Program
Enter 14 to the left of the name of the member you want to compile and bind. If the *PGM object already exists, a Confirm Compile of Member screen (see below) appears; to compile and bind your new version, you must respond Yes to "Delete existing object."

```
                        Confirm Compile of Member

  The following object already exists for the compile operation:

      Object which exists . . . . . . . . :    ADDL
        Library . . . . . . . . . . . . :      SRCLIB
      Object type . . . . . . . . . . . :    *PGM

      Member to compile . . . . . . . . :    ADDL
      File . . . . . . . . . . . . . :      CMDSRC
        Library . . . . . . . . . . . :      ATEST

  Type choice, press Enter.
  Press F12=Cancel to return and not perform the compile operation.

      Delete existing object . . . . . . . .    Y   Y=Yes, N=No




  F12=Cancel
```

Your program will not be ready to run until the system returns a message to you that the processing completed successfully. If the message says that the processing ended abnormally, you must correct program errors and then reselect Option 14.

Run a Program
Select Option 2 (Work with objects) from the PDM screen. The resulting screen will display a list of objects in your library. Enter 16 in the left column adjacent to the program object you want to run. The following figure shows the Work with Objects Using PDM screen. Note that although 16 does not appear as an initial option, pressing F23 would reveal it (and other options, as well).

```
                     Work with Objects Using PDM

Library  . . . . .    QUSRSYS___       Position to . . . . . . . .  _____
                                       Position to type  . . . . .  _____

Type options, press Enter.
   2=Change        3=Copy       4=Delete       5=Display      7=Rename
   8=Display description        9=Save        10=Restore      11=Move ...

Opt  Object    Type      Attribute   Text
__   QAALERT   *FILE     PF-DTA      Data base file for alerts processing
__   QAALHLSN  *FILE     LF          Logical file for alerts processing
__   QAALRCLC  *FILE     LF          Logical file for alerts processing
__   QAALRSCN  *FILE     LF          Logical file for alerts processing
__   QAALRSCT  *FILE     LF          Logical file for alerts processing
__   QAALSOC   *FILE     PF-DTA      Data base file for SOC processing
__   QAEABKMT  *FILE     PF-DTA      System Delivered Education Bookmark F
__   QAEACRSI  *FILE     PF-DTA      System Delivered Education Course Ind
                                                                   More...

Parameters or command
===> _____
F3=Exit            F4=Prompt          F5=Refresh          F6=Create
F9=Retrieve        F10=Command entry  F23=More options    F24=More keys
```

Alternately, you can enter CALL program name on any command line.

Create a *MODULE Object

For most of your work in this course, Option 14 will be the appropriate choice for you to compile and bind your program. However, if you will be working with called programs (Chapter 12), you may want to create a *MODULE object from your source code to bind together with other *MODULEs into a *PGM object. Option 15 (Create module) is the proper choice in this case. Option 15 compiles the source code, but does not bind it. To bind several modules together, use CL command CRTPGM (Create Program).

View or Print Output

Type sp in any option column on any of PDM's screens to obtain a list of your spooled files. (You can also key in WRKSPLF on any command line.) You will see the screen shown on the next page, which includes a list of all spooled output.

```
                        Work with Printer Output
                                              System:     S1034373
User . . . . . .   YAEGER        Name, *ALL, F4 for list

Type options below, then press Enter.  To work with printers, press F22.
   2=Change   3=Hold   4=Delete   5=Display         6=Release   7=Message
   9=Work with printing status    10=Start printing   11=Restart printing

       Printer/
Opt    Output          Status
       Not Assigned
       REMUSRS          Held (use Opt 6)
       GENUSRS2         Held (use Opt 6)
       GENUSERS3        Held (use Opt 6)
       GENUSRS3         Held (use Opt 6)
       GENUSRS3         Held (use Opt 6)
       QSYSPRT          Held (use Opt 6)
       QSYSPRT          Held (use Opt 6)


F1=Help   F3=Exit       F5=Refresh   F6=Completed printed output
F11=Dates/pages/forms      F20=Include system output   F24=More keys
```

You can see the dates, times, and pages of the output by pressing F11.
The screen below shows the result of this action.

```
                        Work with Printer Output
                                              System:     S1034373
User . . . . . .   YAEGER        Name, *ALL, F4 for list

Type options below, then press Enter.  To work with printers, press F22.
   2=Change   3=Hold   4=Delete   5=Display         6=Release   7=Message
   9=Work with printing status    10=Start printing   11=Restart printing

       Printer/
Opt    Output       Date       Time      Pages   Copies  Form Type
       Not Assigned
       REMUSRS      01/08/93   11:22:10     3       1     *STD
       GENUSRS2     01/08/93   11:35:22     4       1     *STD
       GENUSERS3    03/18/93   13:45:30     3       1     *STD
       GENUSRS3     03/24/93   13:52:10     3       1     *STD
       GENUSRS3     03/24/93   13:56:37     3       1     *STD
       QSYSPRT      04/08/93   14:00:14     1       1     *STD
       QSYSPRT      04/08/93   14:01:10     1       1     *STD

                                                                  More...
F1=Help   F3=Exit     F5=Refresh   F6=Completed printer output
F11=Display statuses  F12=Cancel   F20=Include system output   F24=More keys
Printer output REMUSRS moved to printer PRT01.
```

To look at a spooled file, enter 5 adjacent to the file. To delete a
spooled file, enter 4, and then press Enter at the resulting screen to confirm
the deletion request. If you want to print a file, depending on how your system is set up, you may first have to assign the file to a printer by entering 10
adjacent to the file name. At the resulting screen, enter PRT01 — or the
name your instructor provides you.

```
                         Assign Output to a Printer

   Printer output . . :    REMUSRS

This printer output is not assigned to a printer or the number of pages to be
   printed exceeds the limit specified.
To print the output, type the printer name below and then press Enter.

   Printer  . . . . . .  _____    Name, F4 for list
```

You will return to the Work with Printer Output screen, and the message *Attempting to start should appear next to the spooled file you chose to print. Pressing F5 (refresh) will show you the progress the system is making in printing the file.

Display Messages
Type DSPMSG on the command line and press Enter. Or type dm in any option column of your current screen.

Appendix B

Source Entry Utility (SEU)

SEU Overview

RPG IV programs generally are entered into the computer interactively through an AS/400 editor called Source Entry Utility (SEU). An editor is like a limited word processor, in that it lets you easily enter, modify, and delete text. Because the editor has been designed specifically to facilitate entry of program source code, it includes some special features, such as line prompting and syntax checking, that would not be available in a standard word processor.

Source programs are stored as members of a source file. The file generally used to store RPG IV programs is QRPGLESRC; the member type is RPGLE. The name that you supply your program is the name that identifies that member. You can enter SEU by selecting Option 8 from the Programmer Menu, from PDM's Work with Members screen, or by directly entering the command STRSEU (Start SEU) on a command line. You can use SEU to create a new member or to edit, browse, or print an existing member.

When you enter SEU to create a new member, you see a screen like that on the following page. The SEU command line is at the top of the screen; the middle of the screen is used for code entry; and the bottom of the screen reminds you of enabled function keys and their uses and delivers system messages to you.

```
Columns . . . :   1  71            Edit                    BIS264/SOURCE
SEU==>                                                              DEMO
FMT F  FFilename++IPEASFRlen+LKlen+AIDevice+.Keywords++++++++++++++++++++++++
       *************** Beginning of data ********************************
 '''''''
 '''''''
 '''''''
 '''''''
 '''''''
 '''''''
 '''''''
 '''''''
 '''''''
 '''''''
 '''''''
 '''''''
 '''''''
 '''''''
 '''''''
       ***************** End of data ***********************************
   F3=Exit    F4=Prompt   F5=Refresh   F9=Retrieve   F10=Cursor
   F16=Repeat find        F17=Repeat change          F24=More keys
 Member DEMO added to file BIS264/SOURCE.                              +
```

Press Enter to remove the blank lines between the beginning and end of data lines. You are ready to begin entering your program. As you enter your program, SEU tries to detect syntax errors in your code. When you enter a line containing such an error, the error will appear in reverse video and the system provides a brief explanation of the error on the message line of the screen. When you have successfully corrected the error, the entry will display normally.

SEU, like other parts of the AS/400, has lavish on-line help available. The help is cursor-position sensitive. When you find yourself in trouble, or don't know what response is appropriate, try using the Help key.

Using Prompts

SEU can provide you with prompts to facilitate your code entry. To obtain a line prompted appropriately for File Specifications, key IPF (Insert with Prompts for File Specifications) to the left on the Beginning Data line and press Enter. A prompted line appropriate for File Specifications appears at the bottom of the screen. Enter your first File Specification, using the Field Exit key to move from entry to entry. When you have keyed in the first line, press Enter. SEU assigns the line a sequence number and moves it to the main portion of the screen; it also provides another prompted line for your next File Specification.

```
 Columns . . . :    1  71              Edit                         BIS264/SOURCE
 SEU==>                                                                      DEMO
 FMT F    FFilename++IPEASFRlen+LKlen+AIDevice+.Keywords++++++++++++++++++++++++++
          *************** Beginning of data ****************************************
 0001.00          IF   F  100          DISK
 '''''''
 Prompt type . . .     F      Sequence number . . .  '''''''

               File         File          End of        File
 Filename      Type      Designation       File        Addition       Sequence

 File       Record       Limits       Length of       Record
 Format     Length    Processing      Key Field    Address Type

    File
 Organization        Device     Keywords

 Comment



 F3=Exit   F4=Prompt   F5=Refresh         F11=Previous record
 F12=Cancel            F23=Select prompt  F24=More keys
```

Each RPG IV specification form has one or more appropriate prompt formats available in SEU. (A summary of the prompt formats appears below.) To change the prompt format, press F23 and select the new format you want. Once selected, a prompt form will continue until you press F23 for a new prompt, press F12 to cancel the prompt and return to the Edit display, or press Enter without entering anything. This latter method also returns your cursor to the Edit display.

RPG IV Prompt Formats

H	Control (H)
F	File (F)
FX	File (F) (External)
D	Definition (D)
I	Input (I) (Record Identification)
IX	Input (I) (Record Identification-External)
J	Input (I) (Field Description)
JX	Input (I) (Field Description) (External)
C	Calculation (C)
CX	Calculation (C) (Extended Factor 2)
O	Output (O) (File Identification and Control)
OD	Output (O) (Output Disk)
P	Output (O) (Field Description)
*	Comment (*)

Working Within the Edit Display

Sometimes it is more efficient to enter or edit code without the help of the prompts. The list of features below summarizes what you can do in edit display mode and how to do it.

Position Cursor
Use arrow keys to move within a screen; use Roll keys to page up or down between screens.

Move to a Specific Line of Code
Key the sequence number of the line you want to move to over the sequence number of a line currently on the screen and press Enter. The source will be repositioned to display the source code containing the desired line.

Insert Within a Line
The Insert key toggles insertion on.

Delete Within a Line
Use the Delete key to delete individual characters.

   All the bold letter commands described below must be keyed over the sequence number of the line(s) involved in the operation.

Insert a Line
Key an **I** on a line and press Enter. A blank line will appear below the line you are on.

Delete a Line
Key a **D** on the line you want to delete and press Enter.

Delete a Block of Lines
Key **DD** on the first line of the block, move the cursor to the last line of the block, again key **DD**, and press Enter.

Move a Line
Key **M** on the line to be moved, reposition the cursor to the desired location, key either **A** or **B**, and press Enter. The line will be moved either after (A) or before (B) the target line, depending on what you keyed.

Move a Block of Lines
Key **MM** on the first line of the block to be moved, position the cursor to the last line of the block, and key **MM**; then position the cursor to the target line, key **A** or **B**, and press Enter. The block will be moved either after (A) or before (B) the target line, depending on what you keyed.

Copy a Line
Key **C** on the line to be copied, reposition the cursor to the desired location, key either **A** or **B**, and press Enter. The line will be copied either after (A) or before (B) the target line, depending on what you keyed.

Copy a Block of Lines
Key **CC** on the first line of the block to be copied, position the cursor to the last line of the block and key **CC**; then position the cursor to the target line, key **A** or **B**, and press Enter. The block will be copied either after (A) or before (B) the target line, depending on what you keyed.

Repeat a Line
Key an **RP** and press Enter to repeat the line once immediately below the line on which you entered the RP.

Repeat a Line x Times
Key **RPx**, where *x* is any number, and press Enter to repeat the line *x* number of times immediately below the line on which you entered the command.

Prompt an Entered Line
Key **Pf** on the line, where *f* is the prompt format you want, and press Enter.

Insert Prompted Lines
Key **IPf**, where *f* is the prompt format you want, and press Enter. This will return you to prompted mode.

Function Keys in SEU

Several function keys are active within SEU. Those you will use most often are summarized below.

F3
Used to go to the SEU exit screen (described below).

F4
Places the line the cursor is on when the key is pressed into an appropriate prompt format.

F10
Toggles the cursor between the SEU command line and the edit display.

F12
Cancels the current action; generally used to return to display editing from a prompted format.

F13
Takes you to a screen that lets you change the SEU defaults for the current session. Among other things, lets you enable or disable lowercase alphabetic entry.

F15
Splits the screen in two to let you browse a second member or a compile output while working in your source code, or copy code from one member into another.

F23
Displays all possible prompt formats and lets you select the one you want to activate.

SEU's Command Line

To position the cursor on the command line, press F10. Once there, you can enter an SEU command. Some of the possible commands are

SAVE
To save the member without exiting SEU.

CANCEL
To leave SEU without saving and return to the previous menu.

TOP or T
To move to the top of your source member.

BOTTOM or B
To move to the bottom of your source member.

FIND or F
To search for a string of characters in the source member. The string does not need to be enclosed in apostrophes unless it contains blanks, special values, apostrophes, or quotation marks.

CHANGE or C
To change a string of characters to some other string.

Working with a Split Screen

Pressing F15 takes you to a screen that lets you divide your screen into two halves, with your current member on the top and another member or spool file on the bottom.

```
                        Browse/Copy Options

Type choices, press Enter.

    Selection . . . . . . . . . . .    2            1=Member
                                                    2=Spool file
                                                    3=Output queue
    Copy all records . . . . . . .     N            Y=Yes, N=No
    Browse/copy member . . . . . .     SALESRPT      Name, F4 for list
        File . . . . . . . . . . . .   QRPGSRC       Name, F4 for list
            Library . . . . . . . . .  YAEGER        Name, *CURLIB, *LIBL

    Browse/copy spool file . . . .     SALESRPT      Name, F4 for list
        Job . . . . . . . . . . . .    SALESRPT      Name
            User . . . . . . . . . .   YAEGER        Name, F4 for list
            Job number . . . . . . .   *LAST         Number, *LAST
        Spool number . . . . . . .     *LAST         Number, *LAST, *ONLY

    Display output queue . . . . .     QPRINT        Name, *ALL
        Library . . . . . . . . . .    *LIBL         Name, *CURLIB, *LIBL


    F3=Exit       F4=Prompt       F5=Refresh       F12=Cancel
    F13=Change session defaults   F14=Find/Change options
```

At the above screen, if you choose Option 1 (Member), you then should enter the name of the member you want to appear in the lower half of the screen. This option is very useful for copying portions of code from one member to another, or for checking on field names in a database file while entering a program that uses that file. To copy lines from one member to the other in split-screen mode, use the same technique as when you are working within a single member; the arrow keys will take your cursor across the mid-screen boundary. The roll keys affect the member in either the top half or the bottom half of the screen, depending on where your cursor is positioned.

If you choose Option 2 (Spool file), from the Browse Options display, the default values are such that the most recent compile listing of this member is brought into the lower half of the display. This feature is very useful for correcting compile errors, because it lets you scroll through the compile listing and make corrections in your source member based on the errors noted in the listing without the need for a hard-copy version of the compile listing.

```
 Columns . . . :   1  71              Edit                      YAEGER/QRPGSRC
 SEU==>                                                              SALESRPT
        *************** Beginning of data *********************************
0001.00      F***********************************************************************
0002.00      F* This program produces a weekly sales report.  The report
0003.00      F* data come directly from input file SALES.
0004.00      F*    Author: J. Yeager      Date Written: 10/10/92
0005.00      F*
0006.00      F* Indicator 90: End-of-file SALES

 Columns . . . :   1  71              Browse        Spool file . . :    SALESRPT
 SEU==>
        *************** Beginning of data *********************************
0000.01  5738RG1 V2R1M0  910329              IBM SAA RPG/400
0000.02  Compiler . . . . . . . . . . . :    IBM SAA RPG/400
0000.03  Command options:
0000.04    Program  . . . . . . . . . . :    YAEGER/SALESRPT
0000.05    Source file  . . . . . . . . :    *LIBL/QRPGSRC
0000.06    Source member  . . . . . . . :    *PGM



 F3=Exit   F5=Refresh    F9=Retrieve   F10=Cursor     F12=Cancel
 F16=Repeat find         F17=Repeat change            F24=More keys
```

Exiting SEU

When you press F3 to exit SEU, an exit screen (shown on the following page) appears that lets you accept preset default values or change them, as you wish. By changing defaults you can save the member with a name different from that with which you began the editing session, or you can cancel editing changes by specifying N to "Change/create member." You also can get a printout of your member without having to compile it by changing the Print Member option to Y. Note that the "Return to editing" default is N if you exited with no syntax errors in your source, but Y if errors remained. You can exit with errors remaining if you change the default to N.

```
                                    Exit

    Type choices, press Enter.

        Change/create member  . . . . . . .    N           Y=Yes, N=No
          Member  . . . . . . . . . . . .      SALESRPT    Name, F4 for list
          File  . . . . . . . . . . . .        QRPGSRC     Name, F4 for list
            Library . . . . . . . . . . .        YAEGER    Name
          Text  . . . . . . . . . . . . .

        Resequence member . . . . . . . .      Y           Y=Yes, N=No
          Start . . . . . . . . . . . .        0001.00     0000.01-9999.99
          Increment . . . . . . . . . . .      01.00       00.01-99.99

    Print member  . . . . . . . . . . .        N           Y=Yes, N=No

    Return to editing . . . . . . . . .        N           Y=Yes, N=No

    Go to member list . . . . . . . . .        N           Y=Yes, N=No




    F3=Exit    F4=Prompt    F5=Refresh    F12=Cancel
```

Appendix C

Program Testing and Debugging

A major portion of a programmer's time is spent ensuring that the program (s)he has written is, in fact, accurately producing the desired results. This procedure involves carefully checking the program's correctness and fixing any errors the checking uncovers — a process often referred to as "debugging."

Syntax Errors

Program errors fall into one of two broad categories: **syntax errors** and **logic errors**. Syntax errors are errors in your usage of the programming language. Because the system points out these kinds of errors for you, they are simple to detect and easy to correct, once you have mastered the rules of the language in which you are programming.

On the AS/400, SEU detects some kinds of syntax errors as you enter program statements. For example, failing to make a required entry within a specification line, forgetting to right-adjust a numeric entry within its allocated columns, or including an invalid value in a column (e.g., an F instead of an I, O, U, or C for file type on the File Specifications) will cause SEU to display the erroneous entry in reverse video, display an error message on the bottom of the screen, and lock the keyboard. You will need to press the reset key before the system lets you proceed. Moreover, until you correct the error, it will remain in reverse video as a reminder of a problem.

Once you have completely entered your program and have eliminated all syntax errors detected by SEU, your next step is to compile and bind the program. Compiling and binding are processes that translate the statements in your source member into an object of machine-code instructions the AS/400 can then execute. In attempting to complete this translation process, the ILE RPG/400 compiler often detects additional syntax errors unnoticed by SEU.

If your program contains compile errors, the system sends you a message that your job ended abnormally. You can find the cause(s) of the difficulties by printing or displaying the compile listing, a report of the compilation generated by the compiler. A compile listing includes a listing of your program. The compiler numbers the program statements sequentially in increments of 100 and also indicates the date on which the statement was entered (or modified).

Within the program listing, the compiler also indicates how it is interpreting any nesting of structured operators by inserting B at the beginning of the structure, E at the end of the structure, and an X for any ELSE it encounters within the structure. It also prints a digit with each of these codes representing the level of nesting the structure establishes. By cross-checking these digits, you can make sure that the computer has matched the beginnings and ends of the structures as you had intended. You can also request the compiler to indent the program listing so that you can more easily see your logic structures. Ask your instructor how to use this feature on your system.

The compiler also provides a **cross-reference listing** to help you diagnose problems. A cross-reference listing is a list of all fields and indicators used in your program; it logs every program statement within which each of the fields or indicators occurs. The statement defining the field is annotated with D (for define), while any statement within which the field's or indicator's value is changed is annotated with M (for modify). You can use this listing to quickly locate field and/or indicator usage within your program listing.

If your program contains syntax errors, the compiler notes errors by inserting an asterisk and a numeric error code either under the line in error or within the cross-reference listing. At the end of the compile listing, a message summary lists these error codes and provides a message detailing the cause of the problem. Problems vary in severity. A message with a severity of 00 is an informational message noting a condition that will not prevent the program from compiling; errors with severity of 10 or above need to be corrected before the program will compile normally.

Once you have obtained a "clean compile" — that is, once the system has successfully translated your program into machine language and bound the program into a *PGM object — you can begin to check for logic errors your program may contain.

Logic Errors

Logic errors are caused by faulty program design. You detect these kinds of errors by having the computer execute your program and then carefully checking the results of the execution. There are two broad classes of logic errors, sometimes called **runtime errors** and **output errors**.

Runtime Errors

Runtime errors are errors that prevent your program from reaching a normal end. Runtime errors are easy to detect: Either the program abruptly stops in the middle (an abend, or abnormal ending), or the program runs and runs and runs, until finally you or the operator intercedes to terminate the job. (This latter kind of a problem signals an **infinite loop**.) Although detecting the presence of a runtime error is not a problem, sometimes discovering the cause of the error can be difficult. Moreover, the kinds of logic problems that cause abends are different from those that cause infinite loops.

Diagnosing Abends

When your program ends abnormally, the system sends you an error message to inform you of the cause of the problem and where the problem occurred within your program. Sometimes these error messages are not completely clear; by putting your cursor on the message and pressing the Help key you can obtain additional information about the problem. Typical causes of such runtime problems are trying to divide by zero, attempting to carry out a numeric operation on a field that contains non-numeric data, trying to reference an array element beyond the defined limits, or size, of the array, attempting to read past end-of-file, or trying to update a record before you have read a record.

Once you have located the problem statement and determined the nature of the problem, you often have to trace through your program logic to determine how your program allowed that problem to occur. For example, if program statement EVAL C = A / B causes an abnormal ending because of an attempt to divide by zero, you need to determine why field B has a value of zero at the time the system is attempting the division operation. Is B an input field? If so, have you forgotten to read a record before the division? Or, if B is a work field, have you neglected to assign it a non-zero value before the division? Or have you inadvertently assigned 0 to B at the wrong time in your program?

If you cannot locate the cause of the problem, you may find it useful to run the program in debug mode, discussed later in this appendix.

Diagnosing Infinite Loops

If you have had to cancel your job to prevent it from running forever, you know that you have an infinite loop within your program. An infinite loop is a faulty logic structure that causes the computer to repeat the same set of instructions over and over again, without letting the computer break out of the loop. The code below shows two obvious infinite loops.

```
*.. 1 ...+... 2 ...+... 3 ...+... 4 ...+... 5 ...+... 6 ...+... 7 ...+... 8 ...+... 9 ...+...10
CLØNØ1Factor1++++++Opcode(E)+Extended-factor2++++++++++++++++++++++++++++++Comments++++++++++++
CLØNØ1Factor1++++++Opcode(E)+Factor2++++++Result++++++++Len++D+HiLoEq....Comments++++++++++++
C* Two examples of infinite loops.
C                   EVAL      *IN9Ø = *OFF
C                   DOW       *IN9Ø = *OFF
C                   EVAL      Count = Count + 1
C                   ENDDO
C                   ...
C     Loop          TAG
C                   ADD       1             Count
C                   GOTO      Loop
```

In the examples above, the causes of the infinite loops are simple to detect. In the case of the DOW, no statement exists within the loop to change the value of *IN90 to *ON — the condition needed to end the loop. In the second example, the GOTO unconditionally (that is, always) transfers control back to the TAG statement.

Generally, the cause of an infinite loop within a real program is less obvious. The first thing to realize in trying to diagnose the cause of your problem is that you can narrow your focus to the iterative operations in your program: DOW, DOU, and DO. The second thing to realize is that somehow the condition that specifies when the looping should stop is not occurring. Forgetting to include a READ operation, for example, within a DOW loop that continues until end-of-file is reached will result in an infinite loop. Or forgetting to increment a counter in a count-controlled loop based on an operation other than DO will likewise prevent the loop from ever ending.

A common cause of infinite loops that you can easily overlook when modifying older, converted programs is a counter defined too small. Study the example below to see if you can detect the cause of the infinite loop that would result if the program were run.

```
*.. 1 ...+... 2 ...+... 3 ...+... 4 ...+... 5 ...+... 6 ...+... 7 ...+... 8 ...+... 9 ...+...10
CLØN01Factor1++++++Opcode(E)+Factor2++++++Result++++++++Len++D+HiLoEq....Comments++++++++++++
C* A less obvious example of an infinite loop.
C                   Z-ADD     0             COUNT             2 0
C       COUNT       DOUEQ     100
C                   ...
C                   ADD       1             COUNT
C                   ENDDO
```

The example above results in an infinite loop because COUNT never attains the value 100. COUNT is defined as 2 positions (with 0 decimals) in the Z-ADD specification, so the largest value COUNT can store is 99. Adding 1 to 99 causes the resulting value, 100, to be truncated to 00. You can easily avoid such a potential problem by using the modern features of RPG IV. EVAL does not allow high-order truncation; it issues a runtime error to alert you to the problem.

Output Errors

The most insidious kinds of logic errors are those that do not cause abnormal program endings or infinite loops but simply result in incorrect output. Some of these kinds of errors are very obvious: neglecting to print heading lines on reports, for instance, or omitting an output entry that causes an entire column of information to be missing from a report. Other kinds of output errors are less easily detected and require careful checking by hand to discover. You are unlikely to notice errors in complex calculations, for example, if you simply scan the output visually.

Detecting Output Errors

Carefully checking output generated by the computer against the results of your hand calculations is called **desk checking**. How much hand checking is required depends on the complexity of the logic the program expresses.

Generally, you should check out enough sets of data to test each logic branch within your program at least once. That is, if you have written a payroll program that processes workers with overtime hours differently from those workers without overtime, you should hand check at least one worker with overtime hours and one without. The more conditional logic within your program, the more desk checking is required to ensure that your program is processing each case correctly.

Don't forget to check the accuracy of subtotals and grand totals. If you have a large number of columns with totals, generally you do not have to hand calculate the total for all columns; if you are doing all your accumulation in the same place within your program, and the calculations are all set up in the same way, if one column's total is correct, the rest should be correct also — provided that you are using the correct fields in the calculations and referencing the correct accumulators in your Output Specifications.

The final step in output checking is to rigorously compare the computer-generated output with design documents, such as printer spacing charts, to ensure that your output exactly matches the requested format. Are the column headings appropriately centered over the columns? Are the literals spelled correctly (e.g., "Quantity," not "Quanity")? Does the report's vertical alignment exactly match that of the printer spacing chart? Did you edit the output correctly? The programmer's job is to give the designer exactly what (s)he requested. Although concern with these kinds of formatting details may seem "picky," careful attention to detail is one facet of the kind of preciseness required to be a top-rate programmer.

Correcting Output Errors

Once you have discovered an output error, your next job is to discover the cause of the error so you can correct it. A good programmer never makes changes within a program without having a specific reason to make a change. That is, you should try to locate the precise cause of the problem and then fix it, rather than base your changes on hunches or trial and error.

To discover the error, focus your attention initially on those calculations specifically involved in generating the incorrect output. If, after carefully checking these program statements, you still have not found a statement that is incorrect, broaden your search to those portions of the program that may be influencing the output more remotely.

Although it is impossible to list every possible cause of erroneous output, you should be alert to a number of common errors when you are trying to debug your program.

Field Problems

Sometimes variables are defined incorrectly, causing truncation. This problem is most likely to occur with fields used as accumulators or fields that are the result of complex calculations. Another common field-related problem is failure to appropriately initialize or reinitialize fields. Forgetting to reset an indicator, counter, or flag-variable during repetitive processing is a common cause of erroneous output.

Loops
Off-by-one errors, resulting in a count-controlled loop repeating one too few or one too many times, occur frequently in programs. This kind of error stems from incorrectly establishing the conditional test to end the looping process. It often is related to incorrectly initializing the counter field used to control the looping.

For example, both pseudocode examples below, designed to add all the numbers between 1 and 100, are erroneous. The first example would sum the numbers 1 through 101, while the second would add the values 1 through 99.

```
Initialize I to 0
Initialize Sum to 0
WHILE I is less than 101
        Add 1 to I
        Add I to Sum
ENDWHILE

Initialize I to 1
Initialize Sum to 0
WHILE I < 100
        Add I to Sum
        Add 1 to I
ENDWHILE
```

Another common loop problem is failing to enter the loop. When you use a looping operator that tests the condition before executing the steps within the loop, your program may fail to enter the loop. For example, assume you want to read a file sequentially until you locate a desired code value within a record, process that record, and then resume reading until you find the next record with that same code value. The following pseudocode will correctly find the first record containing the desired code, but then will continue to process the same first record infinitely.

```
WHILE not end-of-file
        WHILE code <> desired value and not end-of-file
            Read a record
        ENDWHILE
        Process the record
ENDWHILE
```

The cause of the problem is that once the first appropriate record is located, the code field contains the desired value. As a result, the test of the inner loop will always be false and the inner loop will not be executed, thereby preventing additional records from being read.

IF Logic

Programmers often incorrectly specify the relational comparison used within an IF that is testing for a range of values. For example, if specifications state that pay rate should be less than $45.00, the following pseudocode would be incorrect:

        IF rate > 45
                Perform error routine
        ENDIF

Sometimes output errors are caused by incorrectly nesting IFs. Know how the system matches IFs, ELSEs, and ENDIFs, and check the notation of the compiler listing to make sure the system is interpreting your nested IFs the way you intended.

Another common IF problem is incorrectly using AND, OR, or NOT in compound IFs. NOTs in particular are error-prone. For example, if you want to validate a code field that should have a value of S, H, or R, the pseudocode below would falsely signal valid values as errors:

        IF code NOT = 'S' OR code NOT = 'H' OR code NOT = 'R'
                Perform error routine
        ENDIF

Calculations

Sometimes steps in complex calculations are not executed in the correct order. Also, programmers sometimes overlook the possibility that a calculation may result in a negative value. This can be a difficult problem to locate, because RPG IV prints or displays all values as absolute (unsigned) values unless field editing includes provision for a negative sign; however, during calculations, negative values are handled as negative values.

For example, in figuring income tax withholding, a dependent allowance often is subtracted from gross earnings before applying the withholding tax percentage. If the relationship between gross earnings and number of dependents is such that this subtraction results in a negative value, failure to consider this possibility will cause the tax to be added (subtracting a negative number) to gross earnings; on the payroll register report, the same negative tax liability will appear to be a positive value, unless the tax field is edited with a code specifying that negative signs should print.

Debug

Sometimes despite your best efforts, you may not be able to locate the source of an output error by visually examining your program. Rather than resorting to making random changes in the program to see how they affect your output, you should use the AS/400's debugging facility. A "debugger" lets you trace a program as it is executing, stepping through the program one statement at a time or stopping it at "breakpoints" that you designate so you can examine the values of fields at that point in execution. This procedure often can help you locate program errors that otherwise might elude you.

To run a program in debug mode, you must first enter the CL (Control Language) command STRDBG PGM(program-name), where program-name is the name of the program you are trying to debug. Your program then remains in debug mode until you issue the command ENDDBG. Once in debug mode, you can approach debugging in two ways. First, you can specify "breakpoints," statements within your program where you want execution to halt so you can examine the value of various variables at that point in execution. Or you can follow the flow of control in your program by issuing trace commands.

Breakpoints

Within debug mode, you specify breakpoints with the CL command ADDBKP (Add Breakpoint). The basic format of this command is ADDBKP STMT(statement-identifier), where statement-identifier represents a minimum of one and a maximum of 10 statement identifiers included as parameter values. These statement identifiers can be the statement numbers as they appear on the compile listing or labels (TAG statements) within the program.

ADDBKP STMT(2500 3000 4250) would cause the program to stop successively at statements 2500, 3000, and 4250, in each case just before that statement's execution. Upon stopping, the system shows you the breakpoint display, indicating which breakpoint has been reached and, optionally, the current value of specified program values.

By including an optional parameter with your ADDBKP command, PGMVAR, you can specify up to 10 program variables whose values you want to examine at the breakpoints. ADDBKP STMT(2000) PGMVAR(COUNT TOTPAY) would stop your program just before executing statement 2000 and display the current values of variables Count and TotPay. Pressing the Enter key causes your program to resume execution.

At the breakpoint display, you also can enter additional commands to control the debugging session by pressing F10. You can, for example, add additional breakpoints by issuing another ADDBKP statement, or you can remove breakpoints with the command RMVBKP STMT(statement-identifier). You can specify specific statements to remove, or use *ALL as the STMT parameter value to remove all breakpoints.

You also can issue a DSPPGMVAR (Display Program Variable) to view the contents of variables not specified in an ADDBKP command. The format of this CL command is

```
DSPPGMVAR PGMVAR(var1 var2 ...)
```

where var1 and var2 represent a list of the names of up to 10 program variables you want to examine.

Another useful feature of debug is that you can actually change the value of a variable or variables to determine how your program executes when processing that value. To use this feature, you would generally wait until your program had reached the desired breakpoint and then issue the command

```
CHGPGMVAR  PGMVAR(variable name) VALUE(desired value)
```

where variable name represents the name of the field whose value you want to change and desired value is the value you want that field to assume. You can use this command with character or numeric fields; enclose character values with apostrophes.

Trace Commands

The second approach to using debug is to trace the flow of statement execution. The command ADDTRC (Add Trace) tells the system to trace the flow of the program for the range of statements you specify. The format for this command is

```
ADDTRC STMT(start-statement-identifier                    +
           stop-statement-identifier) PGMVAR(var1 var2...)
```

where the parameter values for STMT indicate the beginning and ending points of the desired trace and PGMVAR includes up to 10 variables whose values are to be tracked during the trace.

Once you have added a trace, as you run your program the system stores the traced statement numbers and the variable values in a special trace file. To view the results of the trace, issue a DSPTRCDTA (Display Trace Data) command. This command displays the statements traced by the most recent trace operation and displays the variables' values within that range of statements. Other associated trace commands are CLRTRCDTA (Clear Trace Data), to clear trace data from a previous trace command, and DSPTRC (Display Trace), to show what traces you have currently defined for the program. Command RMVTRC (Remove Trace) removes all or part of the traces you have specified with ADDTRC.

A special kind of tracing is called "stepping," in which you want all or a portion of your program to execute one line at a time and then stop so that you can examine the logic flow and program variables after each operation. To specify this single-stepping through your program, issue the STRDBG command with additional parameter MAXTRC(1) to specify that only a single trace statement is to be executed before returning control to your terminal.

Thus, to single-step through statements 1000-2000 of program SALESRPT and check the values of fields A and B, you would enter the following commands:

```
STRDBG PGM(SALESRPT) MAXTRC(1)
ADDTRC STMT(1000 2000) PGMVAR(A B)
CALL SALESRPT
. . .
DSPTRCDTA
```

Once you are finished with a debugging session, remember to issue the command ENDDBG to end the session; this command automatically removes all traces and breakpoints.

For additional information about working in debug mode, see IBM's reference manual *CL Programming* (SC41-3721).

As a beginning programmer you sometimes will feel frustrated at your initial inability to locate the cause of program errors. With practice, you will find that you begin to recognize what kinds of logic errors cause various kinds of output errors and as a result, you will be able to correct your programs with increasing ease. And remember, even seasoned programmers make logic mistakes. The sign of an excellent programmer is detecting such problems when they occur, rather than overlooking output errors due to careless or incomplete testing.

Appendix D

Data Files

This appendix contains definitions of the data files used in the programming assignments throughout the book. Most of the assignments focus on three companies to give you a sense of what it is like to develop an application system for a company. An application system is a series of programs that use the same set of data files to record and maintain data important to some facet of the company's business, process that data, permit on-line queries of the data, and produce needed reports. Depending on what programs your instructor assigns you, you will be working with several of the data files described below.

An overview of each company precedes the descriptions of the company's files so you will have a context within which to understand each company's data and program needs. The key fields of each file, if any, are preceded by an asterisk (*).

Case 1: CompuSell

CompuSell is a small mail-order company specializing in computers and computer supplies. The company needs an integrated system of programs to handle its orders and inventory, as well as to generate needed reports for management. An analyst already has done the preliminary design work and determined the files needed as part of the system. The files, and their record layouts, are described below.

CSCSFINP: *Customer Finance File*
This file contains information about customers who are financing purchases.

Record layout of CSCSFINP:

Field	Description	Positions	(Decimal Positions)
*CUSTNO	Customer number	1- 6	(0)
PURAMTE	Purchase amount	7- 12	(2)
DWNPAY	Down payment	13- 18	(2)
PDATE	Purchase date	19- 24	(0) YYMMDD

CSCSTP: *Customer Master File*

This file stores basic information about its customers. A unique customer number is assigned each new customer and serves as that customer's identifier. In addition to storing name, address, and phone information, this file tracks date of last order (for marketing purposes) and balance owed (for billing purposes). (Although most customers are cash customers, occasionally a customer will under- or over-pay on an order).

Record layout of CSCSTP:

Field	Description	Positions	(Decimal Positions)
* CUSTNO	Customer number	1- 6	(0)
CFNAME	First name	7- 16	
CLNAME	Last name	17- 31	
CSTRET	Street address	32- 51	
CCITY	City	52- 66	
CSTATE	State	67- 68	
CZIP	Zip+4	69- 77	(0)
CPHONE	Phone	78- 87	(0)
ORDDAT	Last order date	88- 93	(0) MMDDYY
BALDUE	Balance due	94- 99	(2 implied)

CSINVP: *Inventory Master File*

This file is used to maintain inventory records. When a company adds a new product to its line, the information is recorded in this file. Each item carried has a unique product number. As items are sold, they are subtracted from inventory; as stock comes in from suppliers, the stock is added to inventory. When quantity on hand drops to reorder quantity, the item is reordered from the appropriate supplier. The reorder code field is used to prevent the same item from accidentally being reordered more than once. Supplier code is a supplier identification number assigned by CompuSell; supplier product ID is the supplier's identifier for that product. Current cost reflects the most recent cost paid for the item, while average cost is the average cost of the items in inventory. Selling price is what CompuSell currently charges for the item.

Record layout of CSINVP:

Field	Description	Positions	(Decimal Positions)
* PRODNO	Product number	1- 6	(0)
DESCRP	Description	7- 31	
SELLPR	Selling price	32- 37	(2 implied)
SHIPWT	Shipping weight	38- 41	First 2 positions are pounds; last 2 are ounces

Continued

Record layout of CSINVP *continued*:

Field	Description	Positions	(Decimal Positions)
QTYOH	Quantity on hand	42- 45	(0 implied)
RORPNT	Reorder point	46- 49	(0 implied)
RORQTY	Reorder quantity	50- 53	(0 implied)
RORCOD	Reorder code	54	Blank or R
SUPCOD	Supplier code	55- 57	(0)
SUPPID	Supplier product ID	58- 65	
CURCST	Current cost	66- 71	(2 implied)
AVGCST	Average cost	72- 77	(2 implied)

CSORDP: *Orders File*

This file contains "header" information about each order placed with Compu-Sell. The detailed information about items ordered is stored in CSORPRP.

Record layout of CSPRDP:

Field	Description	Positions	(Decimal Positions)
* ORD#	Order number	1- 5	(0)
ODATE	Date ordered	6- 11	(0)
CUSTNO	Customer number	12- 17	(0)
PAYMNT	Payment included	18- 24	(2)
ORDTOT	Total cost of order	25- 31	(2)

CSORDPRP: *Order/Products File*

This file, in conjunction with file CUSTORD, contains information about customer orders.

Record layout of CSORDPRP:

Field	Description	Positions	(Decimal Positions)
* ORD#	Order number	1- 5	(0)
* PRODNO	Product number	6- 11	(0)
QTYORD	Quantity ordered	12- 15	(0)

CSRCVP: *Goods Received File*

The company uses a file of received goods. Each time goods are received from a supplier, the information is stored in this file until it can be processed in batch to update the inventory file.

Record layout of CSRCVP:

Field	Description	Positions	(Decimal Positions)
* SUPCOD	Supplier code	1- 3	(0)
* SUPPID	Supplier product ID	4- 11	
QTYRCV	Quantity received	12- 15	(0)
COST	Item cost	16- 21	(2)

CSSUPP: *Supplier File*

This file stores information about the suppliers of CompuSell's products.

Record layout of CSSUPP:

Field	Description	Positions	(Decimal Positions)
* SUPCOD	Supplier code	1- 3	
SNAME	Supplier name	4- 28	
CONTAC	Contact person	29- 58	
SSTRET	Street address	59- 78	
SCITY	City	79- 93	
SSTAT	State	94- 95	
SZIP	Zip	96-104	(0)
SPHONE	Phone	105-114	(0)

In addition to the above files, CompuSell will need two "table" files to help it determine what to charge its customers for shipping.

CSZPZNP: *Zip/Zone Table File*

This file will be used to determine the correct shipping zone based on the first three digits of a customer's zip code. Zones range from 2 to 7, depending on zip code. This is a range table file, such that each zip code record represents the highest of a range of zip codes.

Record layout of CSZPZNP:

Field	Description	Positions	(Decimal Positions)
TZIP	3 Zip digits	1- 3	(0)
TZONE	Related shipping zone	4	(0)

CSCHGP: *Charges Table File*

This second "table" file contains shipping charges based on weight and zone. Each record contains a weight and six charges (one each for zones 2-7).

Record layout of CSCHGP:

Field	Description	Positions	(Decimal Positions)
TWGT	Weight in pounds	1- 2	(0)
TCHG2	Charge zone 2	3- 6	(2)
TCHG3	Charge zone 3	7- 10	(2)
TCHG4	Charge zone 4	11- 14	(2)
TCHG5	Charge zone 5	15- 18	(2)
TCHG6	Charge zone 6	19- 22	(2)
TCHG7	Charge zone 7	23- 26	(2)

Case 2: Wexler University

Wexler University is a small midwestern university that wants a system for student records and registration. The system will store information about departments, instructors, courses, sections, students, and enrollment. The files required as part of the system are described below.

WUCRDP: *Earned Credits File*

This file contains a record for each course each student has completed.

Record layout of WUCRDP:

Field	Description	Positions	(Decimal Positions)
*STUNO	Social Security number	1- 9	(0)
DEPT	Course department	10- 12	
CRSNO	Course number	13- 15	(0)
GRADE	Grade	16- 17	
SEMES	Semester taken	18- 20	First two positions YY; third position is semester code, where 1 = Winter; 2 = Summer; 3 = Fall

WUCRSDSP: *Course Description File*

Each course has a description of varying length; the description may include an overview of the course, prerequisites, etc. A description for a given course is represented by one or more records in this file; the records for a given course are sequentially assigned a line number.

Record layout of WUCRSDSP:

Field	Description	Positions	(Decimal Positions)
*DEPT	Course department	1- 3	
*CRSNO	Course number	4- 6	(0)
*LINE	Description line number	7- 8	(0)
CRSDSC	Description	9- 58	

WUCRSP: *Course File*

Each course the university offers is represented by a record in this file. Each course is uniquely identified by a 6-position identification of course department and course number (e.g., CIS264).

Record layout of WUCRSP:

Field	Description	Positions	(Decimal Positions)
*DEPT	Course department	1- 3	
*CRSNO	Course number	4- 6	
CRSTTL	Course title	7- 31	
CREDIT	Credits	32	(0)

WUDPTP: *Department File*

This file contains information about each department of Wexler University.

Record layout of WUDPTP:

Field	Description	Positions	(Decimal Positions)
DEPT	Department code	1- 3	
DNAME	Department name	4- 23	
CHAIR	Name of chair	24- 48	
DOFFIC	Department office	49- 58	
DPHONE	Department phone	59- 68	(0)

WUENRLP: *Current Enrollment File*

A record is entered in this file for each student for each section (s)he is enrolled in. At the end of the semester, scanned grades are added to this file before preparing semester grade reports.

Record layout of WUENRLP:

Field	Description	Positions	(Decimal Positions)
SECT	Section number	1- 5	(0)
STUNO	Social Security number	6- 14	(0)
GRADE	Grade received	15- 16	

WUEXAMP: *Student Exam File*

Record layout of WUEXAMP:

Field	Description	Positions	(Decimal Positions)
STUNO	Social Security number	1- 9	(0)
SFNAME	First name	10- 19	
SLNAME	Last name	20- 34	
EXAM1	Exam 1 grade	35- 37	(0)
EXAM2	Exam 2 grade	38- 40	(0)

Field	Description	Positions	(Decimal Positions)
EXAM3	Exam 3 grade	41- 43	(0)
EXAM4	Exam 4 grade	44- 46	(0)
EXAM5	Exam 5 grade	47- 49	(0)

WUHRLYP: *Hourly Employees File*

Field	Description	Positions	(Decimal Positions)
EMPNO	Social Security number	1- 9	(0)
LNAME	Last name	10- 24	
FNAME	First name	25- 34	
REGHRS	Regular hours	35- 37	(1)
OTHRS	Overtime hours	38- 40	(1)
RATE	Regular pay rate	41- 44	(2)

WUINSTP: *Instructor File*

Each instructor at Wexler University has a record in this file.

Record layout of WUINSTP:

Field	Description	Positions	(Decimal Positions)
IFNAME	First name	1- 10	
ILNAME	Last name	11- 25	
* INSTNO	Social Security number	26- 34	(0)
DEPT	Department	35- 37	
SALARY	Salary	38- 45	(2)
RANK	Academic rank	46	1 = Instructor; 2 = Assistant professor; 3 = Associate professor; 4 = Full professor
SEX	Sex	47	M = male; F = female;
HIRDAT	Date of hire	48- 53	(0) YYMMDD
MARSTS	Marital status	54	M = Married; S = Single; H = Head of house
DEPEND	Number of dependents	55- 56	(0)
TENURE	Tenured faculty	57	Y = yes; N = no
TITLE	Preferred title	58	1 = Dr.; 2 = Mr.; 3 = Mrs.; 4 = Ms.
STREET	Street address	59- 78	
CITY	City	79- 93	
STATE	State	94- 95	
ZIP	Zip	96-104	(0)

WUKEYP: *File of Keys to Tests in WUTSTP*
This file contains the keys (answers) to the tests contained in WUTSTP.
There is one answer key (record) for each test. The file is keyed on Course
ID and Test number; these values match those in the Student Test File.

Record layout of WUKEYP:

Field	Description	Positions	(Decimal Positions)
* TESTNO	Test number	1- 4	(0)
* CRSID	Course ID	5- 10	
ILNAME	Instructor's last name	11- 25	
KEY	Correct answers 1-50	26- 75	

WULOANP: *Faculty Credit Union Loan File*
This file contains records for loan applications to the credit union.

Input record format for WULOANP:

Field	Description	Positions	(Decimal Positions)
* LOANNO	Loan number	1- 5	(0)
CNAME	Customer name	6- 20	
LAMT	Loan amount	21- 27	(2)
ANNRAT	Annual interest rate	28- 31	(4)
YEARS	Years for loan	32- 33	(0)

WUSCTP: *Current Sections File*
Every section of each course currently being offered is represented by a
record in this file. Each section has been assigned a unique number.

Record layout of WUSCTP:

Field	Description	Positions	(Decimal Positions)
* SECT	Section number	1- 5	(0)
DEPT	Course department	6- 8	
CRSNO	Course number	9- 11	
SECTIM	Meeting time	12- 15	(0) HHMM
SECDAY	Meeting days	16- 18	
ROOM	Meeting room	19- 22	
CAP	Maximum enrollment	23- 25	(0)
CURENL	Current enrollment	26- 28	(0)
ILNAME	Instructor's last name	29- 43	

WUSTDP: *Student Master File*

This file contains information about all Wexler University's students who are actively enrolled and those who have graduated within the past five years.

Record layout of WUSTDP:

Field	Description	Positions	(Decimal Positions)
*STUNO	Social Security number	1- 9	(0)
SLNAME	Student last name	10- 24	
SFNAME	Student first name	25- 34	
SMNAME	Student middle name	35- 44	
STREET	Street address	45- 64	
CITY	City	65- 79	
STATE	State	80- 81	
ZIP	Zip	82- 90	(0)
PHONE	Telephone	91-100	(0)
CRDTOT	Credits earned	101-103	(0)
DCODE	District code	104	I = Indistrict; O = Out-of-district; F = International
ADMDAT	Date admitted	105-110	YYMMDD
CLASS	Classification	111	U = Undergraduate; G = Graduate
GRDDAT	Date graduated	112-117	Blanks or YYMMDD
SDEPT	Department of major	118-120	
GPA	Grade point average	121-123	(2)
DEGREE	Degree granted	124-126	

WUTRANSP: *Transcript Request File*

Record layout of WUTRANSP:

Field	Description	Positions	(Decimal Positions)
*STUNO	Social Security number	1- 9	(0)

WUTSTP: *Student Test File*

This file contains student answers to 50-question, multiple-choice tests. The file is keyed on Course ID, Test, and Section number.

Record layout of WUTSTP:

Field	Description	Positions	(Decimal Positions)
*TESTNO	Test number	1- 4	(0)
*SECTN	Section number	5- 9	(0)
*CRSID	Course ID	10- 15	
STUID	Student ID	16- 24	(0)
ANS	Answers 1-50	25- 74	Values A, B, C, D, E

Case 3: GTC, Inc.

GTC is a small regional telephone company that needs an application system to maintain customer accounts, bill for calls, process payments, generate management reports, and so on. Four main files will be needed as part of the system. The files, and their record layouts, are described below.

GTCLSP: *Calls Transaction File*

This file is generated automatically by the telephone switching system. Records accumulate in the file during the month; once a month the file is processed to determine monthly billing. The file is then cleared at the beginning of each new billing period.

Record layout of GTCLSP:

Field	Description	Positions	(Decimal Positions)
CPHONE	Caller's number	1- 10	(0)
CALLED	Called number	11- 20	(0)
CALDAT	Date of call	21- 26	(0) YYMMDD
CALLEN	Length of call (in minutes)	27- 29	(0)
CALTIM	Time of call	30- 33	(0) HHMM based on 24-hour clock
CALCST	Call cost	34- 38	(2)

GTCSTP: *Customer Master File*

This file contains a record for each of GTC's customers.

Record layout of GTCSTP:

Field	Description	Positions	(Decimal Positions)
* CPHONE	Customer phone number	1- 10	(0)
CLNAME	Last name	11- 25	
CFNAME	First name	26- 35	
CSTRET	Street address	36- 55	
CCITY	City	56- 70	
CSTAT	State	71- 72	
CZIP	Zip	73- 77	(0)
CURBIL	Current billing amount	78- 83	(2)
AMTOWE	Amount owed	84- 89	(2)
PAYDAT	Date last payment	90- 95	(0) YYMMDD

GTPAYP: *Payments Transaction File*

This file is generated through OCR and manual entry techniques. Records are used once to update the customer account figures and generate a payment report and then archived.

Record layout of GTPAYP:

Field	Description	Positions	(Decimal Positions)
* CPHONE	Payer's phone number	1- 10	(0)
AMTPD	Amount paid	11- 16	(2)
DATRCV	Date payment received	17- 22	(0) YYMMDD

GTRATP: *Rates Table File*

This is a sequential file used as a table to determine cost of calls to a given area code and exchange.

Record layout of GTRATP:

Field	Description	Positions	(Decimal Positions)
TAREA	Area code called	1- 3	(0)
TEXCH	Exchange called	4- 6	(0)
TCITY	City called	7- 16	
TSTATE	State called	17- 18	
CST1ST	Cost for first minute	19- 20	(2)
CSTADL	Cost for each additional minute	21- 22	(2)

Miscellaneous Files

The files described below are not part of any of the above application systems. They represent "stand-alone" applications included as programming exercises to demonstrate certain programming concepts.

ACP001: *ACME Work File (used in Chapter 4, problem 4)*

Input record format for ACP001:

Field	Description	Positions	(Decimal Positions)
* SOCSEC	Social Security number	1- 9	(0)
NAME	Name	10- 25	
WKDATE	Date worked	26- 31	(0) MMDDYY
HOURS	Hours worked	32- 33	(0)
QTY	Quantity produced	34- 36	(0)

BIDS: *Bids File (used in Chapter 3, problem 4)*

Record layout for BIDS:

Field	Description	Positions	(Decimal Positions)
JOBNO	Job number	1- 4	(0)
PCODE	Paint code	5- 9	(0)
PCOST	Per gallon cost	10- 13	(2)
COVRG	Coverage per gallon	14- 16	(0)
LENFT	Room length, feet	17- 18	(0)
LENIN	Room length, inches	19- 20	(0)
WIDFT	Room width, feet	21- 22	(0)
WIDIN	Room width, inches	23- 24	(0)
HTFT	Room height, feet	25- 26	(0)
HTIN	Room height, inches	27- 28	(0)
PCT	Percent windows, doors	29- 30	(2)

HJSLPP: *Salesperson File (used in Chapter 9, problem 2)*

Record layout for HJSLPP:

Field	Description	Positions	(Decimal Positions)
* SLSMNO	Salesperson number	1- 2	(0)
SNAME	Name	3- 27	
BASPAY	Weekly base pay	28- 33	(2)

HJSLSP: *Sales File (used in Chapter 9, problem 2)*

Record layout for HJSLSP:

Field	Description	Positions	(Decimal Positions)
SLSMNO	Salesperson number	1- 2	(0)
INVNO	Invoice number	3- 7	(0)
AMT	Sale amount	8- 14	(2)

MWC001P: *Meter Reading File (used in Chapter 4, problem 3)*

Record layout for MWC001P:

Field	Description	Positions	(Decimal Positions)
CNAME	Customer name	1- 20	
CUSTNO	Customer number	21- 25	(0)
OLDMTR	Old meter reading	26- 29	(0)
NEWMTR	New meter reading	30- 33	(0)
RCODE	Residency code	34	1 = City resident; 2 = Non-city resident

PIPRESP: *Airline Reservation File (used in Chapter 9, problem 3)*

Record layout for PIPRESP:

Field	Description	Positions	(Decimal Positions)
* DY	Day of week	1	(0)
* FLIGHT	Flight number	2	(0)
RESERV	Seats reserved	3- 4	(0)
FNAME	First name of reserver	5- 14	
LNAME	Last name of reserver	15- 29	
PHONE	Phone number of reserver	30- 39	(0)

PRDSLSP: *Sales Volume File (used in Chapter 9, problem 1)*

This file contains a record for each of the company's products, showing the sales volume for each month.

Record layout for PRDSLSP:

Field	Description	Positions	(Decimal Positions)
PRODNO	Product number	1- 6	(0)
SLS	12 monthly sales*	7- 78	(0)

*Represent 12 monthly total sales figures for that product, arranged sequentially from January to December; each sales figure is a 6-digit integer.

Glossary

abend — the condition in which a program prematurely terminates, or ends abnormally, after issuing an error message indicating the problem that prevented the program from reaching its normal ending point. (Chapters 6; 9; Appendix C)

algorithm — a step-by-step procedure for solving a problem. (Chapter 1)

alphanumeric data — data treated as characters, rather than numbers, regardless of the actual make-up of the data; may be alphabetic, special characters, or digits. (Chapter 1)

alternating format — the form of data entry in tables or arrays in which pairs of related data are entered together. (Chapter 8)

API — Application Programming Interface; a program or command supplied as part of the operating system that lets you access low-level system functions. You can call APIs from within RPG IV programs. (Chapter 12)

array — a data structure similar to a table in that it contains multiple elements defined with a common name; unlike tables, individual elements of arrays may be referenced by using an index. Also unlike tables, arrays can be loaded with values during the course of program execution — called runtime arrays. (Chapter 8)

arrival sequence — the sequence in which database records are accessed in the order in which they were placed in the database file (first-in, first-out), rather than based on the value of a key field. (Chapter 5)

assignment operations — those operations that let you assign a value to a variable. EVAL (Evaluate Expression) is RPG IV's primary assignment operator; other operations sometimes used for assignment include MOVE (Move), MOVEL (Move Left), Z-ADD (Zero and Add), and Z-SUB (Zero and Subtract). (Chapters 3;13)

backward-compatible — a characteristic of RPG that lets you compile and run previously written programs under a new version of the language without rewriting the program. (Chapter 13)

"backwards" sequential access — accessing records in a database file in descending key order through the READP or READPE operations. (Chapter 6)

base string — the factor 2 value of string operations (e.g., SCAN, CHECK, XLATE), which serves as the focus or target of the string operation. (Chapter 11)

based field — a field that is not assigned static storage of its own; instead, its storage location is based on a pointer, whose value may change during program execution. (Chapter 9)

basing pointer — an RPG IV data type used to store addresses of storage locations of variables. (Chapter 9)

batch processing — computer processing in which the computer processes a "batch" of data (typically representing business transactions) without user intervention, in contrast to applications that are interactively controlled by the user during execution. (Chapters 1; 7)

binary — a system of representing values based on powers of 2. For example, decimal value 8 is 1000 in binary. (Chapters 5; 11)

binary data type — numeric data stored directly in base 2 representation, rather than through EBCDIC encoding. (Chapter 5)

bind — a process that prepares a compiled object for execution by linking it with other modules (if needed) and creating a *PGM object. (Chapters 1; 12)

bits (binary digits) — either 0 or 1. A group of eight adjacent binary digits represents one EBCDIC character and equals one byte. *See also* decimal bits; zone bits. (Chapters 1; 11)

built-in function (BIF) — an operation-like feature of RPG IV that returns a value based on the value of its argument. (Chapters 9; 11)

Calculation Specifications — lines in RPG IV programs that detail the procedural processing steps, including calculations, to be performed by your program. Each Calculation Specification line of code must include a C in position 6. (Chapter 2)

CASE logic — a logic construct that allows multiple alternate branches of processing to be specified, in contrast to an IF structure, which allows only a single alternate branch. (Chapter 4)

case sensitive — a condition where uppercase alphabetic letters and their corresponding lowercase versions are treated as different characters. (Chapters 2; 11)

character data type — a declaration that a field will contain alphanumeric data. (Chapter 5)

character field — a field defined to represent alphanumeric characters. (Chapter 2)

character literals — sequences of one or more keyboard characters enclosed within apostrophes and that have fixed, non-numeric values; you can use character literals with character-oriented operations. (Chapter 3)

check-protection — a technique most commonly used in printing checks in which insignificant leading zeros in a number are replaced by asterisks rather than simply suppressed to prevent tampering with the check's face value. (Chapter 2)

combined file — a file that supports both input and output, but as independent operations. Display files are combined files. (Chapter 7)

comment lines — *See* internal documentation. (Chapters 1; 2; 3)

compare string — the factor 1 value of a string operation (e.g., SCAN, CHECK, CHECKR) that contains the value to check for in the base string contained in factor 2. (Chapter 11)

compile — to translate the source code of a program into machine language, or object code. (Chapter 1)

compile-time array — an array whose values are hard-coded at the end of the source program and whose values are bound to the array when the program is compiled. (Chapter 8)

compile-time table — a table whose values are entered at the end of the source program and are bound to the table when the program is compiled. (Chapter 8)

compiler — a special computer program that translates a program written in a high-level programming language (HLL) into machine language that the computer can understand. (Chapter 1)

composite key — a key for a file or record format composed of more than one field. (Chapters 5; 6)

concatenated key — same as composite key. (Chapter 6)

concatenation — a composite or combination of fields, as in a composite (or concatenated) key; also, an operation that joins two character strings in the order specified, forming a single string. (Chapters 5; 11)

conditioning indicator — an indicator in positions 9-11 of a Calculation Specification whose off/on status determines whether or not the calculation is performed. (Chapter 13)

constants — in an RPG IV program, those characters that do not change, representing the actual values that will be processed or printed out on a report; also called literals. (Chapter 2)

continuation line — a line that lets you continue a line of code; you can use continuation lines with File, Definition, Calculation, and Output Specifications for completing keyword and free-form entries that are too long to fit on a single line. (Chapters 2; 3; 8; 9)

control-break problem — a special type of batch processing problem for files whose records are grouped by values of a control field and that require special processing based on a change in the control field's value; generally the special processing involves printing subtotals for each group of records. (Chapter 4)

crossfooting — a term used in accounting to sum across a row of figures to develop a total for that row. (Chapter 8)

cross-reference listing — a list provided by the compiler that logs all fields and indicators used in your program; every program statement within which the fields or indicators occur appear in the listing. Useful for diagnosing problems when debugging programs. (Appendix C)

**CTDTA record — a line in a source member that appends the source code and serves as a delimiter (or separator line) to explicitly identify the table or array whose data follows; used with compile-time tables and arrays. (Chapter 8)

CUA — Common User Access; a set of IBM design standards that were developed to promote standardized user interfaces across platforms. (Chapter 7)

data area — an AS/400 object used to communicate data between programs within a job or between jobs. One program does not have to call another to access the same data if the data resides in a data area. (Chapter 12)

data-area data structures — data structures defined specifically for data areas. See also data area; data structure (Chapter 12)

Data Description Specifications (DDS) — the name given to the RPG IV specification form in which database and display file definitions are developed. (Chapter 5)

data dictionary — a central repository for storing definitions of data independent of programs and widely used in a database approach to data management; on the AS/400, a data dictionary can be developed through a special kind of physical file, called a field-reference file. (Chapters 1; 5)

Data File Utility (DFU) — an AS/400 program that facilitates entering data values into database files without the need for writing an HLL data-entry program. (Chapter 5)

data structure — a contiguous portion of memory, which is then subdivided and referenced in different ways by the data structure's subfields. (Chapters 8; 9)

data type — a defined attribute of a data item that determines what kind of data the item can store and what kinds of operations it can be used with. (Chapters 5; 9)

data validation — attempting to determine that data is correct before accepting it as input. In RPG IV, the four major keywords used for validating user-entered data are VALUES, COMP, RANGE, and CHECK. (Chapter 7)

date data type — an RPG IV data type (type D) used to store dates; its default display format is 10 bytes long, with format yyyy-mm-dd. (Chapter 9)

DBCS (Double-Byte Character Set) graphic data type — an RPG IV data type in which two bytes represent a single character of a graphic character set. (Chapter 9)

debugging — correcting any error found in a computer program. (Chapter 1; Appendix C)

decimal bits — the right-most 4 bits of a byte, numbered 4, 5, 6, and 7; also called low-order or digit bits. *See also* bits. (Chapter 5; 11)

decimal — a system of representing values based on powers of 10. (Chapter 11)

decision operations — the options for sending control to alternate statements within a program. *See also* selection. (Chapter 4)

Definition Specifications — lines used in RPG IV programs for defining data items used within a program; Definition Specifications require a D in position 6. (Chapters 3; 9)

desk checking — checking output generated by the computer against the results of hand calculations. (Appendix C)

detail line — an output line based on data contained in a single record of an input file; the line prints detailed information about the data record being processed. (Chapter 2)

digit bits — the right-most four bits of a byte; also called low-order or decimal bits. *See also* bits. (Chapter 5)

display attributes — special characteristics that can be assigned to fields to affect their appearance on the screen; includes such features as underlining, high intensity, and blinking. (Chapter 7)

display file — files that define the screens that the program presents as it runs. Display files let values keyed by the user in response to the screen be input as data to the program; therefore, display files serve as the mechanism that lets the user and the program interact. (Chapter 7)

dynamic binding — linking (or interconnecting) a calling program object (*PGM) with its called program object (*PGM) when the call is actually executed during runtime; the CALL operation is used with this kind of binding. (Chapter 12)

EBCDIC — Extended Binary Coded Decimal Interchange Code; the data-representation format used by IBM. EBCDIC assigns a unique 8-bit binary pattern to each representable character or digit. The left-most four bits are called zone or high-order bits; the right-most four bits are called digit or low-order bits. In this format, A is less than B, B is less than C, and so on. Lowercase letters are "smaller" than uppercase letters, letters are smaller than digits, and blank is smaller than any other displayable character. (Chapters 4; 5)

edit code — a letter or number that specifies how numeric values are to be formatted to make them more readable upon output; different edit codes evoke different formatting. (Chapter 2)

edit words — an alternative to edit codes for signaling the desired format for numeric output; an edit word supplies a template into which a numeric value is inserted and may include instructions for zero-suppression and insertion of special characters. Edit codes and edit words are never used together for the same field. (Chapter 2)

editor — a computer program designed to let you enter, rearrange, change, and delete source program statements (or other text) interactively. SEU, the AS/400's editor, also performs basic syntax checking as you enter program statements. (Chapter 1; Appendix B)

end-of-file — in sequential record access, when an attempt to read another record fails because no records remain unprocessed. (Chapter 2)

exponentiation — the operation in which a value is raised to a power. (Chapter 3)

extended factor 2 format — a form of the Calculation Specifications in which there is no result entry; instead, positions 36-80 are used for a free-form expression. (Chapter 14)

Extension Specifications — an obsolete RPG specification type, formerly used to define tables and arrays. (Chapter 13)

external documentation — material added to (but not a direct part of) a program that is useful for understanding, using, or modifying the program; external documentation can include such items as system and program flowcharts, user manuals, and operator instructions. (Chapter 1)

externally described file — a file whose records are defined at a field level to the system when the file is created and whose external definition is used by a program referencing that file. (Chapter 5)

field — generally represents the smallest unit of data to be manipulated within a program, such as a customer account number, last name, first name, street address, city, state, zip code, phone number, and so on. *See also* program variable. (Chapter 1)

field definition — the specification of variables to be used within a program by assigning the variable a name, length, and data type. (Chapter 2)

field-definition lines — also called field-description lines; lines in an RPG IV program that describe the content of a given input record for program-described files. (Chapter 2)

field-level keywords — keywords that are associated only with a specific field within a file in DDS Specifications. (Chapter 5)

field-reference file — another name for a centralized data dictionary of the fields in a physical file. *See* data dictionary. (Chapter 5)

figurative constants — implied literals that can be used without a specified length. Figurative constants assume the length and decimal positions of the fields they are associated with. RPG IV's figurative constants are *BLANK (or *BLANKS), *ZERO (or *ZEROS), *HIVAL, *LOVAL, *OFF, *ON, *ALL, and *NULL. (Chapters 3; 9)

file — a named set of records stored or processed as a unit. In RPG IV, files are either physical files or logical files. *See* physical file; logical file. (Chapter 1)

file access — the means by which a file can be read, written to, or updated; methods include sequential and random access. *See* sequential access; random access (Chapter 6)

File Description Specifications — program lines that describe the files your program uses and how the files will be used within the program. File Description Specifications generally begin RPG IV programs, and all file specifications include an F in position 6. Each file used by a program requires its own file specification line. (Chapter 2)

file designation — refers to the way the program will access, or retrieve, the data in an input, combined, or update file. (Chapter 2)

file-information data structure — a special data structure that can be defined for each file used by a program. File-information data structures contain predefined subfields that provide information about the file following I/O operations. (Chapter 9)

file-level keywords — in DDS Specifications, keywords that apply to the file as a whole. (Chapter 5)

file locking — limiting access to a file to one user at a time. (Chapter 6)

File Specifications — a shortened synonym for File Description Specifications. (Chapter 2)

fixed dollar sign — in numeric data, where the dollar sign is positioned in a set column of the output, regardless of the number of significant digits in the number following the sign. (Chapter 1)

fixed-form — *See* fixed-position. (Chapter 2)

fixed format — in File Specifications, an indication that a file's records will be described within the program and that each record of the file has the same, fixed length. (Chapter 2)

fixed-logic cycle — RPG's built-in read-process-write cycle that repeats until all the desired records have been processed. (Chapter 13)

fixed-position — also called *fixed-form*, means that the location of an entry within a program line is critical to its interpretation by the RPG IV compiler. (Chapter 2)

floating dollar sign — in numeric data, where the dollar sign prints next to the left-most significant digit of the number; the position of the dollar sign varies, or floats, depending on the value of the number with which it is associated. (Chapter 1)

Fourth-Generation Languages (4GLs) — languages designed to make programming easier by letting the programmer specify the desired results to be accomplished instead of the detailed processing required to achieve the desired results; often also referred to as non-procedural languages. (Chapter 1)

free-form — a term used to characterize program syntax; free-form implies that the meaning of the code is not dependent on the location of the code within a line (i.e., the meaning is not positionally dependent). (Chapter 3)

full procedural — the term used for a file whose records are explicitly read within the program, as opposed to using the built-in retrieval of RPG's fixed-logic cycle. Such files are identified by an F in position 16 of the entry for file designation on the File Specifications. (Chapter 2)

graphical user interface (GUI) — a visual computer interface that uses icons to represent actual objects; the user accesses and manipulates these icons via a pointing device. The PC Windows environment typifies a GUI. (Chapter 7)

half-adjusting — the term often used to mean "rounding" a numeric answer on the computer. The computer adds half the value of the right-most desired decimal position to the digit immediately to the right of that decimal position before storing the answer in the result field. Because the value added is half the value of the least-significant digit position of the result, the term half-adjust evolved. (Chapter 3)

help-specification format — a format within the Data Description Specifications (DDS) that will associate a specific portion of the screen with a specific record of help text. (Chapter 10)

hexadecimal — a system of representing values based on powers of 16. Digits 0-9 are used to represent 0-9 in hexadecimal; characters A-F are used to represent values 10-15, respectively. Hex B (usually represented as X'0B') is the equivalent of decimal 11, for example. (Chapter 11)

hierarchical decomposition — *See* top-down design. (Chapter 4)

high-level languages (HLLs) — programming languages designed to make it easier for programmers to express instructions to computers; contrasted to low-level languages such as machine language or assembler. Programs written in an HLL need to be translated into machine language, a process called compiling, before the computer can actually execute the program. (Chapter 1)

high-order bits — *See* zone bits; EBCDIC. (Chapter 5)

high-order truncation — the loss of digits from the left end of a result field. (Chapter 3)

index — a value used to reference or indicate an individual element of an array. (Chapter 8)

indicator — an internal switch, or variable, with only two states or values — off or on (or '0' or '1') — used by a program to signal whether a particular event has occurred within the program and to control, or condition, subsequent processing within the program. (Chapters 1; 2; 13)

infinite loop — a loop whose execution continues until you (or a system operator) intervenes to terminate the job that contained the loop. (Appendix C)

input file — a file that contains data to be read by the program. (Chapter 2)

Input Specifications — those specifications that describe the records within the program-described input files and define the fields within the records; they are identified by an I in position 6. (Chapter 2)

integer data — data representing whole numbers. (Chapter 2)

integer numeric field — a numeric field defined with 0 decimal positions, such that it can only store whole numbers. (Chapter 2)

Integrated Language Environment (ILE) — a term IBM introduced with V2R3 of OS/400 to indicate a new approach to interconnecting high-level language (HLL) programs on the AS/400. This approach supports program development using modules written in different HLLs and statically bound into a single application. (Chapters 1;12)

interactive applications — those applications in which a user interacts with the computer directly through a terminal or workstation to control the actions of a computer program as it is running. (Chapters 1; 7)

internal documentation — comments included within the source code of a program to aid in understanding, using, or modifying the program. In RPG IV, coding an asterisk (*) in position 7 designates that line to be a comment. (Chapters 1; 2; 3)

*INZSR — a subroutine which, when included in an RPG IV program, automatically executes at the start of the program; usually used for initializing variables. (Chapter 9)

iteration — a control structure within a program that permits instructions within the program to be repeated until a condition is met or is no longer met; also called "repetition" or "looping." (Chapter 4)

join-logical file — a logical file that combines fields from different physical files into a single record. (Chapter 5)

key field — a field in a record whose contents are used to build access paths to records such that the records appear to be in sequence based on that field's values. (Chapter 5)

key sequence — an access method in which database records are retrieved based on the key field defined for the records. (Chapter 5)

key specifications — DDS specifications that declare which field (or fields) is to serve as the key to the file. (Chapter 5)

keyboard-shift attribute — an entry associated with fields within display files that determines what kinds of data a user can input into that field or be displayed. (Chapter 7)

keywords — in RPG IV and DDS, reserved words with special meanings that are used, often with parameters, to complete definitions or to signal certain attributes. (Chapters 5-9)

leading-decision loop — a program loop in which the test to determine whether or not the instructions within the loop are to be performed is made before the instructions within the loop are executed for the first time. (Chapter 4)

level checking — a feature of the AS/400 that prevents running a program if changes have been made to the definition of a physical or logical file used by that program unless the program is first recompiled. This feature prevents executing a program using an obsolete or inaccurate definition of a database file. (Chapter 5)

level indicator — any of nine indicators, L1-L9, used to detect changes in control fields' values in control-break processing when implementing the fixed-logic cycle. (Chapter 13)

list panels — term referring to the screen display of data from many records for review, selection, and update. (Chapter 10)

literals — *See* constants. (Chapter 2)

local data area (LDA) — a data area created for each job in the system. Each LDA is 1,024 positions long, with type character. *See also* data area. (Chapter 12)

logic errors — program errors caused by faulty program design that cause the program to end abnormally, loop infinitely, or process data incorrectly to produce incorrect output. (Chapter 1; Appendix C)

logical files — files that describe how data appears to be stored in the database. Logical files do not actually contain data records, but rather access paths, or pointers, to records in physical files. Logical files must have one or more fields designated as a key, by which the access paths are identified. (Chapter 5)

low-order bits — the four right-most bits of a byte, also known as decimal or digit bits. *See* high-order bits; EBCDIC. (Chapter 5)

low-order truncation — the loss of digits from the right end of a result field. (Chapter 3)

master files — sets of data or files, of long-term or permanent, importance; such files contain vital information for an organization's ongoing operations. (Chapter 1)

mixed-case entry — a characteristic of programming languages that lets you enter alphabetic characters as either uppercase or lowercase. (Chapter 2; 3)

modular programming — an approach to programming in which small, stand-alone units of code are developed (as opposed to monolithic programs thousands of lines long). (Chapter 12)

multiple-occurrence data structure — similar to a table or an array, a multiple-occurrence data structure enables multiple repetitions of the data structure in storage. (Chapter 9)

named constant — in RPG IV, a constant value that has been provided with a name; this value can then be used throughout the program by referring to it by name, rather than entering the value itself. (Chapter 9)

numeric data — pertaining to non-alphabetic information — i.e., numbers; you can perform arithmetic calculations on numeric data. (Chapter 1)

numeric field — fields that contain numeric values; numeric fields may be used in calculations and edited for output. (Chapters 2; 3)

numeric literals — a number per se whose value remains fixed throughout a program. A numeric literal can be up to 10 positions long and may include the digits 0 through 9, and a decimal point and/or a sign. (Chapter 3)

object code — a program's code translated into executable machine language. (Chapter 1)

operation extender — an extension to an operation that enhances or modifies the effects of the operation. Enclosed within parentheses following the operation code, the extenders include (H), for rounding; (P), for blank padding; (D), for valid date testing; (T), for valid time testing; (Z), for valid timestamp testing. (Chapters 3; 11; 13)

output editing — refers to formatting numeric output values by suppressing leading zeros and adding special characters, such as decimal points, commas, and dollar signs to make the values easier to comprehend for people looking at the output. (Chapters 1; 2)

output errors — logic errors that result in incorrect output when a program is run. (Appendix C)

output file — the destination for writing operations of a computer program. (Chapter 2)

Output Specifications — specifications used to define the desired format of output files when described within a program; they are identified by an O in position 6. (Chapter 2)

overflow indicators — special built-in indicators in RPG IV that signal end-of-page. Overflow indicators include OA, OB, OC, OD, OE, OF, OG, and OV. (Chapter 4)

overlay — in a data structure, a redefinition of a field by an array; the array is defined to occupy the same bytes as the field. (Chapter 8)

packed-decimal data type — the numeric representation of data in EBCDIC format in which only the digit, or low-order, bits of a number are stored, with the sign of the number represented by an additional four bits. The sign bits always occupy the right-most four-bit positions of a packed-decimal value. (Chapter 5)

PARMs — RPG IV's method of designating fields to be shared between calling and called programs (or modules). (Chapter 12)

passing by reference — RPG IV's method for passing a parameter argument between calling and called programs (or modules) by passing the address of the storage location represented by the field, rather than the field's value; changing the parameter field within the called program results in the same change in the parameter field of the calling program. (Chapter 12)

passing by value — A method for passing a parameter argument between calling and called programs (or modules) by passing a copy of the field's value, rather than the address of the storage location represented by the field; changing the parameter field within the called program does not change the parameter field of the calling program. (Chapter 12)

phantom updates — the condition that occurs if two users access the same record for update at the same time and as a result of this concurrent access, one of the user's changes are lost; modern multiuser operating systems are designed to prevent phantom updates. (Chapter 6)

physical files — database files that actually store data records. (Chapter 5)

PLIST operation — an RPG IV declarative operation that identifies a list of parameters to be shared between programs. PLIST requires an identifying entry in factor 1. (Chapter 12)

pointer — a field whose value represents the address of a memory location. (Chapter 9)

pre-runtime array — an array whose values are obtained from a disk file at the start of a program's execution. (Chapter 8)

pre-runtime (pre-execution) table — a table whose values are obtained from a disk file at the start of a program's execution. (Chapter 8)

priming read — an initial read operation before the main process loop of a program, designed to provide the instructions within the loop with their first set of data to process. (Chapter 2)

printer spacing chart (PSC) — a detailed representation of the desired report layout when desired output includes a report. The PSC shows all constants the report should include (e.g., report headings, column headings) and where on the report the constants should appear. Variable information is generally indicated by Xs, where each X represents one character of data. (Chapter 1)

problem definition — the first step in the Program Development Cycle, the process of identifying the problem in terms of the programming specifications. (Chapter 1)

procedural languages — programming languages that require explicit, step-by-step statements or instructions to the computer of the procedure required to produce a specific result or product (e.g., a sales report). (Chapter 1)

procedure pointer — an RPG IV data type that is used to store the address of an entry point of a program module. (Chapters 9; 12)

program design — the second — and crucial — step in the Program Development Cycle, this phase encompasses working out the solution (algorithm) to the problem using sound programming logic prior to expressing the solution in a given programming language. (Chapter 1)

Program Development Cycle — the sequence of activities required to develop a program, including defining the problem, designing the solution, writing the program, entering the program, testing and debugging the program, documenting the program, and maintaining the program. (Chapter 1)

program maintenance — making modifications to a program once it is actually being used, or "in production." (Chapter 1)

program module — an object of type *MODULE that is the result of a compile operation in RPG IV; a program module must be bound (either alone or with other modules) to produce an executable program. (Chapters 1; 12)

program-status data structure — a data structure that can provide information about the program itself and about exceptions/errors that occur during program execution. (Chapter 9)

program variable — a program-defined construct that represents a location in the computer's memory; referencing a variable within a program causes the computer to access the memory location that corresponds to that variable and appropriately manipulate the data value stored at that location. In RPG, the term *field* is usually used instead of *variable*. Such fields, or variables, may represent alphanumeric (character) or numeric data. (Chapter 1)

pseudocode — a tool of program design that uses stylized English to detail the underlying logic needed for a program. (Chapters 1; 2)

*PSSR — a subroutine which, when included in an RPG IV program, automatically executes when a program runtime error occurs. (Chapter 9)

random access — the term applied to file access by just "reaching into" a file and extracting only the specific record you want (as opposed to retrieving database records sequentially). (Chapter 6)

range table — a table in which the entries represent a range of values rather than discreet values. (Chapter 8).

record — a set of one or more related data items grouped for processing. (Chapter 1)

record identifying indicator — an indicator associated with a record format of a primary input file that signals a record was successfully read; turned on/off automatically as part of the fixed-logic cycle. (Chapter 13)

record layouts — descriptions of the record formats of input files to be used by a program, including the beginning and ending positions of data fields within records, the order and length of the fields, and the number of decimal positions for numeric data. (Chapter 1)

record-format descriptions — a term used to describe those entries on Input and Output Specifications that describe one record type of a program-described input or output file. (Chapter 2)

record-level keywords — in DDS, those keywords that apply to a specific record format within a file. (Chapter 5)

record locking — a mechanism for preventing two users from accessing the same database record for update at the same time. RPG IV automatically puts a lock on a record of an Update file when the record is read. Updating that record or reading another record releases the record from the locked state. While the record is locked, other application programs can access the record if they have defined the file as an input file, but not if they have defined it as an update file. (Chapter 6)

recursion — a programming technique in which subroutines execute or invoke themselves, either directly or indirectly through an intermediate subroutine; this technique is not permitted in RPG IV. (Chapter 4)

redundancy — the duplication of data across files. (Chapter 5)

relational codes — in RPG IV programming, one of six two-letter codes used in making a relational comparison between two values. The six codes are GT (Greater Than), LT (Less Than), EQ (Equal To), NE (Not Equal To), LE (Less Than or Equal To) and GE (Greater Than or Equal To). (Chapters 4; 13)

relational comparison — testing a condition to determine the appropriate course of action within a program by making a comparison between two values via one of six criteria: greater than, less than, equal to, not equal to, less than or equal to, and greater than or equal to. (Chapter 4)

relative record number — a value that represents a record's ordinal position within a file or subfile. (Chapter 10)

Report Layout Utility (RLU) — an AS/400 utility to facilitate the design and definition of reports. (Chapter 5)

Report Program Generator (RPG) — a high-level programming language introduced by IBM in the early 1960s. As originally designed, RPG included a fixed-logic cycle that eliminated the need for programmers to detail each processing step required for the computer to execute the program. Another unique characteristic of RPG was its use of a special class of built-in, pre-defined variables called indicators. (Chapter 1)

resulting indicator — an indicator coded in positions 71-76 of Calculation Specifications to signal whether the result of a computation is a positive value, zero, or a negative value. (Chapter 13)

runtime array — an array that obtains or changes its values during the course of program execution, as a result of either input or calculations. (Chapter 8)

runtime errors — errors that prevent your program from reaching a normal end; a runtime error can cause a program to abruptly stop in the middle of execution or cause it to run forever until you (or a system operator) intervene to terminate the job. (Appendix C)

selection — the logic structure that lets you establish alternate paths of instructions within a program; which alternate the program executes depends on the results of a test or condition within the program. (Chapter 4)

sequence — the logic structure that lets you instruct the computer to execute operations serially. (Chapter 4)

sequential access — a method of retrieving or reading records serially, either in key order (if the file is keyed and so noted on the File Specifications) or in arrival or FIFO (First-In-First-Out) order (for non-keyed files). (Chapter 6)

simple logical file — a logical file whose records are based on a single physical file. *See* logical file. (Chapter 5)

source code — the statements/instructions of a program expressed in a high-level language. (Chapters 1; 7)

Source Entry Utility (SEU) — the AS/400 editor you can use to enter your RPG IV program. (Chapters 2; 7; Appendix B)

source member — on the AS/400, a subset of a file that contains a set of source statements/instructions representing a single program. (Chapters 1; 7)

spaghetti code — a program whose flow of control is difficult to follow; usually caused by undisciplined, haphazard transfer of control from one part of the program to another. (Chapters 1; 4; 7)

specific arithmetic operations — single-purpose, fixed-form operations to add, subtract, multiply, divide, or store remainders. Used by previous versions of RPG to perform all arithmetic calculations; their function largely has been replaced by EVAL. (Chapters 3; 13)

stand-alone field — additional fields used to store the results of calculations; so called because these fields are not part of a database record or any other kind of data structure. (Chapter 3)

static binding — linking (or interconnecting) a calling module object (*MODULE) with its called module object (*MODULE) during the binding stage to form a single executable *PGM object; the CALLB operation is used with this kind of binding. (Chapter 12)

structured design — a program development methodology that advocates a systematic approach to program design and emphasizes limiting flow-of-control structures within a program to three basic logic structures: sequence, selection (also called decision), and iteration (also called repetition or looping). (Chapters 1; 4)

subfile control-record format — the record format immediately following the subfile record format that controls the display of the subfile records through the use of special record-level keywords. Column headings for the subfile display also are often included as part of this record format. (Chapter 10)

subfile record format — describes the subfile fields that are to appear on the screen. (Chapter 10)

subfiles — a collection of record data from a database file that is handled as a unit for screen I/O. (Chapter 10)

subroutine — a set of operations coded elsewhere within the calculations of a program and invoked as a unit by referencing the subroutine's name with an EXSR (Execute Subroutine) operation. (Chapter 4)

subschemas — in database terminology, users' views of data. (Chapter 5)

syntax errors — errors in programming caused by misuse of the rules of the programming language that prevent the creation of an object program for the computer to execute. (Chapter 1; Appendix C)

table — conceptually, a collection of data organized into columns and rows. Similar kinds of data are stored within a column, and the data within a row of a table is "related," or belongs together. In RPG IV, one column of such a conceptual table. (Chapter 8)

table look-up — an operation to locate a specified value within a table. In RPG IV, the common use of tables is to look up a value in one table to extract a related value from a second table. (Chapter 8)

time data type — an RPG IV data type (type T) used to store time values; its default display format is 8 bytes long, with format hh.mm.ss. (Chapter 9)

timestamp data type — an RPG IV data type (type Z) used to store combined date/time values; its default display format is 26 bytes long, with format yyyy-mm-dd-hh.mm.ss.mmmmmm. (Chapter 9)

top-down design — the term used for program development that starts with a broad "outline" of the solution followed by successively breaking the big pieces into smaller and smaller units. Also sometimes called hierarchical decomposition. (Chapter 4)

trailing-decision loop — a program loop in which a test based on a comparison is made after the instructions within the loop have been executed; the outcome of the test determines whether or not the instructions within the loop are again executed. (Chapter 4)

transaction files — relatively temporary data files, usually generated during the course of a day's business, that often need to be processed only a single time. (Chapter 1)

truncation — the loss of digits from the right or the left ends of a result field. (Chapter 3)

two-dimensional array — an array that requires two indexes (or subscripts) to determine the identity of a given element of the array; one index points to the row and the second to the column location of the element. (Chapter 9)

typed literal — a literal value enclosed within apostrophes and preceded by a data type code to indicate what type of data the literal represents. (Chapter 9)

user space — a defined, permanent location in storage that is created by an API and used by other APIs. (Chapter 12)

volatile — in terms of programming, refers to data that is frequently changing. (Chapter 8)

Warnier-Orr diagram — a tool of program design that uses a notation relying on brackets to indicate program level and logic structures, such as iteration and decision. (Chapter 1)

zero suppression — the elimination of leading, non-significant zeros when printing or displaying numeric data. For example, 000123 would print as " 123" if zero suppression were in effect. (Chapter 1)

zone bits — the left-most four bits in IBM's EBCDIC coding scheme, bits 0, 1, 2, and 3. *See also* bits; decimal bits; high-order bits; EBCDIC. (Chapters 5; 11)

zoned-decimal data type — the numeric representation of data in EBCDIC format in which a full byte is required to store each digit of a numeric value, except that the zone of the right-most digit is used to store the sign of the data (1111 represents a + sign and 1101 represents a – sign). (Chapter 5)

Index

& (ampersand) separator character, 218

' (apostrophe)
  display files and, 158
  in specifying constants, 27

* (asterisk)
  comment line designation, 34
  as insignificant leading zeros, 38
  multiplication operator, 48
  object types and, 349
  syntax error designation, 370

** exponentiation operator, 48

+ (plus sign)
  addition operator, 48
  character string concatenation, 285
  continuation character, 28, 60, 225
  zoned-decimal representation and, 105

, (comma) separator character, 218

– (minus sign)
  constants and, 28
  continuation character, 60
  floating, 37
  separator character, 218
  subtraction operator, 48
  zoned-decimal representation and, 105

. (period) separator character, 218

/ (slash)
  division operator, 48
  separator character, 218

: (colon)
  character strings and, 280, 281
  separator character, 218

< (less than) relational comparison, 73

<= (less than or equal to) relational comparison, 73

<> (not equal to) relational comparison, 73

= (equal to) relational comparison, 73

> (greater than) relational comparison, 73

>= (greater than or equal to) relational comparison, 73

A

Abends, 130, 144, 242
  diagnosing, 371
  See also Errors

Absolute notation, 228

Access
  random, 135-138
  sequential, 129-134

Accumulators, subtotal, 237

ADD (Add) operation, 51, 317-318
  defined, 317
  forms of, 318

ADDBKP (Add Breakpoint) command, 376

ADDDUR (Add Duration) operation, 219-220
  defined, 219
  duration codes, 219
  use of, 220

Addition, result field size, 52-53

%ADDR function, 223, 275

ADDTRC (Add Trace) command, 377

Algorithms, 9

Alignment, vertical, 25

*ALL figurative constant, 63

ALT keyword, 190

Alternating format, 190-192
  defined, 190
  table definition limitations, 192

Ampersand (&) separator character, 218

AND operator, 75
  conditioning indicators and, 168
  DOW operation with, 81
  with other operations, 76

using, 76
  See also OR operator

ANDxx operation, 320-321

APIs, 303-305, 309
  defined, 303
  QCMDEXC, 304
  QUSCMDLN, 304
  QUSCRTUS, 304
  QUSRLSPL, 303
  QUSRSPLA, 303
  user space, 303

Apostrophes (')
  display files and, 158
  in specifying constants, 27

Application Development ToolSet/400: Report Layout Utility, 116

Application programming interfaces. *See* APIs

Arithmetic operations, 47-51
  ADD, 51
  DIV, 50-51, 55
  format for, 65
  MULT, 51
  MVR, 50-51, 55
  rules of precedence, 48
  specific, 49-51
  SQRT, 50
  SUB, 51
  use example, 56
  See also Operations

Array(s), 196-211
  calculations with, 200-205
  compile-time, 197, 208
  defined, 196
  defining, 196-197
  Definition Specification and, 196-197
  editing, 210
  elements
    corresponding, 201

indicating, 200
indicators as, 210
summing, 201-202
externally described files and, 231
*IN, 210
indexes, 200
variable, 207
look-ups, 208-209
with index, 208
starting, at beginning, 208
using, 209
without index, 208
moving, 202-205
names, 200
printing, 210
operations for, 201-205
output with, 210-211
pre-runtime, 197
printer spacing charts and, 210
RPG III and, 324
runtime
data structures and, 198-199
defined, 197
Definition Specifications and, 197
input data and, 197-200
loading, 199
sorting, 202
tables vs., 211
two-dimensional, 234
uses, 211
using, 205-208
See also Table(s)
Arrival sequence, 100
AS/400
developing programs on, 349-357
libraries, 349
PDM, 352-357
Programmer Menu, 349, 350-351
SEU, 17, 359-367
ASCEND keyword, 185, 195
Asterisk (*)
comment line designation, 34
as insignificant leading zeros, 38
multiplication operator, 48
object types and, 349

syntax error designation, 370

B

Base string, 281
Based fields
defined, 223
manipulating, 224
storage, 225
See also Fields
Basing pointers, 222-223
defined, 222
fixed length, 223
manipulating, 224
storage, 225
See also Pointers
Batch processing, 2, 155
defined, 30
BEGSR operation, 86
Binary
data type, 104
digits. *See* Bits
representation, 289
Bind, 11, 13
Binding, 296-297
defined, 369
dynamic, 296
static, 296-297
Bits, 1
high-order, 104
low-order, 104
patterns of, 288-289
*BLANKS figurative constant, 63
Blank lines, 34, 40
BLINK keyword, 164, 170
Breakpoints, 376-377
adding, 376
defined, 376
removing, 376
Built-in functions (BIFs)
%ADDR, 223, 275
%ELEM, 277, 290
%PADDR, 299
%SIZE, 276-277, 290
%SUBST, 286-287, 290
%TRIM, 286, 290

%TRIML, 286, 290
%TRIMR, 286, 290
defined, 275
Bytes
inspecting, 278-284
number of, 276

C

CABxx (Compare and Branch) operation, 321, 322-323
defined, 322
transfer of control, 323
Calculation Specifications, 17, 29-31, 39
80-column, 336
character literals in, 60
comments in, 55
defined, 17
layout, 31
operations, 31, 32-33
Calculations
with arrays, 200-205
output errors with, 375
See also Arithmetic operations
CALL (Call a Program) operation, 297-298
APIs, 303-305
defined, 297
dynamic binding, 296
flow of control, 296
LR indicator, 298
PARMs, 300, 302
specification, 297
CALLB (Call a Bound Module) operation, 298-299
defined, 298
flow of control, 296
format, 299
PARMs, 300, 302
specification, 299
static binding, 296-297
Calling
external routine, 303
programs, 297-298
RPG program from CL program, 303

sharing data and, 299-302
See also CALL (Call a Program) operation; CALLB (Call a Bound Module) operation
CAnn (Command Attention), 158, 163
coding, 163
CASE logic, 77
coding simplification, 78-80
Case sensitivity, 19, 22
CASxx (Conditionally Select Subroutines) operation, 79-80
layout, 80
CAT (Concatenate) operation, 323-324
CFnn (Command Function), 158, 163
coding, 163
CHAIN (Random Retrieval from a File) operation, 135-136
defined, 135
subfiles and, 269
successful, 135, 138
unsuccessful, 136
Character comparisons, 73
Character fields, 22
maximum length, 46
value assignment, 60-61
See also Fields
Character literals, 60-61
defined, 60
uses, 60
See also Literals
Character strings
base, 281
compare, 280
concatenating, 285
RPG III manipulation of, 323-324
scanning, 280-282
CHECK (Check) operation, 282-284, 290
checking direction, 283
example use, 284
format, 282
indicator, 283
SCAN vs., 283
specification, 283
starting location, 283

uses, 283
CHECK keyword, 166-167
defined, 167
parameter values, 167
Check-protection, 38
CHECKR (Check Reverse) operation, 284, 290
CL commands
ADDBKP, 376
ADDTRC, 377
CLRTRCDTA, 377
CRTBNDRPG, 297
CRTDTAARA, 305
CRTLF, 113
CRTPF, 113
CRTPGM, 297, 355
CRTRPGMOD, 296
CVTRPGSRC, 315-316
DSPPGMVAR, 377
DSPTRC, 377
DSPTRCDTA, 377
ENDDBG, 376
RMVBKP, 376
RMVTRC, 377
STRDBG, 376
STRSEU, 359
CL Programming, 378
CLEAR (Clear to Default Value) operation, 237-238
defined, 237
specification, 238
CLOSE operation, 144
CLRTRCDTA (Clear Trace Data) command, 377
Coding
defined, 10
display files, 155
edit words, 39
indicators, 32
keywords, 163
multiple-level control-break problem, 91
simple logical files, 107
Colon (:)
character strings and, 280, 281

separator character, 218
Combined files, 161
table files as, 196
See also Display files
Comma (,) separator character, 218
Command keys, 164
Commands. *See* CL commands
Comment lines, 34, 40
blank, 35
on calculations, 55
Common User Access (CUA), 177-178, 179
panel layout, 177-178
standards, 178
Communications, interprogram, 295-309
COMP (Compare) operation, 336
COMP keyword, 109, 166-167
defined, 166
format, 166
relational operators, 167
Compare string, 280
Compile errors, 369
correcting, 365
See also Errors
Compile listing, 369-370
cross-reference listing, 370
program listing, 370
Compilers, 1, 13
Compile-time arrays, 197, 208
Compile-time tables, 186-187
alternating format, 190
CTDATA keyword, 186
data entry, 186
defined, 186
PERRCD keyword, 186-187
uses, 187
Compiling, 369
defined, 11
Composite, 100
Composite keys, 103
defined, 136
referencing, 136-138
Concatenation, 100
Conditioning indicators, 168-170, 179

multiple, 168
RPG II, 336
status of, 168
turning on/off, 168
See also Indicators
CONST keyword, 225
Constants
defined, 27
entering, 27-28
named, 225-227, 244
numeric, 225
See also Literals
Control Language (CL), 349
See also CL commands
Control-break logic, 87-92
overview, 87-88
pseudocode, 88
routines, 88-89
sample program, 89-90
Control-break problem, 87
multiple-level, 90
coding, 91
logic, 91-92
Cross-reference listing, 370
CRTBNDRPG (Create Bound RPG
Program) command, 297
CRTDTAARA (Create Data Area)
command, 305
CRTLF (Create Logical File) com-
mand, 113
CRTPF (Create Physical File) command, 113
CRTPGM (Create Program) com-
mand, 297, 355
CRTRPGMOD (Create RPG Module)
command, 296
CTDATA keyword, 186
**CTDATA record, 186, 193
Cursor, blinking, 164, 170
CVTRPGSRC (Convert RPG Source)
command, 315-316

D

Data
character, 103-104

files, 5-6
hierarchy, 5-6
integer, 22
invalid, 170
multicolumn, 193, 194
passing, between programs, 299-302
validation, 166, 170
volatile, 187
See also Data items; Data types
Data areas, 305-309
accessing, 306-309
with data structure, 306, 307
with *NAMVAR DEFINE, 306-309
creating, 305
data structures, 306, 309
defined, 305
explicit I/O of, 307
local (LDAs), 305, 309
retrieving, 307-308
unlocking, 308-309
updating, 308
Data Description Specification (DDS),
101-102, 122, 178
CA03 line, 158
comment lines, 101
defined, 101
field definition lines, 101
fields
beginning position, 118
ending position, 118
key specifications, 101
keywords. *See* Keywords
lowercase characters and, 103
record format descriptions, 101
Data File Utility (DFU), 113
Data items
bytes, inspecting, 278-284
defining, 275
size of, 275-278
See also Array(s); Data structures;
Fields; Literals; Named constants;
Table(s)
Data structures, 198-199, 227-241, 244
data-area, 306, 309
defined, 227

defining, 198, 228
file-information, 239-240
initializing, 235-236
multiple-occurrence, 232-235
names of, 228
overlay, 198
program-status, 241
simple, 228-231
subfields, 228-229
Data types, 217-225
changing, 62, 64
combined files, 161
conversion of, 61-63
data storage and, 103-106
date, 218-219, 244
DBCS, 222, 244
default length, 218
defined, 217
display format, 218
graphic, 222, 244
list of, 217
with literals, 220-221
numeric, 104
pointer, 222-225, 244
separator characters, 218
time, 218-219, 244
timestamp, 218-219, 244
Database design, 116, 122
Database files. *See* Files; Logical files;
Physical files
Date
current, 27
data type, 218-219, 244
display formats, 218
displaying, 168
duration codes, 219
field testing, 279-280
operations, 219-221
separator characters, 218
slashes, 37
See also Time
DATE keyword, 118, 168
DATFMT keyword, 218
DBCS (Double-Byte Character Set),
222, 244

data manipulation, 222
DDS. *See* Data Description Specification (DDS)
DDS Reference, 110, 163, 269
Debug mode, 376-377
Debugging, 369-378
    defined, 10
Decimal representation, 289
Decision operations, 74-80
    See also Selection operations
DEFINE operation
    *LIKE, 317
    *NAMVAR, 306-309
Definition Specifications, 45-46, 64
    in array definitions, 196-197
    continuation line, 184
    defined, 45
    runtime arrays and, 197
    in table definitions, 184
    See also Specifications
DELETE (Delete Record) operation, 140-141
DESCEND keyword, 185
Desk checking, 372
Detail lines, 24, 25-26
Digits, 104
DIM keyword, 185, 190
Display attributes, 165-166
    defined, 165
    list of, 165
    using, 166
Display files, 155-163, 178
    coding, 155
    contents of, 155-156
    defined, 155
    field-level keywords, 164-168
    fields, 157
        defining, 177
        numeric output, 164-165
    file-level keywords, 163-164
    READ/WRITE operations and, 162
    record formats, 156, 159
        DDS, 157, 159
        identifier, 157
    record-level keywords, 164

See also Display attributes; Interactive applications
DIV (Divide) operation, 50-51, 55, 317
Division
    result field size, 53-54
    rounding and, 54-55
DO (Do) operation, 82-84, 92
    counters and, 83
    format, 82-83
    loops, 83-84
Documentation
    external, 10
    internal, 10, 33-34
    overview, 34
Dollar signs
    edit words and, 39
    fixed, 7, 38
    floating, 8, 38, 58
    printing, 38
DOU (Do Until) operation, 81-82, 92
    flowchart, 82
    trailing decision loop, 81
DOUxx operation, 319-321
DOW (Do While) operation, 33, 80-81, 92
    with AND/OR operators, 81
    flow chart, 82
    leading decision loop, 81
    use example, 81
DOWxx operation, 319-321
DSPATR keyword, 165-166
    (PC), 173
    (PR), 172, 174
DSPPGMVAR (Display Program Variable) command, 377
DSPTRC (Display Trace) command, 377
DSPTRCDTA (Display Trace Data) command, 377
Duration codes, 219
Dynamic binding, 296

E

EBCDIC (Extended Binary Coded Decimal Interchange Code), 104, 222

upper limit, 222
Edit codes, 36-38, 40
    associating, 36
    DDS and, 165
    defined, 29
    list, 37-38
    See also Edit words
Edit words, 38-39, 40
    blanks, 210
    coding, 39
    DDS and, 165
    defined, 38
    dollar sign and, 39
    template, 39
    See also Edit codes
Editing, 36
Editor, 10
    defined, 359
    See also Source Entry Utility (SEU)
EDTCDE keyword, 118-119, 164-165
    format, 165
    using, 165
EDTWRD keyword, 118-119, 164-165
    format, 165
    using, 165
%ELEM (Number of Elements) function, 277, 290
    using, 277
ELSE operation, 74
END operation, 320
ENDCS operation, 80
ENDDBG (End Debug) command, 376
ENDDO (End Do Group) operation, 33, 84
ENDIF operation, 74, 76
End-of-file condition, 30
ENDSL operation, 79
ENDSR operation, 86
ERRMSG keyword, 167
    conditioning, 169
    indicator, 167
Error indicators, 242-243
Error messages, 163, 171
    displaying, 173
    uses of, 167

Errors, 11
   compile, 365, 369
   handling, 242-244
   I/O, 144
   logic, 10, 13, 370
   output, 372-375
   program, 243
   runtime, 370-372
   syntax, 10, 11, 13, 369-370
EVAL (Evaluate Expression) operation, 33, 64
   + with, 285
   advantage over arithmetic operators,
      318
   assigning command to parameter,
      304-305
   character assignment, 60-61
   continuation line and, 49
   date/time field value assignment,
      221
   format, 47
   free-form entry, 49
   in numerical field value assignment,
      47
   right-padding, 61
   using, for arithmetic, 48-49
EXCEPT (Calculation Time Output)
   operation, 32, 120, 139
   updating through, 142
   writing records to database file, 139
   writing records to printer file, 120
Exception lines, 25
EXFMT operation, 162
Exponentiation (**) operator, 48
EXPORT keyword, 302
EXSR (Execute Subroutine) operation,
   86
External documentation, 10
Externally described files, 99-122
   advantages, 99
   arrays and, 231
   defined, 99
   printer, 116-120
   programmer efficiency and, 100
   RPG IV programming with, 113-114

See also Logical files; Physical files
EXTRCT (Extract Part of a
   Date/Time Item) operation, 220
   defined, 220
   duration codes, 219
   use of, 220

F
F3 key, 158
Field-reference files, 114
   example illustration, 115
   name of, 115
   using, 115-116
   See also Files
Fields
   character, 22, 46, 60-61
   character manipulation, 284-288
   data type of, 22
   DDS
      beginning position, 118
      ending position, 118
   defined, 5
   defining, 5, 103
      through referencing, 160
   display file, 157
      defining, 177
      numeric output, 164-165
   indicators as, 32
   initializing, 237
   input-capable, protecting, 172
   location of, 22
   name of, 22, 23, 27
   numeric, 22, 46
   overlapping, 231
   PAGE, 27, 118
   result, 52-54
   sizes of, 51-52
      result, 52-54
   stand-alone, 45-46
   UDATE, 27, 118
   work, 316-317
   See also Records
FIFO (First-In-First-Out), 129
Figurative constants, 63, 64
   defined, 63

list of, 63
   See also specific constants
File Description Specifications, 17,
   18-20, 39
   defined, 17
   Device, 20
   File Designation, 20
   File Format, 20
   File Name, 19
   File Type, 19
   layout, 19
   Record Length, 20
   See also Specifications
File formats, 20
File locking, 142-144
   defined, 142
*FILE objects, 349
File-information data structures,
   239-240
   defined, 239
   example code, 240
   linking, 239
   status codes, 240
   See also Data structures
Files
   access, 129-138
   closing, 144
   combined, 161, 196
   data, 5-6
   defined, 5
   designation of, 20
   display, 155-163
   externally described, 99-122
   field-reference, 114
   full procedural, 20
   input, 19, 114
   maintaining, interactively, 170-177
   master, 5
   names of, 19, 21, 24-25
   opening, 144
   output, 19, 138-140
   printer, 116-120
   spooled, 356
   types of, 19
   update, 140-142

See also Logical files; Physical files
Fixed dollar sign, 7, 38
  specifying, 38
Fixed-logic cycle, 4, 25, 343
  control breaks and, 332-336
  detail-time, 332
  interactive applications and, 342
  non-use of, 335-336
  procedural techniques vs., 342
  pseudocode, 331
  RPG II and, 328
  total-time, 332
Fixed-position entries, 17
Floating dollar sign, 8, 38, 58
  specifying, 38
Flow of control, 295-296
Fourth Generation Languages
  (4GLs), 1
Free-form entry, 47, 48
FROMFILE, 187, 188, 190, 196
Full procedural, 20
Function keys
  associating, 158, 163
  SEU, 363-364
Functions. *See* Built-in functions

G

GOTO operation, 72, 321-323
  with IF logic, 322
  RPG II decision logic, 338
  unconditional transfer of control,
    322
  uses, 322
GOTO-less programming. *See* Structured programming
Graphic data type, 222, 244

H

Half-adjusting, 54
  See also Rounding
Heading lines, 25-26, 58
Help, on-line, 269-271
  building, 269
  specifications, 270-271
  subfiles and, 271

Help key, 269, 271
HELP keyword, 269
Help-specification format, 270
Hexadecimal system, 289
  value manipulation, 289
Hierarchical decomposition, 85
High-level languages (HLLs), 1
High-order bits, 104
*HIVAL figurative constant, 63
HLPARA keyword, 270
HLPRCD keyword, 269, 270
Hyphen. *See* Minus sign (−)

I

I/O errors, 144
I/O operations
  resulting indicators and, 144
  RPG IV formats for, 149
  update files and, 140-142
IF logic, output errors with, 375
IF operation, 73, 92
  compound, 375
  with ElSE, 74
  matching, 375
  nested, 76-77, 375
  page overflow and, 78-80
IFxx operation, 319-320
ILE RPG/400 Reference, 218, 221, 239,
  241
IMPORT keyword, 302
*IN array, 210
IN (Retrieve a Data Area) operation,
  307-308
Indexes, array, 200
Indicators, 31-32
  as array elements, 210
  associating, with output line, 329
  coding, 32
  conditioning, 168-170, 179, 336
  defined, 2, 31
  error, 242-243
  as fields, 32
  level, 333-335
  numbered, 211, 328
  overflow, 78

resulting, 32, 339-340
  RPG II and, 336
INFDS keyword, 239
Infinite loops, 370
  diagnosing, 371-372
  example code, 371
  See also Errors; Loops
INFSR keyword, 243
Initialization, 235-239
  data structure, 235-236
  explicit, 237
  field, 237
  subfields, 235-237
  subroutine, 237
Input files, 19, 114
  operations for, 129-138
  See also Files
Input Specifications, 21-23, 39
  Decimal Positions, 22
  defined, 21
  field description entries, 22-23
  Field Location, 22
  Field Name, 22
  File Name, 21
  layout, 21
  record identification entries, 21
  record identifying indicator, 328
  Sequence, 21
  See also Specifications
Integer data, 22
Integrated Language Environment
  (ILE), 296
  defined, 3
Interactive applications, 2
  fixed-logic cycle and, 342
  uses, 179
  See also Display files
Interactive file maintenance, 170-177
Internal documentation, 33-34
  defined, 10
INZ keyword, 235-236
  uses, 235-236
  using, 236
*INZSR subroutine, 237, 238, 244
ITER operation, 84-85

Iteration
  defined, 80
  operations, 80-84
    formats for, 93
    RPG II and, 340-342
Iteration control structure, 71
  illustrated, 72

J

JFILE keyword, 112
JOIN keyword, 112
Join-logical files, 111-112
  defined, 111

K

Key field, 100
  name of, 103
Key lists, 136-137
  partial, 137-138
Key sequence, 100
Keyboard-shift attribute, 157-158
  defined, 157
  value list, 158
Keywords
  ALT, 190
  ASCEND, 185, 195
  BLINK, 164
  CAnn, 163
  CFnn, 163
  CHECK, 166-167
  coding, 163
  COMP, 109, 166
  CONST, 225
  CTDATA, 186
  DATE, 118, 168
  DATFMT, 218
  defined, 102
  DESCEND, 185
  DIM, 185, 190
  DSPATR, 165-166
  EDTCDE, 118-119, 164-165
  EDTWRD, 118-119, 164-165
  ERRMSG, 167, 169
  EXPORT, 302
  field-level, 102, 164-168

  file-level, 102, 163-164
  FROMFILE, 187, 188, 190, 196
  HELP, 269
  HLPARA, 270
  HLPRCD, 269, 270
  IMPORT, 302
  INFDS, 239
  INFSR, 243
  INZ, 235-236
  JFILE, 112
  JOIN, 112
  LIKE, 226-227
  MSGLOC, 163
  OCCURS, 232
  OFLIND, 78, 119
  OVERLAY, 164, 229-230, 256
  PAGNBR, 118
  PERRCD, 186-187, 190
  PRINT, 164
  PROCPTR, 223
  RANGE, 109, 166
  record-level, 102, 164
  REF, 115, 160, 253
  ROLLDOWN, 263
  ROLLUP, 259, 262
  SFILE, 257
  SFL, 253
  SFLCLR, 254-255
  SFLCTL, 254
  SFLDSP, 254
  SFLDSPCTL, 254
  SFLEND, 259-260
  SFLPAG, 254
  SFLRCDNBR, 260, 263
  SFLSIZ, 254
  SKIPA, 119
  SKIPB, 119
  SPACEA, 119
  SPACEB, 119
  TEXT, 103
  TIME, 168
  TIMFMT, 218
  TOFILE, 188, 190, 196
  UNIQUE, 102
  validation, 170

  VALUES, 108, 166, 167
  VLDCMDKEY, 164
KFLD (Define Parts of a Key) operation, 136-137, 267
KLIST (Define a Composite Key)
  operation, 136-137, 267
  declaring, 137
  partial key lists and, 137-138

L

Languages
  Fourth Generation (4GL), 1
  high-level (HLL), 1
  procedural, 1
  RPG, 1-4, 315
Leading decision loop, 81
LEAVE operation, 84-85
Length notation, 228, 229
  supplementing, 229
Level checking, 114
Level indicators, 333-335
  uses, 334
  See also Indicators
LIKE keyword, 226-227
  specification, 226
  uses, 227
List panels, 251
Literals
  character, 60-61
  data types with, 220-221
  hex, 289
  numeric, 46
  typed, 220-221
  See also Constants
Local data areas (LDAs), 305, 309
  *NAMVAR DEFINE operation with,
    305
  See also Data areas
Locking, 142-144
  file, 142-144
  record, 142-144
Logic errors, 370
  defined, 10, 13
  types of, 370

See also Output errors; Runtime errors
Logic structures, 71
  illustrated, 72
Logical files, 100-101, 106-112, 122
  creating, 113
  defined, 100, 106
  join, 111-112
  multiple-record formats, 110-111
  record selection/omission, 108-110
  sequentially reading, 111
  simple, 106-108
    coding, 107
    defining, 106
    limiting access and, 108
    restricting, 107
  See also Physical files
LOOKUP operation, 188-189
  arrays and, 208-209
  indicator, 188
  in range tables, 195
Look-ups
  array, 208-209
    with index, 208
    starting, at beginning, 208
    using, 209
    without index, 208
  multiple data structure, 233
  table, 188-189
    code, 189
    multiple related, 191-194
    single table, 189
    successful, 191
    two related, 189-191
    unsuccessful, 191
Looping, 319-323
Loops, 84-85
  DO, 83-84
  early exits and, 84-85
  infinite, 370, 371-372
  output errors with, 374-375
*LOVAL figurative constant, 63, 131, 237
Low-order bits, 104

M
Maintenance, 10
  interactive file, 170-177
  program
    pseudocode, 174-175
    source code, 175-177
  programming, 33
Master files, 5
Members. *See* Source members
Message line, location of, 163
Messages, displaying
  with PDM, 357
  with Programmer Menu, 351
Minus sign (−)
  constants and, 28
  continuation character, 60
  floating, 37
  separator character, 218
  subtraction operator, 48
  zoned-decimal representation and, 105
Modular programming, 295-296, 309
  advantages, 295
  defined, 295
  using, 302-303
*MODULE objects, 349
  creating, 355
  temporary, 351
Modules
  binding, 355
  calling, 297
    dynamically bound, 297-298
    statically bound, 297, 298-299
MOVE (Move) operation, 61-63, 64, 193, 325
  for changing data types, 61-63
  numeric fields and, 62
  use examples, 62
MOVEA (Move Array) operation, 202-205, 325-326
  defined, 202
  examples, 203-205
  extender (P), 204
  manipulating data field portions and, 205

specification, 202
MOVEL (Move Left) operation, 62-63, 64, 193, 325
MSGLOC keyword, 163
MULT (Multiply) operation, 51, 318
  defined, 318
  forms, 318
Multiple-level control-break problem, 90
  coding, 91
  logic, 91-92
Multiple-occurrence data structures, 232-235
  active occurrence in, 233
  defined, 232
  establishing occurrence in, 232
  look-ups in, 233
  subscripts/pointers and, 232
  two-dimensional array capabilities, 234
  See also Data structures
Multiplication, result field size, 53
MVR (Move Remainder) operation, 50-51, 55

N
Named constants, 225-227, 244
  advantage of, 226
  defined, 225
  defining, 225
  maximum length, 225
  numeric values, 225
  uses, 226
  using, 226-227
  See also Constants
*NAMVAR DEFINE operation, 306-309
Negative values, 8
Nested IFs, 76-77, 375
*NULL figurative constant, 63, 237
Numbered indicators, 211, 328
Numeric fields, 22
  maximum length, 46
  MOVE operation and, 62
  See also Truncation
Numeric literals, 46

decimal points and, 46
defined, 46
examples of, 46
justification, 46
signs and, 46
use restrictions, 46
See also Literals

O

Object code, 11
Object types, 349
OCCUR operation, 232
OCCURS keyword, 232
*OFF figurative constant, 63
OFLIND keyword, 78, 119
*ON figurative constant, 63
On-line help, 269-271
    building, 269
    specifications, 270-271
    subfiles and, 271
OPEN operation, 144
Operation extender, 54
Operations, 31, 32-33
    ADD, 51, 317-318
    ADDDUR, 219-220
    ANDxx, 320-321
    arithmetic, 47-51
    array, 201-205
    BEGSR, 86
    CABxx, 321, 322-323
    CALL, 296, 297-298
    CALLB, 296, 298-299
    CASxx, 79-80, 92
    CAT, 323-324
    CHAIN, 135-136, 138, 269
    CHECK, 282-284, 290
    CHECKR, 284, 290
    CLEAR, 237-238
    CLOSE, 144
    COMP, 336
    date/time, 219-221
    decision, 74-80, 93
    DEFINE, 306-309, 317
    DELETE, 140-141
    DIV, 50-51, 55

DO, 82-84, 92
DOU, 81-82, 92
DOUxx, 319-321
DOW, 33, 80-81, 92
DOWxx, 319-321
ELSE, 74
END, 320
ENDCS, 80
ENDDO, 33
ENDIF, 74, 76
ENDSL, 79
ENDSR, 86
EVAL, 33, 47, 48-49, 60-61, 64, 221
EXCEPT, 32, 120, 139
EXFMT, 162
EXSR, 86
EXTRCT, 220
formats for, 65, 93, 149
GOTO, 72, 321-323
IF, 74, 76-77, 78-80, 92
IFxx, 319-320
IN, 307-308
ITER, 84-85
iteration, 80-84, 93
KFLD, 136-137, 267
KLIST, 136-137, 267
LEAVE, 84-85
LOOKUP, 188-189, 195, 208-209
MOVE, 61-63, 64, 193, 325
MOVEA, 202-205, 325-326
MOVEL, 62-63, 64, 193, 325
MULT, 51, 318
MVR, 50-51, 55
OCCUR, 232
OPEN, 144
OR, 75-76
ORxx, 320-321
OTHER, 79
OUT, 308
PARM, 300-302, 309
PLIST, 300-301, 309
READ, 32-33, 129-130, 162
READC, 266-268
READE, 133, 138
READP, 134

READPE, 134
RESET, 238-239
RETURN, 33
SCAN, 280-282, 290
SELECT, 79, 92
selection, 74-80
SETGT, 132-133
SETLL, 130-131, 138
SETOFF, 340-341
SETON, 340-341
SORTA, 202
SQRT, 50
SUB, 51, 318
SUBDUR, 220
SUBST, 323-324
TAG, 322
TEST, 279-280, 290
TESTN, 278-279, 290
UNLOCK, 143, 308-309
UPDATE, 141-142, 269
WHEN, 79, 92
WHENxx, 319-321
WRITE, 120, 139-140, 162, 269
XFOOT, 201-202
XLATE, 287-288, 290
Z-ADD, 319
Z-SUB, 319
OR operator, 75
    conditioning indicators and, 168
    DOW operation with, 81
    with other operations, 76
    using, 76
    See also AND operator
ORxx operation, 320-321
OTHER operation, 79
OUT (Write Out a Data Area) operation, 308
Output
    checking, 372-373
    editing, 7, 36
    printing, 355-357
    queue, displaying, 351
    viewing, 355-357
Output errors, 372-375
    calculations, 375

correcting, 373-375
defined, 372
detecting, 372-373
field problems, 373-374
IF logic, 375
loops, 374-375
Output files, 19
operations, 138-140
Output Specifications, 23-29, 39-40
Constants, 27-28
continuation form, 28
defined, 23
detail line, 24
Edit Codes, 29
End Position, 28-29
Exception Name, 25
field description entries, 26-29
Field Name, 27
File Name, 24-25
layout, 24, 27, 28
record identification entries, 24-26
Space and Skip Entries, 25-26
Type, 25
See also Specifications
Overflow indicators, 78
Overlay, 198
field definitions, 231
subfields, 229
OVERLAY keyword, 164, 229-230, 256
data name, 230
example use, 229-230
length notation and, 229

P

Packed-decimal data type, 104, 105
%PADDR function, 299
PAGE field, 27, 118
Page overflow, 78-80
PAGNBR keyword, 118
PARM (Identify Parameters) operation, 300-302, 309
data names, 300
factor 2 with, 301
list of, 300
passing and, 301

result field entry, 300
Passing
by reference, 301
by value, 301
Period (.) separator character, 218
PERRCD keyword, 186-187, 190
compile-time tables, 186-187
pre-runtime tables, 187-188
*PGM objects, 296, 297, 349
binding module into, 351
Phantom updates, 142-144
Physical files, 100-101, 122
creating, 113
defined, 100
defining, 102-103
record access, 100
record format, 102
source statements, 102
See also Logical files
PLIST (Identify a Parameter List)
operation, 300-301, 309
PARMs within, 301
specification, 301
Plus sign (+)
addition operator, 48
character string concatenation, 285
continuation character, 28, 60, 225
zoned-decimal representation and,
105
Pointers
basing, 222-223, 224
data types, 222-225
defining, 222-223
procedure, 222-223
Pre-runtime arrays, 197
See also Array(s)
Pre-runtime tables, 186, 187-188
alternating format, 190
defined, 186
FROMFILE keyword, 187
PERRCD keyword, 187
TOFILE keyword, 188
See also Table(s)
Priming read, 31
Print key, 164

enabling, 170
PRINT keyword, 164
Printer files
externally described, 116-120
multiple record formats, 117
See also Files
Printer spacing charts (PSCs), 7
arrays and, 210
dollar signs, 7-8
negative values, 8
sample illustration, 9
Xs, 7
zeros, 7
Procedural languages, 1
Procedure pointers, 222-223
defined, 222
fixed length, 223
See also Pointers
PROCPTR keyword, 223
Program Development Cycle, 9-10, 13
defined, 9
documenting the program, 10
entering the program, 10
maintaining the program, 10
problem definition, 9
solution design, 9, 29
testing/debugging program, 10
writing the program, 10
Program listing, 370
Program variables, 4-5
changing, 377
defined, 4
displaying, 377
See also Fields
Programmer Menu, 349, 350-351
F6, 351
F18, 351
illustrated, 350
Option 3 (Create an object from
source file), 351
Option 4 (Call a program), 351
Option 8 (Edit a source file member), 350
using, 350

See also Programming Development
   Manager (PDM)
Programming
   modular, 295-296
   specifications, 6-9
Programming Development Manager
   (PDM), 349, 352-357
   accessing, 352
   Assign Output to a Printer screen,
     357
   Confirm Compile of Member
     screen, 354
   menu, 352
   Option 2 (Work with objects),
     354-357
   Option 3 (Work with members),
     352-354
   Specify Members to Work With
     screen, 353
   Work with Members Using PDM
     screen, 353
   Work with Objects Using PDM
     screen, 355
   Work with Printer Output screen,
     356
   See also Programmer Menu
Programs
   calling, 297-298
   debugging, 369-378
   developing on AS/400, 349-357
   editing, 350, 352-354
   entering, 10-11, 350, 352-354
   executable, compiling/creating,
     351, 354
   maintaining, 10
   passing data between, 299-302
   running, 351, 354-355
   step flowchart, 12
   testing, 10-11, 369-378
Program-status data structures, 241
   defined, 241
   subfields, 241
   See also Data structures
Pseudocode
   calculation example, 56

defined, 30
fixed-logic cycle, 331
for loading subfiles, 257
maintenance program, 174-175
of two-level control-break problem,
   91
*PSSR subroutine, 243-244
   design logic, 243
   error handling and, 242-244

Q

QCMDEXC API, 304
QRPGLESRC, 359
QUSCMDLN API, 304
QUSCRTUS API, 304
QUSRLSPL API, 303
QUSRSPLA API, 303

R

Random access, 135-138
   composite keys and, 136-138
   defined, 135
RANGE keyword, 109, 166
   with character fields, 166
   defined, 166
Range tables, 194-196
   accessing, 195
   defined, 194
   sequence entry, 195
   See also Table(s)
READ (Read Sequentially) operation,
   31, 32-33, 129-130
   display files and, 162
   errors and, 129-130
READC (Read Next Changed
   Record) operation, 266-268
   use of, 266
READE (Read Equal Key) operation,
   133, 138
READP (Read Prior Record) operation, 134
READPE (Read Prior Equal) operation, 134
Record formats, 6
   display files, 156, 159

DDS, 157, 159
identifier, 157
methods of describing, 7
multiple, 6
   logical files with, 110-111
   printer files with, 117
physical files, 102
subfile, 253-254, 272
   control, 254-255
   footer, 256
See also Records
Record identifying indicator, 328
Record locking, 142-144
   access and waiting problems,
     142-143
   defined, 142
   update procedures and, 143
Records
   accessing with composite key, 136
   adding, 177
   **CTDATA, 186, 193
   defined, 5
   deleting, 140-141
   existence of, 131
   length of, 20
   output, end position, 28-29
   positioning to first, 131
   selection/omission, 108-110
   sequence of, 21
   sequential read of, 133-134
   updating, 141-142, 177
   writing
     to database file, 139
     to printer file, 120
     to screens, 162
   See also Fields; Record formats
Recursion, 87
Redundancy, 99
REF keyword, 115, 160, 253
Relational comparisons, 72-74
   defined, 73
   list of, 73
Relative record number, 256-257
   associating, 257
   defined, 256

Report Layout Utility (RLU), 116
Report Program Generator. *See* RPG
Reserved words, 27
RESET (Reset to Initial Value) operation, 238-239
  defined, 238
  format, 238
  specification, 239
Result fields, 52-54
  for addition, 52-53
  for division, 53-54
  for multiplication, 53
  for subtraction, 53
  See also Fields
Resulting indicators, 32
  automatic on/off, 339
  RPG II, 339-340
  See also Indicators
RETURN (Return to Caller) operation, 33
RMVBKP (Remove Breakpoint) command, 376
RMVTRC (Remove Trace) command, 377
ROLLDOWN keyword, 263
ROLLUP keyword, 259, 262
Rounding, 54-55
  operation extender, 54
RPG
  add-ons, 315
  backward-compatibility, 315
  characteristics, 2
  defined, 1-2
  history of, 1-4
RPG II, 2, 315
  decisions in, 336-338
  familiarity with, 326
  GOTO decision logic, 338
  indicator logic, 337
  indicators and, 336
  iteration and, 340-342
  resulting indicators, 339-340
  RPG IV vs., 327-330
RPG III, 3, 315

arithmetic/numeric assignment, 317-319
  delimiting tables/arrays, 324
  holdovers from, 316
  looping and selecting, 319-323
  moving data in, 325-326
  string manipulation, 323-324
  structured operations, 320-321
  work field definitions, 316-317
RPG IV, 3
  backward-compatibility, 315
  compatibility with, 315-316
  RPG II vs., 327-330
RPG/400, 3
Runtime arrays, 197-200
  data structures and, 198-199
  defined, 197
  Definition Specifications and, 197
  input data and, 197-200
  loading, 199
  See also Array(s)
Runtime errors, 370-372
  defined, 370
  diagnosing, 371-372
  See also Errors

S

SCAN (Scan Character String) operation, 280-282, 290
  CHECK vs., 283
  defined, 280
  effects of, 282
  example use, 281
  result field, 281
  specification, 280
  starting location, 281
  uses, 283
Scope terminators, 320
Screen Design Aid (SDA), 155
Screens
  date/time display, 168
  design, 171
    CUA and, 177-178
  displaying, 156
  I/O, 162

panel layout, 177-178
  panel types, 177
  writing records to, 162
  See also Display files
SELECT (Conditionally Select Operations) operation, 79, 92
Selection control structure, 71
  illustrated, 72
Selection operations, 74-80
  CASxx, 79-80
  formats for, 93
  IF, 74, 76-77
  SELECT, 79
Separator characters, 218
Sequence control structure, 71
  illustrated, 72
Sequential access, 129-134
  defined, 129
Sequential flow of control, 72
SETGT (Set Greater Than) operation, 132-133
  defined, 133
  uses, 133
SETLL (Set Lower Limit) operation, 130-131, 138
  defined, 130
  uses, 131
SETOFF operation, 340-341
SETON operation, 340-341
SEU. *See* Source Entry Utility (SEU)
SFILE keyword, 257
SFL keyword, 253
SFLCLR keyword, 254-255
SFLCTL keyword, 254
SFLDSP keyword, 254
SFLDSPCTL keyword, 254
SFLEND keyword, 259-260
SFLPAG keyword, 254
SFLRCDNBR keyword, 260, 263
SFLSIZ keyword, 254
%SIZE (Number of Bytes) function, 276-277, 290
  examples, 277
  parameters, 276
  using, 276

SKIPA (SKIPB) keywords, 119
Skipping, 26
Slash (/)
    division operator, 48
    separator character, 218
SORTA (Sort an Array) operation,
  202
Source code
    copying portions of, 365
    defined, 11
    entering, 13
    for loading subfiles, 258
Source Entry Utility (SEU), 17, 359-367
    Browse/Copy Options screen, 365
    command line, 359, 364
    commands, 354
    defined, 359
    edit display mode, 362-363
    Edit screen, 360, 361, 366
    entering, 359
    Exit screen, 367
    exiting, 366-367
    function keys, 363-364
    prompt formats, 361
    prompts, 360-361
    screen illustration, 360
    sequence numbers, 360
    split screens, 364-366
    syntax error detection, 360
Source members
    compiling, 354
    defined, 11
    editing, 354
    entering, 354
SPACEA (SPACEB) keywords, 119
Spacing, 25-26
Specifications, 17-31, 39-40
    Calculation, 17, 29-31, 39, 336
    defined, 17
    Definition, 45-46, 64, 184
    example program, 18
    File Description, 17, 18-20, 39
    help, 270
    Input, 21-23, 39, 328
    order of, 35

Output, 23-29, 39-40
Spooled files, 356
SQRT (Square Root) operation, 50
Square root, calculating, 50
Stand-alone fields, 45-46
    defined, 45
    defining, 46
    See also Fields
Static binding, 296-297
Status codes, 241
    checking, 243
    subfield, 241
STRDBG (Start Debug) command,
  276, 376
Strings. See Character strings
STRSEU (Start SEU) command, 359
Structured design, 2-3, 71-72
    defined, 71
    logic structures, 71-72
Structured programming, 71-93
SUB (Subtract) operation, 51, 318
    defined, 318
    format, 318
SUBDUR (Subtract Duration) opera-
  tion, 220
    defined, 220
    duration codes, 219
    use of, 220
Subfields, 228-229, 244
    absolute notation, 228
    checking, 243
    defined outside data structure, 229
    initializing, 235-237
    length notation, 228, 229
    location of, 229
    numeric, 228-229
    overlapping, 231
    overlay, 229
    pre-defined, 241
    status-code, 241
    See also Data structures
Subfile(s), 251-269, 272
    change and, 266-269
    clearing, 254-255
    control record, 254

data transfer, 269
defined, 251
defining, 272
display, 254
display control, 254
ending, 259-260
help specification and, 271
loading, 255-259
    page at a time, 259-265
    pseudocode for, 257
    source code for, 258
for multiple records display, 253
page, 254
READC operation, 266-268
record formats, 253-254, 272
    control, 254-255
    footer, 256
record number, 260
record rolling, 259, 263
relative record number, 256-257
restarting, 264
size, 254, 259
    equals page, 263-265
    much bigger than page, 262-263
    one greater than page, 259-262
uses, 269
Subroutines, 79-80
    BEGSR operation, 86
    coding, 86
    control and, 86
    defined, 79, 86
    defining, 86-87
    ENDSR operation, 86
    *INZSR, 237, 238, 244
    other subroutines and, 87
    *PSSR, 243-244
Subschemas, 100
%SUBST (Substring) function,
  286-287, 290
    format, 286
    using, 287
SUBST (Substring) operation,
  323-324
Subtraction, result field size, 53
Syntax errors, 369-370

asterisk (*) marking, 370
defined, 10, 13, 369
list of, 11
SEU and, 369
severity, 370
See also Errors
System API Reference, 305

T
Table(s), 183-196
alternating format, 190-192
arrays vs., 211
changing values of, 196
compile-time, 186-187
data elements, 184
data order, 185
defined, 183
defining, 184-186
Definition Specifications and, 184
element indication, 185
entering values in, 185-186
example, 183
look-ups, 188-189
code, 189
multiple related, 191-194
single table, 189
successful, 191
two related, 189-191
unsuccessful, 191
multicolumn data, 193, 194
multiple related, 191-194
pre-runtime, 187-188
range, 194-196
representing, 183-184
RPG III and, 324
RPG IV, 184
table name, 185
two related, 189-191
uses, 211
volatile table, 187
See also Array(s)
TAG operation, 322
TEST (Test Date/Time/Timestamp)
operation, 279-280, 290
defined, 279

example use, 280
specification, 279
Testing, 10-11, 369-378
TESTN (Test Numeric) operation,
278-279, 290
defined, 278
indicators, 279
specification, 278
TEXT keyword, 108
Time
data type, 218-219, 244
display formats, 218
displaying, 168
duration codes, 219
field testing, 279-280
operations, 219
separator characters, 218
system, 168
See also Date
TIME keyword, 168
Timestamp data type, 218-219, 244
field testing, 279-280
TIMFMT keyword, 218
TOFILE keyword, 188, 190, 196
Top-down design, 85, 92
control-break logic, 87-92
defined, 85
Trailing decision loop, 81
Transaction files, 5
%TRIM function, 286, 290
%TRIML function, 286, 290
%TRIMR function, 286, 290
Truncation, 51-52
defined, 51
high-order, 51
low-order, 51
See also Numeric fields; Result fields
Two-dimensional arrays, 234
Typed literals, 220-221
defined, 220
examples, 221
using, 221
See also Literals

U
UDATE field, 27, 118
UIM (User Interface Manager), 269
UNIQUE keyword, 102
UNLOCK (Unlock a Data Area) oper-
ation, 143, 308-309
Update files, 140
UPDATE (Modify Existing Record)
operation, 141
function of, 141
subfiles and, 269
Updates
interactive, 170, 171
phantom, 142-144
User space, 303

V
Validation, 166, 170
keywords, 170
VALUES keyword, 108, 166, 167
defined, 166
Variables. See Program variables
Vertical alignment, 25
VLDCMDKEY keyword, 164

W
WHEN operation, 79, 92
WHENxx operation, 319-321
WHILE loops, 30
WRITE (Write a Record to a File)
operation, 120, 139-140
display files and, 162
subfiles and, 269
Writing
to database file, 139
to printer file, 120
to screens, 162

X
X edit code, 38
XFOOT (Sum the Elements of an
Array) operation, 201-202
defined, 201
specification, 202

XLATE (Translate Characters) operation, 287-288, 290
  defined, 287
  example use, 288
  operation extender (P), 288
  specification, 287

Y

Y edit code, 37

Z

Z edit code, 37-38
Z-ADD (Zero and Add) operation, 319
Zero balances, 37
*ZERO figurative constant, 63
Zero suppression, 7
Zone bits, 104
Zoned-decimal data type, 104, 105
  storage length, 106
Z-SUB (Zero and Subtract) operation, 319

Also Published by *NEWS/400*

APPLICATION DEVELOPER'S HANDBOOK FOR THE AS/400

Edited by Mike Otey, a **NEWS/400** *technical editor*

Explains how to effectively use the AS/400 to build reliable, flexible, and efficient business applications. Contains RPG/400 and CL coding examples and tips, and provides both step-by-step instructions and handy reference material. Includes diskette. 768 pages, 48 chapters.

C FOR RPG PROGRAMMERS

By Jennifer Hamilton, a **NEWS/400** *author*

Written from the perspective of an RPG programmer, this book includes side-by-side coding examples written in both C and RPG to aid comprehension and understanding, clear identification of unique C constructs, and a comparison of RPG op-codes to equivalent C concepts. Includes many tips and examples covering the use of C/400. 292 pages, 23 chapters.

COMMON-SENSE C
Advice and warnings for C and C++ programmers

By Paul Conte, a **NEWS/400** *technical editor*

C programming language has its risks; this book shows how C programmers get themselves into trouble, includes tips to help you avoid C's pitfalls, and suggests how to manage C and C++ application development. 100 pages, 9 chapters.

CONTROL LANGUAGE PROGRAMMING FOR THE AS/400

By Bryan Meyers and Dan Riehl, **NEWS/400** *technical editors*

This comprehensive CL programming textbook offers students up-to-the-minute knowledge of the skills they will need in today's MIS environment. Progresses methodically from CL basics to more complex processes and concepts, guiding readers toward a professional grasp of CL programming techniques and style. 512 pages, 25 chapters.

DDS PROGRAMMING FOR DISPLAY & PRINTER FILES

By James Coolbaugh

Offers a thorough, straightforward explanation of how to use Data Description Specifications (DDS) to program display files and printer files. Covers basic to complex tasks using DDS functions. The author uses DDS programming examples for CL and RPG extensively throughout the book, and you can put these examples to use immediately. Focuses on topics such as general screen presentations, the A specification, defining data on the screen, record-format and field definitions, defining data fields, using indicators, data and text attributes, cursor and keyboard control, editing data, validity checking, response keywords, and function keys. A complimentary diskette includes all the source code presented in the book. 446 pages, 13 chapters.

DESKTOP GUIDE TO CL PROGRAMMING

By Bryan Meyers, a **NEWS/400** *technical editor*

This first book of the **NEWS/400** *Technical Reference Series* is packed with easy-to-find notes, short explanations, practical tips, answers to most of your everyday questions about CL, and CL code segments you can use in your own CL programming. Complete "short reference" lists every command and explains the most-often-used ones, along with names of the files they use and the MONMSG messages to use with them. On-line Windows Help diskette available. 205 pages, 36 chapters.

DESKTOP GUIDE TO AS/400 PROGRAMMERS' TOOLS

By Dan Riehl, a **NEWS/400** *technical editor*

This second book of the **NEWS/400** *Technical Reference Series* gives you the "how-to" behind all the tools included in *Application Development ToolSet/400* (ADTS/400), IBM's Licensed Program Product for Version 3 of OS/400; includes Source Entry Utility (SEU), Programming Development Manager (PDM), Screen Design Aid (SDA), Report Layout Utility (RLU), File Compare/Merge Utility (FCMU) — *new in V3R1*, and Interactive Source Debugger — *new in V3R1*. Highlights topics and functions specific to Version 3 of OS/400. On-line Windows Help diskette available. 266 pages, 30 chapters.

DESKTOP GUIDE TO THE S/36

By Mel Beckman, Gary Kratzer, and Roger Pence, **NEWS/400** *technical editors*

This definitive S/36 survival manual includes practical techniques to supercharge your S/36, including ready-to-use information for maximum system performance tuning, effective application development, and smart Disk Data Management. Includes a review of two popular Unix-based S/36 work-alike migration alternatives. Diskette contains ready-to-run utilities to help you save machine time and implement power programming techniques such as External Program Calls. 387 pages, 21 chapters.

IMPLEMENTING AS/400 SECURITY, SECOND EDITION

A practical guide to implementing, evaluating, and auditing your AS/400 security strategy

By Wayne Madden, a **NEWS/400** *technical editor*

Concise and practical, this second edition brings together in one place the fundamental AS/400 security tools and experience-based recommendations that you need and also includes specifics on the latest security enhancements available in OS/400 Version 3 Release 1. Completely updated from the first edition, this is the only source for the latest information about how to protect your system against attack from its increasing exposure to hackers. 389 pages, 16 chapters.

AN INTRODUCTION TO COMMUNICATIONS FOR THE AS/400

By Ruggero Adinolfi; Technical editor, John Enck, a **NEWS/400** *technical editor*

This guide to basic communications concepts and how they operate on the IBM AS/400 outlines the rich mix of communications capabilities designed into the AS/400 and relates them to the concepts that underlie the various network environments. 183 pages, 13 chapters.

INSIDE THE AS/400

An in-depth look at the AS/400's design, architecture, and history

By Frank G. Soltis

The inside story every AS/400 developer has been waiting for, told by Dr. Frank G. Soltis, IBM's AS/400 chief architect. Never before has IBM provided an in-depth look at the AS/400's design, architecture, and history. This authoritative book does just that — and also looks at some of the people behind the scenes who created this revolutionary system for you. Whether you are an executive looking for a high-level overview or a "bit-twiddling techie" who wants all the details, *Inside the AS/400* demystifies this system, shedding light on how it came to be, how it can do the things it does, and what its future may hold — especially in light of its new PowerPC RISC processors. 475 pages, 12 chapters.

JIM SLOAN'S CL TIPS & TECHNIQUES

By Jim Sloan, developer of QUSRTOOL's TAA Tools

Written for those who understand CL, this book draws from Jim Sloan's knowledge and experience as a developer for the S/38 and the AS/400, and his creation of QUSRTOOL's TAA tools, to give you tips that can help you write better CL programs and become more productive. Includes more than 200 field-tested techniques, plus exercises to help you understand and apply many of the techniques presented. 564 pages, 30 chapters.

MASTERING THE AS/400

A practical, hands-on guide

By Jerry Fottral

This introductory textbook to AS/400 concepts and facilities has a utilitarian approach that stresses student participation. A natural prerequisite to programming and database management courses, it emphasizes mastery of system/user interface, member-object-library relationship, utilization of CL commands, and basic database and program development utilities. Also includes labs focusing on essential topics such as printer spooling; library lists; creating and maintaining physical files; using logical files; using CL and DDS; working in the PDM environment; and using SEU, DFU, Query, and SDA. 484 pages, 12 chapters.

OBJECT-ORIENTED PROGRAMMING FOR AS/400 PROGRAMMERS

By Jennifer Hamilton, a **NEWS/400** *author*

Explains basic OOP concepts such as classes and inheritance in simple, easy-to-understand terminology. The OS/400 object-oriented architecture serves as the basis for the discussion throughout, and concepts presented are reinforced through an introduction to the C++ object-oriented programming language, using examples based on the OS/400 object model. 114 pages, 14 chapters.